COLERIDGE
ON THE SEVENTEENTH CENTURY

I have devoted myself to a life of unintermitted reading, thinking, meditating, and observing.

COLERIDGE

COLERIDGE

ON THE

SEVENTEENTH CENTURY

EDITED BY

Roberta Florence Brinkley

INTRODUCTION BY

Louis I. Bredvold

GREENWOOD PRESS, PUBLISHERS   NEW YORK   1968

Dedicated to

PRISCILLA COLERIDGE

Great-great-granddaughter of
Samuel Taylor Coleridge

Preface

This work attempts to bring together with reasonable completeness the many illuminating comments which Coleridge made concerning the seventeenth century, its movements and its writers; to give them as much unity as possible by assembling them around their logical topics; and to establish a reliable text for these materials. In his own proposal for a volume of selections ("beauties") from Leighton's works) Coleridge defended an arrangement according to the relation of thought "inde-pendent of the accidental place of each in the original volumes" and justified this procedure by its result in giving "a connection or at least a propriety of *sequency*, that was before of necessity wanting."[1] It was on this principle that the following excerpts were chosen and or-ganized. The material falls into sections on history, philosophy, theology, science, prose style, and literary criticism, the last including prose works as well as poetry and drama. A further attempt at unifying each section is made in a general introduction for each except the one devoted to prose style, on which the background material needed is to be found in Professor Bredvold's introductory essay. In selecting from Coleridge's notes on the theologians, I found it especially necessary to present the ideas which are of general significance, sacrificing a mass of material which is important primarily to specialists in seventeenth-century the-ology. In purely literary criticism, however, Coleridge's comments nat-urally center upon a particular author and his work.

To look at the seventeenth century through the eyes of a creative critic possessing the background, understanding, and vitality of Cole-ridge is to see beyond one's ordinary range of vision and to gain cer-tain sharply outlined impressions of the period and its writers. Through his "unintermitted reading" Coleridge had gained the background to make correlations with the past and to point out the impact of one writer upon another. The material assembled here is not for seventeenth-century scholars alone; it also provides a convenient reference work for Coleridgeians and affords further insight into the nature and extent of that age's influence upon Coleridge.

Since the sources are widely scattered, bringing them together has meant searching through not only the printed works of Coleridge and

[1] Letter to John Murray, June 18, 1822. Coleridge, E. H., *Letters*, II, 720.

articles in periodicals but also letters, printed and in manuscript, lecture notes, unpublished notebooks and other manuscript materials, marginal notes in books, and even reports of conversations. Many of the printed sources are out of print, not easily procurable, or unknown except to the specialist. In his admiration for the seventeenth century, Coleridge often referred to it brilliantly in annotating books written in other periods or brought it in unexpectedly in association with ideas seemingly remote. Additional marginalia will appear no doubt from time to time as other books from Coleridge's library or the library of some friend of his come back into circulation from the hands of collectors. But the pattern of Coleridge's seventeenth-century criticism is clear from that which is now available, and the story will not be materially changed by fugitive items.

A considerable body of new material is offered, and in the majority of instances where previously printed marginalia have been included it has been possible to re-edit the text from its original source. This is true, for example, for all but four of the fifteen theologians included, and in many cases the re-editing provides almost the equivalent of a new text. Henry Nelson Coleridge in *Literary Remains* sometimes suppressed passages, occasionally even changed the meaning of the original, and frequently revised the wording of a comment in such a way that the flavor of Coleridge's personality is lost. Thomas Poole noticed these things at the time of publication and wrote to Henry Nelson reproving him for misrepresenting Coleridge. The editor admitted toning down certain comments but denied making his uncle "speak of any supposed polities of my own."² The changes are so numerous that to collate the text of the original source with the passage in the *Literary Remains* would increase this volume to an intolerable size; therefore in most instances the reader is given only a cross reference. When selections from Coleridge's own works have been reprinted, the general policy has been to use editions printed during his lifetime.

The manuscript notes have been transcribed *literatim*, with the exception that the Greek has been corrected and accents, which Coleridge so frequently ignored, have been added. Exact transcription adds some interesting details to our knowledge of the characteristics of the period and of Coleridge's own practices. For example, Coleridge used both capitals and italics for emphasis and had various idiosyncrasies and inconsistencies in spelling which in themselves give recognizable flavor to his writing. He employed certain distinguishing marks for reference and a time-saving set of symbols for which he provided a key. He signed especially important notes, and he did not hesitate upon a second

² Letter to Poole, June 15, 1835. British Museum, Add. MSS, 35,344.

reading to contradict the note previously made. He often repeated ideas in almost the same words in many different places. His own books underwent constant revision, and copies sent to friends were often enriched by marginalia. In a letter to George Frere concerning the *First Lay Sermon* he said, "It has passed through many an anxious revisal, and yet you will observe on a mere 'Turning-over of the Pages what a Gleaning the last produced me.'"[3]

Coleridge was often at his best when making annotations as he read. He caught the apt and penetrating thought before it could vanish or become dim,[4] and he could not be prolix because of the restraint imposed by marginal limitations. These notes have an even greater importance, however, for frequently they were made as a part of some projected work which he meant to complete by organizing and transcribing them. Sometimes he spoke of works in this state as already written; they were "in full material existence," he said, ready to "be reduced into formal and actual being."[5]

A further value of these marginal notes is that they reveal Coleridge's critical mind at work and show us the man at home with his books. Books were to him "dear, very dear companions," but he often longed for the author's presence so that he could "*object* to him this and that, express my sympathy and gratitude for this part and mention some facts that self-evidently overset a second, start a doubt upon a third, or confirm and carry [on] a fourth thought."[6] All these things find their way into the marginalia, adding the living tone to the critical note. Sometimes he loses patience with the author and exclaims, "Is the fellow mad!" Seward's notes on Beaumont and Fletcher annoyed him, and opposite one of them he wrote, "Mr. Seward had his brains out." Hurd was no critic for Shakespeare, he felt, and in one place he addressed him: "H. thou right reverend Aspirate, what hast thou to do with sweetest Shakespeare."

Among the writers of the romantic period who were attempting to revive an interest in the older literature, Lamb and Coleridge were particularly active. Much of the initial impetus came from Lamb, whose enthusiasms were convincing and contagious. In a letter to Coleridge dated June 14, 1796, Lamb praised Massinger and quoted him, and on July 1 he again commented, saying, "I writhe with indignation when in books of criticism . . . I find no mention of such men as Massinger, or

3 December, 1816. Gabrielle Festing, *J. Hookham Frere and His Friends* (London: 1899), p. 220.
4 On April 14, 1805, Coleridge wrote, "While I was preparing the pen to write this remark, I lost the train of thought which had led me to it." *Anima*, p. 136.
5 Letter to Allsop, January, 1821. Allsop, *Letters*, I, 161.
6 December, 1804. *Anima*, p. 91.

B. and Fl.''[7] He appealed to Coleridge to ''try and do something to bring our elder bards into more general fame.''[8] Coleridge was interested in doing this, and when he lectured on Shakespeare he frequently made comparisons with Beaumont and Fletcher and Massinger. Finally in 1818 he devoted an entire lecture to Jonson and these three dramatists. By his comments on a number of authors Lamb stimulated Coleridge to read and criticize them. After asking Coleridge a second time whether he had read Walton's *Compleat Angler*, he said, ''Pray make yourself acquainted with it.''[9] He asked specifically for a judgment on Cowley, both on his poetry and on his essays, and inquired if his writing ''be not delicious.''[10] He was excited over Chapman's Homer and as soon as he had finished it, sent off a letter about its ''uncommon excellence.''[11] Coleridge in turn admired it enough to give an annotated copy to Sara Hutchinson in 1807, a volume which after Coleridge's death she discovered had been sent away from Rydal Mount with other books and was trying to recover.[12] Lamb also had More's ''fine poem,'' Donne's poems and Daniel's, Taylor's *Sermons*, Luther's *Table Talk*, and other volumes which Coleridge borrowed and enriched with annotations.

On the other hand, Coleridge introduced Lamb to Quarles, George Wither,[13] and others in whom he was interested. Lamb, finding the lines which Coleridge had copied out from Wither ''most exquisite,'' became so much interested that he wrote a fine critical essay on his poetical works. But Coleridge's enthusiasm for Herbert did not awaken a response in Lamb, who continued to admire Harvey's *Synagogue* more than Herbert's *Temple*. It was Coleridge who suggested Lamb's writing ''the forgery of a supposed manuscript of Burton the anatomist of melancholy,''[14] and who urged him ''to study the works of Dr. Jeremy Taylor.'' Lamb says, 'I have had reason to bless the hour in which he did it,''[15] and in praising Taylor to Robert Lloyd stressed some of the same passages which Coleridge had admired. He also found Coleridge's library useful and when he returned Fuller's works spoke with affection of the ''dear, fine, silly old angel, whom I part from bleeding.''

In the research which compiling this work has required over a number of years I am under obligation to many people, and no summary can be adequate. Especial mention should be made, however, of a grant from the American Philosophical Society and of sabbatical leave from Goucher

7 July 1, 1796. Lamb, *Letters*, I, 32.   8 *Ibid.*
9 Oct. 28, 1796. *Ibid.*, I, 51.   10 Jan. 10, 1797. *Ibid.*, I, 85.
11 Oct. 23, 1802. *Ibid.*, I, 326.
12 Unpublished letter in the possession of A. H. B. Coleridge.
13 July 1, 1796. Lamb, *Letters*, I, 32.   14 March 17, 1800. *Ibid.*, I, 178.
15 April 16, 1801. *Ibid.*, I, 257.

College in 1946-47 which made it possible to spend a concentrated period of time collecting materials in England.

To Professor Louis I. Bredvold of the University of Michigan I am indebted for the idea of making a collection of Coleridge's criticism of the seventeenth century, for frequent encouragement and counsel, for reading the collected materials, and for the introductory essay.

I have enjoyed the hospitality of many libraries; but in expressing my thanks to individual staffs, I have space to name only some of the centers of Coleridge material: the British Museum and Dr. Williams's Library in London, the Central Library in Bristol, the John Rylands Library in Manchester; in the United States, the Henry E. Huntington Library, the Harvard College Library, the Library of Yale University, and the Henry W. and Albert A. Berg Collection of the New York Public Library. I am also deeply indebted to the staff of Duke University Library.

It is a pleasure to record my special indebtedness to many individuals: to Mr. A. H. B. Coleridge, who allowed me to go through the manuscripts and books which he inherited from his father the Reverend G. H. B. Coleridge and who gave me permission to print various materials from this collection and from the British Museum; to Lord Coleridge, who kindly granted me the use of other Coleridge manuscript materials in the British Museum, with the proviso that I clear the use of excerpts from the unpublished *Notebooks* with Miss Kathleen Coburn, of Victoria College, Toronto, who is editing these books; to Miss Coburn, who not only released these excerpts but also granted permission for the reproduction of sections from the *Philosophical Lectures* and who has in many other ways afforded generous co-operation; to Professor S. G. Dunn, Stratford-on-Avon, who put at my disposal his volume of John Donne's *Sermons* with Coleridge's original annotations; to Mr. C. K. Ogden, who permitted me to see and quote from his Coleridge collection; to Professor T. M. Raysor, who gave me permission to reprint selections from his volumes, and who read the entire manuscript; to Professor Earl Leslie Griggs, who released his priority so that I might use excerpts from several unpublished Coleridge letters; to Professor A. A. Suppan, who released priority in the use of the manuscript *On the Divine Ideas* so that I might quote four excerpts; to Dr. Roger Bennett, who turned over to me his transcription of Barron Field's copy of Coleridge's notes in Lamb's copy of Donne's poems; and to four of my colleagues at Duke University—Dr. Robert E. Cushman, who read my introduction to the section on the old divines and made a number of valuable suggestions; the late Dr. Charles W. Peppler, who corrected Coleridge's Greek; Dr. Robert S. Rogers, who checked the Greek in proof;

and Dr. Lewis Patton, who called my attention to the copy of Coleridge's notes on Daniel's poems found in the Abinger papers.

I also wish to thank several libraries for permission to print manuscript materials in their possession. These libraries are specifically noted as the materials appear: the Henry W. and Albert A. Berg Collection of the New York Public Library, the Henry E. Huntington Library, the John Rylands Library, and the libraries of Cambridge, Duke, Harvard, and Stanford universities.

To acknowledge permission from publishers to use excerpts from printed works also expresses my gratitude to the editors of these works: to Constable and Company, E. L. Griggs's *Unpublished Letters of S. T. Coleridge;* to Cornell University Press, Leslie N. Broughton's *Some Letters of the Wordsworth Family;* to Harvard University Press, T. M. Raysor's *Coleridge's Miscellaneous Criticism;* to the Philosophical Library, Kathleen Coburn's *The Philosophical Lectures of Samuel Taylor Coleridge.*

A generous subsidy granted by the Research Council of Duke University has made possible the publication of this book.

Contents

	PAGE
Preface	vii
Short-Title Bibliography	xv
Introductory Essay: Coleridge on the Seventeenth Century *By Louis I. Bredvold*	xxi
The Seventeenth Century	3

Philosophy

INTRODUCTION	39
FRANCIS BACON	41
THOMAS HOBBES	58
JOHN LOCKE	67
FORERUNNERS OF KANT	109

The Old Divines

INTRODUCTION	125
COLERIDGE'S GENERAL COMMENTS	134
RICHARD HOOKER	140
RICHARD FIELD	153
JOHN DONNE	163
JOHN HACKET	205
PETER HEYLYN	223
WILLIAM CHILLINGWORTH	230
THOMAS FULLER	232
ROBERT LEIGHTON	243
JEREMY TAYLOR	258
HENRY MORE	316
RICHARD BAXTER	321
JOHN SMITH	365
ISAAC BARROW	368
GILBERT BURNET	369
EDWARD STILLINGFLEET	375
DANIEL WATERLAND	379

Science

    INTRODUCTION 393

    COLERIDGE'S GENERAL COMMENTS ON SCIENCE 394

    ISAAC NEWTON 399

Literary Prose

    COLERIDGE'S GENERAL COMMENTS ON PROSE STYLE 411

    JOHN DONNE 428

    ROBERT BURTON 431

    JOHN BARCLAY 433

    JOHN SELDEN 436

    SIR THOMAS BROWNE 438

    THOMAS FULLER 463

    JOHN MILTON 471

    JOHN BUNYAN 474

    SAMUEL PEPYS 486

    JOHN ASGILL 493

Poetry

    GEORGE CHAPMAN 503

    SAMUEL DANIEL 506

    JOHN DONNE 519

    BISHOP RICHARD CORBET 530

    GEORGE WITHER 530

    FRANCIS QUARLES 531

    GEORGE HERBERT 533

    JOHN MILTON 541

    RICHARD CRASHAW 612

    SAMUEL BUTLER 614

    HENRY MORE 617

    ABRAHAM COWLEY 626

    CHARLES COTTON 629

    JOHN DRYDEN 630

    SIR RICHARD BLACKMORE 634

Drama

    BEN JONSON 637

    FRANCIS BEAUMONT AND JOHN FLETCHER 649

    PHILIP MASSINGER 673

    JOHN DRYDEN 679

    SIR GEORGE ETHEREGE 679

    WILLIAM CONGREVE 680

    GEORGE FARQUHAR 681

Appendix 683

Index 695

Short-Title Bibliography

[The following short-title bibliography includes the works most frequently cited in the Notes, where they are identified by their short titles. Manuscripts, annotated books, and books referred to only once or twice are cited fully in the footnote reference.]

Allsop, Letters	Thomas Allsop. Letters, Conversations, and Recollections of S. T. Coleridge. 2 vols. London: 1836.
Ashe, Miscellanies	T. Ashe (ed.). Miscellanies, Aesthetic and Literary. London: George Bell & Sons, 1892.
Campbell, Life	James Dykes Campbell. Samuel Taylor Coleridge. A Narrative of the Events of His Life. London: Macmillan Co., 1894.
Coburn, Phil. Lect.	Kathleen Coburn (ed.). The Philosophical Lectures of Samuel Taylor Coleridge. New York: Philosophical Library, 1949.
Coleridge, E. H., Letters	Ernest Hartley Coleridge (ed.). Letters of Samuel Taylor Coleridge. 2 vols. Boston and New York: Houghton Mifflin Co., 1895.
[Coleridge, S. T.]	Samuel Taylor Coleridge:
Aids	Aids to Reflection in the Formation of a Manly Character. London: 1825. (First edition.)
Anima	Anima Poetae. From the Unpublished Note Books of Samuel Taylor Coleridge, ed. Ernest Hartley Coleridge. London: William Heinemann, 1895.
Biog. Lit. C	Biographia Literaria; or Biographical Sketches of My Literary Life and Opinions. 2 vols. London: 1817. (First edition.)
Biog. Lit. S	Biographia Literaria, with His Aesthetical Essays, ed. J. Shawcross. 2 vols. Oxford: Clarendon Press, 1907.

"Blessed are ye."   "Blessed are that sow beside all waters." A Second Lay Sermon, Addressed to the Higher and Middle Classes, on the Existing Dangers and Discontents. London: 1817. (First edition.)

Church and State   On the Constitution of the Church and State, According to the Idea of Each. London: 1830. (First edition.)

Confessions   Confessions of an Inquiring Spirit and Some Miscellaneous Pieces, ed. Henry Nelson Coleridge. London: 1849. (Second edition.)

English Divines   Notes on English Divines by Samuel Taylor Coleridge, ed. Derwent Coleridge. 2 vols. London: 1853.

Essays   Essays on His Own Times; Forming a Second Series of "The Friend," ed. His Daughter [Sara Coleridge]. 3 vols. London: 1850. (First edition.)

Estlin   Unpublished Letters from Samuel Taylor Coleridge to the Rev. John Prior Estlin, communicated by Henry A. Bright. ("Miscellanies of the Philobiblon Society," Vol. XV.) London: 1884.

The Friend   The Friend. A Series of Essays. A New Edition. 3 vols. London: 1818. (Second edition.)

Lit. Rem.   The Literary Remains of Samuel Taylor Coleridge, ed. Henry Nelson Coleridge. 4 vols. London: 1836-39.

Method   Treatise on Method, as published in the Encyclopædia Metropolitana, ed. Alice D. Snyder. London: Constable & Co., 1934.

Monologues   "Monologues of the Late Samuel Taylor Coleridge, Esq., No. II. The Science and Systems of Logic," Fraser's Magazine, XII (December, 1835), 622-28.

Notes Theolog.   Notes Theological, Political, and Miscellaneous

	by Samuel Taylor Coleridge, ed. Derwent Coleridge. London: 1853.
Plot Discovered	*The Plot Discovered; or an Address to the People against Ministerial Treason.* Bristol: 1795. (First edition.)
Sib. Leaves	*Sibylline Leaves.* London: 1817. (First edition.)
Statesman's Manual	*The Statesman's Manual, or the Bible the Best Guide to Political Skill and Foresight; A Lay Sermon Addressed to the Higher Classes of Society.* London: 1816. (First edition.)
Table Talk S	*The Table Talk and Omniana of S. T. Coleridge,* in Shedd, VI.
Table Talk A	*Table Talk and Omniana of S. T. Coleridge with Additional Table Talk from Allsop's "Recollections," and Manuscript Matter not before Printed,* ed. T. Ashe. ("Bohn's Standard Library.") London: George Bell & Sons, 1896.
Theory of Life	*Hints Towards the Formation of a More Comprehensive Theory of Life,* ed. Seth B. Watson. London: 1848. (First edition.)
Collier, *Seven Lect.*	John Payne Collier. *Seven Lectures on Shakespeare and Milton by the Late S. T. Coleridge.* London: 1856.
Cottle, *Recollections*	Joseph Cottle. *Early Recollections, Chiefly Relating to the Late Samuel Taylor Coleridge, during His Long Residence in Bristol.* 2 vols. London: 1837.
Cottle, *Reminiscences*	Joseph Cottle. *Reminiscences of Samuel Taylor Coleridge and Robert Southey.* London: 1847.
Descartes, *Works*	*The Philosophical Works of Descartes,* rendered into English by E. S. Haldane and G. R. T. Ross. 2 vols. Cambridge [Eng.]: University Press, 1911-12.

Gillman, *Life*

James Gillman. *The Life of Samuel Taylor Coleridge*. London: 1838.

Griggs, *Unp. Letters*

Earl Leslie Griggs (ed.). *Unpublished Letters of Samuel Taylor Coleridge.* 2 vols. London: Constable & Co., 1932.

Hume, *Phil. Works*

David Hume. *The Philosophical Works.* 4 vols. Edinburgh and London: 1826.

Knight, *Mem. of Coleorton*

William Knight (ed.). *Memorials of Coleorton, Being Letters from Coleridge, Wordsworth and His Sister, Southey, and Sir Walter Scott to Sir George and Lady Beaumont of Coleorton, Leicestershire, 1803 to 1834.* 2 vols. Edinburgh: 1887.

Lamb, *Letters*

The Letters of Charles Lamb: to which are added those of his sister Mary Lamb, ed. E. V. Lucas. 3 vols. New Haven: Yale University Press, 1935.

Litchfield, *Tom Wedgwood*

R. B. Litchfield. *Tom Wedgwood, the First Photographer. An Account of His Life, His Discovery and Friendship with Samuel Taylor Coleridge, Including the Letters of Coleridge to the Wedgwoods.* London: Duckworth & Co., 1903.

Meteyard, *Group of Englishmen*

Eliza Meteyard. *A Group of Englishmen (1795-1815): Being Records of the Younger Wedgwoods and Their Friends.* London: Longmans, 1871.

Muirhead, *C. as Philos.*

John H. Muirhead. *Coleridge as Philosopher.* London: Allen and Unwin; New York: Macmillan Co., 1930.

Raysor, *Misc. Crit.*

T. M. Raysor (ed.). *Coleridge's Miscellaneous Criticism.* London: Constable & Co., 1936.

Raysor, *Shakes. Crit.*

T. M. Raysor (ed.). *Coleridge's Shakespearean Criticism.* 2 vols. Cambridge: Harvard University Press, 1930.

Richards, *Imagination*   I. A. Richards. *Coleridge on Imagination.* New York: Harcourt, Brace & Co., 1935.

Richards, *Lit. Crit.*   I. A. Richards. *Principles of Literary Criticism.* London: K. Paul, Trench, Trübner, & Co., 1924.

Robinson, *Diary*   *Henry Crabb Robinson's Diary, Reminiscences, and Correspondence,* ed. Thomas Sadler. 2 vols. Boston: 1870.

Sandford, *T. Poole*   Mrs. Margaret E. Sandford. *Thomas Poole and His Friends.* 2 vols. London, New York: Macmillan Co., 1888.

Shedd   W. G. T. Shedd (ed.). *The Complete Works of Samuel Taylor Coleridge.* 7 vols. New York: Harper & Bros., 1854.

Snyder, *Logic*   Alice D. Snyder. *Coleridge on Logic and Learning, With Selections from Unpublished Manuscripts.* New Haven: Yale University Press, 1929.

Southey, *Omniana*   Robert Southey (ed.). *Omniana or Horae Otiosiores* [S. T. Coleridge and Robert Southey]. 2 vols. London: 1812.

Stuart, *Lake Poet Letters*   Mary Stuart (ed.). *Letters from the Lake Poets, Samuel Taylor Coleridge, William Wordsworth, Robert Southey, to Daniel Stuart, 1800-38.* London: Printed for private circulation, 1889.

Taylor, *Crit. Annot.*   William F. Taylor (ed.). *Critical Annotations, Being Marginal Notes Inscribed in Volumes Formerly in the Possession of S. T. Coleridge.* Harrow: Privately printed, 1889.

Turnbull, *Biog. Epist.*   A. Turnbull (ed.). *Biographia Epistolaris: Being the Biographical Supplement of Coleridge's Biographia Literaria. With Additional Letters.* London: George Bell & Sons, 1911.

Watson, *C. at Highgate*   Lucy E. Watson. *Coleridge at Highgate.* London, New York: Longmans, Green & Co., 1925.

Willmott, *C. at Trinity*   Robert Ars Willmott, "S. T. Coleridge at Trinity," in *Conversations at Trinity.* London: 1836.

Wise, *Ashley*   *The Ashley Library, A Catalogue of Printed Books, Manuscripts and Autograph Letters,* collected by Thomas J. Wise. 11 vols. London: Printed for private circulation only, 1922.

Wise, *Two Lake Poets*   *Two Lake Poets. A Catalogue of the Printed Books, Manuscripts and Autograph Letters by William Wordsworth and Samuel Taylor Coleridge,* collected by T. J. Wise. London: Printed for private circulation only, 1927.

Wordsworth, *Letters*   *The Letters of William and Dorothy Wordsworth,* ed. Ernest de Selincourt. Oxford: Clarendon Press. *The Early Letters (1787-1805),* 1935; *The Middle Years,* 2 vols., 1937; *The Later Years,* 3 vols., 1939.

Wordsworth, *Family Letters*   *Letters of the Wordsworth Family,* ed. William Knight. 3 vols. New York: Ginn & Co., 1907.

Wordsworth, *Some Family Letters*   *Some Letters of the Wordsworth Family,* ed. Leslie Broughton. Ithaca, New York: Cornell University Press, 1942.

Coleridge on the Seventeenth Century

by Louis I. Bredvold

English literature of the seventeenth century demands of its readers an unusual catholicity of sympathy and understanding. All past periods of course appear more and more complex when they are examined closely and at first hand, but the seventeenth century can on good grounds claim pre-eminence in the extraordinary complexity, and even confusion, of its many currents and crosscurrents. It was a myriad-minded age. Many of the ideas which in our day pass current as common-sense platitudes—and are little understood because they are not critically examined—were at that time still in an emergent stage, fresh and new and, to old-fashioned minds, not a little dangerous. Sects abounded in religion, politics, philosophy, and literature, and eccentric and apparently unique personalities were usually representative of some movement or other. The connoisseur of rare types will find his devotion to this period amply rewarded. The historian, however, whose task it is to reduce this chaos to a pattern, is in danger of overlooking some of the richness of the age in his eager search for the right formula of historical synthesis. Thus in recent years we have had the age in-terpreted for us in terms of the baroque, of the progressive dissociation of thought and sensibility, of the rise of capitalism, of the changing conceptions of philosophical truth. Such neat syntheses are likely to be oversimple or one-sided, and at times positively untrue, especially when applied to the multitudinous variety of the seventeenth century. But they may be useful for all that, if their limitations are kept in mind. Though they do not give us the complete pattern of the age, they may contribute something towards it, and often they indicate a point of view from which a writer or a school may profitably be studied. To approach sympathetically all the heterogeneous elements of the century, we need all the sources of insight we can find. And the contribution of Cole-ridge, in spite of a definite theoretical bias and a conception of English literary history different from anything now current, remains to this day one of the most important.

It is unfortunate that so little use has been made of Coleridge's comments on the writers of the "Great Age," whom he cultivated so familiarly and read with such deep satisfaction. His criticism of Shakespeare and the other Elizabethan dramatists has always commanded attention and been of epochal significance. But his remarks on the poets and prose writers, the divines and philosophers, have not been similarly drawn into the main current of scholarship and criticism dealing with the period. Some few gems, no doubt, get quoted at second or third hand, but it is not the custom for the student of Hooker, Jeremy Taylor, or even Milton, to consult Coleridge as a part of his task. The difficulties have perhaps been sufficient to discourage many who have made the attempt. Coleridge's commentary on the seventeenth century exists only in fragments, scattered throughout his treatises, his notes, his marginalia, and his letters; much of it is highly doctrinaire and schematic and presupposes in the reader a very special interest and competence in Coleridge's metaphysical speculations. To minimize these difficulties for the student of the seventeenth century—not, it may be emphasized, primarily for the Coleridge specialist—is the purpose of this volume.

To do Coleridge justice, he was capable of saturating his writing with thought, even with his own ever-recurring philosophical concepts, because it was natural for him to apprehend ideas poetically. He was a poet-philosopher. His criticism is neither a pure scientific treatise nor a poem about a poem, but something of both. He expressed his own acute and sensitive perceptions with a suggestive and infectious style, in which ideas are often rather implied than stated. Such, for instance, is his provocative metaphor for Dryden: ''Dryden's genius was of the sort which catches fire by its own motion; his chariot wheels get hot by driving fast.'' Sometimes critical statements which have obviously germinated in his philosophical system nevertheless seem self-sufficient without commentary, and illuminate even for the unphilosophical reader both the ideas and their application to literature. There is deep Coleridgean doctrine in the familiar comparison of Shakespeare and Milton in the *Biographia Literaria*:

While the former darts himself forth, and passes into all the forms of human character and passion, the one Proteus of the fire and the flood; the other attracts all forms and things to himself, into the unity of his own ideal. All things and modes of action shape themselves anew in the being of Milton; while Shakespeare becomes all things, yet for ever remaining himself.

But no accomplished reader of Shakespeare and Milton is obligated by such a passage to pursue erudite studies in metaphysics; his own experience will provide sufficient commentary if he is not in a mood to meditate on first principles. The value of any critic must depend in the first instance upon his perceptions; and most great critics, although their theories may have served them well with certain authors, have been more versatile in their sympathies than their principles might lead us to suppose. Certainly this observation is true of Coleridge. By both his theories and his tastes he was predisposed to prefer the seventeenth century to the eighteenth, but he could also enjoy the latter. Although he disapproved in principle of Addison's style, he read *The Spectator* "with increasing admiration." In the first chapter of *Biographia Literaria* he said excellent things about the school of Pope, and confesses that he had earlier "with the presumption of youth withheld from its masters the legitimate name of poets." When Coleridge was critical of the eighteenth century it was not that he was blind to its merits.

The seventeenth century, however, was his spiritual home, and its controversies and idiosyncrasies, even more than those of German Romanticism, congenially reflected his own tastes and his intellectual bent. But although we are here concerned primarily with Coleridge's relation to the seventeenth century proper, it must be kept in mind that he did not distinguish it sharply, in the modern manner, from the Elizabethan age. Throughout all his comment there is an assumption of a distinct period in English culture extending from the reign of Edward VI to the Revolution of 1688, a period which he believed characterized by traditions of sound thought and great style, and which was therefore a unity in spite of its lapses and its variety. Of the more limited conception of the Renaissance, popularized only after his death by Michelet and Burckhardt, he of course knew nothing; nor can he be said to have anticipated in a significant way any of those divisions and classifications which now organize our literary history in such detail. Not that he was deficient in a sense of history—he knew very well the changes in intellectual and moral climate within this period; he digested the controversies and studied the effect upon them of historical developments—for he always aimed to read the literature of the past with a genuine historical imagination guided by learning. "The man," he once wrote, "who reads a work meant for immediate effect on one age with the notions and feelings of another, may be a refined gentleman, but must be a sorry critic."[1] But beneath all the change and diversity in this long era of seven reigns, Coleridge believed he could see a more important unity of tone, manner, and preconceptions. He did not think of the period as a "movement" which, by biological analogy, had a youth, a maturity, and a senescent decay. The period came to an end simply because the English people, like the rest of Europe, adopted superficial philosophical principles.

To the modern student, familiar with the complexities and perplexities of historical methodology, all this may appear somewhat simple and

1 Shedd, IV, 306.

undeveloped. But for Coleridge, whose admiration for these early writers verged at times on idolatry, it provided the one synthesis that was both necessary and sufficient. English prose style, for instance, falls into two periods, before and after 1688. This subject Coleridge studied all his life both as critic and practitioner, and his ideas regard-ing it seem not to have changed materially after 1800. Already in the autumn of 1802 his letters were mentioning a projected history of English prose style. He declared that he had given much thought to the subject of style in prose and verse and was ready "in a very few weeks to go to Press with a Volume on the Prose writings of Hall, Milton, and Taylor—and shall immediately follow it up with an Essay on the writings of Dr. Johnson, and Gibbon—And in these two Volumes, I flatter myself that I shall present a fair History of English Prose."[2] Of course this volume never went to press, but its contents remained stored up in Coleridge's mind, to be divulged in fragments from time to time, as occasion arose. We may be sure that it would have been a literary manifesto as much as a treatise, with the purpose of demonstrating the superior excellence of "our elder writers."

His own style was consciously modeled on that of the seventeenth century. In a statement in *The Friend*—less an apology than a defense—he admitted his deficiencies as a journalist:

We insensibly imitate what we habitually admire; and an aversion to the epigrammatic unconnected periods of the fashionable Anglo-Gallican taste has too often made me willing to forget, that the stately march and difficult evolu-tions, which characterize the eloquence of Hooker, Bacon, Milton, and Jeremy Taylor, are notwithstanding their intrinsic excellence, still less suited to a periodical essay. This fault I am now endeavoring to correct; though I can never so far sacrifice my judgment to the desire of being immediately popular, as to cast my sentences in the French moulds, or affect a style which an ardent critic would have deemed purposely invented for persons troubled with asthma to read, and for those to comprehend who labour under the more pitiable asthma of a short-witted intellect.[3]

His uneasiness over this difficulty is recorded also in a letter to George Coleridge written October 9, 1809,[4] and he turned to a study of *The Spectator* to learn how to cast his thoughts in a less antique mold. But to no avail. He was not blind to the merits of this model, which he read "with increasing pleasure and admiration." "Yet it must be evident to you," he wrote to Thomas Poole on January 28, 1810,

that there is a class of thoughts and feelings, and these, too, the most important, even practically, which it would be impossible to convey in the manner of

[2] Griggs, *Unp. Letters*, I, 217. Cf. I, 210-11, and *Biog. Lit. S*, I, 36 n.
[3] *The Friend*, Essay III. Shedd, II, 31.
[4] Griggs, *Unp. Letters*, II, 10-11.

Addison, and which, if Addison had possessed, he would not have been Addison. Read, for instance, Milton's prose tracts, and only *try* to conceive them translated into the style of *The Spectator,* or the finest part of Wordsworth's pamphlet.⁵

For anything like a precise statement of Coleridge's ideas about the great English prose of the seventeenth century, it is necessary to piece together fragments from various sources. He seems not to have regarded the influence of Ciceronianism as of primary importance, except perhaps as contributing the element of architectural structure to the style of certain writers. In his lectures of 1818 he discussed this style, which, he said,

arose from the very nature of their language in the Greek writers, but which already in the Latin orators and historians, had betrayed a species of effort, a foreign something, which had been superinduced on the language, instead of growing out of it; and which was far too alien from that individualizing and confederating, yet not blending, character of the North, to become permanent, although its magnificence and stateliness were objects of admiration and occasional imitation. This style diminished the control of the writer over the inner feelings of men, and created too great a chasm between the body and the life; and hence especially it was abandoned by Luther.⁶

Racial theories of literature elicited Coleridge's interest, and he relished in the "elder writers" that native idiom which he felt was as authentic for English as the idiom of Luther's prose for German. In a note to *The Friend* he expresses himself explicitly on this point:

I can scarcely conceive a more delightful volume than might be made from Luther's letters, especially from those that were written from the Wartburg, if they were translated in the simple, sinewy, idiomatic, hearty, mother-tongue of the original. A difficult task, I admit—and scarcely possible for any man, however great his talents in other respects, whose favorite reading has not lain among the English writers from Edward VI to Charles I.⁷

Where, as in his lecture *On Style,* he recognizes that the classical influence differentiates the style of Hooker, Bacon, Milton, and Taylor from the simpler style of "Latimer and our other venerable authors about the time of Edward VI," he nevertheless emphasizes that "in all these the language is dignified but plain, genuine English." Coleridge was sensitive to the continuing traditions of English prose.

It was the style of this period that Coleridge would have championed in his history of English prose. He loved it in all its rich variety, and no one has excelled him in describing with felicity and truth the "individual idioms" of its great writers, from the "classical structure of

⁵ Shedd, II, 130 n.
⁶ Raysor, *Misc. Crit.,* p. 22.
⁵ Coleridge, E. H., *Letters,* II, 557.

Hooker," to the "impetuous, thought-agglomerating flood of Taylor."
The prose of the age of Queen Anne he declared was not, "upon sound
principles of judgment," equal to the best of it. And this appeal to
sound principles implies that Coleridge regarded style and idiom as
something more than a mere literary condiment or a salty preservative.
The superiority of English prose before the Revolution of 1688 lies in
the fact that it was not characteristically composed by agglutination, but
evolved by an organic inner principle. "The unity in these writers is
produced by the unity of the subject, and the perpetual growth and
evolution of the thoughts, one generating and explaining and justifying
the place of another, not, as it is in Seneca, where the thoughts, striking
as they are, are merely strung together like beads, without any causation
or progression."[8]—"This principle of organic continuity is of course as
applicable to verse as to prose. "Who can read with pleasure more
than a hundred lines or so of Hudibras at one time? Each couplet or
quatrain is so whole in itself, that you can't connect them. There is no
fusion—just as it is in Seneca."[9]

Many of Coleridge's notes and marginalia on the poets of the seventeenth century are applications of this organic principle, and they exhibit his acute intelligence combining with his sensitive ear to ascertain
the true poetic meaning as well as the true melody, these being but
two aspects of one experience. A striking illustration of his nice discrimination in these matters appears in his lectures on Shakespeare,
where he indicated the "true reading" of the passage in Genesis: "God

8 Shedd, IV, 340.

9 Shedd, VI, 468. These references to Seneca, and in the lecture "On Style" to
Tacitus, as the archetype of the disconnected and epigrammatic style need not imply
that Coleridge was insensitive to those qualities in his favorite English authors which
recent scholars have attributed to the direct influence of Seneca, Tacitus, and the
Silver Latin writers generally. As has been pointed out above, Coleridge was no
admirer of Ciceronianism, which was unacceptable to the genius of the North;
and perhaps this instinct for the native English tradition may be a salutary cor-
rective to some recent studies of the Senecan influence. See such representative
studies as Morris W. Croll, "Attic Prose in the Seventeenth Century" (Studies in
Philology, XVIII, 1929, 79-128), and "Attic Prose: Lipsius, Montaigne, and Bacon"
(Schelling Anniversary Papers, New York, 1923, pp. 117-50), and George William-
son, "Senecan Style in the Seventeenth Century" (Philological Quarterly, XV,
1936, 321-51). There are important implications for this subject in R. C. Chambers, On the Continuity of English Prose, although Mr. Chambers ends his history
with Sir Thomas More. Coleridge's mention of Seneca in each case implies a reference to the extreme form of this style, much in the spirit of Cowley's "dry chips
of short lung'd Seneca." Lord Monboddo believed that English prose style of the
eighteenth century was more characteristically Tacitean than that of the seventeenth,
and he saw Greek influence in the styles of Hooker, Milton, and Lord Clarendon
(The Origin and Progress of Language, 2d ed., III, 1786 passim). A similar
judgment regarding the style of modern historical writing may be found in
Chateaubriand, Génie du Christianisme, 3ième Partie, Livre III, chap. iii.

said, Let there be light, and there was *light*," not "there *was* light." Coleridge's reading has some merit in eliminating the touch of absurd surprise hinted at in Pope's parody, where a heavy and more than metrical emphasis falls on the verb:

"Let spades be trumps!" she said, and trumps they were.

His notes on prosody, which sometimes seem so heavily labored, are all attempts to indicate the true reading of difficult passages, and they deserve careful scrutiny as coming from a reader gifted with such unusual imagination and sensitivity. Sometimes he relied on his own perceptions to the extent of arbitrarily emending the text of his author. Such audacities the modern reader, accustomed as he is to a science of textual criticism far more rigorous than the ingenious guessing applied to English texts in Coleridge's day, will observe with interest and judge in-dulgently.

His explanations of the irregularities of seventeenth-century prosody are especially fertile in suggestion. In Massinger's verse he discerned "a rich harmony, puzzling the fingers, but satisfying the ear." His sympathetic characterization of the wit of Donne was a major event in the history of that author's reputation: "Wonder-exciting vigour, in-tenseness and peculiarity of thought, using at will the almost boundless stores of a capacious memory, and exercised on subjects, where we have no right to expect it." He observed that in such poems as Donne's, "where the writer *thinks*, and expects the reader to do so, the sense must be understood to ascertain the metre." By meter Coleridge meant not only the beat of the accent, but a complicated polyphonic pattern, including pauses and other quantitative elements. "To read Donne you must measure *Time*, and discover the *Time* of each word by the sense of Passion." English verse, as has been understood since the sixteenth century, is primarily accentual; but all good readers have recognized the presence also of other elements, and Tennyson maintained that he knew the quantitative value of every syllable of every English word except "scissors." In a marginal note to Beaumont and Fletcher, Coleridge insisted on a "modifying of quantity by emphasis, without which our elder poets cannot be scanned." In this note he elaborated his theory sufficiently to elucidate some of his more cryptic fragments:

It is true that quantity, an almost iron law with the Greek, is in English rather a subject for a peculiarly fine ear, than any law or even rule; but, then, instead of it, we have, first, accent; secondly, emphasis; and lastly, retardation, and acceleration of the times of syllables according to the meaning of the words, the passion that accompanies them, and even the character of the person that uses them. With due attention to these,—above all, to that, which requires the most attention and the finest taste, the character, Massinger, for example, might be reduced to a rich and yet regular metre. But then the *regulae* must be first known;—though I will venture to say, that he who does not find a line (not corrupted) of Massinger's flow to the time total of a trimeter catalectic iambic verse, has not read it aright. But by virtue of the last principle—the retarda-tion or acceleration of time—we have the procel*eusmatic* foot $\cup\cup\cup\cup$, and the dispond*aeus* – – – –, not to mention the *choriambus*, the ionics, paeons, and epitrites. Since Dryden, the metre of our poets leads to the sense: in our elder and more genuine bards, the sense, including the passion, leads to the metre. Read even Donne's satires as he meant them to be read, and as the sense and passion demand, and you will find in the lines manly harmony.

Such marginalia need not be expected to settle the heated controversies of the science of prosody; their value is rather that they are rough transcriptions of readings by a genius in both poetry and criticism.

As the reading as well as the writing of poetry is the work of the "esemplastic" or unifying imagination, melody must not be divorced from meaning. Coleridge was sure that the poets of the seventeenth century, whatever their individual faults and shortcomings, also shared the general intellectual excellence of their age. In a passage in *Bi-ographia Literaria* he generalized broadly regarding their modes of poetical conception:

the characteristic fault of our elder poets is the reverse of that, which dis-tinguishes too many of our more recent versifiers; the one conveying the most fantastic thoughts in the most correct and natural language; the other in the most fantastic language conveying the most trivial thoughts. The latter is a riddle of words; the former an enigma of thoughts.

It may be observed that Coleridge does not here pretend to indicate the characteristic virtues of either period, but it is clear enough that he was more ready to pardon the characteristic faults of the seventeenth century, which he indeed regarded as the obverse of their characteristic merits. Their enigmas conveyed thoughts. Early in his life he had been merely amused by the "quaintness" of Herbert's *Temple*, but he learned to read it as a source of comfort. Quarles and Wither he thought were "unkindly underrated" because readers failed to appreciate "their sound hunger and thirst after religion." He examined with special vigilance the speculations of philosophical poets, such as Henry More; yet he could not understand how Southey could so grossly err as to reject More's *Song of the Soul*. He had his favorites also among the much less conceited poems of Drayton and Daniel. His letter urging Charles Lamb to have another look at Daniel's *Civil Wars* is an excellent illustra-tion of his gift for entering imaginatively into the intellectual and poetic character of an author. All his powers were of course supremely en-gaged in his criticism of Shakespeare and Milton.

Great as Coleridge was as a reader, he was also a literary theorist seeking to justify his literary judgments by universal aesthetic principles, and these in turn involved him in metaphysical questions. Everyone will recall how much of his criticism revolves around his favorite antithesis between the mechanical and the organic. "Shakespeare," he says, "is the height, breadth, and depth of Genius; Beaumont and Fletcher the excellent mechanism, in juxtaposition and succession, of talent." Turning only a few pages we find him using the same antithesis to explain the weakness of construction in Beaumont and Fletcher, the inconsistency of Massinger's characterization, and the difference in fundamental poetic conception between Massinger and Shakespeare. In all Ben Jonson's works, he says, "in verse or prose, there is an extraordinary opulence of thought; but it is the produce of an amassing power in the author, and not of a growth from within." By the application of the same principle he places Spenser below Shakespeare and Milton. Coleridge was never weary of reiterating that the greatest poetry and prose, the really true poetry and prose, is more than a product of the associative and mechanical powers of the mind; it evolves by a logic of its own, a logic as severe and inevitable as the syllogism, but of a higher and more complex nature. It is organic, and it springs from an organism. The imagination is the function of this organism in the creation of works of art, and Coleridge labored hard to explain and justify this conception of the creative imagination, to state its metaphysical foundations, to expound its analogies in ethics, religion, and politics, as well as to apply it in his literary judgments. Perhaps he did not entirely succeed in these deep speculations,[10] but some formulation of his conception from his own point of view must be attempted, if only to make clear his habitual mode of approach to the literature and thought of the seventeenth century, these two aspects of the period being to him interrelated and inseparable.

Coleridge is, by common consent, a great psychological observer, whose precision in the statement of the nuances of his own reactions to literature would alone rank him among the foremost critics. But he has also had genuinely devoted readers who have felt that they had exhausted all that is valuable in his criticism by reading it simply as a psychological record. They emphasize quite correctly that Coleridge conceives of the poetic process, in both author and reader, as an organizing activity of the whole organism, under conditions of freedom not experienced in the ordinary routine of life. Because poetry is such a harmonious activity of the whole complex nature of man, it offers a

[10] Although there is now observable a tendency to take him more seriously as a philosophical thinker, as in J. H. Muirhead, *Coleridge as Philosopher.*

greater or more complex satisfaction than any attainable from the partial exercise of our powers in ordinary experience. The antithesis to poetry, Coleridge said, is not prose, but science. And science, so goes the argument of his modern apologists, is the exercise of only a fractional part of our organism, whereas poetry springs from the obscure depths of our natures and moves through every part. In this way Coleridge's theory can be adjusted to modern psychology and be made serviceable as an apologetic for poetry in an age of science.[11]

But this psychological apologetics often turns out to be nothing but biology. Our psychological needs of today are our biological heritage from yesterday. Our psychological defense of poetry leads us to the biological fact that an organism has appetencies of many kinds, and that some of these are satisfied by writing and reading poetry. Such psychological investigations are especially attractive in our scientific age, and as refined by modern research have undoubtedly contributed valuable insight into the poetic process. But they would have satisfied only one side of Coleridge's inquiring mind. He argued insistently that the aesthetic experience has its own unique quality which cannot be defined, or even apprehended, merely as a psychological and biological appetency. He elaborated this distinction in his essay ''On the Principles of Genial Criticism,'' in the ''Fragment of an Essay on Taste,'' and in many other places.

If a man, upon questioning his own experience, can detect no difference in *kind* between the enjoyment derived from the eating of a turtle, and that from the perception of a new truth; if in *his* feelings a taste *for* Milton is essentially the same as the taste *of* mutton, he may still be a sensible and a valuable member of society; but it would be desecration to argue with him on the Fine Arts.

To define the aesthetic experience, Coleridge frequently observed, it is necessary to go beyond psychological description to transcendent philosophical principles.

We have sufficiently distinguished the beautiful from the agreeable, by the sure criterion, that, when we find an object agreeable, the *sensation of* pleasure always precedes the judgment, and is its determining cause. We find it agreeable. But when we declare an object beautiful, the contemplation or intuition of its beauty precedes the *feeling* of complacency, in order of nature at least: nay, in great depression of spirits may even exist without sensibly producing it.[12]

Every aesthetic experience, according to Coleridge, involves a judgment, and this judgment is the immediate and intuitive experience of a value.

[11] See I. A. Richards, *Principles of Literary Criticism* and *Coleridge on Imagination.*

[12] *Biog. Lit.*, S, II, 241.

It gives to our experience of art an element of universality and inevitability which is immediately felt and recognized. It carries its own credentials and is not to be validated by any plebiscite. "A Shakspere, a Milton, a Bruno," according to Coleridge, "exist in the mind as pure *action,* defecated of all that is material and passive. And the great moments that formed them—it is a kind of impiety against a voice within us, not to regard them as predestined, and therefore things of now, for ever, and which were always."[13] Any exploration of the meaning of such an experience must lead beyond psychology and sociology, to metaphysical first principles. "All genius," Coleridge remarked, "is metaphysical; because the ultimate end of genius is ideal, however it may be actualized by incidental and accidental circumstances" (*Table Talk,* August 11, 1832). The creative imagination must therefore be more than an "aggregative and associative power"—its activity is the unfolding of the consciousness of man. It involves the mind of man as well as his instincts and impulses. In *Anima Poetae* Coleridge explains that in both poetry and religion "there is a *synthesis* of intellectual insight . . . and of the proper external object which we call *fact.* . . . It is more than historical fact; it is not made up by the addition of one to the other, but it is the *identity* of both, the co-inherence." Such philosophical language was necessary to Coleridge, not merely because he had what Mr. Richards might possibly call an appetency for metaphysics, but primarily because without such philosophical terminology he could not be articulate about the full content and meaning of his own experience with poetry. His theory of the creative imagination and of the organic nature of its product involves a theory of knowledge and reality; and the "sound principles" on which Coleridge judged such a question as the superiority of the style of the seventeenth century over that of the eighteenth, might present themselves to him in their several aspects as either psychology, aesthetics, or metaphysics.

It has too often been assumed, even by his most devoted readers, that Coleridge's whole philosophical development consisted merely in a liberation from the Associationist psychology of Hartley and a half-competent assimilation of the philosophy of his German contemporaries. In his volume on *Coleridge as Philosopher* Professor J. H. Muirhead has made a notable correction of this misconception and incidentally also given some indications of how the very speculations stimulated by Kant and his followers carried Coleridge back to his favorite writers of the seventeenth century. And in various places Coleridge has himself claimed a philosophical kinship with the seventeenth century in at least three important ways.

[13] *Anima,* p. 73.

First of all, the error of the eighteenth century, the error of Locke, Hume, and the Associationists, was to conceive of the mind of man as purely passive. This false psychology, Coleridge is never weary of contending, was the one pre-eminent source of the evil influence of that century on poetry, ethics, politics, and religion. From this error philosophy was rescued by Immanuel Kant, who showed that our perception of the external world involves activity of the mind as well as passivity, that the constitution of the intelligence is as essentially a part of this experience as the external stimulus acting upon it, and that the assumption of some regulative power in the mind itself is necessary to any orderly thought. This restoration of the rights and authority of the active mind became the starting point of all Coleridge's mature thought. And he based his whole theory of values, in his literary as well as in his homiletic writings, on the Kantian distinction between the Reason and the Understanding.

His conception of this distinction may best be given in his own words, from *The Friend.* Reason, he says, may be defined

as an organ bearing the same relation to spiritual objects, the universal, the eternal, and the necessary, as the eye bears to material and contingent *phenomena.* But then it must be added, that it is an organ identical with its appropriate objects. Thus, God, the soul, eternal truth, &c., are the objects of reason; but they are themselves reason. We name God the Supreme Reason; and Milton says,

—whence the soul
Reason receives, and reason is her being.

Whatever is conscious self-knowledge is reason: and in this sense it may be safely defined the organ of the supersensuous; even as the understanding wherever it does not possess or use the reason, as its inward eye, may be defined the conception of the sensuous, or the faculty by which we generalize and arrange the *phenomena* of perception; that faculty, the functions of which contain the rules and constitute the possibility of outward experience. In short, the understanding supposes something that is understood. This may be merely its own acts or forms, that is, formal logic; but real objects, the materials of substantial knowledge, must be furnished, I might safely say revealed, to it by organs of sense. The understanding of the higher brutes has only organs of outward sense, and consequently material objects only; but man's understanding has likewise an organ of inward sense, and therefore the power of acquainting itself with invisible realities or spiritual objects. This organ is his reason.[14]

But this distinction, newly established by the Critical Philosophy of Kant, Coleridge maintained he found anticipated everywhere in "our elder writers," in Hooker, Bacon, Milton, Shakespeare, and the Cambridge Platonists, to mention only a few. The terminology was not consistent or stabilized, but the meanings are there. "Lord Bacon him-

[14] Shedd, II, 144-45.

self, who in his *Novum Organum* has so incomparably set forth the nature of the difference, and the unfitness of the latter faculty [understanding] for the objects of the former [reason], does nevertheless in sundry places use the term reason where he means the understanding, and sometimes, though less frequently, understanding for reason."[15] Coleridge was impressed by the profundity of an aphorism which he quoted from his favorite divine, Archbishop Leighton: "Faith elevates the soul not only above sense and sensible things, but above reason itself. As reason corrects the errors which sense might occasion, so supernatural faith corrects the errors of natural reason judging according to sense." Leighton's "natural reason" Coleridge regarded as identical with Kant's Understanding. And he must have felt great satisfaction in being able to point out that the explanation of the divine of the seventeenth century is, as he says, " (by a noticeable coincidence) word for word, the very definition which the founder of the Critical Philosophy gives of the understanding—namely, 'the faculty judging according to sense.' "[16] Again, in the *Biographia Literaria* Coleridge appeals, not to Kant, but to his authorities of the seventeenth century: "I have cautiously discriminated the terms, THE REASON and THE UNDERSTANDING, encouraged and confirmed by the authority of our genuine divines and philosophers before the Revolution [of 1688]."[17] Such anticipations of the Kantian philosophy did not of course detract from Coleridge's high estimate of Kant, but, on the contrary, added to Kantianism the high authority of an ancient and sound tradition. It was not the conception of the active mind that was new in philosophy, but the heresy of the Lockean psychology.

In the second place, Coleridge sought to clarify the difference between the Reason and the Understanding by reviving the ancient distinction between "intuition" and "tuition," or, as Milton phrased it, between "intuitive" and "discursive" reason. Here again he appeals to the seventeenth century. "I have followed Hooker, Sanderson, Milton, etc.," he says, in *Biographia Literaria*,[18] "in designating the *immediateness* of any act or object of knowledge by the word *intuition*, used sometimes subjectively, sometimes objectively, even as we use the word, thought, now as *the* thought, or act of thinking, and now as *a* thought, or the object of our reflection." By this reintroduction of ancient terminology, Coleridge brought his theory of knowledge into relation with the idealistic traditions from Plato down to the Cambridge Platonists, and distinguished it from English empiricism, and, to some degree, also from Kant.

[15] *Ibid.*, I, 241.
[17] *Biog. Lit. S*, I, 109.
[16] *Ibid.*
[18] *Ibid.*

The third aspect of Coleridge's indebtedness to the thought of the seventeenth century cannot be explained fully in any brief statement, and it is possible here only to indicate its general nature. It is related to Coleridge's dissatisfaction with the final results of Kant's theory of knowledge. It may be stated in this way, that Kant provided but a poor propaedeutic, or no propaedeutic at all, to the fourth Gospel, with its doctrine of the Logos, so dear to Coleridge. The philosophy of Kant does not permit a man to believe that he can see God. His knowledge is limited to the world of phenomena; the noumena behind these appearances remain unknowable. Moreover, Coleridge complained, the Kantian Ideas of Reason, such as God, freedom, and immortality, are merely regulative of our experience, and can never themselves become the objects of knowledge or be grasped as realities, and thus become constitutive as well as regulative of our knowledge. Coleridge wanted to regard them as realities, and our Reason as the organ of insight into them. Hegel sought to transcend this dichotomy of Kant by his famous trichotomy of thesis, antithesis, and synthesis. Coleridge's thought pursued a path somewhat parallel to that of Hegel. He has much to say about trichotomy, and his homiletic writings and his notes on the English divines have a number of diagrams illustrating this mystery. To put it briefly, Coleridge tried hard to make the Kantian epistemology point to a position beyond itself, a position essentially Platonic. For, although Kant may have been the Moses who led philosophy out of the wilderness of empiricism, he did certainly not, in Coleridge's opinion, succeed in returning himself to the Promised Land.

Coleridge would never classify philosophers into Kantians and non-Kantians. He reserved the primacy here to Plato. "In the only accurate sense of the term," Coleridge wrote to J. Gooden in 1820, "there neither are, have been, or ever will be but two essentially different Schools of Philosophy: the Platonic, and the Aristotelean. To the latter, but with a somewhat nearer approach to the Platonic, Immanuel Kant belonged; to the former Bacon and Leibnitz and in his riper and better years Berkeley."[19] In terms of this antinomy he phrased a penetrating and suggestive comment on Hooker: he called him a "giant of the race Aristotle *versus* Plato. . . . An ample and most ordonnant conceptionist, to the tranquil empyrean of ideas he has not ascended."[20] Coleridge deeply admired Bacon, and in *The Friend* and other places he argues, to the surprise of the modern reader, for "the substantial correspondence of the genuine Platonic doctrine and logic with those of Lord Bacon."[21] In the letter to Gooden already quoted he explains succinctly:

[19] Griggs, *Unp. Letters*, II, 264-65.   [20] Shedd, V, 36.
[21] *Ibid.*, V, 380.

He for whom Ideas are constitutive, will in effect be a Platonist—and in those, for whom they are regulative only, Platonism is but a hollow affectation. Dryden *could* not have been a Platonist—Shakespeare, Milton, Dante, Michael Angelo, and Rafael could not have been other than Platonists. Lord Bacon, who never read Plato's Works, taught pure Platonism in his *great* Work the Novum Organum, and abuses his divine Predecessor for fantastic nonsense, which he had been the first to explode.[22]

Platonism was the guiding and directive impulse also in Coleridge's reading of the divines and in his attempt to find the metaphysical bases of religion. It drew him naturally to the fourth Gospel and to St. Paul.

The first three Gospels show the history, that is, the fulfilment of the prophecies, in the facts. St. John declares explicitly the doctrine, oracularly, and without comment, because, being pure reason, it can only be proved by itself. For Christianity proves itself, as the sun is seen by its own light. Its evidence is involved in its existence. St. Paul writes more particularly for the dialectic understanding; and proves the doctrines which were capable of such proof by common logic.[23]

In such a passage Coleridge is using a Kantian terminology, but for his own purposes; the "pure reason" is not what Kant expounded, but the Logos interpreted in the Platonic tradition. Coleridge's highest praise for the work of Leighton, his favorite British divine, is that it is "Plato glorified by St. Paul."[24] However deeply the philosophy of his German contemporaries may have influenced him, at the most it but provided him with a modern approach to some ancient ways of thinking.

The decline in English literature and religion with the advent of the eighteenth century Coleridge attributed mainly to this lapse of idealistic philosophy as an active force permeating the intelligence of the nation. "Idea," the key word in Platonism, was debased from its technical meaning to stand, in popular use, for merely a concept. "It is *noticeable*," he writes in the margin of Jeremy Taylor, "that this is the only instance I have met in any English classic before the Revolution of the word 'idea' used as synonymous with a mental image."[25] Such an observation, though it may not prove to be literally accurate, may be of immense suggestion to the modern student. We may be better informed than Coleridge regarding the extent to which intellectual security was already broken up in the seventeenth century, and we are more alert than he was to recognize and enjoy this aspect of the period, as furnishing an analogy with our own age. But this contemporaneity in our interpretation is itself a danger, and we may be unduly neglecting the

---

[22] Griggs, *Unp. Letters*, II, 266. Cf. *Table Talk S*, July 2, 1830.

[23] Shedd, VI, 264. However, Paul's Epistle to the Ephesians he calls the "divinest composition of man." *Ibid.*, VI, 321.

[24] *Ibid.*, V, 370.   [25] *Ibid.*, V, 246.

aspect of the seventeenth century which drew Coleridge to it. Professor
Lovejoy has contended that the essential philosophy of Kant was anticipated by the Cambridge Platonists.[26] But Coleridge long ago discovered in Richard Baxter even that principle of trichotomy by means
of which he was able to transcend the difficulties left by Kant's philosophy:

> Among Baxter's philosophical merits, we ought not to overlook, that the
> substitution of Trichotomy for the old and still general plan of Dichotomy in
> the method and disposition of Logic, which forms so prominent and substantial
> an excellence in Kant's Critique of the Pure Reason, of the Judgment, and the
> rest of his works, belongs originally to Richard Baxter, a century before Kant;
> —and this not as a hint, but as a fully evolved and systematically applied
> principle. Nay, more than this;—Baxter grounded it on an absolute idea pre-
> supposed in all intelligential acts: whereas Kant takes it only as a fact in which
> he seems to anticipate or suspect some yet deeper truth latent, and hereafter
> to be discovered.[27]

This extraordinary discovery is introduced here, not to discuss its soundness, but to illustrate Coleridge's susceptibility to the idealistic tenor
of the thought of the seventeenth century, and his readiness to re-
interpret, in the light of more recent critiques of the human intellect,
the convictions and insights of "the rich and robust intellects" of our
elder divines, whose works, he said, were "shot through with refracted
light from the not risen but rising truth."[28] One may say of much of
Coleridge's speculation in philosophy, religion, and literature, what he
himself said of *The Friend*, that he was "upholding some principles both
of taste and philosophy, adopted by the great men of Europe, from the
middle of the fifteenth till toward the close of the seventeenth century."[29]

It will doubtless have been noticed that Coleridge was constantly
lamenting that his critical and philosophical efforts—which we now usually assume to have been representative of his age—had to make their
appeal to an unregenerate and contrary public. Whether he really was
so isolated intellectually is not our problem here. But it is certain that
his philosophy and criticism reflect a type of mind not much in favor
in our day, and in danger of neglect due to our sheer unwillingness to
understand it. To read him intelligently and profitably we must remind
ourselves that his "anticipated sympathies," to borrow an expression

---

[26] Arthur O. Lovejoy, "Kant and the English Platonists," in *Essays Philosophical and Psychological in Honor of William James*, pp. 263-302. The statement
has, however, been assailed as an inadequate interpretation of Kant. See René
Wellek, *Immanuel Kant in England*.

[27] Shedd, V, 355.

[28] *Ibid.*, V, 113.

[29] *Ibid.*, II, 526.

from his marginalia to Donne's sermons, were different from our own. We shall dull the edge of Coleridge's criticism if, in our enthusiasm over his psychological penetration, we allow ourselves to pass lightly over all his philosophical idealism. It may be wise or necessary to translate Coleridge into the idiom of our generation, but not until we have mastered his own idiom.

It is a weakness of our time that descriptive psychology is constantly overreaching itself and attempting the work of criticism, which is beyond its scope and power. In his *The Seventeenth Century Background,* Mr. Basil Willey has analyzed the philosophy of Hobbes.

> Very nearly every statement of Hobbes can be reduced either to hatred and contempt of schoolmen and clerics, or to fear of civil war and love of ordered living in a stable commonwealth. A certain belief is of the kind which discourages enquiry, or weakens the authority of kings, therefore it is false and pernicious. Another belief, on the contrary, favours "speculation of bodies natural," the favourite pursuit in which Hobbes had been interrupted by the civil commotions; or it buttresses the lawful authority of sovereigns—therefore it is true.[30]

This is psychological explanation, and as such is neither new nor profound nor likely to be disputed; the novelty of this treatment of the theme lies in the implied assumption that there is nothing more to be said. The process of direct valuation, the exercise of the normative judgment, is carefully eliminated. Throughout Mr. Willey's book we find the same assumption as to how the question of truth is to be approached; we learn that in as much as all attempts of the seventeenth century to state truth were "dominated by a suasive purpose" their meaning can be exhausted by a psychological analysis of their origins. "What we have to look out for," he says, "in reading the philosophers of Western Europe, is the emotional or social determinant which makes their work what it is"[31]—advice which, so far as it goes, is excellent. The trouble with this as the final and complete method of dealing with "truth" is that it is paralyzing. Something must be added to make it humane and profitable. Psychological insight into a philosopher's mind is not the exact equivalent of, or sufficient substitute for, a philosophical insight into his doctrine. Coleridge dealt with the central doctrine of Hobbes in a passing remark in *The Friend:*

> Hobbes has said, that laws without the sword are but bits of parchment. How far this is true, every honest man's heart will best tell him, if he will content himself with asking his own heart, and not falsify the answer by his notions concerning the hearts of other men. But were it true, still the fair answer would be—Well! but without the laws the sword is but a piece of iron.[32]

[30] *The Seventeenth Century Background,* p. 95.
[31] *Ibid.,* p. 93.   [32] Shedd, II, 160.

This may also be viewed as a psychological observation, but there emerges from the psychology a philosophical evaluation which elucidates the doctrine of Hobbes more than a whole chapter on social determinants. The introspection is characteristic of Coleridge, but equally so is his method of dealing with ideas as ideas and his faith that the human mind has the power to cope critically with them. And the penetration and precision with which he defines the issue must be acknowledged by the adherents of both sides of the debate.

If we approach Coleridge with a willingness to master his ideas and his philosophical idiom, the effort will not be lost. We shall at least follow more accurately his literary perceptions, which were both profound and acute even though sometimes erratic. But it is possible that we may also restore a needed balance to our interpretation of the seventeenth century. We have been too ready, perhaps, to lend to it emphasis derived from our contemporaneous thought, searching with a quick sympathy for any distintegrating processes that might be regarded as anticipations of the modernity of our own generation. Coleridge's sympathies were definitely on the other side, and that is the reason why so much of his criticism seems on the first reading to "date." Throughout it we are exposed to a form of philosophical speculation and exploration which we may have believed to be happily obsolete. But it would be rash to relegate it to the rubbish heap. It recurs even in so modern a poet as Hart Crane, who seems to have read Coleridge with understanding. In his admirable little essay on "Modern Poetry" Crane says: "poetic prophecy in the case of the seer has nothing to do with factual production or with futurity. It is a peculiar type of perception, capable of apprehending some absolute and timeless concept of the imagination with astounding clarity and conviction."[33] These words might be used as a motto for any collection of Coleridge's criticism. This is not the place to settle the many literary and philosophical questions raised by Coleridge, and least of all to examine in detail the soundness of Coleridge's version of philosophical idealism. But a careful student of his criticism will not pass over it lightly, nor will a wise reader ignore this aspect of a great mind. For we shall err profoundly in our literary and philosophical studies if we hastily deny that the desire to escape from the tyranny of the "appetencies" is also one of the persistent "appetencies" in human nature.

[33] *Collected Poems of Hart Crane* (New York: 1933), p. 178.

THE SEVENTEENTH CENTURY

COLERIDGE'S TABLE OF SYMBOLS

Coleridge frequently uses these symbols as short cuts in writing and gives an explanatory table in several places. In addition, he writes §¶ to indicate sections within paragraphs.

= equivalent to

+ together with

× multiplied into: and in moral or spiritual subjects, it signifies a mutual interpenetration: thus the Finite Will × the Reason = Faith; or Faith is the focal energy from the convergency of the Reason and the Will, or the total Act of the entire Man arising from the interpenetration of the Reason and the Will.

χ = disparate from: thus Prudence χ Virtue

✕ = opposite to: thus Sweet ✕ Sour

✗ = contrary to: thus Bitter ✗ Sweet

The Seventeenth Century

INTRODUCTION

In studying the seventeenth century, Coleridge not only read the histories written in the period, but also such eighteenth-century surveys as the work of James Ralph. His continued interest in this field is shown by the fact that he read Miss Lucy Aikens's *Memoirs of the Court of James I*, published in 1822, and her *Memoirs of the Court of Charles I*, 1833. He made himself acquainted with contemporary pamphlets and tracts, with speeches, and with a number of biographies. Among the latter the *Life of Colonel Hutchinson* by his widow Lucy was considered of highest importance, and word of it went around in Coleridge's circle. Thomas Poole recommended it to Josiah Wedgwood. He wrote:

> There is a book lately published which I suppose you have seen; but if you have not I am sure it will give you great pleasure to read. I mean the Life of Col. Hutchinson, one of King Charles Judges, written by his wife, who was a Model for Women. I am sure that the Book will do more good than any which has been published these last twenty years.[a]

Dorothy Wordsworth had to wait for an opportunity to read the book, for her brother and his wife had been reading it, and William "intends to read it over again." She says that William "speaks of it with unqualified approbation."[b]

Always reading critically, Coleridge compared sources and accepted no authority without question. He investigated for himself the problem of authorship of the *Eikon Basilike,* and he felt as free to call attention to errors in the writings of such men as Raleigh, Clarendon, and Burnet as in less famous works. He was also frequently able to use his wide knowledge of church history in clarifying phases of political history.

When his comments on the historical events of the century are assembled, they provide insight into the ferment of liberal movements which characterize the age, and they particularly illuminate the great

[a] July 30, 1807. Quoted by Meteyard, *Group of Englishmen*, p. 331.
[b] Dorothy to Lady Beaumont, Feb. 17 [Postmark], 1807. Wordsworth, *Family Letters*, I, 294.

struggle between the authority of the crown and the liberty of the people. He made an interesting contrast between the prudential motives of the leaders in the time of Elizabeth and the "fulness of grand principle" which marked the patriots in the days of Charles I and Cromwell. He recognized that the just administration of the law and the protection of the individual by law were fundamental and inviolable principles of the English nation and therefore held that Charles I deserved death for using the authority of the king to destroy the law. He saw that there was good in the point of view of both opposing forces in the Civil War and showed that William III owed his success to the fact that a resolution of the conflict was accomplished by combining the best from each side.

In some respects Coleridge's thoughts about history are very modern. He stressed the value of contemporary materials and deplored the fact that many seventeenth-century pamphlets and flying sheets had been destroyed. He therefore emphasized the necessity of compiling a history of Charles I, the Republic, and the Protectorate before such materials completely disappeared. The purpose in studying history, he said, is to discover principles instead of to learn facts. It throws light on the present and aids in anticipating the future, for in the course of history the same principles are seen to recur with similar consequences. In Philosophical Lecture XI, March 8, 1819,[c] he cited the Civil War as one of "three great instructive events in history" which hold "lessons of wisdom and caution." Lamb spoke of Coleridge's own practice of "applying past inferences to modern *data*."[d] One of the most brilliant examples of this is his comparison of the conditions leading to the restoration of Charles II with those connected with the return of the Bourbons.[e] One principle, however, which had been advanced by William III and reiterated by Coleridge was not mastered by England in time to prevent the situation since World War II: this principle was that her place in "the first rank of nations" rested on her "commercial, manufactory, and colonial superiority," and that "such a nation, rather such an *empire*, could not have a separate interest from that of the great European Commonwealth of nations."[f]

---

[c] Coburn, *Phil. Lect.*, p. 318.

[d] Lamb, *Letters*, I, 198.

[e] *Essays*, II, 532-33. See below.

[f] Edwin Berck Dike, "Coleridge Marginalia in Henry Brooke's *The Fool of Quality*," *Huntington Library Bulletin*, I (November, 1931), 161.

Afterwards he remarked on the character of the age of Elizabeth and James I at the commencement, in which intellect predominated, over that of Charles I in which moral feeling prevailed.[1]

In the course of the evening Coleridge among other things remarked, no doubt in a great degree fancifully, upon the singular manner in which the number *three* triumphed everywhere in everything . . .

Three great metaphysicians—Hobbes, Kant, and Hartley.
Three great philosophers—Plato, Aristotle, and Bacon.
Three great epics—the Iliad, the Inferno, and Paradise Lost. . . .
Three great astronomers—Copernicus, Galileo, and Newton.
Three great satirical characters—by Dryden, Pope, and Churchill.
Three remarkable prose sentences—by Raleigh, Hooker, and Milton . . .

He was asked to name the three great satirical characters, and he mentioned either Dryden's Buckingham, or Shaftesbury, Pope's Addison, and Churchill's Fitzpatrick; the three prose sentences were by Raleigh at the close of his "History of the World"; by Hooker in praise of Law, in his "Ecclesiastical Polity"; and by Milton, on the value of good books, in his *Areopagitica*. They were not long, and he repeated them.[2]

The difference between the state of mind in the reign of Elizabeth, and in that of Charles I. is astonishing. In the former period there was an amazing development of power, but all connected with prudential purposes—an attempt to reconcile the moral feeling with the full exercise of the powers of the mind, and the accomplishment of certain practical ends. Then lived Bacon, Burghley, Sir Walter Raleigh, Sir Philip Sidney, and a galaxy of great men, statesmen, lawyers, politicians, philosophers, and poets; and it is lamentable that they should have degraded their mighty powers to such base designs and purposes, dissolving the rich pearls of their great faculties in a worthless acid, to be drunken by a harlot. What was seeking the favor of the Queen, to a man like Bacon, but the mere courtship of harlotry?

Compare this age with that of the republicans: that indeed was an awful age, as compared with our own. England may be said to have then overflowed from the fulness of grand principle—from the greatness

[1] H. C. Robinson's Records, Dec. 5, Thursday, 1811, in Dr. Williams's Library. Also printed by Raysor, *Shakes. Crit.*, II, 216.
[2] Oct. 20, 1811. Collier, *Seven Lect.*, pp. xxix-xxxi. This is similar to Lecture VII, p. 69.

which men felt in themselves, abstracted from the prudence with which they ought to have considered, whether their principles were, or were not, adapted to the condition of mankind at large. Compare the revolution then effected with that of a day not long past, when the bubbling-up and overflowing was occasioned by the elevation of the dregs—when there was a total absence of all principle, when the dregs had risen from the bottom to the top, and thus converted into a scum, founded a monarchy to be the poisonous band and misery of the rest of mankind.[3]

Let us throw ourselves back to the age of Elizabeth, and call up to mind the heroes, the warriors, the statesmen, the poets, the divines, and the moral philosophers, with which the reign of the virgin queen was illustrated. Or if we be more strongly attracted by the moral purity and greatness, and that sanctity of civil and religious duty, with which the tyranny of Charles the First was struggled against, let us cast our eyes in the hurry of admiration, round that circle of glorious patriots— but do not let us be persuaded, that each of these, in his course of discipline, was uniformly helped forward by those with whom he associated, or by those whose care it was to direct him. Then as now, existed objects to which the wisest attached undue importance; then, as now, judgment was misled by factions and parties—time wasted in controversies fruitless, except as far as they quickened the faculties; then, as now, minds were venerated or idolized, which owed their influence to the weakness of their contemporaries rather than to their own power. Then, though great actions were wrought, and great works in literature and science produced, yet the general taste was capricious, fantastical, or groveling; and in this point, as in all others, was youth subject to delusion, frequent in proportion to the liveliness of the sensibility, and strong as the strength of the imagination.[4]

The years previous to Charles & even during the reformation are characterized by an astonishing credulity in men even of ability & research; this may be attributed to the absence of all psychological knowledge—one fearful result was the revival of witchcraft—it ought to humble people that this was not an age of barbarism, but during the revival of letters, at the time of a Galileo, and under a purer and reforming religion.[5]

[3] *Ibid.*, pp. 34-35.
[4] Introduction to Section II of *The Friend*, III, 28-29.
[5] Report of Philosophical Lecture XI, March 8, 1819. British Museum, MSS Egerton, 3057, p. 2.

Of unexampled measures the causes and effects might be deemed uncertain; the prophecies of philosophical prescience too often acquire authority only from their accomplishment. But these Bills though most strange, are not new. Lord Grenville professes to imitate the "precautions of our ancestors"; and the precedents, which he would pursue, are those of Elizabeth and Charles the second. To ascertain therefore what effects they *will* produce, and to what purposes they *will* be employed, we need only revolve the pages of history and discover what effects they *did* produce, and to what purposes they *were* employed. The measures of Elizabeth were imitated by the first James, and deemed safe precedents by the first Charles; who "wisely and spiritedly adopted such provisions and passed such laws, as gave a security to the Monarchy, as the *essential part* and pillar of the Constitution.[6]

And it is in imitation of these illustrious examples, that he (Lord Grenville) as a servant of the Crown, called on their Lordships to pursue similar measures of precaution and safety! ! Such measures, good Lord Grenville, produced that evil commotion, *vulgarly* called, the great REBELLION! The measures and laws of the second Charles followed up by the second James, produced that other commotion, *vulgarly* called, a Revolution.[7]

The interests of the King both in the first and in the second acceptation of the term did indeed require James (& should have impelled Elizabeth) to protect & strengthen the Bishoprics, & with these all the other Church Dignitaries dependent on the Crown by vesting the manors to the former & the tythes to the Latter—but instead of this he & the infatuated Bishops kept up their Ecclesiastic Courts with Lay Chancellors, an impudent Brummagem-brass[8] Counterfeit of Church-Discipline, with even the white of the Blindman's Bell rubbed off; or with enough only remaining to make it look dirty—which gave them no real, diffusive influence as Individuals, while it was yearly weakening the true power of the Episcopacy—Thus while James & his unhappy Successor was [*sic*] doing one right thing by halves, & so that the half remaining leavened the new half & ever rendered it an additional cause of Odium, they entirely neglected the other equally imperious Desideratum, as important in relation to the third Branch of the Legislature as

[6] Coleridge gives as reference: "Lord Grenville's speech, Friday, Nov. 6, 1795, quoted on the authority of the Senator, or Clarendon's Parliamentary Chronicle, page 121 of the third number of the present session."

[7] *Plot Discovered*, pp. 29-30. Reprinted in *Essays*, I, 78-79.

[8] "Brummagem" for Birmingham is still sometimes heard in England. I am indebted to Miss Coburn for this reading.

the former was for the second, & with an ex-parliamentary respect more important than either, viz. the increase of the City & Town Livings, with the Foundation of Lectureships &c. by Act of Parliament. Elizabeth's Policy & Measures as Head of the Church I regard as by far the greatest Draw-back from the Glory of her Character & Government.[9]

Elizabeth had some excuse—nay, in the first years of her reign a justifying cause—viz. the bringing the moderate Romanists, all who retaining both names yet layed the main stress on the *Catholic*, to an outward conformity which in the next generation would probably become an inward consent. But when the Passion or Policy of the Roman Court had put an end to this, and to all rational hope of succeeding by any other than the alone honest way and mean of presenting Truth in it's truest & entirest form, the conduct of James & his Bishops was senseless—and of the latter inexcusable—for they had not James's personal recollections of hard usage. However, the Result was that the Cause of Protestantism was stopt all over Europe. The vast influence which the Church of so great a Monarchy as the British was or under the Plantagenet Breed would have, being wasted in repeating bloody Queen Mary to the Scottish presbyterians, and the English Antiprelatic Episcopalians.[10]

The boasted Scheme, the darling of the loathsome Lackwit, James I, and so much *lauded* to their indelible infamy by his Prelates, for a Union of the Protestant & Romish Pseudo-Catholic Churches, was a mere plot for the old conspiracy of Despotism with Superstition—or as James's Theory justifies us in saying, for realizing the blasphemous superstition of civil autocracy by the less absurd & not more blasphemous Superstition of Papal Hierarchy. It is evident that all James would have required, would have been a renunciation of the Dethroning & regicidal Right of the Pope, and little more than a few quibbling qualifications respecting the Sacramental Mysteries and the Hyperdulia due to the Virgin would have satisfied the majority of the Court Bishops & Arminian Divines. The Resistance even to the Stake of the Scottish Presbyterians, and the abandonment of the Reformed Churches in France & Geneva, were doubtless foreseen with delight by the Puritan Hating & fearing Scot—who even after his providential escape from Fawks could not suppress his Puritans *"worthy of fire."*[11]

[9] Notebook 30, fol. 41 verso-42 recto. British Museum, Add. MSS, 47,527. Printed for the first time.

[10] British Museum, MSS Egerton, 2801, fol. 195. Printed for the first time.

[11] Notebook 30, fol. 19 verso-20 recto. British Museum, Add. MSS, 47,527. Printed for the first time.

We may have good Reason to infer Plots, but that Reason will not discover the Particularities of them; otherwise there could be no Plot at all. But yet I will comply with the Objection, and say that, all the while Coleman corresponded and, as well before as afterwards, in the Reign of King Charles the Second, the Plot was to introduce the Catholic Religion by such means as the Politicians of that Interest thought most conducing, and that was by a Toleration of all dissenting Sects, whereby to destroy the Church of England established, and not by active force, Murders, Poisons, Assignations, and the like; and not to grasp at the secular Power directly, whereof the Friendship they desired to defend them in what they went about. And my Reason for this is, that, after King James the Second became possessed of the Crown, and the whole active force of the Nation was in his Hands, who espoused the Cause of his Religion with all Manner of Zeal, that Method, I mean of Toleration, and no other, was pursued. The King had an Army, but there was no shew then of employing it in that way. The Papists seemed all to decline the Ways of Violence, and went into Chicane and Matters of Law, building upon a supposed Power in the Crown of Dispensing &c. They set up the Papists' Invention, adopted in the English Chancery to procure Elections, and favourable Laws to be made in Parliament. They could not but consider a Nation, so aliened as England was, could not be regained impetuously, but tried with all their Arts and Policies to gain Ground by Steps. I may not doubt that as Fanatics, from Toleration, leaped into comprehension, and then looked up higher for Power to exclude all others, so the Papists had gone from Toleration to comprehension, and, having had Success, would have compassed the Use of all the Powers and Authorities they work with in Roman Catholic Countries. And this was the true Popish Plot; and I doubt not but it is the same, as well of Fanatic as Papist still. It is therefore a Special Note, for all Protestants to consider what transcendent Benefits they enjoy in the true primitive Christian Church established in England, which once broken, the true Exercise and use of Christianity will, to all intents be rescinded, and, early or late, Ecclesiastical Tyranny and Violence, nay downright Atheism, and all manner of Anti-Christian Blasphemy and Heresy will enter and take Possession.[12]

If a Writer, tho' an eminent Member of their own Church, Burnet or Leighton for instance, honestly let out a few unpleasant Truths, it

[12] Transcript of MS by S. T. C., "Toleration of Dissenters in reign of Charles II, a plot to re-introduce Romanism." In the possession of A. H. B. Coleridge, who has given me permission to publish the comment.

is enough to say—For all this we have but the suspicious authority of the prejudiced Burnet. If you ask proofs of this prejudice & Partiality, these very passages are adduced. So if you support a charge against Laud by quoting Bishop Hacket, it is enough to say, that Hacket was the Zealous Friend of Archbishop Williams—when no other perhaps could have come at the information. In short, every man is to be a Liar, who relates ought which the Party do not like to hear—as soon as a possible motive can be drawn from any one of the Relations in which the Relator must have stood in order to be a competent Historian.[13]

The darker charges, that Bishop Hackett thought right to suppress—& the Letters to the H. of Commons which Sir E. Cokes (one of the Committee of 22 appointed to read it) dared read but a line & a half—& then sent it sealed to his Majesty, who read it, threw it into the fire, & returned his thanks to the Committee—all strange![14]

A wise & rightly feeling Historian will find it hard to decide which on the whole was the more despicable & worthless character, of the four Stuart Kings—all cruel, all liars, all morally cowards, and two loathsome; but he will have no difficulty in deciding that no four succeeding Monarchs ever blotted the English Annals before, or since. O favored Land! while other countries date their ruin and degradation from the vices & follies of their kings, for thee they were the means & occasions of, Greatness, Liberty and pure Religion. Inconsist. in Miss Aikens concluding Chapter—James I the best of the 4 owing wholly to his Learning and Love of Learned men and learned Conversation.

It cannot and need not be denied that the Religion common to Luther and Calvin and—the exceptions being so few, and these too doubtful, we may add—to all the *first* Reformers—is more favorable to Whig Ideas of Liberty, than the ever-stretching Arminianism introduced into the English by the Court Prelates of the first James & Charles in it's stead—not, however, from the parity of the Ministry & the substitution or predominance of the Presbyterians for or over the Bishops, but from the Symbolical Character of the former.[15]

[13] Notebook 30, fol. 62. British Museum, Add. MSS, 47,527. Printed for the first time.

[14] Notebook 30, fol. 19 recto. British Museum, Add. MSS, 47,527. Printed for the first time.

[15] Notebook 30, fol. 17 verso-18 recto. British Museum, Add. MSS, 47,527. Printed for the first time.

The Ussean overrators of the Performance of the Negative Duties and the high tone they affect over those who are in all respects as blameless in their lives as themselves, only because they do not choose to write their ordinary notes, and Household Accounts all in Large Capitals. Charles's personal non-immorality had no effect even on his Court & immediate Followers (Profligacy being the general & most approved Mark of Loyalty) (i.e. *Re Nello*-ism) much less on the Nation.[16]

I know no portion of history which a man might write with so much pleasure as that of the great struggle in the time of Charles I.,[17] because he may feel the profoundest respect for both parties. The side taken by any particular person was determined by the point of view which such person happened to command at the commencement of the inevitable collision, one line seeming straight to this man, another line to another. No man of that age saw *the* truth, the whole truth; there was not light enough for that. The consequence, of course, was a violent exaggeration of each party for the time. The King became a martyr, and the Parliamentarians traitors, and *vice versâ*. The great reform brought into act under William the Third combined the principles truly contended for by Charles and his Parliament respectively: the great revolution of 1831 has certainly, to an almost ruinous degree, dislocated those principles of government again. As to Hampden's speech,[18] no doubt it means a declaration of passive obedience to the sovereign, as the creed of an English Protestant individual; to every man, Cromwell and all, would have said as much, it was the anti-papistical tenet, and almost vauntingly asserted on occasions by Protestants up to that time. But it implies nothing of Hampden's creed as to the duty of Parliament.[19]

This is not a logical age. A friend lately gave me some political pamphlets of the time of Charles I. and the Cromwellate. In them the premisses are frequently wrong, but the deductions are almost always legitimate; whereas, in the writings of the present day, the premisses are commonly sound, but the conclusions false. I think a great deal of commendation is due to the University of Oxford, for preserving the

[16] Notebook 30, fol. 19 recto. British Museum, Add. MSS, 47,527. Printed for the first time.
[17] For the other comments on the time of Charles I see under Baxter, *Life of Himself*, Book I, Part I, pp. 25, 40, 66, 71, and Part II, p. 374.
[18] On his impeachment with the other four members, 1642.
[19] May 8, 1833. *Table Talk S*, pp. 448-49.

study of logic in the schools.   It is a great mistake to suppose geometry
any substitute for it.[20]

It was never my purpose, and it does not appear the want of the
age, to bring together the rules and inducements of worldly prudence.
But to substitute these for the laws of reason and conscience, or even
to confound them under one name, is a prejudice, say rather a profanation, which I became more and more reluctant to flatter by even
the appearance of assent, though it were only in a point of form and
technical arrangement.

At a time, when my thoughts were thus employed, I met with a
volume of old tracts, published during the interval from the captivity of
Charles the First to the restoration of his son.   Since my earliest manhood it had been among my fondest regrets, that a more direct and frequent reference had not been made by our historians to the books,
pamphlets, and flying sheets of that momentous period, during which
all the possible forms of truth and error (the latter being themselves
for the greater part caricatures of truth) bubbled up on the surface
of the public mind, as in the ferment of chaos.   It would be difficult to
conceive a notion or a fancy, in politics, ethics, theology, or even in
physics and physiology, which had not been anticipated by the men of
that age: in this as in most other respects sharply contrasted with the
products of the French revolution, which was scarcely more characterized
by its sanguinary and sensual abominations than (to borrow the words
of an eminent living poet) by

A dreary want at once of books and men.

The parliament's army was not wholly composed of mere fanatics.
There was no mean proportion of enthusiasts: and that enthusiasm must
have been of no ordinary grandeur, which could draw from a 'common
soldier, in an address to his comrades, such a dissuasive from acting in
"the cruel spirit of fear!" such and such sentiments, as are contained
in the following extract, which I would rescue from oblivion, both for
the honor of our forefathers, and in proof of the intense difference between the republicans of that period, and the democrats, or rather dema-
gogues, of the present . . .[21]

[20] Jan. 4, 1823.   *Table Talk S*, p. 262.
[21] *The Friend*, Section II, Essay I, III, 68-70.

The eighth tract, 1649, in a volume of tracts relating to the times of Cromwell.[22]

Justice upon the Remonstrance of the Army, by William Sedgwick —highly interesting. I must make myself better acquainted with this W. Sedgwick, who re-excites the regret I have so often felt, that a History of Charles I., the Republic, and Protectorate, were not written with especial reference to the numberless Pamphlets, Books, &c., then published, or while yet there is time.

But, alas, every year destroys its quota; the noble, probably unique, collection of Sir W. Lawson's Predecessor, left out of spite to the Butler, lasted the Grocers, Chandlers, and Druggists of Penrith and Kendal during a destruction of 20 years and more!— W. S. appears an instance of an Independent sublimated into a theosophic Behmenist, greatly to the improvement of his political insight at least. Several passages on the Spirit of Fear, as symptomatic of hollowness and weakness, and the contrary spirit of co-inherence, are almost sublime. Sedgwick's views of immortality seem, however, to coincide with those of Spinoza, rather than with Behmen's. See p. 25, last paragraph, and the three or four following pages.

The Preface to "England's Dust and Ashes raked up; or, the King and People beguiled."

The King therefore cannot be capable of constraint from his vassals; for whom, if they miscarry for want of temper at his correction, he is said, in a qualified sense, to be generally accountable; which could by no means be, if his power were not above all men, and his dominion absolute.

Here we have an open avowal of arbitrary monarchy, which Charles I. encouraged in his followers, while he disavowed it in the public papers, written for him and in his name, but with his full consent and authority, by Clarendon, Falkland and Culpepper.[23]

Hartley Coleridge, NORTHERN WORTHIES, I, 300.

That Charles *wished* to be free of Parliamentary controul there can be no doubt, any profession of his own notwithstanding; for he was a man, a King, and a High-Church-man; but that he was plotting to make himself absolute by force of arms, there is no better proof than the reports of spies, the wild talk of a few hot-brained drunken cavaliers, and the apprehensions of some who had indeed occasion to dread the exercise

[22] *Notes Theolog.*, p. 200. This note appears on a blank page at the end of the volume of tracts.

[23] "Notes Written in a Volume of Tracts Relating to the Civil Wars," *Notes Theolog.*, p. 201.

of his lawful prerogative. To these weak grounds of suspicion, we perhaps may add the secret insinuations of foreign states, particularly France and Sweden, then respectively governed by Richelieu and Oxenstiern, two of the *profoundest politicians* that ever lived.

Is not all this asserted too positively? Charles's letters to the Duke of Hamilton and Lord Strafford tend to impress a contrary belief. It was a confusion of the idea, or ultimate aim, with the historic genesis, in which the idea gradually revealed and realised itself, which misled both Charles and his father. And what James *thought,* Charles acted. Because the crown has been the seed out of which grew the stem, *i.e.* the parliamentary power, James reasoned as if the stem were still included in the seed, whereas the seed had necessarily rotted away in order to reappear as the flower,—the corolla and seed-vessel of the plant. S. T. C.[24]

Notes on "The Royalist's Defence, Vindicating the King's Proceedings in the Late War Made Against Him," p. 48.

By this it appears, that when the two Houses have passed a bill for an Act of Parliament, and to it the King's Royal assent is had, the Parliament's power ends, and then begins the authority of the Judges of the Realm, whose office is (the case being regularly brought before them) first to judge whether the Act itself be good, and, if binding, then to declare the meaning of the words thereof. And so the necessity of having a power upon emergent occasions to make new laws is supplied, and yet the fundamental grounds of the law, by this limitation of the power of the law-maker, with reference to the Judges to determine which Acts of Parliament are binding, and which void, is preserved.

In a state of society, in which the active and influencive portion of the inhabitants was small, scarcely perhaps trebling the number of the members of the two Houses—the right and power here contended for might have been wisely vested in the Judges of the Realm.

It is curious to observe, that the thinner the realm was (the less both the wealth and influence, and the less they were *diffused,*) the greater was the division of the power. It is now almost merged in the House of Commons. Formerly the Convocation, the Judges, &c., shared in it.

The dispensing power, as completory of the Law and supplying the inherent deficiency of all human provisions expressed in determinate words, is so natural and necessary a prerogative of the supreme Executive's trust, that Charles I., richly deserved death for this alone, that he had treacherously and treasonably perverted a power entrusted to

[24] Coleridge's note to Hartley Coleridge's ''Thomas Lord Fairfax,'' *Lives of the Northern Worthies* (3 vols.; London: 1852), I, 300-1.

him for the completion of Law, into a means of destroying Law and of evacuating its essential purpose—viz., the ensurance of the subject against individual will. It was an abuse of terms to say, that the King has the right of dispensing with the Laws. It can only be asserted that the King *had* a dispensing power in such or such a case—or the King has a dispensing power in *this* case. The particular case must be known and specified in order to the determination of the Right—for what is true of all ordinance is eminently true of this—the Reason and ultimate purpose of the ordinances must determine its interpretation.

Since the Revolution we have deemed it necessary to secure this principle, by throwing the *onus probandi* in each instance on the Dispenser, by *presuming* that he had *not* the power; and this is, perhaps, the wisest plan. But the substance is the same: as is evident by the fact, that, in certain emergencies, the Parliament might, and would be bound to, impeach a Minister for not dispensing (advising the King to dispense) with an existing statute.[25]

But this was the κοινὸν ψεῦδος & calamity of that age [Elizabeth's], the equivoque of *the King* including the Powers judicial, & legislative Powers by common law or irrevocable Charters, and the King in contradistinction from the Peers and the Commons, or (too often, during the Stewart Dynasty) with the Person contrasted with the supreme executive function.[26]

It appears from Clarendon's own account, that Charles himself was the first who set on foot and authorized Army-agitators, & petitions from men embodied under arms—Himself the infatuated Beginner of that abhomination which after destroying his own life, baffled every attempt to form a regular free Government, & which served Cromwell himself as the familiar Fiends serve Witches—help them to do what harm they like; but as to any good—whoo! in a whirlwind, & a blue flame, & a stink—what? bid the Devil turn traitor to Hell! It is strange that so wise a man as Clarendon did not notice this sad mistake—as he has done so many others of less, tho' great importance.[27]

[25] "Notes Written in a Volume of Tracts Relating to the Civil Wars," *Notes Theolog.*, pp. 205-6.

[26] Notebook 30, fol. 41 verso. British Museum, Add. MSS, 47,527. Printed for the first time.

[27] Notebook 18, fol. 18 verso. British Museum, Add. MSS, 47,515. Printed for the first time.

Hartley Coleridge, NORTHERN WORTHIES, *I, 341.*

It was a most ungentlemanlike act of the weekly-fast-ordaining
Parliament or their agents to open Charles's letters to his wife, and all
historians who make use of them to blacken his character ought to forfeit the character of gentlemen.

How could a faithful historian avoid it? The Parliament had acted
ab initio on their convictions of the King's bad faith, and of the utter
insincerity of his promises and professions; and surely the justification
or condemnation of their acts must depend on, or be greatly modified by
the question—were these convictions well grounded, and afterwards
proved to be so by evidence, which could without danger to the state be
advanced? What stronger presumption can we have of the certainty
of the evidences which they had previously obtained, and by the year
after year accumulation of which their suspicions had been converted
into convictions. And was Henrietta an ordinary *wife?* Was Charles
to her as Charles of Sweden to his spouse? The Swede's Queen was only
the man's wife, but Henrietta was notoriously Charles's queen, or rather
the He-queen's She-king—a *commander* in the war, meddling with and
influencing all his councils. I hold the Parliament fully justified in the
publication of the letters; much more the historian. S. T. C.[28]

There are three great instructive events in history the reflection on
which perhaps more than on any other part of human history well repays
us by the lessons of wisdom and caution which they imply—I mean the
Reformation, the Civil War, and the French Revolution.[29]

My heart dilated with honest pride, as I recalled to mind the stern
yet amiable character of the English patriots, who sought refuge on the
Continent at the Restoration! O let not the civil war under the first
Charles be paralleled with the French Revolution! In the former, the
chalice overflowed with excess of principle; in the latter, from the
fermentation of the dregs! The former, was a civil war between the
virtues and virtuous prejudices of the two parties; the latter, between
the vices. The Venetian glass of the French monarchy shivered and
flew asunder with the working of a double poison.[30]

LIFE OF HUTCHINSON, *first end-page, recto.*[31]

As the only-begotten Word was incarnate in Christ Jesus, so is the

[28] Hartley Coleridge, *Northern Worthies,* I, 341.
[29] Philosophical Lecture XI, March 8, 1819. Coburn, *Phil. Lect.*, p. 318.
[30] "Satyrane's Letters," II. Shedd, III, 524.
[31] *Memoirs of the Life of Colonel Hutchinson,* Written by his Widow Lucy.

Spirit that procedeth from the divine Word incarnate, as it were, in the written, inspired Word and by the Written Word, with the Spirit and by the Spirit in and thro' the written Word do the Father, the Son and the Spirit manifest the Will, Truth and Wisdom of God to the Redeemed thro' and in the Church.

The Word

The
Written Word   The Spirit   The Church

The
Preacher

The Word is the Prothesis, the written Word the Thesis, The Church the Antithesis, the Spirit in and by the written Word and in and by the Church the Mesothesis, and the Preacher declaring the w. word and representing the Church, the Synthesis. S. T. C.

LIFE OF HUTCHINSON, *"The Life of Mrs. Lucy Hutchinson," p. 3.*

The people, by the plenty of their country, not being forc'd to toyle for bread, have ever addicted themselfes to more generous employments.

Alas! the change! 1831.

Whether the Nation, whose mechanic or a manufacturing class is merely adequate to the supply of it's Learned & Landed Gentry, and it's Agriculturalists, is not a nobler & more prosperous, tho' less powerful, than manufacturies stimulated by a unduly extended Commerce now presents?

LIFE OF HUTCHINSON, *p. 9.*

In matters of faith his reason allwayes submitted to the word of God, and what he could not comprehend, he would believe because 'twas written.

Well may I *believe* what I do not *comprehend,* when there are so many things which I *know* yet do not *comprehend*—my Life, for instance, my Will, my rationality, &c. But let us be on our guard not to confound *com*prehending with *ap*prehending. I do not, even because I *can* not, believe what I do not *ap*prehend—i.e. I cannot assent to the

Published from the original manuscript by Rev. Julius Hutchinson (London: 1806). In describing this book, T. J. Wise says: "None of the notes contained in this volume have yet been presented." (Wise, *Ashley*, VIII, 114). The notes appear, however, in *Notes Theolog.*, pp. 169-77. It is interesting to note that Wise had a copy of this book in his library. Some of the notes, originally written in pencil, have been traced over in ink—see, for example, p. 198. Mrs. Gillman's name appears on the first flyleaf, recto. British Museum, Ashley, 4780.

meaning of words, to which I attach no meaning, tho' I may believe in the wisdom of the Utterer. But this is to believe the veracity of the Doctor, not the truth of the Doctrine. S. T. C.

LIFE OF HUTCHINSON, *p. 11.*

He was as faithfull and constant to his friends as mercifull to his enemies: nothing griev'd him more than to be oblieg'd, where he could not hope to returne itte.

The youthful Reader should be made [to] see, that this was a defect, tho' a defect symptomatic of a noble nature. Besides, except to God, we cannot be obliged without the power of making the right return: for where no more is in our power, to feel, to acknowledge, and duly to appreciate an obligation, is to return it. Nay, God himself accepts our thankfulness & obedience as a *return* for his free gifts & mercies.

LIFE OF HUTCHINSON, *p. 45.*

. . . soe as his shadow, she waited on him every where, till he was taken into that region of light, which admitts of more, and then she vanisht into nothing. ["more" is underlined by Coleridge.]

?None—i.e. of no shadow.

LIFE OF HUTCHINSON, *p. 47. Note continued on p. 48.*

The gentleman that assisted him he converted to a right beliefe in that greate poynt of predestination, he having bene before the Arminian iudgment, till upon the serious examination of both principles, and comparing them with the scriptures, Mr. Hutchinson convinc'd him of the truth, and grew so well instructed in this principle, that he was able to maintaine it against any man.

A most instructive instance of the delusions, consequent on the Logic of Dichotomy: or the antithesis of terms precluding each other or assumed so to do. Ex. gr. Necessity ✕ Freedom, Real ✕ Unreal, Spirit ✕ Body, Cause ✕ Effect. The doctrine of Predestination as built on the assumption that the distinction of the Terms implys a division of the Things—ex. gr. the Divine Reason & the Divine Will. The former is arbitrarily taken as the Antecedent & the *Cause*, the latter, as the *effect*, as a passive Clay, receiving the impression of the former—Deny this, or (as you safely may do) affirm the contrary, namely that the Will is the Antecedent and the Reason the form or Epiphany of the Will—and the whole Argument of Predestination is quashed.

LIFE OF HUTCHINSON, *p. 69.*

If any one obiect the fresh example of Queene Elizabeth, let them remember that the felicity of her reigne was the effect of her submission to her masculine and wise councellors.

But what was the cause of that submission to men chosen? of that choice of men, worthy to be submitted to? This is an old but just Answer to an old Detraction from Elizabeth's personal character.

LIFE OF HUTCHINSON, *p. 74.*

> . . . but yet the parliament shew'd such a wonderfull respect to the king, that they never mention'd him, as he was, the sole author of all those miscarriages, but imputed them to evill councellors, and gave him all the submissive language that could have bene us'd to a good prince, fixing all the guilt upon his evill councellors and ministers of state, which flattery I feare they have to answer for: I am sure they have thereby expos'd themselves to much scandall. *Editor's Note.* This is an oversight of Mrs. Hutchinson's, of which she is seldom guilty. Good policy required then, as it does now, that the king should be held incapable of wrong, and the criminality fixed on ministers, who are amenable to the law. If the patriots of that day were the inventors of this maxim, we are highly obliged to them.

I am yearly more and more inclined to question the expediency of falsehood of any kind and therefore doubt the wisdom of Mr. J. Hutchinson's censure of his high-minded Ancestress. Had the Parliament as soon as the King's own principles and passions were known to be prime movers of his Council declared the same, it might have prevented the Civil war, at all events the apparent inconsistency of their own proceedings.

LIFE OF HUTCHINSON, *p. 115.*

> There was one Mr. Widmerpoole, a man of good extraction, but reduc'd to a small fortune, had declin'd all the splendor of an old house, and sunke into the way of the middle men of the country.

The Ellipsis of the pronoun relative after the conjunction is a frequent and, I think, a graceful idiom in our elder authors. "But reduced" for "but who, reduced."

As a portrait-painter Mrs. H. unites the grace and finish of Vandyke with the life and substantive Reality of Rembrandt. By the bye, among the numerous parts, that make up that most notice-worthy Contrast of the old English Republican, and the modern mongrel-bred Jacobin, one of the most striking is the reverential value of ancient family entertained by the former, with comparative contempt of the court-derived Titles, which the Latter hates because he envies both, both alike.

LIFE OF HUTCHINSON, *p. 196, Editor's note. Coleridge's note continued on p. 197.*

> . . . the road still lay open to Lincoln, but probably Prince Rupert was

too strong and too active to let the besiegers escape any way unless they had acted with better accord amongst each other.

There is something almost fantastic in the thought, that this Prince Rupert whose character of Temerity, Brutality, Insolence, Impetuosity, and *Unreasonableness* i. e. the abandonment of Bristol is given almost in the same words by the Royalist and the Parliamentarian Historians, should have been the Inventor of Mezzo tint Engraving. The Superstition of *Royal Blood* in it's most exclusive intensity, acted on Charles's mind in the instance of this his Nephew, most ruinously for his affairs. If Charles did not authorize, he passively sanctioned, and perhaps inwardly approved of Rupert's *overly* treatment of the Duke of Newcastle and thus baffled & disgusted the chivalrous Loyalty and Devotion which nothing could alienate. Prince Rupert was the Evil Genius of Charles's *Military* Enterprizes.

LIFE OF HUTCHINSON, *p. 197.*

> Indeed, such a blow was given to the parliament interest, in all these parts, that it might well discourage the ill-affected, when even the most zealous were cast downe and gave up all for lost: but the governor, who in no occasion ever lett his courage fall, but, when things were at the lowest, recollected all his force, that his owne despondency might not contribute aniething to his mallicious fortune, at this time animated all the honest men, and expresst such vigor and cheerefullnesse, and such stedfast resolution, as disappointed all the mallignants of their hopes.

Beautiful! A woman only (tho' certainly a Woman κατ' ἐξοχήν) could have so appreciated the true grandeur of masculine virtue.

One great moral Benefit results from the study of History that it tends to free the mind from the uncharitable, the calumniating spirit of party Zeal. Take the warmest Zealot of Charles, the Martyr's cause, & let him only be an *honest* man and with the feelings of a Christian and the reflection, *"But yet* Col. Hutchinson was a Regicide" could not but attemper his Heart, could not but Christianize his antipathies. S. T. C.

LIFE OF HUTCHINSON, *p. 199, Editor's note. Comment continued on p. 200.*

> . . . it is proper here to state, that in the outset all those sects, which have since taken so many various names, joined their forces to repel the encroachments of the *Prelates,*—it would not be fair to say of the *Church of England,* whose characteristic is moderation itself,—but when they had almost crushed the Episcopalians, the Presbyterian ministers began to rise pre-eminent in power, and to shew that though they had changed the name, they by no means intended to diminish the dominion of the hierarchy.

It seems (and if it were so, it is much to be regretted) that the

Editor had not read Baxter's own Life, published by Silvester. The Rev^d. Julius Hutchinson is an honor to the C. of E. O si sic omnes! His kindred Soul would have *felt* Baxter's veracity and integrity: his freer Judgement would have discovered without difficulty the good old *Church*-presbyter's unconscious declinations from verity: & he would not here or elsewhere have used the term, Episcopalians, as synonimous with the Prelatists. Even the phrase, Presbyterian Ministers, and Presbyterian Party, Mr. H. would have found reason to place among the vulgar errors of History. The fingers of one hand would suffice to number all the *proper* Presbyterians in the Parliament at this time, or among the London Ministers. A large number of those who were afterwards ejected on the twice-infamous St. Bartholomew's Day would have been content even to retain the Prelates under the name of Patriarchs (Cant. and York) and Archbishops: indeed as to the main characteristic of the Genevan, or true Presbyterian, Discipline, the introduction of laymen as Deacons & Ruling Elders, they were almost to a man against it. Let it not be forgotten too, that their very intolerancy, to which Mr. H. does not attribute more than be answerably laid to their charge, was the intolerancy of the established Church, inherited from the Refounders of the Church under Elizabeth, & grounded on an interpretation of Schism common to them & the Prelatic and anti-parliamentary Party of the *same* Church. Remember, that the Reformers in the Church before the War, approached far more nearly to a majority, than the Protestants in the Western Church: & if the latter were not Schismatics, neither were the former.

LIFE OF HUTCHINSON, *p. 203.*

> To rayse this siege, Prince Rupert came with a great armie out of the south; the besiegers rise to fight with the prince, and Newcastle drew all his force out of Yorke to ioyne with him, when both armies, on a greate plaine call'd Marston Moor, had a bloody encounter.

This appears to have been forced on Newcastle by Prince Rupert.

LIFE OF HUTCHINSON, *p.253, Editor's note on the publication of the King's letters.*

> The public is in possession of these, they having been printed by the parliament, which some thought a hardship, but surely without reason.

I altogether agree with the Editor and regard the outcry raised by late writers against the indelicacy of publishing the King's correspondence, as sickly sentimental cant. S. T. C.

LIFE OF HUTCHINSON, *p. 270, Editor's note on the story of the questioning by Hutchinson and his wife concerning infant baptism. Coleridge's note continued on p. 271.*

> Surely this shews an unbecoming propensity to speculate in religion; the story is, however, told with candour.

Surely this is the strangest note that ever came from a man of the Editor's sense. Mrs. H., has been speculating in Politics from the very commencement and all to the Editor's approbation and admiration, she and Col. H. speculate on the most unbecomingly speculative part of Theology, God's absolute decrees, and the Editor finds no fault. Now as Parents about to exercise a duty to their own child, they endeavour to square their conduct with the commands of their Redeemer—examine the sacred Scripture to learn what they are, find them in apparent contradiction to the common practice.

LIFE OF HUTCHINSON, *p. 322.*

> The collonell prosecuting the defence of truth and iustice, in these and many more things, and abhorring all councells of securing the young commonwealth, by cruelty and oppression of the vanquisht, who had not laid downe their hate, in delivering up their armes, and were therefore, by some cowards, iudg'd unworthy of the mercy extended to to them, the collonell, I say, disdaining such thoughts, displeas'd many of his owne party, who, in the maine, we hope, might have bene honest, although through divers temptations, guilty of horrible slips, which did more offend the collonell's pure zeale, who detested these sins more in brethren then in enemies.

These and of this sort were the too notorious Practices, the disappointment, disgust, and indignation at which misled Milton for a time into a Supporter and Apologist of Cromwell's violent ejection of the Parliament, and assumption of the Dictatorship under the name of Protector. Good men bore too little and expected too much: and even wise men, comparatively wise, were eager to have an Oak, where they ought to have been content with planting an Acorn. O that Col. Hutchinson and his Co-patriots throughout England could at this period have brought themselves to a conviction of the necessity of a King, under that or some other name, & have joined with Lord Brook & others in offering the Throne to Cromwell, under a solemn national contract!

So, and so only, might England have been a Republican Kingdom— a glorious Commonwealth, with a King as the Symbol of it's Majesty, and the Key-stone of it's Unity. S. T. C.

LIFE OF HUTCHINSON, *p. 344.*

> It is believed that Richard himselfe was compounded with, to have

resign'd the place that was too greate for him; certeine it is that his poore spiritt was likely enough to doe any such thing. The army perceiving they had sett up a wretch who durst not reigne . . .

There is something delightful to me in this illustrious *Woman* in all the contra-distinctive Womanhood breaking forth the high, accomplished, and Christian minded masculine intellect of Mrs. Hutchinson! But in a Woman's Soul, no virtues in a man can atone for Pusillanimity; for either bodily or mental *Cowardice*. Woman cannot look *down* and love: Even her children are *angels* to her, and she clasps her babe to her Bosom with a participation of the Feeling, with which the Catholics describe the Holy Mother to embrace her Godenshrining Child. S. T. C.

"Life of Strafford," p. 226.[32]

At no period was the omnipotence of Parliament a more established doctrine [than in the time of Henry VIII.]. It was not enough that More confessed its power to make or depose a king; he suffered for a treasonable offence, because he would not acknowledge its right to confer a supreme control over men's consciences.

Is not this a contradiction, this very King being an essential part of this omnipotent Parliament? And would Henry have endured such a doctrine as that his Vassals and Subjects had the right to depose him?

"Life of Strafford," p. 269.

In this conjuncture two expedients seem to have been requisite for the prevention of violent civil dissensions; the limitation of the royal prerogative by such accurate and insuperable barriers as would for ever guard the persons and property of the subject from arbitrary encroachments, and the separation of the King's private expenditure from the disbursements of the public, &c. But of these expedients, the separation of the King's expenditure from that of the nation, however simple and obvious it may now appear, does not seem to have then occurred either to the Prince or the people.

Now this appears to me one of those *plausible* silly remarks that even sensible men may sometimes fall on. At a second thought, however, a man of reflection would see, that this *"simple* and *obvious"* expedient involves one or other of two consequences. Either the two Houses of Parliament were to appoint, appropriate, and control the nation's expenditure; or they were not. If the latter, the separation would be nominal only—a mere powerless Act of Parliament! If they were, it would itself be and constitute such a limitation as the boldest Patriot at that time would not have thought of. With no greater patronage

[32] "Life of Thomas Wentworth, Earl of Strafford," in John Macdiarmid, *Lives of British Statesmen* (1807); *Notes Theolog.*, pp. 208-10.

than the Crown *then* possessed, it would have reduced the King to mere Stadtholder.

"Life of Strafford," p. 468.

> Strafford was aware that his life was in the hands of his enemies; that no chance of escape remained; but he was not prepared to expect so sudden a dereliction by his sovereign, &c. &c., and when assured of the fatal truth, he raised his eyes to heaven, and laying his hand on his heart, exclaimed, 'Put not your trust in princes, nor in the sons of men, for in them there is no salvation.'

Canting scoundrel—a hypocrite in his very last act! Nothing indeed can justify the measures of the House of Commons, nothing palliate the baseness of the House of Lords; unless it be the unvaried example of all their predecessors, and the faithful imitation of the same submission to the stronger party by all their successors spiritual and temporal. It was not this remorseless apostate that suffered undeservingly; he deserved a thousand deaths; but England, but Law, and the everlasting principles and grounds of Law in the sense of public justice, that received a deadly wound: and every Bill of Pains and Penalties since then has been a fresh hydra-head sprouting from this wound. Thus is the cycle of retributive Providence completed. What the Gracchi begin, a Bluebeard and a Heliogabalus finish.

"Life of Strafford," p. 472.

> In his address to the people from the scaffold, he assured them that he submitted to his sentence with perfect resignation, &c. &c. He declared that, however his actions might have been misinterpreted, his intentions had always been upright, that he loved Parliaments, that he was devoted to the Constitution, and to the Church of England, &c. &c.

If aught could—but nothing can, nor dare we indeed desire, that anything should—remove the superstition in favour of dying words, this fact and the similar fact in Charles's own scaffold scene are well fitted to produce the effect. Both died with a lie in their mouths. Strafford with his love of Parliaments and devotion to the Constitution by which the King was made dependent on them; and Charles with the delivery of his Icon Basilike as his own work!

It is a mark of a noble nature to be more shocked with the unjust condemnation of a bad man than of a virtuous one—as the sentence of the E. of Strafford.[33]

[33] Notebook 18, fol. 18 verso-19 recto.   British Museum, Add. MSS, 47,515. Printed for the first time.

It must (I am almost ashamed to confess it) have been more than 20 years since I had read the Εἰκὼν βασιλική. I determined therefore, after having skimmed the first 20 pages of Dr. Wordsworth,[34] to give it a careful re-perusal, before I entered on the controversy as to it's true Author. This I have done: and tho' I cannot help conceding to Dr. Walker's[35] argument drawn from the chapter on the Covenant more force or at least a greater plausibility than Dr. Wordsworth is disposed to allow it, it does not sensibly weaken my total and final impression—first, that the work was written by the King—tho' I think it probable that many passages were composed from his recollection of the public papers, published in his name, but (as we learn from Clarendon) written by himself, or Lord Falkland. Second, that the Book was written with the intent and foresight (surely, a very justifiable nay laudable design!) of conciliating the judgement and affections of his subjects, in favor of himself—should the opportunity offer—or at all events of his Children. And doubtless, neither you nor I will be ashamed to regard it as some confirmation of this conjecture, that God did actually bless the work to this end: and that it militated more effectively for his Son's restoration, than all the cowardly crowned heads of Europe and all the tumultuary Plots and Mobbings of the drinking and swearing Cavaliers. But this second point of view, in which I look on the work, sufficiently explains the Chapter on the Covenant—and other passages in a nobler strain, which correspond better to Falkland's præter sæculum liberality and enlargement of Principles than to Laud's Royal Admirer and Partisan; tho' God forbid! that I should scruple to believe, that Adversity, the Mother or Nurse of Reflection, might have led Charles to adopt them, as his own—negatively, at least, and as permissible when circumstances rendered it necesary or highly expedient. A man, whose object is to mediate, soften, bring together *for a time* contending parties, will naturally, and may innocently, go as far as he can—even beyond his wishes, if not beyond his intentions. The example of his Father, James I, in the best, or rather the only, good and wise book, he ever wrote, addressed to himself, the year before James ascended the English Throne, might not improbably have suggested the idea of the Eikon, and the whole work, style and matter, is exactly what we might expect from a man accustomed to peruse and even to make, abstracts of Memoirs and State Papers—Results—Notes of the leading Points, etc.—As to Gau-

[34] In 1824 Christopher Wordsworth, the poet's younger brother, published *Who Wrote* ΕΙΚΩΝ ΒΑΣΙΛΙΚΗ?, which supports the claims of Charles I.

[35] Cf. A. Walker, *A true account of the author of a book entitled* Εἰκὼν βασιλική (1692).

den's[36] writing it, it is hard to say what is *impossible;* but it appears to me, judging wholly from internal Evidence, next to impossible. Alas! is it not a melancholy Reflection, that the Bishops after the Restoration, who affected to idolize this book and it's ostensible Author, should have acted throughout in direct opposition to all it's principles and counsels!!!—But so it is! Experience, like the stern lanthorn of a Ship, casts it's light only on the *Wake*—on the Track already past.[37]

"Life of Clarendon," p. 520.[38]

It is not to be concealed that even Hyde encouraged the attempts of Captain Titus and others to remove Cromwell by assassination.

Nor ought it to be concealed that Hyde suborned assassins against an honester man than Cromwell, the patriot Ludlow. When to this detestable wickedness we add his hardening of Charles I. in his pre-latical superstition, his being an accomplice of the King's in the three contradictory treaties with three different parties at the same time, neither of which the King intended to fulfill, and his total abandon-ment of the religious rights of the subjects to the fury of the Bishops after the Restoration, we must attribute the high praise bestowed on Clarendon by historians, and the general respect attached to his memory chiefly to the infamy of the rest of the Cavalier Faction canonising bad by incomparably worse.

"Life of Clarendon," p. 522.

When the death of Cromwell, and the deposition of his son, enabled the active spirits to resume the business of framing Constitutions, they showed that their political sagacity had undergone no improvement. Without comprehending the distribution of powers, by which the au-thority of rulers is rendered at once effectual and innoxious, their crude discussions turned upon the eligibilty of vesting the supreme power in one man, in a few, or in the people at large; and men seemed ready to lose their lives for theoretical governments, which were either per-nicious or impracticable.

This at least cannot be said of Harrington's scheme: nor should it be forgotten, that Cromwell's Scheme of Representation, eulogised by Clarendon himself, and which would have more than superseded the Revolution, owed its failure not to the ambition of Cromwell, but the narrow prejudices and persecuting bigotry of the Presbyterians, who furthermore brought back the perjured popish Brotheller without con-ditions, and met their due reward.

[36] John Gauden (1605-62), bishop of Worcester, claimed the authorship, and this claim was apparently admitted at the Restoration.

[37] To Rev. S. Mence, July 13, 1825. Griggs, *Unp. Letters,* II, 352-54.

[38] "Life of Edward Hyde, Earl of Clarendon," in John Macdiarmid, *Lives of British Statesmen* (1807); *Notes Theolog.,* pp. 213-16.

"Life of Clarendon," pp. 538-39.

It would have been fortunate for the memory of Clarendon, if the same good sense and benevolence which guided his civil policy had governed his religious opinions. But in these prejudice triumphed over his better judgment; and we find him breathing sentiments, which, in a darker age, would have led him to promote the most cruel persecution. From his early youth he had imbibed the maxim of *No Bishop, no King,* as an infallible truth; and had conscientiously instilled into the mind of his sovereign the doctrine that Episcopacy is the only form of Church Government compatible with Monarchy.

It is sad to think, how dangerous a poison the tone and general spirit of our modern historians instill into the public mind, and (still worse) into the souls of the young men, whose talents, rank, or connections destine them to a public life: a poison, slow indeed and lurking, and therefore the fittest to undermine the moral constitution. What an effect must not [be produced by] the mere attachment of the honours of virtue to wicked statesmen only because they were much less wicked than others! "Conscientiously!" What? was Hyde a poor simple recluse? must not the knowledge, that this tenet was despised as absurd, and detested as base and ruinous by Falkland, Southampton, and a majority of the great and good men who lived and died for the monarchy, have at least so far influenced an honest mind as to prevent him from persecuting with remorseless cruelty thousands, nay, myriads, of men whose only charge was that of holding the same opinion respecting the prelates (for the quarrel was not concerning Episcopacy, such as Archbishop Usher supported, but *Prelacy*), as Falkland? If a conscience sered by party-passions, and the assumption of infallibility, is to be the sufficient reason for calling actions conscientious, for Heaven's sake, say not an unkind word against the Massacre on St. Bartholomew's Day, or the horrors of Bonner and Gardner!

The plausibility of the sophism, No Bishop, no King! rests wholly on the circumstance, that there is *some* truth in the converse, viz.: No King, no Prelate.

Note, that *we* have the whole Good of the learned Bishops in James I & Charles I time as well, nay more distinctly & collectively than the Evil—but the Compatriots of Milton only their foul flatteries, their *Villiers,* their persecutions.[39]

Milton and his great Compatriots were too much Republicans because they were too little Democrats. The universal Habit of the Age, and of

[39] Notebook 30, fol. 15 recto. British Museum, Add. MSS, 47,527. Printed for the first time.

Ages before them, among able educated men to exclude the Many, the
Population, from all concern in political and national economy, as naturally and by a law of God and Right Reason—the Government, and to
confine all share and interest in Government and Legislature to the
Gentry and the Learned, i. e. the Officers and the Authors of the Permanent—(Senatus Populusque were the Nobility, Gentry and Clergy—)
and the confirming source of the History of their Country, which gave
them no other example but of Changes and beneficient Innovations
effected by the FEW, the Mass of the people disregarded, and either
passive or blindly following their Lords,—these go a great way to excuse
them for the error, they committed in aiming at forms of Government
and institutions beyond the moral and intellectual growth of the Nation at large, and (a yet more fatal error) without adverting to their
progress in wealth and influence.   Even their aversion to the gauds of
the Monarchy and Hierarchy, and to the rites and ceremonies which
the first English Reformed Bishop had retained from the Papal Church
in charitable & prudent condescension to the customs, prejudices, and
prepossessions of the People by and large, but which Charles' Prelates
and Oxford Divines were abusively increasing in Love and admiration
for the things themselves—even this aversion had it's main source in their
aristocratic Feeling and Principle.   They despised and condemned them,
as flatterers to the Populace.   Algernon Sidney's Essay on Government
is one continual illustration of this remark.[40]

The independents in Cromwell's time held—That whatsoever they
said or did for the present, under such a measure of light, should oblige
them no longer when a greater measure of light should give them other
discoveries.[41]

QUARTERLY REVIEW, *October, 1813, p. 108.*

> Cromwell, indeed, was frequently favoured with their admonitions,
> and the old Quakers were firmly persuaded that the overthrow of his
> family was a judgment upon him for not interfering more authoritative-
> ly to stop the proceedings against them.

There is much truth in this opinion.   Cromwell's dynasty fell a sacrifice to indecision and cross-catching.[42]

Henry Brooke, THE FOOL OF QUALITY *(1776), III, 3.*

> A number of external successes, also, assisted to persuade us, in those

[40] Notebook 26, fol. 42 recto-43 verso.   British Museum, Add. MSS, 47,524.
Printed for the first time.
[41] Notebook 21, fol. 4 recto.   British Museum, Add. MSS, 47,518.   Printed for the
first time.
[42] *Notes Theolog.,* p. 155.

days, that felicity was to be attained and ascertained upon earth. The regency of Cromwell was administered with the strictest justice at home, while . . . it became revered and formidable abroad.

Alas! and to what a Wretch did the bigotry & intolerant Spirit of the Presbyterians sacrifice their own & the Nation's *Power & Freedom!* Very little Freedom Charles had left them to sacrifice & as to national power that was greater under Cromwell than under any of the favorite Stuart Family.[43]

"His Highness the Lord Protector's Speech to the Parliament, in the Painted Chamber, on Tuesday, the 12th of September, 1654."

And that there was high cause for their dissolving, is most evident, not only in regard there was a just fear of the Parliament perpetuating themselves, but because it was their design; and had not their heels been trod upon by importunities from abroad, even to threats, *I* believe there would never have been thoughts of rising, or of going out of that room, to the world's end.

After reading this cloudy *Tiberian* Speech, and comparing these impudent assertions with the measures and declared intentions of the Republican Parliament, it should be impossible to doubt the baseness of Cromwell. Even supposing some truth in, yet what more can be wished from a Parliament than that they should yield to the desires from abroad?[44]

The Presbyterians hated the Independents much more than they did the bishops, which induced them to co-operate in effecting the Restoration.

The conduct of the bishops towards Charles, whilst at Breda, was wise and constitutional. They knew, however, that when the forms of the constitution were once restored, all their power would revive again as of course.[45]

The elements had been well shaken together during the civil wars and interregnum under the Long Parliament and Protectorate; and nothing but the cowardliness and impolicy of the Nonconformists at the Restoration, could have prevented a real reformation on a wider basis.

[43] Henry Brooke, *The Fool of Quality* (4 vols.; London: 1775-76). From the original notes in the Huntington Library volume but also printed by E. B. Dike, "Coleridge Marginalia in Henry Brooke's *The Fool of Quality*," *Huntington Library Bulletin*, I (November, 1931), 156.

[44] "Notes Written in a Volume of Tracts Relating to the Times of Cromwell," *Notes Theolog.*, p. 196.

[45] June 10, 1830. *Table Talk S*, p. 333.

But the truth is, by going over to Breda with their stiff flatteries to the hollow-hearted King, they put Sheldon and the bishops on the side of the constitution.[46]

The magic rod of fanaticism is preserved in the very adyta of human nature; and needs only the re-exciting warmth of a master hand to bud forth afresh and produce the old fruits. The horror of the peasant's war in Germany, and the direful effects of the Anabaptist's tenets (which differed only from those of jacobinism by the substitution of theological for philosophical jargon) struck all Europe for a time with affright. Yet little more than a century was sufficient to obliterate all effective memory of these events. The same principles with similar though less dreadful consequences were again at work from the imprisonment of the first Charles to the restoration of his son. The fanatic maxim of extirpating fanaticism by persecution produced a civil war. The war ended in the victory of the insurgents; but the temper survived, and Milton had abundant grounds for asserting, that "Presbyter was but OLD PRIEST writ large!" One good result, thank heaven! of this zealotry was the re-establishment of the church. And now it might have been hoped, that the mischievous spirit would have been bound for a season, "and a seal set upon him, that he might deceive the nation no more." But no! The ball of persecution was taken up with undiminished vigor by the persecuted. The same fanatic principle, that under the solemn oath and covenant had turned cathedrals into stables, destroyed the rarest trophies of art and ancestral piety, and hunted the brightest ornaments of learning and religion into holes and corners, now marched under episcopal banners, and having first crowded the prisons of England, emptied its whole vial of wrath on the miserable covenanters of Scotland (*Laing's* History of Scotland.—*Walter Scott's* Bard, ballads, &c.). A merciful providence at length constrained both parties to join against a common enemy. A wise government followed; and the established church became, and now is, not only the brightest example but our best and only sure bulwark, of toleration! The true and indispensable blank against a new inundation of persecuting zeal —ESTO PERPETUA![47]

Name to me any Revolution recorded in History, that was not followed by a depravation of the national Morals. The Roman character during the Triumvirate, and under Tiberius; the reign of Charles the

[46] July 21, 1827. *Table Talk S*, p. 294.
[47] *Biog. Lit. C*, I, 191-92.

Second; and Paris at the present moment; are obvious instances. What is the main cause? The sense of Insecurity.[48]

The faults of the Puritans were many; but surely their morality will, in general, bear comparison with that of the Cavaliers after the Restoration.[49]

State Comp. of England, Ch. I. and II. & the present times. How full of Confidence the Cavaliers, at the outburst of the war—& with what a shew of reason! In each County, what a splendid decisive majority, what a [——?] non-omneity, of Gentry & Nobility on the part of the King!—& with these the majority of the populace in the cities. London itself forming scarcely an exception. So now *perhaps* as to the higher class! but not so now with regard to the populace.[50]

"On the Circumstances that appear especially to favour the return of the Bourbons at this present time."[51]

It was scarcely more than a month before his restoration when Charles the Second appeared to all Europe as much an exile from the hope, as from the possession of his throne. He had neither army, nor treasure, no organized faction in England, no influence in the Continental Courts: he was countenanced by no foreign Power, and Cardinal Mazarine, the then masterspirit of Europe, was intriguing against him. His fortunes were at their lowest ebb; and they returned, as the tide does in our rivers Trent and Parrot, not by any gradual increase, but *in a head,* and like a wall of waters. Had England then sunk in the rank of nations during her commonwealth? And were the inhabitants recalled to loyalty by national pride? Or had her commerce failed? Or was her naval strength giving way? Least of all things. Never had England stood crowned with equal glory; never had she spoken with so commanding a voice to the surrounding Powers! Lord Clarendon, and other contemporary writers, can find no other terms for this sudden restoration, than that it was *miraculous,* and effected by an immediate influence of the Deity. This was the natural language of gratitude and exultation at the time; but it now would be childish. The inferences, which thinking men have since drawn from this event, are these:— That to conduct with splendour the foreign concerns of a revolutionary

[48] *"Blessed Are Ye,"* pp. 103-4. Pickering edition, 1839, p. 405. This edition is bound with *Church and State.*
[49] June 10, 1830. *Table Talk* S, p. 333.
[50] Notebook 28, fol. 54 verso-55 recto. British Museum, Add. MSS, 47,526. Printed for the first time.
[51] *Essays,* II, 532-37.

nation is an easy task, but to settle its domestic troubles, exceeds the strength of the most gigantic genius; and that though a nation may be intoxicated for a while by their glory abroad, yet they will inevitably, sooner or later, be sobered by the sense of insecurity and oppression at home. The Republic of England was splendid and powerful; and the Pretender to the Throne a weak and friendless exile. But the people of England were sick at heart with hope long delayed; it was natural for those, who had been disappointed of liberty, to compound for quiet. "For *liberty* they had fought, but they still found themselves *slaves;* and weary of their military yoke, were easily induced to submit once more to that of the old monarchy, as the lesser evil." (*Vide Ralph's Review of the Reign of Charles II. and James II.,*[52] p. 2.) These inferences we receive, as the fair solution of the apparent miracle, yet not without some addition and some correction. It ought not to be overlooked, that the revolution itself, its rapid change of constitution, and its quick succession of political contrivances, had distempered the people with a craving for novelty, while new constitutions, and new ordinances, became themselves stale and unattractive; and that the only novelty, which remained, of sufficient excitement to ease their craving, was the restoration of their banished sovereign; and the more extraordinary the circumstances of this restoration, the more likely therefore was it to be effected. This addition is not only important in itself, but likewise eminently pertinent to our present purpose, for who among our leaders has not already detected the application? And the correction, which we propose, is on the same ground still more interesting. All the reasoners on this great event have spoken of the weakness and desertion of Charles the Second as circumstances which of themselves were unfriendly to the restoration, though they were more than counterpoised by the national discontents, contempt of transitory constitutions, and dread and hatred of the military despotism. Now we, on the contrary, feel a deep conviction, that this very weakness, this very desertion of the monarch, was a *cause* of his restoration equally powerful with any of those last enumerated; that it was a great co-cause, and necessary condition of his return. For, in the first place, it flattered both the national pride and the national morality; it was an act of its own free choice, a true election, a measure not of compulsion or foreign influence, but of conscience and genuine conviction; secondly, it did from the same reasons present nothing opposite to good policy and the welfare

[52] James Ralph (1705?-62). Historian and journalist, whose chief work was *The History of England during the Reigns of King William, Queen Anne, and King George I. with an Introductory Review of the Reigns of the Royal Brothers Charles and James,* (2 vols.; London: 1744 and 1746).

of the nation.—If Charles came back wholly unassisted by the power of the Continental Courts, he came back of course unintangled in their interests, with no obligations incurred that were likely to set the *gratitude* of the throne at variance with the honour and prosperity of the nation; and, lastly, infatuated as the parliament appeared by its loyalty, yet the whole proceedings of all the parliaments of his whole reign make it amount almost to demonstration, that if Charles the Second had been powerfully backed by the armies and resources of France, Spain, or the Empire, he never would have been received without *terms;* that the discussion of *terms* would have rekindled the disposition to political controversy; that a spirit of Republican enthusiasm, which only slumbered, would have been re-awakened in the army; and that, instead of Charles the Second on the throne, England would have seen General Monk[53] on the scaffold. These are no mere speculations; they are facts of history. Hale,[54] afterwards chief justice, moved in the new parliament, that a committee should be appointed to digest such propositions of terms, as might be sent over to the king. This motion was seconded; but immediately and successfully opposed by Monk, who swore solemnly, that though all was now quiet beyond expectation, he nevertheless could not answer for the army, if any delay whatsoever was put to the sending for the king: and as a sufficient answer to the general expediency of sending over terms, he uttered the following memorable sentences, which appeared so full of unanswerable good sense, that they were followed by a *shout* of assent over the whole house. "I cannot answer for the peace of the army, if there be any delay; and the blood and mischief, that will follow, will be on the heads of those who cause that delay, however plausible the pretext.—But in this instance, there is not even a plausible pretext. What need is there of *sending* over propositions to the king? May you not as well prepare them, and offer them to him when he shall have come over? He has neither army nor treasure to bring with him, wherewith to frighten or corrupt you."

If it were unsafe or imprudent to compare these facts in open and direct terms with the present circumstances of the Bourbons, the resemblance is so close and striking, that we might confidently leave the inference to be drawn by our readers themselves. But it will be more pleasant to our readers to find their own thoughts in our words, and we have, besides, other facts and circumstances, *peculiar* to France, which it belongs to our present purpose to place in their proper light;

[53] George Monk (1608-70) was won over to the Parliamentary cause and gave valuable assistance to Cromwell. Later he returned to the Loyalists and helped in the restoration of Charles.

[54] Sir Matthew Hale (1609-76) was made chief justice in 1671.

and lastly, although we are no adherents or partisans of the present
ministry, yet we do believe that both ministers themselves, and the great
offices in the service of the government, possess too much of the principles and temper of our constitution to regard, with an evil eye, any
truly dispassionate, respectful, and unfactious reasoning, that has been
conceived in the spirit, and expressed with the decency, of an Englishman and a gentleman. Whether the restoration of the Royal Family
of France be the object of our hopes, or of our fears, whether it be an
event which we implore or deprecate, we shall, in the present disquisition, give our readers no opportunity of concluding or even conjecturing;
for we shall confine ourselves to *facts*, and to the deductions that flow
immediately from those facts. *Sedulo curavimus humanas res et actiones
humanas non ridere, non lugere, neque detestari; sed intelligere!*
(Spino. Tract. Pol.) . . .

O Heavens! what a Leash of Patron Saints have the Tory Clergy
fixed on for the Anglican Church!

I. Charles the first, Martyr to the inveterate Vice of Lying, the poor
uxorious Slave of a lewd Virago, and the perjured accomplice in the
atrocity of the Irish Massacre. See Hallam's Constit. History, Vol. II.,
p. 46.

II. Archbishop Laud, the St. Dominic of the semi-protestant High
Church, the vindictive, hot-headed, narrow-minded, superstitious Bigot—
who having sacrificed the peace and prosperity of the Realm to his
Monkish Follies, and kindled the flames of Civil War in three Kingdoms,
died remorseless with a self-approving Conscience.

III. Lord Clarendon—Hypocrite, Liar in all his characters, as Man,
Statesman and Historian, and the Suborner of Assassination, and unless
we transfer the Guilt from the Murdered to his Stiletto, himself virtually and morally an assassin.

What a Trio for High Church Canonization—the beatified Triumvirate of Oxford, and—proh pudor.

The Lawyers ran side by side with the Churchmen in the race of
infamy during the reigns of Charles the Second and his infatuated
Brother. But what Judge, or Barrister professes to think the Bench
or the Bar, interested in defending the conduct and principles of
Scroggs,[55] Sawyer,[56] Showers,[57] Jefferies?[58]

[55] Sir William Scroggs, lord chief justice, 1673-83. He condemned a number of
men connected with the "Popish Plot."

[56] Sir Robert Sawyer (1633-92), attorney general.

[57] Sir Bartholomew Showers (1658-1701), appointed recorder of London by James
II in 1688.

[58] George Jefferies or Jeffreys (1648-89), judge. He presided at the trial of

The High Church Divines stand alone in the abject folly of gratuitously identifying the existing Church of England with the worst members in it's morally and politically most disgraceful period. These dignified Anachronisms of our own Age may with little hyperbole be said to identify the Sun with it's Maculæ, nay, to select the latter as the representative Idols of their Sun-worship. See Apologetic Preface to Fire, Famine, & Slaughter—Coleridge's poetical Works, Vol. I. p. 352 [1829].[59]

Southey, LIFE OF WESLEY, *I, 270.*

> And because of the want of unexceptionable subjects, men of learning, but of tainted opinions, found admittance into the Church, and their zeal was more pernicious than the torpor of the papistical clergy.

Only reperuse the preceding faithful statement of the papistry, superstition, and immorality of the great majority even of the church ministers, how much more of the congregations and parishes throughout the island, during the former half of the Reign of Elizabeth; then compare with this the only not universal Protestantism (the court excepted) at the expulsion of James II., and then ask whether it is possible that the labors of the men, of whom two thousand were ejected by the St. Bartholomew Act, could have been more pernicious to the Church of Christ in Great Britain, than the torpor of the perjured papistical clergy in the time of Elizabeth.[60]

Whenever the CONSTITUTION shall be violated, then the Right of resistance will commence; a Right restricted only by prudence, that is, a knowledge of the means. Such sentiments "amount to legal Treason," exclaims our minister. So said King James the second, and the Pope swore by his infallibility that King James spoke truth! But our ancestors thought otherwise. They thought that the people alone were the rightful vicegerents of God, and that to the people is delegated the divine attributes of "exalting the humble and debasing the mighty." So "the descendant of a long line of Kings" they sent a begging, and a foreigner brought from a petty spot in Germany they placed on the throne of Great Britain and Ireland. May the principles, which gave it to him, preserve it to his descendants! Amen! Amen![61]

Algernon Sidney, Titus Oates, and Richard Baxter. In 1685 he became lord chancellor.

[59] Notebook 38, fol. 7 verso-8. British Museum, Add. MSS, 47,533. Printed for the first time.

[60] Coleridge's note to Southey's *Life of Wesley* (London: 1847), I, 270.

[61] *Plot Discovered*, p. 26. See also *Essays*, I, 75-76.

Henry Brooke, THE FOOL OF QUALITY *(1776), IV, 3-7.*

My father thinks that he [William III] has attachments and views that look something further than the mere interests of the people by whom he has been elected; but he says that those views ought . . . to be indulged, in return of the very great benefits that he has done us.

A common objection to W. IIIrd even among the Whigs; but in fact, it was one of that great & good man's excellencies, that he saw distinctly, that Great Britain must owe her elevation to, and preservation in, the first rank of nations, yea and as the primus inter primates, to her commercial, manufactory, and colonial superiority—and that such a nation, rather such an *empire,* could not have a separate interest from that of the great European Commonwealth of Nations.—that the maintenance of Continental Protestantism, and the full independence & vigor of North Europe, in counterpoise of France always & an antagonism to despotic R. Catholic France, was a vital interest of G. Britain. This the Tory semi-Jacobite high Church Squire Westerns of the Day were too stupid to see, and this even the Whigs, for the greater part, understood but partially. Williams, not fault, but deficiency & misfortune, was that he was not endowed with the power of communicating his superior wisdom to others persuasively, & in a way appropriate to the genius & character of the English of that age. But he was a truly great & good man.[62]

. . . the association [i.e. the Protestant Association] became daily more numerous, and more respectable, and at length, in the year 1795, in grateful memory of their great deliverer William III. they dropt the name of DEFENDERS, to assume that of Orangemen, that whether collected in their lodges as brethren, or called to the field as loyal soldiers, they might hear in the very name, and bear about them in the common badge of their union, a perpetual remembrancer of that tolerant spirit, admitting no principles of persecution, but that of disarming persecutors on principle; and of that heroic devotion to liberty and equal laws, which have rendered the House of Nassau venerable to all Europe, and the name of Orange dear and religious in the heart of every patriotic and loyal

Irish Protestant[63]

[62] From the Huntington Library copy with the original notes, but see also E. B. Dike, ''Coleridge Marginalia in Henry Brooke's *The Fool of Quality,*'' *Huntington Library Bulletin,* I (November, 1931), 161.
[63] *Essays,* III, 721-22.

PHILOSOPHY

INTRODUCTION

Coleridge's reading in seventeenth-century English philosophy was part of an extensive survey made in preparation for writing his *Magnum Opus*. Since he believed that the truth might lie in a synthesis of what was true in all other philosophical systems, he undertook a stupendous amount of critical reading, not only in Latin and Greek but also in German, French, and English philosophical writing. During the long illness of 1800 and 1801 he read widely in the ancient philosophers and the Schoolmen, finding that much which had later been cried up as "new" was new only because it had been forgotten. He therefore grew to be "exceedingly suspicious of *supposed Discoveries* in metaphysics,"[a] and became increasingly aware of the necessity of knowing what had previously been said on a subject in order to establish the starting point for making an original contribution.

As the fragments of his own philosophical work become known, one can see Coleridge's creative mind piecing together a great mosaic, choosing, rejecting, shaping in á new way, and finally going beyond previous designs. When the notebooks are published, scholars in philosophy may be able to show more fully than Muirhead has done that Coleridge had a basis for his claim that a revolution in philosophical thought would have resulted from the completion of the *Magnum Opus*. Such a revolution was a vital matter, for materialistic philosophy was gaining renewed strength. Coleridge's reading showed him that the seventeenth century furnished an example not only of a like spread of materialism but also of a way to combat it by a return to Platonism.

The negative side of the campaign was to discredit the powerful supporters of materialism by showing that they were not great discoverers and that the systems for which they were popular had been previously tried and abandoned. He said:

> It must be my business to tame the vanity of moderns by proving to you, in every case I know of, that those men took up such and such opinions but that those opinions were nothing more than what had been brought forward by such and such of the ancients, as far as they were really philosophical.[b]

The statement was true for Locke and Hobbes in the seventeenth century as well as for Hartley, Hume, and others.

[a] Letter to Poole, Feb. 13, 1801. British Museum, Add. MSS, 35,343, fol. 251 verso. Cf. Griggs, *Unp. Letters*, I, 173.
[b] Philosophical Lecture VIII, Feb. 15, 1819. Coburn, *Phil. Lect.*, p. 263.

Much of Coleridge's commentary on the seventeenth-century philosophers is concerned with presenting evidence that these men had gained fame for "original" ideas which were only restatements; Bacon himself was a "British Plato" who applied to nature the same science of method which Plato had applied to the intellect. Coleridge argued that the *Novum Organum* agreed "in all essential points with the true doctrine of Plato,"[c] but he did not mean that Bacon consciously took the method from Plato. He recognized that Bacon had probably not read the original Greek works of Plato and that his unfair remarks about his great master were based upon translations or commentaries which erroneously interpreted what Plato really said.

Locke and Hobbes, on the other hand, derived directly from Descartes and had their ultimate source in Aristotle. Interleaving an edition of Locke prepared for Cambridge University students, Coleridge wrote opposite Locke's words the "exact same statement" which appeared in Descartes. A reporter of Philosophical Lecture XIII said that Coleridge showed this volume to his audience.[d]

Hobbes's claim as an original thinker was based upon the discovery of the law of association, but in reality he had taken this idea from Descartes. Even before Descartes, others, notably Vives, had defined the law and stated its functions, and Aristotle had first discovered and formulated it. So Hobbes had no claim whatsoever to be called a discoverer.

Two practical motives activated Coleridge in writing out his findings. His friend and patron, Tom Wedgwood, whose studies had been a great stimulus to Coleridge, was engaged on a philosophical work which his friends thought would "revolutionize metaphysics." Coleridge saw that his historical survey would make a valuable introduction for this work. Furthermore, James Mackintosh, a family connection of the Wedgwoods whom Coleridge heartily disliked, had been giving public lectures in which he lauded Locke and Hobbes for their discoveries, and Coleridge wanted to refute these claims.

In letters to the Wedgwoods he first presented the evidence that Locke took his ideas from Descartes. To his great disappointment his friends did not even reply. Adding Hume to his discussion he planned to use the material as the preface for the *Magnum Opus.*[e] The next year, however, Tom Wedgwood and Mackintosh were "hatching a great metaphysical work," and Coleridge was preparing as a preface "a his-

c *The Friend,* Section II, Essay VI, III, 169 n.
d British Museum, MSS Egerton, 3057.
e Letter to Poole, March 16, 1801. British Museum, Add. MSS, 35,343, fol. 265 recto. Cf. Coleridge, E. H., *Letters,* I, 349.

tory of metaphysical opinion"; [f] but by February, 1803, he thought of it as a "History of Metaphysics from Lord Bacon to Mr. Hume, inclusive." [g] When Tom Wedgwood died, Mackintosh was delegated to complete his philosophical work and nothing further was said about Coleridge's historical preface.

From this time on, Coleridge made free use of his collected materials in various published works and in lectures, as will be seen from the excerpts below. He had not, however, given up the idea of a history of philosophy as "introductory and preparative" to the *Magnum Opus*. In a letter to Allsop he said that he already had "the *written materials* and contents" for such a work, though he had to add that these existed as "scraps and *Sibylline* leaves, including margins of books and blank pages." [h] It is in this uncollected state that his history of philosophy has remained.

He recognized that the positive philosophical contributions of the century were of the greatest importance and treated them at length, showing that both in the discovery of the system of trichotomy and in the distinction between the Reason and the Understanding the English thinkers had priority over Kant.

Francis Bacon

We have heard much, far too much, of Lord Bacon's political crimes, while his calumnious misrepresentations of Plato & Aristotle have been imputed to him as merits. Aristotle, indeed, was rightly served, for he was guilty of the same ambitious detractions. I wish that Mr. Gifford would admit into the Quarterly a series of Reviews of our immortal Dead Men—one in each number: or that I had the republication of the Novum Organum with a series of extracts from Plato in the

f Letter from Southey to William Taylor, February, 1802. *A Memoir of the Life and Writings of . . . William Taylor*, ed. J. W. Robberds (2 vols.; London: 1843), I, 398. Also quoted by Campbell, *Life*, p. 128.

g Letter to Samuel Purkis, Feb. 17. Quoted in John Ayrton Paris's *The Life of Sir Humphry Davy* (2 vols.; London: 1831), I, 175. Also quoted by Campbell, *Life*, p. 137.

h Allsop, *Letters*, I, 151, 153.

Notes—I could pledge myself for the proof that whatever is true in the Baconian Logicè realis is precisely Platonic.[1] S. T. C.

That which, contemplated *objectively* (*i.e.* as existing *externally* to the mind), we call a LAW; the same contemplated *subjectively* (*i.e.* as existing in a subject or mind), is an idea. Hence Plato often names ideas laws; and Lord Bacon, the British Plato, describes the Laws of the material universe as the Ideas in nature. Quod in naturâ *naturatâ* LEX, in naturâ *naturante* IDEA dicitur.[2]

An outline of the History of Logic in General. . . . 9th Chap. Lord Bacon, or the Verulamian Logic. 10th Chap. Examination of the same, and comparison of it with the Logic of Plato (in which I attempt to make it probable that, though considered by Bacon himself as the antithesis and the antidote of Plato, it is *bonâ fide* the same, and that Plato has been misunderstood).[3]

The logic of Lord Bacon and of Plato have been considered almost as Philosophical Opposites and Lord Bacon himself, whose opinions concerning the Ancients must not be read with implicit faith, appears to have considered it in this light; in reality however the Novum Organon of our great countryman and the correspondent parts of his other works are only the logic of Plato carried on to its proper consequences and applied to Physics.[4] Plato confined himself to subjects the similitudes and differences of which were evident by simple intuition or rather to such as he too often erroneously considered as intuitive. Bacon demanded a previous analysis; his Philosophy was no doubt different from that of Plato according to his own conception of it—he placed the permanent where Plato placed the fluxionary. Practically no doubt

---

[1] From a copy of the notes in the *Politicus* of Plato. These notes appear in a notebook owned at the present time by A. H. B. Coleridge, and this excerpt is printed with his permission.

[2] *Church and State*, pp. 4-5.

[3] Letter to Godwin, June 4, 1803. Turnbull, *Biog. Epist.*, I, 272.

[4] Coleridge made three separate but almost identical comparisons of Bacon with Plato. The earliest published version is in the *Treatise on Method*, written for publication in the *Encyclopedia Metropolitana*, January, 1818; but this account was so changed in publication that Coleridge included a fuller treatment of the same material in the revised edition of *The Friend* later in the same year. A shortened account was incorporated in Philosophical Lecture XI, delivered March 8, 1819. Since this is a patchwork of sentences from the two previous accounts, it is not included in this collection, and the reader is referred to Coburn, *Phil. Lect.*, pp. 331-37.

he was right, yet I venture to suspect that a still more subtle analysis of the Powers and Objects of Thought will lead to the construction of a third Organon, which will correct the errors of both Philosophers and probably end in deducing the Practice of Bacon from the Metaphysics of Plato. Permit me to repeat however that the Logic of both in the strict sense of the word is the same, both recommending a copious Induction of Particulars and a consequent investigation of their analogies and their points of difference, and an ascending series of Classifications built on this investigation. It must however be confessed that it would be in the highest degree presumptuous to affirm anything positively of the Platonic system as there is too much reason to fear that we do not possess the key to its nomenclature. The works of Plato like the sacred books of the East keep us in continual doubt what is to be understood literally and what figuratively or allegorically. These writers contrive to be dark with excess of light.[5]

Were it not as it is of highest importance from the moral interest of the question it would be indispensable in order to the establishment of logical criterion, by which the true nature of the premises may be distinguished, and rules of undoubted legitimacy in forensic reasoning, when what is subjectively true is likewise practically valid, be prevented from being applied as principles to the determination of objective truth in real Science and Natural philosophy—in order to this end I say which among all the works of modern philosophy Bacon's Novum Organum has the immortal merit of having first fully and worthily set forth, it is indispensable that this last point should be seen with the greatest possible clearness and distinctness. The student must be made to understand, that not the relation of cause and effect applied to certain antecedents and consequents in nature in and for itself was the object of Hume's Scepticism. What Hume doubted was the *necessity* of the connection between A and any given B not included in A, as a necessity of Reason and Insight.[6]

I presume, the passage which hovers before your recollection,[7] is Biogr. Literaria, Vol. 1, p. 58, 59, 60. . .

[5] "This appears to be the first version of Coleridge's attempted reconciliation of Bacon and Plato. Cf. *The Friend* (1818), III. Essays 8 and 9." Snyder, *Logic*, pp. 65-66.
[6] MS Logic, II, 302-3. British Museum, MSS Egerton, 2826. Quoted by Snyder, *Logic*, p. 123.
[7] That of Basil Montagu. From an unpublished letter to Montagu, n.d., in University Library, Cambridge, England, Add. MSS, 4331E. This note is printed with permission of the library and A. H. B. Coleridge.

The same retrograde movement may be traced in the relation which the Authors themselves have expressed towards their readers. From the lofty address and prophetic self-reverence of BACON—"These are the Meditations of FRANCIS OF VERULAM, which that Posterity should possess he deemed their interest" . . . there was a gradual sinking in the etiquette or allowed style of pretension.

The only other passage in my published works respecting Lord Bacon is that in *Friend*, Vol. III. p. 204. Essay VIII.

In one of Goethe's least known Works and in a *Note* too, there is (I distinctly recollect) an elaborate Character of Lord Bacon—and in some one of my Manifold Many-Scraps or Many Scrips in my own Manuscript, alias Manuscrawl, there are sundry additaments, judicia emendata, and over ruling of the Goethian Dicta—& a comparison of Plato and Bacon. Altogether, if I could afford the time, there might be framed out of it a highly polished Character of Lord Bacon, as Man, Statesman, and Philosopher.[8]

Now a law and an idea are correlative terms, and differ only as object and subject, as being and truth.

Such is the doctrine of the Novum Organum of Lord Bacon, agreeing (as we shall more largely show in the text) in all essential points with the true doctrine of Plato,[9] the apparent differences being for the greater part occasioned by the Grecian sage having applied his principles chiefly to the investigation of the mind, and the method of evolving its powers, and the English philosopher to the development of nature. That our great countryman speaks too often detractingly of the divine philosopher must be explained, partly to the tone given to thinking minds by the Reformation, the founders and fathers of which saw in the Aristotelians, or schoolmen, the antagonists of Protestantism, and in the Italian Platonists the despisers and secret enemies of Christianity itself; and partly, by his having formed his notions of Plato's doctrines from the absurdities and phantasms of his misinterpreters, rather than from an unprejudiced study of his original works.[10]

[8] Letter, dated May 1, 1827, to Basil Montagu. From an unpublished letter in University Library, Cambridge, England, Add. MSS, 4331E.

[9] Cf. "Lord Bacon, who never read Plato's Works, taught pure Platonism in his *great* Work, the Novum Organum, and abuses his divine Predecessor for fantastic nonsense, which he had been the first to explode." To J. Gooden, Jan. 14 [1820]. Griggs, *Unp. Letters*, II, 266.

[10] *The Friend*, Section II, Essay V, III, 168-69 n.

THE FRIEND, *Section II, Essay VII.*[11]

> The soul doth give
> Brightness to the eye: and some say, that the sun
> If not enlighten'd by the Intelligence
> That doth inhabit it, would shine no more
> Than a dull clod of earth.
> Cartwright['s *Lady-Errant*, Act III, scene iv.]

It is strange, yet characteristic of the spirt that was at work during the latter half of the last century, and of which the French revolution was, we hope, the closing *monsoon*, that the writings of PLATO should be accused of estranging the mind from sober experience and substantial *matter-of-fact*, and of debauching it by fictions and generalities. Plato, whose method is inductive throughout, who argues on all subjects not only *from*, but *in* and *by*, inductions of facts! Who warns us indeed against that usurpation of the senses, which quenching the "lumen siccum" of the mind, sends it astray after individual cases for their own sakes; against that "*tenuem et manipularem experientiam,*" which remains ignorant even of the transitory relations, to which the "pauca particularia" of its idolatry not seldom owe their fluxional existence; but who so far oftener, and with such unmitigated hostility, pursues the assumptions, abstractions, generalities, and verbal legerdemain of the sophists! Strange, but still more strange, that a notion so groundless should be entitled to plead in its behalf the authority of Lord BACON, from whom the Latin words in the preceding sentence are taken, and whose scheme of logic, as applied to the contemplation of nature, is Platonic throughout, and differing only in the mode: which in Lord Bacon is dogmatic, *i. e.*, assertory, in Plato tentative, and (to adopt the Socratic phrase) *obstetric*. We are not the first, or even among the first, who have considered Bacon's studied depreciation of the ancients, with his silence, or worse than silence, concerning the merits of his contemporaries, as the least amiable, the least exhilarating side in the character of our illustrious countryman. His detractions from the divine PLATO it is more easy to explain than to justify or even than to palliate: and that he has merely retaliated ARISTOTLE's own unfair treatment of *his* predecessors and contemporaries, may lessen the pain, but should not blind us to the injustice of the aspersions on the name and works of that philosopher. The most eminent of our recent zoologists and minerologists have acknowledged with respect, and even with expressions of wonder, the performances of ARISTOTLE, as the first clearer and breaker-up of the ground in natural history. It is indeed scarcely possible to pursue the treatise on colors, falsely ascribed to Theophrastus, the scholar and suc-

[11] *The Friend*, III, 193-203 (Essay VIII in 1837 edition). Cf. *Method*, pp. 37-51.

cessor of Aristotle, after a due consideration of the state and means of science at that time, without resenting the assertion, that he had utterly enslaved his investigations in natural history to his own system of logic (*logicæ suæ prorsus manicipavit*).[12] Nor let it be forgotten that the sunny side of Lord Bacon's character is to be found neither in his inductions, nor in the application of his own method to particular phænomena or particular classes of physical facts, which are at least as crude for the age of Gilbert, Galileo, and Kepler, as Aristotle's for that of Philip and Alexander. Nor is it to be found in his recommendation (which is wholly independent of his inestimable principles of scientific method) of tabular collections of particulars. Let any unprejudiced naturalist turn to Lord Bacon's questions and proposals for the investigation of single problems; to his Discourse on the Winds; or to the almost comical caricature of this scheme in the "Method of improving Natural Philosophy," (page 22 to 48) by Robert Hooke (the history of whose multifold inventions, and indeed of his whole philosophical life, is the best answer to the scheme—if a scheme so palpably impracticable needs any answer), and put it to his conscience, whether any desirable end could be hoped for from such a process; or inquire of his own experience, or historical recollections, whether any important discovery was ever made in this way. For though Bacon never so far deviates from his own principles, as not to admonish the reader that the particulars are to be thus collected, only that by careful selection they may be concentrated into universals; yet so immense is their number, and so various and almost endless the relations in which each is to be separately considered, that the life of an ante-diluvian patriarch would be expended, and his strength and spirits have been wasted, in merely polling the votes, and long before he could commence the process of simplification, or have arrived in sight of the law which was to reward the toils of the overtasked PSYCHE.

We yield to none in our grateful veneration of Lord Bacon's philosophical writings. We are proud of his very name, as men of science: and as Englishmen, we are almost vain of it. But we may not permit the honest workings of national attachment to degenerate into the jealous and indiscriminate partiality of *clanship*. Unawed by such as praise and abuse by wholesale, we dare avow that there are points in the character of our Verulam, from which we turn to the life and labors of John Kepler, as from gloom to sunshine.[13] The beginning and the close of his life were clouded by poverty and domestic troubles, while the

---

[12] *Novum Organum*, Aph. LIV.

[13] This comment reappears almost verbatim in Philosophical Lecture XI, March 8, 1819. Coburn, *Phil. Lect.*, p. 336.

intermediate years were comprised within the most tumultuous period of the history of his country, when the furies of religious and political discord had left neither eye, ear, nor heart for the Muses. But KEPLER seemed born to prove that true genius can overpower all obstacles. If he gives an account of the modes of proceeding, and of the views under which they first occurred to his mind, how unostentatiously and *in transitu*, as it were, does he introduce himself to our notice: and yet never fails to present the living germ out of which the genuine method, as the inner form of the tree of science, springs up! With what affectionate reverence does he express himself of his master and immediate predecessor, TYCHO BRAHE! with what zeal does he vindicate his services against posthumous detraction! How often and how gladly does he speak of Copernicus! and with what fervent tones of faith and consolation does he proclaim the historic fact that the great men of all ages have prepared the way for each other, as pioneers and heralds! Equally just to the ancients and to his contemporaries, how circumstantially, and with what exactness of detail, does Kepler demonstrate that Euclid Copernicises—ὡς πρὸ τοῦ Κοπερνίκου κοπερνικίζει Εὐκλείδης! and how elegant the compliments which he addresses to PORTA![14] with what cordiality he thanks him for the invention of the camera obscura, as enlarging his views into the laws of vision! But while we cannot avoid contrasting this generous enthusiasm with Lord Bacon's cold and invidious treatment of Gilbert, and his assertion that the works of Plato and Aristotle had been carried down the stream of time, like straws, by their levity alone, when things of weight and worth had sunk to the bottom:[15] still in the Founder of a revolution, scarcely less important for the scientific, and even for the commercial world than that of Luther for the world of religion and politics, we must allow much to the heat of protestation, much to the vehemence of hope, and much to the vividness of novelty. Still more must we attribute to the then existing and actual state of the Platonic and Peripatetic philosophy, or rather to the dreams of verbiage which then passed current as such. Had he but attached to their proper authors the schemes and doctrines which he condemns, our illustrious countryman would, in this point, at least, have needed no apology. And surely no lover of truth, conversant with the particulars of Lord Bacon's life, with the very early, almost boyish age, at which he quitted the university, and the manifold occupations and anxieties in which his public and professional duties engaged, and his courtly,—alas! his servile, prostitute, and mendicant—ambition, en-

[14] Giambattista Della Porta, an Italian physician (1540-1615), who gained a wide reputation for various scientific studies.
[15] Repeated in Philosophical Lecture XI. Coburn, *Phil. Lect.*, p. 337.

tangled him in his after-years, will be either surprised or offended, though we should avow our conviction, that he had derived his opinions of Plato and Aristotle from any source, rather than from a dispassionate and patient study of the originals themselves. At all events, it will be no easy task to reconcile many passages in the De Augmentis, and the Redargutio Philosophiarum, with the author's own fundamental principles, as established in his Novum Organum; if we attach to the words the meaning which they *may* bear, or even, in some instances, the meaning which might appear to us, in the present age, more obvious; instead of the sense in which they were employed by the professors, whose false premises and barren methods Bacon was at that time controverting. And this historical interpretation is rendered the more necessary by his fondness for point and antithesis in his style, where we must often disturb the sound in order to arrive at the sense. But with these precautions; and if, in collating the philosophical works of Lord Bacon with those of Plato, we, in both cases alike, separate the *grounds* and essential *principles* of their philosophic systems from the inductions themselves; no inconsiderable portion of which, in the British sage, as well as in the divine Athenian, is neither more nor less crude and erroneous than might be anticipated from the infant state of natural history, chemistry, and physiology, in their several ages; and if we moreover separate the principles from their practical application, which in both is not seldom impracticable, and, in our countryman, not always reconcileable with the principles themselves: we shall not only extract that from each, which is for all ages, and which constitutes their true systems of philosophy, but shall convince ourselves that they are radically one and the same system: in that, namely which is of universal and imperishable worth!—the science of Method, and the grounds and conditions of the science of Method.

THE FRIEND, *Section II, Essay VIII.*[16]

> A great authority may be a poor proof, but it is an excellent presumption: and few things give a wise man man a truer delight than to reconcile two great authorities, that had been commonly but falsely held to be dissonant. Stapylton

Under a deep impression of the importance of the truths we have essayed to develope, we would fain remove every prejudice that does not originate in the heart rather than in the understanding. For Truth, says the wise man, will not enter a malevolent spirit.

To offer or to receive names in lieu of sound arguments, is only less reprehensible than an ostentatious contempt of the great men of

[16] *The Friend,* III, 204 ff. (Essay IX in 1837 edition).

former ages; but we may well and wisely avail ourselves of authorities, in confirmation of truth, and above all, in the removal of prejudices founded on imperfect information. We do not see, therefore, how we can more appropriately conclude this first, explanatory and controversial section of our inquiry, than by a brief statement of our renowned countryman's own principles of Method, conveyed for the greater part in his own words. Nor do we see, in what more precise form we can recapitulate the substance of the doctrines asserted and vindicated in the preceding pages. For we rest our strongest pretensions to a calm and respectful perusal, in the first instance, on the fact, that we have only re-proclaimed the coinciding prescripts of the Athenian Verulam, and the British Plato—genuinam scilicet PLATONIS Dialecticem; et Methodologiam *principialem.*

FRANCISCI DE VERULAMIO

In the first instance, Lord Bacon equally with ourselves, demands what we have ventured to call the intellectual or mental initiative, as the motive and guide of every philosophical experiment; some well-grounded purpose, some distinct impression of the probable results, some self-consistent anticipation as the ground of the *"prudens quæstio"* (the forethoughtful query), which he affirms to be the prior *half* of the knowledge sought, *dimidium scientiæ.* With him, therefore, as with us, an idea is an experiment proposed, an experiment is an idea realized. For so, though in other words, he himself informs us: "neque scientiam molimur tam sensu vel instrumentis, quam *experimentis*; etenim experimentorum longe major est subtilitas quam sensûs ipsius, licet instrumentis exquisitis adjuti: de iis loquimur experimentis, quæ ad intentionem ejus quod quæritur peritè nam secundum artem excogitata et apposita sunt. Itaque perceptioni sensûs immediatæ *et* propriæ *non multum tribuimus*: sed eò rem deducimus, ut *sensus tantum de experimento, experimentum de re judicet."*[17] This last sentence is, as the attentive reader will have himself detected, one of those faulty *verbal* antitheses not unfrequent in Lord Bacon's writings. Pungent antitheses, and the analogies of wit in which the resemblance is too often more indebted to the double or equivocal sense of the word, than to any real conformity in the thing or image, form the dulcia vitia of his style, the Dalilahs of our philosophical Samson. But in this instance, as indeed throughout all his works, the meaning is clear and evident—namely, that the sense

---

[17] "Distributio Operis," *Novum Organum* in *Works of Francis Bacon,* ed. David Mallet (4 vols.; London: 1740), I, 15. "Thus (to take the first instance that occurs), Bacon says, that some knowledges, like the stars, are so high that they give no light. Where the word, 'high,' means 'deep or sublime,' in the one case, and 'distant' in the other." Coleridge's note.

can apprehend, through the organs of sense, only the phænomena evoked by the experiment: vis verò mentis ea, quæ experimentum excogitaverat, de Re judicet: i.e. that power which, out of its own conceptions had shaped the experiment, must alone determine the true *import* of the phænomena. If again we ask, what it is which gives birth to the question, and then ad intentionem quæstionis suæ experimentum excogitat, unde de Re judicet, the answer is: *Lux Intellectûs, lumen siccum*, the pure and impersonal reason, freed from all the various *idols* enumerated by our great legislator of science (*idola tribûs, specûs, fori, theatri*); that is, freed from the limits, the passions, the prejudices, the peculiar habits of the human understanding, natural or acquired; but above all, pure from the arrogance, which leads man to take the forms and mechanism of his own mere reflective faculty, as the measure of nature and of Deity. In this indeed we find the great object both of Plato's and of Lord Bacon's labors. They both saw that there could be no hope of any fruitful and secure method, while forms, merely *subjective*, were presumed as the true and proper moulds of *objective* truth. This is the sense in which Lord Bacon uses the phrases—intellectus humanus, mens hominis, so profoundly and justly characterized in the preliminary (Distributio Operis) of his De Augment. Scient. And with all right and propriety did he so apply them: for this was, *in fact*, the sense in which the phrases were applied by the teachers, whom he is controverting; by the doctors of the schools; and the visionaries of the laboratory. To adopt the bold but happy phrase of a late ingenious French writer, it is the homme *particuliere*, as contrasted with l'homme *generale*; against which, Heraclitus and Plato, among the ancients, and among the moderns, BACON and STEWART[18] (rightly understood), warn and pre-admonish the sincere inquirer. Most truly, and in strict consonance with his two great predecessors, does our immortal Verulam teach—that the human understanding, even independent of the causes that always, previously to its purification by philosophy, render it more or less turbid or uneven, ipsâ suâ naturâ *radios ex figurâ* et sectione propriâ immutat":[19] that our understanding not only reflects the objects *subjectively*, that is, substitutes for the inherent laws and properties of the objects the relations which the objects bear to its own particular constitution; but that in all its conscious presentations and reflexes, it is itself only a phænomenon of the inner sense, and requires the same corrections as the appearances transmitted by the outward senses. But that there is potentially, if not actually, in every rational being, a somewhat, call it what you will, the pure reason, the spirit, lumen siccum, νοῦς, φῶς νοερόν,

---

[18] Dugald Stewart (1753-1828), philosopher.
[19] "Distributio Operis," *Novum Organum* in Mallet, *Works*, I, 15.

intellectual intuition, &c. &c.; and that in this are to be found the in-
dispensible [sic] conditions of all science, and scientific research, whether meditative, contemplative, or experimental; is often expressed, and
everywhere supposed, by Lord Bacon. And that this is not only the
right but the possible nature of the human mind, to which it is capable
of being restored, is implied in the various remedies prescribed by him
for its diseases, and in the various means of neutralizing or converting
into useful instrumentality the imperfections which cannot be removed. There is a sublime truth contained in his favourite phrase—
Idola intellectus. He thus tells us, that the mind of man is an edifice not
built with human hands, which needs only to be purged of its idols and
idolatrous services to become the temple of the true and living Light.
Nay, he has shown and established the true criterion between the ideas
and the idola of the mind—namely, that the former are manifested by
their adequacy to those ideas in nature, which in and through them are
contemplated. "Non leve quiddam interest inter humanæ mentis idola
et divinæ mentis ideas, hoc est, inter placita quædam inania et veras
signaturas atque impressiones factas in creaturis, prout Ratione sanâ et
sicci luminis, quam docendi causâ, interpretem naturæ vocare con-
suevimus, inveniuntur."[20] Thus the difference, or rather distinction between Plato and Lord Bacon is simply this: that philosophy being necessarily bi-polar, Plato treats principally of the truth, as it manifests
itself at the *ideal* pole, as the science of intellect, (i.e. de mundo intelli-
gibili) ; while Bacon confines himself, for the most part, to the same truth,
as it is manifested at the other, or material pole, as the science of nature
(i.e. de mundo sensibili). It is as necessary, therefore, that Plato should
direct his inquiries chiefly to those objective truths that exist in and for
the intellect alone, the images and representatives of which we construct for ourselves by figure, number, and word; as that Lord Bacon
should attach his main concern to the truths which have their signatures
in nature, and which (as he himself plainly and often asserts) may
indeed be revealed to us *through* and *with,* but never *by* the senses,
or the faculty of sense. Otherwise, indeed, instead of being *more* objective than the former (which they are not in any sense, both being in
this respect the same), they would be *less* so, and, in fact, incapable
of being insulated from the "Idola tribûs quae in ipsâ naturâ
humana fundata sunt, atque in ipsâ tribu seu gente hominum: cum
omnes perceptiones tam sensûs quam mentis, sunt ex analogiâ hominis,
non ex analogiâ universi."[21] Hence too, it will not surprise us, that
Plato so often calls ideas LIVING LAWS, in which the mind has its whole

---

[20] *Novum Organum,* Aph. XXII and XXVI. Cf. Aph. CXXIV.
[21] *Novum Organum,* Aph. XLI.

true being and permanence; or that Bacon, vicè versâ, names the laws of nature, *ideas;* and represents what we have, in a former part of this disquisition, called *facts of science* and *central phænomena,* as signatures, impressions, and symbols of ideas. A distinguishable power self-affirmed, and seen in its unity with the Eternal Essence, is, according to Plato, an IDEA: and the discipline, by which the human mind is purified from its idols (εἴδωλα), and raised to the contemplation of Ideas, and thence to the secure and ever-progressive, though never-ending, investigation of truth and reality by scientific method, comprehends what the same philosopher so highly extols under the title of Dialectic. According to Lord Bacon, as describing the same truth seen from the opposite point, and applied to natural philosophy, an idea would be defined as— Intuitio sive inventio, quæ in perceptione sensûs non est (ut quæ puræ et sicci luminis Intellectioni est propria) idearum divinæ mentis, prout in creaturis per signaturas suas sese patefaciant. That (saith the judicious HOOKER) which doth assign to each thing the kind, that which determines the force and power, that which doth appoint the form and measure of working, the same we term a LAW.[22]

We can now, as men furnished with fit and respectable credentials, proceed to the historic importance and practical application of METHOD, under the deep and solemn conviction, that without this guiding Light neither can the sciences attain to their full evolution, as the organs of one vital and harmonious body, nor that most weighty and concerning of all sciences, the science of EDUCATION, be understood in its first elements, much less display its powers, as the nisus formativus of social man, as the appointed PROTOPLAST of true humanity. Never can society comprehend fully, and in its whole practical extent, the permanent distinction, and the occasional contrast, between cultivation and civilization; never can it attain to a due insight into the momentous fact, fearfully as it has been, and even now is exemplified in a neighbour country, that a nation can never be too cultivated, but may easily become an over-civilized, race:[23] while we oppose ourselves voluntarily to that grand prerogative of our nature, A HUNGERING AND THIRSTING AFTER TRUTH, as the appropriate end of our intelligential, and its point of union with, our moral nature; but therefore after truth, that must be found within us before it can be *intelligibly* reflected back on the mind from without, and a religious regard to which is indispensable, both as guide and object to the just formation of the human BEING, poor and rich: while, in a word, we are blind to the master-light, which we have already pre-

[22] Hooker, *Eccl. Pol.* (1682), Book I, p. 2. Adapted from Aph. XXIII.
[23] In later editions there is interpolated at this point: ''never, I repeat, can this sanative and preventive knowledge take up its abode among us.''

sented in various points of view, and recommended by whatever is of highest authority with the venerators of the ancient, and the adherents of modern philosophy.

Turn over the fugitive writings, that are still extant, of the age of Luther; peruse the pamphlets and loose sheets that came out in flights during the reign of Charles the First and the Republic; and you will find in these one continued comment on the aphorism of Lord Chancellor Bacon (a man assuredly sufficiently acquainted with the extent of secret and personal influence) that the knowledge of the speculative principles of men in general between the age of twenty and thirty, is the one great source of political prophecy.[24]

The Lord Chancellor Bacon lived in an age of court intrigues, and was familiarly acquainted with all the secrets of personal influence. He, if any man, was qualified to take the gauge and measurement of their comparative power, and he has told us, that there is one, and but one infallible source of political prophecy, the knowledge of the predominant opinions and the speculative principles of men in general, between the age of twenty and thirty.[25]

Then glancing off to Aristotle, he gave a very high character of him. He said that Bacon objected to Aristotle the grossness of his examples, and Davy now did precisely the same to Bacon; both were wrong; for each of these philosophers wished to confine the attention of the mind in their works to the *form* of reasoning only by which other truths might be established or elicited, and therefore the most trite and commonplace examples were in fact the best.[26]

Mystes, from the Greek μύω—one who muses with closed lips, as meditating on ideas which may indeed be suggested and awakened, but can not, like the images of sense and the conceptions of the understanding, be adequately expressed by words.

Where a person mistakes the anomalous misgrowths of his own individuality for ideas or truths of universal reason, he may, without impropriety, be called a mystic, in the abusive sense of the term; though

[24] *Statesman's Manual,* p. 19.
[25] *The Friend,* Section I, Essay III, I, 315.
[26] April 20, 1811, at Richmond. Recollections communicated by Mr. Justice Coleridge. *Table Talk S,* VI, 525.

pseudo-mystic or phantast would be the more proper designation. Heraclitus, Plato, Bacon, Leibnitz, were mystics in the primary sense of the term; Iamblichus and his successors, phantasts.[27]

> . . . the element of air in the nomenclature of observation (that is, of Nature as it appears to us when unquestioned by art), and azote or nitrogen in the nomenclature of experiment (that is, of Nature in the state so beautifully allegorized in the Homeric fable of Proteus bound down, and forced to answer by Ulysses, after having been pursued through all his metamorphoses into his ultimate form)

Such is the interpretation given by Lord Bacon. To which of the two gigantic intellects, the poet's or philosophic commentator's the allegory belongs, I shall not presume to decide. Its extraordinary beauty and appropriateness remains the same in either case.—C.[28]

Logic, for every general purpose, is, in my opinion, infinitely more useful than geometry, and furnishes a more healthful regimen for the mind; and I say this without in any way undervaluing the importance of mathematics; for I, too, have—

> . . . Mused on Granta's willowy strand,
> The sage of Alexandria in my hand,
> And marked his mystic symbols; the severe
> And cogent truths dwell in my reason's ear.

Nor have I forgotten the words of that illustrious man, by whom SCIENCE was married to POETRY, and in whose writings she always appears in the company of the Graces. Need I mention Lord Bacon? "If the wit be too dull," said he, "they sharpen it; if too wandering, they fix it; if too inherent in the sense, they abstract it." This great principle ought to be kept constantly in sight. Geometry is a means to an end— a series of steps to a temple; many, I fear, there are who never get beyond the steps. The admirable Fuller, of whom Queen's ought to be almost as proud as of Erasmus, has placed the matter in a very clear and proper light, in his character of a learned and accomplished person. "Mathematics," he says, "he moderately studieth to his great contentment, using it as ballast for his soul; yet to fix it, not to stall it, nor suffers it to be so unmannerly as to jostle out other arts." A mere mathematician, made up of unknown quantities, is dreary and melancholy spectacle—a tree without leaves. . . .

[27] "Notes on Isaac Taylor's *History of Enthusiasm*," Shedd, VI, 129-30.
[28] *Hints towards the Formation of a More Comprehensive Theory of Life*, ed. Seth B. Watson (London: 1848), p. 69. Coleridge's note on the passage from the text.

Nothing can be more absurd than this belief of the necessary opposition of poetry to science. In all great poets the reverse is manifest. You see it in Homer, in Dante, and above all, in Milton. Perhaps I ought rather to say, that you *feel* its influence, in shaping the conceptions of the poet, and preserving those fine proportions whose combination makes the harmony of a structure.[29]

We have borrowed & your Mother will send the only English Translation of Bacon's Novum Organum as yet in print. Had you been in town, Montagu would have lent for your perusál Mr. Wood's new Translation but it is in MSS.—But honestly, I must tell, that in my judgement it would be an *unseasonable* application of your time & thoughts—if not a waste of them. You are not sufficiently prepared for that Work by a previous intimacy with the antecedent Schools of Philosophy—especially the *genuine* & the corrupt, Platonic and Aristotelean Schools—And nothing can be more unfair & often untrue, than Lord Bacon's attacks on both the one and the other. Besides, the Aphoristic and fragmentary character of the work, aggravated by Bacon's frequent inconsistencies, is not likely to engender that state of intellect especially desirable for you at this time & for the next year or two of your studies.[30]

There is a noble passage in Lord Bacon on the *serious* [?] manifestation of the craving for permanence in the human mind and feelings—& no more fearful symptom of moral deterioration in a people than the contemptuous disregard of Antiquity.[31]

I must turn from the Critic to refresh myself with the glorious passage (the last §s, ph. but one of the First Book of Lord Bacon's "Of the Advancement of Learning," the English version of the De Augmentis) "Lastly, leaving the vulgar arguments" &c.[32]

In Lord Bacon's New Atlantis there is a sentence which might have been quoted during the Debates on the Marriage Bill by Lord Ellenborough[33] or Canning—"Marriage without consent of Parents they do

[29] Willmott, *C. at Trinity*, pp. 11-12, 13.
[30] To James Gillman, Jr., Aug. 11, 1830. Wordsworth, *Some Family Letters*, pp. 105-6.
[31] Notebook 51, fol. 4 verso. British Museum, Add. MSS, 47,546. Printed for the first time.
[32] *Ibid.*, fol. 13 recto. Printed for the first time.
[33] This debate took place in 1823; Edward Law, Lord Ellenborough (1750-1818), was lord chief justice.

not make void, but they mulct it in the inheritors: for the children of
such Marriages are not admitted to inherit above a Third part of their
parents' Inheritance.''[34]

As I disclaim all necessity of palliating Shakespear's supposed
offenses against morals (& an offense against our manners needs no defense) from the Times in which he lived wch [*sic*] is after all but the
multitude of accomplices—so I hold Bacon's mind in too great awe to
dare offer him the benefit of the Abandoned & despicable Court of James
I.—This conduct under Elizabeth respecting the E. of Essex does not
in my opinion deserve the harsh reprobation it has receive[d]. The
meanness of his behaviour resolves itself, I think, in the general meanness of his submitting to being a Solicitor at all—into the disproportion
of vulgar ambition, and craving for court favor to such and so self-
conscious an Intellect. Far more difficult to bring within the bounds
of moderate Reprehension is his Conduct towards Coke, his Letters of
Advice to James, his promises of abject and treasonable servility in
begging for the Seals, his correspondence with Buckingham &c. It is
indeed possible that Bacon may have actually, I scarcely dare say conscientiously, held the opinion, that the government & stability of the
Realm required a remnant of law-dispensing monarchy, an occasional
ipse volo, sit pro Lege, regia voluntas, & some thing might, in a less man,
be conceded to that notion so universal in thought of the highest ministers of State being not the King's (i. e. State's) but the *Man's* confidential Servants who sustained the name & shew of the never-dying &
impeccable King—so that fidelity obliged them to pursue and uphold
his (the individual's) interests, ex. gr. his power & revenue, even against
those of the People, above all, against Parliament—while their virtue
consisted in not carrying their zeal to a degree hazardous to *his* safety
or popularity. But after all, the Letters are so very base as almost to
embolden me to enquire whether I have not over-rated Lord Bacon's
Genius (To over-rate his Talents is perhaps not possible)—to meet boldly
the Question, whether Lord Bacon does really form the one only known
exception to Baseness in union with a *first-rate Genius?* In order to this,
we must begin by seeking in what the character of Bacon's intellect—
Generalization—a most active associative Power—an opulence in rami-
fication—felicity in observation and the reduction of observances to the

[34] Notebook 3½, fol. 111 recto. ''See Mallett's Folio Edition of Bacon, V.
IInd, p. 448. Mem. Should the preceding Reflection be thought by my executives,
J. H. Green & H. N. C. worth putting into better [—?] for the Press, I would have
the whole passage quoted.'' Coleridge's note.

+ nimis & − nimis—and of particulars to their comprehensive & interpretive *Maxims*—n. b. seldom *Principles*—

These are the Excellencies—The reverse of the Medal may be described in two compartments, his Deficiencies & his Defects. . . .[35]

I meant (last p. & last L. but one)[36] that Bacon might have considered the British Constitution as hanging many and various weights & remoras on the absolute power of the Crown; but not as intending to destroy the spring (Federkraft) or to preclude utterly all and every room for its play. He might regard, for instance, the High Court of Chancery, as a sort of loaded or strongly weighted Safety-pipe of the Royal Steam-power, that ordinarily distributed itself among the preconformed Channels, at once restraining & giving it effect, while the Star-chamber, as a court of High Police, could not in theory have appeared an unplausible Part of a mixed Constitution, when no other Substitute has been found for it but the occasional Suspens. of the Hab. Corp. and a Bill of Indemnity on the meeting of Parliament— and surely no one can censure a Statesman of the Age of James for not hazarding so violent an anomaly, as the latter, at a time when an annual Parliament would probably have been still felt as a burthen by the Nation, and when there were neither a standing army requiring an Annual Meeting Act, nor a National Debt, as securities for it's convocation!

A well-balanced mind cannot, however, but contemplate with complacency the retributive justice in Lord Bacon's Fall—ostensibly punished for comparative Trifles, which explained and precedented, as it was in Bacon's power to have done, would have borne no proportion to the penalty—but really *for* his base and servile compliances with the King [and] his profligate Ganymede, & sacrificed by them as a screen for the latter. It is to be feared that Williams's sagacity saw, & that his Desire of binding the Favorite to him prompted him to suggest, that a far higher Victim than the insignificant Scoundrels, he names in his letter to Buckingham, would be required either to blind or to satisfy the Parliament. Bacon must have been base indeed.[37]

The best plan, I think, for a man who would wish his mind to continue growing, is to find, in the first place, some means of ascertaining for himself, whether it does or no. And I can think of no better than

[35] At this point Coleridge wrote a long irrelevant comment in Italian concerning his nephew Henry Nelson Coleridge.
[36] The reference is to fol. 14 recto.
[37] Notebook 30, fol. 13 recto-15 verso. British Museum, Add. MSS, 47,527. Printed for the first time.

in early life, say after 3 & 20, to procure gradually the works of some two or three great writers—say, for instance, Bacon, Jeremy Taylor, Kant, and the De republica, de legibus, the Sophistes, and Politicus of Plato, and the Poetics, Rhetoric and περὶ πολιτείας of Aristotle—and amidst all other reading, to make a point of re-perusing some one or some weighty Part of some one, of these every four or five years.[38]

I believe in my depth of being, that the three great works since the introduction of Christianity are,—Bacon's *Novum Organum,* and his other works, as far as they are commentaries on it:—Spinoza's *Ethica,* with his Letters and other pieces, as far as they are comments on his Ethics: and Kant's Critique of the Pure Reason, and his other works as commentaries on, and applications of the same.[39]

Thomas Hobbes

Sir James Mackintosh (who amid the variety of his talents and attainments is not of less repute for the depth and accuracy of his philosophical enquiries, than for the eloquence with which he is said to render their most difficult results perspicuous, and the driest attractive) affirmed in the lectures, delivered by him in Lincoln's Inn Hall, that the law of association as established in the contemporaneity of the original impressions, formed the basis of all true phsychology [sic]; and any ontological or metaphysical science not contained in such (i. e. an empirical) phsychology was but a web of abstractions and generalizations. Of this prolific truth, of this great fundamental law, he declared HOBBS to have been the original *discoverer,* while its full application to the whole intellectual system we owe to David Hartley; who stood in the same relation to Hobbs as Newton to Kepler; the law of association being that to the mind, which gravitation is to matter.

Of the former clause in this assertion, as it respects the comparative merits of the ancient metaphysicians, including their commentators, the school-men, and of the modern French and British philosophers from

---

[38] Notebook 23, fol. 23 verso-24 recto.   British Museum, Add. MSS, 47,521. Printed for the first time.

[39] Quoted from notes in Coleridge's copy of Schelling's *Philosophische Schriften,* undated, in Shedd, III, 257 n.

Hobbs to Hume, Hartley and Condillac, this is not the place to speak. So wide indeed is the chasm between this gentleman's philosophical creed and mine, that so far from being able to join hands, we could scarce make our voices intelligible to each other: and to *bridge* it over, would require more time, skill and power than I believe myself to possess. But the latter clause involves for the greater part a mere question of fact and history, and the accuracy of the statement is to be tried by documents rather than reasoning.

First then, I deny Hobbs's claim in toto: for he had been anticipated by Des Cartes, whose work "De Methodo" preceded Hobbs's "De Natura Humana;" by more than a year. But what is of much more importance, Hobbs builds nothing on the principle which he had announced. He does not even announce it, as differing in any respect from the general laws of material motion and impact: nor was it, indeed, possible for him so to do, compatibly with his system, which was exclusively material and mechanical. Far otherwise is it with Des Cartes; greatly as he too in his after writings (and still more egregiously his followers De La Forge,[1] and others) obscured the truth by their attempts to explain it on the theory of nervous fluids, and material configurations. But in his interesting work "De Methodo," Des Cartes relates the circumstance which first led him to meditate on this subject, and which since then has been often noticed and employed as an instance and illustration of the law. A child who with its eyes bandaged had lost several of his fingers by amputation, continued to complain for many days successively of pains, now in this joint and now in that of the very fingers which had been cut off. Des Cartes was led by this incident to reflect on the uncertainty with which we attribute any particular place to any inward pain or uneasiness, and proceeded after long consideration to establish it as a general law; that contemporaneous impressions, whether images or sensations, recall each other mechanically. On this principle, as a ground work, he built up the whole system of human language, as one continued process of association. He showed, in what sense not only general terms, but generic images (under the name of abstract ideas) actually existed, and in what consists their nature and power. As one word may become the general exponent of many, so by association a simple image may represent a whole class. But in truth Hobbs himself makes no claims to any discovery, and introduces this law of association, or (in his own language) discursûs mentalis, as an admitted fact, in the *solution* alone of which, and this by causes purely physiological, he arrogates any originality. His system is briefly this; whenever the

---

[1] Louis de La Forge, a French Protestant theologian, whose *Treatise on the Human Mind* was published in Paris in 1666.

senses are impinged on by external objects, whether by the rays of light reflected from them, or by effluxes of their finer particles, there results a correspondent motion of the innermost and subtlest organs. This motion constitutes a *representation,* and there remains an *impression* of the same, or a certain disposition to repeat the same motion. Whenever we feel several objects at the same time, the *impressions* that are left (or in the language of Mr. Hume, the *ideas*) are linked together. Whenever therefore any one of the movements, which constitute a complex impression, are renewed through the senses, the others succeed mechanically. It follows of necessity therefore that Hobbs, as well as Hartley and all others who derive association from the connection and interdependence of the supposed matter, the movements of which constitute our thoughts, *must* have reduced all its forms to the one law of time. But even the merit of announcing this law with philosophic precision cannot be fairly conceded to him. For the objects of any two ideas[2] need not have co-existed in the same sensation in order to become mutually associable. The same result will follow when one

[2] "I here used the word 'idea' in Mr. Hume's sense on account of its general currency among the English metaphysicans; though against my own judgment, for I believe that the vague use of this word has been the cause of much error and more confusion. The word 'Ιδέα, in its orignal sense as used by Pindar, Aristophanes, and in the gospel of Matthew, represented the visual abstraction of a distant object, when we see the whole without distinguishing its parts. Plato adopted it as a technical term, and as the antithesis to Εἴδωλα, or sensuous images; the transient and perishable emblems, or mental words, of ideas. The ideas themselves he considered as mysterious powers, living, seminal, formative, and exempt from time. In this sense the word became the property of the Platonic school; and it seldom occurs in Aristotle, without some such phrase annexed to it, as according to Plato, or as Plato says. Our English writers to the end of Charles 2nd's reign, or somewhat later, employed it either in the original sense, or platonically, or in a sense nearly correspondent to our present use of the substantive, Ideal; always however opposing it, more or less, to image, whether of present or absent objects. The reader will not be displeased with the following interesting exemplification from Bishop Jeremy Taylor. 'St. Lewis the King sent Ivo Bishop of Chartres on an embassy, and he told, that he met a grave and stately matron on the way with a censer of fire in one hand, and a vessel of water in the other; and observing her to have a melancholy, religious, and phantastic deportment and look, he asked her what those symbols meant, and what she meant to do with her fire and water; she answered, my purpose is with the fire to burn paradise, and with my water to quench the flames of hell, that men may serve God purely for the love of God. But we rarely meet with such spirts which love virtue so metaphysically *as to abstract her from all sensible compositions, and love the purity of the idea*'. Des Cartes having introduced into his philosophy the fanciful hypothesis of *material ideas,* or certain configurations of the brain, which were as so many moulds to the influxes of the external world; Mr. Lock adopted the term, but extended its signification to whatever is the immediate object of the minds attention or consciousness. Mr. Hume distinguishing those representations which are accompanied with a sense of a present object, from those reproduced by the mind itself, designated the former as *impressions,* and confined the word *idea* to the latter." Coleridge's note.

only of the two ideas has been represented by the senses, and the other by the memory.

Long however before either Hobbs or Des Cartes the law of association had been defined, and its important functions set forth by Melanchthon, Ammerbach, and Ludovicus Vives;[3] more especially by the last. Phantasia, it is to be noticed, is employed by Vives to express the mental power of comprehension, or the *active* function of the mind; and imaginatio for the receptivity (vis receptiva) of impressions, or for the *passive* perception . . .

But from Vives I pass at once to the source of his doctrines, and (as far as we can judge from the remains yet extant of Greek philosophy) as to the first, so to the fullest and most perfect enunciation of the associative principle, viz. to the writings of Aristotle; and of these principally to the books "De Anima," and "De Memoria," and that which is entitled in the old translations "Parva Naturalia." In as much as later writers have either deviated from, or added to his doctrines, they appear to me to have introduced either error or groundless supposition.

In the first place it is to be observed, that Aristotle's positions on this subject are unmixed with fiction. The wise Stagyrite speaks of no successive particles propagating motion like billiard balls (as Hobbs;) nor of nervous or animal spirits, where inanimate and irrational solids are thawed down, and distilled, or filtrated by ascension, into living and intelligent fluids, that etch and re-etch engravings on the brain, (as the followers of Des Cartes, and the humoral pathologists in general;) nor of an oscillating ether which was to effect the same service for the nerves of the brain considered as solid fibres, as the animal spirits perform for them under the notion of hollow tubes (as *Hartley* teaches)— nor finally, (with yet more recent dreamers) of chemical compositions by an elective affinity, or of an electric light at once the immediate object and the ultimate organ of inward vision, which rises to the brain like an Aurora Borealis, and there disporting in various shapes (as the balance of plus and minus, or negative and positive, is destroyed or re-established) images out both past and present. Aristotle delivers a just *theory* without pretending to an *hypothesis;* or in other words a comprehensive survey of the different facts, and of their relations to each other without *supposition,* i. e. a fact *placed under* a number of facts, as their common support and explanation; tho' in the majority of instances these hypotheses or suppositions better deserve the name of 'Υποποιήσεις, or *suffictions.* He uses indeed the word Κινήσεις, to express what we call representations or ideas, but he carefully distinguishes them from material motion, designating the latter always by annexing the words

[3] Vives, Juan Luis (Giovanni Ludovico) (1492-1540) was a Spanish philosopher.

Ἐν τόπῳ, or κατὰ τόπον. On the contrary in his treatise "De Anima," he excludes place and motion from all the operations of thought, whether representations or volitions, as attributes utterly and absurdly heterogeneous.[4]

The pleasurable heat which the blood or the breathing generates, the sense of external reality which comes with the strong grasp of the hand, or the vigorous tread of the foot, may indifferently become associated with the rich eloquence of a Shaftesbury, imposing on us man's possible perfections for his existing nature; or with the cheerless and hardier impieties of a Hobbes, while cutting the Gordian knot he denies the reality of either vice or virtue, and explains away the mind's self-reproach into a distempered ignorance, an epidemic affection of the human nerves and their habits of motion.

         Vain wisdom all, and false philosophy![5]

       . . . and themselves[6] they cheat
       With noisy emptiness of learned phrase,
       Their subtle fluids, impacts, essences,
       Self-working tools, uncaus'd affects, and all
       Those blind omniscients, those almighty slaves,
       Untenanting creation of it's God![7]

Even so late as the time of Charles the First and the Republic of England, the words "compelled" and "obliged" were perfectly synonymous. Hobbes and other men of his mind took advantage of this one term and contended therefore, that as everybody acknowledged that men were obliged to do such and such things, and that if a man were *obliged* it was synonymous to say he was *compelled*, there could never arise anything like guilt. For who could blame a man for doing what he was obliged to do since he was compelled to do it. This fortunately puzzled only a few minds but it convinced only those who wished to be convinced, whose crimes and bad conscience found a consolation in this; while the innocent, puzzled, began to say, "There is a defect in our language." In this instance they are two perfectly different things and every man feels them to be different and the best way is to use the word "obliged" when we mean what a man ought to do, and the word "compelled" when we mean what man must do whether he likes it or

[4] *Biog. Lit. C,* I, 96-103.
[5] *The Friend* (1837 edition), Appendix B, III, 312.
[6] Hobbes and Locke.
[7] "Destiny of Nations."

not. And with this single clearing up of the terms the whole basis fell at once, as far at least as *that* argument was convincing.[8]

Thus in the reign of Charles II. the philosophic world was called to arms by the moral sophisms of Hobbs, and the ablest writers exerted themselves in the detection of an error, which a school-boy would now be able to confute by the mere recollection, that *compulsion* and *obligation* conveyed two ideas perfectly disparate, and that what appertained to the one, had been falsely transferred to the other by a mere confusion of terms.[9]

It is most true that such an equivocation did exist, and perhaps in the minds of too many may exist still in the term necessity and till the reign of Charles the second even in the word compulsion. And Hobbes repeatedly speaks of the will as compelled by certain causes where an accurate speaker would now say impelled by such and such motives or tendencies. But this ambiguity has long since ceased to exist among men conversant with the history of this celebrated controversy, and at all entitled to renew it, and its removal having been effected by and in consequence of the controversy furnishes a proof in point, that the most noted Questions in philosophy not only are not mere Logomachies easily reconciled by shewing that though both parties used the same word, yet each understood it in a different sense . . .[10]

And herein I follow the practice of all scientific men, whether naturalists or metaphysicians, and the dictate of common sense, that one word ought to have but one meaning. Thus by Hobbes and others of the materialists, compulsion and obligation were used indiscriminately; but the distinction of the two senses is the condition of all moral responsibility.[11]

Ah! poor Hobbes, he possessed fine talents: in forming his theories, however, he fancied the first link of his chain was fastened to a rock of *adamant;* but it proved to be a rock of *ice.*[12]

All the evil achieved by Hobbes and the whole School of Materialists will appear inconsiderable if it be compared with the mischief effected

[8] Philosophical Lecture V, Jan. 18, 1819. Coburn, *Phil. Lect.*, p. 174.
[9] *Biog. Lit. C*, I, 91 n.
[10] MS Logic, II, fol. 153. British Museum, MSS Egerton, 2826.
[11] "Note on Birch's Sermon," *Lit. Rem.*, II, 366.
[12] "Retrospect of Friendly Communications with the Poet Coleridge," *Christian Observer*, XLV (May, 1845), 260.

and occasioned by the sentimental philosophy of STERNE, and his numerous Imitators. The vilest appetites and the most remorseless inconstancy toward their objects, acquired the titles of *the Heart, the irresistible Feelings, the too tender Sensibility*: and if the Frosts of Prudence, the icy chains of Human Law thawed and vanished at the genial warmth of Human *Nature,* who *could help it?* It was an amiable Weakness![13]

In the most similar and nearest points there is a difference, but for the most part there is an absolute contrast, between Hobbes and Spinoza. Thus Hobbes makes a state of war the natural state of man from the essential and ever continuing nature of man, as not a moral, but only a frightenable, being:—Spinoza makes the same state a necessity of man out of society, because he must then be an undeveloped man, and his moral being dormant; and so on through the whole.[14]

All the different philosophical systems of political justice, all the Theories on the rightful Origin of Government, are reducible in the end to three classes, correspondent to the three different points of view, in which the Human Being itself may be contemplated. The first denies all truth and distinct meaning to the words, RIGHT and DUTY, and affirming the human mind consists of nothing, but manifold modifications of passive sensation, considers men as the highest sort of animals indeed, but at the same time the most wretched; inasmuch as their defenceless nature forces them into society, while such is the multiplicity of wants engendered by the social state, that the wishes of one are sure to be in contradiction to those of some other. The assertors of this system consequently ascribe the origin and continuance of Government to fear, or the power of the stronger, aided by the force of custom. This is the system of Hobbes. Its statement is its confutation. It is, indeed, in the literal sense of the word *preposterous*: for fear presupposes conquest, and conquest a previous union and agreement between the conquerors.[15]

The Contro-distinction of PERSON[16] from THING being the Ground and Condition of all Morality, a system like this of Hobbes's, which be-

[13] *Aids,* pp. 53-54. Cf. Shedd, I, 137.
[14] *Notes Theolog.,* p. 358.
[15] *The Friend,* Section I, Essay I, I, 283-84.
[16] "The former must not be used, as a *Means,* without likewise included in the *End:* the latter may. I may find Sheep, or fell Timber, for my own advantages exclusively; but not so with the Shepherd or Woodcutter, whom I employ. I must

gins by confounding them, needs no confutation to a moral Being. With contradicting Results illegitimately deduced from false Premises, thus *trebly* self-baffled, it, nevertheless, in it's essential points passed into the political creed of a powerful & numerous Party for more than half a Century. It becomes interesting, therefore, not only as a curious Fact in Speculative Philosophy, but likewise as an event in English History. Destined for Oliver Cromwell the Hobbesian Theory was embraced and acted on by the restored Monarch and his Ministers: the amiable Cowley extolled the *superhuman* Genius of it's Author: Swift disseminated it in his own name: and Bolingbroke in his Letter to Sir W. Wyndham, in that to Mr. Pope, and in his Tract on the State of the Nation, has given a summary of it as his own Principles and those of the Tories and High-Church men with whom he acted; as the Truths, the enforcement of which by Law was the grand Object of the Party, which at that time comprized four fifths of the inferior Clergy and Country Gentlemen throughout England. Alas! even the venerable University of Oxford, while she denounced the Author and sundry Tenets extracted from the Leviathan, yet as far as concerns the . . .[17]

[end of page, and no more in book. Not published in *Essays* III, 925ff.]

The first of Hobbes's work, in which association of Ideas is spoken of—is—Cap. xxv. pars 4. Elementorum Philosophiæ &c.—first published 1665—& this a very lame account too of it, & merely deduced from materialism.[18]

That Hobbes translated Homer in English verse and published his translation, furnishes no positive evidence of his self-conceit, though it implies a great lack of self-knowledge and of acquaintance with the nature of poetry. A strong wish often imposes itself on the mind for an actual power: the mistake is favoured by the innocent pleasure derived from the exercise of versification, perhaps by the approbation of intimates; and the candidate asks from more impartial readers that

make them *amends*, i.e. the advantage must be reciprocal. A Slave is a *Person perverted* into a *Thing*: Slavery, therefore, is not so properly a deviation from Justice, as an absolute subversion of all Morality." Coleridge's note.

[17] British Museum, MSS Egerton, 2800, fol. 114. "The Catholic Petition. Letter III. Systems of Toleration. Hobbes. Locke. Warburton. Mendelssohn: continued from the Courier of Wednesday, Sept. 24."

[18] Notebook 22, fol. 92 verso. British Museum, Add. MSS, 47,520. Printed for the first time.

sentence, which Nature has not enabled him to anticipate. But when the philosopher of Malmesbury waged war with Wallis and the fundamental truths of pure geometry, every instance of his gross ignorance and utter misconception of the very elements of the science he proposed to confute, furnished an unanswerable fact in proof of his high presumption; and the confident and insulting language of the attack leaves the judicious reader in as little doubt of his gross arrogance. An illiterate mechanic, who mistaking some disturbance of his nerves for a miraculous call proceeds alone to convert a tribe of savages, whose language he can have no natural means of acquiring, may have been misled by impulses very different from those of high self-opinion; but the illiterate perpetrator of "the Age of Reason," must have had *his* very conscience stupified by the habitual intoxication of presumptious arrogance, and his common-sense over-clouded by the vapours from his heart.[19]

At the time I wrote this essay, and indeed till the present month, December, 1818, I had never seen Hobbes' translation of the Odyssey, which, I now find, is by no means to be spoken of contemptuously. It is doubtless as much too ballad-like, as the later volumes are too epic, but still, on the whole, it leaves a much truer impression of the original.[20]

> Ulysses his estate and wealth were such,
> No prince in Greece, not Argos, nor Epire,
> In Ithaca no twenty, had so much:
> And, if to have it reckoned you desire,
> Upon the continent twelve herds of kine,
> Twelve herds of goats, as many flocks of sheep,
> As many swine-houses replete with swine;
> And here, upon the island's farthest end,
> There be eleven herds of goats
> HOBBES' *Odyssey;*

which, homely as it is throughout and too often vulgar, scarcely falls below the point more than the other translators strain above it. In easy flow of narration, Hobbes has few rivals; and his metre in alternate rhyme is so smooth (*negatively* smooth, I mean,) so lithe, without bone or muscle, that you soon forget that it is metre, and read on with the same kind and degree of interest as if it were a volume of the Arabian Nights.[21]

[19] *The Friend,* Essay IV, I, 46-47.
[20] Note to the above reference.
[21] *Chronological and Historical Assistant to a Course of Lectures on the History of Philosophy* (1818), pp. 5-6; also printed by Coburn, *Phil. Lect.,* p. 72 n.

I had not then seen Hobbes' Version of the Odyssey: which, homely as it is throughout, and too often vulgar, scarcely falls below the right point more than the later translators strain above it. In easy flow of narration, H. has few rivals, and his metre in alternate rhyme is so smooth (i. e. negatively smooth) so *lithe* without bone or muscle, that we soon forget that it is metre and read on with the same sort of interest, as in a Volume of Arabian Nights. Παρὰ δόξαν μὲν ἀλλ᾽ οὐδαμῶς παρὰ λόγον. I dare avow it as my conviction, that Hobbes was a better poet than philosopher, ever confining the view to the *talent* manifested in his philos. works and without averting to the truth or falsehood of the tenets advanced & supported. The best part of his writings, it appears to me, are the independent shrewd & happy remarks scattered thro them.[22]

John Locke

My *Letters* to the Wedgewoods shall be copied out and sent you in the course of the next week. I do not think, they will entertain you very much, those already written, I mean; for they are crowded with Latin Quotations, & relate chiefly to the character or Mr. Locke, whom I think I have *proved* to have gained a reputation to which he had no honest claim; and Hobbes as little to the reputation to which T. Wedgewood, and after him Mackintosh, have laboured to raise him.[1]

It is somewhat unpleasant to me, that Mr. Wedgewood has never answered my letter requesting his opinion of the utility of such a work,[2] nor acknowledged the receipt of the 4 long Letters containing the evidence that the whole of Locke's system, as far as it was a system, & with

[22] This appears as a note to his comment in *The Friend*, Essay IV, I, 46, and is found in the copy presented to Dr. Morris. The above is printed for the first time in its complete form by the kind permission of the New York Public Library, where the book is in the Berg Collection.

[1] "Correspondence of Thomas Poole," I, fol. 251-52. Feb. 13, 1801. Printed by Griggs, *Unp. Letters*, I, 173. Griggs reads "dates and" for "Latin." There are no dates in the letters.

[2] "A work on the originality and merits of Locke, Hobbes, and Hume, which work I mean as a *pioneer* to my greater work." To Poole, March 18, 1801. Coleridge, E. H., *Letters*, I, 349.

the exclusion of those parts only, which have been given up for absurdities by his warmest admirers, pre-existed in the writings of Des Cartes, in a far more pure, elegant, & delightful form. Be not afraid, that I shall join the party of the *Little-ists.* I believe that I shall delight you by the detection of their artifices & how far Locke was the founder of this sect, himself *a perfect Little-ist.*[3]

From the first letter to the Wedgwoods on Locke, Feb. 18, 1801.[4]

In my Biographical Dictionary the writer introduces Locke as "one of the greatest men that England ever produced.["]¹ Mr. Hume, a much more competent Judge, declares that he was "really a great Philosopher." Wolf, Feder, & Platner, three Germans, the fathers or favourers of three different Systems, concur in pronouncing him to be "a truly original Genius," and Mr. Locke himself has made it sufficiently clear both in his Essay, and in his Letters to the Bishop of Worcester,[5] that he did not regard himself as a Reformer, but as a Discoverer; not as an opposer of a newly introduced Heresy in Metaphysics, but as an Innovator upon ancient and generally received Opinions. In his dedicatory Epistle speaking of those who are likely to condemn his Essay as opposite to the received Doctrines, "Truth" (says he) "scarce ever yet carried it by Vote any where at *it's first appearance. New* Opinions are always suspected, and usually opposed, without any other Reason but because they are not already common. But Truth, like Gold, is not the less so, for being *newly brought out of the Mine.*"[6] It would have

---

[3] "Correspondence of Thomas Poole," I, fol. 265. Printed in Coleridge, E. H., *Letters,* I, 351, with the variation of "the long letter containing the evidence" instead of "the 4 long Letters containing the evidences." The entire volume of manuscript letters was to some extent edited by Poole before he gave it to Coleridge's literary executor, and the assumption is that Poole made the insertions to correspond with the facts as he knew them. See Brinkley, "Coleridge on Locke," *Studies in Philology,* XLVI (Oct., 1949), pp. 522-23, where a discussion of the letters is given.

[4] Letters on Locke addressed to the Wedgwoods have been mentioned in various Coleridge materials but have not been printed. Three letters were described by Coleridge, E. H., *Letters,* I, 351 n. These are in the "Correspondence of Thomas Poole," I, fol. 254-55, 258-59, 260-61. This correspondence, passed down in the Poole family, was presented to the British Museum by Bishop Sandford of Gibraltar in 1899. A rough copy of a fourth letter, part of which is written on the back of a first draft of the second, is in the British Museum, Miscellaneous Manuscripts, Egerton, 2801, fol. 18-20. This volume was purchased from E. H. Coleridge in 1895. The present editor is concerned only with the discussion which bears directly on Locke; the letters will be edited in their entirety by E. L. Griggs in the definitive edition of Coleridge's letters.

[5] Edward Stillingfleet (1635-99) was a severe critic of Locke, and the letters which Locke addressed to him explain and defend the *Essay on the Human Understanding.*

[6] Dedicatory Epistle to "The Right Honourable Thomas, Earl of Pembroke and Montgomery." The italics indicate Coleridge's underlining.

been well, if Mr. Locke had stated the Doctrines which he considered as
Errors in the very words of some of the most celebrated Teachers of
those Doctrines & enumerated the Truths of which he considered himself
as the Discoverer. A short Post script to this purpose would have
brought to an easy determination the opinions of those, who (as Harris[7]
& Monboddo,[8] for instance) believe that Mr. Locke has grossly misrepresented the ancient & received opinions, and that the Doctrines which
he holds for Truths of his own Discovery are many of them erroneous
& none original. Exempli gratiâ—in the very commencement of the
work he says "It is an established opinion amongst some men, that there
are in the understanding certain Innate Principles, some primary notions, κοιναὶ ἔννοιαι, Characters as it were stamped upon the mind of
man, which the Soul receives in it's very first being, and brings into the
World with it."[9] His own opinion on the contrary is that there are
but two sorts of ideas and both acquired by Experience, namely, "external objects furnish the mind with ideas of sensible Qualities, which
are all those different Perceptions they produce in us: and the mind
furnishes the Understanding with ideas of it's own operations."[10] Of
course, as Locke teaches that the Understanding is but a Term signifying
the Mind in a particular state of action, he means that the mind furnishes itself; and so he himself expresses the Thought in the preceding
Paragraph, defining Ideas of Reflection by "those, which the mind gets
by reflecting on it's own operations within itself."[11] Now, it would
have been well if Locke had named those who held the former Doctrines,
and shewn from their own Words that the two Opinions (his and their's)
were opposite or at least different. More especially, he should have given
his Readers the Definition of the obscure Word "innate" in the very
Language of the most accurate of such Writers as had used the Word.
Pythagoras, it is said, and Plato, it is known, held the pre-existence of
human Souls, and that the most valuable Part of our knowledge was
Recollection. The earliest of these Recollections Plato calls Ζώπυρα,
living Sparks & Ἐναύσματα, kindle-fuel. These notions he confuses in the
Theætetus, and the Phædrus, and still more at large in the Meno; but
neither in these nor else where asserts, that any Ideas (in the present
sense of the word) could be furnished originally or recollectively otherwise than by the mind itself or by things external to the Mind; i. e.
by Reflection or Sensation. The nihil in intellectu quod non prius in

---

[7] James Harris (1709-80), a follower of Aristotle.
[8] James Burnett, Lord Monboddo (1714-99), the author of *Antient Metaphysics*.
[9] *Essay on the Human Understanding*, I, ii, 1.
[10] *Ibid.*, II, i, 5.
[11] *Ibid.*, II, i, 4.

sensu of the Peripatetics is notorious, and that Aristotle speaks of the
mind in it's first state ὥσπερ [ἐν] γραμματείῳ, ᾧ μηδὲν ὑπάρχει ἐντελε
χείᾳ γεγραμμένον [12] the original of Gassendi's and Hobbes's tabula rasa,
and Mr. Locke's unwritten sheet of Paper. Of Aristotle's complete coincidence in this point with Mr. Locke vide Cap. 18 (of the Anal. Poster.
Lib. I.) entitled De ignorantia secundum negationem, but above all Cap.
xix (Of the Anal. Poster. Lib. II) entitled De cognitione Primorum
Principiorum. The Stoics used the phrase κοιναὶ ἔννοιαι, indeed; but
that they meant nothing opposite to Mr. Locke's opinions is made evident by a passage in the work (attributed to Plutarch) De Plac. Philos.
4. 11., in which are these words "The Stoics regarded the Soul when it
came into the World as an unwritten Tablet." The Realists among the
Schoolmen held a Doctrine strangely compounded óf the Peripatetic &
Plotinian School, that universal Ideas are the Souls of all things. I have
never read Aquinas or Scotus, the two great Defenders of this System;
but it is certain, it was a question of Psychogony not Psychology; the
Soul, whatever it was, could only derive it's thoughts from itself or things
external to itself. The nominalists taught that these abstract Ideas were
mere names; the Conceptualists who *moderated* between these & the
Realists coincided with Mr. Locke fully & absolutely (of this party
were Abelard & Heloisa.) Mr. Hume with his wonted sagacity has
given an able statement of the utter unmeaningness of the assertions
which Mr. Locke had made. "For what is meant by *Innate?* If innate
be equivalent to Natural, then all the Perceptions and Ideas of the
Mind must be allowed to be innate or natural, in whatever sense we
take the latter word and whether in opposition to what is uncommon,
artificial, or miraculous. If by innate be meant, contemporary to our
birth the Dispute seems to be frivolous; nor is it worth while to inquire,
at what time Thinking begins, whether before, at or after our Birth.
Again the word Idea seems to be commonly taken in a very loose sense
even by Mr. Locke himself, as standing for any of our Perceptions, our
Sensations, & Passions, as well as Thoughts. Now in this sense I should
desire to know what can be meant by asserting that Self-love, or Resentment of Injuries, or the Passion betwixt the Sexes is not *innate?*" Note
at the end of Essay II.[13] I had not read this note of Mr. Hume's when
I had written the former part of this sheet; & having read it I should
have desisted from the Subject altogether, had I not heard Mr. Mackintosh affirm in his Lectures, that "the Doctrine of Innate Ideas (a
doctrine unknown to the ancients) was first introduced by Des Cartes,

[12] *De Anima* III. iv. 430ª. 1-2.
[13] David Hume, *The Philosophical Works* (4 vols.; Edinburgh & London: 1826),
IV, sec. 2, 23 n.

& fully overthrown by Locke." Mr. M. must have made a mistake—for Lord Herbert's Work De Veritate (which Mr. Locke himself refers to in the third Chapter of his first book ¶ 15, as that which he had consulted, and in which these innate Principles were assigned) was published in 1624, whereas Des Cartes' Metaphysical Books did not appear till 1641. But laying this aside, yet in what sense can Des Cartes be called the introducer of the Doctrine? The Phrase "innate Ideas" is surely not of Des Cartes' Invention "ἔννοια ἔμφυτος"—πᾶσι τοῖς ζῴοις ἔμφυτός ἐστιν ἡ τῆς ὁμοιότητος θεωρία (Diog. Laer. in the Life of Plato)[14] à pueris tot rerum atque tantarum *insitas* et quasi consignatas notiones quas ἐννοίας vocant—Cic. Tusc. Quæst.[15]—Omnibus cognitio, Deum existere, naturaliter inserta est. Damascenus.[16] Deus attigitur notione innata. Ficinus in versione Iamblichi de Mysteriis.[17] Des Cartes' Heresy therefore must have consisted in the new meaning, he gave to the Word, in something or other Mr. Locke must have conceived Des Cartes's opinions as opposite to his own, for he never loses an opportunity of a sneer or sarcasm at the French Philosopher—and what if it were nevertheless true, that Mr. Locke's whole System, as far as it is a system, pre-existed in Des Cartes? In order to show this, permit me to trace the meaning of the word Ideas.

By *Ideas* Plato, notwithstanding his fantastic expressions respecting them, *meant* what Mr. Locke calls the original Faculties & tendencies of the mind, the internal Organs, as it were, and Laws of human Thinking: and the word should be translated "*Moulds*" and not "*Forms.*" (Cicero assures us, that Aristotle's Metaphysical Opinions differ from Plato's only as a Thing said in plain prose, i. e. worn out metaphors, differs from the same thing said in new & striking Metaphors)—Aristotle affirms to the same purpose Δυνάμει πώς ἐστι τὰ νοητὰ ὁ νοῦς, ἀλλ' ἐντελεχείᾳ οὐδὲν πρὶν ἂν νοῇ[18] in respect of *Faculty* the Thought *is* the Thoughts,

[14] *Life of Plato* iii. 15. The Loeb translation reads (I, 291): "animals have the innate power of discerning what is similar."

[15] *Tusculanæ Quæstiones M. Tulli Ciceronis*, Per D. Erasmus, Rotrodamum diligenter emendatæ (Leydieni: 1535), I, 34: "a pueris tot rerum atq; tantarum insitas et quasi consignatas in animæ notiones quas ἐννοίας vocant Græci haberemus."

[16] Coleridge appears to use the paraphrase of two sentences from St. John of Damascus which occurs in the *Summa Theologica* of St. Thomas Aquinas, Part I, Ques. 2, Art. 1, Objection 1: "*Omnibus cognitio existendi deum naturaliter est inserta.*" St. John's original statements are found in *De Fide Orthodoxa.* Book I, Cap. 1: "*Nemo quippe mortalium est, cui non hoc ab eo naturaliter insitum sit, ut Deum esse cognoscat*"; and Book I, Cap. 3: "*Velut enim jam diximus, insitum nobis a natura est, ut Deum esse noscamus.*"

[17] *Iamblichus de Mysteriis Aegyptiorum, Chaldæorum, Assyreorum*, trans. M. Ficino (Lugduni: 1570), p. 2.

[18] *De Anima* III. iv. 429b. 30-31. The Loeb translation reads (p. 169): "The mind is in a manner potentially all aspects of thought, but is actually none of them until it thinks."

but *actually* it is nothing previous to Thinking. By the usual Process of language Ideas came to signify not only these original *moulds* of the mind, but likewise all that was cast in these moulds, as in our Language the Seal & the Impression it leaves are both called Seals. Latterly it wholly lost it's original meaning, and became synonimous sometimes with *Images* simply (whether Impressions or Ideas) and sometimes with Images in the memory; and by Des Cartes it is used for whatever is immediately perceived by the mind. Thus in Meditatione Tertiâ Des Cartes had said "Quædam ex his (scilicet cogitationibus humanis) tanquam rerum imagines sunt, quibus solis propriè convenit ideæ nomen, ut cum hominem vel chimæram vel cœlum vel Angelum vel Deum cogito."[19] In the Objectiones Tertiæ, which were undoubtedly written by Hobbes, the word Idea is obstinately taken for Image, and it is objected to the passage, "*nullam* Dei habemus imaginem sive ideam."[20] To which Des Cartes answers "Hic nomine ideæ vult tantum intelligi imagines[21] Angeli, nec Dei propriam ideam esse posse; atqui ego passim ubique, ac præcipuè hoc ipso in loco, ostendo me nomen ideæ sumere *pro omni eo quod immediate à mente percipitur*, adeo ut cum volo, et timeo, quia simul percipio me velle et timere, ipsa Volitio, et Timor inter Ideas a me numerentur, ususque sum hoc verbo,[22] quia jam tritum erat a Philosophis &c.;[23] et nullum aptius habebam.[24] Locke in his second Letter to the B. of Worcester gives the same definition and assigns the same reason; he would willingly change the Term "Idea" for a Better, if any one could help him to it. But he finds none that stands so well "*for every immediate object of the mind in thinking, as Idea does.*"[25] As Des Cartes & Locke perfectly coincide in the meaning of the *Term* Ideas, so likewise do they equally agree as to their Sorts and Sources. I have read Mr. Locke's Book with care, and I cannot suppress my feelings of

[19] *Meditationes de prima philosophia. . . . His adjunctæ sunt variæ objectiones doctorum virorum in istas de Deo & anima demonstrationes; Cum Responsionibus Auctoris* (Amsterdam: 1663), Meditation III, p. 16. For translation see Descartes, *Works*, I, 159.

All the works of Descartes to which Coleridge refers below are bound together with separate title pages and pagination in *Opera Philosophica, Editio Quarta* (Amsterdam: 1664). Coleridge's copy of the 1685 edition with his marginal notes is in the library of the University of Vermont.

[20] "Objectiones et responsiones tertiæ," *Meditationes*, p. 97. Descartes, *Works*, II, 67.

[21] At this point Coleridge omits "rerum materialium in phantasia corporea depictas, quo posito facile illi est probare nullam."

[22] The original has "nomine."

[23] Coleridge omits "ad formas perceptionum mentis divinæ significandas, quamvis nullam in Deo phantasiam agnoscamus."

[24] "Objectiones et responsiones tertiæ," *Meditationes*, pp. 97-98. Descartes, *Works*, II, 67-68.

[25] The italics are Coleridge's.

unpleasant doubt & wonder, which his frequent claims to originality raised in me; his apologies for new words as necessary in a system deviating so widely, as his, from the hitherto received opinions;[26] and his repeated Triumphs over his nameless Adversaries for their incapability of instancing any one idea not derived from one or other of the two Sources, which he, Mr. Locke, had pointed out. I will give 4 quotations from 4 very different authors.

1. Φασὶν οἱ σοφοὶ τὴν ψυχὴν τὰ μὲν διὰ τοῦ σώματος αἰσθάνεσθαι οἷον ἀκούουσαν, βλέπουσαν, τὰ δ' αὐτὴν καθ' αὐτὴν ἐνθυμεῖσθαι. (All Philosophers say, that the Soul perceives some things thro' the Body, as when she hears or sees; and some things she herself notices in herself).[27]

2. Intellectio autem dividatur vulgo in Rectam et Reflexam. Recta dicitur quando tantùm aliquid cognoscimus[28] ut in prima apprehensione Hominis, Bovis, Equi &c. Reflexa autem,[29] quâ mens seipsam cognoscit, scilicet se cognoscere et cognoscendi habere potestatem.[30] 3. The mind receiving certain ideas from without, when it turns it's view inward upon itself and observes it's own actions about those Ideas, it has, takes from thence other ideas which are as capable to be the Objects of it's contemplation as any of those, it derives[31] from Foreign Things.[32] Likewise the Mind often exercises an active power in making several combinations: for it being furnished with simple Ideas, it can put them together in several compositions, and so make variety of complex ideas without examining whether they exist so together in nature.[33] 4. Ex ideis aliæ *cogitativæ,* aliæ adventitiæ, aliæ factæ videntur: nam quod intelligam, quid sit res, quid sit veritas, quid sit cogitatio, hæc non aliunde habere videor quam ab ipsâmet meâ naturâ; quod autem nunc strepitum audiam, solem videam, ignem sentiam, a rebus quibusdam extra me positis procedere hactenus judicavi: ac denique Sirenes, Hippogryphes, et similia a me ipso finguntur, *diversas nempe ideas adventitias* vi propriâ *permiscente.*[34] These four quotations

---

[26] Coleridge repeats the "and."

[27] Diogenes Lærtius, *Life of Plato* iii. 12. The Loeb translation reads (I, 289): "There are some things, say the wise, which the soul perceives through the body, as in seeing and hearing; there are other things which it discerns by itself without the aid of the body. Hence it follows that of existing things some are objects of sense and others objects of thought."

[28] Coleridge omits "nec amplius quid inquirimus: sed species Intellectum sistit, ut cum intellectus tantum est in . . ."

[29] Coleridge omits "seu geminata, & quasi reciproca dicitur . . ."

[30] Daniel Sennertus, *Opera Omnia* (Paris: 1641), I, 116.

[31] The text has "received."

[32] Locke, *Essay on the Human Understanding,* II, vi, 1.

[33] *Ibid.,* xxii, 2.

[34] Descartes, Meditation III, *Meditationes,* p. 17. Descartes, *Works,* I, 160. Coleridge makes a few changes in the text. Descartes wrote, "Ex his autem

were evidently written by four men teaching precisely the same doctrine; but of the third and fourth one might almost suspect that the one was a free translation of the other. The first I extracted from Diog. Lært. in the Life of *Plato;* the second from Daniel Sennertus, an adherent of the Aristotelian Philosophy who wrote the passage about the year 1620; the third you will know to be from Mr. Locke, & the fourth is extracted from the Med. Tert. of Descartes, save only that instead of (*cogitativæ*) the word in the original is *innatæ* (cogitativæ in the principia of Des Cartes being used instead of innatæ) and the last sentence, marked with *Italics,* & crotchets)[35] I have inserted with the text from one of Des Cartes' own explanatory notes. Here then we come at Locke's Innate Ideas, and find that the Author defines them not in relation to *Time* but merely in relation to their source, and that they are neither more nor less than Mr. Locke's own Ideas of Reflection—the intellectio reflexa of the Peripatetics, the αὐτὴν καθ' αὐτὴν of Plato. But to place this beyond the possibility of Doubt, I will add another quotation to this Letter of Quotations. At the close of the year 1647 there was published in Belgium a Programma entitled Explicatio mentis humanæ, &c. levelled at Descartes tho' his name is no where mentioned in it. The 12th Article of this Programma is as follows. XII. Mens non indiget ideis vel notionibus[36] innatis: sed sola ejus facultas cogitandi, ipsi, ad actiones suas peragendas, sufficit. To this Des Cartes answers—*In articulo XII* non videtur nisi solis verbis a me dissentire: Cum enim ait, mentem non indigere ideis[37] innatis, et interim ei facultatem cogitandi concedit (puta naturalem sive innatam) re affirmat plane idem, quod ego, sed verbo negat. Non enim unquam scripsi vel judicavi, mentem indigere ideis innatis, quæ sint aliquid diversum ab ejus facultate cogitandi; sed cum adverterem, quasdam in me esse cogitationes, quæ non objectis externis, nec a voluntatis meæ determinatione, procedebant, sed a solâ cogitandi facultate, quæ in me est—ut ideas sive notiones quæ sunt istarum cogitationum formæ ab aliis *adventitiis* aut *factis* distinguerem, *illas innatas vocavi: eodem sensu, quo dicimus, generositatem esse quibusdam familiis innatam, aliis vero quosdam morbos, podagram, vel calculum— non quod ideo istarum familiarum infantes morbis istis in utero matris laborent, sed quod nascantur cum quâdam dispositione sive facultate ad illos contrahendos.*[38]

---

ideis . . . , aliæ à me ipso factæ mihi,'' and after *finguntur* continued ''vel forte etiam omnes esse adventitias possum putare, vel omnes innatas, vel omnes factas, nondum enim veram illarum originem clarè perspexi.''

[35] There are no crotchets in the MS.

[36] Coleridge omits ''vel axiomatis.''

[37] Coleridge omits ''vel notionibus, vel axiomatis.''

[38] ''*Notæ in Programma* quoddam, sub finem Anni 1647 in Belgio editum, cum

The second letter to the Wedgwoods, Feb. 24, 1801.

. . . It has been made appear then, I think, that Des Cartes & Locke hold precisely the same opinions concerning the original Sources of our Ideas. They both taught, nearly in the same words and wholly to the same Purpose, that the Objects of human Knowledge are either Ideas imprinted on the Senses, or else such as are perceived by attending to the passions and operations of the mind; or lastly Ideas formed by Help of Memory and Imagination, either compounding, dividing, or barely representing those originally perceived in the aforesaid ways. This proves no more, I allow, than that Mr. Locke's first Book is founded on a blunder in the History of Opinions, and that Des Cartes and Locke agree'd [*sic*] with each other in a Tenet, common to all the Philosophers before them; but it is far enough from proving the assertion I made in my first Letter, that the whole System of Locke, as far [as] it was a System (i. e. made up of cohering Parts) was to be found in the writings of Des Cartes. But even that, which I have proved, trifling as it may seem, has led me to Reflections on the Rise & Growth of literary Reputation, that have both interested & edified me; nor can it, I suppose, be wholly without effect in the minds of any, who know or remember how much of Locke's Fame rests on the common Belief, that in overthrowing the Doctrine of Innate Ideas he had overthrown some ancient, general, & uncouth Superstition, which had been as a pillar to all other Superstitions. If you ask a person, what Sir Isaac Newton did—the answer would probably be, he discovered the universal action of Gravity, and applied it to the Solution of all the Phænomena of the Universe. Ask what Locke did, & you will be told if I mistake not, that he overthrew the Notion generally held before his time, of innate Ideas, and deduced all our knowledge from experience. Were it generally known that these Innate Ideas were Men of Straw, or scarcely so much as that—and that the whole of Mr. Locke's first Book is a jumble of Truisms, Calumnies, and Misrepresentations, I suspect, that we should give the name of Newton a more worthy associate—& instead of Locke and Newton, we should say, *Bacon & Newton,* or still better perhaps, Newton and Hartley. Neither N. nor H. discovered the *Law,* nor that it was a Law, but both taught & *first* taught, the way to *apply* it universally. Kepler (aye, and Des Cartes too) had done much more for Newton, than Hobbes had done for Hartley even were it all true which it has been fashionable of late to believe of Hobbes.

But I recur to *my* assertion, that Locke's *System* existed in the writings of Descartes; not merely that it is deducible from them, but

hoc Titulo: *Explicatio Mentis humanæ, sive Animæ rationalis,''* Meditationes, pp. 177, 184-85. Descartes, *Works,* I, 442.

that it *exists* in them, *actually, explicitly.* Do me the kindness to believe, my dear Sir! that I am sensible how exceedingly *dull* these Letters must needs be; but if the Facts, which they contain, have not been noticed to you, or by you, they can scarcely be so worthless, *as* to be *overpaid for* by the Reading of a long Letter in close handwriting, tho' this be no trifle to eyes like your's & mine. Without more apology then I proceed to detail my Proofs. In the *Meditations* and the Treatise De Methodo Descartes gives a little History of the rise & growth of his opinions.[39] When he first began to *think* himself out of that state in which he, like every body else, suppose themselves to perceive objects *immediately* without reflecting at all either on their minds or their senses, he saw that those Ideas, which referred him to Objects as externally present, were more vivid & definite than those of memory or imagination, & were not connected with volition. "Experiebar enim, illas absque ullo, meo consensu mihi advenire,[40] et quum multo magis *vividæ* et *expressæ*[41] essent quam ullæ ex iis quas ipse prudens et sciens meditando effingebam, vel memoriæ meæ impressas advertebam, fieri non posse videbatur ut à meipso procederent; ideoque supererat, ut ab aliis quibusdam Rebus advenirent, quarum Rerum cum nullam aliunde notitiam haberem, quàm ex istis ipsis Ideis, non poterat aliud mihi venire in mentem, quàm illas iis similes esse;[42] & seeing that his other Ideas were less vivid than those which referred him to objects as externally present, et ex earum partibus componi, he was led to believe that his mind did nothing more than passively represent the Objects which were within the reach of the Senses. But afterwards, the Differences made by Distance in the Shape of Objects, and his often Detecting of himself in such Speeches as these "Yonder is a man coming," when in truth he saw only a Red or Blue Coat, & perhaps only the Glimmer even of that, forced him to consider that this seemingly intuitive Faith was made up of *Judgements* passed by the Mind in consequence of repeated Experiences, that such Appearances in the Distance would prove that other appearance which we call a man, when he came close to it; and that from hence he had been caused to judge, both that the appearance was a man, and that the Man was at a Distance. These judgements too were often found to have been wrong; he often misunderstood the meaning of these appearances, and he saw clearly that if any one phænomenon,

[39] Coleridge gives a similar account in *Biog. Lit. C*, I, 97 ff.

[40] There is a long omission here: "adeo ut neque possem objectum ullum sentire, quamvis vellem, nisi illud sensus organo esset præsens; nec possem non sentire cum erat præsens; cumque ideæ sensu perceptæ essent multo," etc.

[41] Coleridge omits "et suo etiam modo magis distinctæ."

[42] Meditation VI, *Meditationes*, pp. 37-38. The material in English following this quotation is a paraphrase of p. 38.

however different, were connected with another sufficiently long &
sufficiently often, they would be identified in the mind so as to pass for
intuitions. This he illustrates by the common phrases, I have a pain in
my Limbs, &c. He was led to consider the vast power of association
chiefly by having his curiosity excited concerning the causes, that determined the *place* of Pain, and relates in the fourth Part of the Principia[43] the fact to which he had before alluded in his sixth Meditation—
Cum puellæ cuidam, manum gravi morbo affectam habenti, velarentur
oculi quoties Chirurgus accedebat, ne curationis apparatu turbaretur,
eique post aliquot dies brachium ad cubitum usque, ob gangrænam in eo
serpentem, fuisset amputatum, et panni in ejus locum ita substituti, ut
planè ignoraret se brachio suo privatam fuisse,[44] ipsa interim varios
dolores, nunc in uno ejus manus quæ abscissa erat Digito, nunc in alio
se sentire querebatur. To these he added the old crambe bis cocta of
the Pyrrhonists, of the ordinary Phænomena of Dreams and Deliria, in
which Ideas, became so vivid as to be undistinguishable from Impressions; but he observes in his own defense, "Nec tamen in eo Scepticos
imitabar, qui dubitant tantum ut dubitent, et præter incertitudinem
ipsam nihil quærunt. Nam contra totus in eo eram ut aliquid certi
reperirem."[45] In consequence of his reflection on these and similar
facts he informs us that he found himself compelled to turn his view
inward upon his own frame and faculties in order to determine what
share they had in the making up both of his Ideas and of his Judgements on them. He now saw clearly, that the objects, which he had
hitherto supposed to have been intramitted into his mind by his senses,
must be the joint production of his Mind, his Senses, and an unknown
Tertian Aliquid, all *which* might possibly be developments of his own
Nature in a way unknown to him. The existence of archetypes to his
Ideas was not therefore proveable either by the vividness of any Impression nor by it's disconnection from the Will. Et quamvis sensuum
perceptiones à voluntate meâ non penderent, non ideo concludendum esse
putabam illas à rebus à me diversis procedere, quia forte aliqua esse
potest in meipso facultas, etsi mihi nondum cognita, illarum effectrix.[46]
All such ideas however, as arose in him without his will, & referred him
to something separate from himself, or were *recollected* as such, he
termed *adventitious* and *factitious* when the parts only of any Shape
were remembered by him, but the disposition, or number of those parts

[43] *Principiorum Philosophiæ*, pars quarta CXCVI, p. 216 in *Opera Philosophica*
(1664). Coleridge retells this in *Biog. Lit. C*, I, 93.
[44] Descartes writes "ut eo se privatam esse planè ignoraret." Note Coleridge's
adaptation.
[45] *De Methodo*, Part III, p. 18 in *Opera Philosophica* (1664).
[46] Meditation VI, *Meditationes*, p. 39.

were *imagined* either actively or passively by him, i. e. awake or in dreams. But besides these he found in himself certain Ideas of *Relation*, certain Ideas, or rather modes of contemplating Ideas, of which he had acquired the knowledge by attending to the operations of his own Thoughts, and which did not depend in any degree on his Will. In these he recognized the fountains of Truth, and of Truth immutable, because it did not depend upon the existence of any Archetypes. These Truths in his early works he called Innate Ideas, but in his Principia he dropped this name, & adopted that of res cogitativæ, or experiences acquired by Reflection. By these, according to him, we may acquire the knowledge, that there is a God, and from the Veracity implied in the Idea of an absolutely perfect Being deduce a complete Assurance, that all those Things are real to the belief of the Reality of which our Reason doth truly & inevitably compel us. A clear and distinct Perception therefore of any thing warrants it's Truth & Reality in the relation, in which it is clearly & distinctly perceived. On these grounds he builds the certainty of an external World—(in what *sense* he uses these words, I may have occasion to shew hereafter) and to consider his Ideas in reference to it. Accordingly he divides his Ideas, precisely as Mr. Locke has done, into simple ideas, of one sense, of more than one sense, of Reflexion, & both of Reflexion & Sensation and states the distinction of primary & secondly [*sic*] Qualities, or of Qualities & Powers, in words so exactly corresponding to Mr. Locke's that they might be deemed a free Translation, one of the other—save only that Solidity which Mr. Locke distinguishes from Hardness, & affirms to be a primary Quality of Matter, Des Cartes considers only as a secondary Quality, a mode of Hardness—a mere sensation of Resistance, of course a power not a quality, that same Somewhat which Mr. Locke calls *Motivity* (which by Thinking form according to him the primary Ideas of Spirit, &c) which Des Cartes therefore very consistently excluded from his Idea of Matter: as Mr. Locke *ought* to have done, unless he had been able to shew the difference between Resistance & Impulse, or power of *originating* motion, which last he expressly confines to the Idea of Spirit.[47] The subjects of Perception, Retention, and Discerning, which Locke has skimmed over so superficially & yet not without admixture of error in his 9th, 10th, & 11th Chapters,[48] Des Cartes, in his Dissertation De Methodo, in the fourth Book of his Dioptrics, & in the Pars Prima of his Work De Passionibus, has treated in a manner worthy of the Predecessor of Hartley. In these & the first Book of his Principia you find likewise the whole substance of Locke's 12, 14, 15, 16, 18, 20, 29, 30, 31, 32, & 33rd Chapters. Mr. Locke has given

[47]*Essay on the Human Understanding*, II, iv.
[48] The chapter references here and below are to Book II.

25 folio pages to the explanation of clear, distinct, obscure, confused, real, fantastical, adequate, inadequate, true, & false Ideas; and if I mistake not has exhibited throughout the whole a curious specimen of *dim* writing. Good heavens twenty five folio pages to define half a dozen plain words; and yet I hazard the assertion, that the greater number of these words are explained falsely. Des Cartes took the *words* from the Schools, and defined them only as they occurred.[49] I have taken the trouble to collect & arrange his Definitions. Read them, and when you have a leisure half hour glance your eye over Mr. Locke's four Chapters on the meaning of these Words & compare. Our Ideas, says Des Cartes, are classed & distinguished, not in & for themselves, but in reference to the Judgements of the mind respecting their Relations to each other, to their supposed external Archetypes or Causes, and to Language. Accordingly, Ideas may be divided into simple and complex —that is, into those which we cannot and those which we can analyse. Again, complex Ideas may be subdivded into complex ideas of memory, as a man, a horse, & complex Ideas of Imagination, as a Centaur, a Chimæra. Simple Ideas are said to be CLEAR, when they recur with such steadiness that we can use names intelligibly. James's Ideas of Red & Yellow are two clear Ideas—let a Red and a Yellow Thing be brought before him, & he will say, this is Red & this Yellow, in the same Instance in which others would say it—But his Ideas of Green & Blue are said to be OBSCURE (not that they are not clear in each particular instance in & for themselves, but) because they are so unsteady in relation to their supposed external Cause, that he *sometimes* mistakes Blue for Green, & Green for Blue—not *always,* for then his ideas would be *steady,* consequently, his mistake undiscoverable, or more properly, no mistake at all. Again, a man may have an idea that is clear & steady, yet unintelligible because ANOMALOUS. James's Brother cannot distinguish Purple from Violet—two different external objects produce uniformly *one* effect on *him,* that produce two on his neighbours. When he tells them, he has seen a man in a purple Coat, they know only that he means either Purple or Violet. Simple Ideas can be called neither distinct nor confused. (Mr. Locke instead of saying "the Smell of a Rose & that of a Violet are clear & distinct Ideas" need only have said, they are *two Ideas*).[50] Distinct does not mean, in accurate language, difference merely, but such difference as can be stated in words. When in his preface he says, he has ordinarily preferred the word determinate, & used it instead of clear & distinct, and used it in one sense for simple Ideas, & in another sense for complex Ideas, I may be allowed

[49] Coleridge deleted ''in the place in which he found them.''
[50] For this discussion in Locke see end of II, iii.

to say without petulance that his word is idly chosen (it means too many things to mean any thing *determinately*). A complex idea may be either DISTINCT or CONFUSED. It is said to be distinct, when we distinguish all it's component parts: that is, when we see the Relations which the Ideas, it may be analysed into, bear to each other. An anatomist has a distinct Idea of the Eye; but I have only a CONFUSED one. I do not know all it's component parts, or I have not arranged them in my mind so as to enable me to pass from one to another, still perceiving their Relations as Parts to the Whole, and as Co-parts to each other. When a complex idea passes in the mind for a simple Idea, for instance, when a plain man thinks, he has a *Pain* in his *Limbs*, this is said to be a clear but not a distinct Idea: in other words, it is to *him* a simple Idea. Light to my child is a *clear* but not *distinct* idea, to me a complex but confused one, to Newton it was a distinct complex idea. We are likewise said to have sufficient & insufficient, adequate & inadequate Ideas. (For sufficient & insufficient Mr. Locke uses True & False Ideas, which I think injudicious.) I have a sufficient idea of Winter Cole so far as it enables me to distingiush it from Savoy Cabbage, but insufficient in as much as I cannot distinguish it from Brocoli [*sic*]. The Botanist's Ideas of Plants may be sufficient to distinguish the Genera & Species, but insufficient to distinguish the Individuals of the same Species from each other. Adequate, that is, perfectly sufficient Ideas, belong only to the Supreme Being. To say with Mr. Locke that all simple Ideas are adequate is an error in language. A simple Idea, as a simple Idea, cannot refer to any external Substance representatively: for as Pythagoras said, nothing *exists* but in complexity. A simple Idea can be adequate therefore only in reference to itself: and this is merely affirming that this particular Idea is the same particular Idea, that is, if A be A, then A is A—nor is it a whit more proper to say, that a Mathematician's Idea of a Triangle is adequate, for this is likewise to say, if A is A, then A is A. Adequate is not synonimous with "complete," but with "perfectly coincident": which is absurd to affirm of an Idea with itself.

S .T. Coleridge

Mathematician's Idea of a Triangle is false [Logically?]—it should be, his Idea, Triangle.

From the third letter to the Wedgwoods.[51]

This letter I intend for a miscellaneous Postscript to my last, or if you like, a sort of sermon on a text from Hobbes "Animadverte quam sit ab improprietate verborum pronum hominibus prolabi in errores circa

[51] This letter is postmarked March 27, 1801, but it is inscribed on the back in Poole's hand, February, 1801. "Correspondence of Thomas Poole," I, fol. 260-61.

res." Mr. Locke would have never disgraced his Essay with the first Book, if he had not mistaken innasci for synonimous with connasci, whereas to be "born *in*" and to be "born *at the same time with*," are phrases of very different import. My mind is, for aught I know to the contrary, *connate* with my brain, but a staunch materialist would perhaps deny this, and affirm that the Brain was the elder of the two, and that the mind is *innate in* the brain. Des Cartes chose the word "innascor" because it implied Birth & of course *Subsequence,* & at the same time pointed out the *place* of Birth. He confined it to what Locke calls Ideas of Reflection, merely because he did not wish to innovate on the established Language of metaphysics. But he expressly affirms, that in more accurate Language all ideas are *innate,* "ipsas motuum et figurarum Ideas esse innatas"; the mind is both their Birth-place and their Manufacturer; and we use the term *"adventitious"* quando *judicemus,* has vel illas Ideas, quas nunc habemus cogitationi nostræ præsentes, ad res quasdam extra nos positas referri—non quia res extra nos menti nostræ per organa sensuum illas ipsas Ideas immiserunt; sed quia *aliquid* tamen immittitur, quod menti occasionem dedit ad ipsas per innatam sibi facultatem hoc tempore potius quam alio, efformandas."[52] *Innate* therefore is inaccurately *opposed* to adventitious; but as the word had been in common use, he had adopted it to express those cognitions which the mind gains by attending to it's own passions & operations. These cognitions he elsewhere calls in the language of his age communes notiones and eternæ veritates, the same which Mr. Locke calls intuitive Knowledge, & they are explained by Descartes to the same purport as these Intuitions are explained by Mr. Locke to be those Laws in the conformation of the mind by which all men *necessarily* perceive ideas, in certain *Relations* to each other. These Laws Aristotle calls Δύναμιν σύμφυτον κριτικήν, (φαίνεται δὲ τοῦτο ὕπαρχον πᾶσι τοῖς ζώοις)[53] a power inherent in all living Beings determining the manner in which external objects must act upon them. It is observable, that Des Cartes finding that he had been misunderstood both in the word "innatæ" and in the word "Ideæ" entirely dismissed them from his Principia: for

[52] "*Notæ in Programma,*" *Meditationes,* p. 185, with reference to Art. XIII. Descartes, *Works,* I, 442-43. Coleridge adapts the text which reads: "judicemus, has vel illas ideas, quas nunc habemus cogitationi nostræ præsentes, ad res quasdam extra nos positas referri, non, quia istæ res illas ipsas nostræ menti per organa sensuum immiserunt; sed, quia tamen aliquid immiserunt, quod ei dedit occasionem ad ipsas, per innatam sibi facultatem, hoc tempore potius quàm alio, efformandas."

[53] This sentence is condensed from Aristotle, *An. Post.* ii. 19. 99b 32-34.

ἀνάγκη ἄρα ἔχειν μέν τινα δύναμιν, μὴ τοιαύτην δ᾽ ἔχειν ἢ ἔσται τούτων τιμιωτέρα κατ᾽ ἀκρίβειαν, φαίνεται δὲ τοῦτό γε πᾶσιν ὑπάρχον τοῖς ζώοις, ἔχει γὰρ δύναμιν σύμφυτον κριτικὴν ἣν καλοῦσιν αἴσθησιν.

innatæ he uses cogitativæ or intellectualis, and for Ideæ he uses sometimes notiones, sometimes cognitiones, sometimes motus percepti, & when
he wishes to express himself generally he resigns the *convenience* of a
single Word, which was his first motive for using it, & expresses himself
by a paraphrase, "Quæcunque sub perceptionem nostram cadant." The
word Idea occurs but twice in the first book of the Principia, and then
he uses it only in *reference* to his Meditations. It is a proof to me, of
Mr. Locke's having never *read* the works of Des Cartes, that he adopted
the word Idea; he would never have used this word, if he had seen the
disputes in which it involved the French Philosopher, the anxious Ward-
ing-off of misinterpretation, which he never fails to manifest when he
uses it, by repeated Definitions, & sometimes by marginal Nota benes: and
in his Principia he wisely desisted from the use of the word altogether.
It is likewise to be observed that he uses it steadily in one sense & never
dreamt of introducing such a phrase as *"abstract Ideas.*["]¹ Having
thus seen how grossly Mr. Locke has misunderstood Des Cartes, or perhaps how gossip-like he has taken up upon hearsay a rabble of silly
calumnies respecting him, we shall be the less surprized at the 23rd
Paragraph of the fourth Chapter of his first Book, in which he implies
that Aristotle was an asserter & Patron of connate Principles & Ideas—
Aristotle, whose expressions in reprobation of such a doctrine are even
violent: Quod igitur eas (scil. cognitiones) a naturâ habemus, absurdum
est. Ἄτοπον! is the mildest phrase which he deigns to bestow on such
an hypothesis. If Locke ever looked into the logical or metaphysical
Works of Aristotle, I hazard a conjecture that this strange Blunder of
his in matter of *fact* originated in a Blunder as to the meaning of a
Word. Ἐγγίγνομαι and ἐγγίνομαι are put together in some Lexicons
as one word, and in all the Lexicons which I have consulted, they
are given as synonimous with each other & with ἔνειμι, and all three
are rendered by Insum, innascor. But in philosophical Greek γνώσεις
ἔνουσαι, ἐγγιγνόμεναι and ἐγγινόμεναι have each it's separate meaning
γνώσεις ἔνουσαι (which is mentioned by Aristotle as a possible Hypothesis & disposed of with an "absurdum est["]¹) is equivalent to
connate or inherent Ideas, Mr. Locke's Innate Ideas. γνώσεις ἐγγιγνόμεναι
(which is used by Plato) = Ideas born *in* the mind, or in Mr. Locke's
Language, Ideas derived from Reflection. But γνώσεις ἐγγινόμεναι,
a *favorite* Phrase of Aristotle's, or ingenerated Ideas = Ideas acquired by Experience—cognitiones, quæ a nobis *acquiruntur* as Pacius
rightly translates these passages. Hence Aristotle often has the sentence.
Thus then these cognitions ἐγγίνονται τῇ ψυχῇ —are *ingenerated* in
the Soul—i.e. by the action of external subjects on our senses. I guess

therefore that Mr. Locke carelessly & in a slovenly mood of mind, reading these passages, with a preconceived Opinion that the Peripatetic
Philosophy was a congeries of false Hypotheses & verbal Subtleties, translated the words "are *innate*^['''] (i. e. in *his* sense, *inherent*) in the mind,
herein perhaps relying without scruple on the authority of his Lexicon,
and the common use of the word in common Greek.   I hope, that I am
not treating Mr. Locke with undue disrespect; for if I reject this, and
all similar suppositions, I shall be reduced to the Belief that he charged
upon a truly great man an opinion, which he himself deemed outrageously silly, without having ever read that great man's Works.   Thus too
in that express attack on Des Cartes in the 1st Chap. of his 2nd Book
"Men think not always" by translating the Cartesian "Cogito" by the
word "Think" he prepares his Reader to suppose that Des Cartes had
taught, that we are always *voluntarily* combining Ideas (for this, as Mr.
Locke himself observes) is the meaning of the English word Think.
Now Des Cartes expressly defines his cogitatio, as a general *Term* for
all our consciousness, whether of Impressions, Ideas, or mere Feelings.
Again in the words "think not always" I need not point out to you the
confusion in the word ("always") as combined with ("think not",) if
we should admit Mr. Locke's own account of Time as meaning nothing
more than a *succession* of Thoughts, & that in this Proposition Mr. Locke
in order to rescue himself from absurdity must necessarily bewilder his
Reader in obscure notions of *Relative* Time as contradistinguished from
Absolute.   This whole Reasoning (as far as Des Cartes *Cogito* is not
misconstrued) resolves itself into an equivocation in the word Consciousness, which is sometimes used for present Perception, & sometimes
for the memory of a past Perception; for as to the wild & silly assertions,
with the which this Chapter is so amply stocked, it would be idle to
include them under the term *reasoning*.   These equivocations & these
assertions are happily blended in the two following sentences.   "Those
who do at any time sleep without dreaming can never be convinced that
their Thoughts are sometimes for four hours together busy without their
knowing it."   And "If the Soul doth think in a sleeping man without
being conscious of it, I ask whether during such thinking it has any
pleasure or Pain or be capable of Happiness or Misery?   I am sure, the
Man is not, no more than the Bed or Earth he lies on. (! ! !)[54] For to
be happy or miserable without being conscious of it seems to me utterly
inconsistent & impossible."[55] This is a truly curious passage! First Des
Cartes had expressly defined Thinking by Consciousness—thus, "If the
Soul is conscious without being conscious I ask whether during such

---

[54] Coleridge's exclamation points.
[55] *Essay on the Human Understanding,* II, i, 11.

consciousness it has any consciousness"—or what if a Cartesian should answer To be happy or miserable without being afterwards conscious of *having* been so seems to me either inconsistent or impossible. But if Mr. Locke speaks of *present perception*, how came he to be so sure that a sleeping man is devoid of Feeling? "The man does not remember that he had any." Well (it may be answered,) the natural Deduction from this is, that the man had forgotten it. For to affirm that a man can breathe & turn himself & perform all the usual actions of sleep without any sensation is actually to affirm of men that same absurd Doctrine which Des Cartes is accused of having held concerning the Brutes, & which Mr. Locke in his merry mood calls "a step beyond the Rosicrucians." This silly chapter with many others not much better originated in the little attention, which Locke had given to the Law of Association or explanatory of the Phænomena both of Memory and of Reasoning (for I find by his Preface what I first heard from Mr. Mackintosh, that the trifling Chapter on Association was not introduced till the fourth Edition). It is true, that if we were to judge of Locke's merits by the first Book & the first Chapter in the second Book of his Essay, we should sink him below his proper rank, even more than his present Reputation is above it. Yet if any one had read to me that Chapter on "Men think not always" without mentioning the Author, and afterwards read a passage in his fourth Book, in which it is asserted that Morals are equally susceptible of Demonstration as Mathematics, & then another passage in the conclusion of the eleventh Chapter of Book the third, in which it said, "all the figurative applications of Words, Eloquence hath invented, are for nothing else but to insinuate wrong ideas, move the Passions, and thereby mislead the Judgement; and so indeed are perfect cheats," I should have found myself incapable of believing the Author to be any thing but—what, I reverence even a great *name* too much to apply to Mr. Locke.

It may not be amiss to remark that the opinion of Descartes respecting the Brutes has not been accurately stated. Malbranche indeed positively denies all feeling to Brutes, & considers them as puræ putæ Machines. But Des Cartes asserted only, that the Will and Reason of man was a Something essentially distinct from the vital Principle of Brutes, and that we had no *proof* that Brutes are *not* mere Automatons.[56] Des Cartes, like Hartley & Darwin, held the possibility of a machine so perfect, with & susceptible of Impulses, as to *perform* many

---

[56] For the discussion of the difference between man and the brutes see *Discourse on Method*, Part V, in Descartes, *Works*, I, 106-18; and the letter to Henry More, 1649, *The Philosophy of Descartes in Extracts from his Writing*, selected and translated by Henry A. P. Torrey (New York: 1892), pp. 284-87.

actions of apparent Consciousness without consciousness but the falsehood of a thing possible can never "be *demonstrated*," tho' such demonstration may be superseded by intuitive Certainty. I am *certain* that I
feel; and when I speak of men, I *imply* in the *word* "Men" Beings like
myself; but in the word "Brutes" I imply Beings some way or other
different from my own species, to them therefore I am not entitled to
transfer my intuitive Self-knowledge; consequently, I cannot *prove* i. e.
demonstrate, that any consciousness belongs to them. The strongest expression in all Des Cartes' Writings on this subject is "etsi ratione
careant, et *forte* omni cogitatione."[57] This is, no doubt, egregious
trifling, unworthy of Des Cartes, & hardly to be reconciled with other
parts of his own Works, in which he shews that Nature acts upon us
as Language, and that veracity is involved in the notion of Deity.
However, to assert that a thing is so or so, and to assert that it *cannot*
be demonstrated *not* to be so or so, form articles of Belief widely different from each other. Malbranche asserted that Brutes were machines
devoid of all consciousness, Des Cartes only asserted, that no one could
demonstrate the contrary.

I have abstained purposely from intermingling in these Letters any
remarks of my own, not connected with matters of historical Fact tho'
I was greatly tempted to animadvert on the gross metaphor & at the
same time bold assumption implied in the words *"inherent," "innate,"*
"ingenerated," "object of the mind in thinking," &c. I was likewise
tempted to remark that I do not think the Doctrine of Innate Ideas even
in Mr. Locke's sense of the Word so utterly absurd & ridiculous, as
Aristotle, Des Cartes, & Mr. Locke have concurred in representing it.
What if instead of innate Ideas a philosopher had asserted the existence
of *constituent* Ideas (the metaphor would not be a whit more gross,
nor the hypothesis involved more daring or unintelligible, than in the
former phrases) and I am sure, it would lead to more profitable Experiments & Analyses. In Mr. Locke there is a complete Whirl-dance of
Confusion with the words *we, Soul, Mind, Consciousness,* & Ideas. It is
we as far as it is consciousness, and *soul* & *mind* are only other words for
we (and yet nothing is more common in the Essay than such sentences
as these "I do not say there is no *Soul* in *us* because *we* are *not sensible*
of it in our sleep"[58] &—actions of our *mind unnoticed* by *us*—i. e. (according to Locke's own definition of *mind* & *we*) *"actions of our con-*
sciousness, of which our consciousness is unconscious." Sometimes again
the Ideas are coincident as objects of the mind in thinking, sometimes

[57] *Passiones Animæ*, Part I, Art. L, p. 25 in *Opera Philosophica* (1664). Descartes, *Works*, I, 355-56.
[58] *Essay on the Human Understanding*, II, i, 10.

they stand for the mind itself, and sometimes we are the thinkers, & the mind is only the Thought-Box. In short, the Mind in Mr. Locke's Essay has three senses—the Ware-house, the Wares, and the Ware-house-man. . .

From the fourth letter to the Wedgwoods.[59]

Mr. Locke's third Book is on Words; and under this head [he] should have arranged the greater number of the Chapters in his second Book. Des Cartes has said multum in parvo on the subject of words. He has said the same things as Mr. *Locke;* but he has said them more perspicuously, more philosophically, & without any admixture of those errors or unintelligibilities into which Mr. Locke suffered himself to be seduced by his Essences and Abstract Ideas. Words (according to Des Cartes) are to be considered in three ways—they are themselves images and sounds; 2. they are connected with our thoughts by associations with Images & Feelings; 3. with Feelings alone, and this too is the natural Tendency of Language. For as words are learnt by use in clusters, even those that most expressly refer to Images & other Impressions are not all learnt by us determinately; and tho' this should be wholly corrected by after experience, yet the Images & Impressions associated with the words become more & more dim, till at last as far as our consciousness extends they cease altogether; & Words act upon us immediately, exciting a mild current of Passion & Feeling without the regular intermediation of Images. Nam videmus, verba, sive ore prolata, sive tantum scripta, quaslibet in animis nostris cogitationes & commotiones excitare —& so forth. And if, says Des Cartes, it be objected that these Words do not all excite *images* of the Battles, Tempests, Furies, &c. sed tantum modo *diversas intellectiones;* this is true, but yet no wise different from the manner in which Impressions & Images act upon us. Gladius corpori nostro admovetur, et scindit illud;[60] ex hoc sequitur Dolor qui non[61] minus diversus a gladii, vel corporis locali motu, quam color, vel sonus.[62] Words therefore become a sort of Nature to us; & Nature is a sort of Words. Both Words & Ideas derive their whole significancy from their coherence. The simple *Idea* Red dissevered from all, with which it had ever been conjoined would be as unintelligible as the word *Red;* the one would be a *sight,* the other a Sound, meaning only themselves, that is in common language, meaning nothing. But this is perhaps not in our power with regard to Ideas, but much more easily with regard to Words. Hence the greater Stability of the Language of

[59] This letter is not dated and bears no postmark.
[60] The text has "illud scindit," and then reads below, "corporis quod scinditur."
[61] The text reads "qui sane non minus diversus est."
[62] Descartes, *Principiorum Philosophiæ,* Pars Quarta CXCVII, pp. 216-17 in *Opera Philosophica* (1664). Descartes, *Works,* I, 294.

Ideas. Yet both Ideas & Words wherever they are different from or contrary to our Habits either surprize or deceive us; and both in these instances deceive where they do not surprize. From inattention to this, it is conceivable, quantum in Catoptricis majores nostri aberrarint, quoties in speculis concavis et convexis locum Imaginum determinare conati fuerunt.[63]

With regard to Knowledge, & Truth, & Error & Falsehood I find no essential Difference whatsoever in the opinions of Locke & Des Cartes. Knowledge according to Des Cartes is clear & distinct Perception, & Truth a clear & distinct Perception of the Relations which our Cognitions bear to each other. The causes of error & falsehood are such associations of Ideas with Ideas, of Words with Ideas, & of Words with Words, as are liable to be broken in upon; I associate the idea of a Red Coat with a Soldier; & herein I have not erred; but I have associated with the idea of a Red Coat nothing else but the Idea of a Soldier, & in consequence a feeling of conviction that whenever I see a Red Coat coming, it must be a Soldier, but this is liable to be broken in upon—it is error. The most common sources of error arise according [sic] from misunderstanding the nature of Abstract Ideas, and the confiding in certain propositions & verbal theses, as believing that we had formerly demonstrated them— quod multa putemus a nobis olim fuisse percepta, iisque memoriæ mandatis, tanquam omnino perceptis, assentiamur; quæ tamen revera nunquam percepimus.[64] To which he adds, as a motive for a wise and moderate scepticism, the action of early prejudice on our minds long after we have appeared to ourselves to have completely ridden our minds of them.[65]

If the facts, I have adduced, produce the same effect on you which they have produced on me, you will have been convinced that there is no Principle, no organic part, if I may so express myself, of Mr. Locke's Essay which did not exist in the *metaphysical* System of Des Cartes— I say, the metaphysical, for with his Physics & in them with [——?] his notices of Plenum &c I have no concern. Yet it doth not follow that Des Cartes' System & Locke's were precisely the same. I think, if I were certain that I should not weary-disgust you by these lcng Letters, I could make it evident, that the Cartesian is bonâ fide identical with the Berkleian Scheme, with the Difference that Des Cartes has developed it more confusedly, and interruptedly than Berkley, and probably therefore did not perceive it in his own mind with the same steadiness &

[63] Descartes, *Dioptrice*, Cap. VI, xix, p. 93 in *Opera Philosophica* (1664).
[64] Descartes, *Principiorum Philosophiæ*, Pars Prima XLIV, p. 12 in *Opera Philosophica* (1664). Descartes, *Works*, I, 236.
[65] *Ibid.*, LXXI, LXXII. Descartes, *Works*, I, 249-51.

distinctness . . . So Des Cartes System is a *drossy* Berkleianism—and
it is in consequence of it's dross & verbal Impurities that the System of
Locke is found so completely bodied out in it. If I should not have
been mistaken in this, it would follow that the famous Essay on the
human Understanding is only a prolix Paraphrase on Des Cartes with
foolish Interpolations of the Paraphrast's; the proper motto to which
would be nihil hîc novi, plurimum vero superflui. A System may have
no new Truths for it's component Parts, yet having nothing but Truths,
may be for that very reason a new System—which appears to me to be
the case with the moral philosophy of Jesus Christ, but this, it is admitted on all hands, is not the case with Mr. Locke's Essay. But if it's
Truths are neither new nor unaccompanied by Errors and Obscurities,
it may be fairly asked, wherein does Mr. Locke's Essay merit consist.
Certainly not in his style, which has neither elegance, spirit, nor precision; as certainly not in his arrangement, which is so defective that I
at least seem always in an *eddy*, when I read him (round & round, &
never a step forward) but least of all can it be in his Illustrations, which
are seldom accurate to the eye, & never interesting to the Affections. I
feel deeply, my dear Sir! what ungracious words I am writing; in how
unamiable a Light I am placing myself. I hazard the danger of being
considered one of those trifling men who whenever a System has gained
the applause of mankind hunt out in obscure corners of obscure Books
for paragraphs, in which that System may seem to have been anticipated; or perhaps some sentence of half dozen words, in the intellectual
Loins of which the System had lain Snug [?] in *homuncular* perfection.
This is indeed vile in any case, but when that system is the work of our
Countryman; when the Name, from which we attempt to detract, has
been venerable for a century in the Land of our Fathers and Forefathers, it is most vile. But I trust, that this can never be fairly applied to the present Instance—on the contrary I seem to myself as far
as these facts have not been noticed, to have done a good work, in restoring a name, to which Englishmen have been especially unjust, to
the honors which belong to it . . .

But more than all, these Detections are valuable as throwing
[light?] on the causes & growth of Reputation in Books as well as man.
I hold the following circumstances to have [been] the main efficients of
Mr. Locke's Fame. First & foremost, he was a persecuted Patriot, in
the times of James the Second—closely connected with the Earl of
Shaftesbury, the Earl of Peterborough &c. (and his works cried up by
the successful Revolutionary Party with the usual zeal & industry of
political Faction).[66] 2. The opinions of Gassendi, & Hobbes, had spread

[66] At this point Coleridge deletes "the zealous Antipapists among the Clergy."

amazingly in the licentious & abominable Days of Charles the second & the controversial Reign of his Successor. All knowlege [*sic*], & rational Belief were derived from experience—we had no experience of a God or a future state—therefore there could be no rational Belief. How fashionable these opinions & how popular the argument against Miracles of which Mr. Hume seems to have conceited himself to have been the Discoverer, we need only read the Sermons of South to be convinced of. When the fundamental Principles of the new Epicurean School were taught by Mr. Locke, & all the Doctrines of Religion & Morality, forced into juxta-position & apparent combination with them, the Clergy imagined that a disagreeable Task was fairly taken off their hands—they could admit what they were, few of them, able to overthrow, & yet shelter themselves from the consequences of the admission by the authority of Mr. Locke. These high Church Clergy were no friends to Mr. Locke indeed; but they were popular chiefly among the Ignorant, and their popularity was transient. Besides, a small party violently & industriously praising a work will do much more in it's favor, than a much larger party abusing it can effect to it's disadvantage. But the low Clergy were no small party, & they had all the Dissenters to back. To this must be added the great spread of Arian notions among the Clergy (and it was no secret that Mr. Locke was an Arian) of this however the Clergy in the present Day take no notice; no Parson preaches, no Judge speechifies, no Counciller babbles against Deism, but the great Mr. Locke's name is discharged against the Infidels, Mr. Locke that greatest of Philosophers & yet honest Believer. The effect, the Clergy have had in raising, extending & preserving Mr. Locke's reputation cannot be calculated—and in the mean time the Infidels were too politic to contradict them. The infidels attacked the Christians with Mr. Locke's Principles, & the Christians fell foul on the Infidels with Mr. Locke's authority. 3. Sir Isaac Newton had recently overthrown the whole system of Cartesian Physics & Mr. Locke was believed to have driven the plough of Arius over the Cartesian Metaphysics. This was a complete Triumph of the English over the French—the true origin of the union, now proverbial, of the two names—Newton & Locke. 5. After this came Leibnitz, & the Dispute concerning the Invention of the Infinitesimal &c. and the bitterness & contempt with which the great man was treated not only by Newton's Understrappers but by the whole English Literary Public, has not yet wholly subsided. Now Leibnitz not only opposed the Philosophy of Locke; but was believed & spoken of as a mere reviewer of the exploded Cartesian Metaphysics, a visionary & fantastic Fellow, who had long given Mr. Locke occasion to "fight his

Battles o'er again & twice to slay the Slain."[67]   Leibnitz's notions, of
Plenum; pre-established Harmony &c. were misrepresented with the
most ludicrous blunders by Maclaurin[68] & other Lockists—& Voltaire in
that jumble of Ignorance, Wickedness & Folly, which with his usual
Impudence he entitled a *Philosophical* Dictionary, made it epidemic
with all the no-thinking Freethinkers throughout Europe, to consider
Locke's Essay as a modest common sense System, which taught but little
indeed—& yet taught all that *could* be known & held it up in opposition
to the dreams of the Philosophy of Leibnitz, whose mortal sin in the
mind of Voltaire & his Journeymen was, not his monads, but that intolerable Doctrine of the Theodicèe, that the system of the universe
demanded not only the full acquiescence of the Judgement in it's perfection, but likewise the deepest devotion of Love & Gratitude.   Berkley
who owed much to Plato & Malebranche, but *nothing* to Locke, is at this
day believed to be no more than a refiner upon Locke—as Hume is
complimented into a refiner on Berkley.   Hence Mr. Locke has been
lately called the Founder of all the succeeding Systems of Metaphysics
as Newton is of natural Philosophy & in this sense his Name is revered
tho' his Essay is almost neglected.   Those, who do read Mr. Locke as a
part of Education or of Duty, very naturally think him a great man
having been taught to suppose him the Discoverer of all the plain pre-
adamitical Common sense that is to be found in his Book.   But in general
his Merit like that of a Luther, or a Roger Bacon, is not now an idea
abstracted from his Books, but from History, [——?] the [——?] of
Superstition: his Errors & Inaccuracies are sometimes admitted, only
to be weighed against the Bullion of his Truths, but more often as in
other holy Books are explained away—& the most manifest self-contradic-
tions reconciled with each other on the plea, that so great a man was to be
Judged by the general Spirit of his opinions, & not by the Dead Letters.
Lastly we must [——?] in as the main Pillar of Mr. Locke's reputation
the general aversion from over the name of Metaphysics & the Discussion connected with it arising from the enormous commerce of the
Nation, & the enormous increase of Number in the Profession of the
Law consequent hence, and 2. from the small number of the Universities
& the nature of the Tutorships & Professorships in them, & 3 & principally from the circumstance that the preferment of the Clergy in general is wholly independent of their Learning or their Talents, but
does depend very greatly on a certain passive obedience of Satellites
[?] to the Articles of the Church. . . .

[67] Dryden's "Alexander's Feast," l. 66.

[68] Colin Maclaurin (1698-1746), mathematician and philosopher, friend of Sir
Isaac Newton.

From Philosophical Lecture XIII.[69]

My conscience bears me witness that it is not from any neglect of studying his writings or of seeking for assistance from those who have professed to do so, but sincerity compels me to say that after all the study and all the assistance, I could never discover any one thing to account for that prodigious impression that seems to have been made, either in the novelty of the sentiments or in the system of those which are peculiar to him.

I verily believe myself that the case stood thus: we were becoming a commercial people; we were becoming a free people, in enjoyment, as we had always been in right. Mr. Locke's name, and his services, which of themselves would be sufficient to immortalize him, had connected his name with that of freedom, and that of the revolution from the natural attachment of old and established learned bodies to old and established political bodies which had been their protectors. It was not to be wondered that those who were supposed to teach the philosophy of past times were found mainly amongst those who supported the old forms of government; it was [*also to be expected*] and <*stated*> that the same great revolution was to go on in mind that had been going on in state affairs, and that as King William had completely done away with all the despotism of the Stuarts, so Mr. Locke had done away altogether with the nonsense of the Schoolmen and the universalists.[70] In consequence of which, people read <*him*> who had never once examined the subject or thought about it, and found some monstrous absurdities that they themselves had never heard of before, and they found them most ably confuted. To those absurdities they attributed all they had connected in their own minds with the abuses and miseries of former ages, utterly neglecting the good at that time. They had considered this as a new light stepping into the world; and it is not once or two or three times that I have heard it stated, when I referred to the writers before William the Third, "Oh, you forget there was no light till Locke." Milton, Shakespeare and so on were forgotten. They were poets! But it is clear the reign of good sense came in with Locke.

Now one of the followers of Locke, Hume, who has carried the premises to the natural consequences, has allowed that he did not completely

---

[69] A transcription of shorthand reports of all but the first and last of this set of fourteen lectures is in the possession of the Coleridge family. These reports were made by a reporter whom Hookham Frere engaged. They are full of omissions and errors, and they show little feeling for sentence structure. Occasionally gaps can be filled by reference to manuscript material in the British Museum. For the method of doing this see "The Text," Coburn, *Phil. Lect.*, pp. 14-21. This selection on Locke is from pp. 376-82.

[70] MSS Egerton, 3057, has "Universities."

understand the first book of Locke, what was understood and what overthrown; but I believe it may be traced historically nearer that Descartes
was the first man who made nature utterly lifeless and godless, considered it as the subject of merely mechanical laws. And having
emptied it of all its life and all that made it nature in reality, he referred
all the rest to what he called "spirit," consequently "the faculty of
spirit" in relation to this "matter." What must be then the perception?
What was it then to perceive? What was it not? For mechanical laws
prevented his admission of that. (Not, as the old Platonists would
have said, perceiving the things outward; physiology had advanced too
far to render that attainable.) He therefore conceived what he called
"material ideas." That is, he supposed that as there were in the soul
causative powers which produced images for it, so there were in the
brain certain modes that pre-existed in itself and which determined
it to receive such and such impressions rather than others, and these
he called "material ideas." And in consequence of their origin being
in the organization itself, he had named them "innate ideas," in both
senses; first of all, the true ideas, or spiritual ones, he conceived as
having their birth place in the mind; and secondly, those material ideas
he considered innate, as having their birth place in the organization.
But the Jesuit, Voetius, before Locke wrote, had attacked this on the
ground that Locke proceeds on, but the answer Descartes (who was a
truly great man) makes[71] is this: "I said innate not connate, I spoke of
birthplace not the time. Do you suppose that either I or any man in
his senses, nay, I will add, that any man out of his senses, could imagine
such an absurdity as that men heard *before* they heard, that they had
images *before* they saw? These things are too absurd to be attributed
to any man in his senses, much more to a philosopher." But still admitting that, and taking Descartes without his material hypothesis at
all, nothing can be more simple than what he says or more agreeable
to common sense. And what indeed was not first stated by Descartes it
would <not> be difficult to find anywhere among the Schoolmen in
which you will find the same things said, or among the ancient metaphysicians, which is simply this: that there must be a difference in the
perceptions of a mouse and a man, but this difference cannot be in the
object perceived but in the percipient; that therefore, says Descartes,
we have reason to suppose that there are two sorts of ideas or thoughts.
If, says he, two really be two, (these are Descartes' own words and I am

[71] For this reply see *Answer to Objections*, VII, Quest. 2 in Descartes, *Works*, II,
271. MSS Egerton, 3057, inserts: "to Mr. Locke's fancied refutation of his system
and prove Locke not only to be the refuter but the absolute instigator & only
possessor of any such ideas as he attempted to destroy."

now speaking logically and as a grammarian, not as a mathematician) if there are two, *they show these* differences. One is of those thoughts or images in which we are conscious of being passive; those which are impressed upon us whether we will or no, and those (as appearing to have their causes externally) we call external ideas. But, says he, there are others in which the mind is conscious of its own activity, and tracing its own operations, forms notions which from the place of their origin are all innate ideas. He then goes on with a definition which is noticeable (you may see it in his answer to Voetius) by being word for word the same as Locke's definition of the ideas of reflection, so that in truth the man-of-straw that was to be thrown down never existed, but the real assertion to be opposed was not merely in substance but *totidem verbis* [*identical with*] the idea in Locke's "ideas of reflection."

The abuse of the word "idea" by Descartes and Locke I shall not further speak of, and therefore I simply say, and most happy should I be to stand corrected by any man who could give me better information, that if you only substitute for the phrase the ideas being *derived from* the senses or *imprest upon* the mind, or in any way supposed to be brought in—for nothing can be more mechanical or pagan-like than the phrases used in the *Essay on the Human Understanding*—if for this you only substitute the word *elicit*<*ed*>, namely that there are no conceptions of our mind relatively to external objects but what are *elicited* by their circumstances and by what are supposed to be correspondent to them, there would be nothing found in Locke but what is perfectly just. (But at the same time I must say, nothing but what is perfectly known, has been taught from the beginning of time to the end.) And with regard to the rest, the grammatical part, I think I took the fairest way of convincing myself that a man could. I took the abridgement of his work published at Cambridge for the use of the young men at the University, and having it interleaved, from Descartes and with no other guide, I wrote opposite to each paragraph the precise same thing written before, not by accident, not a sort of hint that has been given, but directly and connectedly the same.[72] The question therefore amounts precisely to this: Mr. Locke's phrases seem to say that the sun, the rain, the manure, and so on, had made the wheat, had made the barley and so forth; but we cannot believe that a man who was certainly a very wise man in his generation could have meant this and that he was only misled in the expressions from his not being made apprehensive of the consequences to be deduced from them. If for this you substitute the

---

[72] In MSS Egerton, 3057, the account reads: "Mr. C. had a copy of Locke's Essay on the Understanding interleaved and against each particular paragraph he wrote what Descartes and others had before promulgated."

assertion that a grain of wheat might remain forever and be perfectly useless and to all purposes non-apparent, had it not been that the congenial
sunshine and proper soil called it forth—everything in Locke would be
perfectly rational. I am only standing in amazement to know what is
added to it, for never have I been able to learn from repeatedly questioning these Lockians what was done. The only answer has been, "Did
he not overthrow innate ideas?"

Locke is no materialist. He teaches no doctrines of infidelity, whatever may be deduced from them. In his controversy with the Bishop of
Worcester, speaking of substance, when the Bishop says substance can
never be brought to an image, . . . that which stands under every
possible image precluded this—what is Locke's answer? "I never
denied the mind could form a just image of itself by reflection and
deduction." So that, in truth, those who have drawn the doctrines of
mere materialism from Locke certainly drew what he never intended
to draw. And with regard to the rest, I remain as before. I have not
yet been able to discover the ground, or any ground, why I should ca-
lumniate all the great men that went before him in compliment to any
one idol, however deserving of praise in other respects, as to say that,
because Locke told us, in defining words, we ought to have distinct
images or conceptions, [and therefore we ought to have an image or a
conception of an idea,] which Cicero never heard of and which was a
strange thing to Plato. But I can very easily understand that <in>
men with far less merit than Locke, and even men who wrote more enter-
tainingly. (For that is a great thing—when a book has once got a character, if it should be so dull that nobody should read it afterwards, it
saves the reputation for centuries; this we have had instances of in
others.)

Many circumstances combined <the names of Locke and Newton> at
the time. The first was that Descartes had had his physical prophecies
and other parts of his mechanical system overthrown by Sir Isaac Newton
but the [metaphysical parts, it was said, by Locke; though rather it
was the case that his (Descartes') epistemological theory of innate ideas
turned up in another form][73] as Locke's ideas of reflection. Therefore
one great man had overthrown the physical parts and another the
metaphysical parts and to that circumstance we owe entirely the custom
of talking of "Locke and Newton," to that accident entirely.

The next thing was that Voltaire and others before him both in
France and in Germany, had held up [Maupertuis and Leibnitz,] a
truly great man, but as a sort of rival to our Newton; and any one who
has read the literary and scientific history of that time well knows that

[73] Adapted from MSS Egerton, 3057, and MSS Egerton, 2801, fol. 19.

nothing in politics would excite more fury than the controversy concerning the arithmetic, as to who was the inventor. This again interested the natural feelings. But Leibnitz supposed [a *plenum*, a pre-established harmony, but he was a visionary, a fantastic fellow and was treated with bitterness and contempt by Newton's understrappers] ;[74] and here again there was another connection made between Locke and Newton. He was opposed to Leibnitz, and the [*calculus of fluxions*] which had been invented by our Newton.

At that time, too, we know well the very great heats that there were between the high church and the low church, and at the same time the existence of a middle party who, while they kept to the church, yet still favored all the tolerant opinions and in general what was termed the most rational way of interpreting the religion. But Locke was . . . while the clergy at large and the religious people found that in an age when the philosophers were beginning to be notorious as infidels, there was a man of true piety who wrote very edifying comments (as they really are) on the Scriptures, and those won *that* party; while the infidels such as Voltaire and others cried him up beyond all bounds. He was the true modest man. He had referred all things to the effects, to mind [as the result of sensation. It is interesting to compare the scepticism of another disciple, Hume][75] who, smiling at Mr. Locke's deductions, said they were merely amulets against priestcraft, take them in the lowest sense (which Locke did not intend).

If you doubt, just refer to the beginning of Hume's essay on *Cause and Effect;* you will find immediately the channels made on Locke's opinions. Everywhere it is <*argued*>, you have no real truth but what is derived from your senses. It is in vain to talk of your ideas of reflection, for what are they? They must have been originally in our senses or there is no ground for them. So many circumstances combined together as to make it a kind of national pride, in the first place, and secondly the interest of almost each of the parties to cry up Mr. Locke. And the effect is shewn more especially that the most ingenious, I think some of the finest works of philosophy for that period, those produced by the great Stillingfleet and others, were not merely put down at once as trash out of fashion but it was said that Stillingfleet had died of a broken heart in consequence of his defeat by Locke; though wherein the man was to become defeated till we can find how Locke differed from others is for other considerations. I can, therefore, say this finally with regard to Locke, that it was at the beginning of a time when they felt one thing :

[74] MSS Egerton, 2801, fol. 19, adapted.

[75] Miss Coburn has filled in a gap in the transcript by adopting MSS Egerton, 2801, fol. 19.

that the great advantage was to convince mankind that the whole process of acting upon their own thoughts or endeavouring to deduce any truth from them was mere presumption, and henceforward men were to be entirely under the guidance of their senses. This was most favourable to a country already busy[76] with politics, busy with commerce, and in which yet there was a pride in human nature, so that a man would not like to remain ignorant of that which had been called the Queen of Sciences; which was supposed above all things to elevate[77] the mind; which had produced a word which a man had overthrown, had [exploded one of the distinctions of rank and title][78] that of a philosopher. What a delight to find it all nonsense! that there was nothing but what a man in three hours might know as well as the Archbishop of Canterbury.[79]

The first book of Locke's Essays (if the supposed error, which it labours to subvert, be not a mere thing of straw, an absurdity which, no man ever did, or indeed ever could, believe) is formed on a σόφισμα Ἑτεροζητήσεως, involves the old mistake of *cum hoc: ergo, propter hoc*.[80]

Nor in this enumeration dare I (though fully aware of the obloquy to which I am exposing myself) omit the noticeable fact, that we have attached a portion even of our national glory (not only to the system itself, that system of disguised and decorous *epicureanism,* which has been the only orthodox philosophy of the last hundred years; but also, and more emphatically) to the name of the assumed father of the system, who raised it to its present "pride of place," and almost universal acceptance throughout Europe. And how was this effected? *Extrinsically,* by all the causes, consequences, and accompaniments of the Revolution in 1688: by all the opinions, interests, and passions, which *counteracted* by the sturdy prejudices of the mal-contents with the Revolution; *qualified* by the compromising character of its chief conductors; not more propelled by the spirit of enterprize and hazard in our commercial towns, than held in check by the characteristic VIS INERTIÆ of the peasantry and landholders; both parties cooled and lessoned by the equal failure of the destruction, and of the restoration, of monarchy; it was effected extrinsically, I say, by the same influences, which (*not* in and of themselves, but *with* all these and sundry other modifications)

[76] MSS Egerton, 3057, reads: "bustling political and economical people."
[77] The report gives the word as "alleviate."
[78] Omission filled in from MSS Egerton, 3057.
[79] MSS Egerton, 3057, concludes "that a few hours could make us fit for the See of Canterbury or place us upon an equality with a life of study."
[80] *Biog. Lit. C,* I, 137.

combined under an especial controul of Providence to perfect and secure the majestic Temple of the British Constitution!—But the very same which in France, *without* this providential counterpoise, overthrew the motley fabrics of feudal oppression to build up in its stead the madhouse of jacobinism! *Intrinsically*, and as far as the philosophic scheme itself is alone concerned, it was effected by the mixed policy and bon hommie, with which the author contrived to retain in his celebrated work whatever the system possesses of soothing <for the indolence, and of flattering> for the vanity, of men's average *understandings*: while he kept out of sight all its darker features, that outraged the instinctive faith and moral feelings of mankind, ingeniously threading-on the dried and shrivelled, yet still wholesome and nutritious fruits, plucked from the rich grafts of ancient wisdom, to the barren and worse than barren fig tree of the mechanic philosophy. Thus, the *sensible* Christians "the angels of the church of Laodicea" with the numerous and mighty Sect of their admirers, delighted with the discovery that they could purchase the decencies and the. *creditableness* of religion at so small an expenditure of faith, extolled the work for its pious *conclusions*: while the Infidels, wiser in their generation than the children (at least than these *nominal* children) of light, eulogized it with no less zeal for the sake of its principles and assumptions, and with the foresight of those obvious and only *legitimate* conclusions, that might and would be deduced from them. Great at all times, and almost incalculable are the influences of party spirit in exaggerating contemporary reputation; but never perhaps "from the first syllable of recorded time" were they exerted under such a concurrence and conjunction of fortunate accidents, of helping and furthering events and circumstances, as in the instance of MR. LOCKE.[81]

As usual he spoke with contempt of *Locke's* Essay. It led to the destruction of Metaphysical Science by encouraging the unlearned to think that with good sense they might dispense with study. The popularity of *Locke's* Essay he ascribed to his political position: he was the advocate of the new dynasty against the old & as a religious writer against the infidel, tho' he was but an Arian! And the *national* vanity was gratified. He & Newton were pitted against Leibnitz. It was to lessen Leibnitz that Voltaire set up Locke. He assented to my remark that Atheism might be demonstrated out of Locke—he praised Stillingfleet as the opponent of Locke's Essay.[82]

[81] *Statesman's Manual*, Appendix E, pp. xlii-xliii.

[82] H. C. Robinson's MS "Diary, Reminiscences, and Correspondence," 1834 vol. of "Reminiscences," p. 433. Dec. 23, 1810. This volume is in Dr. Williams's

I am unable to account for Mr. Locke's popularity; in some degree it may be owing to his having exposed and confuted the absurdities, or rather the absurd part, of the schoolmen. Hume has carried his premises to their natural and inevitable conclusion.[83]

He said that during a long confinement to his room he had taken up the Schoolmen, and was astonished at the immense and acute knowledge displayed by them; that there was scarcely any thing which modern philosophers had proudly brought forward as their own which might not be found clearly and systematically laid down by them in some or other of their writings. Locke had sneered at the Schoolmen unfairly, and had raised a foolish laugh against them by citations from their *Quid libet* questions, which were discussed on the eves of holidays, and in which the greatest latitude was allowed, being considered mere exercises of ingenuity. We had ridiculed their *quiddities,* and why? Had we not borrowed their *quantity* and their *quality,* and why then reject their *quiddity,* when every school-boy in logic must know, that of everything may be asked, *Quantum est? Quale est?* and *Quid est?* the last bringing you to the most material of all points, its individual being. He afterward stated, that in a History of Speculative Philosophy, which he was endeavoring to prepare for publication, he had proved, and to the satisfaction of Sir James Mackintosh, that there was nothing in Locke which his best admirers most admired, that might not be found more clearly and better laid down in Descartes or the old Schoolmen; not that he was himself an implicit disciple of Descartes, though he thought that Descartes had been much misinterpreted.[84]

Of the Moderns, he [Gassendi] has a right to be considered as the main Spring or Fountain head of the Atomistic & Mechanic Scheme: while if you restore to him and Hobbes all the feathers that belonged to them there will remain of Locke's whole philosophic plumage the one or two feathers only which his Followers have been unanimous in the wish to pluck out (ex. gr. his general Triangles &c. See Berkley, Hume, &c. &c.). Grant me Gassendi, Hobbes, Des Cartes De Methodo, and Spinoza; first Tract, Principia Cartesiana, More Geometrico demonstrata: and I will undertake to produce a duodecimo volume containing in a

---

Library, London. The comment appears with considerable variation in Robinson, *Diary,* I, 200.

[83] Allsop, *Letters,* I, 138. A similar statement concerning Hume is in Philosophical Lecture XIII. See above.

[84] April 20, 1811, at Richmond. Recollections communicated by Mr. Justice Coleridge. *Table Talk S,* pp. 525-26.

connected form every principle of the Essay on the Human Understanding, the whole sum and detail with exception only of Locke's Admitted
Errors—nay, all that has been since added by Locke's Followers, on
Association and the application of the same to the principles of Language and of general conceptions.[85]

. . . the PROFOUND Essay on the Human Understanding by the GREAT
LOCK, who therein magisterially informs us that all eloquence, all power
of imagination the similar accompaniments of Justly tho' highly excited,
passions are, if employed in *reasoning*, a *trick*, a *cheat*; & the writers
or orators to be considered as Imposters & Mountebanks. S. T. C. [Note
to "profound"], carefully sounded in all it's depths by me, S. T. C.,
and found at the deepest ancle-high relatively to Des Cartes; but very
muddy: Ergo, profound—for what better proof of it's Depth, than that
no one can see to the bottom of it. [Note to Descartes], from whom &
his immediate disciples all that is true or ingenious in the Essay is
stolen.[86]

Petvin, LETTERS CONCERNING MIND,[87] *first flyleaf, recto and verso.*

At the time, in which these Letters were written, the Haut Ton
philosophique was ascendant, according to which Plato, Aristotle, and
the rest of the unfortunate Ante-Nati, who wrote before "John Locke
had thrown the *first* ray of Light on the nature of the human mind
and the true source of all our Ideas," were mere Dreamers or word-
splitters. Yet still there were many of a better mould, who retaining
their love and veneration of the Ancients were anxious to combine it with
the new Orthodoxy by explaining Aristotle and even Plato *down* into
John Locke. Such was that excellent man, and genuine *Classic* Scholar,
the Poet Gray. Others there were, and Petvin appears to have been one
of the number, who, if they did not *love* the Ancients more than the
former class, *understood* them better: and yet wanted either will or
courage to oppose the reigning Dynasty. These men attempted to recon-

[85] Feb. 11, 1824. From the Clasped Vellum Notebook, pp. 12-13, in the Berg
Collection of the New York Public Library. Printed for the first time by the kind
permission of that library.
[86] Note on flyleaf of *An Historical Apology for the Irish Catholics,* by William
Parnell, Esq. (1807). This pamphlet belonged to Thomas Poole. Information concerning the pamphlet was communicated by Alfred Hart to the *Times Literary
Supplement* (London), May 9, 1935.
[87] John Petvin, *Letters Concerning Mind, To which is added a sketch of universal
arithmetic* (London: 1750). Posthumously published by Petvin's friends. For
an account of this book and the complete transcript of the notes, see "Coleridge on
John Petvin and John Locke," *Huntington Library Quarterly,* VIII (May, 1945),
277-92.

cile the old with the new Authority by a double operation—now, like the former class, lowering down Pl. and Arist. to John Locke, & now pully-ing John Locke up to Plato & Aristotle. The result was, now a confusion in their own thoughts & an inconsistency in their several positions; now & more frequently, an expression of the Truth in lax, inaccurate, & in appropriate Terms. But the general Effect a nearly universal Neglect of Metaphysics altogether, & the substitution of a shallow semi-mechanical Psychology under the pretended *Law* (but in fact no more than a vague generalization) of Association :[88] in which a mode of causation is made the ground & cause and explanation of Causation itself.

But the whole scheme of Locke is an Heterozetesis—by which the Sun, Rain, Air, Soil &c are made to *constitute* the germs (as of Wheat, Oat, or Rye) of the *growth & manifestation* of which they are the efficient *Conditions.*—Instead of the words, "give, convey" and the like, write wherever they occur, "excite, awaken, bring into consciousness" or words equivalent—& little will remain in Locke's Essay to be complained of, but it's dullness & superficiality, its putting up of Straw-men to knock them down again—in short, the making a fuss about nothing, & gravely confuting Nonsense, which no man ever *had* asserted & which indeed no man ever *could* believe—ex. gr. (as Des Cartes says to the Jesuit, Voetius, who had assailed him in the true Locke Style, tho' before Locke's Essay), that men saw before they saw, heard before they heard, & the like 2 + 2 = 5, cross-readings!—

S. T. Coleridge

Petvin, LETTERS CONCERNING MIND—LETTER IV, *pp. 29ff. Comment on p. 35.*

> What is it in general, *to find out Truth;* and *How do we come by it?* To find out Truth is, *to find out general Ideas.* And how are these got into the Mind? By means of *Sense;* Two Ways. The one easily, and as it were of a sudden; the other with more Difficulty, and Expence of Time. [Illustration of the first is knowledge of a triangle; illustration of the second is the application of a general truth previously established to the particular situation of a man named Callias.]

So *very* near to the Truth was this writer that nothing but the Locke-dynasty could have prevented him from seeing, that the difference here is *diversity*—not a difference in *degree* but in *kind.* The proof is, that the Latter (the kind of empirical deduction instanced in Callias)

---

[88] "Substitute-under the pretended Law of Association, which, however, is in fact no *Law* at all, but a mere vague general or *common* Term for Causal connection as far as the same is seen in living & thinking, as distinguished from inanimate Things, thus making one particular mode of causal connection the ground &c.—" Coleridge's own note, which appears on the front board.

remains as unlike the former after the fullest acquaintance with the several facts, as at the first enumeration—while the Former (τὰ νούμενα) never *wax,* nor wane, but are either known wholly or not at all—and at all Times are accompanied by the sense of Universality & Necessity.

It was the fashion, even among Men far above Lockianism, in this age to accommodate Locke to all that they admired in the Ancient Philosophers; as it was the fashion of a lower order of minds, but yet reverencers of the Ancients, to explain all into Mr. Locke. So Gray.

Petvin, LETTERS CONCERNING MIND—LETTER XI, *p. 71.*

> Mr. *Locke* says, we do not think always, But he allows, that we think always when we are awake.

Who told Mr. L. this? Thought & recollectible Thought, are very different positions: & it is the latter only that L. had any right to *negative.*

Petvin, LETTERS CONCERNING MIND—LETTER XV, *pp. 88-89.*

> And here it is plain, that *every self-evident* Principle must be a *general Idea,* because 'tis a *Medium* by which *general Conclusions* are drawn. I should hardly have made so obvious a Remark, but that, as obvious as it is, it seems to have escaped Mr. *Locke,* or not to have been considered by him in a right manner.

At length, Petvin dares *use* his own eyes. But what an instance of the effect of a *great Reputation* on an honest & even superior mind! For with this ground-falsity the *whole* of L.'s system, as far [as] it is System, sinks & is overturned.

Petvin, LETTERS CONCERNING MIND—LETTER XVIII, *pp. 105-6. Note continued at top of p. 106.*

> When we are given to understand by *Pythagoras,* in his mysterious Way, that KNOWLEDGE is the *Harmony* of Ideas, we take no Notice of it, except as it affords us Diversion.—But when we are told by a *Locke,* that KNOWLEDGE is the *Agreement* and *Disagreement of Ideas,* and have it immediately explained to us, without the least Mystery, wherein this Agreement and Disagreement consists, by enumerating the Sorts of it; we are serious, and give up our Attention and Assent, in a manner, together, admiring the Clearness of the Writer.

The Duce! Where lies the difference, excepting that Pythagoras expresses himself more accurately by confining the definition to Locke's first term. For how can *"disagreement of Ideas"* be knowlege? A Knowlege *of* the disagreement of certain Terms as A is always all white: & A is always black is or gives the knowlege that such terms are not exponents of Ideas—but that Knowlege is itself an agreement or Harmony. This on the supposition, that Pythagoras did use the term, "Ideas," whereas more probably he would have said "Numbers"— 2nd. that the Ideas of the (later) Pythagoreans & the Platonists were the same as Locke's Ideas—the identity of which is scarcely more affirmable that [sic] the sameness of a Syllogism & an Apple-dumpling.

Petvin, LETTERS CONCERNING MIND—LETTER XVIII, *p. 106.*

> For this Character [i. e. clearness], I think, is universally given to Mr. *Locke,* considering, as they say, the abstract Nature of his Subject.

Abstract! Aye, with a vengeance! For this is what we complain of in Locke, that he has reduced the whole Intelligible to an Aggregate of Sensory Abstractions! And that an empty warmthless lifeless Idealism is an inevitable deduction from his Principles! But this was the character of the Times. *Locke* was to be cried up, at the very moment that Positions the most subversive of Locke's premises, were admitted as truths.

Locke's Essay on the human Understanding is an enquiry respecting the (by him so called) Ideas, that is, notions, conceptions as the immediate objects of the faculty, and not an enquiry into the constitution of the faculty itself. The categories of Aristotle with the fragments attributed on very suspicious authority to Archideus and the Pythagorean School; but above all the passages elsewhere referred to in the Novum Organum of Lord Bacon may be justly considered as approaches to, and the latter, as anticipations or an implication of the transcendental Logic but as a distinct branch of speculation it did not exist before the publication of the "Critique on the pure Reason" though it must have been more or less clearly present to the Author's mind when he wrote the delightful essay entitled "Dreams of a Ghost-seer illustrated by Dreams of Metaphysics," 1766, the most popular of Kant's works and in the best sense of the word popular.[89]

The Position of the Aristoteleans, Nihil in intellectu quod non prius in sensu, on which Mr. Locke's Essay is grounded, is irrefragable: Locke erred only in taking half the truth for a whole Truth. Conception is consequent on Perception. What we cannot *imagine,* we cannot, in the proper sense of the word, conceive.[90]

The poor Trick attributed to Aristotle (that of stealing his Master's black Horse, and then swearing that it could not be his Master's Horse

[89] MS Logic, II, 328, 329 verso, British Museum, MSS Egerton, 2826. Printed for the first time.
[90] *Aids,* p. 73.

because *that* was piebald) succeeded, I own, in the instance of Locke *versus* Aristotle and Des Cartes, and of Horne Tooke *versus* the Dutch Etymologists but under a conflict of accidental aidances, from factions in Church and State and from a general aversion to Speculative Philosophy, which cannot be supposed in Athens at the period in which the Peripatetic School was founded.[91]

But Plato the philosopher, but the divine Plato, was not to be comprehended within the field of vision, or be commanded by the fixed immovable telescope of Mr. Locke's human understanding.[92]

III. Mem. In my Elements of Discourse after the Etymological Chapter to insert the Essay on Noumena and Phænomena, as a separate Chapter—and not to forget the Noumena Statica ✕ hypostatica—then the history (excluding the biographical Details) of the famous Dispute between the Realists & the Nominalists—this hist. sketch introduced by and brought in proof the ill-consequences of Aristotle's *Universals,* as shown on the preceding Leaf—and the confusion of Abstractions & Generalizations with Laws and Forms of noticing and thinking, whence followed the confusion of Ideas with Categorical conceptions (unbegriffe). In short, there was the same neglect, τῆς προπαιδείας in Aristotle as so long after in our own Locke. Ar. grounded *all* knowledge on Experience, and Locke's work is in fact an Essay on Human Consciousness—and yet no where has Aristotle given a distinct and *genetic* definition or explanation of Experience, or the process of Thought by which he arrived at the fundamental Dogma, that all knowledge is derived from Experience, as Source, & not merely as occasion—and no

[91] Marginal note in W. G. Tennemann's *Geschichte der Philosophie* (Leipzig: 1798-1817), I, first flyleaf verso and second recto. Published by Zimmern in *Blackwood's,* CXXXI (January, 1882), pp. 122-23, but here transcribed from the original.

[92] "Notes on Gray," Shedd, IV, 395-96. The footnote comment below is from *Table Talk S,* p. 336, July 2, 1830. Coleridge frequently makes a similar distinction. "Every man is born an Aristotelian or a Platonist. I do not think it possible that any one born an Aristotelian can become a Platonist; and I am sure no born Platonist can ever change into an Aristotelian. They are the two classes of men, beside which it is next to impossible to conceive a third. The one considers reason a quality, or attribute; the other considers it a power. I believe that Aristotle never could get to understand what Plato meant by an idea. There is a passage, indeed, in the Eudemian Ethics which looks like an exception; but I doubt not of its being spurious, as that whole work is supposed by some to be. With Plato ideas are constitutive in themselves.

"Aristotle was, and still is, the sovereign lord of the understanding;—the faculty judging by the senses. He was a conceptualist, and never could raise himself into that higher state which was natural to Plato, and has been so to others, in which the understanding is distinctly contemplated, and as it were, looked down upon from the throne of actual ideas, or living, inborn, essential truths."

where has Locke given a constitutive Definition (Def. realis ⚥ verbalis) of Consciousness, or any insight respecting it's elements or it's conditions. It is possible that the nature of Experience may by a Reader who is already acquainted with it from other sources be deduced from particular Sentences in the Analytics, Metaphysics, De Anima; but I do not know any position, however frequently and systematically contradicted elsewhere that might not be deduced from some sentence or other in so voluminous, multifarious, and difficult (obscure from excessive compression) a writer as Aristotle—To this add Aristotle's Passion of detracting from his great Master—his gross almost inferring *wilful,* misconception, of Plato's Doctrine of Ideas, which he first confounds with the altogether different Doctrine of Innate Conceptions and thus makes a mish-mash of both, that is true of neither. The latter therefore fall under the same interdict—and are controverted by the same misinterpretations, as the Cartesian *Phrase,* Innate Ideas, was assailed by Locke, and the Leibnitzian Doctrine of Constitutional Forms, Aptitudes, or Predispositions of the Human Mind under the name of Innate Ideas[93] was by Locke's Followers. The Result, or rather the *Consequence,* is obvious, as $2 - 1 = 1$. The mind itself excluded as an active principle, and neither it's productivity admitted nor even its formative power—the Subject, I say, being denied to be the Source either of Shift (Ideas) or of Form (Categories of Sense or of Understanding are nothing but passive receptivity admitted) Arist., I own, as evermore implying an active or spontaneous recipiency; but how this is comprehensible, consistently with the denial of Innate Forms, or even [————?], I am unable to conceive. Nothing of course remains but the outward Nature or Aggregate of Objects. Whatever just and necessary Conceptions exist must therefore have their correspondents in Nature, must express outward Realities. But the so called Universals, ex. gr. Classes, Genera, Species, Height, Depth, Thinness, Largeness, Heaviness, and other Exponents of Relation and Comparison, are just & necessary Conceptions—Ergo each must have it's origin in a Counterpart, in Nature—and hence the Realism of the Schools—a strict & legitimate Consequence of Aristotle's Nihil in intellectu quod non prius in Sensu.[94]

Nor ought we to forget that the Metaphysicians on whom Mr. Hume called were for the far greater part at least avowed disciples of Mr. Locke. Men who no less than himself had exploded the doctrine of in-

[93] "Not indeed happily adopted, but it was the language of that Age & continues to be the L. of the Present." Coleridge's note.
[94] Clasped Vellum Notebook, pp. 28-29. Printed for the first time.

nate ideas and had adopted without limitation the principle of "nihil in intellectu quod non prius in sensu."

If indeed in the sense in which the words are used by Mr. Locke any such doctrine ever existed of which Hume himself expresses his doubts. It is almost incomprehensible how a man of Locke's learning could have attributed the notion to Aristotle of whom it is however insinuated at least. In Des Cartes indeed the words "innata Idea" are found; but accompanied by a definition word for word the same with Mr. Locke's own ideas of reflection. It is curious that the jesuit Voetius had interpreted Des Cartes' phrase in the same way and it is interesting to see with what contempt the philosopher repels a charge almost too ridiculous to need a serious answer, innatas non connatas dixi, Locum non tempus oriundi, &c. and in the same place apologises for the barbarous use of the term Idea on the ground of his having employed it metaphorically. At the same time he observes that strictly speaking all Ideas were necessarily innate, that is, had their immediate birthplace as Images, conceptions, &c. in the mind and that the distinction was merely logical, not metaphysical or philosophical. Hume, in short, took the very same position, that had been previously taken by Berkley in the introduction to his principles of Knowledge and dialogue between Hylas and Philonöus, the crude yet *racy* first fruits of his philosophic speculations and with a more vehement and prolonged preface deepened while he refreshed the footmarks which his Predecessor had left. On the grounds contended for (and which at that time he doubtless considered as having been fully established) by Locke himself did our English metaphysicians attack Locke's Abstract Triangles or the Abstract Idea, Triangle in genere (the main weight of the confutation resting on Mr. Locke's own definitions and usage of the term Idea) and afterwards flashed forth the luminous remark cited at the commencement of this chapter. . . .

The application of the causal connection to the particular phænomena depends beyond doubt on the knowledge given by experience; but it cannot be legitimately concluded from this that the connection itself or that which forms the essence of the notion of cause is likewise derived from experience (given by it I mean) in contradiction from merely occasioned by it or called into definite act and distinct consciousness : for this would have been falling into the same confusion with which Mr. Hume himself so justly charges Mr. Locke's reasoning, or rather the impossible error which Mr. Locke exerts himself to confute in his first book in the essay on the human Understanding . . .[95]

[95] MS Logic, II, 287-88, 297, British Museum, MSS Egerton, 2826. Printed for the first time.

It is seldom, that the most original minds, and who oppose themselves most diametrically to the opinions in vogue, rise above the temptation of procuring a hearing for their own opinions by flattering some dogma then in the ascendant. Thus it was that Hutchinson, Des Cartes, Boyle, and Newton, with Locke, had conspired with the spirit of their times in setting up the idol of Mechanism as the presiding Genius, not only of common sense against the substantial forms of the Scholastic Aristotelians, and the Hierarchs, anima mundis, &c. of the Alchemists; but likewise against the later Antinomian and New-Light Men, as the safeguards of rational Religion. To this Idol Hutchinson sacrificed the consistency of his System—and gave us the old Death out of Life, and lumen de Luce, in short, the πρῶτον ψεῦδος of deducing from mechanism all the mechanism presupposes, in each atom as much as in a world.[96]

Well! this, the student may reply, we can understand and in this sense you have yourself informed us Mr. Locke himself admits the existence of innate conceptions under the name of determinate predispositions of the mind only they must not be called innate Ideas. Though the difference assumed in the present treatise and hereafter to be more fully explained and I trust established between Ideas and Conceptions, and Intuitions, is not at all a point in question in Mr. Locke's Essay, Idea in Locke's use of the word comprehending both the two latter, that is, whatever is the immediate object of the mind; though in point of fact and history, the word Idea was if not invented yet as a *philosophical* term first introduced for the very purpose of expressing the pre-existing principles of particular Thoughts, inasmuch as the ordinary language wanted a word that might contradistinguish these antecedent Principles from their consequent εἴδωλον intuition, image, or *particular* thoughts. But on the other hand, had he not quarrelled with the phrase, Innate Ideas, there would have been nothing for him to have quarrelled with either in Aristotle or Des Cartes, nothing whereon to raise the glory of having overthrown and routed the Logical and Psychological Principles of Des Cartes as his great contemporary Newton had subverted the Physical and Astronomical System of the same Philosopher. But for this accident, I do not say that we should not have heard much of both Mr. Locke and of Sir Isaac Newton, but—we should not have heard so often of Locke and Newton.[97]

[96] Duncan Forbes, *The Whole Works* (2 vols. in 1; Edinburgh: 1755 [?]). In George Frere's copy in the British Museum (C. 60 c. 4.) there is a note to him concerning defacing the book with notes, written by Coleridge on the first blank page at the end of the first volume, dated August, 1817. The note quoted is on the second blank page between the two volumes, verso. Printed for the first time.

[97] MS Logic, II, 383-85. British Museum, MSS Egerton, 2826. Printed for the first time.

It is indeed a singular fact that the distinction between these two judgments [analytic and synthetic] should have remained so generally unnoticed, that the only exception is to be found in Locke's Essay and even here in one passage only viz. the third Chapter of the fourth book. In this Chapter, however, our great Essayist expressly distinguishes two sources of the mind's Judgments, and two sorts of knowledge as resulting therefrom—the first being the agreement or disagreement of the idea with itself that is, analytic Judgments and the other the combination of the two Ideas into one subject that is synthetic Judgments.[98] And he adds that with regard to the latter the power of the mind, acting on it's own reserves, is very limited—, but without particularizing what the limits are, or what the knowledges contained within them. Had he proceeded to this enquiry, he must have been led to the transcendental Logic, that is, a true analysis of the Understanding and not a mere classification of the Ideas; and would have thus rescued the truths, which he actually meant, from the attacks of Berkley and others, to which it was exposed by the impropriety of the expression consequent on the want of distinctness and adequacy in the conception of it.[99]

Time, Space, Duration, Action, Active, Passion, Passive, Activeness, Passiveness, Reaction, Causation, Affinity—here assemble all the mysteries—known, all is known—unknown, say rather, merely known, all is unintelligible; and yet Locke & the stupid adorers of that *Fetisch* Earth-clod, take all these for granted—blinde fenster der blossen Ordnung wegen an einem Gebände verträgt, wo gerade das beste Licht hereinbrechen und die schönste Aussicht seyn sollte.[100]

I dare confess that Mr. Locke's treatise on Toleration appeared to me far from being a full and satisfactory answer to the subtle and oft-times plausible arguments of Bellarmin, and other Romanists. On the whole, I was more pleased with the celebrated W. Penn's tracts on the same subject.[101]

Truly ridiculous as Locke's notion of founding the right of Property on the sweat of the man's Brow being mixed with the Soil, yet taking it

[98] ''The reader will be pleased to observe that Idea and Ideas are here taken in Mr. Locke's sense of the term, as including all the immediate objects of the mind.'' Coleridge's note.
[99] MS Logic, II, 336-37. British Museum, MSS Egerton, 2826. Printed for the first time.
[100] Notebook 12, fol. 50 recto. British Museum, Add. MSS, 47,509. Printed for the first time.
[101] *Table Talk A*, p. 372

as a mere metaphor, and translating it into a general proposition, it is both true & important.[102]

Of Inconsistency honorable to the man tho' not creditable in the Philosopher, such is Berkley's, Locke's and even Leibnitz's.[103]

Dr. Parr, SPITAL SERMON.

> Upon the various effects of superstition, where it has spread widely and thriven long, we can reason from facts. But in the original frame of the human mind, and in the operation of all those usual causes which regulate our conduct or affect our happiness, there seems to be a most active, constant, and invincible principle of *resistance* to the approachments of theism. 'All nature, cries aloud' against them, 'through all her works,' not in speculation only, but in practice.

I never had even a doubt in *my being* concerning the supreme Mind; but understand too sufficiently the difficulty of any intellectual demonstration of his existence, and see too plainly how inevitably the principles of many pious men (Locke, Priestly, Hartley, even Archbishop King) would lead to atheism by fair production of consequences, not to feel in perfect charity with all good men, atheist or theist.[104]

Religion was believed by Newton, Locke, and Hartley, after intense investigation, which in each had been preceded by unbelief.[105]

I see, evidently, that the present is *not* the highest state of society of which we are *capable*. And after a diligent, I may say an intense, study of Locke, Hartley, and others who have written most wisely on the nature of man, I appear to myself to see the point of possible perfection, at which the world may perhaps be destined to arrive.[106]

Give a Dog a bad name: and you hang him or worse, have him hunted with a black kettle at his tail. So has it been with me in relation to the black charge of *Metaphysics*—and then "his jargon about Ideas! Poor Ignoramus! He should be informed, that long before he began to scribble, or even breathe, there was a John Locke who had blown up all his ideal trash!" Nevertheless, S. T. C. begs leave to observe, that he had

---

[102] Notebook 18, fol. 118 recto. British Museum, Add. MSS, 47,515. Printed for the first time.

[103] Notebook 14, fol. 22 verso. British Museum, Add. MSS, 47,511. Printed for the first time.

[104] J. M. G., "Samuel Taylor Coleridge," *Notes and Queries*, 1st. ser., VII (March 19, 1853), 280.

[105] To J. Thelwall, Dec. 17, 1796. Coleridge, E. H., *Letters*, I, 198.

[106] To Rev. George Coleridge, Nov. 6, 1794. Coleridge, E. H., *Letters*, I, 105.

read Locke and read him *all through,* more than once some 25 or 30 years ago—which is more, he ventures to believe, than 19 out of 20 of his compassionate Critics can truly affirm of themselves! S. T. C., 1830.[107]

Swedenborg, Emanuel, DE EQUO ALBO & DE VERBO & EJUS SENSU SPIRITUALI, *p. 11.*

Quod absque ideis intellectus & inde cogitationis de quacunque re nulla perceptio.

Excellent. This single Line fairly outweighs the whole of Locke's Essay on the Hum. Underst.[108]

Forerunners of Kant

INTRODUCTION

One of Coleridge's contributions to the history of philosophy is his discovery that the thinkers of the seventeenth century had anticipated many of the principles attributed to Kant. Since the materials which establish this point are dispersed throughout Coleridge's writings, including marginal notes, it is only when they are assembled that one can see that Coleridge set forth a number of ideas which twentieth-century scholars have reached independently. He would have been in full agreement with Lovejoy's statement that the "Kantian doctrine was destitute of any radical originality . . . the principal developments in post-Kantian philosophy . . . were clearly present in germ, sometimes even in fairly full-blown form, in the writings of Kant's predecessors or contemporaries [the English Platonists]."[a] But he would have been more sweeping in his statement, for he found much earlier, in Bacon and in a number of the old divines, the anticipation of some of Kant's leading ideas. One of the most fundamental of these anticipations was the distinction

[107] *Statesman's Manual,* Coleridge's own copy with marginal notes, British Museum, Ashley, 2850, pp. 52-53. The note was printed by T. J. Wise in *Two Lake Poets* (London: 1927), p. 75.

[108] MS note in edition of London, 1758. British Museum, C.44.g.5.

[a] Arthur O. Lovejoy, "Kant and the English Platonists," in *Essays Philosophical and Psychological in Honor of William James* (New York: Longmans, Green, 1908), p. 265 f.

in the nature and functions of the reason and the understanding.[b] This, he says, "stands foremost among the eminent services rendered to philosophy by Lord Bacon." Kant had only completed and systematized what Lord Bacon had "boldly designed and loosely sketched out in the Miscellany of Aphorisms, his Novum Organum."[c] The distinctions were clearly comprehended in the seventeenth century; it was only through carelessness and lack of steady discrimination that the writers of the period sometimes fell into error.

Coleridge tells us why this distinction is of "inestimable importance." It is basic for the development of philosophy itself and for the applications of philosophy to politics and religion. He says:

> Until you have mastered the fundamental difference, in kind, between the reason and the understanding as faculties of the human mind, you can not escape a thousand difficulties in philosophy. It is pre-eminently the *Gradus ad Philosophiam.*[d]

Observing over a period of thirty years that the failure to master this difference had led to innumerable errors, Coleridge called it "the queen-bee in the hive of error."[e] In his Philosophical Lecture of February 15, 1819, he stated very clearly the political and religious implications:

> Statesmen, who have to manage a constitution founded in the spirit of one philosophy, but who *do* manage it in that directly contrary, or even a clergy, who with one set of opinions are to preach doctrines brought together by men who believe the direct contrary, cannot but produce a state either of dissension or of indifference.[f]

He makes his meaning clear by citing as examples Frederick the Great and Joseph of Austria. In *The Friend* he showed the necessity of discriminating the functions of understanding and reason in order to found a satisfactory constitution; the failure of the first French constitution had "lamentably proved" the results of such lack of insight. In the religious field the mastery of these differences not only established the rationality of religion, but also undermined heresy:

> I have no hesitation in undertaking to prove, that every Heresy which has disquieted the Christian Church, from Tritheism to Socinianism, has originated in and supported itself, by arguments rendered plausible only by the confusion of these faculties, and thus demanding for the

[b] Coleridge worked on expressing this distinction throughout his life. In order to present his thought as a background for this section, a few selections on the subject are given in an Appendix.

[c] Letter to John Taylor Coleridge, April 8, 1825. Coleridge, E. H., *Letters*, II, 735.

[d] May 14, 1830. *Table Talk S*, 313.

[e] *Church and State* in Shedd, VI, 61-62.

[f] Coburn, *Phil. Lect.*, p. 264.

objects of one, a sort of evidence appropriated to those of another faculty.[g]

As unsteady as the seventeenth-century distinction had been, it had enabled the Cambridge Platonists to develop an idealistic philosophy in opposition to the materialism which had spread so rapidly throughout England. In this way, also, they were anticipatory of Kant's emphasis on idealism in answer to Hume. As Lovejoy demonstrates, all the principal tenets of Kant's philosophy were present among the followers of Plato in the seventeenth century, whether these were at Cambridge or at Oxford. Now Coleridge would go still further in explaining this anticipation, for he held that by the age of Epicurus "philosophy had formed its circle and appeared in every possible form."[h] The opinions of individual philosophers since that time "were nothing more than what had been brought forward by such and such of the ancients, as far as they were really philosophical." Therefore when the pendulum of materialism had made its arc and met the counterforce of idealism, the only possibility was a restatement of Platonism adapted to the temper of mind and the conditions of that particular age, and in the light of increased knowledge developed beyond the earlier conceptions, not originated in the new age.

To make this kind of progress possible a new method had been discovered in the seventeenth century. This was the method of trichotomy first set forth by Richard Baxter and applied in his *Methodus Theologiæ* (1675). Up to Baxter's time the old dichotomous method had prevailed —that is, the method of affirmation and negation. According to this principle the truth must lie in one or other of two opposing concepts. Finding this dual system inadequate, Baxter had sought truth in a unity of which the two opposing concepts were but diverse manifestations. Coleridge explains this philosophical method by a chemical analogy: water is the unity, the synthesis, of hydrogen and oxygen; in itself it is neither of the elements, "nor yet is it a commixture of both."[i] Three terms are necessary to designate the members of the triad: *synthesis* (sometimes called *unity* or *identity* by Coleridge) to designate the real substance or being; and *thesis* and *antithesis* to designate the two opposite manifestations of this synthesis. The discovery of the trichotomous method was attributed to Kant, but Coleridge realized that though Kant had used the triad in arranging his categories, he neither made the discovery of trichotomy nor really saw its full importance. Instead of finding two opposites which were the exponents of some one

[g] *The Friend*, Section I, Essay III, I, 306 n.
[h] Coburn, *Phil. Lect.*, p. 263.
[i] *The Friend*, Essay XIII, I, 156 n.

substance in which they existed in unity, his general tendency was to make a triad by means of finding a third thing which would bridge over the still-existing space between the two opposites. It seemed to Coleridge, therefore, that Baxter had hit upon a more vital interpretation than Kant's and that Baxter's method was of extreme importance in the further development of philosophical thought. Coleridge himself used the trichotomous method for explaining such diverse things as the nature of the Trinity or the nature of poetic genius.

REASON AND UNDERSTANDING

The reason & its objects are not things of reflection, association, or *discourse;* the latter word used as opposed to intuition, a use frequent & established in our elder writers, thus Milton "discursive or intuitive." Reason does not indeed necessarily exclude the finite, whether in time or in space, in figure or in number, because it includes them eminenter. Thus the prime mover of the material universe was affirmed in the elder philosophy to contain all motion as its cause, but not to be or suffer motion in itself. The reason is not the faculty of the finite. The faculty of the finite is that, which reducing the confused impressions of sense to its own essential forms, to quantity, quality, relation & inclusively to the forms of actions, reaction, cause & effect, &c. &c., thus raises the material furnished by the senses & sensations into objects of reflection i. e. renders them capable of being reflected on, & thus makes experience possible. Without this faculty the man's representative power would be a delirium, a mere chaos of scudding-cloudage of shapes, and it is therefore most appropriately called the understanding or sub-stantive faculty. Our elder metaphysicians down to Hobbes inclusively, named it ontological exercise, likewise discourse, discursus discursio, from its mode of action as not staying along one object, but running as it were from this to that to abstract, generalize, classify &c. Now when this faculty is employed in the service of the reason to bring out the necessary & universal truths contained in the infinite into distinct contemplation by means of the pure acts of the imagination ex. gr. in the production of the forms of space and time abstracted from all corporeity or of the inherent forms of the understanding itself abstractly from the consideration of particulars—processes which constitute the science of geometry, numeral mathematics, universal logic, & pure metaphysics—in this case the discursive faculty becomes what our Shakspeare, with equal felicity & precision, entitles "discourse of reason."

It is evident then that the reason as the irradiative power of the understanding, and the representative of the infinite[1] i. e. boundless, judges the understanding as the faculty of the finite, and cannot without grievous error be judged by it. When this is attempted, where the understanding in its synthesis with the personal will, usurps the supremacy of the reason, or affects to supersede the reason, it is then what St. Paul calls φρόνημα σαρκός the mind of the flesh σοφία τοῦ κόσμου τούτου the wisdom of this world &c. . . . The result then of this our third subdivision is: The reason is super-finite, and in this relation it hath for its antagonist the *unsubordinated understanding*, the φρόνημα σαρκός, or MIND OF the FLESH.[2]

Sir Thomas Brown, in his Religio Medici, complains, that there are not impossibilities enough in Religion for his active faith; and adopts by choice and in free preference such interpretations of certain texts and declaratons of Holy Writ, as place them in irreconcilable contradiction to the demonstrations of science and the experience of mankind, because (says he) ''I love to lose myself in a mystery, and 'tis my solitary recreation to pose my apprehension with those involved enigmas and riddles of the Trinity and Incarnation;''—and because he delights (as thinking it no vulgar part of faith) to believe a thing not only above but contrary to Reason, and against the evidence of our proper senses. For the worthy knight could answer all the objections of the Devil and Reason (!!) ''with the old resolution he had learnt of **Tertullian**: Certum est quia impossibile est. It is certainly true because it is quite impossible!'' Now this I call ULTRA-FIDIANISM.

Again, there is a scheme constructed on the principle of retaining the social sympathies, that attend on the name of Believer, at the least possible expenditure of Belief—a scheme of picking and choosing Scripture texts for the support of doctrines that have been learned beforehand from the higher oracle of Common Sense; which, as applied to the truths of Religion, means the popular part of the philosophy in fashion. Of course, the scheme differs at different times and in different Individuals in the number of articles excluded; but, it may always be recognized by this permanent character, that its object is to draw religion down to the Believer's intellect, instead of raising his intellect up to religion. And this extreme I call MINIMI-FIDIANISM.

[1] ''*Infinite:*—that is sine finibus, not having, or essentially incapable of having outlines; not bounded, or boundable from without. The reader must be on his guard not to substitute for this, the proper and scientific sense of infinite, the popular meaning of infinite, viz. what is immeasurably vast.'' Coleridge's note.

[2] From Notebook II in the possession of A. H. B. Coleridge, pp. 9-12; but printed as part of the ''Essay on Faith'' in *Lit. Rem.*, IV, 432-33. Changes in wording characteristic of Henry Nelson Coleridge's editing occur throughout.

Now if there be one Preventive of both these extremes more efficacious than another, and preliminary to all the rest, it is the being made fully aware of the diversity of Reason and Understanding. And this is the more expedient, because though there is no want of authorities ancient and modern for the distinction of the faculties and the distinct appropriation of the terms, yet our best writers too often confound the one with the other. Even Lord Bacon himself, who in his Novum Organum has so incomparably set forth the nature of the difference, and the unfitness of the latter faculty for the objects of the former, does nevertheless in sundry places use the term Reason where he means the Understanding, and sometimes, though less frequently, Understanding for Reason. In consequence of thus confounding the two terms, or rather of wasting both words for the expression of one and the same faculty, he left himself no appropriate term for the other and higher gift of Reason, and was thus under the necessity of adopting fantastic and mystical phrases, ex. gr. the dry light (lumen siccum), the lucific vision, &c., meaning thereby nothing more than Reason in contra-distinction from the Understanding. Thus too in the preceding Aphorism, by Reason Leighton means the human Understanding, the explanation annexed to it being (by a noticeable coincidence) word for word the very definition which the Founder of the Critical Philosophy gives of the Understanding—namely, "the Faculty judging according to Sense."[3]

On the contrary, Reason is the Power of universal and necessary Convictions, the Source and Substance of Truths above Sense, and having their evidence in themselves. Its presence is always marked by the *necessity* of the position affirmed: this necessity being *conditional,* when a truth of Reason is applied to Facts of Experience, or to the rules and maxims of the Understanding, but *absolute,* when the subject matter is itself the growth or offspring of the Reason. Hence arises a distinction in the Reason itself, derived from the different mode of applying it, and from the objects to which it is directed: according as we consider one and the same gift, now as the ground of formal principles, and now as the origin of *Ideas.* Contemplated distinctively in reference to *formal* (or abstract) truth, it is the *speculative* Reason; but in reference to *actual* (or moral) truth, as the fountain of ideas and the *Light* of the Conscience, we name it the *practical* Reason. Whenever by self-subjection to this universal Light, the Will of the Individual, the *particular* Will, has become a Will of Reason, the man is regenerate: and

[3] This statement is repeated in a note on Rev. Edward Irving's *Ben Ezra* (1827), p. lxxx. *Lit. Rem.,* IV, 402-3. The aphorism which heads this discussion is: "Faith elevates the soul not only above Sense and sensible things, but above Reason itself. As Reason corrects the errors which Sense might occasion, so supernatural Faith corrects the errors of natural Reason judging according to Sense."

Reason is then the *Spirit* of the regenerated man, whereby the Person is capable of a quickening intercommunion with the Divine Spirit. And herein consists the mystery of Redemption, that this has been rendered possible for us. "And so it is written; the first man Adam was made a living soul, the last Adam a quickening Spirit." (1 Cor. xv. 45.) We need only compare the passages in the writings of the Apostles Paul and John, concerning the *Spirit* and Spiritual Gifts, with those in the Proverbs and in the Wisdom of Solomon respecting *Reason,* to be convinced that the terms are synonymous. In this at once most comprehensive and most appropriate acceptation of the word, Reason is preeminently spiritual, and a Spirit, even *our* Spirit, through an effluence of the same grace by which we are privileged to say Our Father!

On the other hand, the Judgements of the Understanding are binding only in relation to the objects of our Senses, which we *reflect* under the forms of the Understanding. It is, as Leighton rightly defines it, "the Faculty judging according to Sense." Hence we add the epithet *human*, without tautology: and speak of the *human* Understanding in disjunction from that of Beings higher or lower than man. But there is, in this sense, no *human* Reason. There neither is nor can be but one Reason, one and the same: even the Light that lighteth every man's individual Understanding (*Discursus*), and thus maketh it a reasonable Understanding, *Discourse of Reason*—"one only, yet manifold; it goeth through all understanding, and remaining in itself regenerateth all other powers." (Wisdom of Solomon c. viii.) The same Writer calls it likewise "an influence from the *Glory of the Almighty*," this being one of the names of the Messiah, as the Logos, or co-eternal Filial Word. And most noticeable for its coincidence is a fragment of Heraclitus, as I have indeed already noticed elsewhere;—"To discourse rationally it behoves us to derive strength from that which is common to all men: for all human Understandings are nourished by the one DIVINE WORD.[4]

The high importance of Words, and the incalculable moral and practical advantages attached to the habit of using them definitely and appropriately, the ill consequence of the contrary not confined to Individuals, but extending even to national Character and Conduct. The term in question (i. e. the Understanding) an instance of this: and the contra-distinction of this Faculty from the Sense on the one hand and from the Reason (mens *absoluta,* lumen *siccum*) on the other, stands foremost among the eminent services rendered to Philosophy by Lord Bacon. It is indeed the main object of his Novum Organon, and the

⁴ *Aids*, pp. 201-10. Cf. Shedd, I, 236-42.

central Idea of his System. To the unsteadiness in the application of Words; especially the use of "the Reason" and "the Understanding" indifferently for one and the same Faculty, and this too the faculty, the imperfections and narrow limits of which he himself displays with a depth of insight and a clearness of demonstration hitherto unrivalled; and the consequent adoption of mystical phrases, as Lumen Siccum, Visio lucifera, and the like, in order to distinguish the Reason from the Understanding;—to these, aided by some actual and more apparent inconsistencies scattered thro' his numerous Treatises and Outlines, far more than to the Aphoristic form of his great Work, ought we to attribute the undeniable fact, that this pre-eminent Philosopher is more talked of than read and more read than understood, or read to any worthier purpose than that of finding quotations and mottos for ornament or authority.

I have enlarged on this point far beyond the bounds of a mere Chapter of Contents, because the hope and persuasion, that the Work, to which and to the preparation I have devoted so many years of meditation and Research, will, where ever the *desire* exists, supply the *means*, of deriving the full profit from the study of Lord Bacon's Writings, that mine of enkindling Truths and pregnant expressions! this hope, I repeat, came in aid of the Main Object, that I had proposed to myself, and formed my strongest *supplementary* Motive.[5]

Of the three schemes of philosophy, Kant's, Fichte's, and Schelling's (as diverse each from the other as those of Aristotle, Zeno, and Plotinus, though all crushed together under the name Kantean Philosophy in the English talk) I should find it difficult to select the one from which I *differed* the most, though perfectly easy to determine which of the three *men* I hold in highest honour. And Immanuel Kant I assuredly do value most highly; not, however, as a metaphysician, but as a logician who has completed and systematised what Lord Bacon had boldly designed and loosely sketched out in the Miscellany of Aphorisms, his Novum Organum.[6]

The distinctness of the Reason from the Understanding, and the imperfection and limited sphere of the latter, have been asserted by many both before and since Lord Bacon; but still the habit of using Reason and Understanding as synonymes acted as a disturbing force.

[5] British Museum, MSS Egerton, 2801, fol. 34-35. Printed by Snyder, *Logic*, pp. 76-77.

[6] To John Taylor Coleridge, April 8, 1825. Coleridge, E. H., *Letters*, II, 735.

Some it led into mysticism, others it set on explaining away a clear difference *in kind* into a mere superiority in degree: and it partially eclipsed the truth for all.[7]

Hooker, ECCL. POLITY (1682), *Book I, sec. xi, p. 94. Note continued on p. 95.*

In Hooker, and the great Divines of his age, it was merely an occasional carelessness in the use of the Terms, using Reason where they meant the Understanding, and when from other parts of their writings, it is evidently [sic] that they knew and asserted the distinction, nay, the diversity of the things themselves—to wit, that there was in man another and higher Light than that of "the faculty judging according to Sense," i. e. our Understandings. But, alas! since the Revolution it has ceased to be a mere error of language, and in too many amounts to a denial of Reason.[8]

Richard Field, OF THE CHURCH, *Book IV, chap. viii, p. 357.*

In the second the light of divine reason causeth approbation of what they beleeve: in the third sort, the purity of divine understanding apprehendeth most certainely the things beleeved, and causeth a foretasting of those things that hereafter more fully shall be enjoyed.

Here too Field distinguishes the Understanding from the Reason, as *Experience* following *perception* of *sense.* But as perception thro' the mere presence of the object perceived, whether to the outward or inner sense, is not *insight* which belongs to the "Light of Reason," therefore Field marks it by *"purity"* i. e. *unmixed* with fleshly sensations or the idola of the bodily eye. Tho' Field is by no means consistent in his *epitheta* of the Understanding, he seldom confounds the word itself. In theological Latin, the Underst[anding] as influenced by and combined with the affections and desires is most frequently expressed by "cor," the Heart. Doubtless, the most convenient form of appropriating the terms would be to consider the Understanding as the *man's* intelligential faculty, whatever be it's object—the sensible or the intelligible world— while Reason is of the tri-unity, as it were, of the Spiritual, Eye, Light, and Object.[9]

Take one passage among many from the posthumous Tracts (1660) of John Smith, not the least Star in that bright Constellation of Cam-

[7] *Aids*, pp. 245-46. Cf. Shedd, I, 264-65.
[8] From original notes in British Museum, Ashley, 5175. Cf. *Lit. Rem.*, III, 38.
[9] From original notes in the 1628 edition owned by A. H. B. Coleridge. Cf. *Lit. Rem.*, III, 87-88.

bridge Men, the contemporaries of Jeremy Taylor. "While we reflect on our own idea of Reason, we know that our Souls are not it, but only partake of it: and that we have it κατὰ μεθ' ἕξιν and not κατ' οὐσίην. Neither can it be called a Faculty, but far rather a Light, which we enjoy, but the Source of which is not in ourselves, nor rightly by an individual to be denominated *mine.*" This *pure* intelligence he then proceeds to contrast with the *Discursive* Faculty, *i. e.* the Understanding.[10]

BAXTER AND TRICHOTOMY

Speaking of Baxter, he affirmed that he was a century before his time, that he was a logician, and first applied the tri-fold or tri-une demonstration. Heretofore, the two-fold method only was known as the arguing from a positive to a negative, the reality *ergo* the visionary. He also first introduced the method of argument, that the thing or reason given contains a positive and its opposite: *ex. gr.*, reality contains the actual and the potential, as, I sit, the actual, but I have the power, the potentiality of walking.[11]

I have shewn in another work, that* Dichotomy, or the primary Division of the Ground into Contraries, is the necessary form of reasoning, as long as and wherever the intelligential faculty of Man weens to possess within itself the center of it's own system; and vice versâ, that the adoption of Dichotomy under the supposition of it's being the legitimate and only form of distributive Logic, naturally excites, and seems to sanction this delusive conceit of Self-sufficiency in minds disposed to follow the clue of argument at all hazards, and whithersoever it threatens to lead them, if only they remain assured that the thread continues entire . . .

* I had not then known of, nor have I now seen, Richard Baxter's *Methodus Theologiæ;* but from the following sentence in his Life (that invaluable Work published from Baxter's own manuscript by Matthew Silvester) I cannot doubt, but that the merit of substituting Trichotomy for the then, and alas! the still prevailing Method of Dichotomy, which forms the prominent excellence in Kant's Critique of the pure reason, belongs to R. Baxter, a century before the publication of Kant's Work. Nay, it appears that the claim of our Countryman rests on a stronger as well as an elder plea. For Baxter *grounds* the necessity of Trichotomy, as the Principle of Real Logic, on an absolute Idea presupposed

[10] *Aids,* p. 246 n. Cf. Shedd, I, 264 n.
[11] Allsop, *Letters,* I, 133-34.

in all intelligential Acts: whereas Kant adopts it merely as a fact of
Reflection, tho' doubtless as a singular and curious Fact in which he
suspects some yet deeper Truth Latent and hereafter to be discovered.
The passage: "Having long been purposing to draw up a Method of
Theology, I now began it. I never yet saw a scheme, or Method either
of Physics or Theology that gave any satisfaction to my Reason. Tho'
many have attempted to exercise more accurateness in distribution than
all others that went before them, yet I could never see any whose
Confusion or great Defects I could not easily discover; but not so easily
amend. *I had been twenty six years convinced that Dichotomizing will
not do it;* but that the Divine Trinity in Unity hath exprest itself in the
whole frame of Nature and Morality." Baxter's *Life,* Part 3: p. 69.[12]

. *Baxter,* LIFE OF HIMSELF, *Book I, Part III, p. 69.*

I had been Twenty Six Years convinced that Dichotomizing will not do
it; but that the Divine Trinity in Unity hath exprest it self in the whole
Frame of Nature and Morality . . . But he [Mr. George Lawson] had
not hit on the true Method of the *Vestigia Trinitatis* . . .

Among Baxters philosophical merits, we ought not to overlook, that
the substitution of Trichotomy for the old & still general plan of Dichotomy in the Method and Disposition of Logic, which form so prominent
and substantial an excellence in Kant's Critique of the Pure Reason, of
the Judgement, &c. belongs originally to Richard Baxter, a century
before Kant—& this not as a Hint, but as a fully evolved and systematically applied Principle. Nay, more than this, Baxter* *grounded*
it on an absolute Idea *pre*-supposed in all intelligential acts; whereas
Kant takes it only as a *Fact* of Reflection—as a singular and curious
Fact, in which he seems to anticipate or suspect some yet deeper Truth
latent, & hereafter to be discovered.

* On recollection I am disposed to consider *this* alone as Baxter's
peculiar claim. I have not indeed any distinct memory of Giordano
Bruno's *Logice Venatrix Veritatis;* but doubtless the principle of Trichotomy is necessarily involved in the Polar Logic, which again is the same
with the Pythagorean *Tetractys,* i. e. the eternal Fountain or Source of
Nature; & this being sacred to contemplation of Identity, & prior in
order of Thought to *all* division, is so far from interfering with Trichotomy as the universal form of Division (more correctly of distinctive
Distribution in Logic) that it implies it. Prothesis being by the very
term anterior to Thesis can be no part of it—Thus in

[12] MS Logic, II, 37-38. Notebook in the possession of A. H. B. Coleridge. This
excerpt is also printed by Snyder, *Logic,* pp. 128-29. In Coleridge's note to the text
of the Logic he quotes almost verbatim the note which he had made on the back
board of Baxter's *Life.* See below.

Prothesis

Thesis   Antithesis

Synthesis

we have the Tetrad indeed in the intellectual & intuitive Contemplation;
but a Triad in discursive Arrangement, and a Tri-unity in Result.[13]

N. B. The singular circumstance of this three fold division or
Trichotomy obtaining throughout the analysis of the mind, and which
the founder of the critical philosophy contents himself with noticing
as being singular and worthy of notice, and which he supposes himself
to have noticed first, may be found in a much earlier writer, our own
celebrated Richard Baxter. Any attempt to explain it would be out of
its place in the present disquisition. It is a primary datum of the
understanding, the *way in which* we reflect, proved to us by our pure
products of Reflection, as the existence of the *forma formans* must in
every case be manifested by and in the formâ formatâ; but not to be
explained by them. Its purpose is to *account for* the results of Reflection
and it would be preposterous to expect that these should account for it.
Briefly in common Logic the fact has not interest; in Transcendental
Logic it is a necessary element but its explanation belongs to neither
as transcending the faculty of which the one gives the results and the
other the analysis.

It is no more than common justice to this acute and if too often
prejudiced yet always sincere, pious, and single-hearted Divine to say,
that he saw far more deeply into the grounds, nature and necessity of
this division as a Norma philosophiæ and the evils and inconveniences
of the ordinary Dichotomy when carried from its proper province, that
of common Logic, into philosophy and divinity, than Kant did more than
[a] century after. The sacred fire however remained hid under the
bushel of our good countryman's ample folios.[14]

Glossary. To begin[15] with the passage from Kant respecting Trichotomy,
and vindicate Baxter's claim to the merit of this important remark & that
of having grounded it in the necessary Idea of God, by quoting the
passages from his own Life. Then explain the equality asserted by the
Pythagorean School of the Tetractys & the Triad—namely, that the

[13] *Reliquæ Baxterianæ* (1696). Harvard University copy. This note is on the
back board with reference given to Part III, p. 69.

[14] MS Logic, II, 401-2, British Museum, MSS Egerton, 2826. Also see Snyder,
Logic, p. 126.

[15] "Nay, rather begin with the two different possible modes of contemplating a
line, either as formed by the aggregates of it's points, or as a Point producing &c."
Coleridge's note.

former contemplates the Deity as unmanifested, or if we may hazard the expression or indeed any expression of the Inexpressible, as the Monad or Absolute One, not yet unfolded & still containing in itself the Triad—while the Deity, as self-manifested, was contemplated by them as the Triad, in which the Monad was revealed as the first name or position of the Three, Source & principle of all. I hope, I need not disclaim on the part of these ancient sages, the absurd intention of asserting the Deity as actually existing differently in different times; but merely that such the order of Thought in the formation of the *Idea* in the mind. According, the Monad is designated as the semper presuppositum quod nunquam ponitur, and the same Idea is expressed in the Schools of Theology & the philosophizing Greek Fathers of the Church as an eternal generation. It is here introduced, however, as the ground & reality, & so far therefore (as Baxter has implied) the proper explanation of the universal, tho' long neglected, Form of Logic —the logical Tetractys—in which the Monad has it's correspondent in the Prothesis, & the Triad in the Thesis, Antithesis, and Synthesis, according to the following Figure

Prothesis

Thesis   Antithesis

Synthesis

while in the logical Triad, or Trichotomy, which is the form of all manifestation the Prothesis takes the name & place of the Thesis—a rule observed in classification generally & as it were constructively.[16]

[16] Clasped Vellum Notebook, p. 260. Printed for the first time.

THE
OLD DIVINES

INTRODUCTION

Among the outstanding prose writers of the seventeenth century an almost overwhelming number dealt with theology or religious controversy. This was the century of the great divines, and Coleridge's survey of them was comprehensive and thorough, covering Anglicans, Puritans, and liberals. His comments show full understanding of the various positions and throw much light on the opinions both of the men read and of the commentator himself.

Coleridge recognized the literary excellence of these writers, as well as the value of the subject matter, and it is his appraisal of style which holds the greatest general interest today. First of all, these old divines knew how to expound a text, dividing it logically and presenting each part in detail. They were able to extract all the meaning from a passage of Scripture; they did not use it merely as a motto upon which to hang their own opinions. Sometimes the exposition was wiredrawn, Coleridge acknowledged, but it was clear; and granting the premise, one usually found the chain of argument valid. They knew how to direct an argument forcefully and to arrange material so that a series of minor climaxes would rise to some great climax, with the result that one was often convinced by the sheer impact of force. He had but one criticism of arrangement—the frequent lack of symmetry. The weight of quotation and reference and the Latinization of style were no handicap to Coleridge; and the allusiveness was but an added source of enjoyment, though he would have preferred less of the "Patristic leaven." He enjoyed the intellectual appeal of the artificial conceits which often appeared, and found a congenial mental exercise in the wordplay. But it was the imagery characteristic of the writing of this period which afforded him the greatest pleasure, whether it was the magnificent ebb and flow of Donne's amazing figure of the world as a sea or the homely figure of cobwebs in the heart.

In spite of heavy material and two-hour sermons, these divines were able to hold the attention of large audiences of widely varied intellectual ability. Dramatic situations relieved the discussions, and lively satire often gave refreshment in the weary stretches of the theological deserts. The subject matter itself was of vital interest in the seventeenth century, and the huge folio volumes of sermons and controversial writings often ran into a surprising number of editions.

In Coleridge's opinion the diffusion of knowledge before the Restoration by means of sermons was "among the most remarkable facts of history." The divines read "the many works of the wise and great, in many languages, for the purpose of making one book contain the life and virtue of all others, for their brethren's use who have but that one to read."[a] They informed themselves concerning what had been said before on the subject, and could bring the weight of time and authority to open up the difficult points; they did not spin ideas merely out of their own brains as Bishop Stillingfleet said that Locke had done. Their method seems to have formed a model for Coleridge's own procedure in working out his *Magnum Opus,* one section of which was to be a *Theologica,* for he said, "My system, if I may venture to give it so fine a name, is the only attempt I know, ever made to reduce all knowledges into harmony."[b]

In the theological field the seventeenth-century background was especially important to Coleridge, for here he found similarities to his own day. In both centuries different religious sects arose to express the diversity of belief, and religious controversy was widespread. In both centuries the developments in materialistic thought stirred the opposition of religious leaders. In both, also, there were thinkers who tried to find common minimum essentials of belief, realizing that doctrinal divergencies were after all comparatively minor matters—an effort which led to a tolerant attitude. Furthermore, in both, interest was manifested in biblical criticism and in the relation between the Church and the State.

In the seventeenth century the religious controversies were not confined to the heat and vigor of the theologians; lay men and sometimes lay women poured forth "Vindications," "Letters," and "Modest Confutations," with the result that the twentieth-century reader is sometimes confused as to what point the controversialists themselves thought they had established. These were the "Letters to the Editor" of that day, extended to pamphlets and sometimes to folios by vigorous argument. Frequently the combatants descended from the discussion of doctrinal points to personal attack. Coleridge's explanation of the bitter attacks made upon individual divines is fair and interesting. He says that first the Church itself became personified to the antagonist; then the various rulers in the Church were looked upon as if *"they* constituted its personal identity," and therefore Laud, Sheldon, and others had their violent opponents and equally warm partisans, not in themselves but chiefly because they stood for certain Church doctrines and practices which were opposed or advocated.

Students of the seventeenth century are greatly indebted to Coleridge for his extensive comment on the religious issues of the period. He

a *Lit. Rem.,* III, 155-56.
b Sept. 12, 1831. *Table Talk S,* p. 373.

seems to have been the first to grasp the historical importance of the great divines who distinguished the Church at that time, and his contrasts of them with those of the preceding century and his clear analysis of the changes in emphasis within the century itself are a valuable contribution. He classifies the divines before the time of James I as Apostolic or Pauline; these, he says, were concerned with the "mystery of redemption," the relation of man toward "the act and the author." The divines of the first part of the century he terms Patristic, those who believed in the continuity of the Church from Apostolic times and filled their sermons with the names of the Church Fathers and the Saints. Later there arose a third class, which he calls Papal, for these, he said, had a "longing for a Pope at Lambeth" and put more emphasis upon the Church than upon the Scripture, upon organization and ritual than upon spirit. He says very little about the strict Puritans, whose intolerance and emphasis upon dogma were not congenial to him; but he has much to say about the "Platonizing divines," the Cambridge Platonists, whose teachings were particularly in harmony with much of his own thought.

Coleridge not only clearly distinguished the general tendencies in the age, but analyzed the teaching of many individual divines and often pointed out how various leaders within the Church of England yet leaned toward one or another of the "isms" and in some cases even toward Popery. He also showed the impact of their thought upon later times. Hooker, for example, was too far in advance of his age to modify its thought to any great extent; in fact, it was not until half a century had passed that his work became influential and that people appreciated its breadth and tolerance, its emphasis upon reason, and its perception of the wholeness of life. In the conception of the Church as a comprehensive spiritual society Hooker became a forerunner of the Cambridge Platonists.

Coleridge read the seventeenth-century divines intensively when he was attempting to establish a rational basis for the most fundamental articles of faith, and as we read the notes which he wrote on the pages of the old folios we see not only discriminating understanding of the beliefs of these great religious thinkers but also the shaping up of his own convictions. This body of material illustrates the figure so often employed by Coleridge, a Janus looking both ways. The value of Coleridge's work in the theological field cannot be fully estimated until his later notebooks are made available and the marginal notes in his Bible and in the commentaries which he read are brought together and studied in relation to the pertinent printed materials. Any statement, therefore, must be tentative; yet certain important ideas seem to be established.[c] It is not the purpose of this account to do more than present briefly Coleridge's views on certain of the controversial doctrines over which the seventeenth-century divines so hotly argued: the nature of the Trinity, free will, original sin, the Redemption, baptism, and the Eucharist.

In *Paradise Regained* Milton had posed one of the most vital questions of his day: In what sense was Christ the Son of God? The Socinians, with the minor anti-Trinitarian groups, supported the view that Christ was only a holy man. The Trinitarians rose up to "vindicate" the Trinity, and many distinguished names appear among the controversialists—Stillingfleet, Cudworth, Sherlock, Bull, and Waterland. Coleridge called Bull and Waterland the "classical writers on the Trinity," but he pointed out that their arguments were negative: they said that belief in the Trinity was not irrational, that a Christian who denied the Trinity ran into contradictions and absurdities, and that the various sects which had arisen were "unscriptural and contra-scriptural." Positive evidence was needed. Beginning where Bull and Waterland left off, Coleridge undertook to present such evidence.

He rejected the prevalent teaching that God could be "induced" (*a posteriori*) from his material universe, and then set himself to establish that there is a spiritual reality quite as valid to reason as the physical world is valid to the senses. He saw that man's reason could transcend the limits of sensuous reality, for the spiritual nature of man had its own spiritual reality—the things of the spirit seen by the spirit. Following Lord Herbert of Cherbury and the Cambridge Platonists he accepted the verity of a direct, intuitive knowledge of God as the highest truth; yet he held that this knowledge could also be given a rational explication. He adopted the principle that the necessity of a thing must be accepted as a part of its evidence and based the necessity of the Trinity in the nature of God. In religion as in science, he argued, one must start with an hypothesis; and therefore he boldly states, "All we can or need say is, that the existence of a necessary Being is so transcendently Rational, that it is Reason itself—and that there is no other form under which this Being is contemplable but that of a holy and intelligent Will—admit this and all is solved—deny it, all is darkness—substitute any other Form, and we have a chaos of absurdities."[d] Coleridge's major contribution to the discussion of the nature of the Trinity

---

[c] The fullest discussion is in Muirhead, *C. as Philos.* Some additional notes are made available below.

[d] Kant, *Vermischte Schriften* (3 vols.; Halle, 1799). Unpublished marginal note on second flyleaf, recto, of Vol. II. These volumes formerly belonged to the library of Henry Crabb Robinson, and are now in the possession of Mr. C. K. Ogden, who has kindly given me permission to publish this statement.

is this assumption that God is not only supreme Reason as all the leading theologians had said but is also the great I AM of the Scripture, the one self-originating, self-determining Being, a supreme Will. This basic assumption also satisfied the reaching out of the human spirit for a God who is more than cold Reason, a Being with a personality—or as Coleridge distinguished the term when applied to the suprapersonal, "personeity"—for the will is "the Individual in his essential individuality."[e] God is, therefore, "a personal being, having the *causa sui*, or ground and principle of its being in its own inexhaustible causative might."[f] Self-realization is not, however, in itself an objective expression of individuality, and so the second person of the Trinity was necessitated as God's "eternal exegesis" of himself. Through this expression of his self-realized nature in the Son, God's individuality as Father, with all the qualities of fatherhood, is accomplished. The third person of the Trinity is also inevitable from the assumption of God as both Will and Reason, for the fusion of the two originates the Spirit.[g] Here Coleridge is again indebted to Hooker, who, he says, "as far as I understand him, forms the same conception of Spirit as I have done in Aids to Reflection, —namely, as a focal energy from the union of the Will and the Reason."[h] Thus the Being of God, comprised of Will and Reason held in unity by the Spirit necessitates the triune expression of God as Father, Son, and Holy Spirit.[i] For this reason the doctrine of the Trinity is at the very heart of Christianity, and it is essential to believe that the Son is "very God" and coeternal with the Father.

A second controversial question in the seventeenth century concerned the freedom of the will. To Coleridge the answer was inherent in the conception of God, for man made in God's image must have a self-determining will, which is his "intelligent self." Guided by reason, he must be a free agent to exercise his will in making his choices for

[e] Griggs, *Unp. Letters*, II, 387.

[f] Quoted by Muirhead, *C. as Philos.*, p. 229, from a manuscript volume now in the possession of A. H. B. Coleridge. Coleridge is aware of his predecessor in this line of thought. In a note on Field's *Of the Church*, Book III, chap. xxiii, p. 129, he says: "The Leibnitzian Distinction of the Eternal Reason or Nature of God . . . from the Will or Personal Attributes of God . . . planted the Germ of the only possible Solution—or rather perhaps in words less exceptionable, and more likely to be endured in the Schools, or orthodox Theology, brought forward the Truth involved in J. Behmen's too bold Distinction of God and the Ground of God."

[g] See notes on Leighton in *Lit. Rem.*, IV, 161: "The reason in the process of its identification with the will is the spirit."

[h] Notebook 26, fol. 97 verso, commenting on p. 81 of Hooker's *Eccl. Polity*. Printed for the first time. British Museum, Add. MSS, 47,524.

[i] For Coleridge's "formula Fidei De Sanctissima Trinitate, 1830" see *Lit. Rem.*, III, 1-3.

good or for evil. In an interesting note on Luther's *Table Talk* he explains the assistance of the Holy Spirit in making the choice for good:

> When the will placeth itself in a right line with the reason, there ariseth the spirit through which the will of God floweth and actuates the will of man, so that it willeth the things of God, and the understanding is enlivened.[j]

It is in God, therefore, that constantly "we live and move and *have* our Being."[k]

A third great topic of debate was that concerning the nature of original sin. Although Coleridge named Taylor as one of the ablest writers on the subject, he recognized that no clear solution of the mystery was presented as a substitute for the doctrine that sin originated in one specific act of disobedience, with the resulting curse of hereditary guilt. He says that Taylor "flounders backward and forward, now upping and now downing,"[l] and that his difficulty lay in the failure to recognize that spiritual truths were ideas not subject to space and time. Original sin being an idea could not be an historical act or hereditary guilt. Adam must be considered as representative of mankind and his choice as the manifestation in time of the nature of sin.[m] Coleridge dismissed the doctrine of original sin as a "monstrous fiction" and as usual went straight to the heart of the matter, interpreting original sin as sin at its place of origin, that is in man's will. He says: "A sin is an evil which has its ground or origin in the agent, and not in the compulsion of the circumstances."[n] Reason is the law of the will, but corruption of the will has disposed it to disobey its own law and to follow the inclination of the senses as the lower animals do, placing immediate ends above ultimate ends. Coleridge does not attempt to explain *how* this corruption of the will came about, but like Kant leaves ultimate truth as a mystery. He says: "Final causes answer to why? not to how? and who ever supposed that they did?"[o]

This interpretation of the nature of original sin he saw as an aid in clarifying the doctrines of the Incarnation and Redemption (both of which were controversial in the period), for it gave a reasonable ground for their necessity. Redemption is not the expiation of hereditary guilt imposed on the innocent in fulfilment of the arbitrary decree of a stern

[j] *Lit. Rem.*, IV, 6.
[k] Letter to Rev. J. P. Estlin, Dec. 7, 1802. Coleridge, E. H., *Letters*, I, 415.
[l] *Lit. Rem.*, III, 328.
[m] *Aids*, p. 253 n.
[n] *Ibid.*, p. 256. The comment was originally a marginal note by Coleridge. The volume with the note in Coleridge's hand on p. 233 is now in the Brotherton Library at Leeds.
[o] *Anima*, p. 87.

judge; this is but "Old Bailey" theology, placing the "moral Act in the outward Deed," a point of view which Coleridge could not accept. To him an act was only an "index of principles," and it was the inner principle that was important. By assuming human nature Christ redeemed the individual will so that it regained the power to follow its own law of reason and to enter into harmony with the divine will. "This is the true *Atonement*," Coleridge said, "to reconcile the struggles of the infinitely various finite with the *permanent.*"[p] In this line of thought he seems to be following Milton rather than Taylor. Milton had insisted that virtue lay in the choice of good instead of evil by means of the control of right reason over the will. He depicted Christ as one who would "begin to save mankind," and in Books XI and XII of *Paradise Lost* showed the slow progress of Redemption through the whole of biblical history. To Coleridge likewise Christianity was "a growth, a becoming, a progression," and he thought that "history under the form of moral freedom is that alone in which the Idea of Christianity can be realized."[q]

In his remarks on baptism Coleridge is less clear than in what he has to say on other tenets, but it follows from his conception of original sin that he could not agree with Jeremy Taylor and other divines who grounded the necessity for baptism in hereditary guilt. He turned rather to Waterland, and Sara Coleridge thought that in his later years her father "looked upon baptism as a formal and public reception into a state of spiritual opportunities."[r]

In his discussion of the Eucharist Coleridge more nearly follows Taylor, who in *The Real Presence and Spiritual of Christ in the Blessed Sacrament, Proved against the Doctrine of Transubstantiation* gave a spiritual interpretation to receiving the sacrament. Coleridge calls this "the most wonderful of all Taylor's works," yet by means of a simple human analogy given in a marginal note, he illuminates Taylor's spiritual interpretation by clarifying the meaning of the symbol involved. He says:

> The error on both sides, Roman & Protestant, originates in the confusion of Sign or Figure and *Symbol*—which latter is always an essential *Part* of that, of the whole of which it is the representative. Not seeing this, and therefore seeing no medium between the whole Thing and the mere Metaphor of the Thing, the Romanists took the former or positive Pole

[p] *Ibid.*, p. 81.
[q] MS C. Autograph Notebook, 1825, in the possession of the Coleridge family. Coleridge makes this point also in an unpublished note in *Hadad, a Dramatic Poem* by James A. Hillhouse (N. Y. & London: 1825), Yale MS. The note appears above and below the list of Dramatis Personæ.
[r] *Biog. Lit.* in Shedd, III, lxiv.

of the Error; the Protestants the latter or negative Pole. The Eucharist
is a symbolic, i. e. solemnizing and *totum in parte* acting of an act, that
in a true member of Christ's body is supposed to be perpetual. Thus,
the husband & wife exercise the duties of their marriage contract of
Love, Protection, Obedience, &c. all the year long; and yet solemnize it
by a more deliberate and reflecting act of the same Love on the anniversary of their marriage.[s]

It was not only in theology that Coleridge found the seventeenth-
century divines stimulating, but also in the field of biblical criticism.
Unlike Vernon Storr in the present century,[t] he did not date the beginnings of biblical criticism as nineteenth century or find its origin
in German eighteenth-century criticism. He saw that the intellectual
temper of the seventeenth century in England—the emerging freedom
from authority and tradition, the search for truth, the emphasis on
reason, the application of the scientific method to all fields—had nur-
tured a critical approach to the Bible and had developed the same lines
of study as were brought forward by the eighteenth-century Dutch and
German critics, whose works he read and annotated. It was true that
some like Bacon held, "We are obliged to believe the word of God, though
our reason be shocked at it,"[u] but others, placing reason above authority
and blind faith, attempted to find a rational basis for old beliefs and
to define in what sense the Bible was the word of God.

Textual study of the Bible with its revelation of variant readings
had shown that literal inspiration was an impossibility and therefore had
disproved the idea that the Bible text was infallible. The application of
scientific methods to textual criticism gave accuracy and importance to
the findings. The boldest statement denying the inspiration of the Bible
was made in France by Le Clerc, in 1685, in his criticism of Richard
Simon's book, but Coleridge recognized that English scholarship led to
the same conclusion. Literal inspiration was further disproved by the
many parallels between the Bible and the rabbinical writings, which were
being extensively studied in the seventeenth century. That Coleridge
knew these studies and recognized their importance is shown by frequent references to them.

The scientific principle of exactness in terminology also had an impact upon biblical criticism in this period. Edward Potter, a follower
of Waterland, pointed out, for example, that the terms "Jehovah"
and "Logos" must be distinguished because they denote essential dis-

s *Polemicall Discourses* (1674), p. 190. *Lit. Rem.*, III, 344.
t *The Development of English Theology in the Nineteenth Century, 1800-1860*
(London, New York: Longmans, Green, 1913).
u *De Augmentis*, ix, p. 386 (Bohn).

tinctions in the nature of the Deity.*v* Though Coleridge constantly discriminated terms, it is significant that he made the same distinction in almost the same language as that used by Edward Potter.

Of even greater consequence than the advancement of textual crticism in the seventeenth century was the application of the new critical and historical spirit to biblical study. It became evident that the Bible was a history of Christianity in its outward development as well as an explanation of its nature. Like other histories, it contained much legendary and traditional matter and therefore must be studied as any other book would be. Coleridge marks as "excellent" a paragraph in William Sherlock's *Vindication of the Doctrine of the Trinity* (London: 1690; p. 150) where Sherlock states:

> I affirm that natural reason is not the rule and measure of expounding Scripture, no more than it is of expounding other writing. The true and only way to interpret any writing, even the Scriptures themselves is to examine the use and propriety of words and phrases, the connexion, scope, and design of the text, its allusion to ancient customs and usages, or disputes.*w*

Tulloch is, therefore, too sweeping in his statement that Coleridge was the first "plainly and boldly" to demand this type of study.*x* Coleridge's requirements are similar to those of Sherlock: one should have a knowledge of "the Originals, or of the Languages, the History, Customs, Opinions, and Controversies of the Age and Country in which they were written"*y* in order to understand the Scriptures. He recognized that even in his own time commentators were not paying enough attention to these materials. His basic principle was that the Bible be given "the justice you grant to other books of grave authority, and to other proved and acknowledged benefactors of mankind."*z*

In studying the originals, various critics had come to doubt the attributed authorship of certain parts of the Bible.*aa* Just at the end of the seventeenth century Richard Bentley's *The Epistles of Phalaris* (1699) demonstrated the value of internal evidence in establishing authorship and a method for using such evidence. This book was of the greatest importance to biblical critics, and its method was later used by Coleridge himself.

v *A Vindication of Our Blessed Savior's Divinity* (Cambridge: 1714).
w *Lit. Rem.*, IV, 213.
x *Movements of Religious Thought in Britain during the Nineteenth Century* (New York: Scribner, 1888), p. 25.
y *Aids*, p. 293 n.
z *Confessions*, p. 58.
aa In the seventeenth century, for example, Hobbes and Richard Simon had come to doubt the authorship of the Pentateuch.

In the light of these different lines of critical study the seventeenth-century divines sought to find what restatement of inspiration or revelation was possible. Hooker and Chillingworth held that the Bible contained "all truths necessary to Salvation"[bb] though not all that it contained was necessary. John Smith found the answer in revelation as a continuing process, saying that "God is the perpetual source of illumination to all who can live the life of Reason." It was these points of view which Coleridge accepted and restated.

In an age of great sectarianism the more liberal seventeenth-century divines made a valiant attempt to find a basis for unity in religion by reducing the creed to minimum essentials. The Cambridge Platonists led the way in showing that the important thing was the spiritual power in the individual, not a set of dogmas. Therefore they labored to bring about a church which would be broad enough to provide a spiritual community of worshippers even though these might disagree on doctrinal points. Coleridge suggested as a sufficient creed the original *Symbolum Fidei,* or instruction for baptism, which "was elder than the Gospels, and probably contained only the three doctrines of the Trinity, the Redemption, and the Unity of the Church."[cc]

Even without full materials for study, it is clear that in theology, in biblical criticism, and in the broad church movement,[dd] Coleridge not only recognized the significance of the work done by the great divines of the seventeenth century but also felt the impact of their thought in forming his own ideas.

The Old Divines[1]

How pregnant with instruction, and with knowledge of all sorts, are the sermons of our old divines! in this respect, as in so many others, how different from the major part of modern discourses![2]

bb *Confessions,* p. 88.

cc Omniana, *Lit. Rem.,* I, 379.

dd For discussion of this important matter and of the subject of Church control, see *Coleridge and the Broad Church Movement* by C. R. Sanders (Durham, N. C.: Duke University Press, 1942).

---

[1] When the comments on the divines appear as notes on sermons included below, they are omitted from this section. See especially: Donne, pp. 163, 166, 180, 204, Hooker, pp. 143, 144-45.

[2] Jan. 7, 1833. *Table Talk S,* p. 418.

The effects of a zealous ministry on the intellects and acquirements of the labouring classes are not only attested by Baxter, and the Presbyterian divines, but admitted by Bishop Burnet, who, during his mission in the west of Scotland, was "amazed to find a poor commonality so able to argue," &c. But we need not go to a sister church for proof or example. The diffusion of light and knowledge through this kingdom, by the exertions of the bishops and clergy, by Episcopalians and Puritans, from Edward VI. to the Restoration, was as wonderful as it is praiseworthy, and may be justly placed among the most remarkable facts in history.[3]

Now as my first presumptive proof of a difference (I might almost have said, of a contrast) between the religious character of the period since the Revolution, and that of the period from the accession of Edward the Sixth to the abdication of the second James, I refer to the Sermons and to the theological Works generally, of the latter period. It is my full conviction, that in any half dozen Sermons of Dr. Donne, or Jeremy Taylor, there are more thoughts, more facts and images, more excitements to inquiry and intellectual effort, than are presented to the congregations of the present day in as many churches or meetings during twice as many months. Yet both these were the most popular preachers of their times, were heard with enthusiasm by crowded and promiscuous Audiences, and the effect produced by their eloquence was held in reverential and affectionate remembrance by many attendants on their ministry, who, like the pious Isaac Walton, were not themselves men of learning or education. In addition to this fact, think likewise on the large and numerous editions of massy, closely printed folios: the impressions so large and the editions so numerous, that all the industry of destruction for the last hundred years has but of late sufficed to make them rare. From the long list select those works alone, which we know to have been the most current and favorite works of their day: and of these again no more than may well be supposed to have had a place in the scantiest libraries, or perhaps with the Bible and Common Prayer Book to have *formed* the library of their owner. Yet on the single shelf so filled we should find almost every possible question, that could interest or instruct a reader whose whole heart was in his religion, discussed with a command of intellect that seems to exhaust all the learning and logic, all the historical and moral relations, of each several subject. The very length of the discourses, with which these "rich souls of wit and knowledge" fixed the eyes, ears, and hearts

[3] *Aids*, pp. 7-8 n. Cf. Shedd, I, 121 n.

of their crowded congregations, are a source of wonder now-a-days, and (we may add) of self-congratulation, to many a sober Christian, who forgets with what delight he himself has listened to a two hours' harangue on a Loan or Tax, or at the trial of some remarkable cause or culprit. The transfer of the interest makes and explains the whole difference. For though much may be fairly charged on the revolution in the *mode* of preaching as well as in the matter, since the fresh morning and fervent noon of the Reformation, when there was no need to visit the conventicles of fanaticism in order to

> See God's ambassador in the pulpit stand,
> Where they could take notes from his Look and Hand;
> And from his speaking *action* bear away
> More sermon than our preachers use to *say;*

yet this too must be referred to the same change in the habits of men's minds, a change that involves both the shepherd and the flock; though like many other *Effects,* it tends to reproduce and strengthen its own cause.

The last point, to which I shall appeal, is the warmth and frequency of the religious controversies during the former of the two periods; the deep interest excited by them among all but the lowest and most ignorant classes; the importance attached to them by the very highest; the number, and in many instances the transcendent merit, of the controversial publications—in short, the rank and value assigned to *polemic divinity.* The subjects of the controversies may or may not have been trifling; the warmth, with which they were conducted, may have been disproportionate and indecorous; and we may have reason to congratulate ourselves that the age, in which we live, is grown more indulgent and less captious. The fact is introduced not for its own sake, but as a *symptom* of the general state of men's feelings, as an evidence of the direction and main channel, in which the thoughts and interests of men were then flowing.[4]

If the critical canon be adopted which defines eloquence to consist in a continuous flow of clear and beautiful thoughts, in harmonious and carefully arranged language, the divines of the sixteenth and seventeenth centuries, would, perhaps, be deemed inferior to their successors. They very rarely present us with a perfect whole. Their compositions are marked by the liveliest *expression,* but are often destitute of *symmetry.* Their power comes out in the vivid bursts of sublimity, in flashes of indignant satire, in exhortations of overpowering enthusiasm. You will

---

[4] *"Blessed are ye,"* pp. 88-91. British Museum, Ashley, 2853, with original MS notes. Printed in Pickering edition, pp. 395-97.

observe, also, a dramatic spirit and liveliness of painting.   Their sermons abound in, what we may call, effective situations.   For examples
of all these qualities, I would send you to the works of a writer who
flourished in the Elizabethan reign; and who, for his eloquence, obtained
the appellation of the *silver-tongued preacher*.[5]   Two or three passages
occur to me, which seem to be worthy of the highest reputation.   The
first is taken from a sermon, bearing the singular title of *The Trumpet
of the soul sounding to Judgment;* and refers to the few brief years in
which wickedness is permitted to triumph—"When INIQUITY hath
played her part, VENGEANCE leaps upon the stage.   The black guard
shall attend upon you, you shall eat at the table of Sorrow, and the
crown of Death shall be upon your heads, and many glittering faces
shall be looking upon you."   He has here dashed out with a few strokes
of his pen, a picture of almost Miltonic grandeur.   The next is of a
different character:—"When God seeth an hypocrite, he will pull his
vizard from his face, as Adam was stript of his fig-leaves, and show the
anatomy of his heart, as though his life were written in his forehead."
Who has expressed the weakness of the flesh in stronger terms than
these:—"The kingdome of heaven is caught by violence; so soon as we
rise in the morning, we go forth to fight with two mighty giants, the
World and the Devil, and whom do we take with us but a traitor?"[6]

However strong the presumption were in favor of principles authorized by names that must needs be so dear and venerable to a Minister of
the Church of England, as those of HOOKER, WHITAKER, FIELD, DONNE,
SELDEN, STILLINGFLEET, (masculine intellects, formed under the robust
discipline of an age memorable for keenness of research, and iron industry!) yet no undue preponderance from any previous weight in this
scale will be apprehended by minds capable of estimating the counter-
weights, which it must first bring to a balance in the scale opposite![7]

The Church Episcopalians under the Stuart Dynasty took the worst
way of defending Episcopacy; first, jure divino, by Scripture—in which
they made out nothing—and 2ndly, by Church Antiquity and the
Authority of the Fathers in which they either made out nothing to their
purpose, i.e. Diocesan Prelacy, or presented vulnerable Points to the
Romanists and exposed themselves to the charge of inconsistency from
both parties, Papist and Puritan.   Had they supported their cause by
the Right of the State to make use of it's learned Body and it's public

---

[5] Henry Smyth, *Sermons* (1593).
[6] Willmott, *C. at Trinity*, pp. 9-10.
[7] Appendix E, *Statesman's Manual*, p. xli.

Instructors in the manner best suited to & most congruous with it's Constitution, as a particular State—then challenged their adversaries to shew cause, what should deprive the Sovereign Power (in England, the King & two houses of Parliament) as the representative, and in the right of the State, being themselves Christians, from choosing the Pub. Instructors & the members of the permanent Learned Class from Xtn. ministers—or obliged or even permitted these ministers to refuse compliance—the Puritans would have been entangled & silenced by their own doctrines of [— ?] or Metaphysics: Right & Duty of the Civil Magistrate to interfere with Religion.[8]

Two things I disapprove, the one in several of the Divines before the Restoration—the other in only not all of the C. of E. Divines since— The first a boastful and exaggerated display of the Christian Mysteries, as so many conundrums—seemingly in imitation of the Three Paradoxes. Ex. gr. Lord Bacon's Christians Faith—Of these Voltaire & Volney are mere but mischievous Plagiaries. The Conundrum consists in stating the Transcendents of Reason, above or rather alien to, the Understanding, as contradictions to Reason—to that Reason which they *are!* The other is the cowardly and unfair way of stating the arguments of Infidels—which with generous minds in youth is enough to make them infidels a priori.[9]

Strange infatuation! Metaphysics—that is, μετὰ φυσικά, truths that transcend the evidence of the Senses! and this is a terriculum to a professed Believer in a God, a Redeemer, a responsible Will, and a birth in the Spirit to him who saith, I am the Resurrection & the Life—the Life everlasting! Infatuation indeed! Yet scarcely to be called strange, inasmuch as it may be easily explained by the bran, straw and froth which the Idols of the age, Locke, Helvetius, Hume, Condillac, and their Disciples, have succeeded in passing off for metaphysics. But is it not mournful that such commonplace stuff scummed from the mere surface of the Senses should have superseded the works of Luther, Melancthon, Bucer, yea, of Bull, Waterland, and Stillingfleet, in the Libraries of the clergy, even of those who have & use Libraries? I do not mention Richard Baxter, because—tho' of all Divines the nearest to the opinions of the serious ministers of our present Church, he is numbered among the Dissenters—with about as much right, as I might charge a man with

[8] Notebook 25, fol. 106 recto-105 verso (writing back to front). British Museum, Add. MSS, 47,523. Printed for the first time.
[9] Clasped Vellum Notebook, pp. 152-53. Printed for the first time.

desertion, whom I had thrown out of window in the hope of breaking his neck! But this I will say, that in Baxter's "Catholic Faith," and other of his Works, there is enough to *shame*, as well as supersede, whole shelves of later Divines & Metaphysicians, French, Scotch, & English. God knows my heart! there may be & I trust are, many among our Clergy who love, prize, and venerate our Church as earnestly and disinterestedly as I do! But that any man, "on this side idolatry" can love & prize it more, or more sincerely, it is not in my power to believe. For those, however, who suppose, like the Master of Trinity [Wordsworth], or he who wrote "Who wrote Eikon Basilike?" that the character of our venerable Church is identified with that of those Diseases of the Age, Charles I., Laud, & Sheldon, I must submit to be scowled at, as an alien and an adversary.

12 September, 1830 S. T. Coleridge[10]

The opportunity of diverting the reader from myself to characters more worthy of his attention, has led me far beyond my first intention; but it is not unimportant to expose the false zeal which has occasioned these attacks on our elder patriots. It has been too much the fashion, first to personify the Church of England, and then to speak of different individuals, who in different ages have been rulers in that church, as if in some strange way *they* constituted its personal identity. Why should a clergyman of the present day feel interested in the defence of Laud or Sheldon? Surely it is sufficient for the warmest partizan of our establishment, that he can assert with truth,—when our Church persecuted, it was on mistaken principles held in common by all Christendom; and at all events, far less culpable were the Bishops, who were maintaining the existing laws, than the persecuting spirit afterwards shewn by their successful opponents, who had no such excuse, and who should have been taught mercy by their own sufferings, and wisdom by the utter failure of the experiment in their own case. We can say, that our Church, apostolical in its faith, primitive in its ceremonies, unequalled in its liturgical forms; that our Church, which has kindled and displayed more bright and burning lights of Genius and Learning, than all other protestant churches since the reformation, was (with the single exception of the times of Laud and Sheldon) least intolerant, when all Christians unhappily deemed a species of intolerance their religious duty; that Bishops of our church were among the first that contended

[10] John Miller, *Sermons intended to show a sober application of Scriptural Principles to the Realities of Life* (Oxford: 1830). British Museum, C.43 b.11. A presentation copy to Coleridge. The note above also appeared in "Coleridge Marginalia Hitherto Unpublished," *Blackwood's*, CXXXI (January, 1882), p. 113.

against this error; and finally, that since the reformation, when tolerance became a fashion, the Church of England, in a tolerating age, has shewn herself eminently tolerant, and far more so, both in Spirit and in Fact than many of her most bitter opponents, who profess to deem toleration itself an insult on the rights of mankind. As to myself, who not only know the Church-Establishment to be tolerant, but who see in it the greatest, if not the sole *bulwark* of Toleration, I feel no necessity of defending or palliating oppressions under the two Charleses, in order to exclaim with a full and fervent heart, ESTO PERPETUA![11]

Richard Hooker

When in such a work (*the Ecclesiastical Policy*) of such a mind as Hooker's, the judicious author, though no less admirable for the perspicuity than for the port and dignity of his language; and though he wrote for men of learning in a learned age; saw nevertheless occasion to anticipate and guard against "complaints of obscurity," as often as he was to trace his subject "to the highest well-spring and fountain." Which, (continues he) "because men are not accustomed to, the pains we take are more needful a great deal, than acceptable; and the matters we handle, seem by reason of newness (till the mind grow better acquainted with them) dark and intricate." I would gladly therefore spare both myself and others this labor, if I knew how without it to present an intelligible statement of my poetic creed; not as my *opinions*, which weigh for nothing, but as deductions from established premises conveyed in such a form, as is calculated either to effect a fundamental conviction, or to receive a fundamental confutation. If I may dare onée more adopt the words of Hooker, "they, unto whom we shall seem tedious, are in nowise injured by us, because it is in their own hands to spare that labour, which they are not willing to endure."[1]

The *halting* jump that indivisible Point
Or centre wherein Goodness doth consist

[11] An Apologetic Preface to "Fire, Famine, and Slaughter" in *Sib. Leaves*, pp. 108-9.

[1] *Biog. Lit. C*, I, 92.

A chance Pentam. Iambic from Hooker, p. 82. It is rare to meet an idiom of this sort in Hooker—tho' his diction is native English throughout—the language of a thoughtful learned Englishman indeed, but still English, if not our Mother, yet our genuine *Father* tongue . . .

P. S. Hooker (p. 81) distinguishes Spirit from Soul: and so far as I understand him, forms the same conception of Spirit as I have done in Aids to Reflection—namely, as a focal energy from the union of the Will and the Reason—i.e. the *practical* Reason, the Source of Ideas as ultimate Ends—Ah! if Hooker had initiated & as it were matriculated his philosophy with the *prodocimastic* Logic—or previous examination of the *Heights & Measures* in use! S. T. C. 14 Septr. 1826.

P. 89. Eccles. Pol. An exquisite passage on the instinctive *Humanity* of Men.

"A manifest token that we rush after a sort of universal fellowship with all men appeareth in the wonderful delight, men have, some to visit foreign Countries . . . *and in a word, because Nature doth presume, that how many Men there are in the world, so many Gods,* as it were, there are: or at leastwise such they should be towards Men." &c.[2]

I must acknowledge, with some hesitation, that I think Hooker has been a little over-credited for his judgment.[3]

Hooker was an early Questionist, quietly inquisitive.[4]

Hooker, WORKS,[5] *Dedication to Charles II, fol. A2 recto.*

Although I know how little leisure *Great Kings* have to read large Books, or indeed, any, save only *Gods* . . . Yet having lived to see the wonderful and happy *Restauration* of *Your Majesty* to *Your* Rightful Kingdoms, and of this *Reformed Church* to its just Rights, Primitive Order, and Pristine Constitution, by *Your Majesties* prudent care, and unparallel'd bounty . . . whose transcendent favour, justice, merit, and munificence to the *long afflicted Church of England,* is a subject no less worthy of *admiration* than *gratitude* to all Posterity.

[2] Notebook 26, fol. 96 verso-98 recto. British Museum, Add. MSS, 47,524. Printed for the first time.
[3] Aug. 29, 1827. *Table Talk S*, p. 295.
[4] Notebook 21, fol. 36 verso. British Museum, Add. MSS, 47,518. Printed for the first time.
[5] Folio (London: 1682). British Museum, Ashley, 5175. James Gillman's bookplate is on front board. H. N. Coleridge in editing the notes from Hooker for the *Literary Remains* used Keble's edition, 1836. Most of the notes appear in *Lit. Rem.,* III, 18-57, but with so many changes that it has seemed wise to the present editor to establish the original text and the original order of the notes. See below for errors in reference.

? *Little* Kings, I presume, are better off! O how hateful yet alas! how common, is adulation *in the mouth* of a protestant Bishop—when even Dogs, from whom the metaphor is derived, perpetrate with their Tail! Read the first paragraph, so worthy of a Christian Minister—then what follows of "prudent care, unparalleled bounty, transcendent merit," &c. &c.—& reflect on the even generally *suspected* papistry and the *known notorious* profaneness and profligacy of the heartless Brotheller, Charles II!![6]

Hooker, WORKS: *Walton's* LIFE OF MR. HOOKER, *p. 15. Note continued on p. 16.*

Mr. *Travers* excepted against Mr. *Hooker,* for that in one of his Sermons he declared, *That the assurance of what we believe by the Word of God, is not to us so certain as that which we perceive by Sense.*

There is, I confess, a shade of doubt on my mind as to this position of Hooker's. Yet I do not deny that it expresses a truth. The question in my mind is only, whether it adequately expresses *the* truth. The ground of my doubt lies in my inability to compare two things that differ in *kind.* It is impossible that any conviction of the Reason, even where no act of the Will advenes as a co-efficient, should possess the vividness of an immediate object of the *Senses:* for this vividness is given by Sensation. Equally impossible is it that any truth of the supersensuous Reason should possess the *evidence* of the pure Sense. Even the Mathematician does not find the same *evidence* in the results of transcendental Algebra, as in the demonstrations of simple Geometry. But has he less assurance? In answer to Hooker's argument I say, that God refers to our sensible experience to aid our wills by the vividness of sensible impressions, and 2nd to aid our understanding of the truths revealed—not to increase the conviction of their certainty when they have been understood. S. T. C.

Hooker, WORKS: *Walton's* APPENDIX TO THE LIFE OF MR. HOOKER, *p. 27.*

As there could be in Natural Bodies no motion of any thing, unless there were some first which moved all things, and continued Unmoveable; even so in Politick Societies, there must be some unpunishable, or else no Man shall suffer punishment . . .

It is most painful to connect the venerable, almost sacred, name of *R. Hooker* with such a specimen of puerile sophistry—scarce worthy of a Court-Bishop's Trencher-Chaplain in the slavering times of our Scotch Solomon! It is, however, of some value, some *interest* at least, as a striking example of the confusion of an *Idea* with a *Conception.* Every

[6] This note does not appear in *Lit. Rem.*

Conception has it's sole reality in it's being referable to a Thing or Class of Things of which or of the common characters of which it is the reflection. An Idea is a *Power* (δύναμις νοερά) that constitutes it's own Reality—and is in order of Thought, necessarily antecedent to the *Things*, in which it is, more or less adequately, realized—while a conception is as necessarily posterior.[7]

Hooker, WORKS: *Walton's* APPENDIX TO THE LIFE OF MR. HOOKER, *p. 28.*

It is a strange blind story, this of the 3 last books, and of Hooker's live Relict, the Beast without Beauty, instead of Beauty and the Beast. But Saravia?? if honest Isaac's account of the tender, confidential, even confessional Friendship of Hooker and Saravia be accurate—how chanced it, that H. did not entrust the MSS to his friend who stood beside him in his last moments? At all events, Saravia must have known whether they had or had not received the Author's last hand. Why were not Mr. Chark and *the other* Canterbury parson called to account —questioned at least as to the truth of Mrs. Joan's story? Verily, I cannot help suspecting that the doubt cast on the authenticity of the latter books by the High Church Party originated in their dislike of the Contents. In short, 'tis a blind story, a true Canterbury Tale, Dear Isaac! S. T. C.[8]

Hooker, WORKS: ECCL. POLITY, *Preface, sec. 2, pp. 47-48. Note on p. 48.*

Here were the seeds sown of that controversie which sprang up between *Beza* and *Erastus*, about the matter of Excommunication, Whether there ought to be in all Churches an Eldership having power to Excommunicate.

How readily would this and indeed all the disputes respecting the powers and constitution of Church-government have been settled, or perhaps prevented, had there been a[n] insight into the distinct nature & origin of the National Church and the Church under Christ! To the ignorance of this, all the fierce contentions between the Puritans and the Episcopalians under Eliz. and the Stuarts; all the errors and exorbitant Pretensions of the Church of Scotland; and all the Heats and Antipathies of our present Dissenters, may be demonstrably traced. S. T. C.[9]

[7] The reference in *Lit. Rem.*, III, 48-49 is erroneously given to Book VIII of *Eccl. Polity.*

[8] To explain the alleged spuriousness of Hooker's last three books, Walton recounts that after Hooker's death Mrs. Hooker confessed to the Archbishop of Canterbury that Mr. Chark and another minister ''burnt and tore'' many of Hooker's writings, presumably these three books in manuscript.

[9] The text here given differs from the one in *Lit. Rem.*, III, 20. The note appears at the top of p. 48, where the passage to which it seems to refer is also found. The passage in *Lit. Rem.* is on the following page. Furthermore, ''this dispute'' seems irrelevant to the latter, but does apply to the former.

Hooker, WORKS: ECCL. POLITY, *Preface, sec. 3, p. 49.*

> *Pythagoras,* by bringing up his Scholars in speculative knowledge of numbers, made their conceits therein so strong, that when they came to the contemplation of things natural, they imagined that in every particular thing, they even beheld, as it were with their eyes, how the Elements of Number gave Essence and Being to the Works of Nature: A thing in reason impossible, which notwithstanding, through their mis-fashioned pre-conceit, appeared unto them no less certain, than if Nature had written it in the very Foreheads of all the Creatures of God.

I am too little conversant with the Volumes of Duns Scotus, to know whether he is an *exception;* but I can think of no other instance of *metaphysical Genius* in an Englishman.   Judgement, Solid Sense, Invention in Specialties, fortunate Anticipations, and instructive *Fore-tact* of Truth, in these we can shew Giants.   It is evident from this example from the Pythagorean School, that not even our incomparable Hooker could raise himself to the idea, so rich in truth which is contained in the words Numero, Pondere, et Mensura generantur Cæli et Terra. + Ὁ ἀριθμὸς ὑπεραρίθμιος. Had Hooker asked himself concerning *Will,* *Absolute Will* = numerus omnes numeros ponens, numquam positus![10]

Hooker, WORKS: ECCL. POLITY, *Preface, sec. v, p. 54.   Note continued on pp. 55-56.*

> A Law is the Deed of the whole Body Politick, whereof if ye judge your selves to be any part, then is the Law even your Deed also.

A fiction of Law, for the purpose of giving to that, which is necessarily empirical, the form and consequence of a Science—to the reality of which a Code of Laws can only approximate by compressing all liberty and individuality into a Despotism.   As Justinian to Alfred, the Consuls, and Senate of Constantinople to the Lord Mayor, Aldermen, and Common Council of London; so the imperial Roman Code to the Common Statute and Customary Law of England.   The Advocates of Discipline would, according to our present notions of civil rights, have been justified in putting Fact against Fiction; & might have challenged Hooker to shew, first, that the Constitution of the Church in Christ was a congruous subject of parliamentary Legislation; that the Legislators were bonâ fide determined by spiritual views; and that the jealousy and arbitrary Principles of the Queen, aided by motives of worldly state policy, ex. gr. the desire to conciliate the Catholic Potentates by retaining all she could, of the exterior of the Romish

---

[10] The opening sentence in *Lit. Rem.,* III, 21 is toned down to ''I am not so conversant with the volumes of Duns Scotus as to be able to pronounce positively whether he is an exception, but I can think of no other instance of high metaphysical genius in an Englishman.'' Later the position of the Greek phrase is changed.

Church, it's hierarchy, it's Church Ornaments, and it's Ceremonies, were not the Substitutes for the Holy Spirit in influencing the majorities in the two Houses of Parliament. It is my own belief, that the Puritans and the Prelatists divided the Truth between them; and as half-truths are whole Errors, were both equally in the wrong—the Prelatists in contending for a Church in Christ (i. e. the collective number τῶν ἐκκεκλημένων = ἐκκλησία) which only belonged, but which rightfully did belong, to a National Church, as a *component* Estate of the *Realm* (i. e. *Enclesia*) the Puritans in requiring of the Enclesia what was only requisite or possible for the Ecclesia. Archbishop Grindal is an illustrious exception. He saw the *whole* truth, and saw, that the functions of the *E*nclesiastic and those of the *E*cclesiastic were not the less distinct, because both were capable of being exercised by the same Person; & "vice versa," not the less compatible in the same subject because distinct in themselves. The Lord Chief Justice of the King's Bench is a Fellow of the Royal Society.   S. T. C.[11]

Hooker, WORKS: ECCL. POLITY, *Book I, sec. 2, p. 70. Note continued on pp. 70-73.*

> That which doth assign unto each thing the kind, that which doth moderate the force and power, that which doth appoint the form and measure of working, the same we term a *Law*.

See Essay on Method, *Friend* Vol. III.[12] Hooker's words literally and grammatically interpreted seem to assert the antecedence of the *Thing* to it's *kind*, i. e. essential character; & to it's force together with it's *form* and *measure* of working, i. e. to it's specific and distinctive characters—in short, the words assert the pre-existence of the Thing to all it's constituent powers, qualities and properties. Now this is either—I. equivalent to the assertion of a prima et nuda materia, so happily ridiculed by the Author of Hudibras,[13] and which under any scheme of Cosmogony is a mere phantom, having it's whole and sole substance in an impotent effort of the Imagination or sensuous Fancy; but which is utterly precluded by the doctrine of Creation, which it in like manner negatives. Or II[ndly], the words assert a self-destroying Absurdity—viz. the antecedence of a thing to itself—as if having asserted that Water *consisted* of Hydrogen = 77, and Oxygen = 23, I should talk of Water as existing before the creation of Hydrogen and Oxygen. All

---

[11] Cf. *Lit. Rem.*, III, 23-25. In the second sentence there is an error in the reading: "As Justinian to Alfred, and Constantinople, the Consuls and Senate of Rome to the Lord Mayor. . . ." Coleridge marked the passage to indicate the order in which some out-of-place phrases were to be read.

[12] See especially Essay 5; but Essays 4-9 treat this subject also.

[13] Part I, canto i, ll. 151-56.

Laws, indeed, are not constitutive; and it would require a longer train of argument than a note can contain, to shew what *a Thing* is; but this at least is quite certain, that in the order of *thought* it must be posterior to the Law that constitutes it. But such in fact was Hooker's meaning, and the word, Thing, is used prolepticè, in favor of the imagination—as appears from the sentences that follow, in which the Creative Idea is declared to be the Law of the things thereby created. A productive Idea, manifesting itself and it's reality in the Product, is a Law: and when the Product is phænomenal, (i. e. an object of outward Senses) a Law of Nature. The law is Res *noumenon;* the Thing is Res *phœnomenon.* A physical Law, in the right sense of the term, is the *sufficient* Cause of the Appearance,—causa *sub-faciens.* P. S. What a deeply interesting Volume might be written on the symbolic import of the primary relations and dimensions of Space—Long, broad, deep or depth; superficies; upper, under or above and below; right, left, horizontal, perpendicular, oblique. And then the order of Causation, or that which gives intelligibility, and the reverse order of Effects or that which gives the conditions of actual *existence.* Without the higher the lower would want it's intelligibility; without the lower the higher could not have *existed.* The Infant is a riddle of which the Man is the solution; but the Man could not exist but with the Infant as antedent [antecedent?].

Hooker, WORKS: ECCL. POLITY, *Book I, sec. 2, p. 71.*

> In which Essential Unity of God, a Trinity Personal nevertheless subsisteth, after a manner far exceeding the possibility of mans conceit . . .

If "conceit" here means *conception,* the remark is most true: for the Trinity is an Idea, and no Idea can be rendered by a conception. An Idea is essentially inconceivable. But if it be meant, that the Trinity is otherwise inconceivable, than as the divine Eternity & as *every* attribute of God is & must be—*then* neither the *commonness* of the Language here used nor the high authority of the users, can deter me from denouncing it as untrue and dangerous. So far is it from being true, that the Trinity is the only Form, in which an Idea of God is possible—unless indeed it be a Spinozistic or World-God.

Hooker, WORKS: ECCL. POLITY, *Book I, sec. 4, p. 75.*

> But now that we may lift up our eyes (as it were) from the Foot-stool to the Throne of God, and leaving these Natural, consider a little the state of Heavenly and Divine Creatures: Touching Angels, which are Spirits Immaterial and Intellectual . . .

All this disquisition on the Angels confirms my remark, that our admirable Hooker was a Giant of the Race, Aristotle ✕ Plato. Hooker was truly *judicious*—the consummate Synthesis of Understanding and Sense. An ample and most ordonnant Conceptionist, to the tranquil Empyrean of *Ideas* he had not ascended. Of the passages cited from Scripture how few would bear strict scrutiny—either namely 1. Divine Appearance, Jehovah in human form, or 2. the Imagery of Visions, and all Symbolics, or 3. Name of Honor given to Prophets, Apostles, & Bishops: or lastly, mere accommodation to popular notions!

Hooker, WORKS: ECCL. POLITY, *Book I, sec. 4, p. 75.*

> Since their [i. e. fall of the angels] fall, their practices have been the clean contrary unto those before mentioned; for being dispersed, some in the Air, some on the Earth, some in the Water: some amongst the Minerals, Dens and Caves that are under the Earth; they have, by all means, laboured to effect an Universal Rebellion against the Laws, and as far as in them lieth, utter destruction of the Works of God.

Childish; but the childishness of the Age, without which neither Hooker nor Luther could have acted on their contemporaries with the intense and beneficient energy with which, they (God be praised!) did act.

Hooker, WORKS: ECCL. POLITY, *Book I, sec. 4, p. 76.*

> Thus much therefore may suffice for Angels, the next unto whom in degree are Men.

St. Augustine well remarks that only three distinct Genera of living Beings are conceivable:—1. The Infinite Rational; 2. The finite rational; 3. The finite irrational— i. e. God: Man: Animal.[14] Ergo, Angels can only be men with wings on their shoulders. Were our Bodies transparent to our Souls, we should be Angels.

Hooker, WORKS: ECCL. POLITY, *Book I, sec. 10, p. 86. Note continued on p. 87.*

> It is no improbable opinion therefore which the Arch-Philosopher was of, That as the chiefest person in every houshold, was alwayes as it were a King, so when numbers of housholds joyned themselves in Civil Societies together, Kings were the first kind of Governours amongst them.

There are and can be only two Schools of Philosophy, differing in kind and in source.[15] Differences in degree and in accident, may be many; but these constitute Schools kept by different Teachers with different degrees of Genius, Talent, &c.—Auditories of Philosophizers, not different Philosophies. Schools of Philosophy (the love of empty noise) of Psilology, and Misosophy are out of the question. Schools

---

[14] This statement is frequently repeated by Coleridge.
[15] Cf. a similar statement in *Table Talk S*, p. 336, July 2, 1830.

of Philosophy there are but two—best named by the Arch-philosopher of each—viz. Plato and Aristotle. Every man capable of philosophy at all (& there are not many such) is a *born* Platonist or a *born* Aristotelian. Hooker, as might have been anticipated from the epithet of Arch-philosopher applied to the Stagyrite, *sensu monarchico*, was of the latter family—a comprehensive, rich, vigorous, *discreet* and discretive, *Conceptualist*—but not an *Ideist*. S. T. C.[16]

Hooker, WORKS: ECCL. POLITY, *Book V, sec. 19, p. 208. Note continued on p. 209.*

> Of both Translations, the better I willingly acknowledge that which cometh nearer to the very letter of the Original verity: yet so, that the other may likewise safely enough be read, without any peril at all of gain-saying as much as the least jot or syllable of Gods most sacred and precious Truth.

Hooker had far better have rested on the 1. impossibility, 2. the uselessness, of a faultless translation; and admitting certain mistakes and oversights recommended them for notice at the next revision & then asked, what objection such harmless trifles can be to a Church that never pretended to infallibility? But in fact, the age was not ripe enough even for a Hooker to feel, much less with safety to expose, the protestant's idol—i. e. their Bibliolatry.

Hooker, WORKS: ECCL. POLITY, *Book V, sec. 22, p. 218. Note continued on p. 219.*

> Their only proper and direct proof of the thing in question had been to shew, in what sort, and how far mans Salvation doth necessarily depend upon the knowledge of the Word of God; what Conditions, Properties, and Qualities there are, whereby Sermons are distinguished from other kinds of administring the Word unto that purpose; and what special Property or Quality that is, which being no where found but in Sermons, maketh them effectual to save Souls, and leaveth all other Doctrinal means besides destitute of vital efficacy.

Doubtless Hooker was a theological Talus with a Club of Iron against opponents with paste-board Helmets and armed only with Crab-sticks! But yet I too, too often find occasion to complain of him, as abusing his superior strength. For in a good man it is an abuse of his intellectual superiority not to use a portion of it in stating his Christian Opponents' cause, his Brethren's (tho' dissentient, & perhaps erring, yet still Brethren) side of the question, not as *they* had stated and argued it, but as he himself with his higher gifts of logic and foresight could have

[16] The comment on Book I, sec. 11, p. 94 has been transposed to the section on Reason and Understanding, p. 116. Coleridge points out that the great divines of the 17th century "knew and asserted" the distinction.

set it forth. But Hooker flies off to the *General,* in which he is unassailable; and does not, as in candour he should have done, enquire whether the question would not admit of, nay demand a different answer, when applied solely or principally to the circumstances, the condition and the needs of the English Parishes and the Population at large at the particular time, when the Puritan Divines wrote, & he, (Hooker) replied to them. Now the cause tried in *this* way, I should not be afraid to attempt the proof of the paramount efficacy of Preaching on the scheme, & in the line of argument layed down by himself p. 218 to 20. In short, H. too frequently finds it convenient to forget the homely proverb—the proof of the Pudding is in the eating. Whose parishes were the best disciplined, whose Flocks the best fed, the soberest Livers, and the most awakened and best-informed Protestant Christians, those of the zealous *preaching* Divines? or those of the prelatic Clergy with their *Readers?* In whose Churches and Parishes were all the other pastoral duties, Catechizing, Visiting the Poor &c. &c., most strictly practised?

Hooker, WORKS: ECCL. POLITY, *Book V, sec. 65, p. 298. Note continued on p. 299.*

> Thus was the Memory of that Sign which they had in Baptism, a kind of bar or prevention to keep them even from apostasie, whereunto the frailty of Flesh and Blood, over-much fearing to endure shame, might peradventure the more easily otherwise have drawn them.

I begin to fear that Hooker is not suited to *my* nature. I cannot bear round-abouts for the purpose of evading the short cut straight before my eyes Exempli Gratiâ—I find myself tempted in this place to *psha!* somewhat abruptly— and ask: How many in 20 millions of Christian Men and Women ever reverted to the make-believe anticipation of the Cross on their forehead in unconscious infancy by the wetted tip of the Parson's Finger, as a preservative against anger and resentment? "The whole Church of God"! Was it not the same Church which neglecting and concealing the Scriptures of God, introduced the adoration of the Cross, the worshipping of Relics, Holy Water, and, all the other Countless mummeries of Popery? Something *might* be pretended for the material Images of the Cross, worn at the bosom, or hung up in the Bed Chamber. These may and doubtless often do serve as silent monitors; but this lye-falsehood or pretence of making a mark that is not made, is a gratuitous Superstition, that cannot be practised without leading the Vulgar to regard it as a *Charon.* Hooker should have asked—*Has* it hitherto had this effect on Christians generally? Is it likely to produce this effect, and this principally? In common honesty he must have answered—No! Do I then blame the Church of

England for retaining this ceremony? By no means. I justify it as a wise and pious condescension to the inveterate Habits of a People newly dragged rather than drawn out of Papistry; and as a pledge that the Founder & Fathers of the Reformation in England regarded innovation as per se an evil, and therefore requiring for the justification not only a cause but a weighty cause. They did well and piously in deferring the removal of minor spots and stains to the time when the good effects of the more important Reforms had begun to shew themselves in the minds and hearts of the Saints—But *they* do not act either wisely or charitably who would eulogize these Maculæ as Beauty-spots and vindicate as good what their Predecessors only tolerated as the lesser Evil. S. T. Coleridge. 12 Aug. 1826.

Hooker, WORKS: A DISCOURSE OF JUSTIFICATION, WORKS, AND HOW THE FOUNDATION OF FAITH IS OVERTHROWN, *sec. 31, pp. 508-9.*[17]

> But we say, our Salvation is by Christ alone; therefore howsoever, or whatsoever we add unto Christ in the matter of Salvation, we overthrow Christ. Our Case were very hard, if this Argument, so universally meant as it is supposed, were sound and good. We ourselves do not teach Christ alone, excluding our own Faith, unto Justification; Christ alone, excluding our own Works, unto Sanctification; Christ alone, excluding the one or the other unnecessary unto Salvation. . . As we have received, so we teach, that besides the bare and naked work, wherein Christ without any other Associate finished all the parts of our Redemption, and purchased Salvation himself alone; for conveyance of this eminent blessing unto us, many things are of necessity required, as, to be known and chosen of God before the foundation of the World; in the World to be called, justified, sanctified; after we have left the World to be received unto Glory; Christ in every of these hath somewhat which he worketh alone . . .

No where, out of the Holy Scripture, have I found the root and pith of Christian Faith so clearly & purely propounded. God, whose thoughts are eternal, beholdeth the *End:* and in the completed work seeth and accepteth every stage of the process. P. S. I dislike only the word "purchased,"—not that it is not Scriptural, but because a metaphor well and wisely used in the enforcement & varied elucidation of a truth is not therefore properly employed in it's exact enunciation. I will illustrate, amplify, and "divide" the word with Paul; but I will propound it collectively with John. If in this admirable passage aught else dare be wished otherwise, it is the division & yet confusion of Time and Eternity, by giving an *anteriority* to the latter. S. T. C.

I am persuaded, that the *practice* of the Romish Church tendeth to make vain the doctrine of Salvation by Faith in Christ alone; but judg-

---

[17] In *Lit. Rem.* this discourse follows the sermon on faith. See III, 52-53.

ing by her most eminent Divines I can find nothing dissonant from the truth in her express decisions on this article. Perhaps, it would be safer to say: Christ alone saves us, working in us by the Faith which includes Hope and Love. See Ep. to the Gal. Ch. i. v. 20.

Hooker, WORKS: SERMON OF THE CERTAINTY AND PERPETUITY OF THE FAITH IN THE ELECT, *p. 527.*[18]

P. 527. The following truly admirable Discourse is evidently the concluding Sermon of a Series, unhappily not preserved.

Hooker, WORKS, *p. 528. Note continued on pp. 529-30. (P. 528 is numbered as 328).*

> The other, which we call the *certainty of adherence,* is, when the heart doth cleave and stick unto that which it doth believe: This certainty is greater in us than the other . . . [down to] the fourth Question resteth, and so an end of this Point.

Should be written in gold! O may these precious words be written on my heart! 1. That we all need to be redeemed: & that therefore we are all in captivity to an Evil. 2. That there is a Redeemer. 3. That the Redemption relatively to each individual Captive is, if not effected under certain conditions, yet manifestible as far as is fitting for the Soul, by certain signs and consequents, and 4. That these Signs are in myself, that the conditions, under which the Redemption offered to all men is promised to the Individual, are fulfilled in myself—these are the four great points of Faith, in which the humble Christian finds and feels a gradation from full assurance to trembling Hope.[19] Yet the *Will,* the *Act* of trust, is the same in all. Might I not almost say, that it rather increases with the decrease of the consciously discerned evidence? To assert that I have the *same* assurance of mind that I am saved as that I need a Saviour, would be a contradiction to my own feelings, and yet I may have an *equal,* that is, an equivalent assurance. How is it possible that a sick man should have the same certainty of his convalescence as of his sickness? Yet he may be assured of it. So again, my Faith in the skill and integrity of my physician may be complete, but the application of it to my own case may be troubled by the sense of my own imperfect obedience to his prescriptions. The sort of our beliefs & assurances is necessarily modified by their different Subjects. It argues no want of saving faith on the whole, that I cannot have the

---

[18] In *Lit. Rem.* the comments on this sermon are given in III, 49-54.

[19] Cf. *Lit. Rem.,* III, 50-52. Here the order of this sentence is reversed to read "feels a gradation from trembling Hope to full assurance," but the way Coleridge wrote the lines is certainly the way he meant them, as is evidenced by the discussion which follows.

same trust in myself as I have in my God. That Christ's righteousness can save me,—that Christ's righteousness alone can save—these are simple positions, all the terms of which are steady and co-present to my mind. But that I *shall* be so saved,—that of the many called I have been one of the chosen,—this is no mere conclusion of mind on known or assured Premises. I can remember no other discourse that sinks into, and draws up comfort from, the depths of our Being below our own *distinct* consciousness, with the clearness and godly loving-kindness of this truly evangelical, God-to-be-thanked-for Sermon. Yet how large, how important a part of our spiritual life goes on like the Circulation, Absorptions, and Secretions of our bodily life, unrepresented by any specific Sensation, & yet the ground and condition of our total Sense of Existence! S. T. C.

While I feel, acknowledge, and revere the almost measureless superiority of the Sermons of the Divines, who labored in the first, and even the two first Centuries of the Reformation, from Luther to Leighton, over the prudential morals and *apologizing* theology that have characterized the unfanatical Clergy since the Revolution in 1688, I cannot but regret—especially while I am listening to a Hooker—that they withheld all light from the truths contained in the words Satan, the Serpent, the evil Spirit, & this last used plurally.

Hooker, WORKS, *first flyleaf, recto.*

If R. Hooker had written only the precious pages, 328, 329—I should hold myself bound to thank the Father of Light and Giver of all good Gifts, for his existence and the preservation of his Writings. S. T. Coleridge.[20]

[20] Since p. 528 is numbered 328 by error in this Folio and the passages on pp. 528-29 are heavily marked, as well as commented upon above, this praise seems more logically to belong to pp. 528-29 than to pp. 328-29 in the Folio. The latter give an historical account of the custom of fasting; they are not paragraphed; and they bear no mark to indicate Coleridge's approval. Cf. *Lit. Rem.*, III, 48.

Richard Field

Field, OF THE CHURCH.[1] *This letter, dated March 28, 1819, is written on the title page, verso.*

My dear Derwent,

This one Volume thoroughly understood and appropriated will place you in the highest rank of *doctrinal* Church of England Divines (of such as now are) and in no mean rank as a true doctrinal Church Historian.

Next to this I recommend Baxter's own Life edited by Sylvester, with my marginal MSS Notes. Here (more than in any of the Prelatical and Arminian Divines, from Laud to the death of Charles the Second) you will see the strength and beauty of the Church of England—i. e. it's Liturgy, Homilies, and Articles. By contrasting too it's present state with that which such excellent men as Baxter, Callamy, and the so-called Presbyterian or Puritan Divines would have made it, you will bless it as the bulwark of Toleration.

Thirdly, Eichhorn's introductions to the O. & N. Testament, and to the Apocrypha, and his Comment on the Apocalypse (to all which my notes and your own previous studies will supply whatever antidote is wanting)—these will suffice for your *Biblical* Learning, and teach you to attach no more than the supportable weight to these and such like outward evidences of our holy and spiritual Religion.

So having done you will be in point of professional knowledge such a Clergyman as will make glad the heart of your loving Father,

S. T. Coleridge

Field, OF THE CHURCH, *Dedication to the Duke of Buckingham by Nathaniel Field, p. 1. Note in upper margin.*

N. B.—See Book IV. Chap. 7, p. 353, both for a masterly confutation of the Paleyo-Grotian Evidences of the Gospel, & a decisive proof in what light it was regarded by the Church of England in its best age. Like Grotius himself, it is half way between Popery and Socinianism.

[1] The notes here selected as a minimum representation of the comments on Field are reproduced from the original in the possession of A. H. B. Coleridge and are printed by his kind permission. The notes were copied at some time into the 1635 edition, a volume inscribed "The Revd. James Gillman the Gift of his Father," and this edition is in the British Museum, Ashley, 4771.

Field, OF THE CHURCH, *Book I, chap. v, p. 10.*

Aliud est Etymologia nominis & aliud significatio nominis. Etymologia attenditur secundum id à quo imponitur nomen ad significandum: Nominis vero significatio secundum id ad quod significandum imponitur. 2. 2. q. 92. art. 1.

[Marked for insertion as first part of note] An apt Motto for a Critique on Horne Tooke's ἔπεα πτερόεντα. See above.

The best service of Etymology is when the sense of a word is still unsettled, and especially when two words have each two meanings, A = ab, and B =ab, instead of A = a, and B = b. Thus Reason and Understanding, as at present popularly confounded. Here the Etyma, Ratio, the relative proportion of Thoughts and Things, and Understanding, as the power which substantiates phænomena (substat eis) determines the proper sense. But most often the etyma being equivalent, we must proceed ex arbitrio—as Law *compels,* Religion *obliges:* or take up what had been begun in some one derivative. Thus fanciful and imaginative *are* discriminated—& this supplies the ground of choice for giving to Fancy and Imagination, to each it's own sense. Cowley a *fanciful* Writer, Milton an *imaginative* Poet. *Then* I proceed with the distinction—How ill *Fancy* assorts with *Imagination,* as instanced in Milton's Limbo.[2]

Field, OF THE CHURCH, *Book I, chap. v, p. 10. Note continued on p. 11.*

For the expressing of this difference, and the more easie distinction of the two moities of the people of God, the one before, the other after the worke of redemption was performed by Christ, though both rightly and most aptly named the Church of God; yet it hath beene and is religiously observed, that by a kind of appropriation the one is named the *Synagogue,* the other the *Church.*

I should rather express the difference between the Faithful of the Synagogue and those of the Church thus: that the former hoped generally by an *implicit* faith "It shall in all things be well with all that love the Lord—therefore it cannot but be good for us, and well with us to rest with our forefathers." But the Christian hath an *assured* Hope by an explicit and particular Faith—a Hope because it's object is *future* not because it is *uncertain.* The one was in the road journeying towards a friend of his Father's who had promised that he would be kind to him even to the 3rd & 4th generation. He comforts himself on the road, first, by means of the various places of refreshment which that Friend had built for Travellers & continued to supply—& 2ndly by anticipation of a kind reception at the Friend's own Mansion-House. But

[2] *Paradise Lost,* III, 487ff.

the other has received an express invitation to a Banquet, beholds the preparations & has only to wash & put on the proper Robes in order to sit down.

Field, OF THE CHURCH, *Book I, chap. v, p. 11.*

> The reason why our translators, in the beginning, did choose rather to Use the word *Congregation* than *Church,* was not as the adversarie malitiously imagineth, for that they feared the very name of the Church; but because, as by the name of religion and religious men, ordinarily in former times, men understood nothing but *factitias religiones,* as *Gerson* out of *Anselme* calleth them, that is, the professions of Monkes and Fryers.

For the same reason the word *Religion* for ϑρησκεία in 1st James ought *now* to be altered to—Ceremony or Ritual. The old Version[3] has by change of language become a dangerous mistranslation, and furnished a favorite Text to our *moral* Preachers, Church Socinians, and other *christened* Pagans now so rife among us. What was the *substance* of the Ceremonial Law, is but the *Ceremonial* Part of the Christian Religion, but it is *it's* solemn Ceremonial *Law,* and tho' not the *same,* yet *one* with it and inseparable, even as Form and Substance. Such is St. James's Doctrine, destroying at one blow Anti-nominianism and the Popish Doctrine of good works.

Field, OF THE CHURCH, *Book I, chap. xvii, p. 27.*

> But if the Church of God remained in *Corinth,* where there were *divisions, sects, emulations* . . . who dare deny those societies to be the Churches of God, wherein the tenth part of these horrible evils and abuses is not to be found?

It is rare to meet with sophistry in this sound Divine; but here he seems to border on it. For first the Corinthian Church upon admonition repented of it's negligence; and 2, the objection of the Puritans was, that the institution of the Church precluded Discipline.

Field, OF THE CHURCH, *Book II, chap. ii, p. 31. Note on front board.*

> Miscreant used twice in it's original sense of Misbeliever.

Field, OF THE CHURCH, *Book II, chap. iv, pp. 34-35. Note on front board.*

> What a thing is wee desire to know, either by our owne discourse, or by the instructions or directions of another.

Discourse for the discursive acts of the Understanding: even as discursive is opposed to intuitive as by Milton.[4] Thus understand

---

[3] This reads " whole version" in *Lit. Rem.* See James 1:26 ff.
[4] *Paradise Lost,* V, 426 ff.

Shakespear's "Discourse of Reason" i. e. those discursions of Mind which are peculiar to rational beings.

Field, OF THE CHURCH, *Book III, chap. i, p. 53.*

> The first publishers of the Gospell of Christ delivered a rule of faith to the Christian Churches which they founded, comprehending all those articles that are found in that *epitome* of Christian religion, which wee call the Apostles Creed.

This needs proof. I rather believe that the so called Apostles' Creed was really the Creed of the Roman or Western Church (& possibly in it's present form the Catechismal rather than the Baptismal Creed) and that other Churches in the East had creeds equally ancient and from their being earlier troubled with anti-trinitarian Heresies, more *express* in the Divinity of Christ than the Roman.

Field, OF THE CHURCH, *Book III, chap. xx, p. 110.*

> Thus then, though the Fathers did sometimes, when they had particular occasions to remember the Saints, and to speake of them, by way of *Apostrophe* turne themselves unto them, and use words of doubtfull compellation, praying them, if they have any sense of these inferiour things, to be remembrancers to God for them.

The distinct gradations of the process, by which Commemoration and rhetorical Apostrophes passed finally into Idolatry, supply an analogy of mighty force against the heretical Hypothesis of the modern Unitarians. Were it true, *they* would have been able to have traced the progress of the Christo*latry* from the lowest sort of Christo*duly* with the same historical Distinctness against the universal Church, as the Protestants that of Hierolatry against the Romanists. The gentle and soft censures which our Divines during the reign of the Stuarts pass on the Roman Saint worship, or Hieroduly, as an inconvenient superstition, must needs have alarmed the faithful adherents to the Protestantism of Edward VIth. and the surviving Exiles of bloody Queen Mary's times, and their disciples.

Field, OF THE CHURCH, *Book III, chap. xx, p. 111. Note continued on p. 112.*

> The miracles that God wrought in times past by them made many to attribute more to them, then was fit, as if they had a generalitie of presence, knowledge, & working; but the wisest, and best advised never durst attribute any such thing unto them.

To a truly pious mind awefully impressed with the surpassing excellency of God's ineffable Love to fallen Man in the revelation of himself to inner man thro' the Reason & Conscience by the spiritual Light and

Substantiality (for the Conscience is to the Spirit or Reason what the understanding is to the Sense or Substantive power) this consequence of miracles is so fearful that it cannot but redouble his Zeal against that fashion of modern Theologists which could convert Miracle from a Motive to attention and soliciting examination, & at best from a negative condition of Revelation into the positive foundation of Christian Faith.

Field, OF THE CHURCH, *Book III, chap. xxii, p. 116.*

> But if this be as vile a slander, as ever Satanist devised, the Lord reward them that have beene the Authours and devisers of it, according to their workes.

O no! no!—this the good man did not utter from his Heart, but from Passion. A vile, a wicked Slander it was, and is! O may God have turned the Hearts of those who uttered it—or may it be among their unknown Sins done in Ignorance for which the infinite mercies of Christ may satisfy. I am most assured that if Dear Field were now alive, or if any one had but said this to him, he would have replied—I thank thee, Brother! for thy Christian admonition—join in thy prayer—& pray God to forgive *me* my inconsiderate Zeal!

Field, OF THE CHURCH, *Book III, chap. xxiii, p. 119.*

> For what rectitude is due to the specificall act of hating God? or what rectitude is it capable of?

Is this a possible act, the man understanding by the word God what we mean by God?

Field, OF THE CHURCH, *Book III, chap. xxx, p. 143.*

> The twelfth heresie imputed to us is the heresie of *Jovinian,* concerning whom we must observe, that *Augustine* ascribeth unto him two opinions, which *Hierome* mentioneth not, who yet was not likely to spare him, if he might truely have been charged with them. The first, that *Mary* ceased to be Virgine when shee had borne *Christ;* the second that all sinnes are equall.

Neither this nor that is worthy the name of Opinion. It is mere unscriptural, nay, anti-scriptural Gossiping. Are we to blame, or not rather to praise the anxiety manifested by the great Divines of the C. of E. under the Stuarts, not to remove further than necessary from the Romish Doctrines? Yet one wishes a bolder method; (ex. gr. as to Mary's private History after the conception & birth of Christ, we neither know nor care about it).

Field, OF THE CHURCH, *Book III, chap. xxxii, p. 147.*

Touching the second objection, that *Bucer,* and *Calvin* deny originall sinne, though not generally, as did *Zuinglius,* yet at least in the children of the faithfull: If hee had said that these men, affirme the earth doth move, and the heavens stand, hee might have as soone justified it against them, as this hee now saith.

Very noticeable! a similar passage occurs even so late as Sir T. Brown just at the dawn of the Newtonian System and after Kepler— what a Lesson of Diffidence! S. T. C.

4 Dec^r., 1814. Ashley, Box, Bath.

Field, OF THE CHURCH, *Book III, chap. xli, p. 162.*

But hee will say, Cyprian calleth the Roman Church the principall Church whence sacerdotall unity hath her spring.

This is too large a concession. The real Ground of the Priority of the Roman See was that Rome for the first 3 or perhaps four Centuries was the Metropolis of the Christian World. Afterwards for the very same reason the Patriarch of New Rome, i. e. Constantinople claimed it —& never ceased to assert at least a co-equality. Had the Apostolic Foundation been the Cause, Jerusalem & Antioch must have had priority —not to add that the Roman Church was not founded by either Paul or Peter—as is evident from the Ep. to the Romans. S. T. Coleridge.

Field, OF THE CHURCH, *An Appendix to Book III, p. 205. Note continued on pp. 206-7.*

That Transubstantiation is absolute no-meaning, I think demonstrable:[5] and yet I do not hold this the most successful Point of the orthodox Protestant controversialists. The Question is, what is meant in Scripture, as in John VI by Christ's Body, or Flesh, and Blood. Surely, not the visible, tangible, accidental Body, i. e. a cycle of images and sensations in the Imagination of the Beholders; but his supersensual Body, the Noumenon of his Human Nature: which was united to his divine nature. In this sense I understand the Lutheran Ubiquity. But in this passage may not the oblation have meant the alms-offerings always given at the Eucharist?

P. S. If by substance he meant id quod verè est, and if the divine Nature be the sole ens vere ens, then it is possible to give a philosophically intelligible sense to Luther's doctrine of Consubstantiation—at least, to a doctrine that might bear the same name. At all events, the mystery is not greater than, if it be not rather the same as, the Assumption of the Human by Divine Nature. Now to the possible conception

[5] This statement is omitted in *Lit. Rem.*

of this we must accurately discriminate the incompossible negativum from the incompatible privativum—of the latter are all positive Imperfections, as Error, Vice, &c. of the former simple Limitation. Thus if (*per impossibile*) Human Nature could make itself sinless and perfect, it would become or pass into, God—and if God should abstract from Human Nature all imperfections, it might without impropriety be affirmed, even as Scripture doth affirm; that God assumed or took up into himself, the Human Nature. Thus to use a dim similitude & merely as a faint illustration, all materiality abstracted from a circle, it would become space—and tho' not infinite, yet one with infinite Space. The mystery of omnipresence greatly aids this conception—totus in omni parte:—and in truth this is the divine character of all the Christian Mysteries, that they aid each other, and many Incomprehensibles render each of them, in a certain qualified sense, less incomprehensible. S. T. Coleridge

Field, OF THE CHURCH, *An Appendix to Book III, p. 223. Note continued on p. 224.*

> That the Saints doe pray for us *in genere,* desiring God to be mercifull to us, and to doe unto us whatsoever in any kinde he knoweth needfull for our good, there is no question made by us.

To have placed this question in it's true light, so as to have allowed their full force to the Scriptures asserting the communion of Saints and the efficacy of their intercession without undue concessions to the hierolatria of the Romish Church, would have implied an acquaintance with the science of Transcendental Analysis, & an Insight into the philosophy of Ideas not to be expected in FIELD, and which was then only dawning in the mind of Lord Bacon. The proper reply to Brerely would be this—the communion and intercession of Saints is an Idea, and must be kept such. But the Romish church has *changed* it *away* into the detail of particular and individual conceptions, and Imaginations—into Names and Fancies.

N. B. Instead of the Roman Catholic *read* throughout, in this and all other works; and every where and on all occasions unless where the duties of personal courtesy forbid, *say* the Rom*ish* Anti-catholic Church. Rom*ish* to mark that the corruptions in Discipline, Doctrine, and Practice do for the worst and far larger part owe both their origin and their perpetuation to the Court and local Tribunals of the City of Rome, & are not & never have been the Catholic (i. e. universal) Faith of the Roman Empire or even of the whole Latin or Western Church—and Anti-catholic, because no other Church acts on so narrow and excommunicative a principle, or is characterized by such a jealous Spirit of

Monopoly and Particularism counterfeiting Catholicity by a negative Totality and heretical Self-circumscription—cutting off, or cutting herself off from, all the other members of Christ's body. S. T. C., 12 March, 1824.

Note on the last 16 lines of p. 223. It is of the utmost importance, wherever clear and distinct conceptions are of importance, to make out in the first instance whether the Term in question (or the main Terms of the question in dispute) represents a fact or class of facts simply, or some self-established or previously known Idea or Principle, of which the Facts are instances & realizations or which is introduced in order to explain and account for the facts. Now merits as applied to Abraham, the Saints &c. belongs to the former—It is mere nomen appellativum of the Facts.

Field, OF THE CHURCH, *An Appendix to Book III, chap. v, p. 252.*

> The Papists and wee agree that original sinne is the privation of originall righteousness; but they suppose there was in nature without that addition of grace, a power to doe good.

Nothing seems wanting to this argument but a previous definition and explanation of the term, Nature. Field appears to have seen the truth, viz. that Nature itself is a peccant (I had almost said an unnatural) State—or rather, no *State* at all, οὐ στάσις, ἀλλὰ ἀπόστασις.

Field, OF THE CHURCH, *An Appendix to Book III, chap. vi, p. 269.*

> And surely the wordes of *Augustin* doe not import that shee had no sinne, but that shee overcame it, which argueth a conflict; neither doth he say, he will acknowledge shee was without sinne, but that hee will not move any question touching her, in this dispute of sinnes and sinners.

Why not say at once, that this anti-scriptural superstition had already begun? I scarcely know whether to be pleased or grieved with that *edging on* toward the Roman-Catholic Creed, that exceeding, almost scriptural tenderness for the Divines of the 4th, 5th, & 6th Century, which distinguishes the Church of England Dignitaries from Elizabeth (inclusive) to our Revolution in 1688, from other Protestants.

Field, OF THE CHURCH, *An Appendix to Book III, chap. x, p. 279.*

Derwent! Should this page chance to fall under your eye, for my sake read, fag, subdue, and take up into your proper mind this chap. 10 of Free Will. S. T. Coleridge.

Field, OF THE CHURCH, *An Appendix to Book III, chap. x, p. 281.*

> Of these five kindes of liberty, the two first agree only to God, so that in the highest degree τὸ αὐτεξούσιον, that is, freedome of will, is proper

to God only; and in this sense *Calvin* and *Luther* rightly deny, that the will of any creature is, or ever was free.

I add: except as in God, and God in us. Now the latter alone is Will; for it alone is ens super ens. And here lies the mystery, which I dare not openly and promiscuously reveal.

Field, OF THE CHURCH, *An Appendix to Book III, chap. x, p. 281* (second note). *Continued on p. 282.*

Yet doth not Gods working upon the will, take from it the power of dissenting, and doing the contrary; but so inclineth it, that having liberty to doe otherwise, yet shee will actually determine so.

This will not do!—were it true, then either my understanding would be free in a math. proposition or the whole position amounts only to this, that the Will, tho' compelled is still the Will. Be it so! yet not a free Will. In short, Luther and Calvin are right so far—a *creaturely will* cannot be free, but the Will in a rational creature may cease to be creaturely, and the Creature (=ἀπόστασις finally cease, in consequence, and this neither Luther or Calvin seem [*sic*] to have seen. In short, where Omnipotence is on one side, what but utter impotence can remain for the other?—To make freedom possible the Antithesis must be removed. The removal of the *Antithesis* of the Creature to God is the object of the Redemption—and forms the Glorious Liberty of the Gospel. More than this I am not permitted to expose.

Field, OF THE CHURCH, *Book IV, chap. x, p. 358.*[6]

Of the Papists preferring the Churches authority before the Scripture.

Field from the nature and special purpose of his controversy is reluctant to admit any error in the Fathers—too much so indeed. And this is an instance. We all know what we mean by the Scriptures; but who knows what he means by the Church, which is neither Thing nor Person.

Field, OF THE CHURCH, *Book V, chap. lvii, p. 704. Note continued on p. 705.*

A Bishop therefore must be unreproveable, the husband of one wife, watching, sober, modest, harberous . . .

A *beautiful* word which ought not to have become obsolete—"given to hospitality" (our present version) or hospitable does not so affectingly express the φιλόξενος of St. Paul.— κόσμιος should be rendered *courteous*—it is not easy to give the full force of either the Greek, κόσμιος

[6] The comment on Book IV, chap. viii, p. 357 appears in the section on the Reason and the Understanding, p. 117.

or the Latin mundus,—from the double feeling of ornate and world. In his *manners* & in innocent indifferent things he is a man of the *world*, we say: but "unworldly" has quite a different meaning. Gentlemanly in dress and address is the full meaning of κόσμιος .[7]

Field, OF THE CHURCH, *Book V, chap. lvii, p. 705.*

> Wherefore, letting passe the things the Apostle prescribeth, and those other which the Canons adde, of which there is no question, let us come, to the marriage of them that are to bee admitted into the holy Ministry of the Church.

How so? Does the C. of E. admit no Priests under 30 years of age? The great fault of the early Divines of our Church was the too great reverence of the first 4 Centuries. This Milton saw and reprehended.

Field, OF THE CHURCH, *Appendix, Part I, sec. iv, p. 752.*

> And againe hee saith, That every soule, immediately upon the departure hence, is in this appointed invisible place, having there either paine or ease, and refreshing: that there the rich man is in pain, and the poore in a comfortable estate: for, saith hee, why should wee not thinke, that the soules are tormented, or refreshed in this invisible place, appointed for them in expectation of the future Judgement?

This may be adduced as an instance, *specially,* of the evil consequences of introducing the εἴδωλον of Time as an ens reale into spiritual doctrines, thus understanding literally what St. Paul had expressed by figure and adaptation—Hence the doctrine of a middle state & hence Purgatory with all it's abominations; and *generally,* of the incalculable possible Importance of speculative Errors on the happiness & virtue of mankind. S. T. C.

The following are a few loose hints for your consideration. If you meet with "The Church" by Field: a folio of James Ist's time, do not let it pass by you. From 7 to 12 shillings it's common price. I give you my word, as a Gentleman, that *I* could conscientiously subscribe to' all articles of *Faith*, (Discipline, Church-government, & the article on Baptism not included) of our church in their national interpretation.[8]

Field (an excellent Divine of James the First's reign, of whose work, entitled the Church, it would be difficult to speak too highly).[9]

[7] This note and the one following do not appear in *Lit. Rem.* They are printed for the first time.
[8] Letter to Pryce (n.d.). British Museum, Add. MSS, 37,232, fol. 173 recto.
[9] *Aids*, pp. 304-5. Cf. Shedd, I, 302.

John Donne

Donne, SERMONS,[1] *second flyleaf, verso.*

There have been many and those illustrious Divines in our Church from Elizabeth to the present day, who over-valuing the accident of antiquity, and arbitrarily determining the appropriation of the words, ancient, primitive, &c. to a certain date ex. gr. to all before the 4th or 5th or 6th Century, were resolute Protesters against the corruptions and tyrrany of the Romish Hierarch, and yet lagged behind Luther and the Reformers of the first generation. Hence I have long seen the necessity or expedience of a threefold Division of Divines. There are many whom, God forbid I should call *papistic,* or, like Laud, Montague, Heylin,[2] longing for a Pope at Lambeth, whom yet I dare not name Apostolic. Therefore, I divide our Theologians into, 1. Apostolic, or *Pauline;* 2. Patristic; 3. Papal.

Even in Donne (see p. 80) still more in Bishops Andrews and Hackett, there is a strong *patristic* leaven. In Jeremy Taylor, this Taste for the Fathers, and all the Saints and Schoolmen before the Reformation amounts to a dislike of the Divines of the Continental protestant Churches, Lutheran or Calvinistic. But this must in part at least be attributed to Taylor's keen feelings, as a Carlist and Sufferer by the Puritan anti-prelatic Party. S. T. C.

Is it not a lamentable inconsistency that the For. & Brit. Bible Society should exclude all notes and comments, not to offend the handful of infidels under the name of *Unitarians*—and withhold the Scriptures from the R. Catholics, rather than suffer the Apocrypha to be bound up in the same Volume![3]

---

[1] The notes on Donne's *Sermons* are re-edited in their entirety from the original sources. The editor is grateful to Professor S. G. Dunn, Stratford-on-Avon, for his kind permission to copy and print the notes from his folio volume of *The LXXX Sermons* (1640). This is the source of the notes in *Lit. Rem.*, III, although Henry Nelson Coleridge omitted some notes and made many changes throughout. The source of the additional notes in Derwent Coleridge's *Notes on the English Divines* (2 vols.; London: 1853), I, 115-19, is the 1640 folio formerly owned by John Livingston Lowes and now in the Houghton Library, Harvard University. Four notes from the latter source are printed for the first time.

[2] Coleridge's customary spelling of Peter Heylyn's name.

[3] This paragraph was not printed in *Lit. Rem.*

Donne, SERMONS, *third flyleaf, recto.*[4]

An assured faith in a future State and with a distinct appropriation of it to our own person, cannot but be a heightening and enlivening of all other moral and rational Support. It is a grace to be earnestly prayed for by all, a blessing most fervently to be acknowledged with thanksgiving by as many as feel it. Nevertheless, I can well understand how the religious Hebrews before Christ, with very dim and indistinct views of personal immortality—tho' certainly not under a positive negation or disbelief of the same—might derive great consolation and effectual Support from the simple trust in the divine Love? Wisdom. O there is a marvelously tranquillizing power in the mere sense of *Necessity*—that it *must* be. How much more when this is united with the assurance that whatever must be, therefore only *must* be because it *ought* to be—that the necessity is the Offspring of the freest Love and the most perfect Wisdom. The collective impulses and energies of our proper humanity converge and concenter in that inward act uniting the Will and Reason, by which say—Almighty God! Heavenly Father! Thy Will be done!

Donne, SERMONS, *third flyleaf, verso.*

Paragraphs that peculiarly pleased or struck me and opposite to which, in the margins, I have written, R. i.e. recollige. I begin this at the 35th page, but will look over the preceding pages, & therefore leave a space for prefixing the numbers.[5]

P. 35. B. C.
P. 38. C. E.
P. 39. D.
P. 39. E.
   40. B.
   42. C.   D.—all excellent.
   58, 59.
   60.
   69. D. E.   70. A.
   70. D. E.

Donne, SERMONS, *title page, verso.*

It might be noticed, as seeming to affect the privilege of St. John, as the beloved *Apostle,* that to him alone the Church owes the record of the first and the last Miracle of Christ—that at the Marriage Feast

---

[4] This entire note was omitted from *Lit. Rem.*

[5] This material does not appear in *Lit. Rem.* Coleridge never did fill in the space left for references before p. 35.

at Cana, and the raising of Lazarus—one in honor of conjugal Love, the other of Friendship.[6]

I would thus class the Pentad of Operative Christianity:—

Prothesis

Christ, the *Word*

Thesis	*Mesothesis*	*Anti-thesis*
The Written Word	The H. Spirit	The Church

Synthesis

The Preacher

The Papacy elevated the Church to the virtual exclusion or suppression of the Scriptures: the modern Church of England, since Chillingworth, have [*sic*] so raised the Scriptures as to annul the Church—both alike have quenched the Holy Spirit, as the mesothesis of the two, and substituted an alien compound for the genuine Preacher, who should be the Synthesis of the Scriptures and the Church, and the sensible Voice of the H. Spirit.

Donne, SERMONS, *I. Col. 1: 19, 20. P. 1. E. First part of note, verso page opposite.*

> What could God pay for me? What could God suffer? God himselfe could not; and therefore God hath taken a body that could.

God forgive me! or those who first set abroad this strange μετάβασιν εἰς ἄλλο γένος, this Debtor and Creditor Scheme of expounding the mystery of Redemption, or both! But I never can read the words, 'God himself could not; and therefore took *a body* that could' without being reminded of the monkey that took the Cat's paw to take the chestnuts out of the Fire, and claimed the merits of puss's sufferings. I am sure, however, that the ludicrous Images, under which this Gloss of the Calvinists embodies itself to my fancy, never disturb my recollections of the adorable Mystery itself. It is clear, that a Body, remaining a Body, can only suffer *as* a Body: for no faith can enable us to believe that the same thing can be at once A. and −A. Now that the body of our Lord was not transelemented or transnatured by the pleroma indwelling, we are positively assured by Scripture. Therefore, it would follow from this most unscriptural doctrine, that the divine Justice had satisfaction made to it by the suffering of a Body which had been brought into existence for this special purpose, in lieu of the debt of eternal misery due from, and leviable on, the Bodies and Souls of all mankind! It is to this gross perversion of the sublime Idea of the Redemption by the

[6] This paragraph does not appear in *Lit. Rem.*

Cross, that we must attribute the rejection of Redemption by the Unitarian, and of the Gospel in toto by the more consequent Deist.

Donne, SERMONS, *I. P. 2. C.*

And yet, even this dwelling fullnesse, even in this person Christ Jesus, by no title of merit in himselfe, but onely *quia complacuit,* because it pleased the Father it should be so.

This, in the intention of the preacher, may have been *sound*—but was it *safe* Divinity? In order to the latter, methinks, a less equivocal word than Person ought to have been adopted—as the Body and Soul of the Man, Jesus, considered abstractedly from the Divine Logos, who in it took up humanity into deity, & was *Christ* Jesus. Dare we say that there was no self-subsistent, tho' we admit no self-originated, merit in the *Christ?* It seems plain to me, that in this & sundry other passages of St. Paul, the Father means the total triune Godhead!

Donne, SERMONS, *I. P. 3. D. Note continued at top of p. 4.*

Not disputing therefore, what other wayes God might have taken for our redemption, but giving him all possible thanks for that way which his goodnesse hath chosen, by the way of satisfying his justice (for, howsoever I would be glad to be discharged of my debts any way, yet certainly, I should think my selfe more beholden to that man, who would be content to pay my debt for me, then to him that should entreat my creditor to forgive me my debt) for this work, to make Christ able to pay this debt, there was something to be added to him.

It appears to me, that dividing the Ch. of E. into two Æras, the first from Ridley to Field, or Ed. VI. to the commencement of the latter Third of James the First's Reign—and the second ending with BULL and Stillingfleet—we might characterize their comparative excellencies thus: that the Divines of the first Æra had a deeper, more genial, and more practical Insight into the mystery of Redemption, in the relation of Man toward both the Act and the Author, viz. in all inchoative states, the regeneration, & the operations of saving Grace generally: while those of the second Æra possessed clearer & distincter Views concerning the nature & *necessity* of Redemption, in the relation of God toward Man, and concerning the connection of Redemption with the article of the Trinity, and above all, that they surpassed their Predecessors in a more safe and determinate scheme of the divine Economy of the three Persons in the one undivided Godhead. This indeed was mainly owing to Bishop Bull's masterly work de Fide Nicænâ, which in the next Generation Waterland so admirably maintained against the Philosophy of the Arians, the combat ending in the Death & Burial of Arianism, & it's descent & metempsychosis into Socinianism, and thence into modern Unitarianism—and on the other extreme against the *oscillatory* creed of Sherlock, now swinging to Tritheism in the recoil from Sabellianism and again to Sab. in the recoil from Tritheism.

Donne, SERMONS, *I. P. 4. E. Note continued on p. 5.*

First, we are to consider this fulnesse to have been in Christ, and then, from this fulnesse arose his merits; we can consider no merit in Christ himselfe before, whereby he should merit this fulnesse; for this fulnesse was in him, before he merited any thing; and but for this fulnesse he had not so merited. *Ille homo, ut in unitatem filii Dei assumeretur, unde meruit?* How did that man (sayes St. *Augustine,* speaking of Christ, as of the son of man), how did that man merit to be united in one person with the eternall Son of God? *Quid egit ante? Quid credidit?* What had he done? nay, what had he beleeved? Had he eyther faith, or works, before that union of both natures?

Dr. Donne and St. Augustin said this without offence; but I much question whether the same would be endured now by our Bishops & their chaplains. That it is, however, in the spirit of Paul and of the Gospel, I doubt not to affirm; and that this great truth is obscured by the (in my judgement) post-apostolic Christopædia, concerned with the first & prefixed to Luke's Gospel, I am inclined to think.

Donne, SERMONS, *I. P. 5. A.*

What canst thou imagine, he could fore-see in thee? a propensnesse, a disposition to goodnesse, when his grace should come? Eyther there is no such propensnesse, no such disposition in thee, or, if there be, even that propensnesse and disposition to the good use of grace, is grace; it is an effect of former grace, and his grace wrought, before he saw any such propensnesse, any such disposition; Grace was first, and his grace is his, it is none of thine.

One of the many instances in dogmatic Theology, in which the half of a divine Truth has passed into a fearful Error by being mistaken for the whole Truth.

Donne, SERMONS, *I. P. 6. D. Note continued on pp. 7-9.*

Gods justice required bloud, but that bloud is not spilt, but poured from that head to our hearts, into the veines and wounds of our owne soules. There was bloud shed, but no bloud lost.

It is affecting to observe, how this great man's mind sways & oscillates between his Reason, which demands in the word "blood" a symbolic meaning, a spiritual interpretation, and the habitual awe for the *letter*— so that he himself seems uncertain whether he means the physical lymph, serum and globules that trickled from the wounds of the nails & thorns down the face & sides of Jesus—or the blood of the Son of Man, which he who drinketh not, cannot live. Yea, it is most affecting to see the struggles of so great a mind to preserve its inborn fealty to the Reason under the servitude to an accepted article of *Belief*, which was, alas! confounded with the high obligations of Faith;—Faith, the co-adunation of the finite individual will with the universal Reason, by the submission of the former to the latter. To reconcile redemption by the material blood of Jesus with the mind of the Spirit, he seeks to spiritualize the material blood itself in all men! And a deep truth lies hid even in this! But it is a deep subject—the true solution of which may best, God's grace assisting, be sought for in the collation of Paul with John— specially in St. Paul's assertion that we are baptized into the death of Christ, that we may be partakers of his Resurrection & Life. It was not on the visible Cross, it was not directing attention to the blood-drops on his Temples and Sides, that our blessed Redeemer said, *This* is my body—and THIS is my Blood!

Donne, SERMONS, *I. P. 9. A.*

> But if we consider those who are in heaven, and have been so from the first minute of their creation, Angels, why have they, or how have they any reconciliation? . . .

The history and successive meanings of the term Angels in the O. and N. Testaments, and the Idea, that shall reconcile all as so many several forms, & as it were *perspectives*, of one and the same truth—this is still a disideratum in Christian Theology.

Donne, SERMONS, *I. P. 9. D.*

> For, at the generall resurrection, (which is rooted in the resurrection of Christ, and so hath relation to him) the creature shall be delivered from the bondage of corruption, into the glorious liberty of the children of God; for which, the whole creation groanes, and travailes in paine yet. This deliverance then from this bondage, the whole creature hath by Christ, and that is their reconciliation. And then are we reconciled by the blood of his Crosse, when having crucified our selves by a true repentance, we receive the reale reconciliation in his blood in the Sacrament. But the most proper, and most literall sense of these words, is, that all things in heaven and earth, be reconciled to God, (that is, to his glory, to a fitter disposition to glorifie him) by being reconciled to another, in Christ; that in him, as head of the Church, they in heaven, and we upon earth, be united together as one body in the Communion of Saints.

A very meagre and inadequate interpretation of this sublime text! The Philosophy of Life, which will be the corona et finis coronans of the Sciences of Comparative Anatomy and Zoology, will hereafter supply a fuller and nobler comment.

Donne, SERMONS, *I. P. 10. A.*

The blood of the sacrifices was brought by the high priest *in sanctum sanctorum,* into the place of greatest holinesse; but it was brought but once, *in festo expiationis,* in the feat of expiation; but in the other parts of the Temple it was sprinkled every day. The blood of the cross of Christ Jesus hath had his effect *in sancto sanctorum,* . . .

A truly excellent and beautiful paragraph.

Donne, SERMONS, *I. P. 10. C.*

If you will mingle a true religion, and a false religion, there is no reconciling of God and Belial in this Text. For the adhering of persons born within the Church of Rome, to the Church of Rome, our law sayes nothing to them if they come; But for reconciling to the Church of Rome, by persons born within the Allegeance of the King, or for per-swading of men to be so reconciled, our law hath called by an infamous and Capitall name of Treason, and yet every Tavern and Ordinary is full of such Traitors.

A strange transition from the Gospel to the English Statute-Book! But I may observe, that if this statement could be truly made under James the first, there was abundantly ampler ground for it in the following Reign. And yet with what bitter Spleen does Heylin, Laud's Creature, arraign the Parliamentarians for making the same complaint.

Donne, SERMONS, *II. Isa. 7: 14. P. 11. Note continued on pp. 12-14.*

The fear of giving offence, especially to good men, of whose faith in all essential points, we are partakers, may reasonably induce us to be slow, and cautious in making up our minds finally on a religious ques-tion—may & ought to, influence us to submit our conviction to repeated revisals and rehearings. But there may arrive a time of such perfect clearness of view respecting the particular point, as to supersede all fear of man by the higher duty of declaring the whole truth in Jesus. Therefore, now having overpassed six-sevenths of the ordinary period allotted to Human Life, resting my whole & sole hope of Salvation and Immortality on the Divinity of Christ, and the Redemption by his Cross & Passion, and holding the doctrine of the Triune God as very ground and pediment of the Gospel Faith,—I feel myself enforced by conscience to declare & avow, that, in my deliberate Judgement, the Christopædia prefixed to the third Gospel and concorporated with the first, but according to my belief, in it's *present* form the latest of the four, was no part of the Original Gospel, was unknown or not recog-nized by the Apostles Paul and John, and that instead of supporting the doctrine of the Trinity, and the Filial-Godhead of the Incarnate Word, as set forth by John (Ch. i.) and by Paul, it if [it] not be [*sic*] altogther irreconcilable with this faith, doth yet greatly weaken and bedim it's evidence—& by the too palpable contradictions between the narrative in the first Gospel and that attributed to Luke has been a fruitful magazine of doubts respecting the historic character of the Gospels themselves. No learned Jew can be expected to receive this as the true primary sense of the text in Greek in which the Hebrew word does not correspond to Virgin, Virgo, or παρθένος but to Lass ✕ Lad, to Puella ✕ Puer, to νεᾶνις ✕ νεανίας. Accordingly, νεᾶνις is the Greek Term, by which the severely literal Aquila renders. What sign indeed could Mary's pregnancy have been for King Ahaz? Or rather how could that which in it's very nature could only have been known to herself, be called a *Sign* for any one? S. T. Coleridge, October, 1831. P. S. But were it asked of me—I reply—It is a point of religion with me to have no belief one way or the other—I am in this way like St. Paul, more than content not to know Christ himself ὡς κατὰ σάρκα . It is enough for me to know, that the Son of God "became flesh," ἐγένετο σάρξ γενόμενος ἐκ γυναικός—and more than this, it appears to me, was unknown to the Apostles or if known not taught by them as appertaining to saving faith in Him. S. T. C.

Note the affinity in sound of *son* and *sun, Sohn* and *Sonne,* which is not confined to the Saxon and German, or the Gothic dialects generally. And observe *conciliare versöhnen = confiliare, facere esse cum filio,* one with the Son.

Donne, Sermons, *II. P. 17. B, C.*

> That this Mother, in our text, was a Virgin, is a peculiar signe, given, as such, by God; never done but then; and it is a singular testimony, how acceptable to God, that state of virginity is; Hee does not dishonour physick, that magnifies health; now does hee dishonour marriage, that praises Virginity; let them embrace that state that can . . .

One of the sad relics of patristic super-moralization aggravated by papal Ambition, which clung to too many Divines, especially those of the second or third generation after Luther. Luther himself was too Spiritual, of too heroic faith, to be thus blinded by the declamations of the Fathers—whom with the exception of Augustine, he held in very low esteem.

Donne, Sermons, *II. P. 17. E. Note at end of sermon, p. 19.*

> And *Helvidius* said, she had children after.

Helvidius? If there be any meaning in word, the New Testament asserts the same, over and over again.[7] I think I might safely put the

---

[7] The first sentence of this note as given in *Lit. Rem.* is exactly opposite in meaning.

question to any serious, spiritual-minded, Christian—what one inference tending to edification, in the discipline of Will, Mind, or affections he can draw from these speculations of the last two or three pages of this Sermon respecting Mary's pregnancy & parturition? *Can* such points appertain to our faith as Christians which every Parent would decline speaking of before a family & which, if the questions were propounded by another in the presence of my Daughter, aye, or even of my (no less in mind & imagination) innocent Wife I should resent as an indecency?

Donne, SERMONS, *III. Gal. 4: 4 & 5. P. 20.*

> *God sent forth his Son, made of a woman.*

I never can admit that γενόμενον and ἐγένετο, &c. in John and Paul are adequately or even rightly rendered by the English, *made.*

Donne, SERMONS, *III. P. 21. A.*

> What miserable revolutions and changes, what downfals, what break-necks, and precipitations may we justly think our selves ordained to, if we consider, that in our comming into this world out of our mothers womb, we do not make account that a childe comes right, except it come with the head forward, and thereby prefigure that headlong falling into calamities which it must suffer after?

The taste for these forced and fantastic analogies Donne with the greater number of the learned prelatic Divines from James I to the Restoration acquired from that too great partiality for the *Fathers,* from Irenæus to Bernard, by which they sought to distinguish themselves from the Puritans.

Donne, SERMONS, *III. P. 21. C.*

> That now they [the Jews] express a kind of conditionall acknowl-edgement of it, by this barbarous and inhumane custome of theirs, that they alwayes keep in readinesse the blood of some Christian, with which they annoint the body of any that dyes amongst them, with these words, if Jesus Christ were the Messias, then may the blood of this Christian availe thee to salvation.

!! Is it possible that DONNE could have given credit to this absurd legend! It was, I am aware, not an age of critical acumen—Grit, Bran & Flour were swallowed in the unsifted mass of their Erudition—Still that a man like Donne should have imposed on himself such a set of idle tales for facts of History is scarcely credible—that he should have attempted to impose them on others, most melancholy.

Donne, SERMONS, *III. P. 22. D, E.*

> And then, that he takes the name of the son of a woman, and wanes the miraculous name of the son of a Virgin.—Christ waned the glorious

Name of Son of God, and the miraculous Name of Son of a Virgin to [*sic*]; which is not omitted to draw into doubt, the perpetuall Virginity of the Blessed Virgin, the Mother of Christ . . .

Very ingenious; but likewise very presumptious, this arbitrary attribution of St. Paul's *silence* respecting and presumable ignorance of, the virginity of Mary to Christ's own determination to have the fact passed over.

Is "wane" a misprint for "wave" or "waive"? It occurs so often as to render its being an *erratum* improbable, yet I do not remember to have met elsewhere *wane* used for *decline*, and as a verb active.

Donne, SERMONS, *III. P. 22. B.*[8]

. . . but thou shalt feele the joy of his third birth on thy soul, most inexpressible this day, where he is born this day (if thou wilt) without father or mother; that is, without any former, or any other reason than his own meere goodnesse that should beget that love in him towards thee . . .

Qy? does the will in man precede or follow or is it coexistent?

Donne, SERMONS, *III. P. 22. E.*

. . . when it is said, Joseph *knew her not, donec peperit, till she brought forth her Son,* this does not imply his knowledge of her after, no more, then when God sayes to Christ, *donec ponam,* sit at my right hand, till I make thine enemies thy footstoole, that imports, that Christ should remove from his right hand *after.*

Fabling admits no stop | the negative.

Donne, SERMONS, *III. P. 23. A.*

If there were reason for it, it were no miracle, if there were precedents for it, it were not singular; and God intended both, that it should be a miracle and that it should be done but once.

The relation of the first Comet, that had ever been observed might excite doubt in the mind of an Astronomer to whom from the place, where he lived, it had not been visible. But his reason could have been no objection to it. Had God pleased, all women might have conceived without a mate—as many of the Polypi & Planariæ do. Not on any such ground do I decline this as an article of faith—but because I doubt the evidence.

Donne, SERMONS, *III. P. 25. A-E. Second paragraph of comment from third flyleaf, recto, with reference to p. 25.*

Though we may thinke thus in the law of reason, yet . . .

[8] Both this paragraph and the next are omitted in *Lit. Rem.*

It is and has been a misfortune, a grievous and manifold loss & hindrance, for the interests of moral & spiritual truth, that even our best & most vigorous theologians & philosophers of the age from Edward VI. to James II., so generally confound the *terms*, and so *too* often confound the subjects themselves—Reason and Understanding. Yet the diversity, the difference in *kind*, was known to, and clearly admitted, by, many of them: by Hooker, for instance, and it is *implied* in the whole of Bacon's Novum Organum. Instead of the "law of Reason," Donne *meant* and ought to have said—"judging according to the ordinary presumptions of the *Understanding*"—i. e. the faculty which generalizing particular experiences judges of the future by analogy of the past—See "Aids to Reflection" [concerning 1. the manner of Christ's coming; 2. the purpose.]

All the § ph. from B. to E. I most deliberately protest against—& should cite it's dicta with a host of others, as sad effects of the confusion of Reason and Understanding, and the consequent abdication of the former, instead of the bounden submission of the Latter, to a higher light. FAITH. itself is but an Act of the Will assenting to the Reason on it's own evidence without, and even against, the Understanding. This indeed is, I fully agree, to be brought into captivity to the Faith.

Donne, SERMONS, *III. P. 26. A, B.*

And therefore to be *under the Law*, signifies here, thus much, To be a debter to the law of nature, to have a testimony in our hearts and consciences, that there lyes a law upon us, which we have no power in our selves to performe . . .

This exposition of the term, *Law*, in the epistles of St. Paul is most just, and important. The whole should be adopted among the Notes to the Ep. to the Romans, in every *Bible* printed with Notes.

Donne, SERMONS, *III. P. 27. A. Note continued on pp. 28-29.*

And this was his first worke, *to Redeeme,* to vindicate them from the usurper, to deliver them from the intruder, to emancipate them from the tyrant, to cancell the covenant betweene hell, and them, and restore them so far to their liberty, as that they might come to their first Master, if they would; this was *Redeeming.*

There is an absurdity in the notion of a finite divided from and superaddible to the Infinite; of a particular Quantum of Power separated from, not included in, Omnipotence, i. e. the All-Power. But, alas! we too generally use the terms that are meant to express the *Absolute*, as mere *Comparatives* taken superlatively. In one thing only are we permitted & bound to assert a diversity—viz, God and Hades, the Good and the Evil Will. This awful Mystery, this Truth, at once certain and incomprehensible, is at the bottom of *all* Religion; and to exhibit this truth free from the evil phantom of the Manicheans, or the two co-eternal & co-ordinate Principles of Good and Evil, is the Glory of the Christian Religion.

But this mysterious dividuity of the Good and the Evil Will, the Will of the Spirit and the Will of the Flesh, must not be carried beyond the terms Good and Evil. There can be but one *good* Will—the Spirit in all—and even so all evil Wills are one evil Will, the Devil, or evil Spirit. But then the *One* exists for us, as finite intelligences, necessarily in a two-fold relation—Universal and Particular. The same Spirit *within us* pleads *to* the Spirit as without us, and in like manner is every evil mind in communion with the evil spirit. But O Comfort! the Good alone is the *Actual*—the Evil essentially *potential*. Hence the Devil is most appropriately named the *Tempter,* and the Evil hath it's essence in the *Will.* It cannot pass out of it. *Deeds* are called evil in reference to the individual Will expressed in them; but in the great scheme of Providence they are, only as far as they are good—coerced under the conditions of all true Being—and the Devil is the *Drudge* of the All-good.

۰ *Donne,* SERMONS, *IV. Luke 2. Pp. 29 and 30. B. Note continued on pp. 31-32.*

> We shall consider, that that preparation, and disposition, and acqui-
> escence, which *Simeon* had in his epiphany, in his visible seeing of
> Christ then, is offered to us in this Epiphany, in this manifestation and
> application of Christ in the Sacrament; and that therefore every peni-
> tent, and devout, and reverent, and worthy receiver, hath had in that holy
> action his *Now;* there are all things accomplished to him, and his *For,*
> *for his eyes have seen his salvation;* and so may be content, nay, *glad,*
> *to depart in peace.*

O! would that Donne, or rather that Luther before him, had carried this just conception to it's legitimate consequents! that as the Sacrament is the Epiphany for as many as receive it in faith, so the crucifixion, resurrection, and ascension of Christ himself in the Flesh were the Ephiphanies, the sacramental Acts and *Phœnomena,* of the *Deus Patiens,* the visible Words of the invisible Word that was in the Beginning, Symbols in time & historic fact of the redemptive functions, passions, and procedures of the Lamb crucified from the foundation of the World —the incarnation, cross, and passion, in short, the whole life of Christ in the flesh, dwelling a man, among men, being essential & substantive parts of the process, the whole of which—they represented—& on this account proper *Symbols* of the acts & passions of the Christ dwelling *in* man, as the Spirit of Truth, & for as many as in faith have received him

—in Seth and Abraham no less effectually than in John & Paul. (For this is the true definition of a Symbol as distinguished from the *Thing* on one hand, and from a mere metaphor or conventional exponent of a Thing, on the other.) Had Luther mastered this great Idea, this Master-truth, he would never have entangled himself in that most mischievous Sacramentary Controversy or, had to seek a murky hiding hole in the figment of Consubstantiation. S. T. C.

Donne, SERMONS, *III. P. 30. B, C.*

> In the first part then. . . . . More he asks not, less he takes not for any man, upon any pretence of any unconditional decree.

A beautiful paragraph, well worth extracting aye, and re-preaching.

Donne, SERMONS, *IV. P. 34. E. Note continued on pp. 35-37.*

> When thou commest to this seale of thy peace, the Sacrament, pray that God will give thee that light, that may direct and establish thee, in necessary and fundamentall things; that is, the light of faith to see, that the Body and Bloud of Christ, is applied to thee, in that action; But for the manner, how the Body and Bloud of Christ is there, wait his leisure, if he have not manifested that to thee; Grieve not at that, wonder not at that, presse not for that; for hee hath not manifested that, not the way, not the manner of the presence in the Sacrament, to the Church.

O! I have ever felt & for many years thought, that this rem credimus, modum nescimus, is but a poor evasion. It seems to me an attempt so to *admit* an irrational proposition as to have the credit of denying it—or to separate an irrational proposition from it's irrationality. Ex. gr. I admit $2 + 2 = 5$; *how* I do not pretend to know; but in *some* way not in contradiction to the multiplication table. To scriptural operations the very term, *mode,* is perhaps inapplicable for these are *immediate.* To the linking of *this* with that, of A with Z by intermedia; the term, mode, the question how? is properly applied. The assimilation of the Spirit of a man to the Son of God, to God as the Divine Humanity, this spiritual transubstantiation, like every other process of operative grace, is necessarily modeless. The whole question is concerning the transmutation of the sensible Elements. Deny this—and to what does the *modum* nescimus refer. We cannot ask *How* is that done which we declare not done at all. Admit this transmutation and you necessarily admit by implication the whole absurdity of the Romish Dogma, viz. the separation of a sensible thing from the sensible accidents which constitute all we ever meant by the thing.

Donne, SERMONS, *IV. P. 35. B-C.*

When I pray in my chamber, I build a Temple there, that houre; And, that minute, when I cast out a prayer, in the street, I build a Temple there; And when my soule prayes without any voyce, my very body is then a Temple.

Good; but it would be better to regard solitary, family, and templar devotion as distinctions in *sort*, rather than differences in *degree*. All three are necessary. S. T. C.

Donne, SERMONS, *IV. P. 35. E.*

And that more fearfull occasion of comming, when they came onely to elude the Law, and proceeding in their treacherous and traiterous religion in their heart, and yet communicating with us, draw God himselfe into their conspiracies; and to mocke us, make a mocke of God, and his religion too . . .

What then was their guilt who by terror and legal penalties tempted their fellow Christians to this treacherous mockery? Donne should have asked himself this question.

Donne, SERMONS, *IV. P. 37. C.*

You would have said at noone, this light is the Sun, and you will say now, this light is the Candle.

Preached at candlelight.[9]

Donne, SERMONS, *IV. P. 37. C.*

We say the Sacramentall bread is the body of Christ, because God hath shed his Ordinance upon it, and made it of another nature in the use, though not in the substance; Almost 600 years agoe, the Romane Church made *Berengarius sweare, sensualiter tangitur, strangitur, teritur corpus Christi*, that the body of Christ was sensibly handled, and broken, and chewed.

Mem. To rationalize this frightful figment of his Church, Bossuet has recourse to Spinozism, & dares make God the Substance & sole ens reale of all body—& by this very hypothesis baffles his own end and does away all miracle in the particular instance.

Donne, SERMONS, *V. Exod. 4: 13. P. 39. D. Note on third flyleaf, verso.*

It hath been doubted, and disputed, and denied too, that this Text, *O my Lord, send I pray thee, by the hand of him, whom thou wilt send*, hath any relation to the sending of the Messiah, to the comming of Christ, to Christmas-day; yet we forbeare not to wait upon the ancient Fathers, and as they said, to say, that Moses . . . at last . . . determines all in this, *O my Lord* . . . It is a work, next to the great work of the

⁹ This note and the one following omitted in *Lit. Rem.*

redemption of the whole world, to redeem Israel out of Ægypt; And therefore doe both workes at once, put both into one hand, and *mitte quem missurus es, Send him* I know *thou wilt send;* him, whom pursuing thine own decree, thou shouldest send; send Christ, send him now, to redeem Israel from Ægypt.

This is one of the happier accommodations of the Gnosis, i. e. the science of detecting the mysteries of faith in the simplest texts of Old Testament History, to the contempt or neglect of the literal & contextual sense—a sort of Katterfelt solar Miscroscope that discovered in any drop of transparent water scores of animals, each as large as the Conjuror's own black Cat.[10] It was Gnosis, and not knowledge, as our English Testaments absurdly render the words, that Paul warns against, & most wisely, as *puffing* up, inflating the heart with self-conceit, and the head with idle fancies.

Donne, SERMONS, *V. P. 39. E. and p. 40. A.*

But, as a thoughtfull man, a pensive, a considerate man, that stands for a while, with his eyes fixed upon the ground, before his feete, when he casts up his head, hath presently, instantly the Sun, or the heavens for his object—he sees not a tree, nor a house, nor a steeple by the way, but as soon as his eye is departed from the earth where it was long fixed, the next thing he sees is the Sun or the heavens;—so when *Moses* had fixed himselfe long upon the consideration of his own insufficiency for this service, when he tooke his eye from that low piece of ground, Himselfe, considered as he was then, he fell upon no tree, no house, no steeple, no such consideration as this, God may endow me, improve me, exalt me, enable me, qualifie me with faculties fit for this service, but his first object was that which presented an infallibility with it, Christ Jesus himselfe, the Messias himselfe . . .

Beautifully imagined, & happily applied.

Donne, SERMONS, *V. P. 40. B.*

That Germen Iehovæ, as the prophet Esay calls Christ, that Off-spring of Jehova, that Bud, that Blossom, that fruit of God himselfe, the Son of God, the Messiah, the Redeemer, Christ Jesus, growes upon every tree in this Paradise, the Scripture; for Christ was the occasion before, and is the consummation after, all Scripture.

If this were meant to the neglect or exclusion of the primary sense, if we are required to believe that the sacred Writers themselves, had

---

[10] This sentence was omitted in *Lit. Rem.,* and the next was greatly modified. The illustration was again used in the MS of *Confessions of an Inquiring Spirit* (fol. 89 verso), but was deleted: "the former position that all Scripture is inspired would require for it's verification the Alchemy of a Swedenborg, or the solar microscope of a theological Wizard that can discover in a transparent text as many mysteries as that of Katterfelto discovered black cats in a water-drop—in short, no sober interpreter ever asserted it." Gustavus Katterfelto, the Conjuror, died 1799. Among other exhibitions he demonstrated the microscope.

such thoughts present to their minds—it would doubtless throw the doors wide open to every variety of folly and fanaticism. But it may admit of a safe, sound and profitable use, if we consider the Bible, as *one* Work, intended by the Holy Spirit for the edification of the Church in all ages, & having, *as such*, all it's parts synoptically interpreted, the eldest by the latest, &c. Moses, or David, or Jeremiah (we might in this view affirm) meant so and so, according to the context, and the light under which and the immediate or proximate purposes, for which, he wrote—but we, who command the whole scheme of the great dispensation, may see a higher & deeper sense, of which the literal meaning was a symbol or type—& this we may justifiably call the Sense of the Spirit. S. T. C.

Donne, Sermons, *V. P. 41. B.*

> So in our Liturgie . . . we stand up at the profession of the Creed at the rehearsing the Articles of our Faith, thereby to declare to God, and his Church, our readinesse to stand to, and our readinesse to proceed in, that Profession.

Another Church might sit down, denoting a resolve to abide in this profession. These things are indifferent; but charity, love of peace, & on indifferent points to prefere another's liking to our own, and to observe an order once established for order's sake,—these are not indifferent.

Donne, Sermons, *V. P. 42. C-D. Note on third flyleaf, verso.*

> But when the devill comes to say, Doe this, or thou canst not live in the next world, thou canst not be saved, here the devill pretends to be God, here he acts Gods part, and so prevails the more powerfully up us . . .

All excellent.

Donne, Sermons, *V. P. 46. C.*

> Howsoever, all intend, that this is a name that denotes Essence, Beeing: Beeing is the name of God, and of God only.

Rather, I should say the eternal Antecedent of Being; *I* that shall be in that I will to be—the absolute Will—the ground of Being—the self-affirming Actus purissimus.

Donne, Sermons, *V. P. 55. A.*

> S. *Hierome* reades, *Arripite clypeas, buckle your shields;* To you, which was an alarm to them, to arm . . .

? buckle your shields to you:

Donne, SERMONS, *VI.* *Isa. 53:1.* *Pp. 58-59.*

On general and particular Providence—only to the unbelieving heart diverse. A noble passage. The whole (VIth) a noble Sermon—in thought and in diction.

Donne, SERMONS, *VI.* *P. 59. E.*

Therefore we have a clearer light then this; *Firmiorem propheticum sermonem*, sayes S. *Peter; We have a more sure word of the Prophets;* that is, as S. *Augustine* reades that place, *clariorem*, a more manifest, a more evident, declaration in the Prophets, then in nature, of the will of God towards man.

The sense of this text, as explained by the context, is that in consequence of the fulfilment of so large a proportion of the Oracles, the Christian Church has not only additional light given by the Teaching & Miracles of Christ, but even the Light vouchsafed to the old Church (the Prophetic) stronger & clearer.

Donne, SERMONS, *VI.* *P. 60. A.*

He spake personally, and he spake aloud, in the declaration of Miracles; but *Quis credidit filii?* Who beleeved even his report? Did they not call his preaching sedition, and call his Miracles conjuring? Therefore, we have a clearer, that is, a nearer light than the written Gospell, that is, the Church.

True; yet he who should now venture to assert this truth, or even, as I, in my letters on the religious & superstitious veneration of the Scriptures have done,[11] contended for a co-ordinateness of the Church and the Written Word, must bear to be thought a Semi-papist, an Ultra High-Churchman. Still the Truth is the Truth.

Donne, SERMONS, *VI.* *P. 60. C.* *Note on third flyleaf, verso.*

If the slack and historicall Christian say, alas they are but generall things, done for the whole world indifferently, and not applyed to me, which I reade in the Gospell, to this naturall man, to this Jew, to this slack Christian, we present an established Church, a Church endowed with a power, to open the wounds of Christ Jesus to receive every wounded soule, to spread the balme of his blood upon every bleeding heart.

Admirable. Mem. to quote this if ever I publish my letters on the right ☿ to the superstitious veneration of the Scriptures.

Donne, SERMONS, *VI.* *P. 60. E.*

. . . he does not believe a Church. ["a Church" is underlined by Coleridge]

? "Our Report"?

---

[11] In *Lit. Rem.* "as I . . . have done" is omitted. The two final comments on this sermon are also omitted.

Donne, SERMONS, *VII. John 10. P. 62.*

Since the Revolution in 1688 our Church has been chilled and starved too generally by Preachers & Reasoners Stoic and Epicurean—first, a sort of pagan Morality, = Virtue substituted for the Righteousness by faith, & lastly, Prudence, Paleyianism, substituted for Morality. A Christian Preacher ought to preach Christ alone—and all things in him & by him. If he find a death in this, if it seem to him a circumscription, he does not know Christ, as the Pleroma, the Fullness. It is not possible, that there should be aught *true,* or seemly, or beautiful, in thought, will, or deed, speculative or practical, which may not, & which ought not, to be evolved out of Christ and his Faith in Christ—no folly, no error, no evil to be exposed or warred against, which may not and should not be convicted & denounced from it's contrariancy and enmity to Christ. [To the Christian preacher] Christ in all, and all things in Christ— the Christian Preacher should abjure every argument that is not a link in the chain of which Christ is the Staple & staple Ring. S. T. Coleridge

Donne, SERMONS, *VII. P. 64.*

In this page Donne passes into rhetorical extravagance, after the manner of too many of the Fathers from Tertullian to St. Bernard.

Donne, SERMONS, *VII. P. 66. A.*

Some of the later Authors in the Roman Church . . . have noted (*in several of the Fathers*) some inclinations towards that opinion, that the devil retaining still his faculty of free will, is therefore capable of repentance, and so of benefit by this comming of Christ.

If this be assumed, viz. the free-will of the Devil, the consequence would follow—his capability of repenting, & the possibility that he may repent. But then, he is no longer what we mean by the Devil; i. e. he is not *the* evil Spirit, but a wicked Soul.

Donne, SERMONS, *VII. P. 67. Note on third flyleaf, recto.*

God is so omnipresent, as that Ubiquitary will needs have the body of God every where; so omnipresent, as that the Stancarist will needs have God not *only* to be in everything, but to be everything . . .

"The Stancarist"—i. e. as appears by the context, the Pantheist or what we now call Spinosist. Qy. Is this a misprint. The name is utterly new to me.

A noble passage on death bed Repentance, p. 461.[12]

[12] Omitted in *Lit. Rem.*

Donne, Sermons, *VII. P. 68. C. Note continued on p. 69.*

As though God had said *Qui sum, my name is I am,* yet in truth it is *Qui ero, my name is I shall be.*

Nay, I will be or I shall be in that I will to be.

I am that only one who is self-originant, *causa sui,* whose Will must be contemplated as antecedent in idea to his own co-eternal Being or deeper than. But antecedent, deeper, &c. are mere vocabula impropria, words of accommodation, that may suggest the idea to a mind purified from the intrusive phantoms of Space and Time, but falsify and extinguish the truth, if taken as adequate exponents.

Donne, Sermons, *VII. P. 69. C.*

We affirm, that it is not onely as impious and irreligious a thing, but as senselesse and as absurd a thing to deny that the Son of God hath redeemed the world, as to deny that God hath created the world.

A bold but a true Saying. The man who cannot see the redemptive agency in the Creation has but dim appreciation of the creative power.

Donne, Sermons, *VII. P. 69. D, E., p. 70. A. Note on third flyleaf, verso.*

A noble instance of giving importance to the single words of a text, each word by itself a pregnant text. Here, too, lies the excellence, the imitable, but alas! unimitated, excellence of the Divines from Elizabeth to William IIIrd.

Donne, Sermons, *VII. P. 70. D. Note continued on p. 71. Second paragraph of note p. 70. D, E. from third flyleaf, verso.*

O, that our clergy did but know & see that their Tythes &c belong to them, as Officers and Functionaries of the Nationality, as Clerks, & not exclusively as Theologians, and not at all as Ministers of the Gospel; but that they are likewise Ministers of the Church of *Christ,* and that their claims and the powers of that Church, are no more alienated or affected by their being at the same time the established Clergy, than they are by the casual coincidence of being Justices of the Peace, or Heirs to an Estate, or Fundowners. The Romish Divines placed the Church *above* the Scriptures, our present Divines give it no place at all.

Donne and his great Contemporaries had not yet learnt to be *afraid* in announcing and enforcing the claims of the Church, distinct from, and coordinate with, the Scriptures. This is one evil consequence, tho' most unnecesarily so, of the Union of the Ch. of Christ with the National Church, and of the claims of the Christian Pastor and the Preacher with the legal and constitutional Rights & Revenues of the Officers of the National Clerisy. Our Clergymen in thinking of the Tythes, feeling the weakness of their claim as grounded on the Gospel, forget the rights which depend on no human Law.

Donne, SERMONS, *VII. P. 71. A.*

This is the difference betweene Gods Mercy, and his Judgements, that sometimes his Judgements may be plurall, complicated, enwrapped in one another, but his Mercies are always so, and cannot be otherwise; he gives them *abundantius, more abundantly.*

A just sentiment beautifully expressed.

Donne, SERMONS, *VII. P. 71. C.*

Whereas the Christian Religion is, as Greg. Nazianz[en] sayes, *Simplex & nuda, nisi pravè in artem difficilimam converteretur:* it is plaine, an easie, perspicuous truth.

A Religion of *Ideas,* Spiritual Truths, or Truth-powers—not of notions, and conceptions, the factory of the Understanding—therefore simplex, et nuda—i. e. immediate. Like the clear blue Heaven of Italy, deep and transparent—an ocean unfathomable in it's depth, yet ground all the way. Still as meditation soars upwards, it meets the arched Firmament, with all it's suspended Lamps of Light. O let not the simplex et nuda of Greg. Nazianen be perverted to the Socinian, "plain and easy for the meanest understandings!" The Truth of Christ, like the Peace of Christ, passeth *all understanding.* If ever there was a mischievous misuse of words, the confusion of the terms, Reason and Understanding, Ideas and Notions, or Conceptions, is most mischievous, a Surinam Toad with a swarm of Toadlings sprouting out of it's Back and Sides!

Donne, SERMONS, *VIII. Matt. 5:16. P. 77. C.*

Either of the names of this day were Text enough for a Sermon, Purification, or Candlemas. Join we them together, and raise we only this one note from both, that all true purification is in the light.

The illustration of the day, would be censured as quaint by our modern Critics! Would to heaven! we had but even a few Preachers capable of such quaintnesses.

Donne, SERMONS, *VIII. P. 77. D. Note on blank page opposite.*

Every good work hath faith for the roote; but every faith hath not good works for the fruit thereof.

Faith, i. e., fidelity, the fealty of the finite Will and Understanding to the Reason—*the* Light that lighteth every man that cometh into the world, as one with and representative of the Absolute Will, and to the Ideas i. e. Truths and other Truth-powers of the pure Reason, the supersensuous Truths, which in relation to the finite Will, and as meant to determine the Will, are moral LAWS, the voice and dictates of the Conscience—this Faith is properly a state and disposition of the Will, or rather of the Whole Man, the "I," i. e. finite Will self-affirmed. It is therefore the Ground, the Root, of which the Actions, the Works, the Believings, as acts of the Will in the Understanding, are the Trunk and Branches. But these must be in the *Light*. The disposition to see must have Organs, Objects, Direction and an *outward* Light. The three latter of these our Lord gives to his Disciples in this Sermon, preparatorily and as Donne rightly observes, presupposing faith as the ground & root.[13]

Donne, SERMONS, *VIII. P. 78.*

"To every one of us . . . (from him that rides with his hundreds of Torches, to him that crawls with his rush-candle) our Saviour sayes; *Let your light so shine before men* . . .

P. 78 line the first. But the whole page affords a noble Specimen, how a Minister of the Church of England should preach the doctrine of *Good* Works, purified from the poison of the romish doctrine of *Works*, as the Mandioc is envenomated by fire & rendered safe, nutritious, a bread of Life. To Donne's exposition the heroic Solifidian Martin Luther, himself—would have subscribed, hand and heart.

Donne, SERMONS, *VIII. P. 78. C.*

And therefore our latter men of the Reformation, are not to be blamed, who for the most part, pursuing, S. *Cyrils* interpretation, interpret this universall light, *that lightneth every man,* to be the light of nature.

The error here—and it is a grievous error—consists in the word "Nature." There is, there can be no Light of Nature. There may be a Light in or upon it; but this is the Light, that shineth down into the Darkness, i. e. in Nature; and the Darkness comprehendeth it not. All Ideas, i. e. spiritual truths, are supernatural. S. T. Coleridge

Donne, SERMONS, *VIII. P. 79.*

Our faith is ours as we have received it; our worke is ours, as we have done it. Faith ours, as we are possessors of it, the work ours, as we are doers, actors in it.

In this page, Donne rather too much plays the rhetorician. If the Faith worketh the works, what is true of the former, must be equally

[13] A connecting sentence is inserted in *Lit. Rem.*, and the note below follows immediately.

affirmed of the latter—*causa causæ causa causati*. Besides, he falls into something like a confusion of Faith with Belief, taken as a conviction or assent of the judgement. The Faith and the Righteousness of a Christian are both alike his and *not* his—the f. of Christ in him, the r. of Christ in and for him. (See Ep. to the Galatians, Ch. 2. 20.)

Donne was a truly great man; but he did not possess that full, steady, deep yet comprehensive Insight into the Nature of Faith and Works, which was vouchsafed to Martin Luther. But Donne had not attained to the reconciling of distinctity with unity—ours, yet God—God, yet ours.

Donne, SERMONS, *VIII. P. 79. D.*

> *Velle et nolle nostrum est,* to assent, or to dis-assent, is our own.

? too nakedly expressed?

Donne, SERMONS, *VIII. P. 79. D, E. Note continued on p. 80.*

> And certainly our works are more ours then our faith is, and man concurres otherwise in the acting and perpetration of a good work, then he doth in the reception and admission of faith.

Why? because Donne confounds the act of Faith with the assent of the fancy and understanding to certain words and conceptions. With all my reverence for Dr. Donne, I must warn against the contents of the preceding page, as scarcely tenable in Logic, unsound in Metaphysics, and unsafe, slippery Divinity, and principally, that he confounds Faith, essentially an act, the fundamental *Work* of the Spirit, with Belief, which is then only good, when it is the effect and accompaniment of Faith.

Donne, SERMONS, *VIII. P. 80. D. Note continued on p. 81.*

> Because things good in their institution may be depraved in their practise—*ergonè nihil ceremoniarum rudioribus dabitur, ad jurandam eorum imperitiam?*

Some Ceremonies may be for the conservation of Order & Civility, or to prevent Confusion & Unseemliness; others are the natural or conventional language of our feelings, shaking hands, bowing the head &c —and to neither of these two sorts do I object. But as to "from these books," the *ad jurandam imperitiam* &c. &c., I protest against these & the pretexts for them in toto. What? Can any ceremony be more instructive than the words required to explain the ceremony? I make but one exception & that where the truth signified is so vital, so momentous, that the very occasion & necessity of explaining the sign are of the highest spiritual value. Yet, alas! to what gross and calamitous superstitions has not even this visible sign given occasion?

Donne, SERMONS, *VIII. P. 81. E.*

> Blessed S. *Augustine* reports, (if that Epistle be S. *Augustines*) that when himselfe was writing to S. *Hierome, to* know his opinion of the measure and quality of the Joy, and Glory of Heaven, suddenly in his Chamber there appeared *ineffabile lumen,* sayes he, an unspeakable, an unexpressible light, . . . and out of that light issued this voyce, *Hieronymi anima sum.*

This ridiculous Legend is one instance of what I call the *patristic* leaven in Donne, who assuredly had no belief in the authenticity of this letter, but himself considered [it] spurious. But yet it served a purpose. As to Master Conradus, [who could read at night by the light at his fingers' ends,] he must have very recently been shaking hands with Lucifer.

Donne, SERMONS, *VIII. P. 83. D.*

> The Possedi virum à Domino was Eve's Recognition upon the birth of her first son, *Cain, I have gotten, I possesse a man from the Lord.*

"I have got the Jehova-man," is I believe, the true rendering and sense of the Hebrew words. Eve, full of the promise, supposed her first-born, *the* first-born, to be the promised Deliverer.

Donne, SERMONS, *VIII. P. 84. D, p. 90. B, p. 94. A, B, p. 115. A, p. 124. A, B, C, pp. 134, 135.*

Admirable

Donne, SERMONS, *XII. Matt. 5:2. P. 112. B, C, D. Note continued on p. 113.*

The disposition of our Church Divines under James I., to bring back the stream of the Reformation to the channel & within the banks formed in the first six centuries of the Church, and their alienation from the great Patriarchs of Protestantism, Luther, Calvin, Zuinglius, &c. who held the Saints & Fathers of the Ante-papal Church, with exception of Augustine, in light esteem—this disposition betrays itself in this & many other parts of Donne. For here Donne plays the Jesuit, disguising the true fact, viz. that even as early as the third century the Church had begun to paganize Christianity, under the pretext & no doubt in the hope, of Christianizing Paganism. The mountain would not go to Mahomet, & therefore Mahomet went to the Mountain.

Donne, SERMONS, *XII. P. 117. E.*

> And therefore when the Prophet saies, *Quis sapiens, & intelligit haec?*
> *Who is so wise as to finde out this way?* he places this cleannesse which
> we inquire after, in Wisdome. What is Wisdome?

The primitive Church appropriated it of the third *Hypostasis* of the
Trinity—hence *Santa Sophia* became the distinctive name of the Holy
Ghost; and the temple at Constantinople, dedicated by Justinian to the
Holy Ghost, is called the Church, alas! now the Mosk of Sta. Sophia.
Now this suggests, or rather implies, a far better & preciser definition of
Wisdom than this of Dr. Donne's. The distinctive title of the Father, as
the Supreme Will, is the Good, that of the only-begotten Word, as the
supreme Reason, (= Ens realissimum, ὁ ὤν , the BEING) is the True;
and the Spirit proceeding from the Good thro' the True is The Wisdom. Goodness in the form of Truth is Wisdom: or Wisdom is the
pure Will, realizing itself intelligently, or again, the Good manifesting itself as the Truth and realized in the Act. Wisdom, Life, Love,
Beauty, the Beauty of Holiness, are all *Synonyma* of the Holy Spirit.
S. T. C. 6, December, 1831

Donne, SERMONS, *XII. P. 121. A.*

> The Arrians opinion, That God the Father only was invisible, but the
> Son . . . and the Holy Ghost . . . might be seen.

Here we have an instance, one of many—of the inconveniences &
contradictions that arise out of the assumed contrary essences of Body
and Soul—both Substances each independent of the other, yet so absolutely diverse as that one is to be defined by the negation of the other.

Donne, SERMONS, *XV. 1 Cor. 15: 26. P. 144. D. Note continued on p.
145.*

> Who, then, is this enemy? An enemy that may thus far thinke himselfe
> equall to God, that as no man ever saw God, and lived; so no man ever
> saw this enemy and lived, for it is Death.

This borders rather too close on the Irish Franciscan's conclusion
to his Sermon of Thanksgiving: "Above all, Brethren, let us thankfully
laud and extol God's transcendant mercy in putting Death at the end
of Life and thereby giving us all time for repentance!" Dr. Donne was
an eminently witty man in a very witty age; but to the honour of his
judgement let it be said, that though his great wit is evinced in numberless passages, in a few only is it *shewn off.* This § ph. is one of these
rare exceptions.

Donne, SERMONS, *XV. P. 144. E, p. 145. A, B. Note continued on p. 146.*

We begin with this; That the Kingdome of Heaven hath not all that it must have to a consummate perfection, till it have bodies too.

Mem. Nothing in Scripture, nothing in Reason, commands or authorizes us to assume or suppose any bodiless *creature.* It is the incommunicable attribute of God. But all bodies are not *flesh,* nor need we suppose, that all bodies are corruptible. There are celestial bodies. S. T. C.

Alas! in E. A. B. we trace wild fantastic positions grounded on the arbitrary notion of Man as a *mixture* of heterogeneous components— which Des Cartes shortly afterwards carried into it's extremes. On this doctrine the Man is a mere phænomenal *result,* a sort of *Brandy-Sop* or Toddy-punch! It is a doctrine unsanctioned by, & indeed inconsistent with, the Scriptures. It is not that Body + Soul = Man—i. e. Man is not the Syntheton or *composition* of Body & Soul, as the two component units. No! man is the unity, the Prothesis, and Body and soul are the two Poles, the — & +, the Thesis & Antithesis of the Man; even as Attraction & Repulsion are the two Poles on which one and the same magnet manifests itself.

Donne, SERMONS, *XV. P. 145. C. First note at top of title page. Second, p. 144. Third, p. 145.*[14]

They are glorified bodies that make up the kingdome of Heaven; bodies that partake of the good of the State, that make up the State. Bodies, able bodies, and lastly, bodies inanimated with one soule . . . For as God hath made us under good Princes, a great example of all that, Abundance of Men, men that live like men, men united in one Religion, so wee need not goe farre for an example of a slippery, and uncertain being . . .

Capital improvement on our modern political Economists in Donne's definition of a prosperous state: "Man animated with a common soul—abundance of men, but of men that Live like men."

n.b. answer to Bentham's vindication of Usury—or Vindication of the Wisdom of States in the Discouragement of Usury. This done, then to consider the National Debt; i. e. the Funds, as an enormous Encouragement of Usury, first, preventing the dispersion of Capital & removing the national check which trade-gained wealth would not otherwise receive from the unnecessary Price of Land and thus preventing [—?] and colonization, the natural Relief of old Communities.

[14] None of these comments appear in *Lit. Rem.* They are important in showing how Coleridge's mind related what he was reading to contemporary affairs and also in showing his attitude toward Jeremy Bentham.

Capital may be defined in one word & the same number of syllables, viz. Briareus, i. e. 100 arms under one Head, a plurality of Powers directed by one intellect and activated by one will.

Donne, SERMONS, *XV. P. 146. B.*

> For it is not so great a depopulation to translate a City from Merchants to husbandmen, from shops to ploughes, as it is from many Husbandmen to one Shepheard; and yet that hath beene often done.

Ex. gr. in the Highlands of Scotland.

Donne, SERMONS, *XV. P. 148. A.*

> The ashes of an Oak in the Chimney, are no Epitaph of that Oak, to tell me how high or how large that was. It tells me not what flocks it sheltered while it stood, nor what men it hurt when it fell. The dust of great persons graves is speechlesse too, it sayes nothing, it distinguishes nothing: As soon the dust of a wretch whom thou wouldest not, as of a Prince whom thou couldest not look upon, will trouble thine eyes, if the winde blow it thither; and when a whirlewinde hath blowne the dust of the Church-yard into the Church, and the man sweeps out the dust of the Church into the Church-yard, who will undertake to sift those dusts again, and to pronounce, This is the Patrician, this is the noble floure, and this the yeomanly, this the Plebian bran.

Very beautiful.

Donne, SERMONS, *XV. P. 149. C.*

> But when I lye under the hands of the enemie, that hath reserved himselfe to the last, to my last bed; then when I shall be able to stir no limbe in any other measure then a Feaver or a Palsie shall shake them, when everlasting darknesses shall have an inchoation in the present dimnesse of mine eyes, and the everlasting gnashing in the present chattering of my teeth, and the everlasting worme in the present gnawing of the Agonies of my body and anguishes of my minde & when the last enemie shall watch my remedilesse body, and my disconsolate soule there, there, where not the Physitian in his way, perchance not the Priest in his, shall be able to give me any assistance, And when he hath sported himself with my misery . . .

All this is too much on the style of the Monkish Preachers: papam redolet. Contrast with this Job's description of Sheol, and St. Paul's Sleep in the Lord.

Donne, SERMONS, *XV. P. 150. A.*

> Neither doth *Calvin* carry those emphaticall words, which are so often cited for a proofe of the last Resurrection: *That he knows his Redeemer lives, that he knows he shall stand the last man upon earth, though his body be destroyed, yet in his flesh and with his eyes shall he see God,* to any higher sense then so, that how low soever he bee brought,

to what desperate state soever he be reduced in the eyes of the world, yet he assures himself of a Resurrection, a reparation, a restitution to his former bodily health, and worldly fortune which he had before. And such a Resurrection we all know *Job* had.

I incline to Calvin's opinion, but am not decided. "After my skin," must be rendered, according to or as far as my skin is concerned, Tho' the flies & maggots in my ulcers have destroyed my skin, yet still, and in my flesh, I shall see God as my redeemer. Now St. Paul says, Flesh *cannot* inherit the Kingdom of Heaven, i. e. the spiritual world. Besides how is the passage, as commonly interpreted, consistent with the numerous expressions of doubt & even of despondency?

Donne, SERMONS, *XV. Ezek. 37. P. 150. B, C. (Ezekiel's vision).*[15]

I cannot but think, that Dr. Donne by thus antedating the distinct belief of the Resurrection, destroys in great measure the force & sublimity of this vision. Besides, it was but a mongrel Egyptian-catacomb sort of faith, or rather superstition that was [by?] the later Jews entertained.

Donne, SERMONS, *XV. P. 152. Note at end of sermon.*

In fine. This is one of Donne's least estimable Discourses; The worst sermon on the best text.

Donne, SERMONS, *XVI. John 11: 35. P. 153. C.*

The Masorites (the Masorites are the Critiques upon the Hebrew Bible, the Old Testament) cannot tell us, who divided the Chapters of the Old Testament into verses; Neither can any other tell us who did it in the New Testament.

How should they when their Hebrew Scriptures were not divided into Verses? The Jews adopted the invention from the Christians who were led to it in the construction of Concordances.

Donne, SERMONS, *XVI. P. 154. E.*

If they killed *Lazarus,* had not Christ done enough to let them see that he could raise him againe?

Malice, above all Party-malice, is indeed a blind passion, but one can scarcely conceive the Chief Priests such dolts, as to think that Christ could raise &c. Their malice blinded them as to the nature of the Incident, made them suppose a conspiracy between Jesus and the Family of Lazarus, a mock burial, in short; and this may be one, tho' it is not, I think, the principal reason for this greatest miracle being omitted in the 3 other Gospels.

[15] In *Lit. Rem.* this note and the next following are considerably modified.

Donne, SERMONS, *XVI. P. 155. B.*

> Christ might ungirt himselfe and give more scope and liberty to his passions, then any other man; both because he had no Original sin within, to drive him, . . .

How then is he said to have conquered sin in the flesh? Without *guilt*, without *actual* sin, assuredly he was; but ἐγένετο σάρξ and what can we mean by Original Sin relatively to the flesh, but that man is born with an animal life and a material organism that render him *temptible* to evil, that tends to dispose the life of the Will to contradict the Light of the Reason? Did Paul by ὁμοίωμα mean a deceptive resemblance?

Donne, SERMONS, *XVI. P. 155 D.*

> Christ in another place gave such scope to his affections, and to others interpretations of his actions, that his friends and kinsfolks thought him mad, beside himself.

I can see no possible edification that can arise from these ultra-Scriptural speculations respecting our Lord. S.T.C.

Donne, SERMONS, *XVI. P. 157. A.*

> Though the Godhead never departed from the Carcasse . . . yet because the Human Soule was departed from it, he was no man.

Donne was a poor Metaphysician; i. e. he never closely questioned himself as to the absolute meaning of his words. What did he mean by the *"Soul?"* what by the *"Body?"*

Donne, SERMONS, *XVI. P. 157. D.*

> And I know that there are Authors of a middle nature, above the Philosophers, and below the Scriptures, the Apocryphall books.

A whimsical instance of the disposition in the mind for every pair of opposites to find an intermediate, a *mesothesis* for every Thesis and Antithesis. So here, Scripture ✕ Philosophy; and the Apocrypha is philosophy relatively to Scripture, and Scripture relatively to philosophy.

Donne, SERMONS, *XVI. P. 159. B.*

> And therefore the same Author [Epiphanius] sayes, That because they thought it an uncomely thing for Christ to weep for any temporall thing, some men have expunged and removed that verse out of S. *Lukes* Gospel, That Jesus when he saw that City, wept.

This, by the bye, rather *indiscreetly* lets out the liberties, which the early Christians took with their sacred writings. Origen, who, in answer to Celsus's reproach on this ground, confines the practice to the Heretics, furnishes proofs of the contrary himself in his own comments.

Donne, Sermons, *XVI. P. 161. D.*

That world, which findes it selfe truly in an Autumne, in it selfe, findes it selfe in a spring, in our imaginations.

Worthy almost of Shakspere!

Donne, Sermons, *XVII. Matt. 19: 17. P. 163 D & E. Note on title page, verso.*

The words are a part of the Dialogue, of a Conference, betweene Christ and a man who proposed a question to him; to whom Christ makes an answer by way of another question, *Why callest thou me good? &c.* In the words, and by occasion of them, we consider the Text, the Context, and the Pretext: Not as three equall parts of the Building; but the Context, as the situation and Prospect of the house, The Pretext, as the Accesse and entrance to the house, And then the Text it selfe, as the House it selfe, as the body of the building: In a word, in the Text, the Words; In the Context, the Occasion of the words; In the Pretext, the Pretence, the purpose, the disposition of him who gave the occasion.

The Compendium of Christianity and in E. an example of elegant Division of a Subject! Our great Divines were not ashamed of the learned Discipline, to which they had submitted their minds under Aristotle and Tully—but brought the purified products, as sacrificial gifts to Christ. They *baptized* the logic and manly Rhetoric of ancient Greece.

Donne, Sermons, *XVII. P. 164. A, B. Discussion of "the Context."*

Excellent illustration of fragmentary morality, in which each man takes his choice of virtues and vices & mark D. I almost . . . [This sentence is left unfinished.]

Donne, Sermons, *XVII. P. 164. D.*

Men perish with whispering sins, nay, with silent sins, sins that never tell the conscience they are sins, as often as with crying sins.

I almost doubt whether the truth here so boldly asserted is not of more general necessity for ordinary congregations, or general, than the denunciation of the large Sins, that cannot remain *incognito.*

Donne, Sermons, *XVII. P. 165. A.*

Venit procurrens, He came running. Nicodemus came not so, *Nicodemus* durst not avow his comming; and therefore he came creeping, and he came softly, and he came seldome, and he came by night.

But we trust in God, that they *came*. The adhesion, the thankfulness, the love, that arise & live *after* the having come, whether from spontaneous liking, or from a beckoning Hope, or from a compelling Good, are the truest criteria of the man's Christianity.

Donne, SERMONS, *XVII. P. 165. B.*

> When I have just reason to think my superiours would have it thus, this is Musique to my soul; When I heare them say they would have it thus, this is Rhetorique to my soule; When I see their Laws enjoyne it to be thus, this is Logick to my soul; but when I see them actually, really, clearly, constantly do thus, this is a Demonstration to my soule, and Demonstration is the powerfullest proofe. The eloquence of inferiours is in words, the eloquence of superiours is in action.

A just representation, I doubt not, of the general feeling & principle at the time Donne wrote. Men regarded the gradations of society as God's Ordinances, and had the elevation of self-approving Conscience in every feeling and exhibition of respect for those of ranks superior to themselves. What a contrast with the present times! Mem. What a beautiful sentence. The eloquence of Inferiors is in words, the Eloquence of Superiors is in action!!

Donne, SERMONS, *XVII. P. 165. B-C.*

> He came to Christ; hee ran to him; and when he was come, as S. *Mark* relates it, *He fell upon his knees to Christ*. He stood not then Pharisaically upon his owne legs, his own merits, though he had been a diligent observer of the Commandments before. . . .

But I doubt whether in his desire to make every particle *exemplary,* to draw some Christian moral from it, Donne has not injudiciously attributed quasi per prolepsin, merits inconsistent with the *finale* of a wealthy would-be proselyte. At all events, a more natural and perhaps not less instructive, interpretation might be made of the sundry movements of this religiously earnest & zealous Admirer of Christ, & Worshipper of Mammon. O, I have myself known such! However the passage is beautiful as an independent truth. But from D to E all is *pure gold.*

Donne, SERMONS, *XVII. P. 165. D.*

> He was no ignorant man, and yet he acknowledged that he had somewhat more to learn of Christ then he knew yet. Blessed are they that inanimate all their knowledge, consummate all in Christ Jesus, . . .

Without being aware of this passage in Donne, I had expressed the same conviction, or rather declared the same experience, in the Appendix to my first "Lay Sermon" or the Statesman's Manual. O if only one day in a week, Christians would consent to have the Bible as the only Book, & their Ministers labor to make them find all substantial good of all other books in their Bibles! + E. *Mem. Apply this to the Deacons of the Church* in a discourse on the [——?] advantages of the Church as [——?].¹⁶

Donne, SERMONS, *XVII. P. 165. E.*

> I remember one of the Panegyriques celebrates & magnifies one of the Romane Emperors for this, That he marry when he was yong; that he would so soon confine and limit his pleasures, so soon determine his affections in one person.

It is surely some proof of the moral effect, Christianity has produced, that in all protestant countries, at least, a writer would be ashamed to assign this, as a ground of *panegyric;* as if promiscuous intercourse with those of the other sex had been a naturall Good, a privilege, which there was not great merit in foregoing! O! what do not *women* owe to Christianity! As Christians only, do they, or ordinarily *can* they cease to be *Things* for men—instead of Co-persons in one spiritual I AM.

Donne, SERMONS, *XVII. P. 166. A.*

> But such is often the corrupt inordinatenesse of greatnesse, that it only carries them so much beyond other men, but not so much nearer to God.

Like a Balloon, away from earth, but not a whit nearer the arch of Heaven.

Donne, SERMONS, *XVII. P. 166. C. Note on inserted page.*

> When he inquired of Christ after salvation, Christ doth not say, There is no salvation for thee, thou Viper, thou Hypocrite, thou Pharisee . . . when he sayes to him, *Why callest thou me good? There is none good but God,* he only directs him in the way to that end, which he did indeed, or pretended to seek.

There is a praiseworthy *relativeness* & *life* in the morality of our best old Divines. It is not a cold Law in Brass or Stone, but *this* I may & should think of my neighbor—& yet not quite *this* [to?] soothe myself with—*this* I will say *of* a great man, a prince, yet not *to* him; this he will not say to himself.

Donne, SERMONS, *XVII. P. 167. A.*

> Christ was pleased to redeem this man from this error, and bring him to know truly what he was, that he was God. Christ therefore doth not

¹⁶ Two words cannot be deciphered. The sentence was omitted from *Lit. Rem.*

rebuke this man, by any denying that he himself was good; for Christ doth assume that addition himself, *I am the good shepherd.* Neither doth God forbid, that these good parts which are in men should be celebrated with condigne praise. We see that God, as soon as he saw that any thing was good, he said so, he uttered it, he declared it, first of the Light, and then of other creatures. God would be no author, no example of smothering the due praise of good actions. For, surely that man hath no zeale to goodnesse in himself, that affords no praise to goodnesse in other men.

Very fine. But I think, another not however a different, view might be taken respecting our Lord's intention in these words. The young noble, who came to him, had many praiseworthy traits of character; but he failed in the *ultimate* end and aim. What ought to have been valued by him, as *means,* was *loved,* and had a *worth* given to it, as an *end* in itself. Our Lord, who knew the hearts of men, instantly, in the first words, applies himself to this—& takes the occasion by an ordinary phrase of courtesy to make him aware of the difference between a mere relatively good & that which is absolutely good—that which *may* be called good, when regarded as a *means* to good, but which must not be mistaken for, or confounded with that which *is* good, and itself the *End.*

Donne, SERMONS, *XVII. P. 167. B, C, D. B, C are examples of "this recognition of goodnesse"; D, God, as a "land of Gold," the world as "the land of Spices and Perfumes, the dilation of Gods goodnesse."*

All excellent, and D. most so. Thus, thus our old Divines shewed the depth of their love & appreciation of the Scriptures, and thus led their congregations to feel and see the same. This, this is what I have so earnestly endeavored to show, that God is Ens super Ens, the *Ground* of all Being, but therein likewise absolute Being, in that he is the Eternal Self-Affirmant, & the I AM in that I AM: and that the key of this mystery is given to us in the pure idea of the WILL, as the alone *Causa sui.*

O! compare this manhood of our Church Divinity with the feeble dotage of the Paleian School, the Natural Theology, the Watchmaking Scheme, that knows nothing of the Maker but what can be proved out of the Watch—the unknown Nominative case of the Verb Impersonal, Fit et Natura est; The It of *it* rains, *it* snows, *it* is cold, &c. When, after reading the biographies of Isaac Walton and his contemporaries I reflect on the crowded congregations, on the thousands, who with intense interest came to these hour and two hour long Sermons, I cannot but doubt the fact of any true progression, moral or intellectual, in the mind of the Many. The tone, the matter, the anticipated sympathies in the sermons of an age form the best moral criterion of the character of that age.

Donne, SERMONS, *XVII. P. 167. E.*

His name of Jehova we admire with a reverence.

Rather, say, *Jehova,* his name. It is not so properly a name of God, as God, the Name, God's name and God.

Donne, SERMONS, *XVII. P. 169. A.*

Land, and Money, & Honour must be called Goods, though but of fortune, . . .

We should distinguish between the conditions of our possessing good, and the goods themselves. Health, for instance, is ordinarily a condition of that working & rejoicing in and for God, which are *goods* in the end of, themselves. Health, Competent Fortune, & the like are good, as negations of the preventives of Good—as clear *Glass* is good in relation to the Light, which it does not exclude. Health & Ease without the love of God are crown Glass in the Darkness.

Donne, SERMONS, *XVII. P. 170. Note continued on p. 171, verso, a blank page.*

Much of this page consists of Play on words; ex. gr. that which is useful, as Rain, & that which is *of use,* as Rain on a Garden after drouth & much of Sophistry. Pain is not necessarily an *ultimate* evil, as the means of ultimate good, it may be a relative good—but surely that which makes Pain, Anguish, Heaviness, necessary in order to Good, must be Evil. And so the Scripture determines. They are the Wages of Sin; but God's infinite mercy raises them into sacraments, means of Grace. Sin is the only absolute evil—God the only absolute good—but as myriads of things are good relatively thro' participation of God, so are many things evil, as the fruits of evil.

What is the apostasy, or Fall of Spirits? Answer. That that which from the essential perfection of the Absolute Good could not but be *possible,* i. e. have a potential being, but never ought to have been *actual,* did strive to be actual?—but this involved an impossibility & it actualized only it's own potentiality.

What is the consequence of the Apostasy? That no philosophy is possible of Man & Nature but by assuming at once a Zenith and a Nadir, God and Hades. An ascension from the one thro' and with a condescension from the other—or redemption by prevenient, and then auxiliary, Grace.

Donne, Sermons, *XVII. P. 171. B.*

So sayes S. *Augustine, Audeo dicere,* Though it be boldly said, yet I must say it, *Utile esse cadere in aliquod manifestum peccatum, . . .*

No doubt, a sound sense may be forced into these words; but why use words, into which sound sense must be *forced?*—Besides, the subject is too deep and too subtle for a Sermon. Donne is here too deep, & not deep enough. He *treads waters* & dangerous waters. Mem. The familists.

Donne, Sermons, *XVIII. Acts 2: 36. P. 175. B.*

Therefore let all the house of Israel know assuredly, That God hath made that same Iesus, whome ye have crucified, both Lord, and Christ.

Therefore—&c. there is a sufficing reason, or motive, why I should communicate a certain matter to you, or why you should give attention of it.[17]

But Truth is a common interest—it is every man's duty to convey it to his Brother, if only it be first, a truth that concerns or may profit him, & secondly, he be competent to receive it—for we are not bound to *say* the Truth, when we know that we cannot *convey* it, but very probably may impart a falsehood instead, & no falsehoods more dangerous than Truths misunderstood, nay, the most mischievous Errors on record having been Half-Truths taken as the whole.

But let it be supposed, that the matter to be communicated is a Fact of general concernment, a truth of deep and universal Interest, a momentous Truth involved in a most awe-strking Fact, which all reponsible Creatures are competent to understand, and of which no man can safely remain in Ignorance. Now this is the case with the matter, on which I am about to speak; and it being such, I can with good reason say—&c. Therefore let all the House &c.

Donne, Sermons, *XVIII. P. 176. A, B, C.*

For in all the books of the world, you shall never read so civill languages, nor so faire expressions of themselves to one another, as in the Bible.

True Christian Love not only permits, but enjoins Courtesy. God himself, says Donne, gave us the example.

Donne, Sermons, *XVIII. P. 177. C, E.*

C. excellent, and E. of a deeper worth. "No man knows enough," All that is wanting here is to determine the true sense of "knowing"— i.e. that sense, in which it is revealed that to know God is Life Everlasting.

[17] Changed in *Lit. Rem.*

Donne, SERMONS, *XVIII. P. 178. A.*

Now the universality of this mercy hath God enlarged and extended very farre, in that he proposes it even to our knowledge; *Sciant,* let all know it. It is not only *credant,* let all beleeve it; for the infusing of faith, is not in our power: but God hath put it in our power to satisfie their reason, . . .

A problem here affirmatively stated of highest importance, of deepest interest, viz. Faith *so* distinguished from Reason, credat from sciat, that the former is an infused grace "not in our power"; the latter, an inherent quality or faculty, on which we are able to calculate, as man with man. I know not what to say to this. Faith seems to me the co-adunation of the individual Will with the Reason, enforcing adherence alike of Thought, Act, and Affection to the Universal Will, revealed whether in the Conscience, or by the Light of Reason, however the same may contravene, or apparently contradict, the will and mind of the flesh, the presumed experience of the senses & of the Understanding, as the faculty, or intelligential yet animal Instinct, by which we generalize the notices of the senses, and *substantiate* (understand, jacio apparentiæ aliquid *sub*-stare) the *spectra* or *phænomena.* In this sense, therefore, & in this only, I agree with Donne. No man, (says Christ) cometh to me unless the Father leadeth him. The corrupt will cannot without prevenient as well as auxiliary Grace be unitively subordinated to the Reason, & again, without this union of the moral will, the Reason itself is latent. Nevertheless, I see no *advantage* in not saying the *Will,* and but putting for *it* the term Faith. But the sad non-distinction of Reason and the Understanding, throughout Donne, and the confusion of ideas and conceptions under the same term, "rationalus," painfully inturbidates his theology. Till this distinction (of Reason & Understanding, νοῦς χ φρόνημα σαρκός) be seen, nothing *can* be seen aright. Yet Mr. Hare writes of it, as a sort of arbitrary repr. in words much like *sweat* and *perspire* . . . So little had he comprehended me.[18] Till this great truth be mastered and with the Sight that is Insight, other truths may casually take possession of the mind, but the mind cannot possess them. If you know not *this*, you *know*, you can know *nothing;* for if you know not the diversity of Reason from the Understanding, you do not know Reason; and Reason alone is Knowledge.

What follows [p. 178. B.] is admirable, worthy of a Divine of the Church of England, the National and the Christian, and indeed proves, that Donne *felt, was* at least *possessed by,* the truths, which I have labored to enforce, viz. that Faith is the *Apotheosis* of the reason in man; the *Complement* of Reason, the Will in the form of Reason. As

18 This sentence is omitted in *Lit. Rem.*

the Basin-water to the fountain-shaft, such is Will to Reason in Faith. The whole will shapes itself in the image of God in which it had been created, and shoots toward Heaven, S. T. C.

Donne, SERMONS, *XVIII. P. 178. D.*

If we could have been in Paradise, and seen God take a clod of red earth, and make that wretched clod of contemptible earth, such a body as should be fit to receive his breath, an immortall soule . . .

A sort of pun on the Hebrew word, Adam, or red earth; common in Donne's Age, but unworthy of Donne who was worthy to have seen deeper into the Scriptural sense of "the Ground," i. e. Hades, the Multeity, the many absque numero et infra numerum, that which is *below,* as God is that which transcends intellect.

Donne, SERMONS, *XVIII. P. 179. B.*

We place in the Schoole (for the most part) the infinite Merit of Christ Jesus . . . rather *in pacto* than *in persona,* rather that this contract was thus made between the Father and the Son, than that whatsoever that person, thus consisting of God and Man, should doe, should, onely in respect of the person, bee of an infinite value, and extention to that purpose . . .

O this is sad misty divinity! far too scholastical for the pulpit, far too vague and unphilosophic for the study.

Donne, SERMONS, *XVIII. P. 180. A.*

Quis nisi infidelis negaverit apud inferos fuisse Christum? saies S. *Augustine.*

Qy. In what part of Augustine? Pearson asserts the clause, Descends into Hell, not to have been introduced into the (so called) Apostle's Creed, till the sixth Century. And even now the sense of these words is in no reformed Church determined, as an article of faith, or those pronounced heretical, who render them—*verè* mortuus est —either in contra-distinction from a trance, or suspended animation.[19]

Donne, SERMONS, *XVIII. P. 181. E.*

Never therefore dispute against thine own happinesse; never say, God asks the heart, that is, the soule, and therefore rewards the soule or punishes the soule, and hath no respect to the body . . . Never go about to separate the thoughts of the heart, from the colledge, from the fellowship to the body.

Had Donne but once asked himself what he meant by the Body, as distinct from the carcase, he must have detected the fallacy, the mis-

[19] In *Lit. Rem.* the latter part of this note is omitted and the first part modified.

chievous fallacy, of this reasoning. It is not Soul + Body = Man, as
Brandy+ Water = Toddy; but the Unity, Man, that is Soul and Body
as the + and — Poles of the same Magnet.[20]

Donne, SERMONS, *XVIII. P. 182. D.*

Audacter dicam, saies S. Hierome (I say confidently) Cum omnia posset
Deus, suscitare Virginem post ruinam, non potest.

One instance among hundreds of the wantonness of phrase & fancy
in the Fathers. What did Augustine [sic] mean? Quod Deus mem-
branum Hymenis luniformem reproducere nequit? No! That were
too absurd—What then? That God cannot make what has been not to
have been? Well then, why not say that, since that is all you mean?

Donne, SERMONS, *XIX. Rev. 20: 6. P. 183.*

A lively instance how much excellent good sense a wise man, like
Donne, can bring forth on a passage, which he does not understand. For
to say, that it may mean either X or Y or Z is to confess he knows not
what it means. But if it be X. then, &c., if it be Y. then; and lastly if
it be Z. then,—i. e. that he understands X, Y, Z, but does not understand
the text. S. T. C.

Donne, SERMONS, *XIX. P. 185. B.*

Seas of Blood, and yet but brooks, tuns of blood, and yet but basons,
compared with the sacrifices, the sacrifices of the blood of men, in the
persecutions of the Primitive Church. For every Oxe of the Jew, the
Christian spent a man, and for every sheep and Lamb, a Mother and
her childe . . .

Whoo!!! Had the other nine so called Persecutions been equal to
the *tenth,* that of Diocletian, the only need by great efficiency Donne's
assertion would still be extravagant.

Donne, SERMONS, *XXXI. P. 305.*[21]

And the Spirit of God moved upon the face of the waters. The Jews
. . . a very strong winde blew upon the face of the waters.

If the Earth were waste & wilde—and a fluid confused mass—how can
this confusion of Elements be imagined without *winds?* Let Lime meet
with an acid—and then with a stray [—?] will there not be a violent

---

[20] Omitted in *Lit. Rem.* A similar statement occurs in note to Sermon XV, p.
144. E, p. 145. A, B.

[21] This note and all that follow except the final note are from the 1640 folio of
Donne's *Sermons* formerly owned by John Livingston Lowes. The margins have
been so closely trimmed that some words and phrases are lost. These notes are
printed with permission of the Harvard University Library. The notes from pp.
335, 342, 725, and 727 are included in *English Divines*, I, 115-19.

rush of fixed air?[22] Doubtless the Gloss of the Jews is accurate tho'
still it would be in wretched Taste to translate it, as Dr.
Geddes has done, a violent wind—for this may be the cold truth of the *Thing* but
by no means a fair [?] transfusion of the Prophet's meaning—or in the
spirit of the theocratic Theology, which attribute [sic] all things to God
immediately, that were powerful enough to [cut off]

Donne, SERMONS, *XXXII. P. 313. Note continued on p. 314.*

> Now as this death hath invaded every part and faculty of man, under-
> standing, and will, and all (for though originall sin seem to be con-
> tracted without our will, yet *Sicut omnium natura ita omnium voluntatis
> fuere originaliter* in Adam, sayes S. *Augustine.* As the whole nature of
> mankinde, and so of every particular man, was in *Adam,* so also were
> the faculties, and so the will of every particular man in him) so this
> death hath invaded every particular man; Death went over all men,
> for as much as all men had sinned.

As the one and yet all, the synthesis inclusive and yet annihilative of
all & each antithesis is & must ever remain the great mystery of Deity,
so is the original Sin (i. e. *Guilt:* for taken as mere imperfection is it is
[sic] a contradiction or a nullity: for what sin is it in the whole to have
a deficient Vision,—& if that be all the meaning, Sin means only that
man is now born less capacitated morally and intellectually than Adam
was) so, I say, is [the connate will?] of man (a fact) and it's compata-
bility with the free will, the [cut off] *arbitrement* of man (arbitrium as
distinguished from [?] volition) which is likewise a *Fact,* the great
mystery of Human Nature. And they are grievously mistaken, who
suppose that this difficulty rises in [cut off] as will or in any way expands on, the Truth or Falsehood of *Historical* Christianity, and one
proof of this is that those Sects, who least attend to, or care for, the
external Evidences of Revealed Religion are most affected by, & most
hold [?] their feeling for this very Tenet. Their Will is the sole
possible Fountain of all *Virtue* (as distinguished from *Luck*) and that
Fountain is itself polluted—& therefore the Redemption must come
from without. S. T. C.

Donne, SERMONS, *XXXII. P. 318.*

> *Unum inveni, quod cuncta operatur,* I have (saies Plato) found One,
> who made all things; *Et unum per quod cuncta efficiuntur,* And I have
> found another, by whom all things were made; *Tertium autem non
> potui invenire,* A Third besides those two, I could never finde.

[22] When this experiment was first made, the carbon dioxide which was released
was called "fixed air." The use of this analogy reflects Coleridge's interest in
chemistry. It is regrettable that the word after "stray" is lost; only lime and
acid are needed for the reaction.

A False translation of Plato: I have found one who effects all things; & another, which is the *condition*, as it were, the [?] of all agency—i. e. *mind* and *Being;* a third I could never find. We find a third in conceiving the mutual reaction of mind participant of Being on Being, and of Being participant (by effluence from itself) of mind on it's own offspring—and this is the Spirit = air + motion = wind—& these three, three by distinction are by the same necessity of conception indivisibly *one*.

Donne, SERMONS, *XXXIV. Rom. 8: 16. P. 335. Note continued on pp. 336-40.*

But by what manner comes he from them? By proceeding.

If this mystery be considered as words, or rather *sounds* vibrating on some certain ears, to which their Belief assigned a supernatural cause —well and good! What else can be said? Such were the sounds. What their meaning is, we know not; but such sounds not being in the ordinary course of nature, we of course attribute them to something extranatural. But if God made man in his own Image, therein as in a mirror, misty no doubt at best, & now *cracked* by peculiar & inherited defects, yet still our only mirror, & therein to contemplate all we can of God, this word "proceeding" may admit of an easy sense. For if man first used it to express as well as he could a notion found in himself, as man in genere, we have to look into ourselves, and there we may find, that two events of vital Intelligence may be conceived—the first, a necessary and eternal outgoing of Intelligence (Noῦς) from Being (τὸ ὄν) *with* the will as an accompaniment, but not *from* it, as a cause, in *order,* tho' not necessarily in Time precedent—this is true *Filiation.* The second, an act of *the will & Reason,* in their purity strict indentities, & therefore not *begotten* or *filiated* but *proceeding* from intelligent essence and essential intelligence combining in the *act,* necessarily indeed, & co-eternally. For the co-existence of absolute Spontaneity with absolute necessity is involved in the very Idea of *God,* one of whose intellectual Definitions is, the Synthesis, generative ad extra, and annihilative tho' inclusive quoad se, of all conceivable antitheses; even as the best moral Definition—(and, O how much more godlike to us in this state of antithetic Intellect is the moral beyond the intellectual!)—the best moral Definition is—God is LOVE—and this is (to *us,* the high prerogative of the *moral* that all it's dictates immediately reveal the truths of intelligence, whereas the strictly Intellectual only by more distant & cold deductions carries us towards the moral. For what is Love? Union with the desire of union. God therefore is the Cohesion & the oneness of all

Things—and dark & dim is that system of Ethics; which does [not] take "oneness" as the *root* of all Virtue! Being, Mind, Love in action = holy Spirit are ideas distinguishable tho' not divisible, but *Will* is incapable of distinction or division: it is equally implied in 1. vital Being, 2. in essential intelligence, and 3. in effluent Love or holy Action. Now Will is the true principle & meaning of *Identity,* of *Selfness:* even in our common language. The Will, therefore, being indistinguishably one, but the possessive Powers triply distinguishable, do perforce involve the notion expressed by three *Persons* and one *God.* There are three "Personæ *per quas sonat,*" three forms of manifestation co-eternally co-existing, in which the one Will is totally, all in each; the truth of which we may *know* in our own minds, & can understand by no analogy—for the wind ministrant to divers at the same moment, in [—?] to aid the fancy, borrows or rather steals, from the mind the idea of total *in omni parte,* which alone furnishes the analogy—but that both it & a myriad of other material Images do inwrap themselves in this veste non sua, & would be even no objects of conception, if they did not—yea, that even the very words, "conception, comprehension," & all in all languages that answer to them, suppose this transinfusion from the mind (even as if the Sun [?] [cut off] visual, it must first irradiate from itself in order for itself to perceive) is an argument better than all analogy.

Donne, SERMONS, *XXXV. Matt. 12: 31. P. 342. B.*

> First then, for the first terme, *Sin,* we use to ask in the Schoole, whether any action of man's can have *rationem demeriti,* whether it can be said to offend God, or to deserve ill of God: for whatsover does so, must have some proportion with God.

This ¶ appears to me to furnish an interesting Instance of the bad effects, in reasoning as well as morals, of the *"cui boni? cui malo?"* system of Ethics: that system which places the *good* and *evil* of actions in their painful or pleasurable effects on the sensuous or passive nature of sentient Beings; not in the will, the "pure act" itself. For, according to this system, God must either be a passible and dependent Being, i.e not God, or else he must have no Interest, and therefore no motive, or impulse to reward Virtue or punish Vice. (Corollary, the Epicurean Veil of their atheism is itself an implicit Atheism. Nay, the World itself could not have existed; & as it does exist, the origin of Evil (for if Evil means no more than pain in genere, Evil has a true Being in the order of Things) is not only a difficulty of impossible solution, but it is a fact immediately & necessarily implying the non-existence of an omnipotent & infinite goodness, i. e. of God. For to say that I believe in a God, but not that he is omniscient, omnipotent, and all-good, is as mere a contradiction in Terms, as to say, I believe in a circle; but not that all rays from it's centre to it's circumference are equal.

I cannot read the profound truth so clearly expressed in the last Line but four of p. 342, the very next Paragraph ["it does not only want that rectitude, but it should have that rectitude, and therefore hath a sinfull want"] without an uneasy wonder at it's incongruity with the former Dogmata.

Donne, SERMONS, *LXXI. Matt. 4: 18, 19, 20. P. 725. A.*

But still consider, that they did but leave their nets, they did not burne them. And consider too, that they left but nets; those things which might entangle them, and retard their following of Christ, &c

An excellent Paragraph grounded on a mere Pun. Such was the taste of the Age; and it is an awful joy to observe, that not great Learning, great Wit, great Talent, or even (as far as without great virtue that *can* be) no, not even great Genius, were effectual to preserve the man from the contagion, but only the deep & wise enthusiam of moral Feeling. Compare in this light Donne's theological prose with that even of the honest Knox; and above all, compare Cowley with Milton.

Donne, SERMONS, *LXXI. P. 724. Note continued on p. 725.*

It is a sort of sophism peculiar as far as I know, to the reasoning in behalf of Christianity, first, actually tho' perhaps indirectly to assume the Truth of the Gospels, & then from that assumption to prove the assumption. Every A = A. But A is A. Ergo, A = A. If I believe literally all that is written in the Gospels, what more have you, or any uninspired Being, a right to demand of me? If I do not believe them how silly must those arguments be, quoad *me* which take it's Truth for granted? The argumentum in circulo I own is common enough in all parties, but by inadvertence—or at least in particular reasonings not to make it the Queen-axiom of a whole System, and that not by one man, or by men of one age, but by a whole sect of 200 millions for a succession of ages is, as I said, as far as my Knowlege extends, peculiar to the Christian. S. T. C.

Donne, SERMONS, *LXXII. Matt. 4: 18, 19. P. 727. A-E. Note continued on p. 728.*

And yet, though for the better applying of God to the understanding of man, the Holy Ghost impute to God these excesses, and defects of man (laziness and drowsiness, deterioration, corruptiblenesse by ill conversation, prodigality and wastefulnesse, sudden choler, long irreconcilable-nesse, scorne, inebriation, and many others) in the Scriptures, yet in no place of the Scripture is God, for any respect said to be proud; God in the Scriptures is never made so like man, as to be capable of Pride, for this had not beene to have God like man, but like the devill.

It is amusing to see the use w̄ch the Xtian Divines make of the very facts in favor of their own religion, with which they triumphan[tly] batter that of the Heathen; viz. the gross & sinful anthropomorphitism of their representati[ons] of Divinity; & yet the Heathen Philosophers & Priests (Plutarch, for instance) tell us as plainly as Donne or Æquinas can do, these are only accommodations to human modes of conception, (the divine nature in itself is impassible—how otherwise could it be the prime agent but that we name it, abusive, by the effects it produces on our passions. Pain is commonly inflicted in anger—[—?] & for no reason but from this cause, we say God [cut off] . . . wittiest [?] = Donne. Paganism needs a true philosophical Judge. Condemned it will be, more heavily perhaps than by the present Judges, but not from the same Statutes or on the same Evidence.

Donne, SERMONS, *end-page with reference to p. 461.*[23]

If our old Divines, in their homiletic expositions of Scripture, *wire-drew* their Text, in their anxiety to evolve out of the words the fulness of the meaning, expressed, implied, or suggested, our modern preachers have erred more dangerously in the oppposite extreme, making their Text a mere *theme,* or *motto,* for their discourse. Both err in *degree,* the old Divines, especially the Puritans, by excess the modern by defect. But there is this difference to the disfavor of the latter—that the *defect* in *degree* alters the *kind.* It was on God's Holy Word, that our Donnes, Andrewses, Hookers preached, it was *Scripture* Bread that they divided according to the needs & seasons—The Preacher of our Day expounds, or appears to expound his own sentiments & conclusions & thinks himself evangelic enough, if he can make the Scripture seem in conformity with them.

Above all, there is something to my mind at once elevating & soothing in the idea of an order of learned men reading the many words of the wise & great, in many languages, for the purpose of making one book contain the life and virtue of all for their Brethren's who have but that one to read. What then, if that one book be such, that the increase of learning is shewn more and more enabling the mind to *find* them all in it! But such, according to my experience, turned as I am of 3 score, the Bible is—as far as all moral, spiritual, & prudential, private, do-mestic, or political, truths & interests are concerned. The Astronomer, Chemist, Mineralogist, must go elsewhere; but the Bible is the BOOK for the MAN.

[23] This note is taken from Professor Dunn's volume.

Warburton's note on HAMLET, *Act II, Sc. 2. Speech of Polonius.*

Then as to the *jingles,* and *play* on words, let us but look into the sermons of Dr. Donne (the wittiest man of that age), and we shall find them full of this vein: only, there they are to be admired, here to be laugh'd at.

I have (and that most carefully) read Dr. Donne's Sermons and find none of these Jingles. The great art of an orator is to make whatever he talks of appear of importance, this indeed Donne has effected with consummate skill.[24]

I think you will find the original of Langhorne's celebrated line—

The child of misery baptized in tears,

in Donne's Sermon on the First Epistle to the Thessalonians. The prose works of this admirable Divine, are Armouries for the Christian Soldier. Such a depth of intellect, such a nervousness of style, such a variety of illustration, such a power of argument, are to be looked for only in the writings of that race of Giants. Donne's poetry must be sought in his prose. . . .[25]

John Hacket

Hacket, SERMONS: LIFE OF BISHOP HACKET,[1] *p. xliii. Note on flyleaf.*

In the *Quinquarticular* Controversie he was ever very moderate, but being bred under *Bishop Davenant,* and *Dr. Ward* in *Cambridge,* was addicted to *their Sentiments.*

P. 43 two last lines & 44—Could Bishop Marsh ever have read this striking § ph? As to Bishop Tomlins, alias Pitt Prettyman, it would be useless—Plausible Dullness answers the same purpose for him, that the Goliah Armour of Impudence, the Panoply of Brass, did for his ultra-arminian Predecessor, Heylin.

[24] *Shakespeare's Plays,* ed. Lewis Theobald (8 vols.; London: 1773), VIII, 145 n. 28.
[25] Willmott, *C. at Trinity,* p. 15.

---

[1] By Thomas Plume, prefixed to the folio edition of Hacket's *Sermons* (1675). Two notes which are not given in *Lit. Rem.* are here printed for the first time, while the notes in *Lit. Rem.,* III, 171-72 are not reprinted.

Hacket, SERMONS: LIFE OF BISHOP HACKET, *pp. xliv-v.*

While living He would urge for the indissolubleness of Wedlock . . .

Hacket was twice married, and each time happily and to the Woman of his choice. It is easy for such men to talk thus rigidly. Poor Hooker would have held a different Language.

Hacket, SERMONS, *I.*[2] *Luke 2:7. P. 3.*

Moreover as the Woman *Mary* did bring forth the Son who bruised the *Serpents* head, which brought sin into the world by the woman *Eve*, so the *Virgin Mary* was the occasion of Grace as the *Virgin Eve* was the cause of Damnation. *Eve* had not known *Adam* as yet when she was beguiled, and seduced the man; so Mary . . .

A Rabbinical Fable or Gloss on Gen. 3. 1. Hacket is offensively fond of these worse than silly vanities.

Hacket, SERMONS, *I. P. 5. First paragraph of note on first flyleaf, recto; second, on p. 5.*

I come to the third strange condition of the Birth, it was without travel, or the pangs of woman, as I will shew you out of these words, *Fasciis involvit,* that *she wrapt him in swaddling clouts, and laid him in a Manger. Ipsa genitrix, fuit & obstetrix,* says St. *Cyprian* . . .

A very different § ph!, and quite on the *Cross* Road to Rome. It really makes me melancholy—but one of the 1000 instances of the influence of Patristic Learning, by which the Reformers of the Latin Church were distinguished from the Renovators of the Christian Religion.

Can we wonder that the strict Protestants were jealous of the Backsliding of the Arminian Prelatical Clergy & of Laud, their Leader, when so strict a Calvinist as Bishop Hackett could trick himself up in such fantastic rags and lappets of Popish Monkery?—could skewer such frippery patches, cribbed from the Tyring room of Romish Parthenolatry, on the sober gown and cassock of a Reformed and Scriptural Church!

Hacket, SERMONS, *I. P. 7. Note continued on p. 8.*

But to say the truth, was he not safer among the beasts than he could be elsewhere in all the town of *Bethlem?* His enemies perchance would say unto him, as *Jael* did to *Sisera, Turn in, turn in, my Lord,* when she purposed to kill him; as the men of *Keilah* made a fair shew to give *David* all courteous hospitality, but the issue would prove, if God had not blessed him, that they mean to deliver him into the hands of *Saul*

[2] The notes on the *Sermons* appear with some editorial emendations in *Lit. Rem.,* III, 172-83. Only such notes as relate directly to Hacket or to his period are here reprinted from the original notes in a volume in the British Museum, Ashley, 4778.

that sought his bloud. So there was no trusting of the *Bethlemites.* Who knows, but that they would have prevented *Judas,* and betrayed him for thirty pieces of Silver unto *Herod?* More humanity is to be expected from the beasts than from some men, and therefore *she laid him in a Manger.*

Did not the life of Archbp. Williams prove otherwise, I should have inferred from these Sermons, that H. from his first Boyhood had been used to make themes, epigrams, copies of verses, &c. on all the Sundays, Feasts and festivals of the Church; had found abundant nourishment for this humour of Points, Quirks, and Quiddities in the study of the Fathers and Glossers; and remained an under-Soph all his life long. I scarcely know what to say. On the one hand, there is a triflingness, a Shewman or Relique-hawker's Gossip, that stands in offensive Contrast with the momentous nature of the subject, and the dignity of the ministerial office, as if a Preacher, having chosen the Prophets for his theme should entertain his congregation by exhibiting a traditional shaving-rag of Isaiah's with the Prophet's stubble hair on the dried soap-sud. And yet on the other hand there is an innocency in it, a security of Faith, a fullness evinced in the play and plash of it's overflowing, that at other times give one the same sort of pleasure as the sight of Blackberry bushes and Children's Handkerchief-Gardens on the slopes of a rampart, the Promenade of some peaceful old town, that stood it's last siege in the 30 Years' War.

Hacket, SERMONS, *III. Luke 2: 9. P. 27. Note on first flyleaf, recto, under heading: "Sermons—noticeable passages of."*

By this it appears how suitably a beam of admirable light did concur in the *Angels* message to set out the *Majesty* of the *Son* of *God;* and I beseech you observe, all you that would keep a good *Christmas* as you ought, that the glory of *God* is the best celebration of his *Sons Nativity;* and all your pastimes and mirth (which I disallow not, but rather commend in moderate use) must so be manag'd, without riot, without surfeiting, without excessive gaming, without pride and vain pomp, in harmlessness, in sobriety, as if the glory of the *Lord* were round about us. *Christ* was born to save them that were lost, but frequently you abuse his Nativity with so many vices, such disordered outrages; so that you make this happy time an occasion for your loss rather than for your salvation. Praise him in the congregation of the people, praise him in your inward heart, praise him with the sanctity of your life, praise him in your charity to them that need and are in want. This is the glory of *God* shining round, and the most *Christian* solemnizing of the *Birth* of *Jesus.*

A pretty piece of Poetry, and as prettily worded.[3]

[3] In *Lit. Rem.,* III, 178, the comment reads: "The following paragraph is one of Hacket's sweetest passages. It is really a beautiful little hymn."

Hacket, SERMONS: THE FIRST SERMON ON THE RESURRECTION. *Acts 2: 24.*
P. 550.

Thirdly, the necessity of it, *for it was not possible that He should be holden of death.*

One great Error of Textual Divines is their inadvertence to the dates, occasion, object, and circumstances, at & under which the words were written or spoken. Then the simple assertion of one or two *Facts introductory* to the Teaching of Xtian Religion is taken as comprizing or constituting the Xtian Religion. Hence the disproportionate weight laid on the simple fact of the Resurrection of Jesus, detached from the mysteries of the Incarnation & Redemption.

Hacket, SERMONS: THE FIRST SERMON ON THE RESURRECTION. *P. 557. Note at end.*

Let any competent Judge read Hackett's Life of Archbishop Williams, and then these Sermons—and so measure the stultifying, nugifying effect of the Study of the Fathers, and the prepossession in favor of Patristic Authorities on the minds of many of our Church Dignitaries general, in the reign of Charles I.[4]

But would you have a Protestant instance of the superstitious use of Scripture arising out of this dogma? Passing by the Cabala of the Hutchinsonian School as the dotage of a few weak-minded individuals, I refer you to Bishop Hacket's Sermons on the Incarnation. And if you have read the same author's Life of Archbishop Williams, and have seen and felt (as every reader of this latter work must see and feel,) his talent, learning, acuteness, and robust good sense, you will have no difficulty in determining the quality and character of a dogma, which could engraft such fruits on such a tree.[5]

What a delightful and instructive book Bishop Hacket's Life of Archbishop Williams is! You learn more from it of that which is valuable towards an insight into the times preceding the Civil War, than from all the ponderous histories and memoirs now composed about that period.[6]

Hacket, SCRINIA RESERATA,[7] *first flyleaf, verso.*

[4] In *Lit. Rem.,* III, 183, this passage is modified to the extent that the meaning is somewhat changed.
[5] *Confessions,* pp. 51-52.
[6] June 22, 1833. *Table Talk S,* p. 459.
[7] *Scrinia Reserata: A Memorial Offer'd to the Great Deservings of John Williams, D.D.* (1693). British Museum, Ashley, 4779. This book has Gillman's bookplate. Since some notes were omitted from *Lit. Rem.* (see III, 183-202) and others were modified, the notes are reprinted in full from the original.

Prudence installed *as* Virtue, instead of being *employed,* as one of her indispensable Handmaids this the character of the Divines & Statesmen from Henry VIIIth to the Civil War—& the products of this exemplified & illustrated in the Life of Archbishop Williams—is a Work, I could warmly recommend to my dearest Hartley Coleridge. A man bred up to the determination of being *righteous,* both honorably striving, and selfishly ambitious, but all within the bounds & permission of the *Law* (even the reigning system of Casuistry)—in short, a *Legalist* in Morals, and a Worldling in impulses & motives—and yet by pride and innate nobleness of Nature munificent, and benevolent—with all the negative virtues of temperance, chastity, &c.,—take this man on his road to his own worldy aggrandizement, thredding his way thro' a crowd of powerful Rogues, by flattery, professions of devoted attachment, and by actual & Zealous as well as able Services, till at length he has in fact been as great a knave, as the Knaves (Duke of Buckingham, ex. gr.) whose favor & support he had been conciliating—till at last in some dilemma, some strait between Conscience & Fear, and increased confidence in his own political strength, he opposes or hesitates to further some too foolish or wicked project of his Patron Knave, or affronts his pride by counselling a different course (*not* as less wicked but as *more* profitable & conducive to his Grace's Elevation), and is floored or crushed by him, & falls unknown & unpitied—Such that truly wonderful Schol[ar] and Statesman, Archb. Williams. S. T. C.

Hacket, SCRINIA RESERATA, *Part I, sec. 61, p. 50. Note on first flyleaf, verso.*

And God forbid that any other Course should be Attempted. For this Liberty was settled on the Subject, with such Imprecations upon the Infringers, that if they should remove these great Land-Marks, they must look for Vengeance, as if Entail'd by publick Vows on them and their Posterity. These were the Deans Instructions . . .

What a damning Contrast to the despotic Philodespot Laud.[8]

Hacket, SCRINIA RESERATA, *Part I, sec. 80, p. 69. Letter in behalf of the Earl of Southhampton and of John Selden.*

What true Applause and Admiration the King and your Honour have gained for that gracious and most Christian-like Remorse shewed the E. of Southampton . . .

All this *we* (1833) should call abject, base; but was it so in Bp. Williams? In the History of the Morality of a People, Prudence, yea,

[8] In *Lit. Rem.,* III, 184, the comment is toned down to read: "He deserves great credit for them. They put him in strong contrast with Laud."

Cunning, is the earliest *Form* of Virtue—Jacob, Ulysses. Then all the most ancient Fables.

It will require the true philosophic Calm and Serenity to distinguish and appreciate the character of the Morality, of our great men—from Henry 8th to the close of James I—(the motto, nullum numen abest, si sit *Prudentia*) and of that of Charles I to the Restoration. The difference almost amounts to contrast.

Hacket, SCRINIA RESERATA, *Part I, secs. 81-82, pp. 70-71.*

How is it that so deeply read Historian, as Southey is,[9] should not have seen, how imperfect and precarious the rights of personal Liberty were, during this period? or seeing it, do such scanty Justice to the Patriots under Charles I.? The truth is, that from the reign of Edward I. (to go no farther backward) there was a Spirit of freedom in the people at large, which all our Kings in their senses were cautious not to awaken by too rudely treading on it; but for Individuals, as such, there was none till the Conflict with the Stuarts.

Hacket, SCRINIA RESERATA, *Part I, sec. 84, p. 72.*

Of such a Conclusion of State (*quæ aliquando incognita, semper justa*), . . .

This perversion of words respecting the decrees of Providence to the caprices of James and his *beslobbered* Minion, the D. of B., is somewhat nearer to Blasphemy, than even the *Euphuism* of the Age can excuse.

Hacket, SCRINIA RESERATA, *Part I, sec. 85, p. 73.*

Nor, *Tuus, O Jacobe, quod optas Explorare labor, mihi jussa capessere fas est.*

In our times this would be pedantic Wit: in the days of James I. & in the mouth of Archb. Williams it was witty Pedantry. S. T. C.

Hacket, SCRINIA RESERATA, *Part I, sec. 89, p. 75. Note at top of p. 75.*

Our time is but a Span long, but he that doth much in a short Life products his mortality.

Mem. "products" for "produces"—i. e. lengthens out—*ut apud geometros*—but why Bp. Hacket did not say "prolongs" I know not. [*percussio,* corrected to, *percursio*]

Hacket, SCRINIA RESERATA, *Part I, sec. 89, p. 75. First part of note is on first flyleaf, recto; second part is on bottom p. 75.*

See what a Globe of Light there is in natural Reason, which is the same

⁹ The reference to Southey is omitted in *Lit. Rem.*

in every Man; but when it takes well, and riseth to perfection, it is call'd Wisdom in a few.

Common Sense in an uncommon degree is what the world calls Wisdom.

The GOOD affirming itself the WILL ($=$ I AM) begetteth the TRUE: and Wisdom is the Spirit proceeding. But in the popular acceptation of the word, Common Sense in an uncommon degree is what Men mean by Wisdom.[10]

Hacket, SCRINIA RESERATA, *Part I, sec. 92, p. 79.*

> A well-spirited Clause, and agreeable to Holy Assurance, that Truth is more like to win, than lose. Could the light of such a Gospel as we profess be eclips'd with the Interposition of a single Marriage?

And yet Hacket must have lived to see the practical confutation of this shallow Gnathonism in the results of the marriage with the papist, Henrietta of France!

Hacket, SCRINIA RESERATA, *Part I, sec. 96, p. 83.*

> *Floud,* says the Lord Keeper, *since I am no Bishop in your Opinion, I will be no Bishop to you.*

I see the *wit* of this Speech; but the *Wisdom,* the *Christianity,* the *beseemingness in a Judge and a Bishop?* Hem![11]

Hacket, SCRINIA RESERATA, *Part I, sec. 96, p. 83.*

> And after the Period of his Presidency [of the Star Chamber], it is too well known how far the Enhancements were stretch'd. *But the wringing of the Nose bringeth forth blood,* Prov. 30. 33.

Southey[12] might have learnt from this and 50 other passages, that it did not require the factious prejudices of Prynne or Burton to look with aversion on the proceedings of Laud. Bp. Hacket was as hot a *royalist* as a *loyal* Englishman could be, yet Laud was *allii nimis.*

Hacket, SCRINIA RESERATA, *Part I, sec. 97, p. 84. Note continued on top of p. 85.*

> New Stars have appear'd and vanish'd; the ancient Asterisms remain, there's not an old Star missing.

If they had, they would not have been old. This therefore, like many of Lord Bacon's illustrations, have [*sic*] more wit than meaning. But it is a good trick of Rhetoric. The vividness of the Image, *per se,* makes men overlook the imperfection of the Simile: "You see my *Hand*—the

---

[10] The comment in *Lit. Rem.* is from the flyleaf only.

[11] In *Lit. Rem.* the exclamation is translated, "What am I to say of that?"

[12] In *Lit. Rem.* a general "we" is substituted for Southey's name.

hand of a poor puny fellow-mortal: and will you pretend not to see the hand of Providence in this business? He who sees a mouse, must be wilfully blind if he does not see an Elephant.''

Hacket, SCRINIA RESERATA, *Part I, sec. 100, pp. 87-8.*

> To Be subject to the Higher Powers, is a constant and a general Rule; and Reason can discern, that the Supreme Majesty, which unquestionably is in our King, is inviolable. . . .

The Error of the first James, an ever well-intending, well-resolving, but alas! ill-performing Monarch, a kindhearted, affectionate, and fondling old Man, really and extensively learned, yea, and as far as quick Wit, and a shrewd Judgement go to the making up of Wisdom, wise in his generation, and a pedant by the right of pedantry, conceded at the time to all men of Learning, (Bacon, for example) his Error, I say, consisted in the notion, that because the Stalk and Foliage were originally contained in the Seed, and were derived from it, therefore they remained so in point of right after their Evolution. The Kingly Power was the Seed: the H. of Commons and the municipal Charters and Privileges the Stalk & Foliage; the Unity of the Realm, or what we mean by the Constitution, is the Root. Meanwhile the Seed is gone, and reappears as the Crown and glorious Flower of the Plant.[13] But James was an Angel compared with his Son and Grandsons, As Williams to Laud, so James I. to Charles I. S. T. C.

Hacket, SCRINIA RESERATA, *Part I, sec. 102, p. 90.*

> Restraint is not a Medicine to cure epidemical Diseases; for Sin becomes more sinful by the *Occasion* of the Law.

A most Judicious Remark.

Hacket, SCRINIA RESERATA, *Part I, sec. 103, p. 92. Note continued on p. 93.*

> This Blessed King, in all the time I serv'd him, did never, out of deep and just reason of State, and of the bitter Necessity of Christendom, in these latter Times, give way to any the least Connivance in the World towards the Person of a Papist.

It is clear to us, that this illegal or præter legal & desultory toleration by connivance at particular cases; this precarious clemency de-

---

[13] Compare a similar passage of May 15, 1833. *Table Talk S,* p. 455: ''James the First thought that, because all power in the State seemed to proceed *from* the crown, all power therefore remained *in* the crown;—as if, because the tree sprang from the seed, the stem, branches, leaves, and fruit were all contained in the seed. The constitutional doctrine as to the relation which the king bears to the other components of the State is in two words this—He is the representative of the whole of that, of which he is himself a part.''

pending on the momentary mood of the King, and this is a stretch of questioned Prerogative, could neither satisfy nor conciliate the Catholic Potentates abroad but was sure to offend, and alarm the Protestants at home. But on the other hand, it is unfair as well as unwise to censure the men of an age for want of that which was above their age. The true principles, much more the practicable Rules of Toleration, were in James's time obscure to the wisest—but to the many, Laity no less than Clergy, would have been denounced as Soul-murder and disguised Atheism. In fact, and a melancholy fact it is, *Toleration* then first becomes practicable, when *Indifference* has deprived it of all merit. S. T. C. N.B. In the same spirit I excuse the opposite party, the Puritans and *Papaphobists.*

Hacket, SCRINIA RESERATA, *Part I, sec. 104, p. 93.*

> For because he was principally employ'd by his Office to distribute the King's Favours to some the adverse Sect, he was Traduc'd for a Well-willer to the Church of *Rome.* . . .

It was scarcely to be expected that the passions of James's Age would allow of this wise distinction between Papists, the intriguing restless Partizans of a foreign Potentáte, and simple Catholics who preferred the Mumpsimus of their Grandsire to the corrected Sumpsimus of the Reformation! But that in our age this distinction should have been neglected in the calamitious Catholic Bill!

Hacket, SCRINIA RESERATA, *Part I, sec. 105, p. 94. Note on flyleaf, recto.*

> But this invisible Consistory shall be confusedly diffused over all the Kingdom, that many of the Subjects shall to the intolerable exhausting of the Wealth of the Realm, pay double Tithes, double Offerings, and double Fees, in regard of their double Consistory. And if *Ireland* be so poor, as it is suggested, I hold, under Correction, that this invisible Consistory is the principal Cause of the exhausting thereof.

Memorable remark on the evil of the double Priesthood in Ireland.

Hacket, SCRINIA RESERATA, *Part I, sec. 105, p. 94. First part of note on first flyleaf; second part at bottom of p. 94.*

> "Doctor *Bishop* the New Bishop of *Chalcedon,* is come to London privately, and I am much troubled at it, not knowing what to Advise his Majesty as things stand at this present. If you were Shipped with the *Infanta,* the only Counsel were to let the Judges proceed with him presently; Hang him out of the way, and the King to blame my lord of Canterbury or my self for it." Surely this doth not savour of addiction to the Purple-Hat, or the Purple-Harlot.

Striking instance & illustration of the *tricksy* policy which in the 16th Century [*sic*] passed for State-wisdom even with the comparatively wise. But there must be a *Ulysses* before there can be an Aristides and Phocion.

Poor King James's main errors arose out of his superstitious notions of a Sovereignty inherent in the Person—having a sacred Person, tho' in all other respects a very Devil. Hence his yearning for the Spanish Match—& the ill effects of his Toleration became rightly attributed by his subjects to foreign influence—tho' against his own acknowledged Principle, not *on* a Principle.

Hacket, SCRINIA RESERATA, *Part I, sec. 107, p. 96.*

> Four Scholars he Added to the 40 *Alumni* in the College of *Westminster.* For their *Advancement* he provided, and endowed four Scholarships in St. *John's* College, upon their Maturity and Vacancy of those places to be Translated to them. Two Fellowships he Newly Erected in that House, into which only out of those four the best were to be chosen.

I have at times played with the thought that our Bishoprics, like Fellowships, might advantageously be Confined to Single Men if only it were more openly declared to be on grounds of public Expediency;—on no supposed moral superiority of the Single State.

Hacket, SCRINIA RESERATA, *Part I, sec. 108, p. 97. Reference noted on flyleaf [to "High Court Commission"].*

Hacket, SCRINIA RESERATA, *Part I, sec. 108, p. 98.*

> That a Rector, or Vicar, had not only an Office in the Church, but a Free-hold for Life by the Common Law, in his Benefice.

O if Archbishop W. had but seen in clear view what he indistinctly saw, viz. the essential distinction of the Nationality, and it's Trustees and Holders—& the Christian Church and it's Ministers!

Hacket, SCRINIA RESERATA, *Part I, sec. 111, p. 103.*

> I will represent him [the archbishop of Spolato] in a Line or two, that he was as indifferent, or rather dissolute in Practice, as in Opinion. For in the same *Cap. Ar.* 35. this is his Nicolaitan Doctrine. *A pluralitate uxorum natura humana non abhorret; imo fortasse neque ab earum communitate.* Thus leaving all Differences of Religion *indeterminat, & in vago,* he thought it would be his great Honour to be the Conciliator of Christendom.

How so? The words mean only, that the human Animal was not withheld by any natural instinct from plurality or even community of females. It is not asserted that Reason and Revelation do not forbid both the one and the other: or that Man unwithheld would not be a Yahoo, morally inferior to the Swallow. The Emphasis is to be layed, on "natura," not on "humana," i. e. *Humanity* forbids plural and promiscuous intercourse, not however by the *animal* nature of man but by the Reason and Religion that constitute his moral and spiritual Nature. S. T. C.

Hacket, SCRINIA RESERATA, *Part I, sec. 112, p. 104.*

But being thrown out into Banishment, and hunted to be destroy'd as a Partridge in the Mountain, he subscrib'd against his own Hand, which yet did not prejudice *Athanasius* his Innocency.

I have ever said this of Sir John Cheke. I regard his recantation, as one of the *cruelties* suffered by him & later the guilt flying off from him and settling on his Persecutors.

Hacket, SCRINIA RESERATA, *Part I, sec. 151, p. 143.*

I conclude therefore, that his Highness having admitted nothing in these Oaths or Articles, either to the prejudice of the true, or the Equalizing, or Authorizing of the other Religion, but contained himself wholly within the limits of Penal Statutes, and connivences [*sic*] wherein the Estate hath ever Challenged and Usurped a directing Power, hath Subscribed no one Paper of all these against his own, nor (I profess it openly) against the Dictamen of my Conscience.

Three points wanting to render the L. K.'s argument airtight—First, the proof that a King of E. even then had a right to dispense, not with the execution in individual cases of the Laws, but with the Laws themselves in *omne futurum*—i. e. to repeal Laws by his own Act. 2. The proof that such a Tooth & Talon-drawing of the Laws, did not endanger the equalizing and final Mastery of the unlawful Religion— 3. The utter want of all reciprocity on the part of the Spanish Monarch. In short, it is pardonable in Hacket but would be contemptible in any other person, not to see this advice of the Lord Keeper's as a black Blotch on his character both as a Protestant Bishop and as a Councillor of State in a free & protestant Country. S. T. C.

Hacket, SCRINIA RESERATA, *Part I, sec. 152, p. 144.*

Yet Opinions were so various . . .

Was it not required of, at all events usual, for all present at a Council to subscribe their Names to the Act of the Majority? There is a modern case in point—that of Sir Arthur Wellesley's (now Duke of Wellington's) signature to the infamous Convention of Cintra.

Hacket, SCRINIA RESERATA, *Part I, sec. 164, p. 157.*

For to forbid Judges against their Oath, and Justices of Peace (sworn likewise) not to execute the Law of the Land, is a thing unprecedented in this Kingdom. *Durus sermo,* a harsh and bitter Pill to be digested upon a suddain, and without some Preparation.

What a fine india-rubber Conscience Hackett as well as his Patron, must have had! "Policy with Innocency, Cunning with Conscience," head up the Dance to the tune of Tantara Rogues all!

Hacket, SCRINIA RESERATA, *Part I, sec. 198, p. 192.*

I can scarcely conceive a greater difficulty, than for an honest, warm-hearted man of principle, of the present day, so to discipline his mind by reflection on the circumstances, and received moral system of the Stewartan's Age (from Eliz. to the Death of Charles I.), and it's *place* in the spiral line of Ascension, as to be able to regard the D. of B. & Charles the 1st as not *Villains:* and to resolve their acts into passions, consciences warped and hardened by half-truths, and the secular creed of Prudence, as *being* Virtue, instead of one of her handmaids, when interpreted by minds constitutionally & by their accidental circumstances imprudent, rash yet fearful and suspicious; & with Casuists and Codes of Casuistry as their Conscience-Leaders! One of the favorite works, of Charles the I. who died a martyr to his vice of Lying, & Perfidy,[14] was Sanderson *de Juramento* (1655). S. T. Coleridge.

Hacket, SCRINIA RESERATA, *Part I, sec. 200, p. 194. Note continued on p. 195.*

> Wherefore he waives the strong and full defence he had made upon the stopping of an Original Writ, and depreciates all offence by that Maxim of the Law, which admits of a mischief rather than an inconvenience. Which, was as much as to say, That he thought it a far less Evil, to do the Lady the probability of an Injury (in her own sense) than to suffer those two Courts to clash together again, and fall into a new Dispute about their Jurisdiction, which might have produc'd a publick inconvenience, which is most carefully to be avoided.

A tangle of Sophisms. The assumption is that it is better to inflict a private wrong than a public one—We ought to wrong one rather than many. But even then it is badly stated. The principle is true only when the tolerating of the private wrong is the only means of preventing a greater public wrong. But in this case it was the *certainty* of the wrong of one to avoid the *chance* of an *inconvenience* that MIGHT, perchance, be the occasion of wrong to many, and which inconvenience both easily *might* and should, have been remedied by rightful means—by mutual agreement between the Bishop & Chancellor, or by the King, or by an Act of Parliament.

---

[14] The comment on Charles was omitted in *Lit. Rem.*

Hacket, SCRINIA RESERATA, *Part I, sec. 203, p. 198.* *Note continued on p. 199.*

"Truly, Sir, this is my Dark Lanthorn, and I am not asham'd to inquire of a *Dalilah* to Resolve a Riddle; for in my Studies of Divinity I have glean'd up this Maxim, *licet uti alieno peccato;* though the Devil make her a Sinner, I may make good use of her Sin." *Yea*, says the Prince, Merrily, *do you deal in such Ware?* In good Faith, Sir, *says the Keeper*, I never saw her Face.

And Hacket's evident *admiration*, and not merely approbation, of this base Jesuitry! this *Divinity* had taught the Archb^p. licet uti alieno peccato! But Charles himself was a student of *such* Divinity, & yet (as Rogues of a higher rank comfort the *pride* of their Conscience by despising inferior Knaves) I suspect, that the "merrily" was the Sardonic Mirth of bitter Contempt but only because he *disliked* Williams, who was simply a man of his Age—his *base*ness for us, not for his contemporaries or even for his own mind! But the worst of all is the Archbishop's heartless disingenuousness and moon-like *Nodes* towards his kind Old Master the King. How much of *truth* was there in the Spaniard's information respecting the intrigues of the Prince & the Duke of Buckingham? If none, if they were mere Slanders, if the Prince acted the filial part, toward his Father & King, and the Duke the faithful part towards his Master & only too fond and affectionate Benefactor, what more was needed, than to expose the falsehoods? But if Williams knew that there was too great a mixture of truth in the charges, what a cowardly Ingrate to his old Friend to have thus curried favor with the Rising Sun by this base jugglery!

Hacket, SCRINIA RESERATA, *Part I, sec. 209, p. 203.*

He was the Top-sail of the Nobility, and in Power and Trust of Offices far above all Nobility.

James I. was no Fool; and tho' thro' weakness of character an unwise Master, yet not an unthinking Statesman; and I still want a satisfactory solution of the accumulation of offices on the D. of B.

Hacket, SCRINIA RESERATA, *Part I, sec. 212, p. 206.*

Prudent Men will continue the Oblations of their Forefathers Piety. They were ever readier to supply the publick need in the Custody of the Church, than in the Maws of Cormorants. . . .

The danger and mischief of going far back, & yet not half far enough! Thus Williams refers to the Piety of Individuals, our Forefathers, as the origin of Church Property. Had he gone further back & traced to the Source, he would have found these partial Benefactions to have been mere restitutions of Rights co-original with their Property, and as a *National preserve* for thos[e] purposes of *National* Existence the *conditio sine quâ non* of the equity of their *Proprieties:* for without Civilization a People cannot be or continue to be a Nation. But alas! the ignorance of the essential distinction of a National Clerisy, the Enclesia, from the Christian Church, the Ecclesia, has been the Eclipse to the intellect of both Churchmen & Sectarians even from Elizabeth to the present day, 1833.

Hacket, SCRINIA RESERATA, *Part I, sec. 214, p. 208.*

> And being threatened, his best Mitigation was, That perhaps it was not safe for him to deny so great a Lord, yet it was safest for his Lordship to be Denied . . . The King heard the noise of these Crashes, and was so pleas'd, that he thank'd God, before many Witnesses, that he had put the Keeper into that Place: For, says he, *He that will not wrest Justice for Buckingham's Sake, whom I know he Loves, will never be corrupted with Money, which he never lov'd.*

Strange it must seem to us. Yet it is evident that Hacket thought it necessary to raise a mid something, half apology & half eulogy, for the Lord Keeper's timid half-resistance to the insolence & iniquitous interference of the minion Duke! What a portrait of the times!

Hacket, SCRINIA RESERATA, *Part I, sec. 214, p. 208.*[15]

> And because the Lord Keeper had husbanded that Stock Three Years and a half, and lived fairly upon it, and was not the Richer by the sale of one Cursitors Place in all that time, His Majesty Granted him a Suit, by the Name of a New-Years-Gift, after the size of the Liberality of that Good Master, which was enough to keep a Bountiful *Christmas* twice over.

But the dotage of the King in his maintenance of the Man, whose insolence in wresting Justice he himself admits! But how many points, both of the Times, and of the King's personal character, must be brought together before we can fairly solve the intensity of James's Minionism, his kingly Egotism, his weak kind-heartedness, his vulgar coarseness of temper, his systematic jealousy of the ancient Nobles, his timidity &c. &c.

Hacket, SCRINIA RESERATA, *Part I, sec. 214, pp. 208-9. Note on p. 209.*

> His Majesty bemarked that his Grandchildren, then Young and Tender, would be very chargeable to *England* when they grew to be Men . . . If they fall to their studies [advised Williams] design them to the Bishopricks of *Durham* and *Winchester* when they become void . . . The office of Bishop . . . will be more inviolable, when the Branches

---

[15] This is a separate note, not combined with the above as it appears in *Lit. Rem.*

of Your Royal Stock have so great an Interest in it. And such *Provision* is Needful against Schismatical Attempts, both for Religions Sake, and the Publick Weal.

Williams could not have been in earnest in this villainous counsel; but he knew his man. This conceit of dignifying dignities by the simonical Institution of them to Blood Royal was just suited to James's Fool-Cunningness.

Hacket, SCRINIA RESERATA, *Part II, sec. 74, p. 75.*

The body of the Doctrin [*sic*] is worst of all, that it concerns us upon our Loyalty, nay, upon our Salvation (for else Damnation is threatned) to yield not only Passive Obedience (which is due) but Active also . . .

What in the name of common Sense can this mean, i. e. speculatively? *Practically,* the meaning is clear enough, viz. that we should do what we can, so as to escape hanging. But the distinction is for Decorum, so let it pass.

Hacket, SCRINIA RESERATA, *Part II, sec. 75, p. 76.*

This is the Venom of this new Doctrine, that by making us the King's Creatures, and in the state of Minors, or Children, to take away all our Propriety: Which would leave us nothing of our own, and lead us (but that God hath given us just and gracious Princes) into Slavery.

And yet this just and gracious Prince prompts, sanctions, supports and openly rewards this Envenomer, in flat contempt of both Houses of Parliament,—protects and prefers him and others of the same principles and professions on account of these professions! And the Parliament and Nation were inexcusable, forsooth, in not trusting in this man's assurances, or rather the assurances put into his Mouth by Hyde, Falkland, &c., that he had always abhorred these principles!

Hacket, SCRINIA RESERATA, *Part II, sec. 136, p. 144. Note on first flyleaf, recto.*

When they saw he was not Selfish (it is a word of their own new Mint). . .

Singular! From this passage I learn that our so very common word "selfish" is no older than the latter part of the reign of Ch. I.

Hacket, SCRINIA RESERATA, *Part II, sec. 137, p. 145.*

Their (the Presbyterians) politick Aphorisms are far more dangerous, that His Majesty is not the highest Power in his Realms; That he hath not absolute Soveraignty; That a Parliament sitting is co-ordinate with him in it: He may have the title only of Supreme, yet a Senate have an essential part without the Name . . .

He himself repeatedly implies as much: for would he deny that the King with the Lords and Commons is not more than the King without them? or that an act of Parliament is more than a Proclamation!

Hacket, SCRINIA RESERATA, *Part II, sec. 154, p. 161. Note on first flyleaf, recto.*

> What a venomous Spirit is in that Serpent *Milton* . . . a petty School-boy Scribbler, that durst graple in such a Cause with the Prince of the learned men of his Age, Salmasius . . .

A contemporary of Bishop Hackett's designates Milton as the Author of a profane and *lascivious* Poem, entitled Paradise Lost. The Biographers of our divine Bard ought to have made a collection of such passages. A German Biographer in a Life of Salmasius acknowledges that Milton had the better in the conflict in these words: Hans (i. e. Jack) von Milton, not to be compared in Learning and *Genius* with the incomparable Salmasius, yet a shrewd and cunning Lawyer &c.—O sana Posteritas!

Hacket, SCRINIA RESERATA, *Part II, sec. 174, p. 188.*[16]

> Paper Mercuries, well worded, are fine things, but not forcible.

Certainly not for a man who had & was known to have, the incurable vice of Lying. [i. e., Charles]

Hacket, SCRINIA RESERATA, *Part II, sec. 174, p. 188.*

> And to speak to common Reason and Charity, a man whose Paths were Piety, his Governance, Mercy, his Bed Chastity, his Repast Sobriety, his Addresses Humility, how could he set a Ditty to any other Prick'd-Song, but the Tune of Peace?

"Piety"   Jesuitry?
"Mercy"   Nose-slitting & Ear-cropping?
"Chastity"   uxorious dotage?
"Humility"   Duplicity?

Hacket, SCRINIA RESERATA, *Part II, sec. 175, p. 188.*

> What Pardon can we expect from the Censure of a better Age, that we did not stop the Fury of Malcontents, before any drop of Blood was shed? I appeal to Fidelity, Homage, Duty, why did we not instantly raise an Host of Horse and Foot, which Rebels would not dare to encounter?

We! i. e. the Bishops, about a third of the Clergy, & about a third of the Gentry—these decided Kingsmen; add another third of the

---

[16] This and the next two notes do not appear in *Lit. Rem.*

Gentry, desirous to impose even terms on both parties—*They* i. e. 9/10ths of all the rest of the Island. Why did not *we?* Why, because THEY would not let WE.

Hacket, SCRINIA RESERATA, *Part II, sec. 178, p. 191.*

> Dare they not trust him that never broke with them? And I have heard his nearest Servants say, That no man could ever challenge him of the least Lye?

The impudence of this assertion after the publication of Charles's Letters to his Wife! Not a month before his Execution he signed three contradictory treaties with three different parties, meaning to keep neither—and at length died with a Lie—viz. the making himself the Author of Gauden's *Icon. Basil.*[17]

Hacket, SCRINIA RESERATA, *Part II, sec. 180, p. 193.*

> If an Under-sheriff had arrested *Harry Martin* for Debt, and pleaded that he did not imprison his Membership, but his *Martin*-ship, would the Committee for Priviledges be fob'd off with that distinction?

To make this good in analogy, we must suppose that Harry Martin had notoriously neglected all the duties while he perverted and abused all the privileges of Membership: and then I answer, that the Committee of Privileges would have done well and wisely in accepting the Under-sheriff's Distinction, and out of respect for the Membership consigning the *Martin*ship to the due course of Law.

Hacket, SCRINIA RESERATA, *Part II, sec. 180, p. 193.*

> The higher Power under which they lived, was the meer Power and Will of *Cæsar,* bridled in by no Law.

False, if meant *de jure;* and if *de facto,* the plural "powers" would apply to the Parliament far better than, and to Cromwell as well as, to Nero. Every even decently good Emperor professed himself the Servant of the Roman Senate—the very term Imperator as Gravina[18] observes, implies it—for it expresses a delegated and instrumental power. Before the assumption of the Tribunitial character by Augustus, by which he became the representative of the Majority of the People—majestatem

---

[17] In *Lit. Rem.,* III, 201, the note is greatly modified: "What! this after the publication of Charles's letters to the Queen! Did he not within a few months before his death enter into correspondence with, and sign contradictory offers to, three different parties, not meaning to keep any one of them; and at length did he not die with something very like falsehood in his mouth in allowing himself to be represented as the author of the Icon Basilike?"

[18] Giovanni Vincenzo Gravina (1664-1718), author of *De Romano imperio* (1712) and *Origines juris civilis* (3 vols.; 1713).

indutus est—"Senatus consulit, Populus jubet, imperant Consules" was
the constitutional language.

Hacket, Scrinia Reserata, *Part II, sec. 190, p. 204.*

Yet so much dissonancy there was between his Tongue and his Heart,
that he (Tully) triumpht in the murder of *Cæsar,* the only *Roman*
that exceeded all their Race in nobleness and was next to Tully in eloquence. Boast not therefore in Success, which is an advantage to make
Infidels proud: but the abstruse ways of God's Providence, which setteth
up one, and pulleth down another, as he pleaseth, should make us Christians triumph.

There is something so shameless in this self-contradiction, as of itself
to extinguish the charitable Belief, that the Prelatic Royalists were mistaken Reasoners but yet conscientious in their conclusions. For if the
Senate of Rome were not a lawful Power, what could be? and if Cæsar,
the thrice perjur'd Traitor, was neither perjured nor traitor only because he by his Gaulish troops turned a Republic into an arbitrary
Monarchy—with what face, under what pretext, could Hacket abuse
"Sultan Cromwell"?

Hacket, Scrinia Reserata, *Part II, sec. 191, p. 205.*[19]

Treasurers of the Army, Excise-men, Collectors of Taxes, Victuallers
of the Navy, Committee-men, with their Scribes, Officers of all sorts,
abundance of decayed Fortunes, nay Scoundrels, not worth a Groat
before, are swell'd into vast Estates, progging and prowling every way
in purveyance for themselves. . . . So sensible are all men of this
fatal and general empoverishing . . .

What childish womanish contradictions! A Kingdom consists of
A B C X Y Z—Yesterday A B C were rich—today X Y Z—Ergo the Kingdom is impoverished!! Of all the Benefactors *for* whom G. Britain
ought to thank God, James the second stands foremost—Had not his
bigotry made free with the property and exclusive privileges of these
Priests, nothing could [have] saved us from Despotism—The Church
of England detested every form of Freedom.

[19] This note does not appear in *Lit. Rem.*

Peter Heylyn

Heylyn, LIFE OF ARCHBISHOP LAUD,[1] *"A Necessary Introduction," p. 5.*

6. But though the *Presbyters* or *Priests*, were both in *Order* and *Degree* beneath the *Bishops*, and consequently not enabled to exercise any publick Jurisdiction in *Foro judicii*, in the Courts of Judicature: yet they retained their native and original power in *Foro Conscientiæ* in the Court of Conscience, by hearing and confession of a sorrowful and afflicted *Penitent*, and giving him the comfort of *Absolution*, a power conferred upon them in their *Ordination*.

I profess, I do not see any injurious or superstitious consequence of this. Either it *is* or it is *not*, a Sin in the Sight of God—if it is, and the Sinner is impenitent, assuredly his resistance to the admonition of God's appointed Minister is an aggravation: if not, then there is no Sin to be retained. It is merely a mistaken, or uncharitable opinion of the Priest, for which He alone must answer. S. T. C.

Heylyn, LIFE OF ARCHBISHOP LAUD, *"A Necessary Introduction," p. 6. Note continued on top of p. 7.*

Confession made upon such security will be as saving to the *Fame* of the Penitent, as the *Absolution* to his Soul. In which respect it was neither untruly nor unfitly said by a learned Writer, *Dominus sequitur servum*, &c. Heaven (saith he) waits and expects the Priests Sentence here on Earth; for the Priest sits Judge on Earth, the Lord follows the Servant: and what the Servant binds or looseth here on Earth (*Clave non errante*) that the Lord confirms in Heaven.

Clave non errante. If this have any meaning, it means, I presume, that if the Lord was of the same opinion before, this opinion would not be altered by the Priest's expressing the same. Has Christ entrusted every thing to a Bishop *needful for Salvation,* which every Christian is not permitted, nay, which every Christian is not bound to *profess?*

[1] Peter Heylyn, *Cyprianus Anglicus: Or, the History of the Life and Death of the most Reverend and Renowned Prelate, William, by Divine Providence, Lord Archbishop of Canterbury* (London: 1671). British Museum, Ashley, 4776.

The notes in this volume have not previously been printed with the exception of a few selections given in Wise, *Ashley*, VIII, 104. Many of the notes are in pencil and a number of them are signed by Coleridge. On the first flyleaf, verso, is written "Wm. Arundell his book 1691," and the title page is inscribed "J. Watkins." The notes are in three hands, and some of these in ink seem to correspond to those of the two previous owners; they are clearly not in Coleridge's hand. There are no Coleridge notes after Part I, p. 178. The notes which are not by Coleridge are chiefly factual.

Who, being a Christian can avoid feeling the worldly, harsh, *unspiritual* Spirit of this bitter Factionary! I scarcely know a more unamiable Churchman, as a writer, than, Dr. Heylin. S. T. C.

Heylyn, LIFE OF ARCHBISHOP LAUD, *"A Necessary Introduction,"* p. 6. *Note continued at bottom of p. 7.*

8. The like Authority is vested in the Priest or Presbyter at his *Ordination* for officiating the Divine Service of the Church, offering the Peoples Prayers to God, Preaching the Word, and Ministring the *Holy Sacraments* in the Congregation; Which *Offices* though they may be performed by the *Bishops,* as well as the *Presbyters:* yet they perform them not as *Bishops,* but as *Presbyters* only.

How instantly all this High-Priest Mummery would be dissipated by a simple consecutive History of a single Christian Church, Rome for example, from it's first planting. In the most, the first Planter or Collector of the Church would be it's Overseer, Episcopus or Bishop: and the Presbyters would follow. In others the Elders or Presbyters would exist at and as the beginning; and a President, or Chairman, would follow.

Heylyn, LIFE OF ARCHBISHOP LAUD, *"A Necessary Introduction,"* p. 13. *Second note.*

Thirdly, That *Images* are still used in the Lutheran Churches, upon which our first Reformers had a special eye; and that Luther must have reproved Carolostadius for taking them out of such Churches, where before they had been suffered to stand.

Vide. p. 3. "No regard had to Luther"![2]—& yet too according to this High-Church Fanatic Melancthon was called by Royal Letters!

Heylyn, LIFE OF ARCHBISHOP LAUD, *"A Necessary Introduction,"* pp. 18-19. *Note continued on p. 19.*

21. The *Pope* they deprived of that unlimited Supremacy, and the Church of *Rome* of that exorbitant power, which they formerly challenged over them; yet did they neither think it fit to leave the Church without her lawful and just Authority; nor safe to put her out of the protection of the Supream Governour. Touching the first, it was resolved in the 20 Article, *"That the Church hath power not only to decree Rites and Ceremonies, but also in Controversies of Faith,* as the English, *Ecclesia habet Ritus & Ceremonias Statuendi jus, & fidei controversiis Authoritatem,* as it is in the Latin.

Surely, Dr. H. was not so mean a Scholar, as not to know, he was falsely translating the Latin words. He could not have overlooked the so obvious, so prominent Antithesis of *Jus* and *Authoritatem.* The

[2] See below, p. 228, for a long note on this passage from *Notebook* 20.

Church had full power, original *right*, on the one; and a reverend *authority* on the other. S. T. C.

Heylyn, LIFE OF ARCHBISHOP LAUD, *"A Necessary Introduction," p. 19.*

For in the 34. Article it is thus declared, "That whosoever through his private judgment willingly and purposely doth openly break the Traditions and Ceremonies of the Church, which be not repugnant unto the word of God, and be ordained and approved by common Authority, ought to be rebuked openly . . ." More power then this, as the See of *Rome* did never challenge; so less then this, was not reserved unto it self by the Church of *England*.

A Lie! resting on a lying translation and perversion of the 20th Article.

Heylyn, LIFE OF ARCHBISHOP LAUD, *"A Necessary Introduction," p. 24.*

Many of the *Calvinian* party understand nothing by Christ's *Descent* into Hell, but his *Descending* into the Grave; and then his descending into Hell will be the same with his being buried.

Was H. ignorant that this clause did not exist in the Creed till after the 6th Century? It seems to have been levelled against some heretical or infidel assertion that Christ's Death on the Cross was merely a Trance, or state of suspended animation.

Heylyn, LIFE OF ARCHBISHOP LAUD, *"A Necessary Introduction," p. 32.*

It was the Heresie of *Pelagius* to ascribe so much power to the will of man, in laying hold upon the means of his Salvation, *Ut gratiam Dei necessariam non putaret,* that he thought the Grace of God to be unnecessary, of no use at all. And *Luther* on the other side ascribed so little thereunto, that he published a Book, entitled, *De servo Arbitrio,* touching the servitude of the will; in which he held that there was no such thing as *Free-Will*.

I do not believe, that H. understood or has rightly stated Luther's opinion. If there be a *Servum Arbitrium,* then there must be an *Arbitrium*. Luther was Zealous against the pretence of a *free* will in unregenerate man.

Heylyn, LIFE OF ARCHBISHOP LAUD, *Part I, p. 58. 1611.*

And knowing how much the Peace of the Church did depend upon it, he managed a secret Correspondency with King *James* in *Scotland*, insinuating unto him the necessity of conforming the Churches of both Kingdoms in Government and Forms of Worship, and laying down a plot for restoring *Episcopacy* to that kirk, without noise or trouble: which counsel being advisedly followed by King *James* before his coming into England, was afterwards so well pursued (though not without some violent strugling [*sic*] of the *Presbyterians* of that Kingdom that on the 21. day of *October* in the year 1609. the designed Bishops of *Glasgow, Brechen,* and *Gallo-Way* received Episcopal Consecration in the Chappel of *London*-house.

And what was the final result of all this secret priestly plot? Sullen Faction thro' James's reign & the Scaffold of his Successor with Laud for his avant Courier!

Heylyn, LIFE OF ARCHBISHOP LAUD, *Part I, p. 59. 1611.*

But to go forward where we left, *Laud* was no sooner settled in the Presidentship of his Colledge, but he conceived himself advanced, one step at the least, towards a Precedency in the Church, and therefore thought it was high time to cast an eye upon the Court.

The strange manner, in which the Churchmen of this age united ascetic rigor of Life with all the wiles, intrigues, & unquietudes of worldly ambition & thirst of preferment, is highly characteristic.

Heylyn, LIFE OF ARCHBISHOP LAUD, *Part I, p. 157. 1626.*

For on that very day which gives date to the said *Instructions,* the most Learned and Reverent Bishop *Andrews,* Bishop of *Winton* and Dean of his Majesties Chappel-Royal, departed this Life at his *Episcopal* House in *Southwark* . . . A man he was of such extraordinary Abilities, that I shall rather chuse to express his character by the Pen of others than my own. Thus then says own [*sic*] of our late Historians: "This year one lost the stupendiously profound Prelate Doctor Andrews . . ."

Bishop Andrews is one & a prominent instance of the difference between the men of their age and the men of after ages, or rather of all ages. A wise, pious, and right learned man he was; but who would *now* from the perusal of his works, have guessed at these stupendous attributions. S. T. C.

Heylyn, LIFE OF ARCHBISHOP LAUD, *Part I, p. 158. 1627. Note continued p. 159, top, bottom.*

. . . amongst whom *Sibthorp,* Vicar of *Brackly* in *Northamptonshire,* advanced the Service, in a Sermon Preached by him at the Assizes for that County. *The scope of which Sermon was to justifie the Lawfulness of the general Loan, and of the Kings imposing Taxes by his own Regal Power, without consent in Parliament, and to prove, that the people in point of Conscience and Religion ought chearfully to submit to such Loans and Taxes without any opposition.*

What more can we need to Justify the Jealousy, the remonstrance & finally the active resistance of our Ancestors? The Licensing of this Passionate Sermon against the will of the Archbishop was, doubtless, a grievous misdemeanour on the part of Laud, & merited punishment. But unhappily for the Church of England—the consequences are felt

even at this day—the Bishops generally, as well as Laud, saw no difference between the French and Spanish Monarchs, and the limited King
of G. B.

Heylyn, LIFE OF ARCHBISHOP LAUD, *Part I, p. 160. 1627. Note continued top p. 161.*

> The Fleet and Forces before mentioned being in a readiness, and the
> Duke provided for the Voyage, it was not thought either safe or fit that
> the Duke himself should be so long absent, without leaving some assured
> Friend about his Majesty, by whom all practices against him might be
> either prevented or suppressed, and by whose means the Kings affections
> might be alwaies inflamed towards him; To which end *Laud* is first de-
> sired to attend his majesty to *Portsmouth* . . .

And Heylin coolly and complacently relates these damning proofs of
Laud's base creatureship to Buckingham!! And then what must not
both he & the Duke have thought of the King, who needed so much
watching! But above all floats the baseness and true priestly bitterness & worldly-mindedness of Heylin himself. And what an appetite
for persecution the Fellow had!

Heylyn, LIFE OF ARCHBISHOP LAUD, *Part I, p. 170. 1628.*

> For his Majesty looking on him [Manwaring] in that conjuncture
> as one that suffered in his cause, preferred him first to the Parsonage
> of *Stamford-Rivers* in Essex, (void not long after by the promotion
> of Montague to the See of *Chichester*) afterwards to the Deanery of
> *Worcester;* and finally to the Bishopric of St. Davids.

And yet after all this the Royalists. & (O, shame!) still existing
Partizans of the Martyr blame the Parliament for not *trusting* the King!
The Martyr?—Yes, verily; but it was to the vice of Lying.

Heylyn, LIFE OF ARCHBISHOP LAUD, *Part I, pp. 176-177. 1628. Note p.
176.*

> Taken upon suspicion, and questioned about the Murder [i. e., John
> Felton for the murder of Buckingham], he made no scruple to avow it
> as a meritorious Act, of which he had more cause to glory than to be
> ashamed; And being afterward more cunningly handled by one of his
> Majesties Chaplains (sent to him from the Court of purpose to work
> him to it) he confessed plainly and resolvedly, That he had no other
> motive to commit that Murder, but the late *Remonstrance,* in which the
> Duke had been accused for being the Cause of all the Grievances and
> Mischiefs in the Common-wealth.

The naivtè [*sic*] with which Heylin relates this, is exquisite—the
more, that he had before assigned the true cause, that Felton brooded
over the wrong he had suffered from the Duke, in being passed over in

the Service. But the Chaplain, the cunning Isaac! & sent for this very purpose!!

Heylyn, LIFE OF ARCHBISHOP LAUD, *Part I, p. 177. 1628.*

And on the other side, being well assured of that infinite anguish and disconsolation which *Laud* (his now most trusty servant) must needs suffer under, by the most barbarous Assassination of so dear a Friend, he dispatched *Elphiston* his Cup-bearer with a *gracious* Message to comfort him in those disquiets of his Soul; and on the neck of that, a Letter of his own handwriting to the same effect.

And this creature called himself a Protestant! Judge by him of his Master and Patron! It is idle to pretend that Laud's *Affections* were not towards the Papists & the papistic Government, however in some speculative points he might protestantize.

Heylyn, LIFE OF ARCHBISHOP LAUD, *Part I, p. 178. 1628.*

Upon which prudent considerations he moved his Majesty that the Book of Articles might be reprinted; and such a Declaration placed before them as might preserve them from such misconstructions as had of late been put upon them, and keep them to their literal and *Grammatical* sense.

Laud's first Act, as *"the sage"* Premier, to indulge the passions of his Faction by rekindling the theological discords!—and under what circumstances both of the King & Country! One's pity for Charles's fate is lost in one's contempt for his narrow-mindedness, and one's astonishment at his folly and infatuation. S. T. C.

Heylyn's "Necessary Intro. to his life of Laud," concerning p. 3.[3] P. 3. "No regard had to Luther or Calvin." What does this mean? Did any one of the Reformed Churches profess to look otherwise than to the Bible and the Example of the past ages? or will it be pretended by the Modern Heylins, that the Founders of the Reformation and the Framers of the Articles in England did not learn their faith from the earlier Reformers in Germany—did not correspond with them, hold their names & writings in Reverence & consult with them on all momentous matters?

"But the Archbishop knew the man"—Where is the *Proof*, what shadow of evidence had H. to assert this, that Cranmer held Calvin in other than reverence. It is a mere shameless retrojection of his own political and theological Hates on an illustrious Name of the Age before him. P. 4. all Plausible—but how are we to ascertain wherein & at

[3] Notebook 20, fol. 12 recto-13 verso; 15 recto-16 recto. Printed for the first time.

what time Rome had departed from herself, but by the Scriptures? Or if another authority be admitted, viz. that of the Roman Church itself, at what particular date did this authority cease to be rightful? But so it is, as Leighton Ser.ᵐ (Sion's Plea) observed—against the Papists the Eng. Prelates used the Puritan's arguments, and against the Puritan's the Papists—from the same staff, which they themselves had used as a Rod (i. e. against the Romanists) they fled from when thrown by the Puritans, as from a Serpent.—Is it not notorious that the favorite arguments of the Pontifical Divines (no wonder! they are their only plausible ones) are drawn from inconsistencies of Prelatic & Ceremonial Protestantism in Germany. Luther! Confessionals, his Saint's Days & his Quirks of Consubstantiation & the ubiquity of Christ's glorified Body, & in England from the pretence of the Hierarchy to a positive Power in *significant* Ceremonies? and which therefore involves an equal power in matters of Faith.

But this was in truth the great, but perhaps the providential, oversight of the First Reformers. The Corruptions of the Papal Church were so gross, that all who had received but a gleam of Truth into their hearts, were alive to the contrast between the forms and purposes of Scriptural Christianity and the nominal Christianity then enforced.— These they all condemned by conclamations. In the compleatness of their unanimity respecting this cluster of wild grapes they forgot to question each other whether in the principles, on which they severally protested against these gross abuses, they were as concordant as in the protestancy itself they were unanimous—or whether they were as concordant in the grounds, as in the act, of hostility.—On the Continent the Study of the Fathers was chiefly confined to the adherents of Rome.— Luther held them in small Reverence; but in England the Universities produced a large number of great Scholars, men of extensive Learning— who adopted the Protestant cause but were not willing to leave their superior acquirements behind them—which they considered as great guns conquered from the enemy, and which it would be their honor to turn against them—But in order to do this, it was necessary that they should be re-instated in a portion at least of their former Authority, and reverence. But how was this to be done without detracting or at least retracting, from the plenitude and all-sufficiency of the Inspired Scriptures? At the first, the solution was obvious—and to the Learned and Sober-minded among the Reformed not alone satisfactory, but justifying the claims of the Antiquarian and Patrician Divines (πατρὶ ζώντων θεολόγων) to a high Rank in the Church-Militant.

There were a larger number of Texts in the Canonical writings, to which both Parties appealed, but each according to a different interpretation. Nay, there were in what for ages has been vulgarly entitled canonical & generally received as inspired Writings, sundry Books from and against which the Reformers appealed, but which the Romanists contended to be equally unappellable with those acknowledged such by their opponents.—In both these respects, it was an argument of great force to prove, that the Protestants were indeed and literally *Reformers*, & in no respect Innovators or Subverters—that they interpreted the sacred Scriptures, as those had done who lived nearest the time of Men who taught their true meaning by an infallible Light, and while the Language in which the more important Half of the inspired Scriptures, was a living Language—and that to the Books in dispute they both gave and denied exactly what the best informed of the first ages of the Church, and the Church (i. e. Christians collectively) were unanimous in giving or denying.—This was and it could scarcely be otherwise generally satisfactory—tho' even from the beginning there were many unlearned & a few learned Protestants who were afraid of Weapons that had been in familiar use with the Enemy—They feared the Wooden Horse tho' dedicated to their own Minerva.

William Chillingworth

It is now twenty years since I read Chillingworth's book [*The Religion of Protestants, a Safe Way to Salvation*]; but certainly it seemed to me that his main position, that the mere text of the Bible is the sole and exclusive ground of Christian faith and practice, is quite untenable against the Romanists. It entirely destroys the conditions of a church, of an authority residing in a religious community, and all that holy sense of brotherhood which is so sublime and consolatory to a meditative Christian. Had I been a Papist, I should not have wished for a more vanquishable opponent in controversy. I certainly believe Chillingworth to have been in some sense a Socinian. Lord Falkland, his friend, said so in substance. I do not deny his skill in dialectics; he was more than a match for Knott to be sure.[1]

[1] July 25, 1831. *Table Talk S*, p. 361. Edward Knott (1582-1656), a Jesuit whose real name was Matthew Wilson, was the author of *Charity Maintained by Catholics*.

Chillingworth, "The Answer to the Preface" of Charity Maintained
by Catholics, *20.* AD. ¶ *13, in* Religion of Protestants, *p. 41.*²

To the third—*Whether, seeing there cannot be assigned any visible true Church distinct from the* Roman, *it follows not that she erred not fundamentally?* I say, in our sense of the word *fundamental,* it does follow; for if it be true, that there was then no Church distinct from the *Roman,* then it must be either because there was no Church at all, which we deny; or, because the *Roman* Church was the whole Church, which we also deny; or because she was a part of the whole, which we grant. And if she were a true part of the Church, then she retained those truths which were simply necessary to salvation, and held no errors which were inevitably and unpardonably destructive of it; for this is precisely necessary to constitute any man or any church a member of the Church Catholic. In our sense therefore of the word *fundamental,* I hope she erred not fundamentally; but in your sense of the word, I fear she did; that is, she held something to be Divine Revelation, which was not—something not to be, which was.

If idolatry in both its kinds (*i. e.* worshipping the supreme God under an image, and worshipping subordinate gods); if asserting the merits of creatures so as, though not avowedly, to deny, yet, effectively to make vain the sole redemption by, and mediation of, Christ; if the undermining of the one great purpose of the Gospel, by holding out substitutes for *regeneration* (*i. e.* the practical hatred of sin for its exceeding sinfulness) by doctrines of attrition, priestly absolution as operant *in se,* and not merely declaratory; finally, if a general corruption of the moral sense, produced and favoured by the whole compages of its *distinguishing* doctrines and ceremonies, added to a bold alternation and repeal of divine commands, and additions equally bold— as in the Eucharist, in one kind only—the dogmas concerning marriage, purgatory, &c. &c., if these be not *fundamental* errors, what can be? If they be, the Romish Church is *fundamentally* erroneous, therefore *heretical;* and Chillingworth seems to play at fast and loose. Indeed I cannot but regard it as a proof of the [prevalency of] Low-Church Lockian Faction, that this author is extolled as the Ἀρχασπιστὴς *Ecclesiæ Anglicanæ,* and Stillingfleet's most masterly work (A Rational Account, &c.) forgotten or neglected.³

² *The Religion of Protestants, a Safe Way To Salvation, or an Answer to a Booke Entituled Mercy and Truth or Charitie Maintained by Catholiques,* in *Works* (London: 1742).

³ *Notes Theolog.,* p. 74. Because of the theological detail in the notes on Chillingworth only the first and the last notes are included here. Another volume of the same date (from Lord Coleridge's library and now in the British Museum) contains entirely different notes by Coleridge.

Chillingworth, RELIGION OF PROTESTANTS, *p. 383.*

April 23, 1809.

I have been disappointed in this work, which, however, has confirmed my convictions concerning Mr. Locke's taste and judgment.— *Similis simili gaudet.* I have stated my opinion of Chillingworth's great inferiority to Stillingfleet's volume on the same plan—it is great indeed. First, this work appears to me prolix, heavy, full of repetitions, and alike deficient in arrangement and that mode of logical acumen which regards the conveyance of arguments. Secondly, I do not deny but that a man of sound unprejudiced mind could scarcely read this book and remain a Catholic, or rather Romanist; but the same must be said of twenty other works before Chillingworth. But I do affirm that it is even more probable that from Popery he would be led by it to Infidelity, Socinianism at least, than to regular Protestantism, Arminian or Calvinistic; that the concessions made to the Romanist, and the doctrines laid down concerning fundamentals, breathe a principle of Latitudinarianism destructive to all principle; while with a tiresome repetition of argument *ad hominem,* and retortions, there is a deficiency of direct and affirmative evidences and of learning, both Scriptural and from the Fathers.[4]

Thomas Fuller

Fuller, A TRIPLE RECONCILER.[1]

A Triple Reconciler
stating the Controversies

Whether { Ministers have an exclusive power &c
Any persons unordained may preach
The Lord's Prayer ought not to be used
by all Christians

[4] *Notes Theolog.,* p. 80.

[1] Coleridge has copied the title page, a part of the dedication, and various passages. The latter are sometimes condensed and sometimes partly paraphrased, but the meaning is unchanged. These entries are from the Holograph Notebook with entries dated "Aug. 1833," "Nov. 30, 1833," "9 Dec. 1833," and "Thursday night March [27] 1834 Tomorrow Good Friday." This notebook is in the Henry W. and Albert A. Berg Collection of the New York Public Library, and the section on Fuller is published with the permission of the library.

By THOMAS FULLER, B. D.
London
Printed by Will. Bently, for Will. Shears
at the Bible in St. Paul's Churchyard
Anno Dom. 1654

ergo, about 4 years before the Restoration

Mem. In form duodecimo [?] is sent me, and a prized addition to my assemblage of T. Fuller's Works.

Fuller, A TRIPLE RECONCILER: THE EPISTLE DEDICATORY.

Dedicated (in the true spirit of incomparable FULLER, that great intellectual Potter, whose Clay was Wit, whose Wheel was sound Good Sense, with Learning and Charity for the moulding Hands)

To The
Right Honorable and truly virtuous Lady ANNE Viscountess
BALTINGLASS, the blessings of this life and a better.
Madam
This my Book addresseth itself to you, as once the Dove to Noah in the Ark, bringing an Olive Branch with three sprigs in the mouth thereof. It is of a peaceable Nature, and desires to be a Peace-maker betwixt the opposite Parties in the three controversies therein handled. My humble request is, that with NOAH you would be pleased to put forth your hand and receive it into the Ark of your Protection.

Could the most accomplished Gentleman in the drawing Room of Elizabeth, in the days of Leicester and Sir Philip Sidney, have addressed a high-born Dame with more courtly elegance? and the excellent remark on the success to be expected by all Umpires and Arbitrators, that often they lose one, and sometimes both of their Friends, they would intercede between. "I expect the like fate from that Side which doth the most injury."

Fuller, A TRIPLE RECONCILER: THE FIRST RECONCILER, *p. 3.*

The Leprosy of the Jews, as we have not,[2] so [we] have a disease the Jews had not[3]—the last Rod that Heaven[4] made to whip wantonness, [and which he] handselled on the *French* at *Naples,* 2000[5] miles from this place.
How came this Malady to climb and clamber over the high[6] Alps! England being an Island, and as such secured it might seem, how came

[2] This passage is collated with the printed text as a good example of Coleridge's method in copying. "As the Jews had a disease we."
[3] "It is the last Rod."
[4] "God made therewith to whip wantonness."
[5] "two thousand."
[6] "high aspiring Alps? when got into France?"

it to swim over into England?[7] Did wicked Foreigners bring it to her,[8] or wicked[9] Englishmen fetch it from[10] thence? However it was, so it is: and is a disease so much worse than Leprosy, *as Sin is worse than Suffering, and Guilt more deplorable than Affliction.*[11]

Leprosy ✗ Syphilis

Fuller, A TRIPLE RECONCILER: THE FIRST RECONCILER, *pp. 1, 4, 5, 6.*

And the Priest shall look on him, and pronounce him unclean. Leviticus, 13. 3.

Shall *look*—we must not trust to *hearing*—and pronounce—but having examined & ascertained, then *pronounce*—we must not suspend or conceal in matters of public concernment—One of the 10,000 instances of the manner in which our old Divines contrived to extract a moral sense out of the driest club of a text.

So on the next page—Then did not the examining Priest escape infection—a lawful Calling the most infallible Amulet & Counteraction. A man in his Calling is an armed man, or if he lazily follow his Calling, his Armour like Ahabs is loose in the joints, & he may be wounded in the chinks.[12]

Fuller, A TRIPLE RECONCILER: THE FIRST RECONCILER, *p. 10.*

A noticeable Passage. Mem. How many years before the Great Plague?—1664-5 ✗ 1654—
but this, I suspect, a later Edition.

"Here give me leave to take an occasion to raise the gratitude of this City to God. He that with *Fess* passeth for an old Man in *London,* cannot remember it so long without the Plague. This City was never more populated: surely, there being more Hives, there are [as] many Bees. Daily Increase of Houses argues no Decrease of Households.

Secondly,[13] never more sinful—as much Pride as ever, *tho removed from these, whose Births may, and whose State once did countenance Gallantry, to such, who growing great will grow gaudy in an instant."*

Fuller, A TRIPLE RECONCILER: THE FIRST RECONCILER, *p. 11.*

"When God, thrifty of his Miracles, was pleased now and then to drop one down from *Heaven."*

[7] Text reads: "England being an Island secured from the diseases of the continent how came it to swim over into *England,*"
[8] "hither"   [9] "wanton"
[10] "from" not in text.
[11] "transgression worse than affliction." The italics are Coleridge's.
[12] This is a paraphrase and condensation of the text.
[13] This is "Thirdly" in the text and "Secondly" has been omitted.

Epitaph of the present year on the monument to the memory of Dr. Thomas Fuller[14]

A Lutheran Stout, I hold for *Goose-and-Gandry*
Both the Pope's Limbo, and his fiery Laundry.
No wit e'er saw I in Original Sin,
And no Sin find I in Original Wit;
But if I'm all ĭn the wrong, and Grin for Grin
Scorch'd Soul must pay for each too lucky Hit
Oh! Thomas Fuller! Oh![15] So vast thy debt
Thou art not out of Purgatory yet.

1833

Tho' One, Eight, Three, & Three this year is reckond,
And thou, I think, didst die [with ?] Charles the second

Fuller, A TRIPLE RECONCILER: THE FIRST RECONCILER, *p. 12.*

[Whether *Gods ministers* under the *gospel* have a sufficient *commission* to examin, and exclude Persons from the *Sacrament*]

The question concerning the *right* of Ministers to exclude from the Sacrament, and so far as it exists, the expediency of exorcizing treated by Fuller with his Characteristic good sense, & may be read by a Clergyman even at the present day with practical advantage.

The Argument from the whole may be drawn, which Fuller has not drawn—namely, the great advantage, if not necessity, of *a Church*, Episcopal or Synodal, under whose authority and definite regulations the Individual Clergyman may act, in cases where he is conscience obliged to act at all—both as removing the *invidia* from himself, and lessening if not preventing, the personal passions and resentments on the part of the the the Excluded.

The First Reconciler, pp. 34 and 35 with part of 36, most worthy of transcription, and likewise for it's historical interest, and as an exemplification of the intolerable Despotism and inquisitional pretensions of the Presbyterian Clergy, in consent with the Covenanting Church of Scotland, are well worth transcribing: and will leave two or three pages for this purpose.[16]

----

14 "One, Eight, Three, Three, this present year is reckon'd And Fuller died, I think, in Charles the Second" [Coleridge's note].

15 Coleridge wrote above the line "Fuller! much I fear" but did not delete.

16 Coleridge left half of p. 69 through p. 72 blank in the notebook.

Fuller, A TRIPLE RECONCILER: THE FIRST RECONCILER, *p. 40.*

8 lines—"And here . . . peace makers."—and p. 41, the last lines & p. 42—except the last 7 lines.[17]

> "We do freely confess, that there is neither express Precept nor Precedent in the New Testament for the Baptizing of Infants; and yet are confident, that by undeniable consequences from Scripture it will be made appear to be founded thereon."
>
> Fuller's 'Infants' Advocate,' Ch. 8, p. 71.

So thought, so deliberately wrote and published a Divine of the Church of England, eminently learned in a learned Age, and of unquestionable orthodoxy in all the Articles of her Faith, and of avowed attachment to, and affectionate preference of her Forms & Orders—tho' he did not raise them into indispensable conditions of a true Church.

And what have I said more in my "Aids to Reflection"?[18] except indeed that I have shewn that neither Indirect Precept nor Precept could rationally be expected there, and that the *Spirit* of the Word being clear, the Church is authorized to supply the *Letter.*

Fuller, A TRIPLE RECONCILER: THE FIRST RECONCILER, *p. 55.*

> It is scarcely possible for an eager Racer to stop just at the Mark. He must either over-run it; or else never come at it. But when past the Mark (necessarily transported by his own eagerness beyond the Line) he will return to it again, to shew that *that* Place and no other was the true the intended, end of his Endeavors.

O if the English Presbyterians had been sufficiently disempassioned to have availed themselves of this most wise Advice! If the *drunkenness* of the extreme Parties, the *Prelatists,* and the theocratic Scotch Synod archaspistes had permitted the far larger but because more moderate, less active & actively influencive, not Party, but aggregate of Individuals that combined under an able Leader would have formed, a predominating Party—viz. the Episcopalians in Church and King's-men in State, who preferred Bishops yet dreaded Prelates, who respected a *Monarch,* but desired as the best sign and safeguard of their Liberties, a King as the Head and Voice of a Parliament, & as such only, *the King* of England—had permitted those, I say, to act *positively* to the settlement of their own English MEAN, instead of weighing by a dead weight to the bringing about the Restoration, as a rescue from the immediate Evils of Presbyterian Tyranny & Fanatical Monarchy on

---

[17] Coleridge notes other material to be copied and leaves the remainder of p. 73 and p. 74 blank.

[18] *Aids,* "On Spiritual Religion," Aphorism XXIV, pp. 293-315.

the one hand with a *blind Hope* in the Future, in the positive Scale. And doubtless much of the worst part of Charles the Second's *parliamentary* Measures, and no small portion of the Kingdom's endurance of his lawless intermission of Parliaments, must be attributed to the yet working recollections and fears of Presbyterian Insolence & inquisitorial Intrusion.

Even in our excellent Litany (excellent on the whole but not only capable of many improvements but requiring many corrections) there is a lump of the old Leaven remaining—in the prayer for the *Magistrates*, that they may "maintain the Truth."— as Caiaphas against his intention uttered a great prophetic verity, so might Pilate's contemptuous question be in the truest Christian spirit be [*sic*] respected by every Christian *Magistrate, exclusively* in reference to his *Magistratic* function & Duties—"*What is Truth?*" i. e. what have I to do with that?

A Clown presents himself to a duenna of fashion & stales a sad case of Migrain (Hemicranium) in one of her Daughters. Megrims?—quoth the Charwoman—"What is *Megrim?* Go to the Doctor, Man."

Fuller, A TRIPLE RECONCILER: THE FIRST RECONCILER, *p. 74*.

The lurking desire even in the most moderate and unpretending of the Clergy, the Low-Church Liberals from 1600 to 1688, to keep their own offices, the mystery of a Guild, betrayed in the most moderate FULLER—who cautiously allows to the Lay Masters of Families the reading of the Scriptures to their Households, and the *Repetition* of what they had heard from the Pulpit—could not withhold from the more serious ones the *Application* of Scripture Texts; but warns them against the presumption of *Explication*.

I am persuaded, that the present unlimited exercise of the Right of private Judgement is mainly owing to, and dependent on, the existence of the Established Church, and the consequent *Antithesis* of the various Sects, by that antithesis alone working as a Unity: like a number— Masses, having no bond of union with each other but only connected by their common repulsion to some one large Body, which is at the same time attracting them all. Their neighborhood to each other is preserved by the efforts of each to maintain it's utmost distance from the central Enemy, the Common TEMPTER of all whose influence they all feel against their own will, and acknowledge, that they feel, by constantly resenting. Hence "The *dissenting* Interest," and the Gall of Bitterness in the Dissenters collectively, increasing in proportion to the tolerance, and courtesy of the Established Church. A *mouse, rat, Cat, Dog, and Fox* ORGAN; by a common pressure on whose Tails an [*sic*] full concerto of

Squeaks, Growls, Howls, & Yells is produced ad libitum against the *Church.*

Fuller, A TRIPLE RECONCILER : THE SECOND RECONCILER, *pp. 80-81.*[19]

[A lawful calling is partly internal, partly external, the Internal part thereof consisteth in two things.
First, in having a desire and delight to undertake the ministery. . . .
Secondly, in having some competent ability to discharge that *Office,* I say competent: For for these things who are sufficient?]

Competent, I say: for who shall dare affirm that he is *sufficient.*— An excellent and useful distinction of the *Ever-witty,* but tho' less acknowledged yet not less distinguishing quality of the man, eminently, yea in that age of political and theological party-passions *pre*-eminently *Judicious,* FULLER. I thank him for the distinction, & hope, that I shall profit by it.

S. T. C.
30 Novr 1833.

See p. 81. Mem. Fuller is speaking of the office of a Bishop.

Fuller, A TRIPLE RECONCILER : THE SECOND RECONCILER, *p. 81.*[20]

Some Skill in *Greek* and *Hebrew,* that he may competently recover the Scripture in the original. Some Skill in Logic, to analyze the Scripture aright. For tho' [in] the words of the Apostle,[21] *Rightly dividing the word of Truth, theological* Divisions he principally intended giving comfort to whom comfort, terror to whom terror belongs; yet even *logical* division is necessary for the clear parcelling[22] and expounding the Word. Some skill, lastly, in full (not in *vain*) PHILOSOPHY, in order to understand the metaphors of Scripture.

See the "Aids to Reflection" on the distinction between Symbols and Metaphors;[23] and the necessity of Philosophy in order to the not confounding the one with the other, or either with the *literal* (that is, the *Sensuous*) import of the words. *My Words are Spirit,* said our Lord: *and they* (i. e. their Spiritual substance) *are the Truth.*

Fuller, A TRIPLE RECONCILER : THE SECOND RECONCILER, *p. 82.*

Sad were the times in Queen Elizabeth's Reign, when by her Majesty's Injunctions, the Clergy were commanded to read the Chapters over once or twice by themselves, that they might be able to read them distinctly to the Congregation.

[19] The note occurs on the notebook page (p. 62) opposite Coleridge's copy of Fuller's title page.

[20] This note occurs on p. 81 of the notebook.

[21] Coleridge omits the reference, "2. Tim. 2.15," which is given in the text at this point.

[22] auseinandersetzen. [Coleridge's note.]

[23] *Aids,* "On Spiritual Religion," Aphorism VII, pp. 159-61.

Blessed be God, we have an alteration for the better, and latterly there have been plenty of able men, were their parts but sufficiently sanctified —which both brought me to the third part (the first, was a lawful *Calling*, from within, by sincere desire and without by a lawful authority, the second, competence)—namely, the *internal Call* of the Spirit, i. e. Inward Holiness, under the Ministry of Barnabus *"much People were added to the Lord:"* and why? *"For* He was a *good Man, and full of the Holy Ghost, and of Faith."*

P.S. an excellent Subject for a Sermon by a Clergyman on his first undertaking the more regular ministration of a Parish. All duties are relative. I cannot better tell you of yours than by fully explaining what my own are, first, in common with you, as a Christian, and secondly; in relation to you as *your* Minister & Pastor.

Fuller, A TRIPLE RECONCILER: THE SECOND RECONCILER, *p. 86.*

Excellent remark on Jereboam's policy, who tho' he made the meanest of the People Priests as our present Ministry are doing in their Colonial Edicts and Prescripts (even to an avowed preference of the Emissaries from the Churchless Sects) yet well may "the wicked Politician" [be] aware of the necessity of an *Ordination.* Well did he know, that unless some Solemnity were ["]used to separate the Priests, as mean as they were, from Common People, his Religion would quickly be contemned and confounded.["] Therefore "with the sacrifice of a Bullock & seven Rams." 2 Chron. 23.9.—

So Uzzah & Uzziah—Book of Kings.

Fuller, A TRIPLE RECONCILER: THE SECOND RECONCILER, *p. 87.*

The argument from παρακαλεῖται(Mark 3.13) a sound one. Our Lord invited *all* to Salvation; *but he called, whom he would,* out of those, to be his Apostles and ministerial Disciples—"Would that all the Lord's people were prophets"—but Moses knew, that this could not be and the pious Wish (for it is a *Wish* and not to be confounded with a *Prayer*) amounts to this—Would that all the People were as capable of the priestly office as those whom I now select! For *these* could be the Prophets selected from *those."* "If the whole Body were the Eye, where were the Hearing?" 1. Corinth. XII. 17. κηρύσσω and it's Derivatives occur more than 70 times in the New Testament, and always applied exclusively to public persons, appointed Preachers. The two apparent exceptions (Mark 1.45. and Mark VII.36) are no exceptions or rather confirm the Rule—as they refer to the making known of one particular Boon made publicly known by the grateful and rejoicing Receiver: and hence our Translators have properly rendered not "by preach" [sic] but by publish.

Was not our Lord highly gifted? Yet even he waited for a *Call*—
yea, and for the time of a legitimate Call. He did not take out his
Commission till he was past 30 years old, the Age appointed by Law:
and "from that *time* Jesus began to *preach.*"

Fuller, A TRIPLE RECONCILER, *p. 7.*[24]

—Doctrine.

God's ministers ought without fear or favour to perform their office,
neither to be frightened nor flattered. It is observed that Moses first
hanselled this law on his sister Miriam, *Numb.* xii. 15.

Secondly, we find it served by subjects on their sovereign in the case of
King Uzziah, 2 *Chron.* xxvi. 20.

Five years later this would have cost Fuller a rap on his knuckles
from his Bishop.

Fuller, A TRIPLE RECONCILER, *p. 8.*

Sad and sorrowful the condition of a sequestered Leper. Indeed some
of us have been sequestered; and, blessed be God, we have borne our
yoke in our youth, hoping that more freedom is reserved for our old age.

A hope amounting to an anticipation of the fast approaching Restoration, while Cromwell was yet alive. But there were men who hoped for
a restoration of the Established Church under a moderate Episcopacy
from Cromwell himself, and had he dared take the name of King, he
probably would not have disappointed them.

Fuller, A TRIPLE RECONCILER, *pp. 43, 44.*

First, for Barnabas his title was, by his extraction, being a Levite,
Acts xiv. 36, to whom it belonged by their profession to teach the people.
Secondly, he had an *extraordinary call* from God in the second verse
of this chapter; besides, at this time, a civil invitation from the *masters*
of the *synagogue.* Thus his threefold cable cannot be broken, nor any
unlawful invading of the ministerial office be charged upon him.
Thirdly, St. Paul's commission to preach doth appear both by his
ability and authority for the same. His ability (*Acts* xxii. 3)—brought
up at the feet of Gamaliel.
Object. We confess his ability, but deny his authority, &c. &c.
Ans. All is confessed, but let the impartial reader consider, first, that
Paul was a *Pharisee,* the son of a *Pharisee, Acts* xxiii. 6; secondly, let
him also weigh the words of our *Saviour, Matt.* xxiii. 2, 3. *The Scribes
and Pharisees sit in Moses' chair; all therefore whatsoever they bid you
observe, that observe and do; but do not after their works, for they say
and they do not.*

[24] These notes are taken from a transcription made in a notebook of marginalia
owned by A. H. B. Coleridge. They appear in *Notes Theolog.,* pp. 97-99, where the
variations are merely typographical.

Fuller is here trying to support a plain truth on a false or very questionable Pediment. What wonder that he fails? For those, who admitted that Miracles had ceased in the Church, convincing arguments might have been brought. For those who believed immediate calls, no arguments could have been convincing.

Fuller, LIFE OUT OF DEATH, *p. 4.*[25]

> Was not Hezekiah assured that the setting of his sun here in a mortal life should be the rising thereof in a blessed immortality?

Noticeable even in the sensible Fuller this disposition to consider the Bible from Genesis to the Apocalypse *one* book so as to antedate the Gospel and attribute to the good men under the Law not only the *Faith* but the clear and distinct belief and assurance of Christians. Bishop Warburton fell into the contrary extreme.

Fuller, LIFE OUT OF DEATH, *p. 6.*

> Well, the Prophet Isaiah is sent with a welcome counter-message, that Hezekiah's prayer was heard, and a longer lease of life indulged unto him, confirmed with miracles from Heaven of the going back of the sun.

Was not the recovery itself a sufficient sign? The sun of his life had gone backward, if at sixty he was carried back and reimplaced in the strength and health of fifty. Query, a figurative *expression* of a fact, interpreted by the hearers for a distinct fact in itself?

Fuller, LIFE OUT OF DEATH, *p. 11.*

> Sickness is a time to suffer, not to do in: patients are like bees in in winter, no flying abroad to find fresh flowers; either they must starve, or live on that stock of honey which they have provided in the summer time.

A beautiful improvement might be made of this—viz., that God's mercy through Christ *does* supply to his wisest Bees a power of making fresh honey by patience and acknowledgement.

Fuller, LIFE OUT OF DEATH, *p. 14.*

> David therefore allegeth this as an argument to be continued in the land of the living, *Shall the dust praise Thee, O Lord?* that God's service might still be preserved so in him, that his body might not be altogether useless, as in dead folk, but have a portion of praising of God, conjoined with his soul (as the opposite part of the quire) in lauding the Lord.

With an ingenuity worthy of Fuller; but more ingenious than ingenuous. Better say: it was a question to which sinful man might thro' God's mercy hope, but could not of his own merits expect, an affirmative answer. Compare with Ezekiel, *Can these dry bones live?*

[25] *Life out of Death, a Sermon* (London: 1655). Cf. *Notes Theolog.,* pp. 99-100.

Fuller, THE APPEAL OF INJURED INNOCENCE[26] *(1659), Part I, p. 5.*

> Yet there want not *learned Writers* (whom I need not name) of the Opinion that even the *Instrumental* Pen men of the *Scripture* might commit ἁμαρτήματα μνημονικά: though *open* that *window* to *profaneness, and it will be in vain to shut any dores; Let God be true, and every man a lyer.*

It has been matter of complaint with hundreds, yea, it is an old Cuckoo Song of grim Saints, that the Reformation came to it's Close long before it came to it's Completion. But the cause of this imperfection has been fully laid open by no party,—*scilicet,* that in Divines of both Parties of the Reformers, the Protestants and the Detestants, there was the same Relic of the Roman Lues,—the habit of deciding for or against the orthodoxy of a Position, not according to it's truth or falsehood, not on grounds of Reason or of History, but by the imagined Consequences of the Position. The very same principles, on which the Pontifical Polemics vindicate the papal infallibility, Fuller *et sex centum alii* apply to the (if possible) still more extravagant Notion of the absolute truth and divinity of every syllable of the O. and N. Testament.

Fuller, THE APPEAL OF INJURED INNOCENCE, *Part I, p. 21.*

> Sure I am, that one of as much *Meekness,* as some are of *Morosness,* even upright *Moses* himself, in his Service of the *Essential,* and *Increated Truth* (of higher consequence than the *Historical Truth* controverted betwixt us) had notwithstanding a respect to the recompense of Reward. Heb. xi, 26.

In *Religion* the Faith pre-supposed in the respect, and as it's condition, gives to the motive a purity and an elevation, which of itself, and where the recompence is looked for in temporal and carnal pleasures or profits, it would not have.

Southey, LIFE OF WESLEY, *I, 250-51.*[27]

> It is wisely, as well as eloquently said by Fuller the Worthy, in one of his sermons, "Of such as deny, that formerly we had in our Churches all truth necessary to salvation, I ask Joseph's question to his brethren, *Is your father well? the old man—is he yet alive?* So, how fare the souls of their sires, and the ghosts of their grandfathers? are they yet alive? do they still survive in bliss, in happiness? Oh no! they are dead; dead in soul, dead in body, dead temporally, dead eternally, dead and damned, if so be we had not all truth necessary to salvation before their time.

With a mind so sensitively perceptive of the beautiful, as Robert Southey's is, and with his homebred kindliness of heart, an altar for the

---

[26] Bound with *The Church History of Britain. Lit. Rem.,* II, 385-86.

[27] Robert Southey, *Life of Wesley* (London: 1847). Coleridge's note is printed as a footnote on p. 251.

household pieties, it is not strange that the beauty of this passage from Fuller, conjoined with the truth of the position he is supporting, should have hidden from him the weakness of the particular argument which, if valid at all, would have been equally valid in the mouths of the first Saxon converts to the Monk Augustin—or of the Greek and Roman auditors to St. Paul. If R. S. reply, Well! what then? I can only answer, "But did Fuller, did Samuel Wesley, thus extend their charity?"

Robert Leighton

If not with the works, you are doubtless familiar with the name of that "wonderful man" (for such, says Doddridge,[1] I must deliberately call him), Archbishop Leighton. It would not be easy to point out another name, which the eminent of all parties, Catholic and Protestant, Episcopal and Presbyterian, Whigs and Tories, have been so unanimous in extolling. "There is a spirit in Archbishop Leighton I never met with in any human writings; nor can I read many lines in them without impressions which I could wish always to retain," observes a dignitary of our Establishment and F. R. S. eminent in his day both as a philosopher and a divine. In fact, it would make no small addition to the size of the volume, if, as was the fashion in editing the classics, we should collect the eulogies on his writings passed by bishops only and church divines, from Burnet to Porteus.[2] That this confluence of favourable opinions is not without good cause, my own experience convinces me. For at a time when I had read but a small portion of the Archbishop's principal work, when I was altogether ignorant of its celebrity, much more of the peculiar character attributed to his writings (that of making and leaving a deep impression on readers of all classes), I remember saying to Mr. Southey "that in the Apostolic Epistles I heard the last hour of Inspiration striking, and in Arch. Leighton's commentary the lingering *vibration* of the sound." Perspicuous, I had almost said transparent, his style is *elegant* by the mere compulsion of the thoughts and feelings, and in despite, as it were, of the writer's wish to the contrary. Profound as his conceptions often are, and numerous as the passages are, where the most *athletic* thinker will find himself tracing a rich vein from the

---

[1] Phillip Doddridge, editor of Leighton (Edinburgh: 1748).
[2] Beilby Porteus (1731-1808), bishop of London.

surface downward, and leave off with an unknown depth for to-morrow's delving—yet there is this quality peculiar to Leighton, unless we add Shakespeare—that there is always a scum on the very surface which the simplest may understand, if they have head and heart to understand anything. The same or nearly the same excellence characterizes his eloquence. Leighton had by nature a quick and pregnant fancy, and the august objects of his habitual contemplation, and their remoteness from the outward senses, his constant endeavour to see or to bring all things under some point of unity, but, above all, the rare and vital union of head and heart, of light and love, in his own character,—all these working conjointly could not fail to form and nourish in him the higher power, and more akin to reason, the power, I mean, of imagination. And yet in his freest and most figurative passages there is a *subdued*ness, a self-checking timidity in his colouring, a sobering silver-grey tone over all; and an experienced eye may easily see where and in how many instances Leighton has substituted neutral tints for a strong light or a bold relief—by this sacrifice, however, of particular effects, giving an increased permanence to the impression of the whole, and wonderfully facilitating its soft and quiet *illapse* into the very recesses of our convictions. Leighton's happiest ornaments of style are made to appear as efforts on the part of the author to express himself *less* ornamentally, more plainly.

Since the late alarm respecting Church Calvinism and Calvinistic Methodism (a cry of Fire! Fire! in consequence of a red glare on one or two of the windows, from a bonfire of straw and stubble in the church-yard, while the dry rot of virtual Socinianism is snugly at work in the beams and joists of the venerable edifice) I have heard of certain gentle doubts and questions as to the Archbishop's *perfect* orthodoxy— some small speck in the diamond which had escaped the quick eye of all former theological jewellers from Bishop Burnet to the outrageously anti-Methodistic Warburton.[3] But on what grounds I cannot even conjecture, unless it be, that the Christianity which Leighton teaches contains the doctrines peculiar to the Gospel as well as the truths common to it with the (so-called) light of nature or natural religion, that he dissuades students and the generality of Christians from all attempts at explaining the mysteries of faith by *notional* and metaphysical speculations, and rather by a heavenly life and temper to obtain a closer view of these truths, the *full* light and knowledge of which it is in Heaven only that we shall possess. He further advises them in speaking of these

---

[3] William Warburton (1698-1779), bishop of Gloucester, known today rather as editor of Shakespeare and commentator on Pope than for his violent controversies in theology.

truths to proper scripture language; but since something more than this had been made necessary by the restless spirit of dispute, to take this "something more" in the sound precise terms of the Liturgy and Articles of the Established Church. Enthusiasm? Fanaticism? Had I to recommend an antidote, I declare on my conscience that above all others it should be Leighton. And as to Calvinism, L.'s exposition of the scriptural sense of election ought to have prevented the very [suspicion of its presence]. You will long ago, I fear, have [been asking yourself], To what does all this tend? Briefly then, I feel strongly persuaded, perhaps because I strongly wish it, that the Beauties of Archbishop Leighton, selected and methodized, with a (better) Life of the Author, that is, a biographical and critical introduction as Preface, and Notes, would make not only a useful but an interesting POCKET VOLUME. "Beauties" in general are objectionable works—injurious to the original author, as disorganizing his productions, pulling to pieces the well-wrought *crown* of his glory to pick out the shining stones, and injurious to the reader, by indulging the taste for unconnected, and for that reason unretained single thoughts, till it fares with him as with the old gentleman at Edinburgh, who, eat six kittywakes by way of *whetting* his appetite—"whereas" (said he) "it proved quite the contrary: I never sat down to a dinner with so little." But Leighton's principal work, that which fills two volumes and a half of the four, being a commentary on St. Peter's Epistles, verse by verse, and varying of course, in subject, etc., with almost every paragraph, the volume, I propose, would not only bring together his finest passages, but these being afterwards arranged on a principle wholly independent of the accidental place of each in the original volumes, and guided by their relative bearings, it would give a connection or at least a propriety of *sequency*, that was before of necessity wanting. It may be worth noticing, that the editions, both the one in three, and the other in four volumes, are most grievously misprinted and otherwise disfigured. . . .[4]

I have the honor of agreeing with all the thinking Men, with whom I have conversed, in their objection to "Beauties" of this or that writer, taken as a *general* Rule. In the greater number of cases, these collections of striking and shewy passages without any connection given in lieu of that which had been destroyed is almost as injurious to the Original, as the taking out of the Lights of a Titian or a Correggio and presenting them apart from the Shades would be, considered as a specimen of the Picture. And it is in fact no less injurious to the Reader, and one of

[4] To John Murray, Jan. 18, 1822. Coleridge, E. H., *Letters*, II, 717-20.

the most effective recipes for depraving his Taste and weakening his memory. But if, as in all cases, there are any exceptions to the Rule, the Works of Archbishop Leighton form one of the Strongest. I need not enlarge to *you* on the high and peculiar Merits of Leighton—on his persuasive and penetrating eloquence, or the fine Fancy and profound Reflection which seem trying to hide themselves in the earnest simplicity and if I may so express myself, in the cordiality and *conversingness* of his style and manner. The point, on which I mainly rest as to my present purpose, is this: that from the nature and necessity of his principle Work, (A commentary on the I Epistle of St. Peter, Text by Text) the most important and valuable Lights of these precious Volumes, present themselves to the Reader in a far more *un-* or rather *dis*-connected manner, than they would in the Work, I have in view: so much so indeed, that I was first led to take it in hand from the observations of several, to whom I had strongly recommended the original Volumes, that from the abrupt transitions from one subject to other and wholly different, and the continual interruptions of the thread of Interest as well as of Thought had prevented them, some from continuing the perusal, and more from reading him with the satisfaction, they would otherwise have received.

Now the Volume, I have prepared, will be best described to you by the proposed Table—

Aids to Reflection: or Beauties and Characteristics of Archbishop Leighton, extracted from his various Writings, and arranged on a principle of connection under the three Heads, of 1. Philosophical and Miscellaneous. 2. Moral and Prudential. 3. Spiritual—with a Life of Leighton and a critique on his writings, and opinions—with Notes throughout by the Editor.

I have marked out all the passages intended for Extraction in my Copy of Leighton's Works—which, if you think the proposal worth attending to in the first instance, I would leave with you—tho' you are well aware, how much more favorable Impression the passages would make, arranged and in sequence, with the necessary additions, or completions, and the occasional Substitutions of a word or phrase when the words in the original have acquired by association and change of fashions a mean or ludicrous sense.[5]

[5] To Messrs. Taylor and Hessey, Aug. 8, 1823. Griggs, *Unp. Letters*, II, 314-15. In a letter to John Murray postmarked Jan. 26, 1822, Coleridge had accepted Murray's offer to send him a copy of Leighton and had suggested a similar procedure of work.

I find that my Apology for the Life of Leighton, which I believe, whether from vanity or on good ground to *deserve* as a yet more appropriate tho' less expedient Title, that of—The first impartial and philosophical Account & Explanation of the Conflict between the Protestant Hierarchy (from Edward VI to the Revolution) and the Puritans of England with the Presbyterians in Scotland—which how especially it is the vital Center of the History of England might be presumed even from the unexampled interest felt by all ranks in the first Series of Sir Walter Scott's Novels—I find, I say (you must forgive my hasty *parentheses* in my letters, & I will take that you shall find few to be forgiven in my future publications) that the Life will occupy a full half of the Volume. I think it right to apprize you of this—that if you see any objection as to the saleability of the Book, it may be allowed— which however can only be. done by retaining only the Abstract of the main events of Leighton's Life which, however, I could give only as an Abstract from the Lives prefixed to the several Editions of his Works, not worthy to be called even an Apology for a Life—or such an Apology as the fragments of a dry Caterpillar Skin would be for the Life of the Butterfly. Now all my Materials are both ready, and arranged, save only a spot of terra incognita which I hope to colonize out of *Woodrow's*[6] History of the Church—to which, but of far less likelihood, I may add the *"Biographia Scoticana."* But the former I *must* have looked thro' before I dare publish my Life—well aware of the immense importance of the Advice given me in the enclosed Note from that worthy & enlightened man, the Rev[d]. Joseph Hughes, the Secretary of the Brit. & For. Bible Society. In my laborious Collation of Spottiswood,[7] Heylin,[8] Prynne,[9] Wharton,[10] Burnet,[11] Hacket,[12] &c I have had reason to congratulate myself on the having submitted to the Task. Now Woodrow's Work (in two Volumes Folio) is, Mr. Irving assures me, a common book in Scotland—and he was surprised at his disappointment in not

---

[6] Robert Wodrow (1679-1734), professor of divinity in the University of Glasgow and ecclesiastical historian. He wrote *History of the Sufferings of the Church of Scotland from the Restoration to the Revolution* (1721-22).

[7] John Spottiswood (1565-1637), historian, wrote the *History of the Church and State of Scotland . . . to the end of the reign of King James VI.* (1625).

[8] Peter Heylyn (1600-62), especially his *Cyprianus Anglicus, or the History of the Life and Death of Archbishop Laud* (1668) and *Observations on Mr. Hamon L'Estrange's Life of Charles I.* (1656).

[9] William Prynne (1600-69). Prynne was against episcopacy and independency and especially violent against Laud. *A Breviate of the Life of William Laud* (1644).

[10] Henry Wharton (1664-95), *Anglia Sacra* (1691).

[11] Gilbert Burnet (1643-1715), *History of My Own Times* (1723, 1734); *History of the Reformation of the Church of England* (1679).

[12] John Hacket (1592-1670), *Scrinia Reserata: a Memorial offered to the Great Deservings of John Williams, D.D.* (1693).

being able to procure it for me from any of his Scottish Acquaintance and Church-members in London. Neither is it or the Biographia Scoticana, in Sion College or in Dr. Williams's Library in Red Cress Street.—I should be much obliged to you to have it enquired whether it is in the London Institution Library. I trust that it will, at all events, be in the British Museum & have this morning written to Sir H. Davy to be admitted, as a Reader there—. If not, my last resource must be to procure it by Mr. Irving's means from Scotland.—But should it be in any of the London Catalogues, and could be purchased for any tolerable price (for instance, not exceeding five guineas) I would gladly have the sum put to my Account—if the Loan of it for a fortnight could not be obtained—and so too (but with less anxiety) the book entitled, Biographia Scoticana. . . .[13]

Apology for the Life of Archb. L.—or if it were permitted me to trifle on such a theme—Apology for A Life of Archb. L.? Nevertheless the Word is appropriate—and without using it as Watson did in his Apology for the Bible, in a sense which his Readers were sure to misunderstand— yet there is in the act of giving the countenance of his Name and his Virtue to the abhorred plans and measures of Lauderdale, Sharp, and the Royal Brothers that which asks an Apology—and that which his Life asks, what other Life can hope to receive? Abstine a Fabis. Worship the Echo. For inobservance of these principles, Verulam is a Beacon of Smoke, and a Mist floats before Leighton's Pillar of Flame.

We might compare Leighton in his appearance and character as an Archbishop of the short-lived Protestant Episcopal Church of Britain (the Scoto-anglican Church by Law established under the Stuart Dynasty) to the bright Star in Cassiopeia; but with this difference, that in the latter instance the Star disappeared, the Constellation remaining, in the former the Constellation vanished, no longer numbered among the Heavenly Houses, while the Star remains in undiminished Magnitude, and in unwaning tho' solitary Splendor.[14]

[13] From a MS letter to "Messrs Taylor and Hessey, Fleet St.," Sept. 9, 1823, in the Huntington Library, which has given me permission to publish this excerpt from HM 7256.

[14] Robert Leighton, The Whole Works, ed. George Jerment (4 vols.; London: 1820), first flyleaf, recto. This set of Leighton's works containing numerous marginal notes was formerly in the library of Lord Coleridge and is now in the British Museum. These are the volumes used in the preparation of Aids to Reflection: passages are marked and numbered for various aphorisms and many of the notes constitute material incorporated in the printed text. The projected Apology for the Life of Leighton, however, was not published, and this note is printed for the first time.

Likewise as the Volume is offered in Aids of Reflection, it will be but consistent with it's title and main purpose if the introductory Portion tho' biographical should be distinguished rather by new reflections on events and circumstances long known, and so prominent in the history of our native Land in that period of our History (from the Reformation to the Revolution) of which we might affirm with no greater deviation from the letter of the truth than we are used to pardon in general assertions, that our History begins to have a continued and living interest for the present times, at which it first becomes *our* History.[15]

Notice. In the selection of the Extracts that form the remainder of this Volume and of the Comments affixed, the Editor had the following Objects principally in view. First, to exhibit the true and scriptural meaning and intent of several Articles of Faith, that are rightly classed among the Mysteries and peculiar Doctrines of Christianity. Secondly, to shew the perfect rationality of these Doctrines, and their freedom from all just objection when examined by their proper Organ, the Reason and Conscience of man. Lastly, to exhibit from the Works of Leighton, who perhaps of all our learned protestant Theologians best deserves the title of a Spiritual Divine, an instructive and affecting picture of the contemplations, reflections, conflicts, consolations, and monitory experiences of a philosophic and richly-gifted mind, amply stored with all knowledge that Books and long intercourse with men of the most discordant characters can give, under the convictions, impressions, and habits of a Spiritual Religion.[16]

It would, indeed, be more correct to say, that the present Volume owed its accidental origin to the intention of compiling one of a different description, than to speak of it as the same Work . . . Still, however, the selections from Leighton, which will be found in the fundamental and moral Sections of this Work, and which I could retain consistently with its present form and matter, will, both from the intrinsic excellence and from the characteristic beauty of the passages, suffice to answer two prominent purposes of the original plan; that of placing in a clear light the principle, which pervades all Leighton's Writings—his sublime View, I mean, of Religion and Morality as the means of reforming the human soul in the Divine Image (*Idea*); and that of exciting an interest in the Works, and an affectionate reverence for the name and memory, of this severely tried and truly primitive Churchman.[17]

[15] British Museum, MSS Egerton, 2801, fol. 160. Printed for the first time.
[16] *Ibid.*, fol. 175 verso - 176. Printed in *Aids*, p. 150.
[17] *Aids*, "Advertisement to the first edition of *Aids to Reflection*," pp. iii-iv.

Among the Aids to Reflection place the following maxim prominent
—Let distinctness in Expression advance side by side with Distinction
in Thought. For one useless Subtlety in our elder Divines and Moralists
will produce ten Sophisms of Equivocation in the writings of our modern
Preceptors: and for one error in *distinguishing* the indifferent, I would
shew ten mischievous delusions from the habit of *confounding* the diverse.[18]

Are you familiar with Leighton's Works? He resigned his arch-
bishoprick, and retired to voluntary poverty, on account of the persecutions of the Presbyterians, saying, "I should not dare to introduce
Christianity itself with such cruelties, how much less for a surplice, and
the name of a bishop." If there could be an intermediate space between
inspired, and uninspired writings, that space would be occupied by
Leighton. No show of learning, no appearance, or ostentatious display
of eloquence, and yet both may be shown in him, conspicuously and
holily. There is in him something that must be felt, even as the Scriptures must be felt. To Cottle, Bristol [June], 1807.[19]

Leighton, WORKS.[20]

Surely if ever work not in the sacred Canon might suggest a belief of
inspiration,—of something more than human,—this it is. When Mr.
Elwyn made this assertion, I took it as the hyperbole of affection: but
now I subscribe to it seriously, and bless the hour that introduced me
to the knowledge of the evangelical, apostolical Archbishop Leighton.
April, 1814.

Next to the inspired Scriptures, yea, and as the *vibration* of that once
struck Hour remaining on the Air, stands Leighton's Commentary on
the 1 Ep. of Peter.[21]

Leighton, WORKS, *I, 68.*

In spiritual trials that are the sharpest and most fiery of all, when the
furnace is within a man, when God doth not only shut up his loving-
kindness from its feeling, but seems to shut it up in hot displeasure,
when he writes bittter things against it; yet then to depend upon him,
and wait for his salvation, this is not only a true, but a strong and very

[18] British Museum, MSS Egerton, 2801, fol. 165. Printed with only typographical
changes in *Aids,* pp. 36-37.
[19] Cottle, *Reminiscences,* p. 315. Also given by Turnbull, *Biog. Epist.,* II, 13-14.
[20] *The Genuine Works of Leighton,* ed. Erasmus Middleton (4 vols.; London:
1819), *Lit. Rem.,* IV, 156-83. Only those notes are reprinted which especially show
Coleridge's appreciation of Leighton or contribute to controversial topics in theology.
[21] *Lit. Rem.,* IV, 156-57. The second paragraph is transcribed from Notebook
21½, p. 108.

refined faith indeed, and the more he smites, the more to cleave to him. . . . Though I saw, as it were, his hand lifted up to destroy me, yet from that same hand would I expect salvation.

Bless God, O my soul, for this sweet and strong comforter! It is the honey in the lion.[22]

Leighton, WORKS, *I*, 104-5.

> This sweet stream of their doctrine did, as the rivers, make its own banks fertile and pleasant as it ran by, and flowed still forward to after ages, and by the confluence of more such prophecies grew greater as it went, till it fell in with the main current of the Gospel in the New Testament, both acted and preached by the great Prophet himself, whom they foretold to come, and recorded by his Apostles and Evangelists, and thus united into one river, clear as crystal. This doctrine of salvation in the Scriptures hath still refreshed the city of God, his Church under the Gospel, and still shall do so, till it empty itself into the ocean of eternity.

In the whole course of my studies I do not remember to have read so beautiful an allegory as this; so various and detailed, and yet so just and natural.[23]

Leighton, WORKS, *I*, 121.

> There is a truth in it, that all sin arises from some kind of ignorance. . . . For were the true visage of sin seen at a full light, undressed and unpainted, it were impossible, while it so appeared, that any one soul could be in love with it, but would rather flee from it as hideous and abominable.

This is the only (defect, shall I say? No, but the only) omission I have felt in this divine Writer—for him we understand by feeling, experimentally—that he doth not notice the horrible tyranny of habit. What the Archbishop says, is more true of beginners in sin; but this is the foretaste of hell, to see and loathe the deformity of the wedded vice, and yet still to embrace and nourish it.[24]

Leighton, WORKS, *I*, 122.

> He calls those times wherein Christ was unknown to them, *the times of their ignorance*. Though the stars shine never so bright, and the moon with them in its full, yet they do not, altogether, make it day: still it is night till the sun appear.

How beautiful, and yet how simple, and as it were unconscious of its own beauty![25]

[22] *Lit. Rem.*, IV, 162.
[23] *Lit. Rem.*, IV, 163.
[24] *Lit. Rem.*, IV, 163-64.
[25] *Lit. Rem.*, IV, 164.

Leighton, Works, *I, 124.*

> You were running to destruction in the way of sin, and there was a
> voice, together with the Gospel preaching to your ear, that spake
> into your heart, and called you back from that path of death to the
> way of holiness, which is the only way of life. He hath severed you
> from the mass of the profane world, and picked you out to be jewels
> for himself.

O, how divine! Surely, nothing less than the Spirit of Christ could
have inspired such thoughts in such language. Other divines,—Donne
and Jeremy Taylor for instance,—have converted their worldy gifts,
and applied them to holy ends; but here the gifts themselves seem un-
earthly.[26]

Leighton, Works, *I, 138.*

> As in religion, so in the course and practice of men's lives, the stream
> of sin runs from one age to another, and every age makes it greater,
> adding somewhat to what it receives, as rivers grow in their course by
> the accession of brooks that fall into them; and every man when he is
> born, falls like a drop into this main current of corruption, and so is
> carried down it, and this by reason of its strength, and his own nature,
> which willingly dissolves into it, and runs along with it.

In this single period we have religion, the spirit,—philosophy, the
soul,—and poetry, the body and drapery united;—Plato glorified by St.
Paul; and yet coming as unostentatiously as any speech from an innocent girl of fifteen.[27]

Leighton, Works, *I, 158.*

> The chief point of obedience is believing; the proper obedience to truth
> is to give credit to it.

This is not quite so perspicuous and as single-sensed as Archbishop
Leighton's sentences in general are. This effect is occasioned by the
omission of the word "this," or "divine," or the truth "in Christ." For
truth in the ordinary and scientific sense is received by a spontaneous,
rather than chosen by a voluntary, act; and the apprehension of the
same (belief) supposes a position of congruity rather than an act of
obedience. Far otherwise is it with the truth that is the object of
Christian faith: and it is this truth of which Leighton is speaking.
Belief indeed is a living part of this faith; but only as long as it is a
living part. In other words, belief is implied in faith; but faith is not
necessarily implied in belief. *The devils believe.*[28]

[26] *Lit. Rem.,* IV, 164.
[27] *Lit. Rem.,* IV, 164-65.
[28] *Lit. Rem.,* IV, 165.

Leighton, WORKS, *III, 20. Sermon I.*

They shall see God. What this is we cannot tell you, nor can you conceive it: but walk heavenwards in purity, and long to be there, where you shall know what it means: *for you shall know him as he is.*

We say; "Now I see the full meaning, force and beauty of a passage, —we see them through the words." Is not Christ the Word—the substantial, consubstantial Word, ὁ ὢν εἰς τὸν κόλπον τοῦ πατρός, —not as our words, arbitrary; nor even as the words of Nature phenomenal merely? If even through the words a powerful and perspicuous author —(as in the next to inspired Commentary of Archbishop Leighton,— for whom God be praised!)—I identify myself with the excellent writer, and his thoughts become my thoughts: what must not the blessing be to be thus identified first with the Filial Word, and then with the Father in and through him?[29]

Leighton, WORKS, *III, 63. Sermon V.*

In this elementary world, light being (as we hear) the first visible, all things are seen by it, and it by itself. Thus is Christ, among spiritual things, in the elect world of his Church; all things are *made manifest by the light,* says the Apostle, *Eph.* v. 13, speaking of Christ as the following verse doth evidently testify. It is in his word that he shines, and makes it a directing and convincing light, to discover all things that concern his Church and himself, to be known by its own brightness. How impertinent then is that question so much tossed by the Romish Church, "How know you the Scriptures (say they) to be the word of God, without the testimony of the Church?" I would ask one of them again, How they can know that it is daylight, except some light a candle to let them see it? They are little versed in Scripture that know not that it is frequently called light; and they are senseless that know not that light is seen and known by itself. *If our Gospel be hid,* says the Apostle, *it is hid to them that perish:* the god of this world having blinded their minds against the light of the glorious Gospel, no wonder if such stand in need of a testimony. A blind man knows not that it is light at noon-day, but by report: but to those that have eyes, light is seen by itself.

On the true Test of the Scriptures. Oh! were it not for my infirmities, whereby I am so all unlike the white-robed Leighton, I could almost conceit that my soul had been an emanation from his! So many and so remarkable are the coincidences, and these in parts of his works that I could not have seen—and so uniform the congruity of the whole. As I read, I seem to myself to be only thinking my own thoughts over again, now in the same and now in a different order.[30]

[29] *Lit. Rem.,* IV, 171-72.
[30] *Lit. Rem.,* IV, 172-73.

Leighton, WORKS, *III, 73. Sermon V.*

This fifth Sermon excellent in parts, is yet on the whole the least excellent of Leighton's works,—and breathes less of either his own character as a man, or the character of his religious philosophy. The style too is in many places below Leighton's ordinary style—in some places even turbid, operose, and catechrestic;—for example,—"to trample on smilings with one foot and on frownings with the other."[31]

Leighton, WORKS, *III, 104. Sermon VII.*

The seventh Sermon is admirable throughout, Leighton throughout. O what a contrast might be presented by publishing some discourse of some Court divine, (South for instance,) preached under the same state of affairs, and printing the two in columns![32]

Leighton, WORKS, *III, 107. Sermon VIII.*

> In all love three things are necessary; some goodness in the object, either true and real, or apparent and seeming to be so; for the soul, be it ever so evil, can affect nothing but which it takes in some way to be good.

Postscript. The lines in p. 107, noted by me, are one of the myriad instances to prove how rash it is to quote single sentences or assertions from the correctest writers, without collating them with the known system or express convictions of the author. It would be easy to cite fifty passages from Archbishop Leighton's works in direct contradiction to the sentence in question—which he had learnt in the schools when a lad, and afterwards had heard and met with so often that he was not aware that he had never sifted its real purport. This eighth Sermon is another most admirable discourse.[33]

Leighton, WORKS, *III, 12. Sermon IX.*

> The mind, φϱόνημα. Some render it the prudence or wisdom of the flesh. Here you have it, the carnal mind; but the word signifies, indeed, an act of the mind, rather than either the faculty itself, or the habit of prudence in it, so as it discovers what is the frame of both those.

I doubt. φϱόνημα signifies an act: and so far I agree with Leighton. But φϱόνημα σαϱκός is 'the flesh' (that is, the natural man,) in the act or habitude of minding—but those acts, taken collectively, are the faculty—the understanding.

[31] *Lit. Rem.*, IV, 175.
[32] *Lit. Rem.*, IV, 176.
[33] *Lit. Rem.*, IV, 176, 177.

How often have I found reason to regret, that Leighton had not clearly made out to himself the diversity of the reason and the understanding![34]

Leighton, WORKS, *IV, 105. Lecture IX.*

They always seemed to me to act a very ridiculous part, who contend, that the effect of the divine decree is absolutely irreconcilable with human liberty; because the natural and necessary liberty of a rational creature is to act or choose from a rational motive, or spontaneously, and of purpose: but who sees not, that, on the supposition of the most absolute decree, this liberty is not taken away, but rather established and confirmed? For the decree is, *that such an one shall make choice of, or do some particular thing freely. And whoever pretends to deny, that whatever is done or chosen, whether good or indifferent, is so done or chosen, or, at least, may be so, espouses an absurdity.*

I fear, I fear, that this is a sophism not worthy of Archbishop Leighton. It seems to me tantamount to saying—"I force that man to do so or so without my forcing him." But however that may be, the following sentences are more precious than diamonds. They are divine.[35]

Leighton, WORKS, *IV, 152. Lecture XV.*

The Platonists divide the world into two, the sensible and intellectual world. . . . According to this hypothesis, those parables and metaphors, which are often taken from natural things to illustrate such as are divine, will not be similitudes taken entirely at pleasure; but are often, in a great measure, founded in nature, and the things themselves.

I have asserted the same thing, and more fully shown wherein the difference consists of symbolic and metaphorical, in my first Lay Sermon; and the substantial correspondence of the genuine Platonic doctrine and logic with those of Lord Bacon, in my Essays on Method, in the Friend.[36]

Leighton, WORKS, *IV, 245. Lecture XXIV.*

Ask yourselves, therefore, *what you would be at,* and with what dispositions you come to this most sacred table.

In an age of colloquial idioms, when to write in loose slang had become a mark of loyalty, this is the only L'Estrange vulgarism I have met with in Leighton.[37]

Leighton, WORKS, *IV, p. 252. "Exhortation to the Students."*

Study to acquire such a philosophy as is not barren and babbling, but solid and true; not such a one as floats upon the surface of endless verbal controversies, but one that enters into the nature of things: for

[34] *Lit. Rem.,* IV, 178.
[35] *Lit. Rem.,* IV, 180-81.
[36] *Lit. Rem.,* IV, 181-82.
[37] *Lit. Rem.,* IV, 183.

he spoke good sense that said, "The philosophy of the Greeks was a mere jargon, and noise of words."

If so, then so is all philosophy: for what system is there, the elements and outlines of which are not to be found in the Greek schools! Here Leighton followed too incautiously the Fathers.[41]

Leighton, WORKS, *IV, 6. "An Exposition of the Creed."*[42]

Whether natural reason may evince the creation of the world, we will not dispute.

Here and throughout these Volumes bear in mind that by "natural Reason," "human Reason," "the Reason of man," &c. Leighton means the power or faculty of Reasoning, i. e. of drawing conclusions from premises of Sense and Reflection. In it's highest and proper import, Reason does not *evince,* but *contain, present,* and affirm, Truths— ἡ ἀλήθεια ἄχϱονα.

Leighton, WORKS, *IV, 11. "An Exposition of the Creed."*

The mediation was not a bare matter of word, but there was such a wrong done as required a satisfaction should be made.

It never ceases to be a perplexer to my mind, how such an Intellect as Leighton's could have consented with the systematists in confounding St. Paul's elucidation by various analogies of the beneficent *Effects* of the New Creation with a proper description of the mysterious Efficient itself.

Leighton, WORKS, *IV, 215. Lecture V.*

If even the mathematical demonstrations are examined by the strict rules and ideas of Aristotle, the greatest part of them will be found imperfect and defective.

Either these Demonstrations are not mathematical, or they must be strictly demonstrative. In either case, it is plain that Leighton had not made himself master of the subject: as indeed few were before the appearance of Kant's Critique of the Pure Reason. S. T. C.

Leighton, WORKS, *IV, 306. Lecture XVII.*

They [the philosophers] sometimes, it is true, drop such expressions as these, "That there can be no good disposition of the mind without God;" and, "That in order to be happy, the soul must be raised up to divine things": they also tell us, "That the wise man loves God most of

[41] *Lit. Rem.,* IV, 183.

[42] This note and those following from Vol. IV are from the Jerment edition previously described and are printed for the first time. Several notes either very theological or very short are omitted.

all, and for this reason is the most happy man." But these expressions they drop only at random, and by the bye.

A most illogical and uncandid way of treating the ancient Platonists & Stoics. How *at random?* and with what truth can it be said of Plato, Xenophon, Isocrates, Seneca, Epictetus, that they drop moral & religious truths only *obiter* or *by the bye.* This spirit of bigotry & detraction so unworthy of Leighton flows, in general, from the mean conception of Christianity, as a System of *Teaching*—a mere Code of Prudential and Moral *Instruction.*

Leighton, WORKS, *IV, 396. "Exhortation to the Students."*

Two grievous faults I find in these Exhortations. 1. The disheartening, cheerless, monkish, anti-Lutheran Gloom and ascetic or rather Manichæan Morals: 2. the indefiniteness of the contemptuous Declamation, Exh. after Exh. against Science, Learning, Philosophy, &c. In common candour L. should have informed his Pupils beforehand that they were wasting their time & labor,—if his contempt extended to the whole of their academic courses:—& if not, then he ought after they were compleated, to have particularized what he thought unworthy of bring further pursued.

Leighton, WORKS, *IV, end-page.*

[Faults of Leighton, with references to be used in the projected biography]

p. 196. Life of L.

p. 300. Life—Defect in Leighton. Commonplace Depreciation of the Greek and Roman Philosophers.

p. 360. Life—Railing against Scientific & Scholastic Theology.

p. 373. Life—Ascetic Calumniation of Human Life.

Leighton, WORKS, *IV, 113, 114.*

Archbishop Leighton's Works, in 4 Volumes Octavo, by Revd. Erasmus Middleton. Vol. IV [pp. 113, 114]. . . . The defect of Archb. Leighton's Reasoning is the taking Eternity as a *sort* of Time—a Baron Major, a Baron of Beef or Quarter of Lamb, out of which and *off* which Time is cut as a Brisket, or Shoulder—while even in common discourse without any design of sounding the depth of the Truth or of Weighing the words expressing it in the Hair-balance of Metaphysics, it would be more convenient to consider Eternity as the Antitheton of Time—as simul et totum to pars and successive.[43]

[43] Notebook 21½, fol. 51 recto and verso. Printed for the first time.

'If we could conceive a region of intellect between reason and revelation to have been previously unoccupied, we might say that the Archbishop had taken possession of that region.[44]

He thought favorably of Lord Rochester's conversion as narrated by Burnet; spoke of Jeremy Taylor in exalted terms, and thought the compass of his mind discovered itself in none of his works more than in his "Life of Christ," extremely miscellaneous as it was. He also expressed the strongest commendation of Archbishop Leighton, whose talents were of the loftiest description, and which were, at the same time, eminently combined with humility. He thought Bishop Burnet's high character of Leighton justly deserved, and that his whole conduct and spirit were more conformed to his Divine Master, than almost any man on record.[45]

Jeremy Taylor

I am, and ever have been, a great reader—and have read almost everything—a library-cormorant. I am deep in all out of the way books, whether of the monkish times, or of the puritanical æra—I have read & digested most of the Historical Writers; but I do not like History. Metaphysics & Poetry, & Facts of Mind— (i. e. Accounts of all the strange phantoms that ever possessed your philosophy—dreamers from Thoth, the Egyptian to Taylor, the English Pagan) are my darling Studies.[1]

Man of Genius—of two classes
1. Those who secrete their emotions or odoriferous Realism in one distinct product—the seed, the fruit, the blossom, this or that gland—and
2. Those, in whom the virtue is in all, in root, stem, leaves, & flowers —Jer. Taylor, Fuller, Shakespear are of this later class.[2]

[44] Thomas A. Methuen, "Retrospect of Friendly Communications with the Poet Coleridge," *Christian Observer*, XLV (May, 1845), 260.
[45] Report of conversation in Cottle, *Reminiscences*, p. 334.

[1] To John Thelwall, Nov. 19, 1796. This letter is in the Pierpont Morgan Library, and this excerpt has been reprinted by the kind permission of the trustees of the library. It appears also in E. H. Coleridge, *Letters*, I, 180-81.
[2] Notebook 41, fol. 78 recto. British Museum, Add. MSS, 47,536. Printed for the first time.

It must surely have been after hearing of or witnessing some similar event or scene or wretchedness,[3] that the most eloquent of our Writers (I had almost said of our Poets) Jeremy Taylor, wrote the following paragraph, which at least in Longinus's sense of the word, we may place among the most *sublime* passages in English Literature.

He that is no fool, but can consider wisely, if he be in love with this world we need not despair but that a witty man might reconcile him with tortures, and make him think charitably of the rack, and be brought to admire the harmony that is made by a herd of evening wolves when they miss their draught of blood in their midnight revels. The groans of a man in a fit of the stone are worse than all these; and the distractions of a troubled conscience are worse than those groans: *and yet a careless merry sinner is worse than all that.* But if we could from one of the battlements of Heaven espy, how many men and women at this time lie fainting and dying for want of bread, how many young men are hewn down by the sword of war; how many poor orphans are now weeping over the graves of their father, by whose life they were enabled to eat; if we could but hear how many mariners and passengers are at this present in a storm, and shriek out because their keel dashes against a rock, or bulges under them; how many people there are that weep with want, and are mad with oppression, or are desperate by a too quick sense of a constant infelicity; in all reason we should be glad to be out of the noise and participation of so many evils. This is a place of sorrows and tears, of great evils and constant calamities: let us remove hence, at least in affections and preparations of mind. *Holy Dying*, ch. i. s. 5, with omissions—Ed.[4]

Jeremy Taylor, the Spenser of Prose[5]

And why should I not call Taylor a poet? Is not *The Holy Living and Dying*, a sacred and didactic poem, in almost as wide a sense of the word as the *Commedia* of Dante? What Bard of ancient or modern times has surpassed, in richness of language, in fertility of fancy, in majesty of sentiment, in grace of imagery, this Spenser of English prose?

To Taylor belonged the "believing mind" of Collins. With the romance of the early chroniclers he was deeply imbued. The spirit of discovery had then made little progress; and the knowledge actually acquired only served to kindle the darkness into a faint and uncertain twilight that magnified every object. In the "Lion-haunted Inland" was still supposed to lie

A mystic city, goal of high emprise.—Chapman.

[3] The story of Maria as retold by Coleridge in Essay I, "The Second Landing Place," in *The Friend*, II, 267-300.
[4] *The Friend*, II, 281 n.
[5] Willmott, *C. at Trinity*, pp. 20-27.

And its golden towers often flashed through the waking dreams of the poetical enthusiast. Nor think me too ardent in my admiration of this glory of our Church.

Only take one or two specimens from the best known of his works, and say in what they are inferior to the sublimest poetry. The following is a picture:—

> All the succession of time, all the changes in nature, all the varieties of light and darkness; the thousand thousand accidents in the world, and every contingency to every man and to every creature, doth preach our funeral sermon, and calls us to look how the old sexton, Time, throws up the earth and digs a grave, where we must lay our sins or our sorrows, and sow our bodies till they rise again in a fair or an intolerable eternity.

The next might be copied from the note book of Spenser. The "full eyes of childhood" is one of the finest images in the language.

> Reckon but from the spritefulness of youth, and the fair cheeks and full eyes of childhood, to the loathsomeness and horror of a three days' burial. For so have I seen a rose newly springing from the clefts of its hood; at first it was fair as the morning, and full with the dew of heaven as a lamb's fleece; but when a ruder breath had forced open its virgin modesty, and dismantled its too youthful and unripe retirements, it began to put on darkness, and decline to softness and the symptoms of a sickly age; it bowed the head and broke the stalk, and at night, having lost some of its leaves and all its beauty, it fell into the portion of weeds and outworn faces.

What pen has uttered sweeter things on children, or the delights of the domestic hearth. His sermon on the Marriage-Ring is more beautiful than any pastoral.

> No man can tell but he that loves his children, how many delicious accents make a man's heart to dance in the pretty conversation of those dear pledges;—their childishness,—their stammering,—their little angers, —their innocence,—their imperfections,—their necessities,—are so many little emanations of joy and comfort to him that delights in their persons and society.

He looked out upon nature with the eye and heart of a poet, and in the following passage seems to have anticipated Thomson in one of the most beautiful stanzas of the *Castle of Indolence*.

> I am fallen into the hands of publicans and sequestrators, and they have taken all from me. What now? Let me look about me. They have left me sun, and moon, and fire, and water; a loving wife, and many friends to pity me, and some to relieve; and I can still discourse, and unless I list, they have not taken away my merry countenance, and my cheerful spirit, and a good conscience; they have still left me the providence of

God, and all the promises of the Gospel, and my religion, and my hopes
of heaven, and my charity to them too; and still I sleep, and digest, and
eat, and drink; I read and meditate; I can walk in my neighbours'
pleasant fields, and see the varieties of natural beauties, and delight
in all that in which God delights; that is, in virtue and wisdom, in the
whole creation, and in God himself.

Thomson has all the fervour of the poet, without the chastened submission of the Christian:—

> I care not, Fortune, what you me deny;
> You cannot rob me of free nature's grace,
> You cannot shut the windows of the sky,
>   Through which Aurora shows her brightening face.
> You cannot bar my constant feet to trace
> The woods and lawns, by living streams, at eve:
> Let health my nerves and finer fibres brace,
> And I their toys to the great children leave:
> Of fancy, reason, virtue,—nought can me bereave.

How pleasant would it be to go on thus, if my memory would enable
me, gathering choice specimens of his sublimity, pathos, and picturesque
truth; collecting the precious stones of which his charms are strung;
for even his ornaments are never chosen for their lustre alone; and in
the most gorgeous festivals and riotous enjoyments of his imagination, a
Hand is perceived writing on the wall. His learning and fancy are only
the handmaids and attendants of his piety; and those precious essences
which he extracts from the Tree of Knowledge, are all poured over the
feet of his Divine Master.

It is only when he shackles his fancy with rhyme, that his vein of
poetry ceases to flow. He is a poet everywhere except in verse. Yet how
acutely sensitive was his ear to all sweet sounds. Not even Milton, in
the bright and happy days of his youth, when he wrote *L'Allegro* and
Il Penseroso, breathed a more passionate love of the pealing organ, or
more deeply lamented the "drowsy dulness in devotion," brought in by
the Puritans, or prayed with greater ardour for the "solemn melody
and the raptures of warbling sweet voices out of cathedral choirs," which
Taylor said were wont to raise the spirit, and as it were, carry it up into
heaven.

The inferiority of his verses may, indeed, have resulted from want of
practice and study; for, even in the noblest works of the Muse, much of
the credit is due to the ingenuity and skill of the architect. His poems
are few, but I remember one or two passages which appear to possess
considerable merit.

That bright eternity
Where the Great King's transparent throne
Is of an entire jasper-stone;
There the eye
O' the chrysolite,
And a sky
Of diamonds, rubies, chrysophrase,
And above all, Thy holy face,
Make an eternal clarity:
When Thou thy jewels dost bind up, that day
Remember us, we pray,
That where the beryl lies,
And the crystal 'bove the skies,
There Thou may'st appoint us place
Within the brightness of Thy face.
And our soul
In the scroll
Of life and blissfulness enrol,
That we may praise Thee to eternity.
Full of mercy, full of love,
Look upon us from above,
Thou who taught'st the blind man's night
To entertain a double light,
Thine and the day's (and that thine too).
The lame away his crutches threw;
The parched crust of leprosy
Returned into its infancy.
The dumb amazed was to hear
His own unchain'd tongue strike his ear.
O let thy love our pattern be,—
Let thy mercy teach one brother
To forgive and love another,
That copying thy mercy here,
Thy goodness may hereafter rear
Our souls into thy glory, when
Our dust shall cease to be with men.

It is very astonishing, that among the eighteen prose authors, whom Pope selected as authorities for an English Dictionary, the name of Taylor is not found. Forgotten it could not be, for we are expressly told by Spence, that the "list was talked over several times, and quite settled." Sir Walter Raleigh, it is said, was rejected twice, as being too affected. Had the poet ever perused the concluding chapter of the History of the World? For the omission of Taylor I can assign no reason. Certainly from no other writer could be gathered such stores of dignified and impressive words. No path of ancient or modern learning, however sequestered or untrodden, was unknown to him. His memory brought up treasures from the hidden deep; and never did a soldier of the Holy Cross issue forth in a more gorgeous equipment to fight for the Sepulchre of Christ. But the resplendent sword was of celestial temper, and that costly armour was mighty against the dart of the enemy as any coat of iron mail;—it protected while it shone.

The writings of PLATO, and Bishop TAYLOR, and the Theoria Sacra of BURNET, furnish undeniable proofs that poetry of the highest kind may exist without metre, and even without the contradistinguishing objects of a poem.[6]

Jeremy Taylor's "Holy Dying," he affirmed, is a perfect poem, and in all its particulars, even the rhythm, may be compared with Young's "Night Thoughts."[7]

Jeremy Taylor is an excellent author for a young man to study for the purpose of imbibing noble principles, and at the same time of learning to exercise caution and thought in detecting his numerous errors.[8]

The writings of Bishop Jeremy Taylor are a perpetual feast to me. His hospitable board groans under the weight and multitude of viands. Yet I seldom rise from the perusal of his works, without repeating or recollecting the excellent observation of Minucius Felix: *Fabulas et errores ab imperitis parentibus discimus; et quod est gravius, ipsis studiis et disciplinis elaboramus.*[9]

I begin with *Original* Sin. And for this purpose I have selected the Aphorism from the ablest and most formidable Antagonist of this Doctrine, Bishop JEREMY TAYLOR, and from the most eloquent work of this most eloquent of Divines. Had I said, of Men, the soul of Cicero would forgive me, and Demosthenes nod assent.[10]

Can we wonder, then, that a mind, a heart, like Taylor's, should reject, that he should strain in his faculties to explain away, the belief that this Calamity [original sin], so dire in itself, should appear to the All-merciful God a rightful cause and motive for inflicting on the wretched Sufferers a Calamity infinitely more tremendous? nay, that it

[6] *Biog. Lit. C*, II, 10.
[7] Dec. 23, 1819. Robinson, *Diary*, I, 200.
[8] Aug. 29, 1827. *Table Talk S*, VI, 295.
[9] *Table Talk A*, p. 351.
[10] *Aids*, p. 250. Cf. Shedd, I, 267.

should be incompatible with Divine Justice *not* to punish it by everlasting torment? Or need we be surprised if he found nothing, that could reconcile his mind to such a belief . . . Lastly, might it not be presumed, that so enlightened, and at the same time so affectionate, a Divine would even fervently disclaim and reject the pretended justifications of God grounded on flimsy analogies drawn from the imperfections of human ordinances and human justice-courts—some of very doubtful character even as human Institutes, and all of them just only as far as they are necessary, and rendered necessary chiefly by the weakness and wickedness, the limited powers and corrupt passions, of mankind? The more confidently might this be presumed of so acute and practised a Logician, as Jeremy Taylor, in addition to his other extra-ordinary Gifts, is known to have been, when it is demonstrable that the most current of these justifications rests on a palpable equivocation: viz. the gross misuse of the word Right. . . .

That Jeremy Taylor, therefore, should have striven fervently against the Article so interpreted and so vindicated, is (for me, at least,) a subject neither of Surprise nor of Complaint. It is the doctrine which he *substitutes,* it is the weakness and inconsistency betrayed in the defence of this substitute, it is the unfairness with which he blackens the established Article—for to give it, as it had been caricatured by a few Ultra-Calvinists during the fever of the (so-called) *quinquarticular* Controversy, was in effect to blacken it—and then imposes another scheme, to which the same objections apply with even increased force, a scheme which seems to differ from the former only by adding fraud and mockery to injustice: these are the things that excite my wonder, it is of these that I complain![11]

But to return, or turn off, to the good old Bishop. It would be worth your while to read Taylor's "Letter on Original Sin," and what follows. I compare it to an old statue of Janus, with one of the faces, that which looks towards his opponents, the controversial phiz in highest preservation,—the force of a mighty one, all power, all life,—the face of a God rushing on to battle, and, in the same moment, enjoying at once both contest and triumph; the other, that which should have been the countenance that looks toward his followers, that with which he substitutes his own opinion, all weather eaten, dim, useless, a *Ghost* in *marble,* such as you may have seen represented in many of Piranesi's astounding engravings from Rome and the Campus Martius. Jer. Taylor's discursive intellect dazzle-darkened his intuition. The principle of be-

[11] *Aids,* pp. 265-68. Cf. Shedd, I, 277-79.

coming all things to all men, if by *any* means he might save *any*, with
him as with Burke, thickened the protecting epidermis of the tact-nerve
of truth into something like a callus. But take him all in all, such
a miraculous combination of erudition, broad, deep, and omnigenous; of
logic subtle as well as acute, and as robust as agile; of psychological insight, so fine yet so secure! of public prudence and practical *sageness*
that one ray of *creative Faith* would have lit up and transfigured into
wisdom, and of genuine imagination, with its streaming face unifying
all at one moment like that of the setting sun when through an inter-
space of blue sky no larger than itself, it emerges from the cloud to sink
behind the mountain, but a face seen only at *starts*, when some breeze
from the higher air scatters, for a moment, the cloud of butterfly fancies,
which flutter around him like a morning-garment of ten thousand colours
—(now how shall I get out of this sentence? the tail is too big to be
taken up into the coiler's mouth)—well, as I was saying, I believe such a
complete man hardly shall we meet again.[12]

Let such of my Readers as possess the Volume of Polemical Discourses, or the opportunity of consulting it, give a thoughtful perusal to
the pages from 869 to 893 (*Third Edition enlarged,* 1674). I dare anticipate their concurrence with the judgment which I here transcribe from
the blank space at the end of the Deus Justificatus[13] in my own Copy;
and which, though twenty years have elapsed since it was written, I have
never seen reason to recant or modify. ''This most eloquent Treatise
may be compared to a Statue of Janus, with the one face, which we must
suppose fronting the Calvinistic Tenet, entire and fresh, as from the
Master's hand; beaming with life and force, a witty scorn on the Lip,
and a Brow at once bright and weighty with satisfying reason! the
other, looking toward the '*something to be put in its place,*' maimed,
featureless, and weather-bitten into an almost visionary confusion and
indistinctness.''[14]

Above all, they must not seek to make the mysteries of faith what
the world calls *rational* by theories of original sin and redemption borrowed analogically from the imperfection of human law-courts and the
coarse contrivances of state expedience.
Among the numerous examples with which I might enforce this
warning, I refer, not without reluctance, to the most eloquent, and one

[12] To John Kenyon, Nov. 3 (1814). Coleridge, E. H., *Letters,* II, 640-41.
[13] See p. 293.
[14] *Aids,* p. 275. Cf. Shedd, I, 283-84.

ɔf the most learned of our divines; a rigorist, indeed, concerning the
authority of the Church, but a Latitudinarian in the articles of its faith;
who stretched the latter almost to the advanced posts of Socinianism, and
strained the former to a hazardous conformity with the assumptions of
the Roman hierarchy. With what emotions must not a pious mind peruse
such passages as the following:—"Death reigned upon . . . Michael to
David." (Taylor's Polem. Tracts, p. 711).[15]

But, confining my remark exclusively to the doctrines and the practical deductions from them, I could never read Bishop Taylor's Tract
on the doctrine and practice of Repentance, without being tempted to
characterize high Calvinism as (comparatively) a lamb in wolf's skin,
and strict Arminianism as approaching to the reverse.[16]

Armin. ✗ Calvinism [Coleridge quotes his own note to *Vindication,*
sec. 39, p. 671]. Arm. is cruel to individuals for fear of damaging the
race by false hopes and improper confidences: while Cal. sounds horrible
for the race but is full of consolation to the individual penitent.

The oftener I read and meditate (& how few days are there in which
I do not read and meditate) on J. Taylor's Writings, the more forcibly
does the justice of the preceding Note strike me. And it is so marvellous,
such a hungry dry corrosive Scheme ot Monacho-manichæan Ethics in
so rich, so genial, so tender a Soul as Bishop Taylor's! That he should
have strangled the philosophy of Love by the parasite method of rank
weeds, the Logic of Casuistry.[17]

By the Church of England, I mean the Liturgy, Articles, and Homilies, supported by the Fathers of the Church; from Whittaker, Hooker,
Donne, Sanderson, Hammond, &c., Bull, Stillingfleet, and Waterland;
and I exclude such of her illustrious Divines as were condemned by the
great majority of Divines in their own time, as to the points, and those
only, on which they were condemned. Thus I should appeal with confidence to Jeremy Taylor on all points of discipline, and in the Eucharist: for in those he was the "os et lyra Ecclesiæ;" but not on points
of original sin, nor on the extent of Christ's merit: for on these Bishop
Sanderson and others of his dear friends dropped a tear. He was the
Origen of our Church. There was much in him to be forgiven; but a

15 *The Friend,* Essay, II, III, 108.
16 *Ibid.,* p. 111.
17 Notebook 26, fol. 2 verso. British Museum, Add. MSS, 47,524. Printed for
the first time.

thousand excellencies demand our forgiveness of the former, as the best form in which we can shew our gratitude for the latter. His faith in the article of the Tri-unity was, I doubt not, far more sound than many of his expressions and concessions were cautious, or strictly defensible; but in his tremendous book on Repentance, he transcended not only all the Arminians of his own party, but even the most ascetic writers of the Romanists themelves. It is remarkable that it is the least eloquent of all his works, and the most prolix; without splendor, without unction, —herein contrasted with the tracts which contain the kindred error of Pelagianism ("Letter to a Lady on Original Sin," with those to the Bishop of Worcester) which are the most eloquent of his works—in my humble opinion the most eloquent in our whole language. His "Liberty of Prophesying" contains likewise many indiscreet passages. In his advocation of the Antipædobaptists, he raised a spirit which he himself afterwards tried hard to lay with very doubtful success. Tillotson, Hoadly, and the whole sect of Syncretists and Coalitionists, I utterly reject; however, these writers are of double strength when quoted against the Tomlinists, Pelagians, and the other Prettymen, alias-ers and Isthmus Divines of the present and preceding generation. Even as Eusebius may be fairly challenged as suspicious testimony, when an evidence is brought from him in favour of the systems that diminish the Redeemer's glory; but it is of double power against them: for the concessions of a witness are strong in proportion as his partiality is evident. "Confessio reluctantis bis credibilis, quum vim veritatis demonstrat. Sacrificator, i. e. sacra est quia sacrificium *voluntatis* conscientiæ." The Romanists err in placing the Fathers on a level with the Sacred Scriptures, and the later Fathers with those of the first four centuries,—nay, in giving them the preference, and in subordinating both to the Church. The Reformed churches, both at home and abroad, have erred in altogether rejecting, or at least in grossly underrating, the testimony of the Fathers in general, with an undue partiality in favour of Augustin,—in rejecting the distinction between power in articles of faith, and those forms of church constitution and government. N. B.—Authority is contra-distinguished from power; the King's proclamation has authority, not power. Cæteris paribus, it is my duty to obey it, and it must be on strong grounds, and after the most serious consideration, that I can innocently disobey it. The Church of England is the golden medium. To the Bible it appeals as its only law; to the united suffrage of the first centuries, as its best and safest comment.[18]

[18] "Thoughts on the Church," *The Christian Observer*, XLV (June, 1845), 328-29.

Taylor's was a great and lovely mind; yet how much and injuriously was it perverted by his being a favorite and follower of Laud, and by his intensely Popish feelings of church authority. His Liberty of Prophesying is a work of wonderful eloquence and skill; but if we believe the argument, what do we come to? Why, to nothing more or less than this, that—so much can be said for every opinion and sect, so impossible is it to settle anything by reasoning or authority of Scripture—we must appeal to some positive jurisdiction on earth, *ut sit finis controversiarum*. In fact, the whole book is the precise argument used by the Papists to induce men to admit the necessity of a supreme and infallible head of the church on earth. It is one of the works which pre-eminently gives countenance to the saying of Charles or James II., I forget which: —"When you of the Church of England contend with the Catholics, you use the arguments of the Puritans; when you contend with the Puritans, you immediately adopt all the weapons of the Catholics." Taylor never speaks with the slightest symptom of affection or respect of Luther, Calvin, or any other of the great reformers—at least, not in any of his learned works; but he *saints* every trumpery monk or friar, down to the very latest canonizations by the modern Popes. I fear you will think me harsh, when I say that I believe Taylor was, perhaps unconsciously, half a Socinian in heart. Such a strange inconsistency would not be impossible. The Romish church has produced many such devout Socinians. The cross of Christ is dimly seen in Taylor's works. Compare him in this particular with Donne, and you will feel the difference in a moment. Why is not Donne's volume of sermons reprinted at Oxford?

In the reign of Edward VI., the Reformers feared to admit almost anything on human authority alone. They had seen and felt the abuses consequent on the Popish theory of Christianity; and I doubt not they wished and intended to reconstruct the religion and the church, as far as possible, upon the plan of the primitive ages. But the Puritans pushed this bias to an absolute bibliolatry. They would not put on a cornplaster without scraping a text over it. Men of learning, however, soon felt that this was wrong in the other extreme, and indeed united itself to the very abuse it seemed to shun. They saw that a knowledge of the Fathers, and of early tradition, was absolutely necessary; and unhappily, in many instances, the excess of the Puritans drove the men of learning into the old Popish extreme of denying the Scriptures to be capable of affording a rule of faith without the dogmas of the church. Taylor is a striking instance how far a Protestant might be driven in this direction.[19]

[19] June 4, 1830. *Table Talk S*, VI, 328-30.

But if their answer be, Yes! we do suppose and believe this efficiency in the baptismal act—I have not another word to say. Only, perhaps, I might be permitted to express a hope that, for consistency's sake, they would speak less slightingly of the *insufflation*, and *extreme unction*, used in the Romish Church; notwithstanding the not easily to be answered arguments of our Christian Mercury, the all-eloquent Jeremy Taylor, respecting the latter,—"which, since it is used when the man is above half dead, when he can exercise no act of understanding, *it must needs be nothing. For no rational man can think, that any ceremony can make a spiritual change without a spiritual act of him that is to be changed; nor that it can work by way of nature, or by charm, but morally and after the manner of reasonable creatures.*" Taylor's *Epist. Dedic. to his Holy Dying,* p. 6. . . . To be *called* irrational, is a trifle: to be so, and in matters of religion, is far otherwise: and whether the irrationality consists in men's believing (*i. e.* in having persuaded themselves that they believe) *against* reason, or *without* reason, I have been early instructed to consider it as a sad and serious evil, pregnant with mischiefs, political and moral. And by none of my numerous Instructors so impressively, as by that great and shining Light of our Church in the æra of her intellectual splendour, Bishop Jeremy Taylor: from one of whose works,[20] and that of especial authority for the safety as well as the importance of the principle, inasmuch as it was written expressly ad populum, I will now, both for its own intrinsic worth, and to relieve the attention, wearied, perhaps, by the length and argumentative character of the preceding *discussion,* interpose the following Aphorism.[21]

In Jeremy Taylor's *Holy Living* I have met a passage completely coinciding with, and so far sanctioning the view of Infant Baptism, in the *Aids to Reflection,* viz., that the assertion of regeneration in the Baptismal Service is symbolical, and prospective, and instructs the members of the Church to *feel* and *act* toward the babe by anticipation of a lively and assured hope AS IF it were already a Christian by individual faith and election.[22]

N.B.—In the "Logos" to reperuse Taylor's Works, especially his Sermons, in order to expose the errors and the sources of the errors, of Judaizing Christianity—or to return to the beggarly Elements.—Till the

[20] *Worthy Communicant,* chap. iii, sec. 5 (see n. 88).
[21] *Aids,* pp. 332-33. Cf. Shedd, I, 319-20.
[22] To Lady Beaumont, Saturday, March 18, 1826. Knight, *Mem. of Coleorton,* II, 248.

Light of Immortality was brought by Christ, the God of the Jews must of necessity have combined 1. the general Laws of the Universe (*Dei Sapentia sive essentia*). 2. the Laws of the Jurisprudence of a particular Station—and both unmodified by Religion & Morality in their contradistinctive Character. But it is really shocking to hear Christian Divines talk in the same way, that a Jewish High-Priest might have done unblameably—But the lust of sacerdotal Power is at the bottom of all this—In all but a *mundane* Religion, *not of this world.*—i. e. in all but true Xtnty Priests are Magistrates, Powers, Agents—in Xtnty only Teachers, Persuaders, Comforters.[23]

Taylor, POLEMICALL DISCOURSES,[24] *note at the top of first flyleaf, recto.*

N. B. In the Marginal MSS Annotations the following marks or abbreviations are used.

= equivalent to

+ together with

X multiplied into: and in moral or spiritual subjects, it signifies a mutual interpenetration: thus the Finite Will X the Reason = Faith; or Faith is the focal energy from the convergency of the Reason and the Will, or the total Act of the entire Man arising from the interpenetration of the Reason and the Will.

)(= disparate from: thus Prudence)(Virtue

⨉ = opposite to: thus Sweet ⨉ Sour

⨉ = contrary to: thus Bitter ⨉ Sweet

[23] Notebook 22, fol. 63. British Museum, Add. MSS, 47,520. Printed for first time.

[24] Jeremy Taylor, *Collection of Polemicall Discourses* (London: 1674). This is the third edition enlarged, containing the original notes. British Museum, Ashley, 5174. The volume bears James Gillman's bookplate, and there is a note to Charles Lamb on the verso of the title page of *Episcopacy Asserted*. At the time that the notes were made, Coleridge had not seen the Heber edition. The notes given in *Lit. Rem.*, pp. 303 ff., are from Heber's edition, but whether Coleridge transcribed them or, as in other cases, they were transcribed by someone else cannot be determined unless the volumes come to light. Except for the customary modifications and omissions made by Henry Nelson Coleridge in his editing, the notes are essentially the same in content. That Coleridge later read Heber is indicated by the following note in Charles James Blomefield's *A Charge delivered to the Clergy of His Diocese* (1830):

"On the first perusal of the late Bishop Heber's Life of Jer. Taylor, I was surprized at, and still regret, his unqualified condemnation of Taylor's short treatise on Confirmation. So far from agreeing with Heber on his almost dissenting like views of this ordinance, it appears to me indispensable in a Church which practices Infant Baptism. See Aids to Reflections, on Baptism. S. T. C."

Since the order of Taylor's discourses is very different in the 1674 edition and the Heber edition, footnote references to *Lit. Rem.* are given for convenience in making comparisons. Coleridge's explanation of symbols does not appear in *Lit. Rem.*

THE OLD DIVINES/JEREMY TAYLOR

Taylor, POLEMICALL DISCOURSES, *second, note, first flyleaf, recto.*

I have not seen the late Bishop Heber's Edition of J. Taylor's
Works; but I have been informed, that he did little more than contribute the *Life,* and that in all else it is a mere London Bookseller's
Job. This (if true) is greatly to be regretted. I know no writer whose
works more *require*—I need not say, deserve—the annotations, aye, the
occasional *Animadversions,* of a sound and Learned Divine. One thing,
is especially desirable in reference to that most important, because (with
the exception perhaps of the Holy Living & Dying) the most popular,
of Taylor's Works, viz. The Liberty of Prophesying: and this [is] a
careful collation of the different Editions, particularly of the *first*
printed before the Restoration, and the last published in Taylor's Life-
time, and after his promotion to the Episcopal Bench. Indeed, I regard this as so nearly concerning Taylor's character as a *man,* that if
I find that it has not been done in Heber's Edition, and if I can find a
first Edition in the British Museum, or Sion College, or Dr. Williams'
Library, I will, God permitting, do it myself. There seems something
cruel in giving the name, *Ana*baptist, to the English Anti-pædo-baptists;
but still worse in connecting this most innocent Opinion with the mad
Jacobin ravings of the poor Wretches, who were called Anabaptists, in
Munster, as if the latter had ever formed part of the Baptist's Creeds.
In short, the Liberty of Prophesying is an admirable Work, in many
respects—and calculated to produce a much greater effect on the Many
than Milton's Treatise on the same Subject; on the other hand, Milton's
is throughout *unmixed truth;* and the Man, who in reading the two
does not feel the contrast between the single-mindedness of the one, and
the strabismus in the other, is—*in the road of Preferment.* S. T. C.

Taylor, POLEMICALL DISCOURSES, *"Epistle Dedicatory to Christopher
Lord Hatton," fol. a verso. Note continued on page following.*

   And the breath of the people is like the voice of an exterminating Angel,
   not so killing but so secret.

   "So," i. e. in such wise. It would be well to note, after what time the
"*as*" became the requisite correlative to "so," and even, as in this instance the preferable Substitute. We should have written "as" in both
places probably; but at all events in the latter, transplacing the sentences "*as* secret, tho' not so killing": or, "not so killing but quite as
secret." It is not generally true, that Taylor's Punctuation is arbitrary,
or his Periods reducible to the post-revolutionary standard of Length by
turning some of his Colons or Semi-colons into Full stops. There is a
subtle yet just and systematic Logic followed in his pointing, as often

as it is permitted by the higher principle because the proper and primary purpose of our stops, and to which alone from their paucity they are adequate—that, I mean, of enabling the Reader to prepare and manage the proportions of his Voice and Breath. But for the (ὡς ἐμοί γε δοκεῖ) true scheme of punctuation see the *blank* page overleaf which I will try to disblank into a prize of more worth than can be got at the E.O.'s and Little-goes of Linley Murray.[25]

Taylor, POLEMICALL DISCOURSES : APOLOGY FOR AUTHORIZED AND SET FORMS OF LITURGY, *Preface, sec. 6.*

> Not like women or children when they are affrighted with fire in their clothes; we shak'd off the coal indeed, but not our garments lest we should have exposed our Churches to that nakedness which the excellent men of our sister Churches complained to be among themselves.

O what convenient things Metaphors and Similes are! So charmingly indeterminate! On the general reader the literal sense operates. *He* shivers in sympathy with the poor shiftless matron, the Church of Geneva. To the *Objector* the answer is ready—It was speaking metaphorically! and only meant, that she had no Shift on the outside of her Gown, that she made a Shift without an Over-all. Compare this § 6 with the manful, senseful irrebuttable § 4—a Folio Volume in a single Paragraph! But Jeremy Taylor would have been *too* great for man, had he not occasionally fallen below himself.[26]   S. T. C.

Taylor, POLEMICALL DISCOURSES : APOLOGY, *Preface, sec. 10.*

> And since all that cast off the *Roman* yoke, thought they had title enough to be called Reformed, it was hard to have pleased all the private interests and peevishness of men that called themselves friends, and therefore that only in which the Church of *Rome* had prevaricated against the word of God, or innovated against Apostolical tradition, all that was par'd away.

["*Against*" is underlined]. Aye, here is the *Ovum* (as Sir Everard Home says)—the proto-parent of the whole Race of Controversies between Protestant & Protestant—and each had Gospel on their side. Whatever is not *against* the word of God, is *for* it—thought the Founders of the Church of England. Whatever is not *in* the word of God, is a word of man, a will-worship, presumptuous and usurping—thought the Founders of the Churches of Scotland & Geneva. The one proposed·to themselves to be Reformers of the Latin Church, i. e. to bring it back to the *form*, which it had during the four first Centuries : the latter to be

---

[25] *Lit. Rem.,* III, 205 n., says: "The page however remains a blank. But a little essay on punctuation by the Author is in the Editor's possession, and will be published hereafter."

[26] Cf. *Lit. Rem.,* III, 218.

the Renovators of the Christian Religion, as it was preached and instituted by the Apostles & immediate Followers of Christ thereunto especially inspired. When the Premises are so different, who can wonder at the difference in the conclusions?[27] S. T. C.

Taylor, POLEMICALL DISCOURSES: APOLOGY, *Preface, sec. 26.*

> For if we deny to the people a liberty of reading Scriptures, may they not complain as *Isaac* did against the inhabitants of the land, that the Philistines had spoiled his well, and the fountains of living water; If a free use to all of them, and of all Scriptures were permitted, should not the Church her self have more cause to complain of the infinite licentiousness and looseness of interpretations, and of the commencement of ten thousand errors, which would certainly be consequent to such permission? Reason and Religion will chide us in the first, reason and experience in the latter. . . The Church with great wisdom hath first held this torch out, and though for great reasons intervening and hindering, it cannot be reduced to practice, yet the Church hath shewn her desire to avoid the evil that is on both hands, and she hath shewn the way also, if it could have been insisted in.*

N. B. If there were not at the time, this Preface or this § ph. at least, was written or published, some design on foot or sub linguâ, of making advances to Catholicism for the purpose of conciliating the Catholic Courts of Austria, France and Spain in favor of the Cavalier and Royalist Party at home and abroad—this must be considered as a useless & worse than useless Avowal. The Papacy at the height of it's influence never asserted a higher or more anti-protestant Right than this of dividing the Scriptures into permitted and forbidden portions. If there be a Functionary of divine institution, synodical or unipersonal, who under the name of "The Church" has the right under circumstances of it's own determination to forbid all but such and such *parts* of the Bible, it must possess potentially and under other circumstances a Right of withdrawing the whole Book from the unlearned, who yet can *not* be altogther unlearned—for the very prohibition supposes them able to do what a few Centuries before the majority of the Clergy themselves were not qualified to do—i.e. read their Bible throughout. Surely it would have been politic in the writer to have left out the sentence marked *, which his puritan adversaries could not fail to translate into the Church's shewing her teeth tho' she dared not bite. I regret these passages—neither our incomparable Liturgy, nor this full, masterly, and unanswerable defence of it, requiring them.[28]

[27] Cf. *Lit. Rem.*, III, 218-19.
[28] Cf. *Lit. Rem.*, III, 220-21.

Taylor, Polemicall Discourses: apology, *sec. 2, p. 1.*

> And it may be when I am a little more used to it, I shall not wonder at a *Synod,* in which not one Bishop sits (in the capacity of a Bishop) though I am most certain this is the first example in *England* since it was first Christened.

Is this *quite* fair? Is it not (at least *logically* considered and at the *commencement* of an argument) too like a petitio principii or presumptio rei litigatæ? The Westminster Divines were confessedly not *Prelates,* but there were many in all other points orthodox and affectionate members of the Establishment, who with Bedell, Lightfoot, and Archbishop Usher, held them to be Bishops in the primitive sense of the Term, & who yet had no wish to make any other change in the hierarchy than that of denominating the existing English Prelates *Arch*-Bishops. They thought, that what at the bottom was little more than a question of *names* among Episcopalians, ought not to *have* occasioned such a Dispute; but yet the evil having taken place, they held a change of names not too great a sacrifice, if thus the things themselves could be preserved, and Episcopacy maintained against the Independents & Presbyterians.[29]

Taylor, Polemicall Discourses: apology, *sec. 5, pp. 2, 3.*

> The *Directory* takes away that Form of Prayer which by the authority and consent of the obliging power of the Kingdom, hath been used and enjoyned ever since the Reformation.

It is a thing of no present importance; but as a point of History, Qy. were there any Divines in the Westminster Assembly who adopted by anticipation the notions of the Seekers, Quakers &c. Baxter denies it. I understood the controversy to have been, whether the examinations, at the *admission* to the ministry, superseded or no the *necessity* of any directive Models, besides those found in the sacred Volumes? If not *necessary,* whether there was any greater expedience in providing by authority forms of *prayer* for the minister, than forms of *sermons?* *Reading,* whether of prayers or sermons, might be discouraged without encouraging *unpremeditated* praying and preaching. But the Whole Question as between the Prelatists and the Assembly Divines has, like many others, been best solved by the Trial. A vast majority among the Dissenters themselves consider the antecedents to the sermon, with exception of their congregational Hymns, as the defective part of their public service, and admit the superiority of our Liturgy.

P. S. It seems to me, I confess, that the controversy could never have risen to the height, it did, if *all* the parties had not thrown too far

[29] Cf. *Lit. Rem.,* III, 222.

into the backround the distinction in nature and objective, between the three equally necessary species of Worship—Public, Family, and Private (or solitary) Devotion. Tho' the very far larger proportion of the Blame falls on the Anti-Liturgists; yet on the other hand, too many of our Church divines (among others that *Exemplar* of a Churchman & a Christian, the every way excellent George Herbert) were scared by the growing fanaticism of the Geneva Malcontents into the neighborhood of the opposite Extreme; and in their dread of enthusiasm, will-worship, insubordination, & indecency, carried their preference of the established *public* forms of Prayer almost to superstition, by *exclusively* both using & requiring them even on their own sickbeds. This most assuredly was neither the intention or the wish of the first compilers. However, if they erred in this, it was an error of filial love excused and only not sanctioned, by the love of Peace & Unity, and their keen sense of "the Beauty of Holiness" displayed in their Mother Church. I mention this the rather, because our Church, having in so incomparable a way provided for our *public* Devotions; and Taylor having enriched us with such and so many models of *private* Prayer and devotional Exercise; (from which, by-the-bye, it is most desirable that a well-arranged collection should be made—a *selection* is *requisite* rather from the opulence, than the inequality, of the store)—we have nothing to wish for but a collection of *Family* and *Domestic* Prayers and Thanksgivings, equally (if that be not too bold a wish!) appropriate to the special object, as the *Common* Prayer book is for the Christian *Community,* & the Collection from Taylor for the Christian in his *closet* or at his *bed-side.* Here again our author would himself furnish abundant materials for this work, for surely, since the Apostolic age, never did the Spirit of Supplication move on the deeps of a human soul with a more genial life, or more profoundly impregnate the rich gifts of a happy nature (naturel) than in the person of Jeremy Taylor![30] To render the fruits available for all, we need only a combination of Christian Experience with that finer sense of propriety, which we may venture to call *devotional Taste,* in the Individual choosing, or chosen, to select, arrange, and methodize; and no less in the Dignitaries appointed to revise and sanction the Collections. With one other exception, perhaps: a scheme of *Christian* Psalmody fit for *all* our Churches, & which should not exceed 150 or 200

[30] "All our modern prayers seem tongue-tied. We appear to be thinking more of avoiding an heretical expression or thought than of opening ourselves to God. We do not pray with that entire, unsuspecting, unfearing, child-like profusion of feeling, which so beautifully shines forth in Jeremy Taylor and Andrewes, and the writings of some of the older and better saints of the Romish church, and particularly of that remarkable woman St. Theresa." Jan. 12, 1834. *Table Talk* S, VI, 501.

Psalms & Hymns. Surely, if the Church does not hesitate in the *titles* of the Psalms & of the Chapters of the Prophets, to give the Xtn. sense & application, there can be no consistent objection to do the same in it's spiritual Songs. The effect on the morals, feelings, and information of the People at large is not to be calculated. It is this more than any other single cause that has saved the Peasantry of Protestant Germany from the contagion of Infidelity.[31]

Taylor, POLEMICALL DISCOURSES: APOLOGY, *sec. 32, p. 8. Note on pp. 8-14.*

And yet because the Holy Ghost renewed their memory, improved their understanding, supplied to some their want of humane learning, and so assisted them that they should not commit an error in fact or opinion, neither in the narrative nor dogmatical parts, therefore they writ *by the Spirit.*

And where is the proof? and to what purpose, unless a distinct and plain Diagnostic were given of the *divinities* & the *humanities?* And even then, what would it avail unless the Interpreters & Translators, not to speak of the Copyists in the first & second Centuries, were likewise assisted by inspiration? As to the larger part of the prophetic Books, and the whole of the Apocalypse, we must receive them as inspired Truths, or reject them as inventions or enthusiastic delusions. But in what other Book of Scripture does the Writer assign his own work to a miraculous dictation or infusion? Surely, the contrary is implied in Dr. Luke's Preface. Does the hypothesis rest on one possible construction of a single passage in St. Paul's? And that construction too resting on a καί not found in the oldest MSS?—when the context would rather lead us to understand the words as parallel with the other assertion of the apostle, that all good works are given from God? Finally, will not the certainty of the competence & single-mindedness of the writers suffice? And this too confirmed by the high probability, bordering on certainty, that God's *especial* Grace worked in them? and that an especial Providence watched over the preservation of writings, which, we know, both are and have been of such pre-eminent importance to Christianity —& yet by natural means?[32]

Taylor, POLEMICALL DISCOURSES: APOLOGY, *sec. 59, p. 15.*

So that let the devotion be never so great, set forms of prayer will be expressive *enough* of any desire, though importunate as extremity itself.

[31] Cf. *Lit. Rem.*, III, 223-25.

[32] In *Lit. Rem.*, III, 229-30, a comment is added here which in the original belongs to sec. 45, p. 12. The above comment and the comment on pp. 17-18 below give one of Coleridge's clearest statements on his own belief concerning the great controversy over the inspiration of the Scripture.

This and much of the same import in this Treatise, is far more than Taylor, mature in experience and softened by afflictions, would have written. Besides, it is in *effect*, tho' not in logic, a deserting of his own strong and unshaken ground of the means and ends of *Public Worship*.[33]

Taylor, POLEMICALL DISCOURSES: APOLOGY, *sec. 69, pp. 17-18. Note on p. 18.*

This and the next section are too much in the vague, mythical style of the Italian & Jesuit Divines, and gives to these a greater advantage against our Church, than it gains over the Sectarians in it's support. We well know, who & how many, the compilers of our Liturgy were, under Edw. VI.; & know too well, what the weather-cock Parliaments were, both then & under Eliz. by which the compilation was made law. The argument therefore should be *inverted*—not the Church (= AB; DC; FL; &c.) compiled it, ergo, it is unobjectionable; but (& truly we may say it) it is so unobjectionable, so far transcending all, we were entitled to expect from a few men in that state of Information & under such difficulties, that we are justified in concluding, that the Compilers were under the guidance of the Holy Spirit. But the same Order holds good even with regard to the Scriptures. We cannot rightly affirm they were inspired; therefore, they must be believed; but that they are worthy of belief, excellent in so universal a sense to ends commensurate with the whole moral (ergo the whole actual) world, that as sure as there is a Moral Governor of the world, they must have been, in some sense or other, & that too an *efficient* sense, *inspired*. Those who deny this, must be prepared to assert, that if they had what appeared to them good historic evidence of a Miracle, in the world of the Senses, they would receive the hideous immoral doctrines of Mahomet and Brahma, and thus to disobey the express commands both of the Old & New Testament. Tho' an angel should come from Heaven & work all miracles, yet preach another Doctrine, we are to hold him accursed.[34]

Taylor, POLEMICALL DISCOURSES: APOLOGY, *sec. 80, p. 20. Note continued on p. 21.*

Now then I demand whether the Prayer of *Manasses* be so good a Prayer as the *Lords Prayer?* Or is the prayer of *Judith*, or of *Tobias*, or of *Judas Macchabeus*, or of the son of *Sirach*, is any of these so good? Certainly no man will say they are; and the reason is, because we are not sure they are inspired by the Holy Spirit of God.

How inconsistent Taylor often is! the result of the system of *economizing* truth! The true reason is the inverse—the Prayers of Judith

---

[33] Cf. *Lit. Rem.*, III, 230.   [34] Cf. *Lit. Rem.*, III, 230-31.

&c. are not worthy to be compared with the Lord's Prayer—therefore
neither is the spirit, in which they were conceived, worthy to be compared with the spirit, from which the Lord's Prayer proceeded: &
therefore with all fullness of satisfaction we receive the latter, as indeed
& in fact our Lord's Dictation.

P.S. In all men & in all works of great genius the characteristic
fault will be found in the characteristic excellence. Thus, in Taylor,
Fullness, Overflow, Superfluity. His arguments are a procession of all
the Nobles and Magnates of the Land in their grandest, richest, and
most splendid *Paraphernalia*: but the total Impression is weakened by
the multitude of Lacqueys and ragged Intruders running in & out between the ranks. As far as the Westminster Divines were the Antagonists to be answered (and excepting those & these who like Baxter,
Calamy, & Bishop Reynolds, contended for a reformation or correction
only of the Church Liturgy, there were none worth answering) the
Question was *not* whether the use of one & the same set of Prayers on
all days in all churches was *innocent,* but whether the exclusive imposition of the same was comparatively *expedient* & conducive to edification?
Let us not too severely arraign the judgement or the intentions of the
good men who determined for the negative. If indeed we confined ourselves to the comparison between our Liturgy, & any or all of the proposed Substitutes for it, we could not hesitate; but those good men, in
addition to their prejudices, had to compare the lives, the conversation,
and the religious affections and principles, of the Prelatic and Anti-
prelatic Party, in general! And do not we ourselves, *now* do the like?
Are we not, & with abundant reason, thankful that Jacobinism is
rendered comparatively feeble and it's deadly venom neutralized, by the
profligacy & open Irreligion of the majority of it's Adherents? Add the
recent *cruelties* of the Star-chamber under Laud (I do not say the
intolerance: for that, which was common to both parties, must be construed as an error in both, rather than a crime in either)—and do not
forget the one great inconvenience, to which the Prelatic Divines were
exposed from the very position which it was the peculiar Honor of the
Church of England to have taken & maintained—viz. the golden *mean*:
for in consequence of this their arguments as *Churchmen* would often
have the appearance of contrasting with their grounds of controversy,
as *Protestants*—and we shall find enough to sanction our Charity as
Brethren, without detracting a tittle from our Loyalty, as members of
the established Church. As to *this* "Apologie," the Victory, doubtless,
remains with Taylor, on the whole; but to have rendered it *full* and
triumphant, it would have been necessary to do what perhaps could not
at that time, & by Jeremy Taylor, have been done with prudence—

videlicet, not only to *disprove* in part, but likewise in part to *explain*, the alledged difference of the spiritual fruits in the ministerial Labors of the high and low Party in the Church (for remember that at this period both parties were *in* the Church, even as the Evangelical, Reformed and Pontifical Parties before the establishment of a Schism by the actually schismatical Council of Trent)—& thus to Demonstrate that the differences to the disadvantage of the Established Church as far as they were real, were as little attributable to the Liturgy as the wound in the Heel of Achilles to the Shield & Breast-plate which his immortal mother had provided for him from the Forge divine.[35]

Taylor, POLEMICALL DISCOURSES: APOLOGY, *sec. 88, p. 22.*

> And I rather make the inference from the preceding argument, because of the cognation one hath with the other; for the Apostles did also in the consecration of the Eucharist, use the Lords Prayer, and that together with the words of institution was the only form of consecration, saith St. *Gregory;* and St. *Hierome* affirms, that the Apostles by the command of their Lord, used this prayer in the benediction of the elements.

This § 88 is an instance of impolitic management of a cause, into which J. T. was so often seduced by the fertility of his Intellect and the opulence of his erudition. An antagonist by exposing the improbability of the Tradition (and most improbable it surely is!) and the little credit due to St. Gregory and Saint Jerome (not forgetting a Miltonic Sneer at their Saintship), might draw off the attention from the unanswerable parts of Taylor's Reasoning & leave an impression of his having been confuted.[36]

Taylor, POLEMICALL DISCOURSES: APOLOGY, *sec. 90, p. 23.*

By-the-bye, one cause of the small impression, (small in proportion to their vast superiority in Knowledge and Genius) which J. T. and his Compeers made on the religious part of the community by their *controversial* Writings during the life of Ch. I. is to be found in their predilection for *patristic* Learning & Authority. This *originated* in the wish to baffle the *Papists* at their own weapons; but it could not escape notice, that the latter, tho' regularly beat, were yet not so beat, but that they always kept the field: & when the same mode of warfare was employed against the Puritans, it was suspected as papistical.[37]

[35] Cf. *Lit. Rem.,* III, 232-34.
[36] Cf. *Lit. Rem.,* III, 237-38.
[37] Cf. *Lit. Rem.,* III, 239.

Taylor, POLEMICALL DISCOURSES: APOLOGY, *sec. 92, p. 24. Note continued on p. 25.*

Now here dear Jer. Taylor begins to be *himself:* for with all his astonishing complexity yet versatile agility of Powers, he was too good & of too catholic a spirit to be a good Polemic! Hence he so continually is now breaking, now varying, the thread of the argument: and hence he is so again and again forgetting that he is reasoning against an Antagonist, and falls into conversation with him as a friend—I might almost say, into the literary chit-chat of a rich genius and an unwithholding Frankness whose *sands* are seed-pearl. Of his controversies, those against Popery are the most powerful because there he had subtleties & obscure Reading to contend against, & his Wit, Acuteness, and omnifarious Learning found stuff to work on: those on Original Sin [are] the most eloquent. But in all alike it is the Digressions, Overgrowths, parenthetic *obiter et in transitu* sentences, and above all, his anthropological Reflections and Experiences (ex. gr. the inimitable account of a religious Dispute, from the first collision to the spark, and from the spark to the "World in flames," in his Dissuasive from Popery)—these are the costly gems which glitter, loosely set, on the chain armor of his polemic Pegasus, that expands his wings chiefly to fly off from the field of Battle—the stroke of whose Hoof the very Rock cannot resist, but beneath the stroke of which the opening Rock sends forth an Hippocrene! The work in which all his powers are confluent, in which deep, yet gentle, the full stream of his genius winds onward, & still forming peninsulas in it's winding course, distinct parts that are only not each a perfect Whole—or in less figurative style—(yet what Language that does not partake of poetic eloquence can convey the characteristics of a Poet & an Orator?) the work, which I read with most admiration but likewise with most apprehension and regret, is the Liberty of Prophesying. If indeed, like some Thessalian drug, or the Strong Herb of Anticyra, that helps & harms,

> Which life and death have seal'd with counter-charms;

it could be administered by special Prescription; it might do good service as a narcotic for Zealotry, or a solvent for Bigotry.[38]

Taylor, POLEMICALL DISCOURSES: APOLOGY, *p. 36. Note at end, continued on title page of* THE SACRED ORDER.

Such is the substance of this Tract. What the Author proposed to prove, he has satisfactorily proved. The faults of the Work are:—
1. The intermixture of weak & strong arguments, and the frequent inter-

---
[38] Cf. *Lit. Rem.*, III, 242-44.

ruption of the stream of his Logic by doubtful, trifling, and impolitic interruptions, arguments resting in premises denied by the antagonists, and yet taken for granted—in short, appendages that cumber, accessions that subtract, and confirmations that weaken: non cogitabat,ὅσῳ πλέον ἥμισυ παντός. 2. That he commences by a proper division of the subject into two distinct branches, 1. Extempore Prayer as opposed to set forms, & 2. The Directory as prescribing a form opposed to the existing Liturgy. But that in the sequel he blends & confuses & intermingles one with the other, & presses most and most frequently on the first point, which a vast majority of the Party, he is opposing, had disowned & reprobated no less than himself: & which, tho' easiest to confute, scarcely required confutation.[39]

Taylor, POLEMICALL DISCOURSES: OF THE SACRED ORDER AND OFFICES OF EPISCOPACY, *Dedication, p. [40].*

> But the interest of the *Bishops* is conjunct with the prosperity of the *King,* besides the interest of their own security, by the obligation of secular advantages. For they who have their livelihood from the *King,* and are in expectance of their fortune from him, are most likely to pay a tribute of exacter duty, than others, whose fortunes are not in such immediate dependency on His *Majesty.*

The Cat out of the Bag! Consult the whole Reign of Charles the first & second and the first years of James the second. J. T. was at this time (blamelessly for himself and most honorably for his patrons) ambling on in the high road of Preferment: and to men so situated, however sagacious in other respects, it is not given to read the signs of the Times! Little did J. T. foresee, that to indiscreet avowals, like these, on the part of the Court Clergy, the exauctoration of the Bishops, & the temporary overthrow of the Church itself, would be in no small portion attributable. But the scanty measure & obscurity (if not rather, for so bright a Luminary, the occultation) of his Preferment after the Restoration, is a problem, of which perhaps his virtues present the most probable solution . . .
[*In fine.*]
Like all Taylor's dedications & dedicatory Epistles—easy, dignified, and pregnant. The happiest synthesis of the Divine, the Scholar, and the Gentleman was perhaps exhibited in him & Bishop Berkley.[40]

Taylor, POLEMICALL DISCOURSES: OF . . . EPISCOPACY, *Introduction, p. 3.*

> His next onset was by *Julian,* and *occidere presbyterium,* that was his Province. To shut up publick Schools, to force Christians to ignorance,

[39] Cf. *Lit. Rem.,* III, 246-47. Latin and Greek omitted. Coleridge quotes Hesiod, *Works and Days,* I. 40.
[40] Cf. *Lit. Rem.,* III, 207-8.

to impoverish and disgrace the *Clergie,* to make them vile and dishonorable, these are his arts; and he did the devil more service in this fineness of undermining, than all the open battery of ten great Rams of persecution.

What felicity, what vivacity of expression! Many years ago Mr. Mackintosh gave it as an instance of *my* perverted taste, that I had *seriously* contended that in order to form a style worthy of Englishmen, Milton and Taylor must be studied instead of Johnson, Gibbon, and Junius: and now I see by his introductory Lecture given at Lincoln's Inn, & just published, he is himself imitating Jeremy Taylor—rather copying his semi-colon punctuation—as closely as he can. Amusing to see, how by the time they are at the half-way of the long-breathed Period, the asthmatic Thoughts drop down & the rest is—Words! I have always been an obstinate Hoper: and even this is a datum & Symptom of Hope to me, that a better, an ancestral spirit, will appear & is forming in the rising generation.[41]

Taylor, POLEMICALL DISCOURSES: OF . . . EPISCOPACY, *Introduction, p. 44.*

> *First,* Because here is a concourse of times; for now after that these times have been called the *last* times for 1600 years together, our expectation of the *Great revelation* is very near accomplishing. . . .

Rather, a whimsical consequence, that because a certain party had been deceiving themselves 16 centuries, they were likely to be in the right at the beginning of the 17th! But indeed I question whether in all Taylor's voluminous writings there are to be found three other ¶s. so vague, and *misty-magnific* as this is. It almost reminds me of the "very cloudy and mighty alarming" in Foote.[42]

Taylor, POLEMICALL DISCOURSES: THE REAL PRESENCE AND SPIRITUAL OF CHRIST IN THE BLESSED SACRAMENT, PROVED AGAINST THE DOCTRINE OF TRANSUBSTANTIATION, *title page, recto.*

Perhaps the most wonderful of all Taylor's Works. He seems, if I may so say, to have *transubstantiated* his vast Imagination and Fancy into Subtlety not to be evaded, acuteness to which nothing remains unpierceable, and indefatigable agility of argumentation. Add to these an exhaustive Erudition—& that all these are employed in the service of Reason & Common Sense—whereas in some of his Tracts he seems to wield all sorts of Wisdom and Wit in defense of all sorts of Folly and Stupidity. But these were *ad popellum* [*sic*] & by virtue of the "falsitas

[41] Cf. *Lit. Rem.,* III, 209-10.
[42] Cf. *Lit. Rem.,* III, 210.

dispensativa" which he allowed himself—ψεύδεος φιλαλήθους οἰκονομία. S. T. C.[43]

Taylor, POLEMICALL DISCOURSES: THE REAL PRESENCE, *Epistle Dedicatory*, *R.*

> But for our dear afflicted Mother, she is under the portion of a child, in the state of discipline, her government indeed hindered, but her Worshippings the same, the Articles as true, and those of the Church of Rome as false as ever.

O how much there is in these few words—the sweet and comely Sophistry, not of J. Taylor, but of Human Nature. Mother! Child! State of Discipline! Government hindered!! (i. e. Scourgings hindered, Dungeonings in Dens foul as those of Hell, mutilation of Ears and Noses, and flattering the King, mad with assertions of his divine right to govern pillage and murder without a Parliament). Those pretty Babes of Grace, Laud and Sheldon, with the &c. Oath! The best apology will ever be that those whom they persecuted were as great Persecutors as themselves, and perhaps less excusable.[44]

Taylor, POLEMICALL DISCOURSES: THE REAL PRESENCE, *sec. I. 7, p. 184. Note continued, on p. 185.*

> So, when it is said, *Flesh and blood shall not inherit the Kingdom of God,* that is, *corruption shall not inherit:* and in the resurrection our bodies are said to be spiritual, that is, *not in substance,* but in *effect* and operation.

This is, in the first place, a *wilful* interpretation; and 2nd, it is absurd: for what sort of *Flesh* and *Blood* would incorruptible Flesh and Blood be? As well might we speak of marble F. and B. But in Taylor's mind, as seen throughout, the Logician was predominant over the Philosopher, and the Fancy *outbustled* the pure intuitive Imagination.[45]

Taylor, POLEMICALL DISCOURSES: THE REAL PRESENCE, *sec. I. 11, p. 185. Note continued on p. 186.*

But Jeremy Taylor was a Semi-materialist, & tho' no man better managed the *logic* of Substance and Accidents, he seems to have formed no clear metaphysical notion of their actual meaning . . .[46]

Taylor, POLEMICALL DISCOURSES: OF THE SIXTH CHAPTER OF ST. JOHN'S GOSPEL, *sec. III, p. 227.*

> The purpose of which discourse is this, that no notices are more evident and more certain than the notices of sense; but if we conclude

[43] Cf. *Lit. Rem.*, III, 334-35.
[44] Cf. *Lit. Rem.*, III, 337. "Pillage and murder" omitted.
[45] Cf. *Lit. Rem.*, III, 339.   [46] Cf. *Lit. Rem.*, III, 342.

contrary to the true dictate of senses, the fault is in the understanding, collecting false conclusions from right premises: It follows therefore that in the matter of the Eucharist we ought to judge that which our senses tell us.

Very unusually lax reasoning for J. T., whose Logic is commonly legitimate even where his Metaphysic is unsatisfactory. What Romanist ever asserted that a Communicant's Palate deceived him, when it reported the Taste of Bread or of Wine in the Elements?[47]

Taylor, POLEMICALL DISCOURSES: ST. JOHN, *sec. XII, 16-17, pp. 255-56. Note on p. 255.*

All most excellent; but O that T's stupendous Wit, Subtlety, Acuteness, Learning, & inexhaustible copiousness of argumentation would but tell us what *he* means by eating Christ's *Body* by faith—Mem. *his body*, not his Soul or Godhead. Eat a *body* by faith!![48]

Taylor, POLEMICALL DISCOURSES: A DISSUASIVE FROM POPERY, *Introduction, Part II, p. 357.*

But yet because I will humor J. S. for this once; even here also the Disswasive relies upon a first and self-evident principle as any is in Christianity; and that is, *Quod primum verum.*

I am surprised to meet such an assertion in so acute a Logician and so prudent an Advocate as Jeremy Taylor. . . .[49]

Taylor, POLEMICALL DISCOURSES: DISSUASIVE, *Introduction, Part II, p. 366. Note continued on p. 367.*

When he talks of being infallible, if the notion be applied to his Church, then he means infallibility, *antecedent, absolute, unconditionate,* such as will not permit the Church ever to erre.

Taylor himself was infected with the Spirit of Casuistry, by which saving Faith is placed in the understanding, and the Moral Act in the outward Deed. How infinitely safer the true *Lutheran* Doctrine, "God can not be mocked." Neither will Truth, as a mere conviction of the Understanding, save, nor Error condemn. To *love* Truth sincerely is spiritually to *have* Truth: and an Error becomes a personal error not by it's aberration for Logic or History but so far as the causes of such error are in the Heart, or may be traced back to some antecedent unchristian Wish or Habit. To watch over the secret movements of the Heart, remembering ever how deceitful a thing it is, and that God can not be mocked tho' we may easily dupe ourselves; these as the *Groundwork;* with prayer, study of the Scriptures, and tenderness to all around

[47] Cf. *Lit. Rem.*, III, 350-51. [48] Cf. *Lit. Rem.*, III, 354.
[49] Cf. *Lit. Rem.*, III, 356.

us, as the *Consequents;* are the Christian's Rule & supersede all books of Casuistry: which latter serve only to harden our feelings and pollute the imagination. To judge from the Roman Casuists, nay (I mourn to say) from T's own Doctor Dubitantium, one would suppose that a man's points of belief, and smallest determinations of outward conduct, however pure and charitable his intentions and however holy or blameless the inward source of those intentions or convictions in his past & present state of moral Being, were like the performance of an electrical experiment, and blow a man's salvation into atoms from a mere unconscious mistake in the arrangement & management of the apparatus. See Livy's account of Tullus Hostilius's experiment to draw Lightning from the Clouds. *Ceremoniis* non rite peractis, *Jupiter* enraged shot him dead. Before *God,* our Deeds (which for *him* can have no value) gain acceptance, in proportion as they are evolutions of our spiritual Life. He beholds our Deeds in our Principles. For *Men* our Deeds have *value* as efficient causes, *worth* as symptoms. They infer our Principles from our Deeds. Now as Religion, = the Love of God, can not subsist apart from Charity = the Love of our Neighbor, our conduct must be conformable to both.[50]

Taylor, POLEMICALL DISCOURSES: DISSUASIVE, *Part II, Book I, sec. 1, pp. 387-88. Note on p. 388.*

> The Churches have troubled themselves with infinite variety of questions, and divided their precious unity, and destroyed charity, and instead of contending against the Devil and all his crafty methods, they have contended against one another, and excommunicated one another, and anathematiz'd and damn'd one another; and no man is the better after all, but most men are very much the worse; and the Churches are in the world still divided about questions that commenc'd twelve or thirteen ages since; and they are like to be so for ever, till *Elias* come . . .

I remember no passages of the Fathers nearer to inspired Scripture, than this & similar ones of J. Taylor, in which quitting the acute Logician he combines his Heart with his Head, & utters general & inclusive & reconciling Truths of Charity & Common Sense . . .[51]

Taylor, POLEMICALL DISCOURSES: DISSUASIVE, *Part II, Book I, sec. 1, p. 388.*

> But if you mean the Catholick Church; then if you mean her abstracted separate Being, from all particulars, you pursue a cloud and fall in love with an Idea, and a child of fancy.

N. B. Here J. T. uses *idea* as opposed to image or distinct phantasm; & this is with few exceptions his general sense. And even then exceptions

[50] Cf. *Lit. Rem.,* III, 358-60.   [51] Cf. *Lit. Rem.,* III, 362.

are only metaphors from the general sense—i. e. images so faint, indefinite, and fluctuating as to be almost *no Images*—i. e. Ideas. As we say of a very thin Body—it is a *Ghost* or *Spirit*: the lowest degree of one kind being expressed by the opposite kind.[52]

Taylor, POLEMICALL DISCOURSES: DISSUASIVE, *Book I, Part II, sec. 1, p. 403.*

> *The Spirit of Prophecy* is also a pretty sure note of the true Church, and yet, in the dispute between *Israel* and *Judah, Samaria* and *Jerusalem,* it was of no force, but was really in both . . . I deny not but there have been some Prophets in the Church of *Rome* . . . but (as *Ahab* said concerning *Micaiah*) these do not prophesie good concerning *Rome,* but evil: and that *Rome* should be reformed *in ore gladii cruentandi* was one of the Prophesies . . .

¶ 12. an exquisite specimen of grave and dignified Irony, telum, quod cedere, simulat, retorquentis. In *contrast* with this stands ¶ 15. overleaf, which is a coarse tho' not unmerited *Sneer:* or as a German would have expressed himself "an of-Jeremy-Taylor-unworthy, tho' not-of-the-Roman-Catholic-papicolar-Polemics-unmerited Sneer."[53]

Taylor., POLEMICALL DISCOURSES: DISSUASIVE, Part II, Book I, sec. 2, p. 409.

> From this principle as it is promoted by the *Fanaticks,* they derive a wandring, unsetled, and a dissolute religion . . .

The evils of the Fanatic Persuasion here so powerfully, so exquisitely, stated and enforced by our all-eloquent Bishop, supply no proof or even presumption against the Tenet of the Spirit rightfully expressed. . . .[54]

Taylor, POLEMICALL DISCOURSES: DISSUASIVE, Part II, Book I, sec. 2, p. 419.

> St. Paul's way of teaching us to expound Scripture is, that he that prophesies should do it κατ' ἀναλογίαν πίστεως, according to the Analogy of faith.

Yet in his Liberty of Proph. [s. iv. 4.] Taylor turns this way into mere Ridicule. I love thee, Jeremy! but an arrant theological *Barrister* that thou wast, tho' thy only Fees were thy Desires of doing good in *question*[*ibus*] *singulis.*[55]

Taylor, POLEMICALL DISCOURSES: DISSUASIVE, Part II, Book I, sec. 10, pp. 472, 473, 474, 475.

The following note in reference to Sect. 10. As a general remark,

[52] Cf. *Lit. Rem.,* III, 362-63.   [53] Cf. *Lit. Rem.,* III, 363-64.
[54] Cf. *Lit. Rem.,* III, 367-68.   [55] Cf. *Lit. Rem.,* III, 374.

applicable to very many parts of Taylor's controversial writings, both
against the Anti-prelatic & those against the Romish, Divines, tho' suggested by the following Chapter—namely to those, in which our incomparable Church-Aspist attempts, not always successfully, to demonstrate
the difference between the dogmas and discipline of the ancient Church,
and those which the Romish Doctors vindicate by them—I would say
once for all, that it was the fashion of the Arminian Court Divines of
Taylor's age, i. e. of the High-Church party, Headed by Archbp. Laud
to extol and (in my humble judgement) egregiously to overrate, the
example and authority of the first four, nay, of the six first centuries:
and at all events to take for granted the evangelical and apostolical
character of the Church to the death of Athanasius. Now so far am I
from conceding this, that before the first Council of Nice, I believe myself to find the Seeds and Seedlings of all the worst corruptions of the
Latin Church of the 13th Century—and not a few even before the close
of the second. One pernicious error of the Primitive Church was the
conversion of the ethical Ideas, indispensable to *Science* of morals and
religion into fixed practical Laws & Rules for all Christians in all
stages of spiritual growth and under all circumstances—and with this
the degradation of free & individual Acts into corporate Church Obligations. Another not less pernicious was the gradual concentration of the
Church into a Priesthood and the consequent tendency of the reciprocal
functions of Love & Admonition & Counsel between Christian & Christian exclusively *official*, & between Disparates, viz. the Priest and the Lay-
man.[56]

Taylor, POLEMICALL DISCOURSES: DISSUASIVE, *Part II, Book II, sec. 6,
p. 548.*

> However, if you will not commit down-right idolatry, as some of their
> Saints teach you, then you must be careful to observe these plain dis-
> tinctions, and first be sure to remember that when you worship an image,
> you do it not *materially* but *formally;* not as it is *of such a substance,*
> but as it is *a sign;* next take care that you observe what sort of image
> it is, and then proportion your right kind to it, that you do not give
> *latria* to that where *hyperdulia* is only due; and be careful that if
> *dulia* only be due that your worship be not *hyperdulical. . . .*

A masterly specimen of grave dignified Irony. Indeed Jer. Taylor's
works would be of more service to an English Barrister than those of
Demosthenes, Æschines, and Cicero taken together.[57]

---

[56] Cf. *Lit. Rem.,* III, 376-78.
[57] Cf. *Lit. Rem.,* III, 380.

Taylor, POLEMICALL DISCOURSES: DISSUASIVE, *Part II, Book II, sec. 7, p. 550. Note continued on p. 551.*

A man cannot well understand an Essence, and hath no *Idea* of it in his mind, much less can a Painters Pencil do it.

Noticeable, that this is the only instance I have met in any English Classic before the Revolution of the word "Idea" used as synonimous with a mental Image. Taylor himself has repeatedly placed the two in opposition; but even here I doubt that he has done otherwise. I rather think he meant by the word "Idea" a notion under an indefinite & confused Form, such as Kant calls a Schema, or vague outline—an imperfect embryo of a concrete, to the individuation of which the mind gives no conscious attention, just as when I say—*anything*—I may imagine a poker or a plate; but I pay no *attention* to it's being this rather than that—and the very image itself is so wandering & unstable that at this moment it may be a dim shadow of the one, & in the next of some other thing. In this sense, Idea is ✕ Image in opposition of *degree* instead of kind; yet still contra-distinguished, as is evident by the sequel—Much less can a Painter's Pencil do it—For were it an Image, individui et concreti, then the Painter's Pencil could do it as well as his Fancy, or better. S. T. C.[58]

Taylor, POLEMICALL DISCOURSES: UNUM NECESSARIUM, *chap. v, sec. 3, p. 663.*

Of the moral capacity of sinful Habits.

Probably from the Holiness of his own Life, Taylor has but just fluttered about a bad Habit; not fully described it. He has omitted, or rather described contradictorily, the case of those with whom the objections to Sin are all strengthened, the dismal consequences more glaring & always present to them as an avenging *fury,* the Sin loathed, detested, hated; and yet, spite of all this, nay, more for all this, perpetrated. Both Lust and Intemperance would furnish too many instances of these most miserable victims.[59] Ὀπιοφάγοι, &c.

Taylor, POLEMICALL DISCOURSES: UNUM NECESSARIUM, *chap. v, sec. 5, p. 682.*

[Taylor paraphrases passage from *De Ecclesiasticis Dogmatibus.*] That sins are taken off by repentance, though it be but in the last breath of our life, we believe without doubting. He that thinks otherwise is not a Christian but a Novatian. If we have time, our sins are taken away by amendment of life; but if we die presently, they are taken off by humble confession.

[58] Cf. *Lit. Rem.,* III, 380-81.
[59] Cf. *Lit. Rem.,* III, 302-3, where the Greek "opium-eaters" is omitted.

This is one of the very many instances that confirm my opinion that Calvinism—(Archb. Leighton's for instance) compared with Taylor's Arminianism is as the Lamb in the Wolf's skin to the Wolf in the Lamb's skin. The one is cruel in the phrases, the other in the doctrine. S. T. C.[60]

Taylor, Polemicall Discourses: Unum necessarium, *chap. v. sec. 6, p. 691.*

It was not well with thee when thou didst first enter into the suburbs of Hell by single actions of sin, &c.

Aye! this *is* excellent indeed: and worthy of a Guardian Angel of the Church. But when Jer. Tayl. escapes from the Mononomian Romäism, which netted him in his too eager recoil from the Antinomian Boar, brought forth & foddered (as *he* imagined) in Calvin's Sty,—when from this wiry Net he escapes into the Devotional and the Dialectic, as into a green Meadow-land with springs and rivulets & sheltering groves where he leads his Flock like a Shepherd—then it is that he is most himself— then only he is *all* himself, the *whole* Jeremy Taylor! Or if there be one other subject graced by the same total *Heautophany*, it is in the pourings forth of his *profound* Common Sense on the ways & weaknesses of men & conflicting Sects—as for instance—in the admirable Birth, Parentage, Growth, and Consummation of a religious Controversy in his Dissuasive from Popery; p. 460.[61]

Taylor, Polemicall Discourses: unum necessarium, *chap. vi, sec. 5, p. 732.*

Origen said enough to be mistaken in the Question. Ἡ ἀρὰ τοῦ Ἀδὰμ κοινὴ πάντων ἐστὶ καὶ τὰ κατὰ τῆς γυναικὸς, οὐκ ἔστι καθ' ἧς οὐ λέγεται. Adams curse is common to all. And there is not a woman on earth to whom may not be said those things which were spoken to this woman.

Origen's words ought to have prevented all mistake: for he plainly enough overthrows the phantom of hereditary guilt, and as to guilt from a corruption of nature it is just such guilt as the carnivorous appetites of a weaned Lion, or the instinct of a brood of Ducklings to run to water. What then is it? 1. Guilt, and therefore seated in the Will. 2. Common to all men, and the beginning of which no man can determine in himself or in others. How comes this? It is a mystery, as the will itself. *Deeds* are in time & space, therefore have a beginning. Pure *action*, i. e. the

[60] Cf. *Lit. Rem.*, III, 303-4. In the note to sec. 39, p. 671, Coleridge wrote: "Arminianism is cruel to individuals for fear of damaging the race by false hopes and improper confidences; while Calvinism is horrible for the race, but full of consolation to the suffering individual."
[61] Cf. *Lit. Rem.*, III, 306-7.

Will, is a Noumenon, & irreferable to time. Thus Origen calls it neither hereditary nor original, but universal Sin. The curse of Adam is common to all men, because what Adam did, we all do: thus of Eve. You may substitute any women in her place, and the same words apply. This is the true solution of this unfortunate Question. The πρῶτον ψεῦδος is in the dividing the will from the acts of the will. The will is *ego-agens*.[62]

Taylor, POLEMICALL DISCOURSES: UNUM NECESSARIUM, *p. 739. Note on first end-page, recto.*

. . . 3. Then came the Persecutions of the Arminians in Holland—then the struggle in England against the Arminian Laud & all his Party, terrible persecutors in their turn of the Calvinists & Systematic Divines—then the Civil War & the persecutions of the Church by the Puritans in *their* Turn—and just in this state of heated feelings did Taylor write these works, which contain dogmas subversive of true Christian faith—viz. the *Unum Necessarium,* or Doctrine and Practice of Repentance, which reduces the cross of Christ to nothing; the VIth Chapter of the same, & the after Defences of it in his Letters on Original Sin to a Lady, & to the Bishop of Rochester; & the Liberty of Prophesying, which, putting Toleration on a false ground, has left no ground at all for right or wrong in matters of Christian faith.

In the marginal notes, which I have written in these several Treatises, I appear to myself to have demonstrated that Taylor's System has no one advantage over the Lutheran in respect of God's attributes; that it is bonâ fide Pelagianism (tho' he denies it—for let him detail that Grace, which Pelagius would not accept, because incompatible with Free Will & Merit, & profess his belief in it thus detailed; & every one of his arguments against absolute Decrees tell against himself); and lastly, that it's inevitable *logical* consequences are Socinianism & *quæ sequuntur*. In Tillotson the face of Arminianism looked out fuller, & Christianity, is represented as a mere arbitrary Contrivance of God—yet one without reason. Let not the surpassing Eloquence of Taylor dazzle you, nor his scholastic retiary versatility of Logic illaqueate your good sense! Above all, do not dwell too much on the apparent Absurdity or Horror of the Dogma, he opposes; but examine what he puts in it's place; and receive candidly the few hints I have admarginated for your assistance. . . .[63]

---

[62] Cf. *Lit. Rem.*, III, 312-13. This important statement identifying the will as the act, and the deed as a result of the will acting is basic in Coleridge's philosophy.
[63] Cf. *Lit. Rem.*, III, 296-98.

Taylor, POLEMICALL DISCOURSES: UNUM NECESSARIUM, *chap. vii, "A Further Explication of the Doctrine of Original Sin." Note on blank page opposite beginning of chapter, p. 746.*

In this most eloquent Treatise one may detect sundry logical Lapses, sometimes in the statement, sometimes in the instances, and once or twice in the conclusions. But the main and pervading Error lies in the treatment of the subject *in genere* by the forms and rules of Conceptual Logic; which deriving all its material from the Senses, and borrowing it's forms from the Sense (αἴσθησις καθαρά) or intuitive faculty is necessarily inapplicable to spiritual Mysteries, the very definition or contra-distinguishing character of which is that they transcend the Sense, and therefore the Understanding—which, as Archbishop Leighton and Immanuel Kant excellently define the term, is "the Faculty that judges according to Sense." In the "Aids to Reflection,"[64] I have shewn that the proper function of the Understanding or Mediate Faculty is to collect individual or sensible Concretes into Kinds and Sorts (*Genera et Species*) by means of their Common Characters (*Notæ Communes*); and to fix and distinguish these Conceptions (i. e. generalized Perceptions) by Words. Words are the only *immediate* Objects of the Understanding. Spiritual Verities, or Truths of Reason *respective ad realia*, and herein distinguished from the merely *formal* or so called Universal Truths, are differenced from the Conceptions of the Understanding by the immediatecy of the knowledge, and from the immediate Truths of Sense, i. e. from both pure and mixt intuitions, by not being *sensible*, i. e. not representable by figure, measurement, or weight; nor connected with any affection of our Sensibility, such as color, taste, odors, & the like. And such knowledges we, when we speak correctly, name Ideas.

Now Original Sin, i. e. Sin that has it's origin in itself, that is, in the Will of the Sinner, but yet in a state or condition of the Will not peculiar to the Individual Agent but common to the Human Race, is an *Idea:* and one Diagnostic, or contra-distinguishing Mark, appertaining to all *Ideas*, is—that they are inexpressible by adequate words—an Idea can only be expressed (more correctly, *suggested*) by two contradictory Positions. Ex. gr. The Soul is all, in every Part—Nature is a Sphere, whose Center is every where, & it's Circumference no where, &c. &c. Hence not a few of Bp. Taylor's objections grounded on his expositions of the doctrine prove nothing more than that the Doctrine concerns an *Idea*. But besides this, Taylor every where assumes the consequences of Original Sin as superinduced on a pre-existing Nature in no essential respect differing from our present Nature—for instance, on a Material

[64] Cf. Shedd, I, 206-27.

Body, with it's internal Appetites, it's passivity to material Agents, in short, on an animal *nature* in man. But this *nature,* as the antagonist of the Spirit or Supernatural Principle in man, *are* the Original Sin— the product of the Will indivisible from the Act producing it—just as in pure Geometry the mental construction is indivisible from the constructive Act of the Intuitive Faculty. Original Sin as the Product is a known Fact, concerning which we *know* by the Light of the Idea itself, that it must originate in a self-determination of a Will. That which we do not know is, *how* it originates. But this we cannot explain—first, from the necessity of the Subject, viz. the Will, and secondly, because it is an *Idea*—but all Ideas are inconceivable. It is an *Idea,* because it is not a Conception.[65]

Taylor, POLEMICALL DISCOURSES: UNUM NECESSARIUM, *chap. vii, sec. 1, p. 750.*

> . . . that which remained was a reasonable soul fitted for the actions of life, and of reason, but not of any thing that was supernatural.

What T. calls Reason, *the Friend* called Understanding; and gave the name Reason to that which Taylor would have called Spirit.

Taylor, POLEMICALL DISCOURSES: UNUM NECESSARIUM, *chap. x, sec. 1, p. 820. Note continued on p. 821.*

P. S. I have written but a few marginal Notes to this long Treatise: for the whole is to my feeling and apprehension so *Romish,* so Antipauline, so unctionless, that it makes my very heart as dry as the Desert Sands when I read it. Instead of partial animadversions, I should prescribe the Chapter on the Law & the Gospel, in Luther's Table Talk, as the general Antidote. S. T. Coleridge.[66]

Taylor, POLEMICALL DISCOURSES: VINDICATION OF THE DIVINE ATTRIBUTES IN THE QUESTION OF ORIGINAL SIN, *Obj. IV, p. 884.*

> But if Original Sin be not a sin properly, why are children baptized? And what benefit comes to them by Baptism? I answer, as much as they need, and are capable of.

The eloquent man has plucked just Prickles enough out of the Dogma of Original Sin to make a thick & ample Crown of Thorns for his opponents; and yet left enough to tear his own clothes off his back & pierce thro' the leather jerkin of his closeliest-wrought Logic. In this answer to Ob. 4. he reminds me of the renowned Squire who first scratcht out his eyes in a quick-set Hedge, leapt back and scratcht them in again. So. J. T. first pulls out the very eyes of the Doctrine, leaves it blind &

⁶⁵ Cf. *Lit. Rem.,* III, 314-16.   ⁶⁶ Cf. *Lit. Rem.,* III, 325.

blank, and then leaps back into it & scratches them in again, but with a most opulent Squint that looks a 100 ways at once & no one can tell which it really looks at.[67] S. T. C.

Taylor, POLEMICALL DISCOURSES: VINDICATION, *Obj. V, p. 890.*

The consequent of this discourse must needs at least be this; that it is impossible that the greatest part of mankind should be left in the eternal bonds of Hell by *Adam;* for then quite contrary to the discourse of the Apostle, there had been abundance of sin, but a scarcity of grace.

And yet J. T. will not be called a Pelagian! Why? Because without Grace superadded by Christ no man could be saved—i. e. all men must go to Hell—this not for any Sin, but from a Calamity, the consequences of another man's Sin, of which they were even ignorant. God would not condemn them, the Sons of Adam, of *Sin;* but only inflicted on them an *evil,* the necessary effect of which was that they should all troop to the Devil! And this is J. T.'s Defence of God's justice! The truth is, J. T. was a Pelagian, believed that without Christ thousands, Jews & Heathens, lived wisely & holily, & went to Heaven; but this he did not dare say out, probably not even to himself; and hence it is that he flounders backward & forward, now upping & now downing.[68] S. T. C.

Taylor, POLEMICALL DISCOURSES: VINDICATION, *p. 893 [end].*

This eloquent Treatise may be compared to a Statue of Janus, with one face fixed on certain opponents, full of Life & Force, a witty scorn on the Lip, a brow at once bright and weighty with satisfying Reason— the other, looking at "the something instead" of that which had been confuted, maimed, noseless, & weather-bitten into a sort of visionary confusion, & indistinctness. It looks like this—aye, & very like that—but how like it is, too, such another thing![69] S. T. C.

Taylor, POLEMICALL DISCOURSES: AN ANSWER TO A LETTER *written by the Right Rev. the Lord Bishop of Rochester, concerning the chapter of original sin, in the "Unum Necessarium," p. 902.*

Strange Trinity—God, Necessity, and the Devil! But Taylor's Scheme has far worse consequences than Calvin's: for it makes the whole Scheme of Redemption a theatrical Scenery. Just restore our bodies and corporeal passions to a perfect *equilibrium* & fortunate instinct, & there being no guilt or defect in the Soul, the Son of God, the Λόγος & Supreme Reason, might have remained unincarnate, uncrucified. In short, Socinianism is as inevitable a deduction from Taylor's Scheme as Deism or Atheism is from Socinianism. S. T. C.[70]

[67] Cf. *Lit. Rem.,* III, 325-26. [68] Cf. *Lit. Rem.,* III, 327-28.
[69] Cf. *Lit. Rem.,* III, 327-28. [70] Cf. *Lit. Rem.,* III, 331-32.

Taylor, Polemicall Discourses: second letter to the bishop of rochester, *p. 910. Note continued on p. 911.*

To this it is answered as you see: there is a double guilt; *a guilt of person, and of nature.* That is taken away, *this* is not: for, Sacraments are given to Persons, not to Natures.

I need no other passage but this to convince me, that J. T., the angle in which the two apices of Logic and Rhetoric meet, consummate in both, was yet no Metaphysician. Learning, Fancy, Discursive Intellect, tria juncta in uno, and of each enough to have alone immortalized a man! But yet οὐδὲν μετὰ φύσιν —images, conceptions, notions, such as leave him but one rival Shakespear—but no *Ideas.* J. Taylor was a Gassendist. O that he had but meditated in the silence of his spirit on the mystery of an ɪ ᴀᴍ—he would have seen that a Person, quoad Person, can have nothing *common* or generic—& where this finds place, the Person is corrupted by intrasusception of a Nature, which *becomes* evil thereby, and on this relation only is an evil Nature. The Nature itself, like all other works of God, is good; and so is the Person in a yet higher sense of the word, Good, like all offsprings of the most high. But the combination is evil, & thus not the work of God—and one of the main ends & results of the doctrine of Original Sin is to silence & confute the blasphemy that makes God the Author of Sin, without avoiding it by fleeing to the almost equal blasphemy, a blasphemy against the Conscience, that Sin in the sense of Guilt does not exist.[71]

Taylor, Polemicall Discourses: the liberty of prophesying, *Epistle Dedicatory, first page (K kkk₂).*

O! had this work been published when the Lie-Martyr, Charles, Archbp. Laud, whose Chaplain Taylor was, and the other Star-chamber Inquisitors were sentencing Prynne, Bastwick, Leighton to punishments that have left a brand-mark on the Church of England, the sophistry might have been forgiven for the sake of the motive—which would *then* have been unquestionable! Or if Jer. Taylor had not retracted, after the Restoration; if he had not, as soon as the Episcopal Church had gained the power and resumed the practice of the foulest Persecution, most basely disclaimed and disavowed the principle of Toleration, and apologized for the Publication by declaring it to have been a *ruse de guerre,* currying pardon for his past Liberalism by charging—& most probably *slandering,* himself with the guilt of falsehood, treachery, & hypocrisy; his *character* as a man would at least have been stainless! Alas! alas! most dearly do I love Jer. Taylor! most religiously do I venerate his Memory! But this was too foul a Blotch of the Episcopal Leprosy to

[71] Cf. *Lit. Rem.,* III, 333-34.

be forgiven. He who pardons such an Act in such a man, partakes of it's guilt. S. T. Coleridge.[72]

Taylor, POLEMICALL DISCOURSES: LIBERTY, *sec. I, p. 941.*

Of the nature of Faith, and that its duty is compleated in believing the Articles of the Apostles Creed.

As beautifully written, as it was charitably conceived. Yet how vain the attempt! J. T. ought to have denied that Christian Faith is *at all* intellectual primarily; but only probably—as cæteris paribus it is *probable* that a man with a pure Heart will believe an intelligent Creator. But the Faith resides in the predisposing Purity of the Heart—i. e. in the obedience of the Will to the uncorrupted Conscience. For take Taylor's instances & I ask, whether the *words* or the sense be meant? Surely, the latter. Well then, *I* understand, & so did the dear Bishop, by these texts the Doctrine of a Redeemer, who by his agonies & death actually altered the relations of the spirits of all men to their maker, *redeemed* them from Sin & Death Eternal. He *brought* Life & Immortality into the world. But the Socinian uses the same texts—and means only that a good & gifted teacher of pure morality died a martyr to his opinions, & his resurrection proved the possibility of all men's rising from the Dead. He *did* nothing;—he only taught & afforded Evidence. Can two more diverse opinions be conceived? God here— mere man there. Here a Redeemer from Guilt & Corruption, & a *satisfaction* for offended Holiness—there a mere declarer that God imputed no guilt wherever, with or without a Christ, the Person had repented of it. What could J. T. say for the *necessity* of his Sense (which is mine) but what might be said for the necessity of the Nicene Creed? . . .[73]

Taylor, POLEMICALL DISCOURSES: LIBERTY, *sec. I. 7, p. 942. Note on p. 943.*

In the pursuance of this great truth, the Apostles or the holy men, their Contemporaries and Disciples, composed a Creed to be a Rule of Faith to all Christians, as appears in *Irenæus, Tertullian, St. Cyprian, St. Austin, Ruffinus,* and divers others; which creed, unless it had contained all the intire object of faith, and the foundation of Religion, &c.

Jeremy Taylor does not appear to have been a critical Scholar. His Reading had been *oceanic;* but he read rather to *bring out* the growths of his own fertile & teeming mind than to inform himself respecting the products of those of other men's. Hence his reliance on the broad assertions of the Fathers. Yet it is strange that he should have been ignorant that the Ap. Creed was growing piecemeal for 5 centuries.[74]

[72] Cf. *Lit. Rem.,* III, 250. [73] Cf. *Lit. Rem.,* III, 248-49.
[74] Cf. *Lit. Rem.,* III, 251.

Taylor, POLEMICALL DISCOURSES: LIBERTY, *sec. II, p. 949.*

For heresie is not an error of the understanding, but an error of the will.

Most excellent! To this J. T. should have adhered; and to it's converse. Faith is not an accuracy of Logic, but a rectitude of Heart.[75]

Taylor, POLEMICALL DISCOURSES: LIBERTY, *sec. II, p. 949.*

And, indeed, if we remember that S. *Paul* reckons heresie amongst the works of the flesh, and ranks it with all manner of practical impieties, we shall easily perceive that if a man mingles not a vice with his opinion, if he be innocent in his life, though deceived in his doctrine, his errour is his misery, not his crime; it makes him an argument of weakness, and an object of pity, but not a person sealed up to ruine and reprobation.

O admirable! How could Taylor, after this, preach & publish his Sermon in defence of Persecution—at least against Toleration!![76]

Taylor, POLEMICALL DISCOURSES: LIBERTY, *sec. VIII, p. 1009.*

Such as makes no invasion upon their great reputation, which I desire should be preserved as sacred as it ought.

The vision of the Mitre dawned on Taylor; and his recollection of Laud came to the assistance of the Fathers—of whom in his heart Taylor entertained a very mean opinion. How could such a man do otherwise? I could forgive them their wagon-loads of Nonsense, and even their Lies; but their accursed appetite for making Heresies, & thus occasioning the neglect or destruction of so many valuable Works! Origen's for instance.[77]

Taylor, POLEMICALL DISCOURSES: LIBERTY, *sec. XI, p. 1016.*

Of some Causes of Errour in the exercise of Reason, which are inculpate in themselves.

It is a lamentable misuse of the term, Reason—thus to call by that name the mere faculty of guessing and babbling. The making Reason a Faculty, instead of a Light, and using the term, as a mere synonime of the Understanding, & the consequent ignorance of the true nature of IDEAS, and that none but IDEAS are objects of FAITH—are the grounds of all J. T.'s important errors.[78]

Taylor, POLEMICALL DISCOURSES: LIBERTY, *sec. XI, p. 1016.*

But men may understand what they please, especially when they are to expound Oracles.

[75] Cf. *Lit. Rem.,* III, 257-58.   [76] Cf. *Lit. Rem.,* III, 258.
[77] Cf. *Lit. Rem.,* III, 269-70, which adds, "This I can not forgive or forget."
[78] Cf. *Lit. Rem.,* III, 272.

If this sentence had occurred in Hume or Voltaire!

Taylor, POLEMICALL DISCOURSES: LIBERTY, *sec. XI, p. 1018.*

And then if ever Truth be afflicted, she shall also be destroyed.

Here & in many other passages of his other works J. T. very unfairly states this argument of the anti-prelatic Party. Not that the Church of England was *afflicted* (the Puritans had been themselves much more afflicted by the Prelates) but that having themselves yelled for War, and appealed to the decision of the Sword, the cause was determined against them. But in fact it is false, that the Puritans ever did argue as Taylor represents them. Laud & his Confederates had begun by incarcerating, scouring, and inhumanly mutilating their fellow protestants for not acceding to their whims & fancies, and proceeded to goad & drive the King to Levy war against his Parliament; and the parliamentary Party very naturally cited their defeat & the overthrow of the Prelacy as a Judgement on their bloodthirstiness, not as a proof of their error in questions of Theology.[79]

Taylor, POLEMICALL DISCOURSES: LIBERTY, *sec. XI, p. 1019.*

All that I shall say, . . .

An admirable § ph! Taylor is never more himself, never appears greater or wiser, than when he enters on this topic—viz. the many & various causes beside truth which occasion men to hold an opinion for truth.[80]

Taylor, POLEMICALL DISCOURSES: LIBERTY, *sec. XIII, p. 1028.*

It is characteristic of the Man and the Age, Taylor's high-strained reverential epithets to the names of the Fathers, and as rare and naked mention of Luther, Melancthon, Calvin—the least of whom was at least equal to St. Augustin, & worth a brigade of the Cyprians, Firmilians, &c. And observe! always SAINT Cyprian![81]

Taylor, POLEMICALL DISCOURSES: LIBERTY, *sec. XVI, p. 1036.*

The Religion of Jesus Christ is the form of sound Doctrine and wholesome words, which is set down in Scripture indefinitely, actually conveyed to us by plain places, and separated as for the question of necessary or not necessary by the Symbol of the Apostles.

I cannot refrain from again expressing my surprize at the frequency and the undoubting positiveness of this assertion in so great a Scholar, so profound a *Patrician,* as Jer. Taylor. He appears bonâ fide to have

[79] Cf. *Lit. Rem.,* III, 273.   [80] Cf. *Lit. Rem.,* III, 273-74.
[81] Cf. *Lit. Rem.,* III, 276.

believed the absurd fable of this Creed having been a Pic-nic to which each of the 12 Apostles contributed his *Symbolum!* Had J. T. taken it for granted so completely and at so early an age that he read without attending to the various passages in the Fathers & Eccles. historians, &c. that shew the gradual formation of this Creed? It is certainly *possible;* and I see no other solution of the Problem. S. T. C.[82]

Taylor, Polemicall Discourses: liberty, *sec. XVIII, p. 1042, paragraph 9.*

Judge not lest ye be judged. The dread of these words is, I fear, more influential on my spirit than either the duty of Charity or my sense of Taylor's high merits in enabling me to struggle against the strong inclination to pass the sentence of *Dishonesty* on the Reasoning in this § ph. Had I met the passage in R. Baxter, or in Bishop Hall, it would have made no such unfavorable impression. But Taylor was so acute a Logician, and had made himself so completely Master of the Subject, that it is hard to conceive him blind to sophistry so glaring. I am myself friendly to Infant Baptism, but for that reason feel more impatience of any unfairness in it's Defenders.[83]

Taylor, Polemicall Discourses: liberty, *sec. XX, p. 1074. Second paragraph of notes on first end-page, recto.*

And although they have done violence to all Philosophy and the reason of man, and undone and cancelled the principles of two or three Sciences, to bring in this Article; yet they have a Divine Revelation whose literal and grammatical sense, if that sense were intended, would warrant them to doe violence to all the Sciences in the Circle. And indeed that Transubstantiation is openly and violently against natural reason is no Argument to make them disbelieve it, who believe the mystery of the Trinity in all those niceties of explication which are in the School (and which now-a-days pass for the Doctrine of the Church), with as much violence to the principles of natural and supernatural Philosophy as can be imagined to be in the point of Transubstantiation.

This is one of the many passages in Taylor's works which lead me to think that his private opinions were favorable to *Socinianism.* Observe! not to modern Unitarianism, as taught by Priestly and Belsham. And doubtless, Socinianism would much more easily bear a doubt, whether the difference between it and the orthodox faith was not more in *words* than in the things meant, than the Arian Hypothesis. A mere Conceptualist at least might plausibly ask, whether either party, the Athanasian or the Socinian, had a sufficiently distinct conception of what the one meant by the hypostatical Union of the Divine Logos with the Man,

[82] Cf. *Lit. Rem.,* III, 279-80.   [83] Cf. *Lit. Rem.,* III, 280.

Jesus, or the other of his plenary, total, perpetual, & continuous Inspiration, to have any well grounded assurance, that they do not mean the same thing.

Last line but 9—"would warrant them to do violence to all the Sciences in the Circle." No one knew better than Jeremy Taylor that this apparent Soar of the hooded Falcon, Faith, to the very Empyrean of Bibliolatry amounted in fact to a Truism of which the following syllogism is a fair illustration. . . .[84]

Taylor, POLEMICALL DISCOURSES: A DISCOURSE ON CONFIRMATION, *p. 1080. Note opposite title page.*

Of all Jer. Taylor's works, the Disc. of Conf. seems to me the least judicious; and yet that is not the right word either. I mean, however, that one is puzzled to know for what class of Readers or Auditors it was intended. He announces his Subject as one of such lofty claims; he begins with positions taken on such high ground, no less than the superior dignity and spiritual importance of Confirmation above Baptism itself, whether considered as a Sacramental Rite & Mystery distinct from Baptism, or as it's completory and crowning Part (the finis coronans opus) that we are eager to hear the proof. But Proofs differ in their value according to our previous valuation of Authorities. What would pass for a very sufficient Proof, because grounded on a revered Authority, with a R. Catholic, would be a mere fancy-medal and of no currency with a Bible Protestant. And yet to Protestants, & those too Laymen (for we can hardly suppose that J. T. thought his Episcopal Brethren in need of it) must this Discourse have been intended and in this point of view, surely never did so wise a man adopt means so unsuitable to his end, or frame a discourse so inappropriate to his Audience . . .[85]

Taylor, POLEMICALL DISCOURSES: CONFIRMATION, *Epistle Dedicatory, A₂ verso.*

And amidst these and very many more inconveniences, it was greatly necessary that God should send us such a KING.

O sorrow and shame! Why, Why, O Genius! didst thou suffer thy darling Son to crush the fairest flowers of thy garland beneath a tight Mitre!![86]

[84] Cf. *Lit. Rem.*, III, 291-92.
[85] Cf. *Lit. Rem.*, III, 381-82.
[86] *Lit. Rem.*, III, 384. Another note to this passage—almost in the same words —occurs on the second end-page, recto.

Taylor, POLEMICALL DISCOURSES, *note on back board.*

P. S.—there is one error of very ill consequence to the reputation of the Christian Community, which Jer. Taylor shares with the Romish Divines, viz., the quoting of opinions and even of rhetorical Flights, from the writings of this and that Individual, with Saint prefixed to his name, as expressing the Faith of *the Church*, during the five or six first Centuries! Whereas it would not, perhaps, be very difficult to convince an unprejudiced Man and a sincere Christian, of the impossibility, that even the decrees of the General Councils should represent the Catholic Faith, i. e. the Belief essential to, or necessarily consequent on, the faith in Christ common to all the Elect.[87]

Taylor, WORTHY COMMUNICANT,[88] *first flyleaf.*

Alas! Alas! that the accident of Jeremy Taylor's Father having been a Barber and Perruquier at Cambridge (his Mother at least having been the wife of a Barber &c? Edmund Spencer?? Possible. *Mem.*) and he consequently reared up in the dread & super-reverence of the Hierarchs, should have enslaved such a Mind to the so called FATHERS of the 3rd, 4th and 5th Centuries! That the man who wrote Chapter IVth p. 197-257 should have been an Admirer and Partizan of Archbishop Laud! —and one of the Sainters of that demure Jesuit, Charles Ist!!

Taylor, WORTHY COMMUNICANT, *p. 6.*

So we sometimes espy a bright cloud formed into an irregular figure; when it is observed by unskilful and fantastick travellers, looks like a Centaure to some, & as a Castle to others . . . and all the while it is nothing but a shining cloud . . .; so it is in this great Mystery of our Religion.

Surely never before or since did a wise man pitch on a more unlucky and injudicious Simile!—"and all the while *it*" (that is, the irreg. Figure, that is the mystery of the Lord's Supper) "is nothing but &c."!

Taylor, WORTHY COMMUNICANT, *p. 11.*

Upon this account some say that we receive nothing in the B. Eucharist, but we commemorate many blessed things which we have received.

Zwinglius & the Swiss Sacramentaries.

[87] Cf. *Lit. Rem.*, III, 391.
[88] Jeremy Taylor, *The Worthy Communicant , . . . to which is added a Sermon never printed with the Folio Volume of Sermons* (London: 1674). These notes are printed for the first time from a copy formerly in the library of Lord Coleridge and now in the British Museum. The volume has been severely cut, so that many of the notes are incomplete; but even so they add to our knowledge of Coleridge.

Taylor, WORTHY COMMUNICANT, *p. 21.*

The meaning of which mysterious and Sacramental expressions, when they are reduced to *easie* and *intelligible*[89] significations, is plainly this.

Why then did inspired Wise men use mysterious expressions if their meaning could have been fully expressed in "easy and intelligible words"? In receding from the Romanists Taylor often lays the Doctrine open to the Quakers: as in the words from St. Austin *Believe him & you have eaten him.* What could a Quaker [cut off]

Taylor, WORTHY COMMUNICANT, *p. 22.   Note continued on p. 23.*

And all our prayers are by the aids and communications of the spirit of Christ . . . and so Christ is our food—so he becomes life unto our souls.

All comes to this at last. Is the Soul an Ens per se? Or an accident of the Body, either as a *quality* of the Stuff or a property of the Composition? If the former, is it a body—i. e. extended, & thus invisible only by defect or disproportion of the visive power? Or is it dimensionless, [cut off] Soul be an Ens reale vel substantiale and yet not an Ens materiale seu corporeum. What are *Truths?* Are they acts of the Soul? And [cut off]

Taylor, WORTHY COMMUNICANT, *p. 26.*

Christ always was, is, and shall be the food of the faithful. . . . And this [Sacrament] is not done to make this mystery obscure but intelligible and easie.

This too bold assertion was necessary to sustain Taylor's argument. But could he be in earnest? That which had [—?] all & overwhelmed the faith of [cut off] make so familiar a truth more easy & intelligible. I could sooner believe Transubstantiation.

Taylor, WORTHY COMMUNICANT, *p. 27.*

St. John having thus explicated this mystery in general, of our eating the flesh and drinking the blood of Christ.

Propounded; but not explicated. There are two extremes, the Sensual and the Notional: & the aim of the Gospel is to subvert both.

Taylor, WORTHY COMMUNICANT, *p. 28.*

Believe and repent: is the word in Baptisme . . .; repentance is expressly included in the new covenant, but was not in the old.

What then do the solemn Promises of the Prophets & their invitation to repentance mean?

[89] Words underlined by Coleridge.

Taylor, WORTHY COMMUNICANT, *p. 28.*

. . . and when by the operation of the holy spirit, the waters are re-formed to a divine *Nature* or efficacy, the baptized are made clean.

Here comes the Water again, reformed to a magical efficacy! By whom could the excellent author mean to be read? For the unlearned it is far too learned: for the Learned far too loose [cut off] of Logicians.

Taylor, WORTHY COMMUNICANT, *p. 32.*

It appears to me that between Protestants there is but one Question concerning both Sacraments. Are they as a Button, Cockade, or Epaulette which a Sovereign having ordered to be worn as an outward mark that the Wearers are under the oath of allegiance to him (Sacramentum imperiale) protects & rewards those, who wear it in obedience to his command, *for* their obedience? Or are they as a medicine which a Father has commanded a sick child to take, themselves the efficient means of the reward? Between Romanists & Protestants the Question is—Is the Lord's Supper an instrument of Grace in the hand of God?—or God in the instrument of Grace. Here the order of argument is—1. Is there any *real* difference in the two propositions. 2. If so, is there a medium discoverable? 3. If not, which of the two is the Scripture Truth.

Taylor, WORTHY COMMUNICANT, *p. 85.*

Christ would give himself to none but to them who are ready to give themselves for him.

This should have been explained: otherwise it might seem to contradict the fore-asserted use of the Sacrament [cut off]

Taylor, WORTHY COMMUNICANT, *p. 97.*

For it is worth observing, that there being in the Old Testament thirteen Types and Umbrages of this holy Sacrament, eleven of them are of meat and drink.

I should like to know, *by what authority* these 13 and no more are to be understood as types intended to teach [cut off]

Taylor, WORTHY COMMUNICANT, *p. 152.*

. . . for faith is the principal that there is intended; for the whole analogy of the discourse drawn forth from its clouds and allegory, infers only the necessity of being Christs disciple . . .

If it be allowed to a Bishop of the Church of England to call the express words of Christ, more solemnly re-iterated in the very face of offence taken at them even by such as had been before his Followers, than any other—if it be fit for a Bishop to call such words *"clouds and allegory"* that must be allegorized away—why complain of the Socinians? But if Christ had meant no more, how strange that he did not tell his Disciples, I mean no more than you have often heard [cut off] the necessity of Faith in men if so repulsive a metaphor to express so plain a precept & one so often given before? and still stranger that he should afterwards appoint a sacrament. [cut off]

Taylor, WORTHY COMMUNICANT, *end of chap. iii, sec. 2, p. 156.*

Taylor often speaks of the primitive Church, & yet 9 times out of 10 he can only mean the latter half of the second, and the 3rd & 4th Centuries, for of the 90 years that followed the Death of St. John we have no records of importance. Now of the Church from 145 A.D. I can by no means think so highly as he does or seems to do, and in the interim between 200 & 400 the *germs* of all the after corruption may be traced. He who has read their farrago of miracle-stories & can defend their honesty without derogating from their understanding, or their understanding without detracting from their honesty, can do—wonders!

Taylor, WORTHY COMMUNICANT, *p. 161. Note continued on pp. 162-63.*

In order to this, it is highly considerable that the greatest argument to prove our Religion is the goodness, and the holiness of it.

But might not a pious Jew object sophistry to this? Might he not assert, that the same effect would result from a faithful adherence to the Law & the Prophets? What more in morals can a man do "than to do justice and to love mercy and to walk humbly with the Lord his God?" Might not a pious Deist demonstrate that the same Duties are commanded by Reason & Conscience? How can that be the greatest argument which is simply negative: which proves that Xtnity may be revealed, but cannot prove of itself that it was revealed. Had it not commanded all these things must be, that Christians are able to obey these dictates common both to Religion & to Reason, better than by Reason they could have done. As a Christian, I believe this: and doubtless, the experience of such supernatural aidance is itself a miracle that cannot fail of convincing the individual himself. But how can we prove this? How can we argue to others on this ground? Not by facts, I fear. We should be deminded of the φεῦ! καὶ ταῦτα Χριστιανοὶ Χριστιανούς of the Slave Trade,—Wars, Prostitution, Inquisition &c. and then the additional difficulty of settling the . . . [cut off] total result, which itself requires Faith. S. T. C.

Taylor, WORTHY COMMUNICANT, *p. 169. Note continued on p. 170.*

> For so said God, when he caused his name to be proclaimed to the host of Israel; *The Lord God Merciful and gracious:* he caused to be added, *and that will by no means quit the guilty.*

This to the end of the § ph. is not more fearful than true. But is it *all* the truth? I trust not. It is so base and perilous a question that I shrink inwardly from the agitation of it. But may not *infirmities* and sad constraints or tyrannous temptations, from the organic injuries and deranged functions from former errors & evil [cut off; cont. p. 170] and detested so that the poor Sinner would die rather than *commence* such a course, he too striving by Means & Sacrifices to compensate for the ill by all the *free* parts of his Will—may it not admit of a trembling Hope that the communion with the flesh and blood of the Divine Humanity & the merits & intercession of Christ may cause these fetters of the Old Man to drop off with the Body—that the Disease [cut off] have been punished on the road thereto? According to J. Taylor's Scheme, which has all the Hardness of the Romish doctrine, without [cut off]

Taylor, WORTHY COMMUNICANT, *p. 177.*

> But as he that shuts the eye hard . . . ; So is he that blinds the eye of his reason, and pretends to see by an eye of faith . . . sees like a man in his sleep, and grows as much the wiser as the man that dreamt of a *Lycanthropy*, and was for ever after wisely wary not to come near a River.

Unless Lycanthropy here means Hydrophobia, I do not understand the connection of the last sentence. The Passage is cited in Johnson's Dictionary under the word Lycanthropy but not explained. A man bitten by a rabid animal believed to fancy himself turned into the animal that had bitten him [cut off][90]

Taylor, WORTHY COMMUNICANT, *p. 181. Note continued on p. 182.*

> He hath told us, This is his body: This is his bloud: believe it, and so receive it.

Taylor here recommends a mode of Faith of which I cannot form the remotest conception. If we attach to the words Blood & Flesh the common [cut off; cont. p. 182] and if we do not attach that sense, and yet dare not enquire for any other, wherein do the words differ from Abra in Cadabra—when all by Belief must consist in the Belief.

[90] Cf. another use of "lycanthropy" by Taylor: "For the soul may be alive, and yet not feel; as it may be alive and not understand; so our soul, when we are fast asleep, and so Nebuchadnezzar's soul when he had his lycanthropy." Letter from Taylor to Evelyn, Aug. 29, 1657. Evelyn, *Diary and Correspondence*, ed. William Bray (Bohn ed., 4 vols.; London: 1894-1900), III, 98. See Dan. 4.

Taylor, WORTHY COMMUNICANT, *p. 181, comment on flyleaves.*[91]
This = Bread is my Flesh: and this = Wine is my Blood. Such
is the Position. Now either the emphasis is to be laid on the pronoun
my: and then the words might signify—These to *me* are the same as
Flesh and Blood are to men in general—which again might be interpreted, I as the co-eternal Word, or Son, have, in myself, properly,
neither Flesh or Blood, but in reference to you whatever sustains &
nourishes you, in body or in soul, are my flesh & blood—Thus it might
refer to what some of the Fathers deemed the first incarnation of the
Logos, the creation of the Universe of things finite—& the use of the
words would be to instruct the Apostles, that his *Body,* as a *phænomenon,*
was transitory like theirs, & that the Breaking on the Cross was itself
symbolical—while the real Passion & Act extended thro' creation, of
all which (as far as it is ὄντως ὄν, and not phantasms of the Percipient)
Christ's Body is the Noumenon or Hypostasis.
   2. Or both parts of the Proposition are understood as the *phænomena:*
and then to say that the phænomenon Bread is the Phænomenon Flesh,
is a contradiction both in . . . [cut off] as A is NOT B; but A IS B which
yet might sound a mystery to the Head, if it were uttered with great
pomp, and a weighty emphasis on the "not" and the "*is*" so as to
give them the semblance of antithesis, instead of contradiction. (In the
first interpretation Bread & Wine are regarded as Phænomena; Flesh &
Blood as Noumena, and it is no contradiction in *Reason* to say that B
is the Noumenon of A. The second is palpably a contradiction.)
   Or 3rd, A is used in the ordinary sense, without any distinction of
Noumenon & Phænomenon, the things, *Bread & Wine,*—and in like
manner B, but with this difference that the copula *is* is taken in the
sense of signifies or may remind you of—as—Tie two knots in your hand-
kerchief & remember that the First *is* a Pound of Tea at Twining's, and
the second *is* the Coat which my Taylor will have made by that time.
   Or lastly, it is more than remembrancive or commemorative, & means
—that spiritual Support, & Benefit which is effected for Mankind in general by the breaking of my Body & the shedding of my Blood shall be
present & communicated to each in particular who shall in faith break
bread & drink the Wine in imitation of the former. Thus a Sovereign
might promise protection to every man, who *drank his Health.* [cut
off] This Glass is the King and whoever [cut off] The third may be
believed exclusively—the 4th Conjointly with the third, as a concomitant
—and both may be combined with the first. I myself am inclined to

[91] Cf. this discussion with letter to Cottle, 1807. Turnbull, *Biog. Epist.,* II, 10-18.

adopt the first, involving the 4th & admitting the third as an accessional Use. Thus a Letter, which I was ordered to deliver, may remind me of the Letter, and of it's various contents and connexions.

Bishop Taylor expresses himself so laxly as to appear to contradict himself. I can believe without knowing the *How?* but not without knowing the *What?* Take two Instances. First, This Oak Tree is a Fish. Here I know what I mean by an Oak and a Fish; and for that reason know that the proposition is either false, or that Oak does not mean an Oak or Fish a Fish—and then all I can possibly believe is that the person who said—An Oak is a Fish—had some other meaning which from my reverence for his known Wisdom & Veracity I doubted not was wise & true. In other words, I believe that a something, which you know & I do not, is true—or I believe that you know more than I do. The second Instance shall be, my will acts on my living powers. How I neither fully comprehend any one word—and still less the whole proposition, but I know what I mean by each word & by the whole [cut off] . . . believe it.

In general, the more I reflect on this work, the stronger is my conjecture that the doctrine of Work, i. e. Roman or Pagan Christianism is at the foundation. The demands seem every while to lie between two intolerable Theses: either that God's Justice is merciless and disproportionate to the capabilities of our Nature—or the Cross of Christ is of no effect. For if in order to use any of the means of Grace, (since if not this one, why any?—Prayer for instance?) the man must be fit to die, and have already conquered Sin, in a very subordinate degree, can it be deemed a mean of Grace in any other sense than as Angels might need it—for they too go on from Grace to Grace. Surely, true Sanctification is an effect and a part of the Redemption, not a Cause. Redemption is a free gift—not Wages, no, nor even Reward. If a man earnestly desire & struggles to pray entirely for Faith & it's consequents he may [cut off]

Taylor, WORTHY COMMUNICANT, *p. 210.*

> And indeed, that forgiveness is the best which is the most perfect negative; that is, *in malice be children;* whose pretty quarrels though they be fierce as a sudden spark, yet they are as innocent as the softest part of their own flesh, and as soon out as that sudden spark.

This is one among the (thank God) numerous instances in which J. Taylor's genial Nature, and exquisitely tender Sense of the Beautiful, flung him, like the Flying Fish, above the emprisoning [cut off]

Taylor, WORTHY COMMUNICANT, *p. 218. Note continued on p. 219.*

It was noted as a pitiful thing of Brutus . . . that he cried out most passionately in the words of the Greek tragedy to *Jupiter* to take revenge of young *Octavius.*

But wherein worse than David & other Psalmists in their vehement maledictory prayers? Might not a Patriot [cut off] freedom from pitiful Self-love invoke the divine justice on the treacherous & selfish Authors of his & their Country's Ruin? At all events, let [cut off]

Taylor, WORTHY COMMUNICANT, *p. 265.*

He that giveth honour to a fool (saith *Solomon*) *is like him that bindeth a stone in a sling.*

The meaning is plain enough, and far deeper, methinks than that which the Vulgate would substitute. He that giveth honor to a fool, means to make use of him for some mischievous or hostile purpose. He is the pebble in the Sling of his Flatterer. S. T. Coleridge. 7 Aug. 1826.

Taylor, WORTHY COMMUNICANT, *p. 294. Note continued on p. 265.*

As soon as we are smitten with the terrours of an afflicted conscience . . . we are not instantly worthy and fit to communicate. Attrition is not a competent disposition to the blessed Sacrament . . .; unless it be contrition, it is not a state of favour and grace, but a disposition to it.

But this is dangerous doctrine unless it be added, that there Attrition with a sense of it's imperfection and an earnestly [*sic*] desire to raise it into contrition, and that into a Love of God, is itself a beginning & a mode of Contrition [cut off] be an end, & a reward, but could not be, as it is, a means & an aid for all ranks of sincere tho' imperfect Christians.

Taylor, WORTHY COMMUNICANT, *p. 300. Note continued on p. 301.*

But this is no invitation for them to come who feel such a lukewarmness and indifference of spirit and devotion, that they have more reason to suspect it to be an effect of evil life, rather than of infirmity. . . .

But this is the very truth of the Fact, as related by St. Paul himself. He bids them not dare to pervert the Sacrament to carnal intemperance but no where gives prohibitions resembling these of Bishop Taylor's which savor far too strong of Popery. But I have long since convinced myself that [cut off] rigorous Semblance. Arminianism, a hard & rigid System with a smiling plausible Exterior.

Taylor, WORTHY COMMUNICANT, *p. 301.*

[Those excluded from the Sacrament according to St. Dionysius.] *And to conclude they who are not yet perfectly united to God alone.*

Here we discover one of the germs of Popery—it afterwards developed itself into the exclusion of the Laity from the Cup—they were not perfectly united to Christ, forsooth. How different from Christ's own invitation. Come unto me, all ye that are weary and *heavy-laden!*

Taylor, WORTHY COMMUNICANT, *p. 302. Note continued on p. 303.* [*Account of the penitentials*]

But it is known that this austerity of the Fathers in 2d & 3rd Centuries was the cause of the following Corruptions, & Laxity—& being utterly *non*-scriptural if not *anti*-scriptural, could not have been enforced but by pretences to an equal authority with that of the Apostles. And this, indeed, was the case. An anathema was pronounced on those, who trusted the written word of an Apostle in preference to the living Word of their Presbyter or Bishop. And how could Taylor justify to himself [cut off] accompanying them with an account of the horrible state of morals & Religion in their times? Fruits of Repentance were demanded—by whom? [cut off]

Taylor, WORTHY COMMUNICANT, *p. 304.* [*Danger of admitting sinners to the Communion*]

Thus, one Evil generates another. The Clergy turned the Eucharist into a sort of magic & then complained that Sinners perished by relying [cut off]

Taylor, WORTHY COMMUNICANT, *p. 306.*

It is clear from the rhetorical style that St. Chr.[ysostom] was addressing careless or presumptuous Communicants, not humble & heart-smitten Sinners. But Taylor is in this work so slippery a writer, that I know not when & whether I have hold of him. For instance, nothing can be more different in spirit than his first Quotation from Dionysius,[92] p. 301 & his last from Gennadius.[93] Compare only the last 9 lines of the former with the second period of the later and therefrom without [cut off]

---

[92] *Concerning the Ecclesiastical Hierarchy,* cap. 3. Several works were printed under the name of Dionysius the ''Areopagite,'' who was converted by St. Paul.

[93] *De dogmatibus Ecclesiasticis,* cap. 53. ''And therefore although he be bitten [or grieved] with sin, let him for the future renounce all will to sin . . . let him come to the Eucharist without doubting.'' Gennadius was priest of Marseilles about 493.

THE OLD DIVINES/JEREMY TAYLOR

Taylor, WORTHY COMMUNICANT, *last flyleaves, reference to pp. 22-23.*

The common mode of reasoning is, Christ has called the Faith in him the eating of his Flesh & drinking of his Blood: for Truth, Knowledge, and Religion are exprest by similar metaphors in various parts of the Old Testament. Now I should draw a different conclusion, namely, that Christ has positively declared the participation in his Flesh and Blood indispensable to Redemption—therefore, that all effective Truth, & saving Knowlege subsisted in this communion—whatever it may be. That it is not the *phœnomenon*, Flesh and Blood, we know: for no evidence can go beyond evidence itself. But it may be the Noumenon, the Ens vere ens, of which the Bread & Wine may be as adequate Phænomena, or sensuous Exponents, as the visible Body of Jesus was. No wise man uses a metaphor without a reason. In other words, a metaphor ought to be a noto ad ignotum. Now that Truth is to the mind what Bread & Wine, or generally, meat and Drink is to the body, needs only to be so said: if there be nothing in the nature of Truth which requires to be further known. The : is not without the ∴ [cut off] us that Truth to the Mind and Food to the Body were much more nearly connected, than our abstract Philosophy dreamt of—that matter was more spiritual, and spirit more material, than the distinctions of the Schools, & the Logic of Philosophers, had taught us—then he would have exprest his meaning in the very words of Scripture. When therefore Taylor affirms that to partake of Christ's Body is to have a lively Faith in him &c., I answer in his own words "This is something but much too little" —For what is a lively Faith? To be one with Christ. To be in him as he is in his Father. What are the means by which we become one with Christ? He himself says by assimulating our vital being to his Humanity by taking him as Food.

The main purport of this remark is that to eat the flesh and to drink the blood of Christ is far less intelligible than to believe in him & obey him: therefore, that the latter could be elucidated by the former, which yet must have been the purpose, if the words were mere metaphors. For the end of all metaphors is to [cut off]

P. S. Most worthy of notice it seems to me, that Christ has said that to eat his flesh and to drink his Blood are the indispensable Terms or Means of Spiritual & Everlasting Life. But he has no where said, as far as I remember, that it is indispensably necessary for us to believe in any one *particular* instance that we are *then* eating his Flesh and drinking his Blood. It seems quite sufficient to believe, that if we have a lively Faith in him, obey his commands and to the utmost of our power put on the mind and affections that were in Christ, we shall sometime

or other discover, that we have in some appropriate sense been eating
& drinking Christ.

The Romanists indeed would quote the words of the sacramental
Institution; but the Protestants understand them, as merely saying—Let
these, i. e. Bread & Wine, *represent,* or as the Reformed interpret the
text, Let these be *Remembrancer's* of this spiritual Mystery. Bread &
Wine or Wine & Water as the daily & most general Food & Beverage of
the Roman Empire were the proper & best representatives of bodily
sustenance in toto—as these were the symbols, the [cut off] of spiritual
Assimilation.

A Comparison of Milton and Taylor.[94]

But it seemed to me worthy of consideration, whether the mood of
mind, and the general state of sensations, in which a Poet produces such
vivid and fantastic images [as in "Fire, Famine, and Slaughter"], is
likely to co-exist, or is even compatible with that gloomy and deliberate
ferocity which a serious wish to realize them would presuppose. . . .[95]

Or, to take a case more analagous to the present subject, should we
hold it either fair or charitable to believe it to have been Dante's serious
wish, that all the persons mentioned by him, (many recently departed,
and some even alive at the time,) should actually suffer the fantastic
and horrible punishments, to which he has sentenced them in his *hell* and
purgatory? Or what shall we say of the passages in which Bishop
Jeremy Taylor anticipates the state of those who, vicious themselves,
have been the cause of vice and misery to their fellow-creatures. Could
we endure for a moment to think that a spirit, like Bishop Taylor's,
burning with Christian love; that a man constitutionally overflowing
with pleasurable kindliness; who scarcely even in a casual illustration
introduces the image of woman, child, or bird, but he embalms the
thought with so rich a tenderness, as makes the very words seem beauties
and fragments of poetry from Euripides or Simonides;—can we endure
to think, that a man *so* natured and so disciplined, did at the time of
composing this horrible picture, attach a sober feeling of reality to the
phrases? or that he would have described in the same tone of justification, in the same luxuriant flow of phrases, the tortures about to be

[94] In a letter to John Murray, July 4, 1816 (*A Publisher and His Friends,* ed.
Samuel Smiles, 2 vols.; London and New York: 1891, I, 304), Coleridge wrote:
"I have often thought that there might be set on foot a review of old books, *i.e.* of
all works important or remarkable . . . I would not take the works chronologically,
but according to the likeness or contrast of the *kind* of genius—*ex. gr.* Jeremy
Taylor, Milton (his prose works), and Burke—Dante and Milton (poetry)—Scaliger
and Dr. Johnson." The comparison of Milton and Taylor is found in An Apologetic
Preface to "Fire, Famine and Slaughter," *Sib. Leaves.*

[95] An Apologetic Preface, p. 91.

inflicted on a living individual by a verdict of the Star-Chamber? or the still more atrocious sentences executed on the Scotch anti-prelatists and schismatics, at the command, and in some instances under the very eye of the Duke of Lauderdale, and of that wretched bigot who afterwards dishonored and forfeited the throne of Great Britain? Or do we not rather feel and understand, that these violent words were mere bubbles, flashes and electrical apparitions, from a magic cauldron of a fervid and ebuliant [sic] fancy, constantly fuelled by an unexampled opulence of language? . . .[96]

The passage from Jeremy Taylor to which I referred, is found in his second Sermon on Christ's Advent to Judgement;[97] which is likewise the second in his year's course of sermons. Among many remarkable passages of the same character in those discourses, I have selected this as the most so.

> But when this Lion of the tribe of Judah shall appear, then Justice shall strike, and Mercy shall not hold her hands; she shall strike sore strokes, and Pity shall not break the blow. As there are treasures of good things, so hath God a treasure of wrath and fury, and scourges and scorpions; and then shall be produced the shame of Lust and the malice of Envy, and the groans of the oppressed and the persecutions of the saints, and the cares of Covetousness and the troubles of Ambition, *and the insolencies of traitors and the violences of rebels,* and the rage of anger and the uneasiness of impatience, and the restlessness of unlawful desires; and by this time the monsters and diseases will be numerous and intolerable, when God's heavy hand shall press the *sanies* and the intolerableness, the obliquity and the unreasonableness, the amazement and the disorder, the smart and the sorrow, the guilt and the punishment, out from all our sins, and pour them into one chalice, and mingle them with an infinite wrath, and make the wicked drink off all the vengeance, and force it down their unwilling throats with the violence of devils and accursed spirits.

That this Tartarean drench displays the imagination rather than the discretion of the compounder; that, in short, this passage and others of the same kind are *in a bad taste,* few will deny at the present day. It would, doubtless, have more behooved the good bishop not to be wise beyond what is written, on a subject in which Eternity is opposed to Time, and a death threatened, not the negative, but the *positive* Opposite

[96] *Ibid.,* pp. 94-95. The remainder of the comparison is quoted consecutively, pp. 98-104.

[97] Second sermon on "Christ's Advent to Judgement," *The Works of Jeremy Taylor,* ed. by Reginald Heber (15 vols.; London: 1822), V, 22. Coleridge omits parts of the passage. After "shall appear" read "upon his own mountain, the mountain of the Lord, in his natural dress of majesty, and that justice shall have her chain and golden fetters taken off'"; then continue as printed. After "break the blow," seven lines are omitted, and after "treasures of good things" about four lines are omitted, enumerating the treasures.

of Life; a subject, therefore, which must of necessity be indescribable
to the human understanding in our present state. But I can neither find
nor believe, that it ever occurred to any reader to ground on such passages a charge against BISHOP TAYLOR's humanity, or goodness of heart.
I was not a little surprized therefore to find, in the Pursuits of Literature and other works, so horrible a sentence passed on MILTON's moral
character, for a passage in *his* prose writings, as nearly parallel to
this of Taylor's as two passages can well be conceived to be. All his
merits, as a poet, forsooth—all the glory of having written the PARADISE
LOST, are light in the scale, nay, kick the beam, compared with the
atrocious malignity of heart, expressed in the offensive paragraph. I
remembered, in general, that Milton had concluded one of his works on
Reformation, written in the fervour of his youthful imagination, in a
high poetic strain, that wanted metre only to become a lyrical poem. I
remembered that in the former part he had formed to himself a perfect
ideal of human virtue, a character of heroic, disinterested zeal and
devotion for Truth, Religion, and public Liberty, in Act and in Suffering, in the day of Triumph and in the hour of Martyrdom. Such spirits,
as more excellent than others, he describes as having a more excellent
reward, and as distinguished by a transcendent glory: and this reward
and this glory he displays and particularizes with an energy and
brilliance that announced the Paradise Lost as plainly, as ever the
bright purple clouds in the east announced the coming of the Sun.
Milton then passes to the gloomy contrast, to such men as from motives
of selfish ambition and the lust of personal aggrandizement should,
against their own light, persecute truth and the true religion, and wilfully abuse the powers and gifts intrusted to them, to bring vice, blindness, misery and slavery, on their native country, on the very country
that had trusted, enriched and honored them. Such beings, after that
speedy and appropriate removal from their sphere of mischief which
all good and humane men must of course desire, will, he takes for
granted by parity of reason, meet with a punishment, an ignominy, and
a retaliation, as much severer than other wicked men, as their guilt and
its consequences were more enormous. His description of this imaginary
punishment presents more distinct *pictures* to the fancy than the extract
from Jeremy Taylor; but the *thoughts* in the latter are incomparably
more exaggerated and horrific. All this I knew; but I neither remembered, nor by reference and careful re-perusal could discover, any
other meaning, either in Milton or Taylor, but that good men will be
rewarded, and the impenitent wicked punished, in proportion to their
dispositions and intentional acts in this life; and that if the punishment
of the least wicked be fearful beyond conception, all words and descrip-

tions must be so far true, that they must fall short of the punishment that awaits the transcendently wicked. Had Milton stated either his ideal of virtue, or of depravity, as an individual or individuals actually existing? Certainly not! Is this representation worded historically, or only hypothetically? Assuredly the latter! Does he express it as his own *wish*, that after death they *should* suffer these tortures? or as a general consequence, deduced from reason and revelation, that such *will* be their fate? Again, the latter only! His wish is expressly confined to a speedy stop being put by Providence to their power of inflicting misery on others! But did he name or refer to any persons, living or dead? No! But the calumniators of Milton *daresay* (for what will calumny not dare say?) that he had LAUD and STRAFFORD in his mind, while writing of remorseless persecution, and the enslavement of a free country, from motives of selfish ambition. Now, what if a stern anti-prelatist should *daresay*, that in speaking of the *insolencies of traitors and the violences of rebels*, Bishop Taylor must have individualized in his mind, HAMPDEN, HOLLIS, PYM, FAIRFAX, IRETON, and MILTON? And what if he should take the liberty of concluding, that, in the after-description, the Bishop was feeding and feasting his party-hatred, and with those individuals before the eyes of his imagination enjoying, trait by trait, horror after horror, the picture of their intolerable agonies? Yet this Bigot would have an equal right thus to criminate the one good and great man, as these men have to criminate the other. Milton has said, and I doubt not but that Taylor with equal truth could have said it, "that in his whole life he never spake against a man even that his skin should be grazed." He asserted this when one of his opponents (either Bishop Hall or his nephew) had called upon the women and children in the streets to take up stones and stone *him* (Milton). It is known that Milton repeatedly used his interest to protect the royalists; but even at a time when all lies would have been meritorious against him, no charge was made, no story pretended, that he had ever directly or indirectly engaged or assisted in their persecution. Oh! methinks there are other and far better feelings, which should be acquired by the perusal of our great elder writers. When I have before me on the same table, the works of Hammond and Baxter; when I reflect with what joy and dearness their blessed spirits are now loving each other: it seems a mournful thing that their names should be perverted to an occasion of bitterness among *us*, who are enjoying that happy mean which the *human* TOO-MUCH on both sides was perhaps necessary to produce.

> The tangle of delusions which stifled and distorted the growing tree of our well-being has been torn away; the parasite-weeds that fed on its very roots have been plucked up with a salutary violence. To us there

remain only quiet duties, the constant care, the gradual improvement, the cautious unhazardous labours of the industrious though contented gardener—to prune, to strengthen, to engraft, and one by one to remove from its leaves and fresh shoots the slug and the caterpillar. But far be it from us to undervalue with light and senseless detraction the conscientious hardihood of our predecessors, or even to condemn in them that vehemence, to which the blessings it won for us leave us now neither temptation nor pretext. We ante-date the *feelings,* in order to criminate the *authors,* of our present liberty and toleration. *The Friend,* p. 54.

If ever two great men might seem, during their whole lives, to have moved in direct opposition, though neither of them has at any time introduced the name of the other, Milton and Jeremy Taylor were they. The former commenced his career by attacking the Church-Liturgy and all set forms of prayer. The latter, but far more successfully, by defending both. Milton's next work was then against the Prelacy and the then existing Church-Government—Taylor's in vindication and support of them. Milton became more and more a stern republican, or rather an advocate for that religious and moral aristocracy which, in his day, was *called* republicanism, and which, even more than royalism itself, is the direct antipode of modern jacobinism. Taylor, as more and more skeptical concerning the fitness of men in general for power, became more and more attached to the prerogatives of monarchy. From Calvinism, with a still decreasing respect for Fathers, Councils, and for Church-Antiquity in general, Milton seems to have ended in an indifference, if not a dislike, to *all* forms of ecclesiastic government, and to have retreated wholly into the inward and spiritual church-communion of his own spirit with the light, that lighteth every man that cometh into the world. Taylor, with a growing reverence for authority, an increasing sense of the insufficiency of the Scriptures without the aids of tradition and the consent of authorized interpreters, advanced as far in his approaches (not indeed to Popery, but) to Catholicism, as a conscientious minister of the English Church could well venture. Milton would be, and would utter the same, to all, on all occasions: he would tell the truth, the whole truth, and nothing but the truth. Taylor would become all things to all men, if by any means he might benefit any; hence he availed himself, in his *popular* writings, of opinions and representations which stand often in striking contrast with the doubts and convictions expressed in his more philosophical works. He appears, indeed, not *too severely* to have blamed that *management* of truth (*istam falsitatem dispensativam*) authorized and exemplified by almost all the fathers: Integrum omnino Doctoribus et cœtus Christiani Antistitibus esse, ut dolos versent, falsa veris intermiscéant et imprimis religionis hostes fallant, dummodo veritatis commodis et utilitati inserviant.

The same antithesis might be carried on with the elements of their several intellectual powers. Milton, austere, condensed, imaginative, supporting his truth by direct enunciation of lofty moral sentiment and by distinct visual representations, and in the same spirit overwhelming what he deemed falsehood by moral denunciation and a succession of pictures appalling or repulsive. In his prose, so many metaphors, so many allegorical miniatures. Taylor, eminently discursive, accumulative, and (to use one of his own words) *agglomerative;* still more rich in images than Milton himself, but images of Fancy, and presented to the common and passive eye, rather than to the eye of the imagination. Whether supporting or assailing, he makes his way either by argument or by appeals to the affections, unsurpassed even by the Schoolmen in subtlety, agility, and logical wit, and unrivalled by the most rhetorical of the fathers in the copiousness and vividness of his expressions and illustrations. Here words that convey feelings, and word that flash images, and words of abstract notion, flow together, and whirl and rush onward like a stream, at once rapid and full of eddies; and yet still, interfused here and there, we see a tongue or islet of smooth water, with some picture in it of earth or sky, landscape or living group of quiet beauty.

Differing, then, so widely, and almost contrariantly, wherein did these great men agree? wherein did they resemble each other? In Genius, in Learning, in unfeigned Piety, in blameless Purity of Life, and in benevolent aspirations and purposes for the moral and temporal improvement of their fellow-creatures! Both of them wrote a Latin Accidence, to render education more easy and less painful to children; both of them composed hymns and psalms proportioned to the capacity of common congregations; both, nearly at the same time, set the glorious example of publicly recommending and supporting general Toleration, and the Liberty both of the Pulpit and the Press! In the writings of neither shall we find a single sentence, like those *meek deliverances to God's mercy,* with which LAUD accompanied his votes for the mutilations and loathsome dungeoning of Leighton and others!—no where such a pious prayer as we find in Bishop Hall's memoranda of his own Life, concerning the subtle and witty Atheist that so grievously perplexed and gravelled him at Sir Robert Drury's till *he prayed to the Lord, to remove him,* and behold! his prayers were heard; for shortly afterward this philistine-combatant went to London, and there perished of the plague in great misery![98] In short, no where shall we find the least approach, in the lives and writings of John Milton or Jeremy Taylor, to that guarded gentleness, to that sighing reluctance, with which the holy Brethren of the Inquisition deliver over a condemned heretic to the civil magistrate, recommending him to mercy, and *hoping* that the magistrate will treat the erring brother with all possible mildness!—the magistrate, who too well knows what would be his own fate, if he dared offend them by acting on their recommendation. . . .

Henry More

We may now proceed to our reflections on the *Spirit* of Religion. The first three or four Aphorisms I have selected from the Theological Works of Dr. Henry More, a contemporary of Archbishop Leighton's, and, like him, held in suspicion by the Calvinists of that time as a Latitudinarian and Platonizing Divine, and probably, like him, would have been arraigned as a Calvinist by the Latitudinarians (I cannot say, Platonists) of this Day, had the suspicion been equally groundless.[1]

More, WORKS,[2] *first flyleaf, recto and verso.*

There are three principal causes to which the imperfections and errors in the theological schemes and works of our elder Divines, the Glories of our Church, men of almost unparalleled Learning, Genius, the rich and robust Intellects from the reign of Elizabeth to the death of Charles the second, may, I think, be reasonably attributed. And striking, unusually striking instances of all three abound in this Volume—& in the works of no other Divine are they more worthy of being regretted. For hence has arisen a depreciation of Dr. Henry More's theological writings, which yet contain more original, enlarged and elevating views

---

[98] Joseph Hall, *Observations of Some Specialities of Divine Providence in the Life of Joseph Hall, Bishop of Norwich.* Written with His Own Hand. *Works* (Oxford: 1837), I, xviii-xix.

[1] *Aids*, p. 139. Cf. Shedd, I, 197.
[2] Henry More, *Theological Works* (London: 1708). British Museum, Ashley, 5176. This copy has the bookplate of James Gillman. With the omission of one complete note and part of another, the notes from More were published with a few changes, one of which altered the meaning, in *Lit. Rem.*, III, 156-67. The notes are not reprinted in full, but those which have been selected give the text as it appears in the original notes.

of the Christian Dispensation, than I have met with in any other single
Volume. For More had both the philosophic and the poetic Genius,
supported by immense erudition. But unfortunately, the two did not
amalgamate. It was not his good fortune to discover, as in the preceding Generation William Shakspear discovered, a mordaunt or common Base of both: and in which both, viz. the poetic and philosophic
Power blended into one.

These Causes are,—

I[st] and foremost, the want of that logical προπαιδεία docimastica, that
Critique of the human intellect, which previous to the weighing and
measuring of this or that, begins by assaying the weights, measures, and
scales themselves—that fulfilment of the heaven-descended *Nosce teip-
sum,* in respect to the intellective part of Man, which was Commenced
in a sort of tentative broad-cast way by Lord Bacon in his Novum
Organum, and brought to a systematic Completion by Immanuel Kant
in his Critik der reinen Vernunft, der Urtheilskraft, & der metaphysiche
Anfangsgründe der Naturwissenschaft. From the want of this searching
Logic there is a perpetual confusion of the Subjective with the Objective,
in the arguments of our Divines, together with a childish or anile overrating of Human Testimony, and an ignorance in the art of sifting it,
which necessarily engendered Credulity.

2. The ignorance of Natural Science, their Physiography scant in
fact and stuffed out with fables, their Physiology embrangled with an
inapplicable Logic and a misgrowth of Entia Rationalia, i. e. substantiated Abstractions; and their Physiogony a Blank, or Dreams of Tradition & such "intentional Colors" as occupy space but cannot fill it.
Yet if Christianity is to be the Religion of the World, if Christ be that
Logos or Word that was in the beginning, by whom all things *became;*
if it was the same Christ, who said, Let there be *Light;* who in and by
the Creation commenced that great redemptive Process, the history of
Life which begins in it's detachment from Nature and is to end in it's
union with God—if this be true, so true must it be, that the Book
of Nature and the Book of Revelation, with the whole history of Man as
the intermediate Link, must be the integral and coherent Parts of one
great Work. And the conclusion is: that a scheme of the Christian Faith
which does not arise out of, and shoot it's beams downward into, the
scheme of Nature, but stands aloof as an insulated Afterthought, must
be false or distorted in all it's particulars. In confirmation of this
position, I may challenge any opponent to adduce a single instance in
which the now exploded falsities of physical Science, thro' all it's revolutions from the second to the 17th Century of the Christian æra, did

not produce some corresponding warps in the theological systems and dogmas of the several periods.

III. The third and last cause, and especially operative in the writings of this Author, is the presence and *regnancy* of the false and fantastic Philosophy yet shot thro' with refracted Light from the not yet risen but rising Truth, a Scheme of Physics and Physiology compounded of Cartesian Mechanics, Empiricism (for it was the credulous Childhood of Experimentalism) and a corrupt mystical theurgical Pseudo-platonism, which infected the rarest minds under the Stuart Dynasty. The only not universal Belief in Witchcraft and Apparitions, and the vindication of such monster follies by such men as Sir M. Hales, Granville, Baxter, Henry More, and a host of others, are melancholy proofs of my position. Hence, in the first Chapters of this Volume, the most idle & fantastic Inventions of the ancients are sought to be made credible by the most fantastic hypotheses and analogies. See page 67, first half of.

To the man who has habitually contemplated Christianity as interesting all rational finite Beings, as the very "Spirit of Truth," the application of the Prophecies as so many *Fortune-tellings,* and Soothsayings, to particular Events & Persons, must needs be felt as childish—faces seen in the Moon, or the sediments of a Teacup. But reverse this—and a Pope, and a Bonaparte can never be wanting—the Molehill becomes an Andes. On the other hand, there are few writers whose works could be so easily defecated as More's. Mere Omission would suffice—& perhaps one half (an unusually large proportion) would come forth from the Furnace, pure Gold; if but a 4th, how great a Gain! S. T. Coleridge.

More, WORKS: AN EXPLANATION OF THE GRAND MYSTERY OF GODLINESS, DEDICATION.

Servorum illius omnium indignissimus.

Servus indignissimus, or omnino indignus, or any other *positive* Self-abasement before God, I can understand; but how an express avowal of unworthiness, *comparatively* superlative can consist with the Job-like integrity and sincerity of Profession, especially required in a solemn address to Him, to whom all Hearts are open—this I do not understand —in the case of such men as Henry More, Jer. Taylor, or R. Baxter &c. were, and by *comparison* at least, with the multitude of evil doers must have believed themselves to be. S. T. C.

More, WORKS: GRAND MYSTERY, *Part I, Book V, chap. xiv, sec. 3, p. 117.*

This makes me not so much wonder at that Passage of Providence which allowed so much Virtue to the Bones of the Martyr *Babylas,* once Bishop of *Antioch,* as to stop the mouth of *Apollo Daphneus,* when *Julian* would have enticed him to open it by many a fat Sacrifice: To say nothing of several other memorable *Miracles* that were done by the Reliques of Saints and Martys [*sic*] in those times.

Strange lingering of childish credulity in the most learned & in many respects *enlightened* Divines of the Prot. Epis. Church even to the time of James II. The Popish controversy at that time made a great clearance tho' even at this day the *Oxford* men *harken* after the four first Centuries & have not *heartily* forgiven Conyers Middleton. S. T. C.[3]

More, WORKS: GRAND MYSTERY, *Part I, Book V, chap. xvi, sec. 5, pp. 130-31. Note on p. 131.*

We now proceed to the trumpets.

It would be no easy matter to decide, whether Mede + More was at a greater distance from the meaning, or Grotius from the poetry of this Chapter [Chap. XI, Revelation] whether M. was more wild, or G. more tame, flat, and prosaic.

More, WORKS: GRAND MYSTERY, *Part I, Book VI, chap. xv, sec. 4, p. 180.*

With his semi-Cartesian, semi-platonic, semi-Christian notions, Henry More makes a sad Jumble in his assertion of chronochor-'istorical Xtnty.

One *decisive* reference to the Ascension of the visible & tangible Jesus from the surface of the Earth upward thro' the clouds, pointed out by him in the writings of Paul, or in the Gospel (or either of the three Facciamenti) beginning as certainly did [*sic*] and as in the Copy according to Mark it now does with the baptism of John, or in the writings of the Apostle John, would have been more effective in flooring Old Nic of Amsterdam and his Familiars, than Volumes of such "may be's" "perhapses," and "should be rendered."

More, WORKS: GRAND MYSTERY, *Part I, Book VIII, chap. ii, sec. 6, p. 259.*

I must confess our Saviour compiled no Books, it being a piece of Pedantry below so Noble and Divine a Person . . .

Alas! all this is *woefully beneath* the dignity of Henry More! and *shockingly against* the Majesty of the High & Holy so very unnecessarily compared with Hendrick Nikolas of Amsterdam, Mercer![4]

More, WORKS: GRAND MYSTERY, *Part I, Book X, chap. xiv, sec. 6, pp. 372-73.*

If it be thus with you, I dare appeal unto your own Conscience whether

[3] The last clause of this excerpt is not given in *Lit. Rem.*

[4] Known for *The Family of Love.*

you keep so precisely to *the Light within you,* but that you have consulted with that blind Guide, *H. Nicolas,* and tasted the treacherous Sops of his abhorred Passover, whose fanatick Boldness has led the Dance to this mad Apostacy.

A new Sect naturally attracts to itself a portion of the madmen of the Time, and sets another portion into Activity as Alarmists and Oppugnants. I cannot therefore pretend to say what More might not have found in the writings or heard from the mouth of some Lunatic who called himself a Quaker. But I do not recollect in any work of an acknowledged "Friend" a *denial* of the Facts narrated by the Evangelists, as having really taken place in the same sense, as any other Facts of History. If they were *Symbols* of *Spiritual* Acts and processes (as Fox and Penn contended) they must *have been,* or happened: else, how could they be Symbols? It is too true, however, that the positive Creed of the Quakers is and ever has been extremely vague and misty. The Deification of the Conscience under the name of "The Spirit" seems the main article of their Faith; and of the rest they form no opinion at all, considering it neither necessary or desirable. I speak of Quakers in general. S. T. C.

But what a lesson of experience does not this Chap. 13. [*sic*] of so great and good a man as H. More afford to *us,* who know what the Quakers really are! Had the Followers of G. Fox, or any number of them collectively, acknowledged the mad notions of this H. Nicolas? If not [note ends here]

More, WORKS: A MODEST ENQUIRY INTO THE MYSTERY OF INIQUITY, *Part II, Book II, chap. ii, p. 621.*

A Confutation of Grotius upon the Seventeenth Chapter of the Apocalypse.

Q[y]. Has or has not Grotius been overrated? If G. applied these words to Epiphanius in honest earnest and not ironically, he must have been greatly inferior in sound sense and critical tact both to Joseph Scaliger and to Rhenferd. Strange! that to H. More, a Poet & a man of fine Imagination it should never have occurred to ask himself whether this "Scene["]: Patmos, with which the Drama commences, was not a *part* of the Poem, & like all other parts to be interpreted symbolically? That the poetic—& I see no reason for doubting, the real—date of the Apocalypse is under VESPASIAN, is so evidently implied in the 5 Heads preceding (for Vitellius, Otho, and Galba were abortive Emperors) that it seems to me quite lawless to deny it. That Λατεῖνος is the meaning of the 666, and the treasonable character of this, are both shewn by

Irenæus's pretended rejection & his proposal of the perfectly senseless Titan instead.

Mem. To read over again the 4 or 5 last pages of Dr. H. More's Alazonomastix—and to ask—What these Differences constitutive or demonstrative of "this and that Church" are, of which he speaks so contemptuously. Are they such doctrines, such beliefs and disciplines as impede or even prevent that devotion to the articles of faith and practice controverted by no church, but admitted by all in common? May they not be such as to render it impossible or at least in the highest degree improbable that any man believing and acting on them should have that *Light* and that *Life* of Christian Faith & Morals, to which More would have an exclusive Devotion? Examine each of those Christian Virtues singly, and see what it supposes, what it requires in a Soul possessing it.[5]

Richard Baxter

Baxter, LIFE OF HIMSELF, *first series of notes.*[1]

In the notes, I have been bold enough marginally to write in this book, it will, I trust, be seen, that I am a bigot to no party. Highly do I approve of Baxter's conduct, affectionately admire and bless his peace-seeking spirit, and coincide with him as to the necessity of Church discipline in a Christian Church; but, on the other hand, I think his objections to the Liturgy, &c. &c., mistaken altogether, and even captious. His own system would have introduced an Hierocracy unexampled and insufferable, which yet he was the last man on earth to have meant or wished.

Baxter, LIFE OF HIMSELF, *Book I, Part I, p. 116.*

He had written a scornful book against the ministry, called *Jus Divinum Presbyterii*, and after two more against the Scripture and

[5] Notebook 40, fol. 76. British Museum, Add. MSS, 47,535. Printed for the first time.

[1] *Reliquiæ Baxterianæ: or Mr. Richard Baxter's Narrative of the most memorable Passages of his Life and Times.* (London: 1696.) Since the original notes for this reading have not been located, only the most illuminating notes have been reprinted from Derwent Coleridge's *English Divines*, II, 5-48. For Miss J. Mitford's summary of these notes in a MS Notebook, see British Museum, Add. MSS, 32,566, pp. 9-12.

against me, one called *Fides Divina,* the other's title I remember not: his assertion to me was, that no man is bound to believe in Christ that doth not see confirming miracles himself with his own eyes.

Ay! but this was a natural consequence, honoured Baxter! of thy own step, who didst first introduce into England the Grotian *ab extra* mode of defending Christianity, which either leads to this conclusion or to Socinianism.

Baxter, LIFE OF HIMSELF, *Book I, Part I, p. 123.*

But fain they would have had my controversial writings (about Universal Redemption, Predetermination, &c., in which my judgment is more pleasing to them) ; but I was unwilling to publish them alone, while the practical writings are refused. And I give God thanks that I once saw times of greater liberty (though under an usurper) ; or else as far as I can discern, scarce any of my books had ever seen the light.

A just though severe sarcasm: for observe Baxter and his writings were at least as inimical to Cromwell as to the Diocesans; nay, far, far more so. But the reign of Charles II. is the one great foul blotch of the Church of England.

Baxter, LIFE OF HIMSELF, *Book I, Part II, p. 193.*

And on the other extreme, Cromwell himself, and such others, commonly gave out that they could not understand what the magistrate had to do in matters of religion: and they thought that all men should be left to their own consciences, and that the magistrate could not interpose but he should be ensnared in the guilt of persecution.

One among a thousand proofs of Cromwell's attachment to the best interests of human nature!

Baxter, LIFE OF HIMSELF, *Book I, Part II, p. 197.*

10. Though it be not of necessity, yet would it be of great conveniency and use, if the magistrate would be with us, or appoint some substitute to represent him in all our assemblies, that he may be a witness of our proceedings, and see that we do no wrong to the Commonwealth, and avoid all suspicions that may be occasioned by rumours: but principally that he may see how far it is meet for him in any case to second us by his power, &c.

The magistrate's duty is not to punish or attempt to prevent *all* acts that may indirectly and in their remote consequences *injure* society: for if this were admitted, the statute *de Hereticis comburendis* might be justified: but such acts as are directly incompatible with the *peace* and *security* of society, leaving all else to the influences of religion, education, sympathy, necessity of maintaining a character, &c. But Baxter's error was the error of his age, with the exception of a handful of Quakers, Independents, and philosophic Deists.

Baxter, LIFE OF HIMSELF, *Book I, Part II, p. 197, paragraph 50.*

When Cromwell's faction were making him Protector, they drew up a thing which they called *The Government of England,* &c. Therein they determined that all should have liberty or free exercise of their religion, who professed faith in God by Jesus Christ. After this he called a Parliament, which examined this instrument of Government; and when they came to those words, the orthodox party affirmed, *That if they spake* de re, *and* not *de nomine,* 'Faith in God by Jesus Christ' could contain no less than the fundamentals of religion: whereupon it was purposed that all should have a due measure of liberty who professed the *fundamentals.* Hereupon the Committee, &c. &c.

The ¶ 50 proves the danger of any, even the most moderate, test of religious faith.

Baxter, LIFE OF HIMSELF, *Book I, Part II, pp. 197-98.*

My own judgment was this, that we must distinguish between the sense (or matter) and the words; and that it's only the sense that is primarily and properly our fundamentals; and the words no further than as they are needful to express that sense to others, or represent it to our own conception: that the word 'Fundamentals' being metaphorical and ambiguous, the word 'Essentials' is much fitter; it being nothing but what is essential or constitutive of true religion, which is understood by us usually when we speak of fundamentals: that *quoad rem* there is no more essential or fundamental in religion but what is contained in our baptismal covenant,—I believe in God the Father, Son, and Holy Ghost, and give up myself in covenant to him, renouncing the Flesh, the World, and the Devil.

Baxter often expresses himself so as to excite a suspicion that he was inclined to Sabellianism.

Baxter, LIFE OF HIMSELF, *Book I, Part II, pp. 242-43. "The Bishops' Answer to the First Proposals of the London Ministers who attempted the work of reconcilement, &c.", paragraph 8.*

And we cannot but wonder that the administration of government by one single person should by them be affirmed to be so liable to corruptions, partialities, tyrannies, and other evils, that for the avoiding thereof it should be needful to have others joined with him in the power of government; which if applied to the civil state is a most dangerous insinuation, and we verily believe what experience and the constitutions of kingdoms, armies, and even private families sufficiently confirmeth (in all which the government is administered by the authority of one single person, although the advice of others may be requisite also, but without any share in the government), that the government of many is not only most subject to all the aforesaid evils and inconveniences, but more likely also to breed and foment perpetual factions, both in Church and State, than the government by one is or can be. And since no government can certainly prevent all evils, that which is liable to the least and fewest is certainly to be preferred.

What a base appeal to the plan and passion of Charles II. for arbitrary power and despotic monarchy! what a wicked soothing and fomenting of it! From the furious insolent spirit of this answer, I suppose it to have been drawn up by or under Sheldon.

Baxter, Life of Himself, *Book I, Part II, bottom of p. 243.*

The reign of Charles I. was at once the glory and the shame of the English Diocesan Church; glory for the vast and various learning and stupendous talents of its Prelates and dignified Clergy; shame, for their atrocious cruelties, and rapid approximations to the superstitions, though not to the doctrinal errors of Popery. But the reign of Charles II., subtracting that which had attained its full growth in his father's life, was the mere infamy of the Church—a leprosy, some white discolorations from which are still eating, like a dry rot, into the walls of the Temple.

Baxter, Life of Himself, *Book I, Part II, p. 244.*

> Upon all which consideration it is, that officers in the court, freemen in cities and corporate towns, masters and fellows of colleges in the Universities, &c., are required, at their admission into their several respective places to give oaths for well and truly performing their several respective duties, their liableness to punishment in case of nonperformance accordingly notwithstanding. Neither doth it seem reasonable that such persons as have themselves with great severity prescribed and exacted antecedent conditions of their communion not warranted by law, should be exempted from the tie of such oaths and subscriptions as the laws require.

What a vindictive unchristian spirit of recrimination breathes here! Those who had the chief hand in drawing up the proposals, had opposed the former tyranny as firmly as that now impending.

Baxter, Life of Himself, *Book I, Part II, p. 271.*

> If all presentments and appeals be made to the Bishop and his consistory alone, it will take from us the parish discipline which is granted us, and cast almost all discipline out of the Church. As is most apparent, &c.

The incompossibility of Christian discipline with a Church established by Law, and all the permitted acts of which have the force of penal or compulsory Laws, has always appeared to me the objection that bears hardest on Church Establishment. Where Law begins, Discipline ends.

This Baxter did not at all times see clearly. But the Diocesan form of an Established Church, as it exists in England, adds to this inherent incongruity all possible external impediments. And yet

Old Church! with all thy faults I *love* thee still.—

Yea, with a filial, though not with a blind, adherence.

Baxter, LIFE OF HIMSELF, *Book I, Part II, p. 276, paragraph 108.*

> After all this a day was appointed for his Majesty to peruse the declaration as it was drawn up by the Lord Chancellor, and to allow what he liked and alter the rest, upon the hearing of what both sides should say: accordingly he came to the Lord Chancellor's house, and with him the Duke of Albemarle, and Duke of Ormond (as I remember), the Earl of Manchester, the Earl of Anglesey, the Lord Hollis, &c., and Dr. Sheldon then Bishop of London, Dr. Morley then Bishop of Worcester, &c.

This was the incendiary! this Sheldon the most virulent enemy and poisoner of the English Church. Alas! she still feels the *taint* in her very bones. I look on Gardner as canonisable compared with Sheldon.

Baxter, LIFE OF HIMSELF, *Book, I, Part II, p. 277.*

> Thereupon he read, as an addition to the declaration, that "others also be permitted to meet for religious worship, so be it, they do it not to the disturbance of the peace; and that no Justice of Peace or officer disturb them." When he had read it, he again desired them all to think on it, and give their advice: but all were silent. The Presbyterians all perceived, as soon as they heard it, that it would secure the liberty of the Papists, &c.

Another sad proof of the bad effects of imperfect theory respecting religious toleration. How easy would it otherwise have been to have excepted and excluded the Papists, not as religionists, but as having an actual temporal magistracy, under the false name of spiritual, obstinately independent of the supreme power, and owning a foreign Sovereign.

Baxter, LIFE OF HIMSELF, *Book I, Part II, p. 278.*

> And here you may note, by the way, the fashion of these times and the state of the Presbyterians: any man that was for a spiritual serious way of worship (though he were for moderate episcopacy and Liturgy), and that lived according to his profession, was called commonly a Presbyterian as formerly he was called a Puritan, unless he joined himself to Independents, Anabaptists, or some other sect which might afford him a more odious name.

I suspect that it would have puzzled the mild and kindhearted old man sorely, if he (Baxter, I mean), had been asked: Well! and what would you have done with these sectaries, Independents, Socinians, &c. Hang them? Banish them? Dungeon them? The admission that even an avowed *Atheist* may, *for that cause only*, be rightfully punished by the civil magistrate, doth, by incontestable consequence justify and legitimate the whole fire and faggot system, *de Hereticis cujuslibet generis et omnium specierum.* Even now unlimited toleration is only a thing, half *fashion*, half religious indifference. The *common* arguments in favour of it, such as those adduced by Locke, had been fairly and fully and repeatedly confuted by both Romish and Protestant Divines; and the *true* grounds it would not perhaps *even now* be quite safe for a writer to bring forwards. We owe the blessing wholly to God, with no intervention or instrumentality of Human Wisdom.

Baxter, LIFE OF HIMSELF, *Book I, Part II, p. 279, paragraph 116.*

> Before this I was called to preach at Court before the King (by the Lord Chamberlain, who had sworn me his Chaplain, and invited me under that name): and after sermon it pleased his Majesty to send the Lord Chamberlain to require me to print it. And the Earl of Lauderdale told me, that when he spake to the King of the great number of citizens that wrote it in characters, and said that some of them would publish it, the King answered, "I will prevent that, for I will have it published." Yet when this sermon came abroad, Dr. Thomas Pierce went up and down raging against me, for calling myself on the title-page 'his Majesty's Chaplain,' which if I had not it would have been taken as a contempt, and for saying it was printed by his Majesty's special command: and he renewed all the railings which in print he had lately vented against me.

Who dare presume himself secure from the sin of calumnious bigotry, (except by the opposite extreme of irreligious indifference,) when such men could be capable of such wicked outrages? But an infatuated ἀνακτοδουλεία, an absolute Carololatreia, strongly marked in his fine Latin epitaph on Charles the First, combined with a raging zeal for Diocesan Episcopacy to overset him.

Baxter, LIFE OF HIMSELF, *Book I, Part II, p. 280, paragraph 117.*

> That the reader may understand this the better, by knowing the occasion of his malice, this Mr. Thomas Pierce, being a confident man, and having written somewhat in defence of Grotius, as a judicious, peaceable Protestant, in opposition to some passages in my *Christian Concord,* where I warn the Episcopal party to take heed of Grotianism that was creeping in upon them. I did thereupon write a little collection out of the late writings of Grotius, especially his *Discussio Apologetici Rivetiani,* to prove him to have turned Papist; and that Popery was indeed his religion, though he communicated with no Church; for he expressly pleadeth for our consenting to the Council of Trent, and all other general Councils, as the Churches Law, &c.

This surely must have been some mistake of Baxter's. That Grotius sighed for a reconciliation of the Roman and Protestant Churches is well known; but that he should go beyond the French Catholics, and even the Spanish, is to me incredible. Baxter seems not to have read the works themselves, but to have relied on the authority of the French author of *Grotius Papizans*.

Baxter, LIFE OF HIMSELF, *Book I, Part II, p. 280. Second note.*

> But Mr. Pierce was vehemently furious at my book, and wrote a volume against me full of *ingenuous* lies and railings; for he had no better way to defend Grotius or himself.

One of the very few improvements in our language since the time of the Restoration is the separation of 'ingenious' and 'ingenuous.' The prior writers confound them.

Baxter, LIFE OF HIMSELF, *Book I, Part II, p. 282. "Baxter's Letter to the Lord Chancellor upon the offer of a Bishopric."*

> My Lord,—Your great favour and condescension encourages me to give you more of my sense of the business which your Lordship was pleased to propound. I was, till I saw the Declaration, much dejected, and resolved against a Bishopric as unlawful. But finding there, more than on October 22, his Majesty granted us, in the Pastor's *consent*, &c., the Rural Dean with the whole ministry enabled to exercise as much persuasive pastoral power as I could desire (who believe the Church hath no other kind of power, *unless communicated from the magistrate*), &c.

Even this says the Inquisition! But what right has a Christian pastor to admit, much less to invite, the *Wolf* of temporal power, even against the scabbiest sheep of his flock? Oh! this, this was the dire error that ruined the otherwise good cause of these good men!

Baxter, LIFE OF HIMSELF, *Book I, Part II, p. 354.*

> So to receive one another as Christ received us, to the glory of God the Father, and this not to doubtful disputation (or not to judge their doubtful thoughts), and not to despise or judge one another, but to take each other for such as do what we do to the Lord, and let every man be fully persuaded in his own mind; and so as to distinguish the points that we differ about from those in which God's kingdom doth consist, in which whosoever serveth Christ is acceptable to God, and should be approved of men; and so as to follow the things that edify and make for peace, and not lay a stumbling-block or occasion of falling in our brother's way, or destroy him by the uncharitable use of our liberty, knowing it is sin to him that esteemeth it sin; but to forbear ourselves to use those things in controversy whereby our brother stumbleth or is offended, because he is damned if he use them doubtingly; and therefore

to have the belief of their lawfulness to ourselves before God, and to bear with the infirmities of the weak, and please them to their edification, and not to please ourselves, that so being like-minded one towards another, that with one mind and one mouth we may glorify God: We say, Thus to receive is not consistent with the denial of communion in the Sacrament for those faults. But such was the receiving required by the Apostle, *Rom.* xiv. xv.—*Ergo,* &c.

This is a most beautiful paragraph, and the more so to a *true* taste for the seeming carelessness of its construction, like the *happily* dishevelled hair of a lovely woman.

Baxter, LIFE OF HIMSELF, *Book I, Part II, p. 354. Second note.*

He that can seriously ponder all these expressions, and the scope of the Holy Ghost, and yet can believe that all this receiving is but such as consisteth with forbidding them communion in the Lord's Supper, which then was so great a part of the daily communion of the Church, and also may consist with the further process against people and ministers to excommunication, and prohibition to preach the Gospel, which is now pleaded for in our case, is of so strange a temperature of understanding, as that we can have little hope by any Scripture evidence to convince him.

Most true! Alas, that the *best* of all national churches should have had an era so disgraceful as that of the Restoration!

Baxter, LIFE OF HIMSELF, *Book I, Part II, p. 369.*

Some have maintained that the Lord's Day is kept merely by Ecclesiastical constitution, and that the day is changeable.

So did the learned and saintly martyrs full of faith; yea, Luther himself. Selden too condemns the sabbatical transferred to the dominical day, as the basest of Judaic superstitions. The best argument for the cheerfully serious observation of Sunday in rest, meditation, sober recreation, &c. is, that there *can* be no sound argument against it, or for the change of the day or interval. I consider it, in our present state, as a *command* of natural religion, favoured, though not compelled, by the Gospel revelation. Were an angel to trumpet it from the clouds, the duty of observing it could not be more manifest to my reason than it already is.

Baxter, LIFE OF HIMSELF, *Book I, Part II, p. 370.*

Some have absolutely denied original sin, and so evacuated the cross of Christ, as in a disputation at Oxon.

Bishop Jeremy Taylor doth. If ever book was calculated to drive men to despair, it is Bishop Jeremy Taylor's on Repentance. It first opened my eyes to Arminianism, and that Calvinism is *practically* a far, far more soothing and consoling system.

Baxter, LIFE OF HIMSELF, Book I, Part II, p. 384.

By this means there was a great unanimity in the ministers, and the greater number were cast out: and as far as I could perceive, it was by some designed that it might be so. Many a time did we beseech them that they would have so much regard to the souls of men, and to the honour of England, and of the Protestant religion, as that without any necessity at all they would not impose feared perjury upon them, nor that which conscience and common esteem, and Popish adversaries, would all call perjury: that Papists might not have this to cast in our teeth, and call the Protestants a perjured people, nor England or Scotland perjured lands. Oft have we proved to them that their cause and interest required no such thing, &c. It seemed to be accounted the one thing necessary, which no reason must be heard against, that the Presbyterians must be forced to do that which they accounted public perjury, or to be cast out of trust and office, in Church and Commonwealth. And by this means a far greater number were laid by than otherwise would have been, and the few that yielded to conformity they thought would be despicable and contemptible as long as they lived. A noble revenge, and worthy of the actors.

What Baxter suspected is now known to be true. The new acts were imposed by Sheldon's advice for the express purpose of ejecting all the old godly ministers, and to put in their places another generation, that might (as they effectively did), "wean the people from making *a fuss* about religion;" *i. e.* from thinking or caring about it.

Baxter, LIFE OF HIMSELF, Book I, Part II, p. 387.

These sects are numerous; some tolerable, and some intolerable, &c. &c. Many of them (the Behmenists, Fifth-Monarchy men, Quakers, and some Anabaptists) are proper Fanatics, looking too much to revelations within, instead of the Holy Scriptures.

Baxter makes the usual mistake of writing *Fanatic* when he clearly means *Enthusiast.* The Field-Methodists are fanatics, *i. e. circà fana densâ turbâ concalefacti;* those who catch heat by crowding together round the same *Fane.* Fanaticism is the *fever* of *superstition.* Enthusiasm, on the contrary, implies an undue (or when used in a good sense, an unusual) vividness of ideas, as opposed to perceptions, or of the obscure inward feelings.

Baxter, LIFE OF HIMSELF, Book I, Part II, p. 411.

They say, That all the world confesseth that a vow obligeth *in re necessariâ,* to that which is antecedently a duty: but they propound it to consideration, whether all these things following, which are in the Covenant, are certainly no duties antecedently.

The first instance in which I have found Baxter *unfair*. See the covenant itself, p. 391, and you will find the oath, not for the preservation of the reformed religion in general, but for the *preservation* of the reformed religion in *Scotland*, and the reformation of the English Church —in other words, for the substitution of the Knoxo-Calvinistic Scoto-Genevan form of Synodical Presbytery for the Episcopal government of the Anglican Church.

Baxter, Life of Himself, *Book I, Part II, p. 438.*

> To these sad and heavy accusations we answered,—1. The Covenant bound us to our best to reform, but did not bind us to sin, that is, to forsake all Christian Churches among us and all public worship, when we cannot reform as we desire. As I am bound to amend all the disorders and faults of my own prayers, but not to give over praying till I can amend them. Nay, the Covenant bindeth us to come to the assemblies, &c. &c.

It is impossible to read Baxter without hesitating which to admire most, the uncommon clearness (perspicuity and perspicacity) of his understanding, or the candour and charity of his spirit. Under such accursed persecutions he feels and reasons more like an angel than a man.

Baxter, Life of Himself, *Book I, Part III, pp. 8-9. "Queries upon the Oxford Oath."*

Much as I love the Church of England, I have no hesitation in asserting (as my belief) that nothing in the history of the Inquisition was equally *wicked*, as the conduct of Sheldon and the Court, after the Restoration.

Baxter, Life of Himself, *Book I, Part III, p. 12.*

> Note especially that of the eighth quære, which implyeth divers instances of cases, in which Grotius, Barclay, Bilson, &c., say, that it is lawful to take arms against the King, he seemeth only to grant it, and maketh it but like a cavil, to suppose that those cases ever came into the Parliament's thoughts: and I am much in that of the good man's mind. But if they will swear me to an universal, while they forget particular exceptions, that will not make the oath lawful to me. For, 1st. It is not certain to me, that they would have excepted those things if they had remembered them. 2nd. Much less can I tell which, and how many things they would have excepted. 3rd. And how could the wit of man devise words more exclusive of all exceptions, than to say, 'It is not lawful on any pretence whatsoever?' Are those in the eighth quære 'no pretences whatsoever?'

N.B. But here Baxter confounds the drawers up, or worders, of the oath, with the two Houses of Parliament, who, with the King, were the

Imposers. Still, however, I could no more have taken the oath than Baxter: because it was meant to mean something beyond the former oaths, and whatever that might be, was for Diocesan Prelacy and Despotism. Oh it was a disgraceful era, both in Church and State! How grateful ought we to be for our present truly blessed Constitution in the latter, and for the mild and liberal spirit in the former! If not what a Christian Church should be, yet the Church of England injures only itself. It neither oppresses, annoys, nor interferes with those who dissent from it.

Baxter, LIFE OF HIMSELF, Book I, Part III, p. 46.

I found that *the uncharitable conceit, that the parishes are worse than they, doth tend to make them as bad as they are thought.*

Oh that this no less wise than amiable remark were more and more generally felt and acted upon! This is the sublime moral of Shakspeare's Shylock and Edmund.

Baxter, LIFE OF HIMSELF,[2] flyleaf.

P. 87. ¶ 4 especially valuable.

Mem. Among the grounds for recommending the perusal of our elder writers, Hooker, Taylor, Baxter, in short almost any of the Folios composed from Edward VI to Charles II

1. The overcoming the habit of deriving your whole pleasure passively from the Book itself, which can only be effected by excitement of Curiosity or of some Passion. Force yourself to reflect on what you read, § ph by § ph, and in a short time you will derive your pleasure, an ample portion at least, from the activity of your own mind. All else is Picture Sunshine.

2. The conquest of party and sectarian Prejudices, when you have on the same table the works of a Hammond[3] and a Baxter, and reflect how many & how momentous their points of agreement; how few and almost childish the differences, which estranged and irritated these good men!

Let us but reflect, what their blessed Spirits now feel at the retrospect of their earthly frailties: and can we do other than strive to feel

[2] These notes are selected from the volume containing the original notes, a volume formerly belonging to George Frere, which is now in the Harvard College Library. They are reproduced with the kind permission of the Harvard library. A few notes have not previously been published, and a number have been modified in *Lit. Rem.*, IV, 76-156. The date of the folio used for *Lit. Rem.* (1699) must be a misprint, for the notes are apparently the same as those of the 1696 folio. Another folio of 1696 with the same notes copied in a different hand with many gross errors is in the British Museum, Ashley, 4772. An entirely different set of notes is given as a "first series" by Derwent Coleridge in *English Divines*, II, 5-119.

[3] Henry Hammond (1605-60), Royalist divine.

as they now *feel,* not as they once felt?—So will it be with the Disputes between good men of the present day: and if you have no other reason to doubt your Opponent's goodness than the point in Dispute, think of Baxter and Hammond, of Milton and Jer. Taylor, and let it be no reason at all!—

3. It will secure you from the narrow Idolatry of the Present Times and Fashions: and create the noblest kind of Imaginative Power in your Soul, that of living in past ages, wholly devoid of which power a man can neither anticipate the Future, nor even live a truly human life, a life of reason, in the Present.

4. In this particular work we may derive a most instructive lesson that in certain points, as of Religion in relation to Law, the "Medio tutissimus ibis" is inapplicable. There is no *Medium* possible; and all the attempts, as those of Baxter, tho' no more were required than, "I believe in God thro' Christ," prove only the mildness of the Proposer's Temper, but as a rule would be either = 0, at least exclude only the two or three in a century that make it a matter of religion to declare themselves Atheists; or just as fruitful a rule for a Persecutor as the most complete set of Articles that could be framed by a Spanish Inquisition. For to "believe" must mean to believe aright, and "God" must mean the true God, and "Christ" the Christ in the sense and with the attributes understood by Christians who are truly Xtians. An established Church with a Liturgy is the sufficient solution of the problem de jure Magistratus. Articles of Faith are superfluous, for is it not too absurd for a man to hesitate at subscribing his name to doctrines which yet in the more aweful duty of Prayer & Profession, he dares affirm before his maker? They are therefore *merely* superfluous—not worth re-enacting, had they never been done away with—not worth removing now that they exist.

5. The characteristic Contra-distinction between the Speculative Reasoners of the age before the Revolution and those since then is this: The former cultivated metaphysics without, or neglecting, empirical Psychology; the latter cultivate a mechanical Psychology to the neglect and contempt of Metaphysics. Both therefore almost equi-distant from true Philosophy. Hence the belief in Ghosts, Witches, *sensible* Replies to Prayer &c. in Baxter, and a 100 others. See p. 81; and look at Luther's Table Talk, &c &c.

6. The earlier part of this Volume is most interesting as materials for medical History. The [—?] state of medical Science in the reign of Charles the First almost incredibly low![4]

[4] Note on the recto of the continuation of the end-paper and the recto of the flyleaf.

The saddest error of the theologians of this age is, ὡς ἐμοί γε δοκεῖ, the disposition to urge the histories of the miraculous actions & incidents in and by which Christ attested his Messiahship to the Jewish Eye-witnesses in fulfilment of Prophecies, which the Jewish Church had previously understood & interpreted as marks of the Messiah, before they have shown what and how excellent the Religion itself is—*including* the miracles, as for *us* an harmonious part of the internal or self-evidence of the Religion. Alas! and even when our Divines do proceed to the Religion itself, as to a something which no man could be expected to receive except by a *compulsion* of the senses, which by force of Logic is propagated from the Eye-witnesses to the Readers of the Narratives in 1820—(which Logic, viz. that the evidence of a Miracle is not diminished by lapse of ages, tho' this includes loss of documents &c—which logic, I say, whether it be legitimate or not, God forbid! that the truth of Christianity should depend on the decision!—) even when our Divines do proceed to the Religion itself, on what do they chiefly dwell? On the doctrines peculiar to the Religion? No!—these on the contrary are either evaded, or explained away into metaphors, or resigned in despair to the next world where Faith is to be swallowed up in Certainty!

But the worst product of this epidemic error is the fashion of either denying or undervaluing the evidence of a future state, and the survival of individual Consciousness, derived from the Conscience, and the holy instinct of the whole Human Race. Dreadful is this—for the main force of the Reasoning by which this scepticism is vindicated, consists in reducing all legitimate conviction to *objective* proof—whereas in the very essence of Religion & even of morality the evidence & the preparation for its reception, must be *subjective*. "Blessed are they that have *not* seen yet believe." And dreadful it appears to me especially, who in the impossibility of not looking forward to consciousness after the dissolution of the body (Corpus *phænomenon*) (See p. 347 of my Aids to Reflection) have thro' life found (next to divine Grace) the strongest & indeed only efficient Support against the still-recurring temptation of adopting—nay, *wishing* the truth of—Spinoza's notion, that the survival of consciousness is the highest prize & consequence of the highest Virtue—and that of all below this mark the lot after Death is self-oblivion & the cessation of individual Being. Indeed, how a Separatist or one of any other Sect of Calvinists, who confines Redemption to the comparatively small numbers of the Elect can reject this opinion, & yet not run mad at the horrid idea of an innumerable multitude of imperishable self-conscious Spirits everlastingly excluded from God, is to me inconceivable.

Deeply am I persuaded of Luther's Position—that no man can worthily estimate, or feel in the depth of his being, the incarnation & crucifixion of the Son of God who is a stranger to the *Terror* of Nature, the *Terror* of Immortality, as ingenerate in Man—while it is yet unquelled by the faith in God, as the Almighty Father![5]

Baxter, LIFE OF HIMSELF, *Book I, Part I, p. 14.*

And the result of all my Studies was as followeth: Kneeling I thought lawful, and all meer Circumstances determined by the Magistrate, which God in Nature or Scripture hath determined of only in the General. The Surplice I more doubted of; but more inclined to think it lawful: And though I purposed, while I doubted, to forbear it till necessity lay upon me, yet could I not have justified the forsaking of my Ministry for it; (though I never wore it to this day).

I am not enough read in Puritan Divinity to know the particular objections to the *Surplice,* over & above the general prejudice against all the Retenta of Popery.[6]

Baxter, LIFE OF HIMSELF, *Book I, Part I, p. 23, paragraph 35.*

All these Assistances were at hand before I came to the immediate Evidences of Credibility in the Sacred Oracles themselves.

This is as it should be. That is: first, the evidence à priori, securing the rational probability: and then the historical proofs of it's reality. Pity that Baxter's Chapters in The Saint's Rest should have been one and the earliest occasion of the inversion of this process—the truth of which is the Grotian Palagian Religion, or Minimum of Faith—its maxim being Quanto minus, tanto melius.

Baxter, LIFE OF HIMSELF, *Book I, Part I, pp. 25-26.*

Some thought that the King should not at all be displeased and provoked, and that they were not bound to do any other Justice, or attempt any other Reformation but what they could procure the King to be willing to. And these said, When you have displeased and provoked him to the utmost, he will be your King still! and when you have sate to the longest, you must be dissolved at last: you have no power over his Person, though you have power over Delinquent Subjects: And if he protect them by Arms, you must either be ruined your selves by his displeasure, or be engaged in a War: Displeasing him is but exasperating him; and would you be ruled by a King that hateth you? Princes have great Minds, which cannot easily suffer Contradiction and Rebukes: The more you offend him, the less you can trust him; and when mutual Confidence is gone, a War is beginning: And if it come to a War, either you will conquer or be conquered or come to Agreement. If you are

[5] Note on the verso of the title page.
[6] This passage is omitted in *Lit. Rem.*

conquered, you and the Commonwealth are ruined, and he will be absolute, and subdue Parliaments, and Govern as he pleaseth. If you come to an Agreement, it will be either such as you *force* him to, or he is *willing* of: If the latter, it may be easilier and cheaper done before a War than after: If the *former,* it will much weaken it: And if you Conquer him, what the better are you? He will still be King: You can but force him to an Agreement; and how quickly will he have power and advantage to violate that which he is forced to; and to be avenged on you all for the displeasure you have done him: He is ignorant of the Advantage of a King that cannot foresee this. These were the Reasons of many that were for pleasing the King.

Never was a stronger case made out in justification of the Regicides! Never a more complete exposure of the inconsistency of Baxter's own party! Either the Execution of this incurable Despot was constitutional or passive obedience was an absolute Duty. I do not recollect a clearer case in History, not one, in which a plain Principle grounded on universal Reason & the constituent maxims of the Constitution was ever more distinctly confirmed by the after Events & Occurrences.[7] For observe, that in case of an agreement with Charles all those classes, which afterwards formed the main strength of the Parliament & ultimately decided the contest in it's favor, would have been politically inert, with little influence & no actual power—I mean, the Yeomanry, & the Citizens of London—while a vast majority of the Nobles and landed Gentry, who sooner or later must have become the majority in Parliament, went over to the King at once. Soon with these the whole systematized force of the High Church Clergy, & all the rude ignorant vulgar, in high & low life, who detested every attempt at moral reform—& it is obvious that the king could not want opportunities to retract & undo all that he had conceded under compulsion. But that neither the Will was wanting, nor his Conscience at all in the way, his own Advocates, Clarendon & others, have supplied damning proofs.

Baxter, LIFE OF HIMSELF, *Book I, Part I, p. 27.*

> And though Parliaments may draw up Bills for repealing Laws, yet hath the King his Negative Voice, and without his Consent they cannot do it; which though they acknowledged, yet did they too easily admit of Petitions against the Episcopacy and Liturgy, and connived at all the Clamours and Papers which were against them.

How so! If they admitted the King's right to deny, they must admit the Subject's right to intreat.

---

[7] In *Lit. Rem.* the statement is tempered to: "'This paragraph goes to make a case in justification of the Regicides which Baxter would have found it difficult to answer. Certainly a more complete exposure of the inconsistency of Baxter's own party cannot be. . . .'"

Baxter, LIFE OF HIMSELF, Book I, Part I, p. 27.

> Had they only endeavoured the Ejection of Lay Chancellors, and the reducing of the Diocesses to a narrower Compass, or the setting up of a Subordinate Discipline, and only the Correcting and Reforming of the Liturgy, perhaps it might have been borne more patiently.

Did B. find it so himself? And when too he had Charles's formal & recorded promise?

Baxter, LIFE OF HIMSELF, Book I, Part I, p. 27.

> The Bishops themselves who were accounted most moderate (Usher, Williams, Morton) and many other Episcopal Divines with them, had before this in a Committee at *Westminster,* agreed on certain Points of Reformation, which I will give you afterward. . . . But when the same Men saw that greater Things were aimed at, and Episcopacy it self in danger, or their Grandeur and Riches at the least, most of them turned against Parliament, and were almost as much displeased as others.

[Underlines "or their Grandeur and Riches at least" and notes:] This and in this place is unworthy of Baxter. Even he, good man! could not wholly escape the Jaundice of Party.

Baxter, LIFE OF HIMSELF, Book I, Part I, p. 33.

> And abundance of the ignorant sort of the Country, who were Civil, did flock in to the Parliament, and filled up their Armies afterward, meerly because they heard Men *swear* for the Common Prayer and Bishops, and heard others *pray* that were against them; and because they heard the King's Soldiers with horrid Oaths abuse the name of God and saw them live in Debauchery, and the Parliaments Soldiers flock to Sermons, and talking of Religion, and praying and singing Psalms together on their Guards.

God's mercy to an age that owns Jacobins were Infidels and a scandal to all sober Christians![8]

Baxter, LIFE OF HIMSELF, Book I, Part I, p. 34.   Note continued on p. 35.

> They said to this . . . , That as all the Courts of Justice do execute their Sentences in the *King's Name,* and this by his *own Law,* and therefore by his *Authority,* so much more might his Parliament do. . . .

A very sound argument is here disguised in a false analogy, an inapplicable Precedent, and a sophistical form. Courts of Justice administer the total of the supreme power retrospectively involved in the name of the most dignified part. But here a Part, as a Part, acts as the Whole, where the Whole is absolutely requisite—i. e. in passing Laws; and again as B. and C. usurp a power belonging to A. by the determina-

---

[8] This passage is omitted in *Lit. Rem.*

tion of A. B. and C. The true argument is, That Charles had by acts of his own ceased to be a lawful King &c.

Baxter, LIFE OF HIMSELF, Book I, Part I, p. 40.

2. And that the Authority and Person of the King were inviolable, out of the reach of just Accusation, Judgment, or Execution by Law; as having no Superiour, and so no Judge.

But according to Grotius, a King waging war against the lawful Co-partners of the *summa Potestas* ceases to be their King, and if conquered, forfeits to them his former share, and surely if the King had been victor, he would have taken the Parliament's share to himself. If it had been the Parliament, and not a mere Faction with the Army that tried and beheaded Charles, I could not doubt the lawfulness of the Act.

Baxter, LIFE OF HIMSELF, Book I, Part I, p. 41.

For if once Legislation (the chief Act of Government) be denied to be any part of Government at all, and affirmed to belong to the People as such, who are no Governors, all Government will hereby be overthrown.

Here Baxter falls short of the Subject, and does not see the full consequents of his own prior (most judicious) positions. Legislation in it's high and most proper sense belongs to God only. A People *declare* that such and such they hold to be laws i. e. God's will.

Baxter, LIFE OF HIMSELF, Book I, Part I, p. 59.

For the very time that I was bleeding the Council of War sate at *Nottingham,* where (as I have credibly heard) they first began to open their Purposes and act their Part: and presently after they entered into their Engagement at *Triploe-Heath.* And as I perceived it was the Will of God to permit them to go on, so I afterward found that this great Affliction was a Mercy to my self; for they were so strong and active, that I had been likely to have had small Success in the Attempt, but to have lost my Life among them in their Fury. And thus I was finally separated from the Army.

It is easy to see from B's own account that his party ruined their own cause and that of the Kingdom by their tenets concerning the right and duty of the civil magistrate to use the sword against such as were not of the same Religion with themselves.

Baxter, LIFE OF HIMSELF, Book I, Part I, pp. 66-7.

And therefore how they could refuse to receive the King, till he consented to take the Covenant, I know not: unless the taking of the Covenant had been a Condition on which he was to receive his Crown by the

Laws or Fundamental Constitution of the Kingdom (which none pretendeth). Nor know I by what power they can add anything to the Coronation Oath or Covenant, which by his Ancestors was to be taken, without his own Consent.

And pray, how and by whom were the Coronation Oaths first imposed? The Scottish Nation, in 1650, had the same right to make a bargain with the Claimant of their Throne, as their Ancestors had. It is strange, that Baxter should not have seen, that his objections would apply to our Magna Charta. So he talks of a Constitution, & "unless it be part of the fundamental Law," &c.—just as if these had been aboriginal or rather sans origin, and not as indeed they were, extorted and bargained for by the people. But throughout it is plain, that Baxter repeated, but never appropriated the distinction between the King = the Executive Power, and the Individual Functionary. What obligation lay on the Scottish Parliament & Church to consult the man, Charles Stuart's personal Likes and Dislikes? The Oath was to be taken by him as their King. Doubtless, he equally disliked the whole Protestant Interest—& if the Tories and C. of Eng. Jacobites had recalled James II. would Baxter think them culpable for imposing on him an oath to preserve the Protestant Church of England & the severe penalties on his own Church-fellows?

Baxter, LIFE OF HIMSELF, *Book I, Part I, p. 71.*

And some Men thought it a very hard Question, Whether they should rather wish the continuance of an Usurper that will do good, or the restitution of a Rightful Governour whose Followers will do hurt. But for my part I thought my Duty was clear, to disown the Usurper's Sin, what Good soever he would do; and to perform all my Engagements to a Rightful Governour, leaving the Issue of all to God.

And who shall dare unconditionally condemn those who judged the former to be the better alternative? especially those who did not adopt Baxter's notion of jus divinum personal and hereditary in an Individual whose Father had broke the Compact on which the claim [rests?].

Baxter, LIFE OF HIMSELF, *Book I, Part I, p. 80. Note continued on p. 81.*

Many a time I have been brought very low, and received the Sentence of Death in my self, when my poor, honest, praying Neighbours have met, and upon their fasting and earnest Prayers I have been recovered. Once when I had continued weak three Weeks, and was unable to go abroad, the very day that they prayed for me, being *Good-Friday*, I recovered, and was able to Preach, and Administer the Sacrament the next Lord's Day, and was better after it, &c.

Strange that the common manuals of School Logic should not have secured Baxter from the repeated Blunder of *Cum hoc: ergo propter hoc:* But still more strange that his Piety should not have revolted against degrading PRAYER into medical Quackery!

Before the Revolution, Metaphysics without experimental Psychology: & we here see the results. Since the Revolution Experimental Psychology without Metaphysics: & we now *feel* the Results.

In like manner from Plotinus to Proclus, (i e. from Commodus[9] to Justin[10]) Philosophy as a substitute for Religion: during the dark Ages Religion as superseding Philosophy: & the effects are equally instructive. The great Maxim of Legislation, intellectual or political is *Subordinate, not exclude.* Nature in her ascent leaves nothing behind: but at each step subordinates & glorifies. Mass, Crystal, Organ, sensation, sentience, reflection.

Baxter, LIFE OF HIMSELF, *Book I, Part I, p. 84.*

> For all the Pains that my Infirmities ever brought upon me, were never half so grievous an Affliction to me, as the unavoidable loss of my time, which they occasioned, I could not bear (through the weakness of my Stomach) to rise before Seven a Clock in the morning. . .

Alas! in how many respects does my Lot resemble Baxter's! But how much less have my bodily Evils been, & yet how very much greater an impediment have I suffered them to be! But verily Baxter's Labors seem miracles of supporting Grace! Ought I not therefore to retract the note p. 80? I waver.

Baxter, LIFE OF HIMSELF, *Book I, Part I, p. 87.*

> For my part, I bless God, who gave me even under an Usurper whom I opposed, such Liberty and Advantage to preach his Gospel with Success, which I cannot have under a King to whom I have sworn and performed true Subjection and Obedience; yea, which no Age since the Gospel came into this Land, did before possess, so far as I can learn from History. Sure I am, that when it became a matter of Reputation and Honour to be Godly, it abundantly furthered the Successes of the Ministry. Yea, and I shall add this much more for the sake of Posterity, that as much as I have said and written against Licentiousness in Religion, and for the Magistrate's Power in it, and though I think that Land most happy, whose Rulers use their Authority for Christ, as well as for the Civil Peace; yet in Comparison of the rest of the World, I shall think that Land happy that hath but bare Liberty to be as good as they are willing to be; and if *Countenance* and *Maintenance* be but added to *Liberty,* and tollerated Errors and Sects be but forced to *keep the Peace,* and not to oppose the Substantials of Christianity, I

---

[9] Lucius Aelius Aurelius Commodus, Roman Emperor (180-192).
[10] Justinian I, Byzantine Emperor (527-565).

shall not hereafter much fear such Toleration, nor despair that Truth will bear down Adversaries.

Most valuable and citable ¶! Likewise it is a happy instance of the Force of a cherished Prejudice in an honest mind—*practically yielding* to the truth, but yet with a speculative, *"Though I still think,"* &c.

Baxter, Life of Himself, *Book I, Part I, p. 99.*

> He [i.e. Cromwell] thought that if the war was lawful, the Victory was lawful; and if it were lawful to fight against the King and conquer him, it was lawful to use him as a conquered Enemy, and a foolish thing to trust him when they had so provoked him, (whereas indeed the Parliament professed neither to fight against him, nor to conquer him).

Nonsense.[11]

Baxter, Life of Himself, *Book I, Part I, p. 99.*

> He thought that the Heart of the King was deep, and that he resolved upon Revenge, and that if he were King, he would easily at one time or other accomplish it; and that it was a dishonest thing of the Parliament to set men to fight for them against the King, and then to lay their Necks upon the block, and be at his Mercy.

And was not this the truth? See Laing's History of Scotland, Vol. i.[11]

Baxter, Life of Himself, *Book I, Part I, p. 114.*

> But though my *fears* are never so great, that a man dissembleth and is not sincere, yet if I be not able to bring in that Evidence to invalidate his Profession, which *in foro Ecclesiæ* shall prove it to be *incredible* I ought to receive him as a credible Professor, though but by a *Humane,* and perhaps most *debile* Belief.

And of course, therefore, with a most debile Love.[11]

Baxter, Life of Himself, *Book I, Part I, p. 129. Note continued on p. 130.*

> And at first I took more upon my Author's Credit, than now I can do: And when an Author was highly commended to me by others, or pleased me in some part, I was ready to entertain the whole; whereas now I *take* and *leave* in the same Author, and dissent in some things from him that I like best, as well as from others.

On these points, I have come to a Resting-place. Let such Articles, as are either to be recognized as *facts* (ex. gr. Sin = Evil having it's origination in a Will; & the reality of a responsible & (in whatever sense freedom is pre-supposed in responsibility) of a free will in man) or acknowledged as Laws (ex. gr. the unconditional bindingness of the

---

[11] The three passages referred to this footnote are omitted in *Lit. Rem.*

Practical Reason) or to be freely affirmed as necessary thro' their moral interest, their indispensableness to our spiritual Humanity (ex. gr. the personëity, holiness, & moral government & providence of God): Let these be vindicated from absurdity, from all self-contradiction, and contradiction to the pure Reason, & restored to simple Incomprehensibility.[12] He who seeks for more, knows not what he is talking of: he, who will not seek even this, is either indifferent to the truth of what he professes to believe, or he mistakes a general determination not to disbelieve for a positive and especial Faith—which is only our faith as far as we can assign a *reason* for it.—O how unprofitable it is to move an inch to the right or left in any point of spiritual & moral concernment, without seeing the damage caused by the confusion of the Reason with Understanding. S. T. C.

Baxter, LIFE OF HIMSELF, *Book I, Part I, p. 135.*

> Therefore I confess I give but halting credit to most Histories that are written, not only against the *Albigenses* and *Waldenses,* but against most of the Ancient Hereticks, who have left us none of their own Writings, in which they speak for themselves, and I heartily lament that the Historical Writings of the ancient Schismaticks and Hereticks (as they were called) perished, and that partiality suffered them not to survive, that we might have had more Light in the Church-Affairs of those times, and been better able to judge between the Fathers and them.

It is greatly to the credit of Baxter that he has here anticipated those merits which so long after gave deserved celebrity to the name and writings of Beusobre and Lardner, and still more recently of Eichhorn, Paulus & other Neologists.

Baxter, LIFE OF HIMSELF, *Book I, Part I, p. 136.*

> And therefore having my self now written this History of my self, notwithstanding my Protestation that I have not anything wilfully gone against the Truth, I expect no more Credit from the Reader than the self-evidencing Light of the matter, with concurrent rational Advantages, from Persons, and Things, and other Witnesses, shall constrain him to.

I may not unfrequently doubt Baxter's memory or even his competence in consequence of his particular modes of thinking; but I could almost as soon doubt the Gospel Verity as his *veracity.*

Baxter, LIFE OF HIMSELF, *Book I, Part I, p. 138 (blank).*

The Book following (Lib. I. Part II) is interesting and most instructive as an instance of Syncretism, even when it has been under-

[12] This is an unusually comprehensive summary of a point of view which Coleridge often states in scattered discussions.

taken from the purest and most laudable motives & from impulses the most Christian—it's Epicurean *clinamen,* & yet utter failure in it's object, that of tending to a common center. The experience of 18 centuries seems to prove that there is no practicable medium between a Church Comprehensive (which is the only meaning of a Catholic Church *visible*) in which A in the North or East is allowed to advance *officially* no doctrine different from what is allowed to B in the South or West; and a co-existence of independent Churches, in none of which any further Unity is required but that between the Minister and his Congregation, while this again is secured by the election and continuance of the former depending wholly on the will of the latter.

Perhaps, the best state possible, tho' not the best possible state, is where both are found, the one established by maintenance, the other by permission: in short, that which we now enjoy. In such a state no Minister of the former can have a right to complain for it was at his own option to have taken the latter—et volenti nulla fit injuria. For an individual to demand the freedom of the Independent Single-church when he recives 500£ a year for submitting to the necessary restrictions of the Church General is *impudence* and Mammonolatry to boot.

S. T. C. ⁜ See above.

⁜ Since the Mss. note below was written, I have seen or believed myself to see cause for qualifying the opinion there expressed. More especially since I have had the honor and happiness of a familiar acquaintance with the Rev^d^. Edward Irving, I have acknowledged a true medium between the Church of E. and the Independent Scheme—viz. the Division or Separation of *Election* and *Selection,* the former belonging to the congregation, the latter to the Assembled Ministers.[13]

Baxter, Life of Himself, *Book I, Part II, p. 188.*

> Or if they would not yield to this at all, we might have Communion with them as *Christians,* without acknowledging them for Pastors.

Observe the inconsistency of Baxter. No Pastor, no Church; no Church, no Christ. And yet he will receive them as *Christians*—much to his honor as a Christian, but not much to his Credit as a Logician.

Baxter, Life of Himself, *Book I, Part II, p. 194.*

> By the Establishment of what is contained in these Twelve Propositions or Articles following, the Churches in these Nations may have a Holy Communion, Peace and Concord, without any Wrong to the Consciences or Liberties of Presbyterians, Congregational, Episcopal, or any other Christians.

[13] This passage is omitted in *Lit. Rem.* and in *English Divines.*

Painfully instructive are these proposals from so wise and peaceable a Divine as Baxter. How mighty must be the force of an old Prejudice when so acute a Logician was blinded by it to such palpable inconsistencies. On what ground of Right could a Magistrate inflict a penalty, whereby to compel a man to *hear* what he might believe dangerous to his soul, on which the Right of burning the refractory individual might not be defended?

Baxter, LIFE OF HIMSELF, *Book I, Part II, p. 203.*

Not so much for my own sake, as others; lest it should offend the Parliament, and open the Mouths of our Adversaries, that we cannot our selves agree in Fundamentals; and lest it prove an occasion for others to sue for an Universal Toleration.

That this apprehension so constantly haunted, so powerfully actuated, even the mild and really tolerant Baxter, is a strong proof of my old opinion, that the Dogma of the right and duty of the civil magistrate to restrain and punish religious avowals by him deemed heretical, universal among the Presbyterians and Parliamentary Church-men, joined with the persecuting spirit of the Presbyterians, was the main cause óf Cromwell's despair & consequent unfaithfulness concerning a Parliamentary Commonwealth.

Baxter, LIFE OF HIMSELF, *Book I, Part II, p. 222.*

I tried, when I was last with you, to revive your Reason, by proposing to you the Infallibility of the Common Senses of all the World; and I could not prevail though you had nothing to answer that was not against Common Sense. And it is impossible any thing controverted can be brought nearer you, or made plainer than to be brought to your Eyes and Taste and Feeling: and not yours only, but all Mens else. Sense goes before Faith. Faith is no Faith but upon Supposition of Sense and Understanding; if therefore Common Sense be fallible, Faith must needs be so.

This is one of those two-edged arguments, which (not indeed *began,* but) began to be *fashionable,* before and just after the Restoration. . . .

Baxter, LIFE OF HIMSELF, *Book I, Part I, p. 222. Note on p. 224.*

But methinks yet I should have hope of reviving your Charity. You cannot be a Papist indeed, but you must believe, that out of their Church (that is out of the Pope's Dominions) there is no Salvation; and consequently no Justification and Charity, or saving Grace. And is it possible you can so easily believe your religious Father to be in Hell; your prudent, pious Mother to be void of the Love of God, and in a state of Damnation, &c.

This argument ad affectum cavitatis p. 222 is beautifully and forcibly stated; but defective by the omission of the point—"*not* for unbelief or misbelief of any article of Faith! but simply for not being a member of this particular Part of the Church of Christ. For it is possible that a Christian might agree in all the articles of Faith with the Roman Doctors against those of the Reformation, and yet if he did not acknowledge the Pope as Christ's Vicar, & held Salvation possible in any other Church, he is himself excluded from Salvation." Without this great distinction, Lady Anne Lindsay might have replied to Baxter—So might a Pagan Oratory have said to a Convert from Paganism in the first ages of Christianity. So indeed the Advocates of the old Religion *did* argue. What? can you bear to believe, that Numa, Camillus, Fabricius, the Scipios, the Catos, that Tully, Seneca, that Titus and the Antonini are in the Flames of Hell, the accursed Objects of the Divine Hatred? Now whatever *you* dare hope of *these*, as Heathens, we dare hope of *you* as Heretics.

Baxter, LIFE OF HIMSELF, *Book I, Part II, p. 224. "The Answer to the Lady Anne Lindsay's Letter to Her Mother."*

But this is not the worst; You consequently Anathematize all Papists by your Sentence: for Heresies by your own Sentence cut off Men from Heaven: But Popery is a bundle of Heresies: Therefore it cuts off Men from Heaven. The *minor* I prove, &c:

This introduction of a syllogistic form in a letter to a young lady is whimsically characteristic.

Baxter, LIFE OF HIMSELF, *Book I, Part II, p. 225. Note continued on p. 226.*

You say, [*The Scripture admits no private Interpretation*]. But 1. You abuse the Text and your self with a false interpretation of it, in these Words. An interpretation is called private, either as to the *Subject Person*, or as to the *Interpreter:* You take the Text to speak of the latter, when the Context plainly sheweth you that it speaks of the former: The Apostle directing them to understand the Prophecies of the Old Testament, gives them this Caution, That none of the Scriptures that are spoken of Christ the publick Person must be interpreted, as spoken of *David* or other private Persons only, of whom they were mentioned but as Types of Christ.

It is strange that this sound and irrefragable argument has not been enforced by the Church Divines in their controversies with the modern Unitarians as Capp, Belsham, & others, who refer *all* the prophetic texts of the Old Test. to historical personages of the then time exclusive of all double sense.

I unthinkingly have called this *strange*, but I now recollect that the Romanists' sense of the Text is adopted in our 39 articles,—being one of the very few pitch-stains of Papistry, which our Reformers had not at that time discovered in their robe of Faith.[14]

Baxter, LIFE OF HIMSELF, *Book I, Part II, p. 226. Note continued on p. 227.*

As to what you say of [*Apostles still placed in the Church*]: When any shew us an immediate Mission by their Commission, and by Miracles, Tongues, and a spirit of Revelation and infallibility prove themelves Apostles, we shall believe them.

This is one of those two-edged arguments which Baxter & Jer. Taylor imported from Grotius, & which have since become the universal *Fashion* among Protestants. I fear, however, that it will do us more hurt by exposing a weak part to the *learned* Infidels than service in our combat with the Romanists. I venture to assert most unequivocally that the N. T. contains not the least proof of the *Linguipotence* of the Apostles, but the clearest proofs of the contrary: and I doubt, whether we have even as decisive a victory over the Romanists in our Middletonian, Farmerian and Douglasian Disputes concerning the Miracles of the two first centuries & their assumed contrast *in genere* with those of the Apostles and the Apostolic Age, as we have in most other of our Protestant controversies. *Mem.* These opinions of Middleton & his more cautious Followers are no part of *our* Church Doctrine. This passion for Law Court Evidence began with Grotius.

Baxter, LIFE OF HIMSELF, *Book I, Part II, p. 246.*

We conceived there needs no more to be said for justifying the Imposition of the Ceremonies by Law established then what is contained in the beginning of this Section. . . . Inasmuch as lawful Authority hath already determined the Ceremonies in question to be decent and orderly, and to serve to Edification; and consequently to be agreeable to the General Rules of the Word.

To a self-convinced and disinterested Lover of the Church of England, it gives an indescribable horror to observe the frequency with which the Prelatic Party after the Restoration appeal to *the Laws,* as of equal authority with the express words of Scripture—as if the Laws, by them appealed to, were other than the vindictive Determinations of their own furious Partisans; as if the same appeals might not have been made by Bonner and Gardiner under Philip & Mary.—Why should I speak of the inhuman sophism that, because it is silly in my neighbor to

[14] The last paragraph is not in *Lit. Rem.*

break his egg at the broad end when the Squire & the Vicar have declared their predilection for the narrow end, therefore it is right for the Squire and the Vicar to hang and quarter him for his silliness.

Baxter, LIFE OF HIMSELF, *Book I, Part II, p. 248. Note continued on p. 249.*

> To you it is *indifferent* before your *Imposition:* and therefore you may without any regret of your own Consciences forbear the *Imposition,* or perswade the Law-makers to forbear it. But to many of those that dissent from you, they are *sinful,* &c.

But what is all this, good worthy Baxter, but saying and unsaying? If they are not indifferent, why did you concede them such? In short, nothing can be more pitiably weak than the conduct of the Presbyterian Party from the first capture of Charles I. Common sense required either a bold denial that the Church had power in ceremonies more than in doctrines, or that Parliament was the Church (since it is our Parliament that *enacts* all these things)—or if they admitted the authority lawful, and the ceremonies only (in their mind) *inexpedient*—good God! can self-will more plainly put on the cracked mask of tender conscience, than by refusal of obedience? What intolerable presumption, to disqualify as ungodly and reduce to null the majority of the Country, who preferred the Liturgy, in order to force the long-winded Vanities of bustling God-orators on those who would fain hear prayers, not spouting!

Baxter, LIFE OF HIMSELF, *Book I, Part II, p. 250.*

> Otherwise the poor undone Churches of Christ will no more believe you in such Professions, than we believed that those Men intended the King's *just* Power and *Greatness,* who took away his Life.

Or like Baxter joined the armies that were showering Cannon Balls and bullets around his inviolable person! When ever by reading the Prelatical writings and Histories, I have had an over-dose of anti-prelatism in my feelings, I then correct it by dipping into the works of the Presbyterians, &c., and so bring myself to more charitable thoughts respecting the Prelatists, and fully subscribe to Milton's assertion, that PRESBYTER was but OLD PRIEST writ large!

Baxter, LIFE OF HIMSELF, *Book I, Part II, p. 257. Note continued on pp. 258-59.*

> The *Not-abating* of the *Impositions* is the casting off of many hundreds of your Brethren out of the Ministry, and of many thousand Christians out of your Communion: But the *abating* of the Impositions, will so offend you, as to silence or excommunicate none of you at all: For

e. g. we think it a Sin to Subscribe, or swear canonical Obedience, or use the transient Image of the Cross in Baptism, and therefore these must cast us out: . . .

As long as independent single Churches, or voluntary synodical were forbidden and punishable by penal Law, this argument remained irrefragable: The imposition of such trifles under such fearful threats was the very bitterness of spiritual Pride and vindictiveness;—after the law passed by which things became as they now are, it was a mere question of expediency for the national Church to determine in relation to its own comparative Interests. If the Church chose unluckily, the injury has been to itself alone.

Is it not strange that such men as Baxter should not see that the Ring, surplice, &c. are *indifferent* according to *his own confession,* yea, mere trifles in comparison with the peace of the Church; but that it is no trifle, that men should refuse obedience to lawful authority in matters indifferent, and prefer Schism to offending their *Taste,* and *Fancy?* The Church did *not* contend for a trifle, not for an indifferent matter, but for a principle on which all order in society must depend. *Second Thoughts.* True, provided the Church enacts no ordinances that are not necessary or at least plainly conducive to order or (generally) to the ends for which it is a Church. But surely this cannot be said of the Cross in Baptism or the Judaical conceit implied in the Surplice, or the arranging of the Communion Table as a sacrificial *altar.*[15] Besides the point which the King had required them to consider was not what ordinances it was right to obey, but what it was *expedient* to enact or not to enact.

Baxter, LIFE OF HIMSELF, *Book I, Part II, p. 272.*

Therefore we humbly crave that your Majesty will here declare, [That it is your Majesty's pleasure that none be punished or troubled for not using the Book of Common Prayer, till it be effectually reformed by Divines of both Perswasions equally deputed thereunto.]

The dispensing power of the Crown not only acknowleged, but earnestly invoked! Cruel as the conduct of Laud and that of Sheldon to the Dissentients was, yet God's justice stands clear towards them, for they demanded that from others, which they themselves would not grant. They were to be *allowed* at their own fancies, to denounce the ring in marriage, and yet empowered to endungeon thro' the Magistrate the honest and peaceable Quakers for rejecting the outward ceremony of Water in Baptism as manifestly seducing men to take it as a substitute for the spiritual reality tho' the Quakers no less than themselves appeal

[15] This sentence is omitted in *Lit. Rem.*

to Scripture authority, the Baptist's contrast of Christ's, with the water Baptism.

Baxter, LIFE OF HIMSELF, Book I, Part II, pp. 308 ff. Baxter's exceptions to the Common Prayer Book. . . . Note on p. 310.

But to write seriously on so serious a subject, it is mournful to reflect, that the influence of the systematic Theology then in fashion with the anti-prelatic Divines, whether Episcopalians or Presbyterians, had quenched all *fineness* of mind, all *flow* of Heart, all Grandeur of Imagination in *them;* while the victorious Party, the prelatic Arminians, enriched as they were with all Learning and highly gifted with Taste and Judgement had emptied Revelation of all the *doctrines* that can properly be said to have been *revealed*—and thus equally caused the extinction of the Imagination and quenched the Life in the Light by withholding the appropriate Fuel and the Supporters of the sacred Flame.— So that between both parties our transcendent Liturgy remains like an ancient Greek Temple, a Monumental Proof of architectural Genius, of an age long departed, when there were Giants in the Land!

Baxter, LIFE OF HIMSELF, Book I, Part II, p. 337.

. . . and as I was proceeding, here Bishop *Morley* interrupted me according to his manner, and vehemency crying out . . . and the Bishop (whether in Passion or Design I know not) interrupted me again and mouthed out the odiousness of my Doctrine again and again. . . . I attempted to speak, and still he interrupted me in the same manner.

The Bishops appear to have behaved insolently enough. Safe in their knowledge of Charles's Inclinations they laughed in their sleeves at his *Commission.* Their best answer would have been to have pressed the Anti-impositionists with their utter forgetfulness of the possible nay, very probable differences of opinions between the Ministers and their Congregations—a vain Minister might scandalize a sober congregation with his extempore prayers or his open contempt of their kneeling at the Sacraments, &c. By what right if he acts only as an Individual? And then what an endless source of disputes and preferences of this Minister or of that!

Baxter, LIFE OF HIMSELF, Book I, Part II, pp. 365-67.

Mr. Kenyon yesterday, 1 Sept. 1825, observed that R. S. could not *mediate,* and that I could not *militate:* that even when it was Southey's purpose to sit as an Arbiter, he was sure, before he was aware, to stand up as a Partisan, and drop the Scales in order to wield the Sword, while I was so engaged in tracing the diverging branches to a common Trunk both for Right and Wrong that both Parties took to the sword against me. S. saw all Difference as Diversity, while I was striving to reduce supposed Contraries into compatible Opposites, whose worst error consisted in their reciprocal Exclusion of each other. So S. found positive falsehoods where I saw half-truths, and found the falsehood in the partial Eclipse. S. = a Greyhound. S. T. C. = a Pointer.

I have amplified our common Friend's Observation in my own metaphorical way; but I give the conclusion in his own words. "In short, Southey should write Books, and you write notes on them." It may serve to confirm this Judgement if I[16] mediate here between Baxter & the Bishops: Baxter had taken for granted, that the King had a right to promise a revision of the Liturgy, Canons & Regiment of the Church, and that the Bishops ought to have met him and his Friends as Diplomatists on even ground. The Bishops could not with discretion openly avow all they meant; and it would be High Church Bigotry to deny that the spirit of Compromise had no Indwelling in their Feelings or Intents. But nevertheless it is true that they thought more in the spirit of the English Constitution than Baxter & his Friends. This, thought they, is *the* LAW of the Land, *quam nolumus mutari;* and it must·be the King with and by the advice of his Parliament, that can authorize any part of his Subjects to take the question of it's Repeal into consideration. Under other circumstances a King might bring the Bishops and the Heads of the Romish party together to plot against the Law of the Land. No! we would have no other Secret Committees, but of Parliamentary Appointment. We are but so many Individuals. It is in the Legislature that the Congregations, the party most interested in this Cause, meet collectively in their Representatives. Lastly, let it not be overlooked, that the root of the Bitterness was common to both Parties, —viz., the conviction of the vital importance of Uniformity—and this admitted, surely an undoubted majority in favor of what is already Law must decide *whose* uniformity it is to be.

Baxter, LIFE OF HIMSELF, *Book I, Part II, p. 368. Note continued on p. 369.*

> We must needs believe, that when your Majesty took our Consent to a Liturgy, to be a Foundation that would infer our Concord, you meant not that we should have no Concord, but by consenting to this Liturgy without any considerable Alteration.

This is forcible Reasoning; but which the Bishops could fairly leave for the King to answer: The contract, tacit or expressed, being between him and the anti-prelatic Presbytero-Episcopalian Party, to which

[16] The passage in *Lit. Rem.* begins at this point.

neither the Bishops nor the Legislature had acceded or assented. If Baxter & Calamy were so little imbued with the spirit of the Constitution, as to consider Charles the Second as *the Breath of their Nostrils,* and this dread Sovereign Breath in it's passage gave a Snort for a Snuffle, (or having led them to expect a Snuffle surprized them with a Snort), let the reproach be shared between the Breath's fetid Conscience and the Nostrils' Naso-ductility. Breath's Father died a martyr to the vice of Lying: Breath inherited the vice but chose to shift the martyrdom on the Fools that believed him[17]—the Traitors to the Liberty of their Country who were swarming and intriguing for favor at Breda when they should have been at their post in Parliament or in the Lobby preparing *Terms & Conditions*—! Had all the ministers that were afterward ejected, and the Presbyterian Party generally exerted themselves, heart and soul, with Monk's Soldiers, & in collecting those whom Monk had displaced, and, instead of carrying on treasons against the *Government de facto* by mendicant negotiations with Charles, had taken open measures to *confer* the Scepter on him, as the Scotch did,—whose stern and truly loyal conduct has been most unjustly condemned—the Schism in the Church might have been prevented, and the Revolution superseded.

P. S. In the above, I speak of the Bishops, as *men* interested in a litigated Estate. God forbid! I should seek to justify them, as Christians!

Baxter, LIFE OF HIMSELF, *Book I, Part II, p. 369.*

> Quære. Whether in the Twentieth Article these Words are not inferred, *Habet Ecclesia auctoritatem in Controversiis fidei.*

Strange, that the evident antithesis between *power* in respect of ceremonies and *authority* in points of faith, should have been overlooked.

Baxter, LIFE OF HIMSELF, *Book I, Part II, p. 370.*

> Some have broacht out of *Socinus* a most uncomfortable and desperate Doctrine, *That late Repentance,* that is upon the last Bed of Sickness, *is unfruitful,* at least to reconcile the Pentitent to God.

This, no doubt, refers to Jeremy Taylor's work on Repentance,—& is but too faithful a description of it's character.

---

[17] This sentence is omitted in *Lit. Rem.* In Notebook 38, Coleridge calls Charles I a "Martyr to the Inveterate Vice of Lying." See above in "The Seventeenth Century."

Baxter, LIFE OF HIMSELF, *Book I, Part II, p. 373.*

> A little after the King was beheaded, Mr. *Atkins* met this Priest in *London,* and going into a Tavern with him, said to him in his familiar way [*What business have you here? I warrant you come about some Roguery or other.*] Whereupon the Priest told it him as a great secret, [*That there were thirty of them here in London, who, by Instructions from Cardinal* Mazarine, *did take care of such Affairs, and had sate in Council, and debated the Question, Whether the King should be put to death or not,* and: *that it was carried in the Affirmative, and there were but two Voices for the Negative, which was his own, and anothers. And that for his part, he could not concur with them, as foreseeing what misery this would bring upon his Country.*] Mr. *Atkins* stood to the Truth of this, but thought it a violation of the Laws of Friendship to name the Man.

Richard Baxter was too thoroughly *good* for any experience to make him worldly wise. Else how could he have been simple enough to suppose that Mazarine left such a question to be voted pro & con, & decided by 30 Emissaries in London! And, how could he have reconciled Mazarine's having any share in Charles's Death with his own masterly account, p. 98, 99, 100? Even Cromwell, tho' he might have prevented, could not have effected, the sentence. The Regicidal Judges were not his *Creatures.* Consult the Life of Colonel Hutchinson.

Baxter, LIFE OF HIMSELF, *Book I, Part II, p. 374. Note continued on p. 375.*

> Since this, Dr. *Peter Moulin* hath in his Answer to *Philanax Anglicus,* declared that he is ready to prove, when Authority will call him to it, that the King's Death and the Change of the Government, was first proposed both to the *Sorbonne;* and to the Pope with his Conclave, and consented to and concluded for by both.

The Pope in his Conclave had about the same influence on Charles's fate as the Pope's Eye in a Leg of Mutton. The Letter intercepted by Cromwell was Charles's Death warrant. Charles knew his power; & Cromwell and Ireton knew it likewise, and knew, that it was the Power of a Man who was within a yard's Length of a Talisman, only not within an arm's length, but which in that state of the public mind could he but have once grasped, would have enabled him to blow up Presbyterian & Independent. If ever a lawless Act was defensible on the principle of Self-preservation, the murther of Charles might be defended. I suspect that the fatal delay in the publication of the Eikon Basilike is susceptible of no other satisfactory explanation. In short, it is absurd to burthen this Act on Cromwell or his Party. The guilt, if guilt it was, was consummated at the Gates of Hull—i. e. the first moment, that Charles was treated as an Individual, Man against Man.

Whatever right Hampden had to defend his life against the King in Battle, Cromwell & Ireton had in yet more imminent danger against the King's Plotting. Milton's reasoning on this point is unanswerable —& what a wretched hand does Baxter make of it!

Baxter, LIFE OF HIMSELF, *Book I, Part II, p. 435.*

> That the Minister be not bound to use the Cross and Surplice, and read the Liturgy himself, if another (by whomsoever) be procured to it: So be it he preach not against them.

Wonderful that so good and wise a man as Baxter should not have seen that in this the Church would have given up the best, perhaps the only efficient Preservative of her Faith. But for our blessed and truly apostolic & scriptural Liturgy, our Churches' Pews would long ago have been filled by Arians and Socinians, as too many of their Desks and Pulpits already are.

Baxter, LIFE OF HIMSELF, *Book I, Part III, p. 67.*

> They think while you [the Independents] seem to be for a *stricter Discipline* than others, that your way (or usual Practice) tendeth to extirpate Godliness out of the Land: by taking a very few that can talk more than the rest, and making them the Church, &c.

Had Baxter had as judicious Advisers among his theological, as he had among his legal, friends; & had he allowed them equal influence with him; he would not, I suspect, have written this irritating and too *ego*metrical ¶. But B. would have disbelieved a prophet who had foretold that the whole Orthodoxy of the Nonconformists would be retained & preserved by the *Independent* Churches in England—after the Presbyterian had almost without exception become first, Arian, then Socinian, & finally Unitarian—i. e., the demi-semi-quaver of Xtianity, taking lax Arminianism for the Semi-breve.

Baxter, LIFE OF HIMSELF, *Book I, Part III, p. 69. See p. 119.*

Baxter, LIFE OF HIMSELF, *Book I, Part III, p. 181.*

> About that time I had finished a book called *Catholick Theologie;* in which I undertook to prove that besides things unrevealed, known to none, and ambiguous words, there is no considerable difference between the *Arminians* and *Calvinists,* except some very tolerable difference in the point of perseverance.

What Arminians? *what* Calvinists? It is possible that the guarded Language and Position of Arminius himself may be interpreted into a "very tolerable" compatibility with the principles of the milder Calvinists, such as Archbishop Leighton—that true Father of the

Church of Christ! But I more than doubt the possibility of even approximating the principles of Bishop Jeremy Taylor to the fundamental doctrines even of Leighton—much more those of Cartwright, Twiss, Owen.

Baxter, LIFE OF HIMSELF, *Book I, Part III, p. 191.*

> But after this when I had ceased Preaching, I was (being newly risen from Extremity of pain) suddenly surprised in my house by a poor violent Informer, and many Constables and Officers, who rusht in and apprehended me, and served on me one Warrant to seize on my person for coming within five miles of a Corporation, and five more Warrants, to distrain for an Hundred and ninety pounds, for five Sermons, &c.

I cannot express how much it grieves me, that our Church Clergy should still think it fit and expedient to defend the measures of the High Church men from Laud to Sheldon and to speak of the ejected Ministers, Calamy, Baxter, Gouge, Howe, &c, &c, &c as Schismatics, Factionists, and Fanatics, or Pharisees—thus to flatter some half dozen dead Bishops wantonly depriving our present Church of the Authority of perhaps the largest collective number of learned and zealous, discreet & holy Ministers that one Age & one Church was ever blest with, and whose Authority in *every* considerable point is in favor of our Church and against the present Dissenters from it.—And this seems the more impolitic, when it must be clear to every student of the History of these times, that the unmanly Cruelties inflicted on Baxter and others were, as Bishops Ward, Stillingfleet & others saw at the time, part of the popish Scheme of the Cabal, to trick the Bishops and dignified Clergy into rendering themselves & the established Church odious to the Public by Laws, the execution of which the King, the Duke, Arlington & the popish Priests directed towards the very last man that the Bishops themselves (the great majority at least) would have molested.

Baxter, LIFE OF HIMSELF, *Appendix II, p. 37.*

> If you think not only Imposition to be essential, but also that nothing else is essential, or that all are true Ministers that are ordained by a lawful Bishop per *manuum impositionem*, then do you egregiously *tibi ipsi imponere*.

Baxter, like most scholastic logicians, had a sneaking affection for Puns. The cause is: the necessity of attending to the primary sense of words, i. e. the visual image or general relation expresst, & which remains common to all the after-senses, however widely or even incongruously differing from each other in other respects. . . .

Baxter, LIFE OF HIMSELF, *Appendix II, p. 45.*

Then that the Will follow the practical Intellect whether right or wrong that is no precept, but the Nature of the Soul in its acting, because that Will is *potentia ceca, non nata, ad intelligendum, sed ad volendum vel nolendum intellectum.*

This is the main fault in Baxter's Metaphysics: that he so often substantiates Distinction into dividuous Self-subsistents. So, here. A will not intelligent is no *Will.*

Baxter, LIFE OF HIMSELF, *end-pages.*

The Power of the Soul by it's own act of Will is, I admit, great for any one occasion or for a definite time—yea, it is marvellous. But of such exertions and such an even frame of Spirit as Baxter's were, under such unremitting and almost unheard of bodily derangements and pains, as Baxter's and disappointments in life, I do not believe a human soul capable, unless substantiated or successively potentiated by an especial Grace. S. T. C.[18]

There are two Senses in which the words, Church of England, may be used—first, with reference to the *Idea* of the Church as an Estate of this Christian and Protestant Realm,[19] comprizing the interests of a permanent learned Class, i. e., the Clergy; 2, these of the proper, i. e., *infirm* Poor, from age or sickness; and 3, the adequate proportional instruction, of all in all classes, by public Prayer, recitation of the Scriptures, by expounding, preaching, catechizing, and *schooling,* and last, not least, by the example and influence of a Pastor and a School Master placed, as a germ of civilization and cultivation, in every Parish throughout the Realm. To this Ideal, the reformed Church of England, with its marriable & married Clergy, would have approximated, if the Revenues of the Church, as they existed at the Death of Henry VIIth., had been rightly transferred by his Successor—Transferred I mean, from Reservoirs, which had, by degeneracy on one hand, and progressive improvement on the other, fallen into ruin, & in which those Revenues had stagnated into contagion or uselessness,—tranferred from what had *become* PUBLIC Evils to their original & inherent Purpose of *Public* Benefits,—instead of their sacrilegious alienation by transfer to *private* Proprietors. That this was *impracticable,* is *historically* true; but no less true is it *philosophically,* that this impracticability, arising wholly from *moral* causes (viz. the loose Manners and corrupt Principles of a great majority in all classes during the Dynasty of the Tudors) does not prevent this wholesale Sacrilege, from deserving the character of the first and deadli-

[18] This passage is omitted in *Lit. Rem.*
[19] ''Protecting against the Papal usurpation,'' is inserted in *Lit. Rem.*

est Wound inflicted on the CONSTITUTION of the Kingdom: which term, in the body politic, as in bodies natural, expresses not only what is & has been evolved, but likewise whatever is *potentially* contained in the seminal principle of the particular Body, & would in it's due time have appeared but for the emasculation in it's infancy.—This, however, is the first sense of the words, Church of England.

The second is the Church of England as now by Law established, & by the Practice of the Law actually existing. That in the first sense it is the Object of my Admiration and the earthly Ne Plus Ultra of my religious Aspirations, it were superfluous to say; but I may be allowed to express my conviction, that on our recurrence to the same Ends and Objects (the restoration of a National and Circulating Property in counterpoise of individual Possession, disposable & heritable) tho' in other power and by other means perhaps (Mr. Brougham's Motion, June 28, 1820 promises a *beginning*),[20] the Decline or progress of this country depends. In the second sense of the Words I can sincerely profess, that I love & honor the Church of England, *comparatively*, beyond any other Church established or unestablished now existing in Christendom; and it is wholly in consequence of this deliberate and most affectionate filial Preference, that I have read this work; and Calamy's[21] Historical Writings, with so deep and so melancholy an Interest. And I dare avow that I cannot but regard as an Ignorant Bigot every Man who (especially since the publicity & authentication of the contents of the Stuart Papers, Memoirs & Life of James II, &c.) can place the far later furious High Church Compilations & Stories of Walker & others in competition with the veracity & general Verity of Baxter & Calamy; or forget that the great Body of Non-conformists to whom these great & good Men belonged, were not Dissenters *from* the established Church willingly, but an orthodox & numerous Portion of the Church.—Omitting then the wound received by Religion generally under Henry 8th & the shameless secularizations clandestinely effected during Elizabeth's & the first James's Reign, I am disposed to consider the three following as the grand evil Epochs of our present Church. I. The introduction (& after-predominancy) of Latitudinarianism under the name of Arminianism, & the Spirit of a conjoint Romanism ※ and Socinianism at the latter Half or towards the close of the reign of James the First: Montague, Laud, & their confederates. 2. the ejection

[20] Mr. Brougham presented before Parliament a "Plan for the Education of the Poor" under the patronage of the Church. His speech was called "one of the most elaborate and instructive ever delivered in parliament." (*Annual Register*, 1820, Part II, p. 49.)
[21] Edmund Calamy (1600-66), a Puritan divine who took part in the anti-Episcopal pamphlet-writing against Bishop Hall.

of the 2,000 Ministers after the Restoration, with the other violences into which the Churchmen made themselves the Dupes of Charles, James, the Jesuits, and the French Court. (Vide Stuart Papers) It was this that gave consistence and enduring strength to Schism in this country, prevented the *pacation* of Ireland, and prepared for the separation of America at a far too early period for the true interests of either Country. 3. The surrender by the clergy of the Right of taxing themselves, & the Jacobitical Follies that combined with the former to put it in the power of the Whig Party to deprive the Church of her *Convocation*,—a bitter disgrace & wrong, to which most unhappily the People were rendered indifferent by the increasing contrast of the Sermons of the Clergy from the Articles & Homilies of the Church; but a wrong which already has avenged, & will sooner or later be seen to avenge itself on the State & the Governing Classes that continue this Boast of a short-sighted Policy—the same Policy that in our own memory would have funded the Property of the Church, & by converting the Clergy into salaried Dependents on the Government pro tempore, have deprived the Establishment of it's fairest honor, that of being neither enslaved to the Court nor to the Congregations—the same, alas! which even now pays and patronizes a Board of Agriculture to undermine all landed property by a succession of false, shallow, and inflammatory Libels against Tythes.

These are my weighted Sentiments: and fervently desiring, as I do, the perpetuity and prosperity of the Establishment, zealous for it's rights and dignity, preferring it's Forms, believing it's Articles of Faith, and holding it's Book of Common Prayer and it's translation of the Scriptures among my highest privileges as a Christian & an Englishman, I trust that I may both entertain and avow these sentiments without forfeiting any part of my claim to the name of a faithful Member of the Church of England. S. T. Coleridge, Highgate, June, 1820. P. S. As to Warburton's Alliance of the Church and State, I object to the *Title* (Alliance), and to the matter and mode of the reasoning. But the Interdependence of the Church and the State appears to me a Truth of the highest practical importance. Let but the Temporal Powers protect the subjects in their just rights as subjects merely: and I do not know of any one point, in which the Church has the right or the necessity to call in the Temporal Power as it's ally for any purpose *exclusively* ecclesiastic. The right of a Firm to dissolve it's Partnership with any one Partner, breach of contract having been proved, and publicly to announce the same, is common to all men as social beings.

✕ i.e. Romanism, or if you please, Laudism, or Lambethism in Temporalities & Ceremonials, and of Socinianism in Doctrine, retaining the words but a rejecting or interpreting away the sense and substance of the Scriptural Mysteries. This Spirit has not indeed manifested itself in the articles of the Trinity, since Waterland gave the death-blow to Arianism, & so left no Alternative to the Clergy, but the actual Divinity or mere Humanity of our Lord; & the latter would be too impudent an avowal for a Public Reader of our Church Liturgy; but in the articles of Original Sin, the necessity of Regeneration, the necessity of Redemption in order to the possibility of Regeneration, of Justification by Faith, and of prevenient and auxiliary Grace; all I can say with sincerity is, that our Orthodoxy seems so far in an improving state, that I can hope for the time when Churchmen will use the term *Arminianism* to express a habit of Belief opposed not to Calvinism, or the works of Calvin, but to the Articles of our own Church, and to the Doctrine in which *all* the first Reformers agreed.

N. B. By Latitudinarians, I do not mean the particular tenets of the Divines so called, such as Dr. H. Moore, Cudworth, & their Compeers, relative to Toleration, Comprehension, and the general Belief that in the greater number of points then most controverted, the pious of all parties were far more nearly of the same mind than their own imperfection, and the imperfection of Language allowed them to see. I mean the disposition to explain away the articles of the Church on the pretext of their inconsistence with right Reason—when in fact it was only an incongruity with a *wrong understanding*, the faculty which St. Paul calls φρόνημα σαρκός. the rules of which having been all abstracted from objects of Sense (Finite in Time and Space), are logically applicable to Objects of the Sense alone. This I have elsewhere called the *Spirit* of Socinianism, which may work in many whose tenets are anti-Socinian.

Law is—Conclusio per regulam generis singulorum in genere isto inclusorum. Now the Extremes and Inclusas are contradictory terms. Therefore Extreme Cases are not capable Subjects of Law à priori, but must proceed on knowlege of the Past, and anticipation of the Future, and the fulfilment of the anticipation is the proof, because the only possible determination, of the accuracy of the Knowlege. In other words, the Agents may be condemned or honored, according to their intentions, and the apparent source of their motives; (so we honor Brutus), but the extreme case itself is tried by the Event.

Pray read with great attention Baxter's Life of himself. It is an inestimable work. I may not unfrequently doubt Baxter's memory, or even his competence, in consequence of his particular modes of thinking; but I could almost as soon doubt the Gospel verity as his veracity.[22]

If facts are required to prove the possibility of combining weighty performances in literature with full and independent employment, the works of Cicero and Xenophon among the ancients; of Sir Thomas More, Bacon, Baxter, or to refer at once to later and contemporary instances, DARWIN and ROSCOE, are at once decisive of the question.[23]

QUARTERLY REVIEW, *X (October, 1813), 96, 97.*

> It is easy to talk of toleration, and say that the Church should have tolerated these schismatics: they would not tolerate the Church. "We intended not," says Baxter, "to dig down the banks or to pull up the hedge and lay all waste and common, when we desired the prelates' tyranny might cease. We must either tolerate all men to do what they will, which they will make a matter of conscience or religion, and then some may offer their children in sacrifice to the devil, and some may think they do God service in killing his servants; or else you must tolerate no error or fault in religion, and then you must advise what measure of penalty you will inflict. My judgment I have always freely made known: I abhor unlimited liberty or toleration of all."

Southey did not advert to Baxter's use of the word "Religion," which meant with him the *Regula Fidei*, or Apostles' Creed; and this, too, limited to an open opposition to the words of the Creed. Whoever could conscientiously use the words was not to be further questioned.

This is a most unfair quotation from Baxter, who was the nearest to absolute toleration of all theologians. He proposed that all persons admitted as Church members should be ready to declare, that they desired what was prayed for in the Lord's Prayer, believed what was declared in the Apostles' Creed, and held themselves bound to obey what was enjoined by the Ten Commandments, and that all beyond should be free to each.[24]

And Baxter was of all Anti-tolerationists the least intolerant—say rather, that he used and understood the word "Toleration" in a different sense from the present—for he pleaded for subscription only to the Belief, Lord's Prayer, and ten Commandments, in order to the higher Magistracies, and for Presbyters added no more than, I believe all articles of faith necessary for salvation contained in the canonical

---

[22] July 12, 1827. *Table Talk S,* VI, 292. Cf. p. 17 and see Baxter's *Life of Himself,* p. 136 above, where the the second sentence occurs verbatim.

[23] *Biog. Lit.,* I, 225.

[24] *Notes Theolog.,* pp. 146-47.

Scriptures, and promise that I will use all means in my power to discover the true sense of the words, and that I will interpret accordingly.[25]

One among the countless internal evidences & features of truth, that I find in the Gospel—& this strangely at variance with the fashionable "Evidences," which Grotius first brought into fashion (followed in England first, I believe, by Richard Baxter and Bishop Jeremy Taylor) is the justly subordinate and accessory character assigned to his miracles by our Lord.[26]

Baxter tried to reconcile the almost irreconcilable tenets of Calvinism and Arminianism. He more than any other man was the cause of the restoration, and more than any other sectarian was he persecuted by Charles II.

He is borne out in all his statements by Mrs. Lucy Hutchinson, that most delightful of women and of regicidesses. No doubt the Commons had a right to punish the weak and perfidious King, inasmuch as he first appealed to the God of Battles.[27]

In the life of Baxter written by himself, speaking of the great obligations he had to the Schoolmen, he particularly instances this, that ever afterwards they rendered all indistinctness of means intolerable to him. It enforced on him, it introduced into his mind the necessity of having every position as far back as either duty permitted or it was not demonstrably beyond further pursuit.[28]

Baxter, CATHOLICK THEOLOGIE,[29] *flyleaf.*

How large a proportion of this Volume would have been superseded by a previous reduction of a few words, ex. gr. Thing, Cause, Power &c.[30] to a fixed sense,—in the Writer's thoughts! Year after year, yea, day after day, I see more clearly or feel more livelily the importance

[25] Notebook 21½, fol. 45 recto. British Museum, Add. MSS, 47,519. Printed for the first time.
[26] Notebook 47, fol. 27 recto. Comment on the Gospel of John 11:23. British Museum, Add. MSS, 47,542. Printed for the first time.
[27] Allsop, "Heads of Conversation," in *Letters,* I, 133-34.
[28] Philosophical Lecture XI, March 8, 1819. Coburn, *Phil. Lect.,* p. 317.
[29] Richard Baxter, *Catholick Theologie* (London: 1675). These notes, except the one from the flyleaf and a facsimile of the note on the Preface (a2), which are given by T. J. Wise (*Ashley,* VIII, 108-9), are here printed for the first time. At the top of the first flyleaf is the name of Anne Gillman; the bookplate is that of A. Steinmetz. British Museum, Ashley, 4777.
[30] "Mind" is crossed out and "Power" substituted.

of the *Noetic* Tetrad and the Logical Pentad, as the fundamental Form of all Thinking—and of Trichotomy in all *real* definition.

Instead of the dichotomy Real ÷ Unreal—or Thing: which are mere *words*—for what *is* cannot be Nothing opposed—and Reality can have no opposite, we shall say—

Reality in finite existence has two forms, actual and potential—the latter as truly *real* as the former—

$\odot$ irrelative $+$ relative in

Correspondent antithesis to $-$. $-$ relative in correspondent antithesis to $+$.

$$\odot \text{ Real}$$
$$+ \text{ Actual} \quad - \text{ Potential}$$

In God alone the Actual and the Real are one and the same, as the divine Reality excludes all potentiality.

Actus purissimus sine ulla potentialitate.

Baxter, Catholick Theologie, *Preface, A$_2$ recto. Note continued on verso.*

> Rom. 10. 9, 10. If thou confess with thy mouth the Lord Jesus, and believe in thy Heart that God hath raised him from the dead, thou shalt be saved: For with the Heart man believeth unto Righteousness, and with the Mouth confession is made to salvation.

Few points in the Christian Theology of more interest, and scarcely any that have attracted less attention, than the Energetic & Pauline Sense of the Term, *Saved.* Perhaps, I should have said, *Senses:* for the total Work of Redemption, a regenerated Spirit born spiritually unto Christ, may be intended by Salvation, tho' I do not at present recollect any special instance in the New Testament. But generally "Saved" is taken in a narrower Sense—viz. as the first admission within the pale of the alone saving Church, as the condition & inceptive of Redemption —not superseding the expediency, & where means are afforded, the necessity of a growth in the Faith, of an expansion of the Belief.

Baxter, Catholick Theologie, *Preface, a verso and a$_2$ recto.*

> But in 1640, the *Oath* called [Et Cætera] being offered the Ministry, forced me to a yet more *searching Study* of the case of our *Diocesane Prelacie* (which else I had never been like to have gainsaid.) At a meeting of Ministers to debate the case, it fell to Mr. *Christopher Cartwrights* lot and mine to be the Disputers; and the issue of all (that and my studies) was, that I setled in the approbation of the Episcopacy asserted by *Ignatius,* yea, and *Cyprian,* but such a dissent from the *English* frame, as I have given account of in my *Disputations of Church Government.*

In an honest and intelligent mind this is the first & inevitable Consequent of the Ignorance respecting the true nature & purpose of a National Church and it's Prelacy: and of it's essential distinction from the Christian Church and it's Episcopacy. But what are distinct, yea different, need not therefore be separated. Two distinct trusts and functions may be vested in and exercised by the same Person: nay, the perfection of the lower of the two Trusts may depend on this union. But bear in mind, that the Error in this case was common to both Parties—to the persecutors who demanded as Bishops what they ought to have asked only as Prelates, no less then to the resisting Puritans—while the blame lies heavier ✕ on the former.

S. T. Coleridge.

✕ This may be easily shewn. For the *aggression* was on their part who repressed in the name of Christ what they were entitled to demand only in the name of *Cæsar* & consequently respecting the *temporalities* of the National Church exclusively: and not on those who resisted or remonstrated against a Power assumed in the name of Christ, which they clearly saw, Christ so far from having delegated to others had never assumed for himself.

Baxter, CATHOLICK THEOLOGIE, *Preface, a₂ verso. Note continued at top of a₃ recto.*

> And though *Camero's* moderation and great clearness took much with me, I soon perceived that his Resolving the cause of sin into necessitating objects and temptations, laid it as much on God (in another way) as the Predeterminants do. And I found all godly mens Prayers and Sermons run quite in another strain, when they chose not the Controversie as pre-engaged.

For *me* this would be as weighty an argument as it was for Baxter— possibly, even a more convincing one, thro' my conviction that in prayer and earnest practical enforcement of the truths of Godliness, the Spirit acts more *collectively,* is more total and entire, than it can be in any simply *intellectual* Effort—The *intellection,* being indeed a noble *part* of our Humanity but yet only a *part,* & therefore with the *deficiency* of a fragment—which the mistaking the part for a whole converts into *defect* & positive error.

Baxter, CATHOLICK THEOLOGIE, *Preface, a₃ verso.*

> And now looking daily in this posture, when God calleth me hence, (summoned by an incurable Disease to hasten all that ever I will do in this World,) being uncapable of prevailing with the present Church dis-

turbers, I do apply my self to posterity, leaving them the sad warning of their Ancestors distractions, as a Pillar of Salt, and acquainting them what I have found to be the cause of our Calamities, and therein will find the Cure themselves.

Who having the heart of a Christian can in the present day read the writings of Baxter, and not feel the deaf'ning & hard'ning effects of party-passion: which did make, & which alone could make, so many minds insensible or hostile!

Baxter, CATHOLICK THEOLOGIE, *Preface, c recto.*

14. And it greatly promoteth Schisms that good people are *unacquainted with Church-history,* and know not how just such *Opinions and Schisms* as *their own* have in former ages *risen,* and how they have *miscarryed* and *dyed,* and what have been their *fruits.*

A most just Remark! O if instead of the chopped straw of their prudential discourses on given Texts, Like Schoolboys' *Themes,* our Clergy would labor to *instruct* their Congregations—teach them what they are—and what their Fore-fathers were—and how both the one & the other came to be that which they were or are! From the neglect of this, how languid is Protestantism!

Baxter, CATHOLICK THEOLOGIE, *Preface, c verso.*

1. Christ first laid down the *Description* and *Measure* of *Christianity,* in the *Baptismal Covenant;* and ordained that all should be accounted *Christians in foro Ecclesiæ* who by Baptism were solemnly devoted to him, in a professed Belief and Covenant, Dedication and Vow to God the *Father, Son,* and *Holy Ghost:* These he would have called *Christians* or his *Disciples,* and this is their *Christening* and so ever called in the Church. 2. And next he made it his new (that is *Last*) and *Great Command,* that *All his Disciples should Love each other,* and live in eminent *Unity and Peace:* which he accordingly wrought them to by the first pouring out of his Spirit, Act. 2. & 3. & 4.

Alas! this very text is regarded by sundry learned men as a proof of the post-apostolic Date of the Gospel, in which it occurs: and as a departure from the the more simple form given in the Acts of the Apostles.

Baxter, CATHOLICK THEOLOGIE, *Preface, c₂ recto.*

And what cannot be *done* by *Light* and *Love,* is not to be done by them [i.e., ministers] at all: the Magistrate and not they, must use the Sword; but not to make men *believers* (for he cannot).

This again is most true—that the truth in Christ should be *propounded, declared, offered*—To as many as receive it, offer lovingly every aid & furtherance—but do not attempt to DISPUTE men into it.

Baxter, CATHOLICK THEOLOGIE, *Preface, c₂ recto, continued on verso.*

> It is to me a certainty, that the Apostles made and used the Creed for sense and substance as the very summary and test of Christianity, long before any Book of the New Testament was written (about twelve years, and almost sixty-six before the whole.) [Here Baxter gives eight reason for his certainty.]

All this may be substantially true; but for *Certainty,* I cannot receive it. Nay, I am persuaded that the so called Apostles' Creed was consequent on the conversion of the Gentiles, and intended as a form of instruction for pagan Catechumens preparatory for Baptism. How could John or Paul have sanctioned the first clause of the Creed, who both expressly attribute the making of the Heaven and Earth to the Son?

Baxter, CATHOLICK THEOLOGIE, *Part I, sec. I. 3, p. 2. Note continued at bottom of pp. 3, 4.*

> ※ 3. We neither have, nor can have here in flesh any one proper *formal Conception* of the *Divine Nature,* that is formally suited to the truth in the object: But only Metaphorical or Analogical Conceptions; borrowed from things better known.

How many perplexities and even contradictions would this good and great Man have escaped, had he rightly distinguished an Idea from a Conception, and rigorously observed the distinction! A *Conception* of God, whether in or out of the flesh, is an Absurdity; but the *Idea,* God (for a temptation to error lurks in the phrase, *Idea* of God) is for Man, yea, as the form, norm, ground, and condition of all other Ideas may be affirmed to constitute his Reason. See Aids to Reflection—p. 6—R.B. has, with many others, been misled by translating the familiar ἔσοπτρον "Glass," instead of "Mirror."

The apostle alludes to the Mirrors used in the Mysteries, & which are still frequently discovered in the tombs of the Ancients, & indicate that the Deceased had been an initiated person.

Baxter, CATHOLICK THEOLOGIE, *Part I, sec. V. 64, 65, p. 8. Note continued at bottom of pp. 9, 10.*

> The *Possibility* and *Futurity* of things, are not accidental notions, or relations of the things themselves; but are *termini diminuentes,* as to the *Things,* and are spoken of *Nothing.* To say that a *Thing May be* or *Will be,* which now is not, is to say that *now* it *is nothing.*
> 65. *Nothing* is no *Effect;* and therefore hath no *Cause:* Therefore things *Possible* and *Future* as such, have no *Cause.*

64. 65.—Surely, this is a mere misuse of the Equivoque in the word *"Thing"*—and the delusion would at once clear off on a just definition of "Being," or "Reality"—under which "Thing" would be subsumed

as a *Mode.*—Again—Cause is a vague term. Substitute *"ground"*—
and the fallacy of the assertion in ¶ 65 becomes evident. The Child beginning to walk *will* every now and then Stumble. Who would venture
to assert, that there was no *ground* of this? For in reason tho' not in
the sensuous Fancy Negations are as true causes as positives. The
Frost burns, as truly as the Fire, tho' in both Cases the Heat is the
Efficient. But the merely *logical* character of the Category, "Cause"
had not been disclosed to Baxter.

Baxter, CATHOLICK THEOLOGIE, *Part I, sec. V. 67, 68, p. 9.*

> 67. Therefore also God is no Cause of any Eternal Possibility or fu-
> turity.
> 68. Therefore the *Possibility* and *futurity* of things (conceived as an
> effect) hath no *Eternal Cause:* For there is nothing Eternal but God.

68. a direct contradiction of ¶ 67. The production of finite, i. e. of
non-absolute, Spirits was an eternal possibility: Evil or the Self-will
was a consequent *eternal possibility* & Baxter merely plays on the word
"thing."

Baxter, CATHOLICK THEOLOGIE, *Part I, sec. V. 87, p. 11.*

> It's strange how some Learned men confound *Things and Nothings*
> and the *Notions* and *Names* of *Nothings* with the *Nothings* named.

But excellent Baxter falls into the opposite error—and reduces
into *Nothings* all that tho' they are, yet are not *things*—i. e. units that
fill a space *exclusively*—or which he can imagine as so doing. The
ground of his Error is the attribution of degreelessness to Reality.

Baxter, CATHOLICK THEOLOGIE, *Part I, sec. V. 87, p. 12.*

> But *Bradwardine* saith, that God *knoweth illa vera complexa quæ*
> *voluntatem divinam præcedunt, per solam suam essentiam, sicut alia vera*
> *incomplexa; illa vero quæ voluntatem ejus sequuntur, non scit Deus per*
> *illa complexa neque per aliquid à voluntate, ejus semota, sed per suam*
> *voluntatem, vel per suam substantiam cum voluntate,* &c. More pre-
> sumption still! He saith God knoweth *complexa sed non complexe;*
> And who knoweth what sense those words have?

But then, whispers the Spinosist? what do you *mean* by God? The
incomprehensible? This is what *we* contend & you call us Atheists for
we contend that as God is the Ground of all Motion yet not moving,
so he is the Ground of all intelligence but not intelligent i. e. God is the
term by which we express the relation of cause and effect universally.
But surely this is not the God, whom Christians adore!—Not the Eternal
I AM! not the *Father* of Spirits! Not the Holy, the Merciful God!—
But all these perplexities would have cleared away before a right view
of the diversity of the *Reason* and the Understanding.

John Smith

Smith, SELECT DISCOURSES,[1] *p. 459.*

A Christian's conflicts and conquests. By the devil we are to understand that apostate spirit which fell from God, and that is always designing to hale down others from God also. The old Dragon (mentioned in the Revelation) with his tail drew down the third part of the stars of heaven, and cast them to the earth.

How much it is to be regretted, that so enlightened and able a divine had not philosophically and scripturally enucleated this so difficult, yet important question,—respecting the personal existence of the Evil Principle; *i. e.*, whether as τὸ δεῖον of paganism is ὁ θεός in Christianity, and so the τὸ πονηρόν is to be ὁ πονηρός? and whether this is an express doctrine of Christ, and not merely a Jewish dogma left undisturbed to fade away under the increasing light of the Gospel, instead of assuming the former, and confirming the position by a verse from a poetic tissue of visual symbols—a verse alien from the subject, and by which the Apocalypt enigmatised the Neronian persecutions and the apostacy through fear occasioned by it in a large number of converts! S. T. C.

Smith, SELECT DISCOURSES, *p. 463.*

When we say, the Devil is continually busy with us, I mean not only some apostate spirit as one particular being, but that spirit of apostasy which is lodged in all men's natures; and this may seem particularly to be aimed at in this place, if we observe the context: as the Scripture speaks of Christ not only as a particular person, but as the divine principle in holy souls. Indeed the devil is not only the name of one particular thing, but a nature.

May I venture to suspect that this was Smith's own belief and judgment! And that his conversion of the *Satan*, i. e. *circuitor*, or minister of police (which our Sterne calls the Accusing Angel) in the Prologue to Job into the Devil was a mere condescension to the prevailing prejudice? Here, however, he speaks like himself and like a true religious philosopher, who felt that the personality of Evil Spirits is a

[1] John Smith, *Select Discourses* (London: 1660). The two first notes on *Select Discourses* were given by W. E. A. Axon in "Coleridge on the Spirit of Apostacy." *The Nation*, LXXXIV (June 20, 1907), 563. The notes are dated March. 1824. Shedd has reproduced them in IV, 326-27.

trifling question, compared with the personëity of the Evil Principle. This is indeed most momentous.

Smith, SELECT DISCOURSES.[2]

It would make a delightful and instructive essay, to draw up a critical and (where possible) biographical account of the Latitudinarian party at Cambridge, from the close of the reign of James I. to the latter half of Charles II. The greater number were Platonists, so called at least, and such they believed themselves to be, but more truly Plotinists. Thus Cudworth, Dr. Jackson (chaplain of Charles I., and vicar of Newcastle-on-Tyne), Henry More, this John Smith, and some others. Taylor was a Gassendist, or *inter Epicureos evangelizantes*, and, as far as I know, he is the only exception. They were all alike admirers of Grotius, which in Jeremy Taylor was consistent with the tone of his philosophy. The whole party, however, and a more amiable never existed, were scared and disgusted into this by the catachrestic language and skeleton half-truths of the systematic divines of the Synod of Dort on the one hand, and by the sickly broodings of the Pietists and Solomon's-Song preachers on the other. What they all wanted was a pre-inquisition into the mind, as part organ, part constitutent, of all knowledge, an examination of the scales, weights and measures themselves abstracted from the objects to be weighed or measured by them; in short, a transcendental aesthetic, logic, and noetic. Lord Herbert was at the entrance of, nay, already some paces within, the shaft and adit of the mine, but he turned abruptly back, and the honour of establishing a complete προπαιδεία of philosophy was reserved for Immanuel Kant, a century or more afterwards.

From the confounding of Plotinism with Platonism, the Latitudinarian divines fell into the mistake of finding in the Greek Philosophy many anticipations of the Christian Faith, which in fact were but its echoes. The inference is as perilous as inevitable, namely, that even the mysteries of Christianity needed no revelation, having been previously discovered and set forth by unaided reason.

The argument from the mere universality of the belief, appears to me far stronger in favour of a surviving soul and a state after death, than for the existence of the Supreme Being. In the former, it is one doctrine in the Englishman and in the Hottentot; the differences are accidents not affecting the subject, otherwise than as different seals would affect the same wax, though Molly, the maid, used her thimble, and Lady *Virtuosa* an *intaglio* of the most equisite workmanship. Far

[2] The remaining notes are reprinted from *Lit. Rem.,* III, 415-19.

otherwise in the latter. *Mumbo Jumbo,* or the *cercocheronychous Nick-Senior,* or whatever score or score thousand invisible huge men fear and fancy engender in the brain of ignorance to be hatched by the nightmare of defenceless and self-conscious weakness—these are not the same as, but are *toto genere* diverse from, the *una et unica substantia* of Spinosa, or the World-God of the Stoics. And each of these again is as diverse from the living Lord God, the creator of heaven and earth. Nay, this equivoque on God is as mischievous as it is illogical; it is the sword and buckler of Deism.

Of the Existence and Nature of God.

Besides, when we review our own immortal souls and their dependency upon some Almighty mind, we know that we neither did nor could produce ourselves, and withal know that all that power which lies within the compass of ourselves will serve for no other purpose than to apply several pre-existent things one to another, from whence all generations and mutations arise, which are nothing else but the events of different applications and complications of bodies that were existent before; and therefore that which produced that substantial life and mind by which we know ourselves, must be something much more mighty than we are, and can be no less indeed than omnipotent, and must also be the first architect and δημιουργός of all other beings, and the perpetual supporter of them.

A Rhodian leap! Where our knowledge of a cause is derived from our knowledge of the effect, which is falsely (I think) here supposed, nothing can be logically, that is, apodeictically, inferred, but the adequacy of the former to the latter. The mistake, common to Smith, with a hundred other writers, arises out of an equivocal use of the word 'know.' In the scientific sense, as implying insight, and which ought to be the sense of the word in this place, we might be more truly said to know the soul by God, than to know God by the soul.

So the Sibyl was noted by Heraclitus as μαινομένῳ στόματι γελαστὰ καὶ ἀκαλλώπιστα φθεγγομένη, 'as one speaking ridiculous and unseemly speeches with her furious mouth.'

This fragment is misquoted and misunderstood: for γελαστά it should be ἀμύριστα, unperfumed, inornate lays, not redolent of art.—Render it thus:

Not her's
To win the sense by words of rhetoric,
Lip-blossoms breathing perishable sweets;
But by the power of the informing Word
Roll sounding onward through a thousand years
Her deep prophetic bodements.

Στόματι μαινομένῳ is with ecstatic mouth.

Isaac Barrow

I received last night two Volumes of Dr. Barrow—the admirable Passage on Wit, in which Lady Beaumont had put a paper, is an old friend & favorite of mine. Beyond any other passage in any Language it carries along a regular Admiration with a still increasing Surprize, till the mind rests at length in pure *Wonder*.—I pray, that I may read these excellent Sermons to such an effect, as will be considered by her Ladyship as the best possible Thanks.[1]

Barrow greatly inferior to all his great Predecessors, from Hooker to Taylor, in dignity of Style. Perhaps from aversion to the Puritans, a desire in all innocent ways to affect *liveliness* as a mark of a loyal Churchman, was the foundation of this woeful degeneracy. It is strange the very men, such as Barrow, & *Sa. Theoria Burnet*, who wrote with more than ancient majesty in Latin, should in English be as pert as their subjects & ideas would permit their words to be.—What an instructive Lesson on Style does not Burnet's own Translation of his Sacra Theoria furnish? And thus Barrow—L'Estrange or Tom Brown could not write it more *pertly* than this great man at times, while his Thoughts are always grave & fortunate. Tr. of Pope's Suprem: p. 78. When our Lord was apprehended by the Soldiers, presently *up* was his Spirit, & *out* went his Sword in defence of him. And at the Transf. he fell to propose about making an abode there.[2]

"Makes on merrily & carelessly" for "goes on"—

Barrow[3]

Nov. 25, 1802.

Examine minutely the nature, cause, birth & growth of the *verbal* Imagination of which Barrow is almost the Ideal.[4]

[1] To Sir George Beaumont, Oct. 16, 1803. Wordsworth, *Some Family Letters*, pp. 101-2.

[2] Notebook 16, fol. 25 verso-26 recto. British Museum, Add. MSS, 47,513. Printed for the first time.

[3] Notebook 8, fol. 39 verso. British Museum, Add. MSS, 47,518. Printed for the first time.

[4] Notebook 8, fol. 40. Also printed *Anima*, p. 26, expanded.

I have been reading Barrow's treatise "On the Pope's Supremacy," and have made a note on the *L'Estrangeism* of his style whenever his thoughts rendered it possible for the words to be pert, frisky and vulgar —which, luckily, could not be often, from the gravity of his subjects, the solidity and appropriateness of his thoughts, and that habitual geometrical *precision* of mind which demanded the most appropriate words. He seems to be below South in dignity; at least, South never sinks so low as B. sometimes.[5]

Gilbert Burnet

Burnet, BEDELL,[1] *p. 8.*

In requital of the Instruction he received from P. *Paulo* in the *Italian* Tongue, he drew a Grammar in the *English* Tongue for his use, and for some others that desired to learn it, that so they might be able to understand our Books of Divinity, and he also translated the *English* Common-prayer Book into *Italian.*

——[illegible] is non extant.

Burnet, BEDELL, *pp. 12-14. Comment on flyleaf.*

Here I must add a passage, concerning which I am in doubt whether it reflected more on the sincerity, or on the understanding of the *English* Ambassadour. The breach between the Pope and the Republick was brought very near a Crisis; so that it was expected a total separation, not only from the Court, but the Church of *Rome,* was like to follow upon it. It was set on by P. *Paulo* and the Seven Divines with much zeal, and was very prudently conducted by them. In order to the advancing of it, King *James* ordered his Ambassadour to offer all possible

---

[5] Notebook 21, folio. 86. Also printed in *Anima,* "Sunday morning, Nov. 13, [1803], ½ past 2," p. 47. For other comments on Barrow see the section "Prose Style."

[1] Gilbert Burnet, *The Life of William Bedell* (London: 1692). This edition with the original marginalia is in the Albert M. Bender Room, Stanford University Library, which has given me permission to print the material. This volume has Robert Southey's signature and 1809 upon the title page. Two penciled notes are not in Coleridge's hand, but are possibly Southey's. On p. 208 there is a cross reference to p. 336 penciled, and on p. 224, which, on account of a section of material bound out of place, is opposite p. 336, there is penciled "turn to page 208." On p. 362 there is a marginal "faux pas" penciled. All other notes are by Coleridge, and some are signed notes. Cf. *Lit. Rem.,* IV, 71-76, where the majority of the notes with some editorial variations are printed from an edition of 1810.

assistance to them, and to accuse the Pope and the Papacy as the Chief
Authors of all the mischiefs of Christendome. . . . P. *Paulo* and the
Seven Divines pressed Mr. Bedell to move the Ambassadour to present
King *James's* Premonition to all Christian Princes and States, then
put in *Latine,* to the Senate, and they were confident it would produce
a great effect. But the Ambassadour could not be prevailed upon to do
it at that time, and pretended that since S. *James's* day was not far off,
it would be more proper to do it on that day. If this was only for the
sake of a Speech that he had made on the conceit of S. *James's* Day
and K. *James's* Book, with which he intended to present it, that was a
weakness never to be excused. But if this was only a pretence, and
that there was a design under it, it was a crime not to be forgiven.
All that *Bedell* could say or do to persuade him not to put off a thing
of such importance was in vain; and indeed I can hardly think that
Wotton was so weak a Man as to have acted sincerely in this matter.
Before S. *James's* day came, which I suppose was the First of *May,*
and not the Twenty-fifth of *July,* the difference was made up, and that
happy opportunity was lost; so that when he had his audience on that
Day, in which he presented the Book, all the answer he got, was, That
they thanked the King of *England* for his good will, but they were
now reconciled to the Pope, and that therefore they were resolved not
to admit of any change in their Religion, according to their agreement
with the Court of *Rome.*

P. 13, 14 contain a weak & unhandsome attack on Wooten, [*sic*] who
doubtless had discovered that the presentation of "the Premonition"
previously to the reconciliation, as publicly completed, but after it had
been privately agreed on, between the Court of Rome & the Senate of
Venice, would embarrass the Latter: whereas, delivered, as it was, it
shewed the King's & his Minister's Zeal for Protestantism, and yet
supplied the Venetians with an answer not disrespectful to the King.

Besides, what is there in Wooten's whole Life (a man so disinterested, and who retired from all his Embassies so poor) to justify the
remotest suspicion of his *Insincerity?* What can this word mean less or
other than that Sir H. W. was either a crypto-papist, or had received a
bribe from the Romish Party? Horrid accusations!—Burnet was notoriously rash & credulous; but I remember no other instance in which
his Zeal for Reformation joined with his credulity has misled him
into so gross a calumny. It is not to be believed, that Bedell gave any
authority to such an aspersion of his old & faithful Friend & Patron,
further than that he had related the fact, & that he & the Minister
differed in opinion as to the prudence of the measure recommended.
How laxly too the story is narrated! The exact date of the recommendation by P. Paul & the Divines should have been given—then the date
of the public annunciation of the reconciliation between the Pope & the

V. Rep.—and lastly, the day on which Wooten did present the book;— for even this Burnet leaves uncertain.

Burnet, BEDELL, *pp. 16-17. Cross reference in Coleridge's hand to pp. 161-62.*

Burnet, BEDELL, *pp. 26-27. Comment on third flyleaf, recto.*

In all that time no notice was even taken of him [Bedell], though he gave a very singular evidence of his great capacity. For being provoked by his old acquaintance *Wadsworth's* Letters, he writ upon the points in controversie with the Church of *Rome,* with so much learning and judgment, and in so mild a strain, that no wonder if his Book had a good effect on him for whom it was intended: It is true he never returned and changed his Religion himself, but his Son came from *Spain* into *Ireland,* when *Bedell* was promoted to the Bishoprick of *Kilmore* there, and told him, That his Father commanded to him to thank him for the pains he was at in writing it: he said, It was almost always lying open before him, and that he had heard him say, He was resolved *to save one.* And it seems he instructed his Son in the true *Religion,* for he declared himself a Protestant on his coming over. The Book was printed, and dedicated to the late King, while he was Prince of *Wales,* in the year 1624. The true Reasons that obstructed *Bedell's* preferment seem to be these; He was a Calvinist in the matter of Decrees and Grace; and Preferments went generally at that time to those who held the other Opinions. He had also another Principle, which was not very acceptable to some in power; he thought, Conformity was an exact adhering to the Rubrick; and that adding any new Rite or Ceremony, was as much Nonconformity, as the passing over those that were prescribed: So that he would not use those Bowings or Gesticulations that grew so much in fashion, that Mens affections were measured by them. . . .

R. Southey has given me a bad character of this Son of the unhappy Convert to the Romish Church—he became, it seems, a spy on the Catholics, availing himself of his Father's Character among them—a crime which would indeed render his Testimony null and more than null —it would be a presumption of the contrary. It is clear from his Letter to Bedell that the Convert was a very weak man. I owe to him, however, a compleat confirmation of my old persuasion concerning Bishop Hall, whom from my first perusal of his works I have always considered as one of the *Blots* (alas! there are too many) of the Biography of the Church of England—a self-conceited, coarse-minded, persecuting, vulgar Priest, and (by way of anti-climax) one of the first corrupters and *epigrammatizers* of our English Prose Style. It is not true, that Sir Thomas Brown was the prototype of Dr. Johnson, who imitated him only as far as Sir T. B. resembles the majority of his Predecessors—i. e., in the pedantic preference of Latin Derivatives to Saxon Words of the very same force. In the balance & construction of his periods Dr. Johnson has followed Hall: as any intelligent reader will discover by an attentive Comparison. S. T. C.

Burnet, BEDELL, *p. 89.*

For the selling of Indulgences is really but a commutation of Penance.

Most true! but "if Penance" in Purgatory.[2]

Burnet, BEDELL, *p. 158.*

Yea, will some Man say, But that which marreth all is the Opinion of *merit and satisfaction.* Indeed that is the *School Doctrine.*

Alas! So far from this being the case with 99 out of an 100 in Spain, Italy, Sicily, & Catholic Germany, it is the Gospel Tenets that are the true *School Doctrine*—i. e. confined to the books & objects of the Learned among them.

Burnet, BEDELL, *p. 161.*

But many errours, and much ignorance so it be not *affected*, may stand with True Faith in Christ; and when there is true *Contrition* for one sin, (that is, *because it displeaseth God*) there is a general and implicite repentance for all *unknown sins.* God's Providence in the general revolt of the *ten* Tribes, when *Elias* thought himself left alone, had reserved *seven* thousand, that *had not bowed to the image of Baal:* and the like may be conceived here, since especially, the Idolatry practised under the obedience of Mystical *Babylon,* is rather in false and will-worship of the true God, and rather commended, as profitable, than enjoyned as absolutely necessary, and the corruptions there maintained are rather in a *superfluous* addition than *retraction* in anything necessary to salvation.

This good man's Charity joined[3] with his Love and tender recollections of Father Paul, Fulgento, and the Venetian Divines, has led him to a far, far too palliative a statement of Roman Idolatry. Not what his Pope had yet ventured to thunder forth from his Anti-Sinai, but what he & his Satellites, the Regulars, enforce to the preclusion of all true worship, in the actual practice, life long, of an *immense* majority in Spain, Italy, Bavaria, Austria, &c. &c.—this must determine the point. What they *are*, not what they would persuade Protestants is their essentials of Faith—this is the main Thing.

Burnet, BEDELL, *p. 163.*

This point may give some light in a *Question* that is on foot among learned and good Men at this day, Whether the *Church of* Rome *be a*

[2] This note does not appear in *Lit. Rem.*
[3] Printed as "jarring."

true Church or no? where I think surely if the matter be rightly declared, for the terms there will remain no question. As thus, whether *Babylon pretending to be* the Church of *Rome*, yea the *Catholick Church*, be so or not? or this, *Whether the people of Christ that are under that Captivity be a true Church or no?* either of both wayes if declared in these terms, the matter will be soon resolved.

Strange it seems, that so good & learned a man should swallow unchew'd Cyprian! Definition of a true Church! In what part of the N.T. did he find the Sacerdos = Priest as the *essential* of a church, except as far as every true Christian is a Priest? I ask, what a Priest can do, but what every Christian either ought to do, or may do?—To Baptize is allowed by all Churches; to administer the Sacrament—is this denied? —Yes, or no? If yes, how can the Eucharistic *Form* be *necessary*—ex. gr. in a large ship at sea, the chaplain having died? Are we saved by *Faith?* and yet not saved by Faith unless a Ceremony be performed?[4]

Burnet, BEDELL, *p. 164.*

I answer, under correction of better judgments, they have the Ministry of Reconciliation by the Commission which is given at their Ordination; being the same which our Saviour left in his Church, *Whose sins ye remit, they are remitted, whose sins ye retain, they are retained.*

And *could* B. Bedell believe, that this was committed to every Priest, & to Priests exclusively?[5] Believe, that the mere *will* of a Priest could have any effect on the everlasting Weal or Woe of a Christian? Even to the immediate Disciples & Apostles could the text mean more than this—Wherever you discover, by the spirit of knowlege, which I will send into you, Repentance & Faith, you shall declare Remission of sins—& the sins shall be remitted—and where the contrary exists, your declaration of exclusion from Bliss shall be fulfilled. Did Christ say, that true Repentance & actual Faith would not save a Soul, unless the Priests verbal Remission was superadded?

Burnet, BEDELL, *"Copies of Certain Letters," pp. 315-16.*

Excuse me, Sir, whether you call our Ancestors the first Christian Inhabitants of this Isle, or the ancient Christians of the Primitive Church, neither those, nor these were Roman Catholicks; Namely, the Fathers of the *African* Council, and amongst these S. *Augustine*: And therefore by Pope *Boniface* his Sentence,[6] be undoubtedly damned, for taking upon them, by the *Devil's instinct* (if we are to believe another Pope Boniface) to wax proud against the Church of *Rome*. Such

4 This note does not appear in *Lit. Rem.*
5 The first "that-clause" is omitted in *Lit. Rem.*
6 Boniface. 2 Epist. ad. Eulatium.

Catholicks, if ye mean *the most of* Christendome *be at this Day;* beware of putting your self upon that Issue.

O that the *Romanists* would weigh and apply to themselves that aphorism from Hesiod so productive in wise, so prolific in witty, applications—

νήπιοι, οὐδ' ἴσασιν, ὅσῳ πλέον ἥμισυ παντὸς

i. e. *their* factitious πᾶν !![7]

Burnet, BEDELL, *end-page.*

If it were in my power, I would have this book printed in a convenient form, and distributed thro' every House, at least, thro' every Village and Parish throughout the kingdom. A volume of *Thought,* and of moral Feelings, the offsprings of Thought, crowd upon me, as I review the different parts of this admirable man's Life and Creed. Only compare *his* conduct to James Waddesworth (probably some ancestral Relative of my honoured Friend, W. Wordsworth: for the name in Yorkshire, from whence his Father came, is pronounced Wadsworth) with that of the priest-power, far, far too highly rated, Bishop Hall—his Letter to Hall tenderly blaming his (Hall's) bitterness to an old friend mistaken, & then his Letter to that Friend defending Hall—What a picture of goodness! I confess, in all Ecclesiastical History I have read of no man so spotless: tho' of hundreds in which the Biographers have painted them as masters of perfection: but the *moral tact* soon feels the truth. S. T. C.

Read Bedell's Life & his Letters to Wadsworth—delightful & excellent throughout—the very model of Judicious & truly Christian Controversy. I remember nothing comparable with it. Especially remember the beautiful impersonation of the C. of E., that of the C. of Rome under the character of Solomon's contending Mothers—as to salvation out of the Church.[8]

In the horror of individual atrocities, in the exclusive choice and selection of the victims, in all but opportunity and consequent extent, might not the Armagh outrages be identified with the massacre of the two hundred thousand Protestants in the reign of the unhappy Charles? Was it possible to read and not to re-apply the memorable words of an eye-witness and sufferer in that massacre, of Bishop Bedell, the confi-

[7] This note does not appear in *Lit. Rem.* Quotation from Hesiod, *Works and Days,* l. 40.

[8] Notebook 18, fol. 128 verso-129 recto. British Museum, Add. MSS, 47,515. Printed for the first time.

dential friend of USHER and of Father Paul,[9] whose warm and impartial charity, whose meek and saintly virtues, checked, though they could not control the wolfish spirit even of priest-maddened savages. "The priests and people of the Romish Communion," *he observes*, "enjoyed not only an impunity but were as public in the use of their religion as others were in the use of that which was established by law; so that they wanted nothing but empire, and a power to destroy all that differed from them."[10]

Edward Stillingfleet

Stillingfleet, ORIGINES SACRÆ,[1] *p. 248.*

If *Epicurus* should *contend* still that the *Sun* and *stars* are no *bigger* than they *seem* to be, will it hence *follow* that there can be no *rational demonstration* of the *contrary?*

It cannot be doubted by any man versed in the real system of Epicurus that he meant hereby to affirm that we see only the impressions from the objects, which are what they are, & not the physical magnitude of the realities, the existence of which we *deduce* from these Impressions. Berkely affirms the same, yet never doubted the truth of Newton's Principia. S. T. C.

Stillingfleet, ORIGINES SACRÆ, *p. 253. Note continued on p. 254.*

The subject of this *Hypothesis* is that a *power* of *miracles* is the clearest *evidence* of a Divine *Testimony*, which will appear from these following *considerations*.

This seems mere trifling—for what is a miracle worked in a Desert? De rebus non exist[entibus] et non app[arentibus] eadem est ratio: and the true criterion of a miracle is not quomodo efficitur, sed quid efficit—in order to prove any important deduction, it must be shewn—1.

---

[9] "The upright, intrepid, and philosophical Historian of the Council of Trent." See Burnet, *Bedell*, p. 67.

[10] "To Mr. Justice Fletcher, Letter V," *Essays*, III, pp. 717-18.

---

[1] Edward Stillingfleet, *Origines Sacræ* (London: 1675). This book belonged to Thomas Poole. It is now in the British Museum, and these notes were transcribed from it. The notes were printed in the *Athenæum*, I (March 27, 1875), pp. 422-23, and reprinted for private circulation, Glasgow, 1875. The British Museum call number is C. 45. d. 35.

That God will not suffer any man to be deceived, however ignorant, but by his own wilful negligence, 2. That a false miracle may always be detected, but that a true miracle may not in after times be made to appear false by probable reasons—which, indeed, is involved in the former. I believe in the miracles of Christ because I believe *in* Christ; not vice versâ. They are not the foundation of my Faith, but the result & condition of it. The perception of Heat is no proof *de se* of the Sun; yet it could not be the Sun if it gave no Heat. It is a generic *condition*, not the differential specific *proof*, and this is indeed, the express doctrine of Scripture itself. S. T. C.

Stillingfleet, ORIGINES SACRÆ, *p. 253.*

> The *Devil* no question may, and doth often deceive the world, and may by the *subtility* and *agility* of his *nature,* perform such things as may amuse the *minds* of *men,* and sometimes put *them* to it, to find a *difference* between *them* and real miracles, if they only make their *senses* judges of them.

If Satan, as an invisible Spirit, should lift a man up to the Clouds, surrounding him with Light by his power as a Spirit, or God effect the same by his power as God, how are the Laws of Nature suspended more or less in one instance or the other? I speak it with reverence—yet, how many most learned & pious men have declared it impious to doubt of the former fact. See Dr. Hen. More on Atheism. It is a perilous and painful task for a man to find himself engaged by conscience & a zeal for Christian Truth in the confutation of an error when the error is of such a kind that it cannot be confuted but by adopting language & using arguments, which have been or may be used by an acute Infidel—altho' it is the Error which gives to the Infidel's arguments *all* their strength, & to his general system it's sole plausibility. S. T. C.

Stillingfleet, ORIGINES SACRÆ, *p. 255 (translating Tertullian).*

> They [the devils] *first possess the bodies themselves . . . and affect it with various distempers, afterwards upon using the strange remedies prescribed by Æsculapius, they forsake their station, and the person is cured.*

I ask any and every modern *rational Divine* of the Church of England, and of the School of Tillotson & Paley, does he believe that every statue of Æsculapius had an inspiring Devill? And if he says no! what does he think of Tertullian? and yet, if such a passage had been found in St. Paul—yes! he could reply—but the Doctrines, the occasions, &c. Well! this is just what I say, with Bishop Hall—That to us the doctrine must prove the Miracle, not the M. the D.

Stillingfleet, ORIGINES SACRÆ, *p. 329.*[2] *Note continued on pp. 330-31.*

Lactantius excellently manifests that *Philosophy* could never do so much *good* in the *world* as *Christianity* did, because that was not *suited* at all to *common capacities,* and did require so much *skill* in the *Arts* to prepare *men* for it, which it is impossible all should be well *skilled* in, who yet are as capable of being *happy,* as any others are. And yet how *inefficacious* the *precepts* of *Philosophy* were, appears by the *Philosophers* themselves.

Cannot the Philosophers quote as many instances as can reasonably be expected from men who did not make plebeian Sects? And are not the lives of nominal Xtians as offensive to Xtianity, as those of nominal Philosophers to Philosophy? And is not the number in each proportionate to that of the Professors? Nay! are there not more bad Christians in proportion? Why? because the very habits of Speculation remove men farther from Temptation, or disarm it. This is not meant as an argument in favour of Philos. against Xtnty; but to overthrow its dangerous enemy, false Reasoning in it's favour. And why is Philosophy for ever to be set up as the Rival rather than as the Friend & natural Companion of Christianity? What is Xtianity but divine & preeminent Philosophy, a stream, in whose depths the Elephant may *swim,* and in whose practical & saving Truths the Lamb may *ford?* Besides, who shall dare say of yon river, such and such a wave came from such and such a fountain? What Scholar (& by scholars the vulgar are taught) shall say—Such a conviction, such a moral feeling, I received from St. John, such and such from Seneca, or Epictetus? S. T. C.

Stillingfleet, ORIGINES SACRÆ, *p. 438. Note continued on p. 439.*

Though God be *essentially* and *necessarily good,* yet the *communications* of this *goodness* are the effect of his *Will,* and not meerly of his *nature.*

Well! but is not the *Will* of God identical with his Nature? Is it not naturally good or beneficent? Is there in Eternity a distinguishable moment, that one moment should possibly be preferred to another? And where is the danger to Religion, if we make preservation a perpetual creation, & interpret the first words of Genesis as we must do (if not Socinians) the first words of St. John—From all eternity God created the Universe—And the Earth became waste & void &c.? It might have been a Comet—it might have been, as to its whole surface, ruined by a Comet. It is a rule of infinite importance that the Scriptures always speak, not *ad rem in seipsâ sed quoad hominem.* It is a moral & religious, not a physical, revelation, & in order to render us good moral agents, not accurate natural speculators, to make us know ourselves & our rela-

[2] In the *Athenæum* the page reference for this note is given as 320.

tions both present & future, not to make us knowing in nature—without industry or intellectual exercitation. S. T. C.

Stillingfleet, Origines Sacræ, *p. 473 [quoting Epicurus].*

The Blessed and Immortal Being, neither hath any imployment himself nor troubles himself with others.

I cannot but suspect that Epicurus meant by this only a Sneer at the Anthropomorphitic Gods. You allow, that Jupiter is the King of Gods, the Supreme God—now such a Being as you believe Jupiter, would be wearied & disgusted under such constant occupations. No doubt, Epicurus was in toto an *Atheist.*

Stillingfleet, Origines Sacræ, *p. 521 [translating Claudian].—*

Rufinus' death doth clear the Gods, and set
My mind at ease.

More than all I admire the *force & elegance* of the Bishop's Translation. He would have been a *dead hand* at a Travesty.

Stillingfleet, Origines Sacræ, *p. 540.*

I grant as far as the *Flood extended,* all these were destroyed; but I see no reason to extend the *destruction* of these byond that *compass* and *space* of *earth* where man inhabited.

The Author forgets that fluids must find their level—and that Water overspreading the whole of Asia 40 feet above the highest mountains must necessary [*sic*] have been at an equal height every where, except as far as the Moon & the Equator act & counteract.

Stillingfleet, Origines Sacræ, *p. 543.*

. . . many causes concurred to the making of this *Deluge;* first, the air was *condensed* into *clouds,* and those fell down with continued force and violence, not breaking into drops, but all in a body . . .

Excellent Chemist! if he can turn air into water, why not rather turn earth? It is nearer at hand.

Stillingfleet, Origines Sacræ, *p. 544.*

For, as that judicious Historian, Sir *W. Rawleigh* observes . . . take then the highest mountain of the World, *Caucasus, Taurus, Teneriff,* or any other, and I do not find saith he, that the highest exceeds thirty miles in *height.*

!—3½. Thirty miles! Is the man mad? The highest point of the Andes is not 4. Sir W. R. must have confounded the *Height* of a mountain with the Length of a made road up it's summit. Thus Etna is about 2 miles high—the road from it's base to the crater about 35.

Stillingfleet, ORIGINES SACRÆ, *p. 552.*

So that if we take a *perch* to contain 10 *Hebrew cubits* . . . the whole capacity of the *Ark* will be about 450 cubical perches.

I have seen many calculations as to the *capacity* of the Ark; but none as to it's Tonnage & Burthen. A Ship may contain some million pounds of quicksilver—can it *carry* as much?

Stillingfleet, ORIGINES SACRÆ, *p. 552.*

Sir *W. Rawleigh* gives a prudent *caution,* that men ought not to take *animals* of a *mixt nature,* as Mules or *Hyænas,* nor such as differ in size and shape from each other as the *Cat* of *Europe* and Ownce of *India,* into the several *species* of *animals.*

What! did Sir W. R. believe that a male & female ounce (& if so, why not 2 Tigers, & Lions, &c?) would have produced in course of generations a Cat—or a Cat a Lion? This is Darwinizing[3] with a vengeance. By this mode of reasoning he might have reduced Noah's Sto-[wage] to at most half a dozen, so beautiful is the gradation of the species & genera of animals from men to mice.

Daniel Waterland

He spoke of Dr. Channing. It was an unspeakable misfortune that he should have turned out a Unitarian after all. On this, he burst into a declamation on the folly and ignorance of Unitarianism,—its high unreasonableness; and taking up Bishop Waterland's book, which lay on the table, he read with vehemence two or three pages written by himself in the fly-leaves,—passages too, which, I believe, are printed in the "Aids to Reflection."[1]

In my Marginal MSS Notes on Waterland's Vindication &c. I have taken occasion to show the great inconveniences, to which the Fathers of the Church from Justin Martyr to Augustine exposed that Truth of Truths by substituting the Formula of the *Trias* for that of the *Tetractys*—merging the Prothesis in the Thesis & confounding the

---

[3] Dr. Erasmus Darwin is referred to.

---

[1] R. W. Emerson, *English Traits* (Boston: 1885), p. 14.

identity and Ipseity—ὁ δεός trans-articulan [John 1.18] with the ὁ ϑεός, the Father.[2]

Bull and Waterland are the classical writers on the Trinity.[3]

L'Abbé Claude Fluerry, ECCLESIASTICAL HISTORY, *trans. by H. Herbert (London: 1728), II, 52.*

Besides, the question which they here treat as trifling was nothing less than to determine whether JESUS CHRIST was God or a creature.

A very just remark of the Abbés. No one has shown the vital importance of this controversy with more force and evidence than our own Dr. Waterland.[4].

Waterland, VINDICATION.[5] *Note on blank pasted on cover and continued on flyleaves 1, 2, and 3, recto; titleleaf, verso; margins of first three pages of the Preface.*

It would be no easy matter to find a tolerably competent Individual who more venerates the writings of Waterland than I do, and long *have* done. But still in how many pages do I not find reason to regret, that the Total Idea of the 4 = 3 = 1,—of the adorable Tetractys, eternally self-manifested in the Triad, Father, Son, and Spirit,—was never in it's cloudless Unity present to him. Hence both he, & Bishop Bull too often treat it as a peculiarity of positive Religion, which is to be cleared of all *contradiction* to Reason, & then, thus *negatively* qualified, to be actually received by an act of the mere Will; Stet pro Ratione Voluntas. Now, I affirm that the article of the Trinity *is* Religion, *is* Reason, and the universal Formula of all Reason—& that there neither is nor can be, *any* Reasons, any Religion, but what is or is an expansion of the Truth of the Trinity. In short, that all other pretended Religions, Pagan or pseudo-Christian (ex. gr. Sabellian, Arian, Socinian) are in themselves *Atheism,* tho' God forbid, I should call or even think the men so denominated Atheists. I affirm a Heresy often, but never dare denounce the Holder an *Heretic.* S. T. Coleridge. On this ground only can it be

[2] Notebook, New Series, No. 52, p. 29. Printed for the first time.
[3] July 8, 1827. *Table Talk S,* VI, 289.
[4] This note is printed by the kind permission of the Harvard College Library.
[5] Daniel Waterland, *A Vindication of Christ's Divinity* (Cambridge: 1719). The notes selected for re-editing have been taken from the original notes in the volume formerly in the library of Lord Coleridge and now in the British Museum. Several notes are new; others have been corrected. Cf. *Lit. Rem.,* IV, 221-41. Coleridge refers to the first note and sums it up in Notebook 52, fol. 13-14 recto, saying, ''Here let follow my MSS note on the blank side of the title-page of Waterland's Vindication. . . .''

made comprehensible, how any honest & commonly intelligent man can
withstand the proofs & sound logic of Bull & Waterland—that they
failed in the first place to present the *Idea* itself of the great Doctrine,
which they so ably advocated. Take *myself*, S. T. C., as a humble Instance. I was never so befooled as to think that the Author of the 4th
Gospel or that St. Paul ever taught the Priestleyan Psilanthropism, or
that Unitarianism (presumptuously, nay absurdly, so called) was the
doctrine of the New Testament generally. But during the 16 months of
my aberration from the Catholic Faith, I presumed that the tenets of the
Divinity of Jesus, the Redemption, &c. were irrational and that what
was contradictory to the Reason, could not have been revealed by the
Supreme Reason. As soon as I discovered that these doctrines were not
only consistent with Reason, but themselves *very Reason,* I returned at
once to the literal interpretation of the Scripture—& to the Faith.
S. T. C.

The Will = the absolute subjectively.

Mem. Every Generation has it's one or more overrated men.—Dr.
Johnson in George the Third's—Dr. S. Clark in George the First's—
Lord Byron being the star[6] now in the ascendant.

In all religious and moral use of the word, God, taken absolutely
(i.e. not *a* God or *the* God, but God), a *relativity,* a *distinction* in kind
ab aliquo[7] quod non est Deus, is so *essentially* implied, that it is a matter
of perfect indifference, whether we assert a World without God, or make
God the World. The one is as truly Atheism as the other. In fact, for all
moral and practical purposes, they are the same position, differently
expressed—whether I say, God is the World, or the World is God, the
inevitable conclusion, the sense and *import* is—there is no other God
than the World, i. e. there is no other *meaning* to the term, God. Whatever you may mean by, or choose to believe of the *World,* that and that
alone you mean by or believe of *God.* Now I very much question
whether in any other sense Atheism, i. e. speculative Atheism, is possible
—for even in the Lucretian coarsest & crudest scheme of the Epicurean
Doctrine a hylozoism, a *potential* life, is clearly implied, and in the celebrated "lene clinamen" becoming actual—Bravadoes[8] articulating breath
into a blasphemy of Nonsense, to which they themselves attach no connected meaning & the wickedness of which is alone intelligible, there
may be, but a La Place, a La Grange, would & with justice, resent and
repeal the imputation of a belief in Chance, or a denial of Law, Order,
and Self-balancing Life and Power in the World. Their error is, that

[6] Coleridge first wrote "Idol" and then deleted it.
[7] *Lit. Rem.,* "omni."
[8] *Lit. Rem.,* "Desperadoes."

they make them the proper, underived attributes *of* the World. It follows then, that Pantheism = Atheism and that there is no other Atheism actually existing or speculatively conceivable, but Pantheism. Now I hold demonstrable, that a consistent Socinianism following it's own consequences must come to Pantheism, and in ungodding their Saviour goddify Cats and Dogs, Fleas and Frogs, &c. &c. There is, there can be, no medium between the Catholic Faith (Trinitarianism) and *Atheism* disguised in the self-contradictory term, Pantheism: for every thing God, and no God are identical positions.

Waterland, VINDICATION, *Query II, p. 43. Note on end-pages and top of p. 43.*

> As Son of God, He was really God; and as *Son* of the Almighty, He was *Almighty,* in his *own right,* as *Tertullian* expresses it: And therefore might as justly bear the Stile and Title of *Lord God, God of Abraham,* . . . after he condescended to act in another and to discover his personal Relation.

And *why* did not Dr. Waterland, why did not his great Predecessor in the glorious Controversy, Bishop Bull, contend for a revisal of our law-established Version of the Bible; but especially of the New Testament? Either the unanimous belief and testimony of the 5 or 6 first Centuries, grounded on the elevated declarations of John, Paul, & the Writer of the Epistle to the Hebrews, were erroneous or at best doubtful —& then why not wipe them off? Why these references to them?—Or else they were (as I believe, & both Bull & Waterland believed) the *very truth*—& then why continue the translation of the Hebrew into English at second hand thro' the medium of the Septuagint? Have we not adopted the Hebrew word, *Jehovah?* Is not then κύριος, i. e. Lord, of the Septuagint a Greek Substitute in countless instances for *Jehovah?* Why not then restore the *original* Word? And both in the Old Testament religiously render Jehovah by *Iehovah,* & every text of the New Testament referring to the Old by the Hebrew Word in the Text referred to? Had this been done, Socinianism would have been scarcely possible.

Why? I will tell you WHY. Because that great Truth, in which is contained all treasures & all possible knowlege was still *opake* even to Bull & Waterland—because the *Idea* itself—that Idea idearum, the one substratum Truth which is the Form, *Measure,* and Involvement of all Truths, was never present to them in it's entireness, Unity, and transparency. They most ably vindicated the doctrine of the Trinity, *negatively,* against the charge of positive irrationality. With equal ability they shewed the contradictions, nay the Absurdities involved in the rejection of the same by a professed Christian. They demonstrated the utter unscriptural and contra-Scriptural nature of Arianism, and of Sabellianism & Socinianism.

But the self-evidence of the Truth, as a universal of the Reason, as the Reason itself, as a *Light* which revealed itself by it's own essence as Light, this they had not had vouchsafed to them. Strange, how little use has been made of that profound and most pregnant Text, v. 18 of Chap. 1. of John's Gospel.[9]

Waterland, VINDICATION, *Query XV, pp. 227-28. Note continued on pp. 229-33.*

It is an usual Thing with many (Moralists may account for it), when they meet with a difficulty which They cannot readily answer, immediately to conclude that the Doctrine is False; and to run directly into the opposite Perswasion; not considering that They may meet with much more weighty Objections there, than before; or that They may have reason sufficient to maintain and believe many Things in *Philosophy* or *Divinity,* tho' They cannot answer every Question which may be started, or every Difficulty which may be raised against them.

O, if Bull and Waterland had been first Philosophers, and then Divines, instead of being first, *manacled,* or say *articled* Clerks of a Guild —if the clear free intuition of the Truth had led them to the Article, & not the Article to *the defence* of it as not proved to be *false,* how different would have been the result! Now we only feel the inconsistency of Arianism, not the *Truth* of the doctrine attacked. Arianism is confuted—and so, that I will not reject orthodoxy for these reasons. It *may* still be true. But that it *is* true, because the Arians have hitherto failed to prove it's falsehood, is no logical conclusion. The Unitarian may have better luck; or if he fail, the Deist.

Waterland, VINDICATION, *Query XVI, p. 234.*

But God's *Thoughts are not our Thoughts.*

i. e. as I would interpret the text—the *Ideas* in and by which God reveals himself to Man, are not the same with, and are not to be judged by, the *Conceptions* which the Human Understanding generalizes from the notices of the *Senses,* common to man & the Animals (Dog, Elephant, Beaver &c.) endowed with the same Senses. Therefore I regard this § ph. p. 233, 234, as a specimen of admirable special Pleading *ad hominem,* in the Court of Eristic Logic, but condemn it, as a wilful Resignation, or temporary self-deposition, of the Reason. I will *not* suppose, what my

---

[9] In *Lit. Rem.* this comment from top of p. 43 was transferred to the notes on Query XIX. See IV, 234.

Reason declares to be no *position* at all, & therefore an impossible *Subposition.*

Waterland, Vindication, *Query XVI, pp. 235-36.*

> Let us keep to the *Terms* we began with; lest by the changing of Words we make a change of *Ideas,* and alter the very state of the Question.

This misuse, or rather this omnium-gatherum Expansion & consequent extenuation of the word, Idea, and Ideas, may be regarded as a Calamity inflicted by Mr. Lock on the Reigns of Wm. IIIrd., Queen Anne, & the two first Georges. S. T. C.

Waterland, Vindication, *Query XVI, pp. 237-38. Note continued on pp. 238-40.*

> *Sacrifice* was one instance of Worship required under the Law; and it is said;—*He that Sacrificeth unto any God, save unto the Lord only, He shall be utterly destroyed,* Exod. 22. 20. Now suppose any person, considering with Himself that only *absolute* and *soveraign* Sacrifice was *appropriated* to God, by this Law, should have gone and *sacrificed* to other Gods, and have been convicted of it before the Judges. The Apology He must have made for it, I suppose, must have run thus: "Gentlemen, tho' I have sacrificed to other Gods, yet, I hope you'l observe, that I did it not *absolutely:* I meant not any *absolute* or *supreme* Sacrifice (which is all that the Law forbids) but *relative* and *inferior* only. I regulated my *Intentions* with all imaginable care; and my *esteem* with the most critical Exactness. I *consider'd* the other Gods, whom I sacrificed to, as *inferior* only, and *infinitely* so; reserving all *soveraign* Sacrifice to the *supreme* God of *Israel.*" This, or the like Apology must, I presume, have brought off the Criminal with some applause for his Acuteness, if your Principles be true. Either you must allow this, or you must be content to say, that not only *absolute supreme* Sacrifice (if there be any Sense in that Phrase), but *all Sacrifice* was, by the Law, *appropriate* to God only &c. &c.

How was it possible for an Arian to answer this? But it was impossible; and Arianism was extinguished by Waterland, but in order to the increase of Socinianism; & this, I doubt not, Waterland foresaw. He was too wise a man to suppose that the exposure of the folly & falsehood of one *form* of Infidelism would cure or prevent Infidelity. Enough! that he made it more bare-faced—I might say, *bare-breeched,* for modern Unitarianism is the *Sans cullotterie* of Religion.

Waterland, Vindication, *Query XVI, p. 239.*

> You may imagine that Acts of *religious* Worship are to derive their Signification and Quality, from the *intention* and *meaning* of the Worshippers: whereas the very reverse of it is the Truth.

Truly excellent. Let the Church of E. praise God for her Saints—a more glorious Calendar than Rome can shew!

WATERLAND, VINDICATION, *Query XVI, p. 251.*

The Sum then of the case is this: If the Son could be included as being *uncreated,* and very God; as *Creator, Sustainer, Preserver* of all Things, and one with the Father; then He might be worship'd upon their [the Ante-Nicene Fathers'] Principles, but otherwise could not.

Every where in this invaluable Writer I have to regret the absence of a distinct *Idea* of the ı AM, as the *proper* Attribute of the FATHER: & hence, the ignorance of the proper Jehovaism of the Son—& hence while we worship the Son together with the Father, yet that we *pray* to the Father only, thro' the Son.

Waterland, VINDICATION, *Query XVII, p. 254. Note continued on p. 255.*

And we may never be able perfectly to comprehend the Relations of the three Persons, *ad intra,* amongst themselves; the ineffable Order and Oeconomy of the ever-blessed Co-eternal Trinity.

Comprehend? No! For how can any Spiritual Truth be comprehended? Who can *com*prehend his own Will or his own Personëity (i. e. his "I")[10] or his own Mind, i. e. his Person, or his own *Life?* But we can distinctly *a*pprehend them.[11]

Waterland, VINDICATION, *Query XVIII, p. 269. Note continued on pp. 270-71.*

From what hath been observed, it may appear sufficiently, that the divine Λόγος was our King, and our God long before; that He had the same Claim and Title to religious Worship that the Father Himself had; only not so distinctly reveal'd.

Here I differ *toto orbe* from W., and say with Luther and Zinzendorf, that before the Baptism of John the Logos alone had been distinctly revealed; & that first in Christ He declared himself a Son, viz. the co-eternal only-begotten Son, and then revealed the Father. Indeed the want of the *Idea* of the 1 = 3 could alone have prevented Waterland from inferring this from his own Query II, p. 28 to p. 38 in this Volume. See MSS note at the end of the Book. S. T. C.

Waterland, VINDICATION, *Query XVIII, pp. 273-75.*

Again the want of the Idea. The Father *cannot* be revealed except in and tho' the Son, his eternal Exegesis. The contrary position is an

[10] In *Lit. Rem.* the pronoun is given as "I-ship" followed by "(Ichheit)." Also, two more sentences are given there.

[11] Two more sentences are added in *Lit. Rem.,* IV, 232. These are adapted from p. 308.

absurdity. The Supreme Will, indeed the Absolute Good knoweth *himself* as the Father, but the Act of Self-Affirmation, the ɪ ᴀᴍ in that ɪ ᴀᴍ, is not a manifestation *ad extra*, not an ἐξήγησις.

Waterland, VINDICATION, *Query XIX, p. 279. Note continued on pp. 280-83.*

> That the Father (whose Honour had been sufficiently secured under the *Jewish* Dispensation, and could not but be so under the *Christian* also) being as much concern'd for the *Honour* of his Son, had been pleased to commit *all Judgment* to Him . . .

Here again! This contradiction of Waterland to his own principles is continually recurring; yea, and in one place he involves the very Tritheism, of which he was so victorious an Antagonist, viz. that the Father is Jehovah, the Son Jehovah, and the Spirit Jehovah—thus making Jehovah either a mere synonime of *God*, whereas he himself rightly renders it, ὁ ὤν which St. John every where (and St. Paul no less) makes the *peculiar* name of the Son—μονογενὴς υἱός, ὁ ὤν ἐν κόλπῳ τοῦ πατρός —or affirms the same absurdity, as if he had said the Father is the Son, and the Son, the Son, & the Holy Ghost the Son; yet there are not *three* Sons but *one* Son. S. T. C. N. B. ὁ ὤν is the *Verbal Noun* of ὅς ἔστι not of Ἐγὼ Εἰμί.

Waterland, VINDICATION, *Query XXI, pp. 307-8.*

> For, indeed, this Controversy, manag'd upon the Foot of meer Reason; terminates at length in that single Question, *Whether the Essence of God be above Comprehension, or no.*

One can neither assent to, or dissent from, this position of Waterland's without a strict definition of "to *com*prehend." The Idea, God, like all other *Ideas*, rightly so called and as contra-distinguished from "Conceptions" as not properly *above* Comprehension, as *alien* from it. It is = smelling, a sound.

Waterland, VINDICATION, *Query XXI, p. 316. Note continued on pp. 317-18.*

> The *Simplicity* of God is another Mystery . . . When we come to inquire, whether *all extension*, or *all plurality, diversity*, Composition of *Substance* and *Accident*, and the like, be consistent with it, then we discover how *confused* and *inadequate* our *Ideas* are.

Surely, the far larger part of these assumed difficulties rests on misapplication either of the *Senses* to the Sense, or of the Sense to the Understanding, or of the Understanding to the Reason—in short, on asking Images where only Theorems can be, or Theorems for Thoughts, (= Conceptions or Notions) or lastly, Conceptions for *Ideas*. S. T. C.

Waterland, VINDICATION, *end of Query XXXI, p. 488.*

Without detraction from the inestimable Services of the Fathers from Tertullian to Augustin, respecting the fundamental Articles of the Christian Faith; yet commencing from the 5th Century, I dare claim for the Reformed Church of England the honorable Name of the Ἀρχασπιστής of Trinitarianism, and the foremost Rank among the Churches, Roman or Protestant. The Learned R. Catholic Divines themselves admit this, & make a merit of the reluctance with which they neverthless admit it, in respect of Bp. Bull.

Waterland, VINDICATION, *note on back board.*

In all important controversies let the Terms be predisposed *negatively*, i. e. exclude and preclude all that is *not* meant—and then the *positive* meaning, i. e. what *is* meant, will be the Result—the post- Definition, which is at once the Definition and the *Impletion*, the Circumference and the Area.

I admit however that Dr. Waterland has done good service in reducing the controversy to the question—Shall we accept the Homoüsian Doctrine? Or reject the Christian Scriptures & the Tradition of the Church, as the Rule of our Faith?[12]

Waterland, IMPORTANCE,[13] *chap. i, p. 18.*

> It is the Property of the Divine Being to be unsearchable: And if he were not so, he would not be *divine*. Must we therefore reject the most certain Truths concerning the *Deity*, only because they are *incomprehensible*, when every thing almost belonging to him must be so of course?

It is strange, that so sound, so admirable a Logician as Waterland, should have thought "unsearchable" & "incomprehensible" synonimous or at least equivalent terms! & this, tho' St. Paul hath made the privilege of the full-grown Christian "to search out the deep things of God himself."

Waterland, IMPORTANCE, *chap. iv, p. 123.*

> As soon as the miraculous gifts, or gift of discerning spirits, ceased.

I know of no one point in the New Testament that perplexes me as much as these (so-called) 'miraculous gifts.' I feel a *moral* repugnance to the reduction of them to natural and acquired talents, ennobled and made energetic by the *life* and convergency of faith; and yet on

---

[12] This comment does not appear in *Lit. Rem.*

[13] *The Importance of the Doctrine of the Holy Trinity* (1734). The volume with the original notes is in the British Museum, C. 43. b. 24. With a few omissions and some changes in editing the notes are printed in *Lit. Rem.*, IV, 241-58. The notes selected for reproduction here are from the original MS.

no other scheme can I reconcile them with the idea of Christianity, or the particular supposed, with the general *known* parts. But, thank God! it is a question that does not in the least degree *affect our faith* or practice. But I mean, if God permit, to go through the Middletonian controversy as soon as I can procure the loan of the book, or have health enough to become a reader at the British Museum.

Waterland, IMPORTANCE, *chap. iv, p. 26.*

> And what if, after all, *spiritual* censures (for of such only I am speaking) should happen to fall upon such a Person, he may be in some measure hurt in his *Reputation* by it, and that is all: And possibly hereupon his Errors before *invincible* through Ignorance, may be removed by wholesome *Instruction* and *Admonitions,* and so he is befriended in it.

Dr. Waterland is quite in the Right, so far; but the penal Laws, the *temporal* inflictions—would he have called for the Repeal of these? Milton saw this Subject with a mastering Eye—saw that the aweful power of Excommunication was degraded and weakened even to impotence by any of the least connection with the Law of the State.

Waterland, IMPORTANCE, *chap. vi, p. 257. Note continued on p. 258.*

> *And the light shineth in darkness, and the darkness cometh not upon it.* So I render the Verse, conformable to the rendering of the same *Greek* Verb, by our Translators, in another place in the same Gospel. The Apostle, as I conceive, in this fifth Verse of his first Chapter, alludes to the prevailing Error of the Gnostics.

O sad! sad! How must the Philosopher have been eclipsed by the shadow of antiquarian erudition, in order that a mind like Waterland's could have sacrificed the profound universal import of "comprehend" to an allusion to a worthless dream of heretical nonsense, the mushroom of the Day! Had W. ever thought of the relation of his own Understanding to his Reason? But alas! the identification of these two *diversities*— of how many errors has it been the ground & occasion!

Waterland, IMPORTANCE, *chap. vi, p. 259.*

I still cannot but feel that [in] Waterland's anxiety to show the anti-heretical force of John's Gospel & Epistles, he has overlooked their Catholicity, their applicability to all countries, all times—the truth, independently of all temporary accidents & errors—which Catholicity alone constitutes their claim to Canonicity—i. e. to be *Canonical, inspired* writings.

Waterland, IMPORTANCE, *chap. vi, p. 268. Note continued on p. 270.*

It grieves me to think that such giant archaspistæ of the Catholic Faith, as Bull and Waterland, should have clung to the intruded Gloss

[I John v. 7] which in opulence and continuity of the Evidences, as displayed by their own *Master*-minds, would have [been] *superfluous*— had it not been worse than superfluous—viz. senseless in itself, and interruptive of the profound sense of the Apostle.

Waterland, IMPORTANCE, *chap. vi, p. 292.*

> Le Clerc would appear to doubt, whether the Persons pointed to in *Justin*, really denied Christ's *divine Nature* or no. It is as plain as possible that they did.

No, No! Le Clerc is no favorite of mine: and Waterland is a prime Favourite. Nevertheless, in this instance, I too doubt with Le Clerc, & more than doubt.

Waterland, IMPORTANCE, *chap. vi, p. 387.*

> Quoting Whitby: "In such Doctrines as were rejected by the *universal Church* as *Heresies, Austin* saith truly, that it was sufficient Cause to reject them."

It would be of use, if some able & wise [———?] would explain and vindicate the term "the universal Church" against the plausible tho' sophisticated argument from the evidence of the Heretical churches themselves.

Waterland, IMPORTANCE, *chap. vii, p. 389.*

It is sufficient Reason for rejecting such *Novelties,* and *Interpretations* which they are founded upon, that the Christian World, in the best and purest Times, either knew nothing of them, or rejected them.

As excellent means of raising *a presumption* in the mind of the falsehood of Arianism & Socinianism, and thus of preparing the mind for a docile reception of the great *Idea* itself, I admit & value the testimonies from the writings of the early Fathers. But, alas! the increasing dimness, ending in the final want, of the *Idea* of this all-truths-including Truth of the Tetractys eternally manifested in the Triad—this, this is the ground & cause of all the main Heresies from Semi-Arianism recalled by Dr. S. Clark to the last setting ray of departing Faith in the necessitarian Psilanthropism of Dr. Priestly! S. T. C.

Waterland, IMPORTANCE, *chap. vii, p. 412 ff. Note on first end-page, recto.*

I cannot help thinking that Waterland's Defence of the Fathers aginst Barbeyrac, is below his great powers, and characteristic vigor of judgement. It is enough that the Fathers of the 3 first centuries were the Lights of their age & worthy of all reverence for their good gifts— but it appears to me impossible to deny their *credulity;* their *ignorance*

in the interpretation of the Old Testament, or their hardihood in asserting the truth of whatever they thought it for the interest of the Church,
& for the good of Souls, to have believed as true.   A whale swallowed
Jonas; but a believer in all the assertions & narrations of Tertullian and
Irenæus would be a more wonder-working Jonas, or John-Ass!   For he
must have swallowed Whales.   S. T. C.

Waterland, IMPORTANCE.   *Note opposite.*   A CRITICAL HISTORY OF THE
ATHANASIAN CREED *in the list of "Books printed for W. Innys and R.
Manley."*

How could W. the chosen Elisha, Scholar & compeer of Bishop Bull,
have even *tolerated* this blundering Creed of some red-hot Monk, who
understood the writings of the great Athanasian, just as much as Hun
[————?] & any Sinner Saved, understood St. Paul![14]

[14] This note does not appear in *Lit. Rem.* Printed for the first time.

SCIENCE

Science

INTRODUCTION

Coleridge's study of science has received little attention, but it plays an important part among his varied interests. Medicine first attracted him. During his school days his brother Luke came as a young surgeon to the London hospital, and on Saturdays Coleridge would follow him around the hospital absorbed in watching procedures. From this experience grew the desire to be apprenticed to a surgeon, and in preparation he read many books of medicine in both Latin and Greek.

His serious later concern with science grew out of his perception that some understanding of scientific principles was basic for either his projected epic or his system of philosophy. He lists the necessary scientific studies preliminary to writing an epic as "mathematics, mechanics, hydrostatics, optics, and astronomy, botany, metallurgy, fossilism, chemistry, geology, anatomy, medicine."[a]

He attended lectures by Dr. Beddoes, who, through the generosity of Tom Wedgwood, had established the Pneumatic Institute at Bristol. One of the attractions to Germany was that he might study chemistry and anatomy; and when he was at the University of Göttingen, he had the opportunity of hearing Blumenbach's lectures in biology. Upon his return to England, he frequently observed the experiments of Humphrey Davy, who had joined Beddoes, and together with Southey and Poole volunteered for the experiments with nitrous oxide.[b] After he moved to Keswick he wrote to Davy asking for suggestions for setting up a small chemical laboratory with William Calvert, saying, "You know how long, how ardently I have wished to initiate myself in chemical science."[c]

In his study of science Coleridge followed his usual method of approach to a subject by surveying what had previously been done. He pointed out the slow acceptance of the Copernican theory and the way in which the belief in alchemy had been retained by reputable scientists. He gave a concise account of the great scientific movements from the beginning of the seventeenth century, showing that in each era one con-

[a] Letter to Cottle, May, 1797. Turnbull, *Biog. Epist.*, I, 130-31.
[b] Letter to Poole, May 6, 1796. Turnbull, *Biog. Epist.*, I, 78.
[c] Feb. 3, 1801. Coleridge, E. H., *Letters*, I, 346.

trolling principle was looked upon as explaining all science. After Gilbert, for example, all things were explained by means of magnetic influence; then came the great developments in mathematics and everything was explained by the mechanic philosophy; this in turn was superseded by the dominance of chemistry, which ultimately gave way to that of electricity.

The individual scientists to whom he devoted special attention were Kepler and Newton. Pushing back to the source of principles, he argued that Kepler was the great originator of ideas which were only further developed by Newton. Even the law of gravity, always associated with Newton's name, had been "fully conceived" by Kepler.

Coleridge began his study of Newton with the *Optics* but said he was determined to understand all of Newton before he was thirty. It may have been the study of the *Optics* which sent him to Goethe, Schelling, Steffens, and Oken, all of whom had supported the theory of polarity in opposition to the Newtonian optics. The annotated works of these writers, now in the British Museum, give signposts along the road of Coleridge's developing thought. He was himself dissatisfied wtih Newton's work; and adopting the theory of polarity, undertook to advance the work in light and color. His contribution in this field cannot be appraised until the unpublished notebooks and certain philosophical letters, especially those to Tulk, become available for comparative study with the marginalia referred to above.

In the light of modern research it is especially interesting to find that Coleridge warned against attempting to solve the mystery of life itself and especially stressed the danger of the encroachment of science on alien territory.

GENERAL COMMENTS

I have noticed two main evils in philosophizing. The first is, the absurdity of demanding proof for the very facts which constitute the nature of him who demands it—a proof for those primary and unceasing revelations of self-consciousness, which every possible proof must pre-suppose; reasoning, for instance, pro and con, concerning the existence of the power of reasoning. Other truths may be ascertained; but these are certainty itself, (all at least which *we* mean by the word) and are the measure of every thing else which we deem certain. The second evil is that of mistaking for such facts mere general prejudices, and those opinions that, having been habitually taken for granted, are dignified with the name of COMMON SENSE. Of these, the first is the more injurious to the *reputation,* the latter more detrimental to the *progress* of philosophy. In the affairs of common life we very properly appeal to common sense; but it is absurd to reject the results of the microscope from the negative testimony of the naked eye. Knives are sufficient for the table and the market,—but for the purposes of science we must dissect with the lancet.

As an instance of the latter evil, take the truly powerful and active intellect, Sir Thomas Brown, who, though he had written a large volume in detection of vulgar errors, yet peremptorily pronounces the motion of the earth round the sun, and consequently the whole of the Copernican system, unworthy of any serious confutation, as being manifestly repugnant to *Common Sense:* which said *Common Sense,* like a miller's scales, used to weigh gold or gases, may, and often does, become very gross, though unfortunately not very uncommon, nonsense.[1]

And every man now can say, ''Common sense dictates to us that the small speck we call this earth is not the centre of the whole universe round which the other stupendous bodies move, but itself goes round the larger orb; and this to an extent to which we are unaware.'' This we are almost all taught. You will scarcely find a person in this country ignorant of the truth of what was thought such uncommon sense, even absurd, in a time so recent as that of Charles the second, so that Sir Thomas Browne, one of the ablest men of the age, declared it to be such uncommon nonsense that it was a proof there was no idea so absurd but some philosopher had taught it. This has become the common sense of the village, and of the cottage. Such is the protruded state of progression in society, and it applies not only to thoughts but to words, which on all occasions a man may observe.[2]

There is a similar, but still more intolerant and contemptuous anathema of the Copernican System in Sir T. Brown, almost two centuries later than Luther. Tho' the Problem is of no difficult solution for reflecting minds, yet for the Reading Many it would be a serviceable Work to bring together and exemplify the Causes of the extreme and universal credulity, that characterizes sundry periods of History (ex. gr., from A. D. 1400 to 1650)—and credulity involves Lying and Delusion—for by a seeming paradox Liars are always credulous, tho' credulous persons are not always Liars. *Most often tho'.*

It would be worth while to make a collection of the judgments of

[1] Southey, *Omniana,* I, 305-7. Cf. *Table Talk A,* pp. 371-72.
[2] Philosophical Lecture VI, Jan. 25, 1819. Coburn, *Phil. Lect.,* pp. 200-1.

eminent men in their generation respecting the Copernican or Pythagorean scheme. One writer (I forget the name) inveighs against it as Popery, and a Popish stratagem to reconcile the minds of men to Transubstantiation and the Mass. For if we may contradict the evidence of our senses in a matter of natural philosophy, *a fortiori*, or much more, may we be expected to do so in a matter of faith.[3]

Kepler and Newton, substituting the idea of the infinite, for the conception of a finite and determined world, assumed in the Ptolemaic Astronomy, superseded and drove out the notion of a one central point or body of the Universe: and finding a centre in every point of matter, and an absolute circumference no where, explained at once the unity and the distinction that co-exist throughout the creation by focal instead of central bodies, the attractive and restraining power of the sun or focal orb in each particular system, supposing and resulting from an actual power, present in all and over all, throughout an indeterminable multitude of systems—and this, demonstrated as it has been by science, and verified by observation, we rightly name the true system of the heavens.[4]

It is a wonderful property of the human mind, that when once a momentum has been given to it in a fresh direction, it pursues the new path with obstinate perseverance, in all conceivable bearings, to its utmost extremes. And by the startling consequences of this blind confidence it is first awakened to a sense of its error, and then it either falls back on its former position or receives some new impulse, which it follows with the same eagerness, and admits to the same monopoly.
. . . The idea of a true natural philosophy, by the convergence of the speculative and the practical to a common apex, was evolved by the genius of our BRITISH PLATO; the principles of observation and the

[3] Luther's *Table Talk* (London: 1652), chap. lxx, p. 503. British Museum, Ashley, 4773. "I am now advertised (said *Luther*) that a new Astrologer is risen, who presumeth to prove that the earth moveth and goeth about, not the Firmament the Sun Moon nor the Stars, like as when one sitteth in a Coach or in a Ship and is moved, thinketh he sitteth still and resteth, but the earth and trees go, run and move themselves. Therefore thus it goeth, when we give up ourselves to our own foolish fancies and conceits. This fool will turn the whole art of astronomy upside-down, but the Scripture showeth and teacheth him another lesson, when Joshua commanded the sun to stand still, and not the earth."
    The first paragraph of Coleridge's comment above is from Luther's *Table Talk;* I do not know the source of the second paragraph and have reprinted from *Lit. Rem.,* IV, 61-62.
    Another comment on Sir Thomas Browne's belief in the Ptolemaic astronomy is found in Field's *On the Church* (1628), chap. xxxii, p. 147. See Section on Field.
[4] *Church and State*, pp. 137-38.

means and conditions of legitimate experience unfolded; with the true nature and necessity of experiment as an organ of reason, not less distinguished from the blind or dreaming industry of the alchemists, than successfully opposed to the barren subtleties of the schoolmen.

But scarcely was the impulse given, ere the same propensity was betrayed; that of reducing all to the one that chanced to exercise a predominant attraction. Thus Gilbert, a richly gifted contemporary of Bacon, had no sooner investigated and multiplied the facts and phenomena of the magnet, but all things in "heaven and earth, and waters under the earth," were resolved into magnetic influences. Shortly after, a new light was struck by Harriott, followed up by Des Cartes and others; and the restoration of ancient geometry to its lawful rank and dignity, aided by the modern invention of algebra, transferred the ascendancy to the science of mechanics, which ended in placing the mechanical, or atomic philosophy, on the philosophic throne.

How widely the domination spread, and how long it continued (if, indeed, it can be said even now to have abdicated its pretensions), who needs be told, who is superficially acquainted with the history of philosophy during the last two centuries? The sublime discoveries of Kepler, perfected by Newton, with the no less fruitful than wonderful application of the higher mathethis to the movement of the celestial bodies, and to the laws of light, by the English philosopher, gave almost a religious sanction to the corpuscular system and mechanical theory. It became synonymous with philosophy itself—it was the sole portal at which truth was permitted to enter. The living body was considered as a hydraulic machine, the subjects of the medical art were explained, and its antidotes and operations justified, and too often directed by the laws of gravity and motion. Or, if chemistry was admitted to a share in the solution of the phenomena, and the suggestion of the remedies, it was a chemistry which, as far as its theory is concerned, was itself but a branch of mechanics, working exclusively by imaginary wedges, angles, and globes. In a book on "the Principles of Philosophy," by La Forge, an immediate disciple of Des Cartes (which, with other works of the same era, and no dissimilar contents, I happen to possess), the reader may see the phenomena of sleep at once solved and exhibited in a copperplate engraving, with all the figures which the blood-globules assume, squeezed or expanding, during their passage through tubes of varying diameter; and the results obtained by mathematical calculus, or demonstrated intuitively, *more geometrico,* by diagrams. In short, from the age of Des Cartes to that of Hartley and Le Sage, not only all external nature, but the subtlest mysteries of organisation, life—nay, of the intellect and moral being, were conjured within the magic circle of mechanical forces, and controlled by mathematical formula. By this time a new light had been struck, a new object of pursuit disclosed, by the discoveries in electricity; and it would be no very gross exaggeration to say, that the whole frame of natural philosophy was soon adjusted to electrical theories and electrical hypotheses. That these did not long retain the undivided attention of the age, was owing to the momentous discoveries that immediately followed: of the principal gases by Priestly and Scheele, the composition of water by Cavendish, and the doctrine of latent heat by Black. The scientific world was prepared for a new dynasty, though without avowedly withdrawing its allegiance from the former, *i. e.* the mechanic philosophy. Accordingly, as soon as Lavoisier had excited the expectation of reducing the infinite variety of chemical phenomena to the actions, re-agencies, and interchanges of a few elementary substances, the hope shot up almost instantly, and full of faith, that this had been effected. Henceforward, chemistry became the common road to all departments of knowledge.

It would betray either gross ignorance, or bigotry aggravated into ingratitude, to pretend that the new path so brilliantly opened had not been followed up with increasing splendour; or, to borrow the language of our Verulam, that its fructifying influence has not been in full proportion to its illuminating radiance. Least of all can a Briton, and a contemporary, forget for a moment what the glory of his country owes to the names of Davy, Wollaston, and Hatchett. But neither can he, as a faithful historian, fail to observe that the most momentous, the most truly philosophical discoveries and principles, have not been derived from the school of Lavoisier; nor can they be regarded as continuations of the mechanic system, or of a chemistry grounded on the corpuscular philosophy. And of this alone is it our purpose to speak. As little, too, can its exclusive tendency escape notice; the natural consequence of the enthusiasm with which it has been cultivated, and which, scarcely less than our political revolutions, characterise the spirit of the age.

Many and important are the improvements in all the provinces of physics, and the arts and sciences properly physical. But many likewise, and inauspicious, have been the inroads of the new conquerers into alien territories; and strange alterations have been attempted in homage to an art unsettled, in the very ferment of imperfect discoveries, and without a theory, or with a theory maintained only by toleration and compromise. Can a more striking proof be required than the fact that men of strong minds and undoubted talents have hoped, and repeatedly attempted to penetrate by the clue of chemical experiment, the secret recesses, the sacred adyta of organic life, without being aware that chemistry must needs be at its extreme limit when it has reached the threshold of a higher power.[5]

I have looked into a ponderous Review of the Corpuscular Philosophy by a Sicilian Jesuit, in which the acrimonious Father frequently expresses his doubt, whether he should pronounce Boyle or Newton more impious than *presumptuous*, or more presumptuous than impious. They had both attacked the reigning opinions on most important subjects, opinions sanctioned by the greatest names of antiquity, and by the general suffrage of their learned Contemporaries or immediate Predecessors. Locke was assailed with a full cry for his presumption in having deserted the philosophical system at that time generally received by the Universities of Europe; and of late years Dr. Priestly bestowed the epithets of *arrogant* and *insolent* on Reid, Beattie, &c., for presuming to arraign certain opinions of Mr. Locke, himself repaid in kind by many of his own countrymen for his theological novelties. It will scarcely be affirmed, that these accusations were all of them just, or that any of them were fit or courteous. Must we therefore say, that in order to avow doubt or disbelief of a popular persuasion without arrogance, it is required that the dissentient should know himself to possess the genius, and foreknow that he should acquire the reputation, of Locke, Newton, Boyle, or even of a Reid or Beattie?[6]

Isaac Newton

Galileo was a great genius, and so was Newton; but it would take two or three Galileos and Newtons to make one Kepler. It is in the order of Providence, that the inventive, generative, constitutive mind— the Kepler—should come first; and then that the patient and collective mind—the Newton—should follow, and elaborate the pregnant queries and illumining guesses of the former. The laws of the planetary system are, in fact, due to Kepler. There is not a more glorious achievement of scientific genius upon record, than Kepler's guesses, prophecies, and

[5] *Monologues*, pp. 622, 624-26. Cf. *Theory of Life*, pp. 28, 29-33 and Shedd, I, Appendix C. In these accounts there are some variations in wording, but the ideas are the same.

[6] *The Friend*, General Introduction, Essay IV, I, 39-40.

ultimate apprehension of the law of the mean distances of the planets as connected with the periods of their revolutions round the sun. Gravitation, too, he had fully conceived; but, because it seemed inconsistent with some received observations on light, he gave it up, in allegiance, as he says, to Nature. Yet the idea vexed and haunted his mind; *"Vexat me et lacessit,"* are his words, I believe.[7]

When, however, after a short interval, the Genius of Kepler, expanded and organized in the soul of Newton, and there (if I may hazard so bold an expression) refining itself into an almost celestial Clearness, had expelled the Cartesian Vortices, then the necessity of an active power, of positive forces present in the Material Universe, forced itself on the conviction. For as a Law without a Law-giver is a mere abstraction; so a *Law* without an Agent to realize it, a *Constitution* without an abiding Executive, is, in fact, not a Law but *an Idea!*[8]

In the system of gravity, Newton only developed the idea of Kepler. He advanced a step, and there he fixed his followers. Kepler would have progressed, or have been stationary in act at least.[9]

What a thing, what a living thing is not Shakespeare—and in point of real utility I look on Sir Isaac Newton as a very puny agent compared with Milton—and I have taken some pains with the comparison and disputed with transient conviction for hours together in favour of the former.[10]

Newton *was* a great man, but you must excuse me if I think that it would take many Newtons to make one Milton.[11]

My opinion is this—that deep Thinking is attainable only by a man of deep Feeling, and that all Truth is a species of Revelation. The more I understand of Sir Isaac Newton's works, the more boldly I dare utter to my own mind, & therefore to *you*, that I believe the Souls of 500 Sir Isaac Newtons would go to the making up of a Shakespere or a Milton. But if it please the Almighty to grant me health, hope,

[7] Oct. 8, 1830. *Table Talk S*, VI, 350-51.
[8] *Aids*, pp. 393-94. Cf. Shedd, I, 360-61.
[9] Allsop, *Letters*, I, 127.
[10] To Southey, Aug. 11, 1801. Griggs, *Unp. Letters*, I, 180.
[11] July 4, 1833. *Table Talk S*, VI, 469.

and a steady mind, (always the 3 clauses of my hourly prayers) before my 30th year I will thoroughly understand the whole of Newton's Works—at present, I must content myself with endeavouring to make myself entire master of his easier work, that on Optics. I am exceedingly delighted with the beauty and newness of his experiments, & with the accuracy of his *immediate* Deductions from them—but the opinions founded on these Deductions, and indeed his whole Theory is, I am persuaded, so exceedingly superficial as without impropriety to be deemed false. Newton was a mere materialist—*mind*, in his system is always passive,—a lazy Looker-on on an external World. If the mind be not *passive*, if it be indeed made in God's Image, & that too in the sublimest sense—the Image of the *Creator*—there is ground for suspicion, that any system built on the passiveness of the mind must be false, as a system.[12]

Even where, as in the Optics of Sir I. Newton, or rather in that part of the Newtonian optics which relates to colour, the premises are derived from experiment, the facts must have been proved before the scientific reasoning begins. In reference both to the process and to the result or product of science and as far as the knowledge is scientific, there is no difference in the character of the premises. Whether self evident, or the evident result of some other science grounded on self evident truths, or prepared for the occasion by observation, or experiment, the premises occupy the same place & exercise the same function as premises of a science. For if they were not (*expostulata* and *prœconcessa*) demanded on the one side & preconceded on the other, the science could not have commenced; it would have perished in birth.[13]

Sir Isaac Newton at the end of the last edition of his Optics, supposes that a very subtile & elastic fluid, which he calls æther, is diffused thro' the pores of gross bodies, as well as thro' the open spaces that are void of gross matter; he supposes it to pierce all bodies, and to touch their least particles, acting on them with a force proportional to their number or to the matter of the body on which it acts. He supposes likewise, that it is rarer in the pores of bodies than in open spaces, & even rarer in small pores and dense bodies, than in large pores and rare bodies; & also that its density increases in receding from gross matter;

[12] To Thomas Poole, March 23, 1801. British Museum, Add. MSS, 35,343, fol. 265 verso-266. Printed in *Letters*, I, 351-52.
[13] Coleridge, *On the Divine Ideas*, pp. 219-21. Printed for the first time by the kind permission of the Huntington Library from HM 8195.

so for instance as to be greater at the $\frac{1}{100}$ of an inch from the surface of any body, than at its surface; & so on. To the action of this æther he ascribes the attractions of gravitation & cohæsion, the attraction & repulsion of electrical bodies, the mutual influences of bodies & light upon each other, the effects & communication of heat, & the performance of animal sensation & motion. David Hartley from whom this account of æther is chiefly borrowed, makes it the instrument of propagating those vibrations or confygurative motions which are ideas. As it appears to me, no hypothesis ever involved so many contradictions: for how can the same fluid be both dense & rare in the same body at one time? yet in the Earth as gravitating to the Moon, it must be very rare; & in the Earth as gravitating to the Sun, it must be very dense. For, as Andrew Baxter well observes, it doth not appear sufficient to account how this fluid may act with a force proportional to the body to which another is impelled, to assert that it is rarer in great bodies than in small ones: it must be farther asserted that this fluid is rarer or denser in the same body, whether small or great, according as the body to which that is impelled is itself small or great. But whatever may be the solidity of this objection, the following seems unanswerable.

If every particle thro' the whole solidity of a heavy body, receive its impulse from the particles of this fluid, it should seem that the fluid itself must be as dense as the very densest heavy body, gold for instance; there being as many impinging particles in the one, as there are gravitating particles in the other which receive their gravitation by being impinged upon: so that, throwing gold or any heavy body upward, against the impulse of this fluid, would be like throwing gold *thro'* gold; and as this æther must be equally diffused over the whole sphere of its activity, it must be as dense when it impels cork as when it impels gold: so that to throw a piece of cork upward, would be as if we endeavoured to make cork penetrate a medium as dense as gold: & tho' we were to adopt the extravagant opinions which have been advanced concerning the progressions of pores, yet however porous we suppose a body, if it be not all pore, the argument holds equally; the fluid must be *as* dense as the body in order to give every particle its impulse.

It has been asserted that Sir Isaac Newtons philosophy leads in its consequences to Atheism; perhaps not without reason, for if matter by any powers or properties *given* to it, can produce the order of the visible world, & even generate thought; why may it not have possessed such properties by *inherent* right? & where is the necessity of a God? Matter is, according to the mechanic philosophy, capable of acting most wisely & most beneficently without consciousness of Wisdom or Benevolence; & what more does the Atheist assert? if matter could possess these properties, why might it not possess them from all eternity? Sir Isaac Newtons Deity seems to be alternately operose & indolent, to have delegated so much power as to make it inconceivable what he can have reserved. He is dethroned by Vice-regent second causes. We seem placed here to acquire a knowledge of *effects.* Whenever we would pierce into the *Adyta* of Causation, we bewilder ourselves— and all, that laborious Conjecture can do, is to fill up the gaps of Imagination. We are restless, because *invisible* things are not the objects of vision—and philosophical Systems, for the most part, are received not for their Truth, but in proportion as they give to Causes a susceptibility of being *seen,* whenever our visual organs shall have become sufficiently powerful.[14]

I am anxious to leave the specific objections of the Mathematicians to Goethe's Farbenlehre as far as it is an attack on the *assumptions* of Newton. To me, I confess, Newton's assumptions, first, of a *Ray* of Light, as a physical synodical *Individuum,* secondly that 7 specific individua are co-existent (by what copula?) in this complex yet divisible Ray; thirdly, that the Prism is a mere mechanic Dissector of this Ray; and lastly, that Light, as the common result, is = confusion; have always, and years before I ever heard of Goethe, appeared monstrous *Fictions!*[15]

Oken, L., Erste Ideen zur Theorie des Lichtes *(Jena: 1808), p. 14.*
Es ist nichts leichter, als *Newtons* Optik zu widerlegen, ohne allen Apparat, mit einigen Prismen von ganz gemeinen Glase, mit Linsen, gefärbtem Papier nebst einem finstern Zimmer ist alles abgethan; mehr aber wird erfodert, um die wahre Theorie des Lichtes durch Versuche zu beweisen, weil das Licht nicht in einem bloss mechanischen Brechen, Ablenken, Zerstreuen der Stralen besteht, sondern in einem chemischen Act, der bis ins Innerste der Materie wirkt und sie verändert, nicht etwas bloss durch Erwärmung, also Ausdehnung; sondern durch geistige Action durch Polarisirungen, aus denen chemische Änderungen hervorgehen. Ich spreche hier stark und hart aber nicht ungerecht gegen *Newton,* nur um die Gelehrten mit Ernst auf die bisher gänze Theorie des Lichtes aufmerksam zu machen. In der Folge werde ich *Newtons* Lehre ganz ruhig widerlegen.

Good heavens! how much more good would Oken have done, how much more both wit and wisdom would have been displayed, if instead

[14] This comment appears in the first edition of Southey's *Joan of Arc* but is transcribed from British Museum Add. MSS, 28,016, fol. 26 verso-29. Only the last paragraph is in Coleridge's hand; the remainder is in Southey's hand. The note is to *Joan of Arc,* II, 1. 34: "Their subtle fluids, impacts, essences."
[15] To Ludwig Tieck, July 4, 1817. Griggs, *Unp. Letters,* II, 201.

of this rough Railing and *d—n-your-eyes-you-lie* Ipsedixits, he had *begun* with this "quite quiet confutation of the Newtonian Doctrine," especially it being so very easy a task! Goethe (not indeed "*ganz ruhig*") had attempted it in detail both by impeachment of Newton's Experiments, and by Counter-experiments of his own. And yet G. himself confesses, that he had not succeeded in convincing or converting a single Mathematician, not even among his own friends and Intimates! That a clear and sober Confutation of Newton's Theory of Colors is practicable, the exceeding unsatisfied state, in which Sir I. Newton's first Book of Optics leaves my mind—strongly persuades me. And it is Oken's mountebank Boasting and Threatening that alone makes me sceptical as to his own ability to perform the promise, here given by him. S. T. C. P. S. I readily admit, that the full exhibition of another Theory adequate to the Sum of the Phænomena, and grounded on more safe and solid principles, would virtually be the best confutation—but no one who knows [left unfinished]

Oken, ERSTE IDEEN, *p. 40.*

Goethe, & then Schelling & Steffens, had opposed to the Newtonian Optics the ancient doctrine of Light and Shadow on the grand principle of Polarity—Yellow being the positive, Blue the negative, Pole, Red the Culmination and Green, the Indifference. Oken follows them—but stop! He waits till they are out of sight—Hangs out a new Banner (i. e. metaphors) and becomes a Leader himself.[16]

S. T. C.

de Boyer, KABBALISTISCHE BRIEFE, *IV, 114-15.*

In truth sage and wise Abukibak, the greatest Geometricians have been obliged to abandon in Physics their principal demonstration. We see for instance one example in Newton: although Geometry showed him the infinite divisibility of matter, as a Physicist he dared not acknowledge it; he felt what a repugnance he had to the divisibility of matter not stopping at a certain point. He admitted the atoms of Epicurus; and sustained that it was impossible to divide into several parts what had originally been made one by the disposition of God himself.

What philosophic mathematician ever supposed Geometry to be anything else, than a system of the conceivable and inconceivable in the mind's constructive Intuitions? It is *wholly* ideal. Newton's solid atoms are utter aliens from Geometry, in which the mind exclusively contemplates it's own energies; and *applies* them not otherwise, than hypothetically. Newton erred by introducing *Dogmatic Realism* into

[16] Comments printed for the first time from volume in the British Museum, c. 44. g. 4.(1).

the *Ideal World.* Solid atoms are not an *hypothesis,* as Gravity is; but a mere *Hypopoësis.*[17]

Various are the difficulties that oppose themselves to my comprehension of the Newtonian Theory of Comets. Some of these admit seemingly of a more natural solution on the Helvetian Hypothesis (= the old Aristotelian idea rectified and expanded by it's adaptation to the Copernican System) that the substance of Comets is meteoric and their curve of motion a parabola. For the moment, therefore, they throw some weight into the Helvetian Scale: tho' I have not the smallest doubt that all against all, the latter would kick the beam. Some of these difficulties relate to the facts of the disturbances of the cometary path by the attraction of the orbs, nearest which it must have passed, having been often *assumed,* but never *proved*—and vice versâ that the Comet, which passed so close to Jupiter and to one of the Jovial Satellites, had a *nucleus* calculated as equal in magnitude to Jupiter itself. The same Comet had an alarming Perihelium to our Moon. And yet neither the Jovial nor the Tellurial Satellite suffered the slightest perturbation. But this is of little comparative weight with me, being conscious that I have not enough mathematico-astronomical science to appreciate rightly the force or weakness of the Objection. I turn therefore to the physical phænomena, and here I cannot hesitate a moment in assigning the preference to your view of the Cauda, as a circumambient atmosphere of prodigious expansion, deriving it's apparent form and direction from it's relative position to the Sun and the solar radiance. But here too it is that I am puzzled—and namely by the following argument. If the vapor be self-luminous, and analogous to electric matter, the solution, in the form above stated at least, will no longer apply. The Solar Rays can in this case be causative of the direction, size and increased Splendor of the Tail &c., by *chemical excitement,* of which we have no proof or tenable analogy. On the other hand, that the phænomenon does somehow or other depend on the proximity of the Sun is a *matter of fact*—but if self-luminous, the very contrary *ought to* be the fact: and this will remain a most weighty objection to the *self-luminous* hypothesis, till some valid proof shall be given of an *evocative* action: the solar light not *constituting,* but *exciting* and *evolving,* the varying luminosity of the cometary atmosphere. And on this supposition the apparent position of the Tail must be the *real* one. If then to avoid this complex difficulty, I deny it's self-luminous nature

[17] Jean Baptiste de Boyer, Marquis D'Argens, *Kabbalistische Briefe* (8 vols. in 2; Danzig: 1773). British Museum, C. 43. a. 2. Part IV, pp. 114-15. Comment is printed for the first time.

and adhere to your scheme, I am encountered by another objection—and it is of this that I crave a solution from your sounder and more extended knowledge of these subjects. The reflective power of æriform matter is *inversely* as the rarity—the rarity on the other hand in a direct ratio to the expansion, and of a continuous increase (i. e. diminution of density) so stupendous that according to the Newtonian Calculus a cubic Inch of Air at the surface of our Earth would at the distance of a thousand miles suffice to fill the whole Area within the orbit of Saturn. Yet what is this to an expansion of 50, nay according to Schröter of more than 100,000,000 of miles, as affirmed of the luminous Tails of certain Comets? How is it conceivable, that a vapor of such rarity (an arithmetical denomination of which would require an x = o as the quotient of the density at the end of the first hundred Leagues— so that long before we had reached half-way thro' the Fan-tail we should have in secula seculorum)—how is it possible, I say, that a vapor of such rarity should *reflect* light or even perceptibly obey the projectile or the gravitating force?

I cherish, I must confess, a *pet* system, a bye blow of my own Philosophizing, but it is so unlike to all the opinions and modes of reasoning grounded on the Atoms, Corpuscular and mechanic Philosophy, which is alone tolerated in the present day, and which since the time of Newton has been universally taken as synonimous with Philosophy itself—that I must content myself with caressing the heretical Brat in private under the name of Zoödynamic method—or the doctrine of *Life*.[18]

But the patient wisdom of the experimental philosophy teaches its disciples that investigation is in all cases a sacred duty: and the conviction of this truth actuated the two great masters of this philosophy in a manner most apposite to our argument. Sir Isaac confessed that he had once seriously studied astrology, and Boyle did not conceal that he had formerly been attached to alchemy and natural magic.[19]

The immortal Newton, to whom more than to any other human being Europe owes the purification of its general notions concerning the heavenly bodies, studied Astrology with much earnestness, and did not reject it till he had demonstrated the falsehood of all its pretended grounds and principles.[20]

[18] To the editor of *Blackwood's*, Add. MSS, 34,225, fol. 187.
[19] To the author of "A Letter to Edward Long Fox, M. D.," *Athenæum*, May 2, 1908, p. 542.
[20] *Statesman's Manual*, Appendix C, p. xxiii.

To invent was different from to discover. A watchmaker invented a time-piece; but a profound thinker only could discover. Sir Isaac Newton, when he thought upon the apple falling from the tree, discovered but did not invent the law of gravitation; others, following this grand idea, carried elementary principles into particles, and elucidated chemistry. Sir Isaac Newton, having once found that a body fell to the centre, knew that all other appearances of nature would receive a consequence, agreeably to the law of cause and effect; for it was a criterion of science, that when causes were determined, effects could be stated with the accuracy of prophecy.[21]

We praise Newton's clearness and steadiness. He *was* clear and steady, no doubt, while working out, by the help of an admirable geometry, the idea brought forth by another. Newton had his ether and could not rest in—he could not conceive—the idea of a law. He thought it a physical thing after all. As for his chronology, I believe, those who are most competent to judge, rely on it less and less every day. His lucubrations on Daniel and the Revelations seem to me little less than mere raving.[22]

In the Hebrew poets each thing has a life of its own, and yet they are all our life. In God they move and live and *have* their being; not *had,* as the cold system of Newtonian Theology represents, but *have.*[23]

Robinson, WORKS, *IV, 17.*[24]

> First: this donation implies, that in the opinion of the donors, the Bible is a *plain,* easy book . . .

! ! What if I were to call Newton's "Principia" a *plain,* easy Book, because certain passages were axiomatic, & because the results were evident to common-sense? What? The Pentateuch? the Solomon's Song! The Prophets in general, & Ezekiel in particular! What? the Ecclesiastes? The praise of Jael? of Ehud? of David? What? St. John's Gospel, & his Revelations? the *apparent* Discordances of the Evangelists in the most important affirmation, that of the Resurrection?

---

[21] Lecture VIII of Surrey Institute Lectures, 1812-13. Reported in the *Gazette.* Printed by Raysor, *Shakes. Crit.,* II, 289.

[22] Oct. 8, 1830. *Table Talk S,* VI, 351.

[23] To W. Sotheby, Sept. 10, 1802. Coleridge, E. H., *Letters,* I, 406.

[24] Robert Robinson, *Miscellaneous Works* (4 vols.; Harlow: 1807) with Coleridge's notes is in the Huntington Library, which has given me permission to excerpt the two notes here printed for the first time.

What? St. Paul's Epistles, declared by a contemporary Apostle, dark and hard? are these parts of a plain & easy Book? . . . .

Robinson, WORKS, *IV, 19.*

> Secondly: the donation of a Bible only, implies, that each reader hath *a right of private judgment.* This is another just notion, truly scriptural, and entirely protestant. To give a man a book to read, and to deny him the right of judging its meaning, seems the summit of absurdity.

Doubtless!—but may there not be folly in giving a child (and an ignorant man is a child in knowledge) a book, he cannot understand, without any assistance to enable him so to do? To an ignorant man I would not give Newton at all: for not only he cannot understand it, but he may do very well without it. To the same man I would give the Bible, though a very large part would be worse than unintelligible, for it would be misintelligible—yet as it does concern him, I would give it, only with "all the means & appliances to boot," that would preclude a dangerous misinterpretation.

S. T. C.

The commercial spirit, and the ascendency of the experimental philosophy which took place at the close of the seventeenth century, though both good and beneficial in their own kinds, combined to foster its corruption. Flattered and dazzled by the real or supposed discoveries which it had made, the more the understanding was enriched, the more did it become debased; till science itself put on a selfish and sensual character, and *immediate utility,* in exclusive reference to the gratification of the wants and appetites of the animal, the vanities and caprices of the social, and the ambition of the political, man was imposed as the test of all intellectual powers and pursuits. *Worth* was degraded into a lazy synonyme of *value;* and the value was exclusively attached to the interest of the senses.[25]

[25] *Statesman's Manual,* Appendix C, p. xvi.

LITERARY PROSE

Prose Style

When there are few literary men, and the vast $\frac{999999}{10000000}$ of the population are ignorant, as was the case of Italy from Dante to Metastasio, *from causes I need not here put down, there will be a poetical* language; but that a poet ever uses a word as poetical—that is, formally—which he, in the same mood and thought, would not use in prose or conversation, Milton's Prose Works will assist us in disproving. But as soon as literature becomes common, and critics numerous in any country, and a large body of men seek to express themelves habitually in the most precise, sensuous, and impassioned words, the difference as to mere words ceases, as, for example, the German prose writers. Produce to me *one* word out of Klopstock, Wieland, Schiller, Goethe, Voss, &c. which I will not find as frequently used in the most energetic prose writers. The sole difference in style is that poetry demands a severe keeping— it admits nothing that prose may not often admit, but it oftener rejects. In other words, it presupposes a more continuous state of passion.[1]

Wonderfulness of Prose

Not having my Pocket Book I take note here of what has just struck my feeling namely, that taking for granted the Pherecydean[2] origin Prose must have struck men with greater *admiration* than Poetry. In the latter it was the language of passion and emotion—it is what they themselves spoke and heard in moments of exultation, indignation, &c. But to hear an evolving Roll, or a succession of Leaves, talk continually the language of deliberate Reason in a form of continued preconception, of a Z already possessed when A was being uttered—this must have appeared god-like. I feel myself in the same state, when in the perusal of a sober, yet elevated and harmonious succession of sentences and periods, I abstract my mind from the particular passage, and sympathize with the wonder of the common people, who say of an eloquent man:—he talks like a Book![3]

[1] *Anima*, p. 229.
[2] Pherecydes of Syros was the teacher of Pythagoras.
[3] Copied by E. H. Coleridge in a notebook now in possession of A. H. B. Coleridge. Printed in *Lit. Rem.*, II, 372-73.

Every man's language varies, according to the extent of his knowledge, the activity of his faculties, and the depth or quickness of his feelings. Every man's language has, first, its *individualities;* secondly, the common properties of the *class* to which he belongs; and thirdly, words and phrases of *universal* use. The language of Hooker, Bacon, Bishop Taylor, and Burke, differ from the common language of the learned class only by the superior number and novelty of the thoughts and relations which they had to convey.[4]

Observe the superior truth of language, in Greek, to Theocritus inclusively; in Latin, to the Augustan age exclusively; in Italian, to Tasso exclusively; and in English, to Taylor and Barrow[5] inclusively.[6]

That our elder writers to Jeremy Taylor inclusively *quoted* to excess, it would be the very blindness of partiality to deny. More than one might be mentioned, whose works might be characterized in the words of Milton, as "a paroxysm of citations, pampered metaphors, and aphorising pedantry." On the other hand, it seems to me that we now avoid quotations with an anxiety that offends in the contrary extreme.[7]

He [Coleridge] presumes to dissent from men of established reputation, or even to doubt of the justice, with which the public laurel-crown as symbolical of the *first* class of genius and intellect, has been awarded to sundry writers since the revolution, and permitted to wither around the brows of our elder benefactors, from Hooker to Sir P. Sidney, and from Sir P. Sidney, to Jeremy Taylor and Stillingfleet.[8]

When however facts or matter of fact are concerned, the Student would find it neither uninstructive nor unamusing to compare (I will not send him so far back as to the Masters of the School, no nor even to the systematized divines of the fifteenth or the former half of the sixteenth century) let him compare a volume of Miscellaneous Tracts published during the interval from the death of Elizabeth to the restora-

[4] *Biog. Lit. C*, II, 53.

[5] Isaac Barrow (1630-77), an Anglican divine of the Caroline period and Master of Trinity College, Cambridge.

[6] July 12, 1827. *Table Talk S*, VI, 292.

[7] *The Friend*, General Introduction, Essay VII, I, 80-81.

[8] Gillman's *Life*, p. 190. Quoted from "To My Readers" in the first number of *The Friend*, June 8, 1809.

tion with a similar volume from the last century. I am much mistaken if there should not be found at least as marked a superiority in the logical connection of the sentences, in the correct use of conjunctions, and other exponents of the connecting acts in the mind, in short as marked a superiority in the propriety of the statement and the legitimacy of the consequences on the part of the elder writers, as there is of good sense and accurate observation in those of our contemporaries.[9]

When I think of the vigour and felicity of style characteristic of the age, from Edward VI. to the Restoration of Charles, and observable in the letters and family memoirs of noble families—take, for instance, the Life of Colonel Hutchinson, written by his widow—I cannot suppress the wish—O that the *habits* of those days could return, even though they should bring pedantry and Euphuism in their train![10]

On Style[11]

Another and a very different species of style is that which was derived from, and founded on, the admiration and cultivation of the classical writers, and which was more exclusively addressed to the learned class in society. I have previously mentioned Boccaccio as the original Italian introducer of this manner, and the great models of it in English are Hooker, Bacon, Milton, and Taylor, although it may be traced in many other authors of that age. In all these the language is dignified but plain, genuine English, although elevated and brightened by superiority of intellect in the writer. Individual words themselves are always used by them in their precise meaning, without either affectation or slipslop. The letters and state papers of Sir Francis Walsingham are remarkable for excellence in style of this description. In Jeremy Taylor the sentences are often extremely long, and yet are generally so perspicuous in consequence of their logical structure, that they require no reperusal to be understood; and it is for the most part the same in Milton and Hooker.

Take the following sentence as a specimen of the sort of style to which I have been alluding:—

Concerning Faith, the principal object whereof is that eternal verity which hath discovered the treasures of hidden wisdom in Christ; concerning Hope, the highest object whereof is that everlasting goodness

[9] My reading is from MSS Egerton, 2826, fol. 151-52, but the selection has been printed by Snyder, *Logic*, p. 114.
[10] To Mr. Blackwood, October, 1821. Letter III, "Literary Correspondence," Shedd, IV, 422 n.
[11] *Lit. Rem.*, I, 233-41.

which in Christ doth quicken the dead; concerning Charity, the final object whereof is that incomprehensible beauty which shineth in the countenance of Christ, the Son of the living God: concerning these virtues, the first of which beginning here with a weak apprehension of things not seen, endeth with the intuitive vision of God in the world to come; the second beginning here with a trembling expectation of things far removed, and as yet but only heard of, endeth with real and actual fruition of that which no tongue can express; the third beginning here with a weak inclination of heart towards him unto whom we are not able to approach, endeth with endless union, the mystery whereof is higher than the reach of the thoughts of men; concerning that Faith, Hope, and Charity, without which there can be no salvation, was there ever any mention made saving only in that Law which God himself hath from Heaven revealed? There is not in the world a syllable muttered with certain truth concerning any of these three, more than hath been supernaturally received from the mouth of the eternal God.

Eccles. Pol. I. s. 11.

The unity in these writers is produced by the unity of the subject, and the perpetual growth and evolution of the thoughts, one generating, and explaining, and justifying, the place of another, not, as in Seneca, where the thoughts, striking as they are, are merely strung together like beads, without any causation or progression. The words are selected because they are the most appropriate, regard being had to the dignity of the total impression, and no merely big phrases are used where plain ones would have sufficed, even in the most learned of their works.

There is some truth in a remark, which I believe was made by Sir Joshua Reynolds, that the greatest man is he who forms the taste of a nation, and that the next greatest is he who corrupts it. The true classical style of Hooker and his fellows was easily open to corruption; and Sir Thomas Brown it was, who, though a writer of great genius, first effectually injured the literary taste of the nation by his introduction of learned words, merely because they were learned. It would be difficult to describe Brown adequately; exuberant in conception and conceit, dignified, hyper-latinistic, a quiet and sublime enthusiast; yet a fantast, a humourist, a brain with a twist; egotistic like Montaigne, yet with a feeling heart and an active curiosity, which, however, too often degenerates into a hunting after oddities. In his *Hydriotaphia,* and, indeed, almost all his works the entireness of his mental action is very observable; he metamorphoses every thing, be it what it may, into the subject under consideration. But Sir Thomas Brown with all his faults had a genuine idiom; and it is the existence of an individual idiom in each, that makes the principal writers before the Restoration the great patterns or integers of English style. In them the precise intended meaning of a word can never be mistaken; whereas in the later writers, as especially in Pope, the use of words is for the most part purely arbitrary, so that the context will rarely show the true specific sense, but only that something of the sort is designed. A perusal of the authorities cited by Johnson in his dictionary under any leading word, will give you a lively sense of this declension in etymological truth of expression in the writers after the Restoration, or perhaps, strictly, after the middle of the reign of Charles II.

The general characteristic of the style of our literature down to the period which I have just mentioned, was gravity, and in Milton and some other writers of his day there are perceptible traces of the sternness of republicanism. Soon after the Restoration a material change took place, and the cause of royalism was graced, sometimes disgraced, by every shade of lightness of manner. A free and easy style was considered as a test of loyalty, or at all events, as a badge of the cavalier party; you may detect it occasionally even in Barrow, who is, however, in general remarkable for dignity and logical sequency of expression; but in L'Estrange,[12] Collyer,[13] and the writers of that class, this easy manner was carried out to the utmost extreme of slang and ribaldry. Yet still the works, even of these last authors, have considerable merit in one point of view; their language is level to the understandings of all men; it is an actual transcript of the colloquialism of the day, and is accordingly full of life and reality. Roger North's[14] life of his brother, the Lord Keeper, is the most valuable specimen of this class of our literature; it is delightful, and much beyond any other of the writings of his contemporaries.

From the common opinion that the English style attained its greatest perfection in and about Queen Anne's reign I altogether dissent; not only because it is in one species alone in which it can be pretended that the writers of that age excelled their predecessors; but also because the specimens themselves are not equal, upon sound principles of judgment, to much that had been produced before. The classical structure of Hooker—the impetuous, thought-agglomerating flood of Taylor—to these there is no pretence of a parallel; and for mere ease and grace, is Cowley inferior to Addison, being as he is so much more thoughtful and full of fancy? Cowley, with the omission of a quaintness here and there, is probably the best model of style for modern imitation in general. Taylor's periods have been frequently attempted by his admirers; you may, perhaps, just catch the turn of a simile or single

[12] Sir Roger L'Estrange (1616-1704), journalist and pamphleteer.
[13] Joseph Collyer, the elder, died in 1776. He was a translator and compiler and edited his wife's translation of Klopstock's *Messiah*.
[14] Roger North (1653-1734), lawyer. His brother Francis was Lord Keeper.

image, but to write in the real manner of Jeremy Taylor would require as mighty a mind as his. Many parts of Algernon Sidney's treatises afford excellent exemplars of a good modern practical style; and Dryden in his prose works, is a still better model, if you add a stricter and purer grammar. It is, indeed, worthy of remark that all our great poets have been good prose writers, as Chaucer, Spenser, Milton; and this probably arose from their just sense of metre. For a true poet will never confound verse and prose; whereas it is almost characteristic of indifferent prose writers that they should be constantly slipping into scraps of metre. Swift's style is, in its line, perfect; the manner is a complete expression of the matter, the terms appropriate, and the artifice concealed. It is simplicity in the true sense of the word.

After the Revolution, the spirit of the nation became much more commercial, than it had been before; a learned body, or clerisy, as such, gradually disappeared, and literature in general began to be addressed to the common miscellaneous public. The public had become accustomed to, and required, a strong stimulus; and to meet the requisitions of the public taste, a style was produced which by combining triteness of thought with singularity and excess of manner of expression, was calculated at once to soothe ignorance and to flatter vanity. The thought was carefully kept down to the immediate apprehension of the commonest understanding, and the dress was as anxiously arranged for the purpose of making the thought appear something very profound. The essence of this style consisted in a mock antithesis, that is, an opposition of mere sounds, in a rage for personification, the abstract made animate, far-fetched metaphors, strange phrases, metrical scraps, in every thing, in short, but genuine prose. Style is, of course, nothing else but the art of conveying the meaning appropriately and with perspicuity, whatever that meaning may be, and one criterion of style is that it shall not be translateable without injury to the meaning. Johnson's style has pleased many from the very fault of being perpetually translateable; he creates an impression of cleverness by never saying any thing in a common way. The best specimen of this manner is in Junius,[15] because his antithesis is less merely verbal than Johnson's. Gibbon's manner is the worst of all; it has every fault of which this peculiar style is capable. Tacitus is an example of it in Latin; in coming from Cicero you feel the *falsetto* immediately.

In order to form a good style, the primary rule and condition is, not to attempt to express ourselves in language before we thoroughly know

[15] The Letters of Junius appeared in the *London Public Advertiser*, Jan. 21, 1769-Jan. 21, 1772. Politically important as an attack on the ministry of the Duke of Grafton, they were especially admired by Coleridge for their style.

our own meaning;—when a man perfectly understands himself, appropriate diction will generally be at his command either in writing or speaking. In such cases the thoughts and the words are associated. In the next place preciseness in the use of terms is required, and the test is whether you can translate the phrase adequately into simple terms, regard being had to the feeling of the whole passage. Try this upon Shakspeare, or Milton, and see if you can substitute other simpler words in any given passage without a violation of the meaning or tone. The source of bad writing is the desire to be something more than a man of sense,—the straining to be thought a genius; and it is just the same in speech making. If men would only say what they have to say in plain terms, how much more eloquent they would be! Another rule is to avoid converting mere abstractions into persons. I believe you will very rarely find in any great writer before the Revolution the possessive case of an inanimate noun used in prose instead of the dependent case, as 'the watch's hand,' for 'the hand of the watch.' The possessive or Saxon genitive was confined to persons, or at least to animated subjects. And I cannot conclude this Lecture without insisting on the importance of accuracy of style as being near akin to veracity and truthful habits of mind; he who thinks loosely will write loosely, and, perhaps, there is some moral inconvenience in the common forms of our grammars which give children so many obscure terms for material distinctions. Let me also exhort you to careful examination of what you read, if it be worth any perusal at all; such examination will be a safeguard from fanaticism, the universal origin of which is in the contemplation of phenomena without investigation into their causes.

I am now,[16] therefore, to state the inference which it was my object to draw from the facts above given. To the spirit of exclusive pursuit, and the tendency to contemplate all knowledge through the medium of some predominant form, we may attribute the gradual decline of the sciences which by the ancients, and down to the close of the fifteenth century by our own forefathers, were eminently, and only not exclusively, honoured with the name of *philosophic*, as to its main and continuous cause. It was at the Restoration, however, that the effect became more strikingly manifest, and its operation enforced and accelerated by concurrent causes. In describing the errors and injurious results of the scholastic system, I have precluded, I trust, the suspicion of a wish to detract from the well-merited honours, or the high and, in very deed, indispensable importance of experimental philosophy, in the sense in

[16] *Monologues,* pp. 626-28.

which it was understood and explained by Bacon in his *Novum Organum*. It is not even my purpose to blame that eagerness in collecting single and detached facts, so noticeable in the earlier transactions of the Royal Society, then newly established. "It might or it might not be a necessary preliminary of a true reformation, but neither, on the other hand, can it be denied that this devotion to the fractional materials of knowledge, as so many independent and integral truths—the opposition which then first became fashionable of facts to theory, the former name being confined to things cognisable by the sense—and, lastly, the exaltation of this knowledge as the ground and substance of all truth, did, to use the words of a profound thinker, "by engrossing men's thoughts and fixing their minds so much on corporeal objects, not a little indispose them, however undesignedly, for moral and intellectual matters." BERKELEY's *Siris*. The illustrious bishop pursues the subject into its moral results; for my purpose it is sufficient to remark, that this diversion of the mind from objects purely intellectual (the attention to which implies an effort of the soul) to objects of sense, could not but— and actually did—weaken the connective powers of the understanding, and insensibly induce a habit both of thinking and of writing unconnectedly. The conjunctions, in the largest sense of the term, are the true λογοι, the *verba viventia* of languages. How, indeed, can it be otherwise, seeing that all connexion is of necessity given by the mind itself. It is well known, that the gradual deterioration of Greek literature may be traced through the successive writers by the increasing omission of the particles, which schoolboys are, or were, taught to call expletives. The collation of a few pages in Plato or Xenophon, with an equal number of Achilles Tatius,[17] or even of Herodian,[18] will sufficiently explain and exemplify the position. I have said, that many causes concurred to a common effect. The pursuits of the *virtuosi*, as the naturalists of Charles the Seconds time were entitled, and the diffusion of Materialism and the Epicurean philosophy, in a more decorous shape, by the followers of Gassendi, and without disguise by our own, Hobbes, fought in close alliance with the French taste, introduced at the same time alike into life and literature. The philosophers and theologians—we might say, the prose-writers generally—from the reign of Henry VIII. to the Restoration were faulty in the other extreme; too abundant in Latinisms, too artificial in the structure of their periods, and in the logical cement by which they bound together. The prevailing foible was to be stately, methodical, and connected in excess; and the

---

[17] Achilles Tatius of Alexandria (c. A.D. 450), Greek rhetorician, known for clarity and conciseness of style.
[18] Herodianus (third century A.D.), Greek historian.

fashion was longest retained and most affected by the parliamentary party, the Puritan divines, and adherents of systematic theology. Hence it happened, after the return of the Stuarts, wit, point, and an imitation of colloquial ease, and the desultory character and successive flashes of genial, or rather jovial conversation, were not only objects of admiration and the criterion of genius, but marks of loyalty. Thus, by the too common transition *in contraria*, a style was introduced, of which, in its final consummation, it has been not untruly observed, that an ancient critic would have deemed it purposely invented for persons troubled with the asthma to read. It cannot but be injurious to the human mind never to be called into effort; the habit of receiving pleasure without any exertion of thought, by the mere excitement of curiosity and sensibility, may be justly ranked among the worst effects of habitual novel-reading. It is true, that these short and unconnected sentences are easily and instantly understood; but it is equally true that, wanting all the cement of thought as well as of style, all the connexions, and (if you will forgive so trivial a metaphor) all the *hooks-and-eyes* of the memory, they are as easily forgotten; or, rather, it is scarcely possible that they should be remembered.

Nor is it less true, that those who confine their reading to such books dwarf their own faculties, and finally reduce their understandings to a deplorable imbecility: many facts might be mentioned, as furnishing fair instances and striking illustrations. Like idle morning visitors, the brisk and breathless periods hurry in and hurry off in quick and profitless succession; each, indeed, for the moments of its stay, prevents the pain of vacancy, while it indulges the love of sloth: but, altogether, they leave the mistress of the house (the soul, I mean) flat and exhausted, incapable of attending to her own concerns, and unfitted for the conversation of more rational guests.[19]

Report of Lecture XIV, 1818.[20]

The influence of national character on language is exemplified in the literature of the Eastern nations, in that of the Greeks, of our own and of the Northern Nations.

The Greek writings are distinguished by long sentences, formed, as it were, architecturally; each part is built on the preceding; and the whole sentence would lose by changing the arrangement. The modern construction among ourselves is more simple. The sentences are short,

[19] In the latter part of this selection Coleridge repeats almost *verbatim* what he had written in *The Friend*. See selection below from Essay III, I, 24-26.

[20] From the *Tatler*, May 23, 1831; reprinted in the *Athenæum*, March 16, 1889, pp. 345-46, and in Raysor, *Misc. Crit.*, pp. 221-26.

but preserve a consistency with each other. Such is the prose-writing of Chaucer.

A more popular style followed; but the confusion resulting from the civil wars prevents us from seeing the transition. In Luther we have a striking example of the popular style,—popular in the highest sense of the term, addressing the intellect of the reader, and readily understood wherever good sense is the habit of the mind. A similar style, with less genius, may be found in Latimer and other writers of Edward VI's time and the preceding reign.

After the Restoration came the classic style. A true relish of this style presupposed a taste and cultivation in the reader somewhat corresponding to it, for it was too learned to be popular. Boccaccio it is true was popular; but we can account for the exception in him by the fascination of his subjects. Hooker, Bacon, Milton, and Jeremy Taylor are distinguished ornaments of the classic style.

[The Lecturer here read an extract from Sir Francis Walsingham, Minister in Queen Elizabeth's time. He characterized it as plain, sober language, but distinguished by talent; void of affectation, and of clear meaning. It bore evidence that the writer had thought before he attempted to communicate. The subject was Honesty.]

Jeremy Taylor reconciles the architectural and the classic styles. His sentences are of great length, yet do not require review in order to understand them; the words are judiciously chosen, and the sentence grows with the importance of the subject.

[Two admirable extracts were read in illustration—the first on Original Sin, the other on the Progress of Disputes.]

The style next in succession was of a very different nature. The new stylists represented a person who tries to recollect all the good things he has heard during the last three months, that he may give utterance to them all together. They strung together sparkling points, unrelieved by intermediate plainness. Their writings bear marks of recollection, not of reflection. In the writings of Taylor, &c., uncommon and foreign words are not unfrequently used, but they are used only when no others could be found so expressive of the author's meaning. Sir Thomas Browne appears to be the first who used uncommon words for their own sake. Mr. C. confessed that Sir Thomas, with all his imperfections, was a favourite of his. He described him as a sublime and quiet enthusiast, as bearing some resemblance to Montaigne, but entering into his speculations with more intenseness of purpose than the French writer. His writings bear the stamp of an original and amiable mind. The only imitable quality of them is their entireness, or plenitude of illustration.

[A passage from Sir T. B.'s 'Treatise on Urn Burial' was read.]
Barrow and his contemporaries next come under consideration.
Their predecessors offended by pedantry. It now became a mark of
loyalty to pass into the other extreme, and everything must appear free
and unlaboured.

Hence proceeded occasional quaintness and sometimes even ludicrous-
ness. For instance in Barrow's 'Sermon on Spiritual Monarchy,' the
action of St. Peter in cutting off the ear of the High Priest's servant, is
thus stated—''Up rose his blood, and out popped his sword.'' Sir
Roger L'Estrange and Jeremy Collier carried this plainness to excess.
The style of the period was infected with a sort of slang or black-
guardism. Notwithstanding these defects, there is much to approve in
the writers in question. Their style is purely English, full of idioms,
and partakes of the passions of man in general.

[An extract from Roger North's Life of his brother, the Lord Keeper,
followed in illustration.]

The liveliness of the thoughts was well conveyed by the words.

It was the opinion of some that the first perfect models of good
writing were produced after the Revolution. We had, however, perfect
models before,—of the architectural style in Hooker, of the impetuous
in Taylor, of elegant simplicity in Cowley; with some abatement, Algernon Sydney and Dryden were also good models.

[Here Cowley's account of Oliver Cromwell's funeral was in part
extracted.]

The style of Cowley is most fitted for imitation; it is distinguished
by variety of excellence.

Our great poets, Chaucer, Spenser, Milton, Dryden, &c., were all good
prose-writers; they seemed to have kept their thoughts on separate
shelves, so as to avoid that injudicious mixture of poetry with prose
which disgusts us in less skilful writers. The style of Swift may be
considered perfect; by no defects it reminds us of itself.

After the Revolution, we became commercial, and our style suffered
considerably. It was not learned, nor plain, nor popular; the thoughts
were commonplace, but the manner was strange. The first object seemed
to be,—not to speak naturally.

[Mr. C. illustrated this part of his subject by extracts from Mr.
Phillip's speech in the case of Guthrie v. Sterne,[21] and exposed the
absurdities and false eloquence contained in it. The instances he selected were of false antithesis, confusion of metaphor, bathos, and sheer
nonsense.]

[21] Charles Phillips, *Collected Speeches* (London: 1817).

Mr. Coleridge then gave a few instructions which he conceived might be usefully adopted to write and talk respectably.

We should not express ourselves till we feel that we know clearly what we mean to express. The want of previous reflection is the cause of much incoherent and unconnected writing and talking.

Adverting to the opinion of a Greek writer (Strabo, I believe) that none but a good man could be a great poet, the Lecturer concurred with him, and thought, moreover, that moral excellence was necessary to the perfection of the understanding and the taste. The good writer should be a lover of what is common to all his fellow creatures, rather than of what makes them unequal; he should look to fame rather than to reputation. Fame is the approbation of the wise of successive generations; reputation is no more than the echo of hastily formed opinions. Many contemptible works have had great reputation; few works greatly reputed at first, have afterwards ripened into fame.

We should use no words nor sentences which can be translated into simpler words with the same meaning.

Shakespeare and Milton are distinguished by their appropriate use of words. You cannot change a word without injury to the effect.

The first two lines of Dryden's translation of Juvenal's Tenth Satire were contrasted with Johnson's imitation of the same passage.

Johnson takes up six lines, and does not well express his meaning after all.

Dryden's two lines are,—

> Look round the habitable globe: how few
> Know their own good, or knowing it, pursue.

Johnson's six are,—

> Let observation, with extensive view,
> Survey mankind, from China to Peru;
> Remark each anxious toil, each eager strife,
> And watch the busy scenes of crowded life;
> Then say how hope and fear, desire and hate,
> O'er spread with snares the clouded maze of fate,
> Where wavering man, &c.

The great source of bad writing is a desire in the writers to be thought something more than men of sense. Language is made a sort of leap-frog. Our Poetry runs after something more than human; our Prose runs after our Poetry; and even our conversation follows in the pursuit.

At a dinner of twenty persons, when your health is proposed, you are supposed to return thanks in a set speech. Metaphors are used, not to illustrate, but as substitutes for plain speaking.

The frequent rendering of abstractions into persons is also a growing evil, as in the following line:—

Come, I shed Compassion's tear,

which is the same as saying that Mrs. A. sheds Mrs. B's tear.

Sound sense and sound feeling are necessary to a good writer. Accuracy is akin to Veracity. They who are accustomed to weigh the meaning of words before they utter them are much less likely to disregard truth in greater matters, than those who, from neglecting accuracy, lose the sense of its importance. We should habituate ourselves to see the relation of our thoughts to each other; we should consider pleasure derived without any effort as enervating, and therefore undesirable. That only is permanent which appeals to something permanent in our natures.

Cavalier Slang[22]

A good lecture upon style might be composed, by taking on the one hand the slang of L'Estrange, and perhaps even of Roger North, which became so fashionable after the Restoration as a mark of loyalty; and on the other, the Johnsonian magniloquence or the balanced metre of Junius; and then showing how each extreme is faulty, upon different grounds.

It is quite curious to remark the prevalence of the Cavalier slang style in the divines of Charles the Second's time. Barrow could not of course adopt such a mode of writing throughout, because he could not in it have communicated his elaborate thinkings and lofty rhetoric; but even Barrow not unfrequently lets slip a phrase here and there in the regular Roger North way—much to the delight, no doubt, of the largest part of his audience and contemporary readers. See particularly, for instances of this, his work on the Pope's supremacy. South is full of it.[23]

The style of Junius is a sort of metre, the law of which is a balance of thesis and antithesis. When he gets out of his aphorismic metre into a sentence of five or six lines long, nothing can exceed the slovenliness of the English. Horne Tooke[24] and a long sentence seem the only two antagonists that were too much for him. Still the antithesis of Junius is a real antithesis of images or thought; but the antithesis of Johnson is rarely more than verbal.

[22] July 3, 1833. *Table Talk S,* pp. 467-68.
[23] Robert South (1634-1716), chaplain in ordinary to Charles II, famous for introducing humor into sermons.
[24] Horne Tooke (1736-1812), author of *Diversions of Purley.*

The definition of good prose is—proper words in their proper places —of good Verse—the most proper words in their proper places. The propriety is in either case relative. The words in prose ought to express the intended meaning, and no more; if they attract attention to themselves, it is, in general, a fault. In the very best styles, as Southey's, you read page after page, understanding the author perfectly, without once taking notice of the medium of communication; it is as if he had been speaking to you all the while. But in verse you must do more;— there the words, the *media,* must be beautiful, and ought to attract your notice—yet not so much and so perpetually as to destroy the unity which ought to result from the whole poem. This is the general rule, but, of course, subject to some modifications, according to the different kinds of prose or verse. Some prose may approach towards verse, as oratory, and therefore a more studied exhibition of the *media* may be proper; and some verse may border more on mere narrative, and there the style should be simpler. But the great thing in poetry is, *quocunque modo,* to effect a unity of impression upon the whole; and a too great fulness and profusion of point in the parts will prevent this. Who can read with pleasure more than a hundred lines or so of Hudibras at one time? Each couplet or quatrain is so whole in itself, that you can't connect them. There is no fusion—just as it is in Seneca.

THE FRIEND has reprinted the following Biographical sketch, partly indeed in the hope that it may be the means of introducing to the Reader's knowledge, in case he should not have formed an acquaintance with them already, two of the most interesting biographical Works in our language, both for the weight of the matter, and the *incuriosa* felicitas of the style. I refer to Roger North's Examen, and the Life of his brother, the Lord Chancellor North. The pages are all alive with the genuine idioms of our mother-tongue.

A fastidious taste, it is true, will find offence in the occasional vulgarisms, or what we now call *slang,* which not a few of our writers, shortly after the restoration of Charles the Second, seem to have affected as a mark of loyalty. These instances, however, are but a trifling drawback. They are not *sought for,* as is too often and too plainly done by L'Estrange, Collyer, Tom Brown,[25] and their imitations. North never goes out of his way either to seek them or to avoid them; and in the main his language gives us the very nerve, pulse, and sinew of a hearty healthy conversational *English.*

This is THE FRIEND's first reason for the insertion of this Extract.

[25] Tom Brown (1663-1704), miscellaneous writer, often satirical.

His other and principal motive may be found in the kindly good-tempered spirit of the passage. But instead of troubling the Reader with the painful contrast which so many recollections force on my own feelings, I will refer the character-makers of the present day to the Letters of Erasmus and Sir Thomas More to Martin Dorpius, that are commonly annexed to the Encomium Moriæ; and then for a practical comment on the just and affecting sentiments of these two great men, to the works of Roger North, as proofs how alone an English scholar and gentleman will permit himself to delineate his contemporaries even under the strongest prejudices of party spirit, and though employed on the coarsest subjects. A coarser subject than L.C.J. Saunders cannot well be imagined; nor does North use his colors with a sparing or very delicate hand. And yet the final impression is that of kindness.[26]

Barrow often debased his language merely to evidence his loyalty. It was, indeed, no easy task for a man of so much genius, and such a precise mathematical mode of thinking, to adopt even for a moment the slang of L'Estrange and Tom Brown; but he succeeded in doing so sometimes. With the exception of such parts, Barrow must be considered as closing the first great period of the English language. Dryden began the second. Of course there are numerous subdivisions.[27]

Doubtless too, I have in some measure injured my style, in respect to its facility and popularity, from having almost confined my reading of late years, to the works of the Ancients and those of the elder Writers in the modern languages. We insensibly imitate what we habitually admire; and an aversion to the epigrammatic unconnected periods of the fashionable *Anglo-gallican* taste has too often made me willing to forget, that the stately march and difficult evolutions, which characterize the eloquence of Hooker, Bacon, Milton, and Jeremy Taylor, are, notwithstanding their intrinsic excellence, still less suited to a periodical Essay. This fault I am now endeavouring to correct; though I can never so far sacrifice my judgement to the desire of being immediately popular, as to cast my sentences in the French moulds, or affect a style which, an ancient critic would have deemed purposely invented for persons troubled with asthma to read, and for those to comprehend who labour under the more pitiable asthma of a shortwitted intellect. It cannot but be injurious to the human mind never to be called into effort: the habit of receiving pleasure without any exertion of thought, by the mere ex-

[26] *The Friend,* ''Second Landing Place,'' Essay II, II, 307-8.
[27] July 5, 1834. *Table Talk S*, VI, 520-21.

citement of curiosity and sensibility, may be justly ranked among the worst effects of habitual novel reading. It is true that these short and unconnected sentences are easily and instantly understood: but it is equally true, that wanting all the cement of thought as well as of style, all the connections, and (if you will forgive so trivial metaphor) all the *hooks-and-eyes* of the memory, they are as easily forgotten: or rather, it is scarcely possible that they should be remembered.—Nor is it less true, that those who confine their reading to such books dwarf their own faculties, and finally reduce their understandings to a deplorable imbecility: the fact you mention, and which I shall hereafter make use of, is a fair instance and striking illustration. Like idle morning visitors, the brisk and breathless periods hurry in and hurry off in quick and profitless succession; each indeed for the moments of its stay prevents the pain of vacancy, while it indulges the love of sloth; but all together they leave the mistress of the house (the soul I mean) flat and exhausted, incapable of attending to her own concerns, and unfitted for the conversations of more rational guests.[28]

Habits of abstruse and continuous thought and the almost exclusive perusal of the Greek Historians and Philosophers, of the German Metaphysicians and Moralists, and of our English writers from Edward VI, to James II, have combined to render my sentences more *piled up* and *architectural*, then is endurable in so illogical an eye as the present, in which all the cements of style are dismissed, and the popular book is only a sequence of epigrams and aphorisms on one subject. Too often my Readers may justly complain of involution and *entortillage* in my style, tristem nescio quam et inflexam antiquitatem.[29]

All the defects, you have mentioned, I am perfectly aware of, and am anxiously endeavouring to avoid. There is too often an *entortillage* in the sentences & even the thoughts, which nothing can justify; and, always almost, a stately piling up of *story* on *story* in one architectural period, which is not suited to a periodical Essay, or to Essays at all (Lord Bacon, whose style mine more nearly resembles than any other, in his greater works, thought Seneca a better model for his Essays) but least of all suited to the present illogical age, which has in imitation of the French, rejected all the *cements* of language; so that a popular

---

[28] *The Friend*, General Introduction, Essay III, I, 24-26.
[29] To George Coleridge, Oct. 9, 1809. Griggs, *Unp. Letters*, II, 10-11. Read "illogical an age" for "illogical an eye" above, a correction from my reading of the transcript of the original letter made by E. H. Coleridge.

Book is now a mere bag of marbles, i. e. aphorisms and epigrams on one subject.[30]

The Friend—the first six numbers at least—is partly chargeable with obscurity and heaviness of movement in it's periods—too often with entortillage or intertwisting both of the thoughts and the sentences.[31]

Very shortly however, I shall present you from the Press with my opinions in full on the subject of Style both in prose and verse—and I am confident of one thing, that I shall convince you that I have thought much and patiently on the subject, and that I understand the whole strength of my Antagonist's Cause. For I am now busy on the subject —and shall in a very few weeks go to Press with a Volume on the Prose writings of Hall, Milton, and Taylor—and shall immediately follow it up with an Essay on the writings of Dr. Johnson, and Gibbon—And in these two Volumes I flatter myself that I shall present a fair History of English Prose. If my life and health remain, and I do but write half as much and as regularly, as I have done during the last six weeks, these will be finished by January next—and I shall then put together my memorandum Book on the subject of poetry. In both I have sedulously endeavoured to state the Facts, and the Differences, clearly and acutely—and my reasons for the Preference of one style and another are secondary to this. Of this be assured, that I will never give anything to the world in propriâ personâ, in my own name, which I have not tormented with the File. I sometimes suspect, that my foul Copy would often appear to general Readers more polished than my fair Copy— Many of the feeble and colloquial Expressions have been industriously substituted for others, which struck me as artificial, and not standing the test—as being neither the language of passion, nor distinct Conceptions.[32]

[30] To Thomas Poole, Oct. 9, 1809. British Museum, Add. MSS, 35,343, fol. 365. Printed in Coleridge, E. H., *Letters*, II, 551.
[31] To Samuel Purkis, Oct. 18, 1809. Griggs, *Unp. Letters*, II, 20.
[32] To Tom Wedgwood, Oct. 20, 1802. Griggs, *Unp. Letters*, I, 217. Cf. Cottle, *Reminiscences*, pp. 330-31.

John Donne

Donne, LETTERS.[1] *"To Sir. H. G."*

I send not my letters as tribute, nor interest, nor recompence, nor for
commerce, nor as testimonials of my love, nor provokers of yours, nor
to justifie my custom of writing, nor for a vent and utterance of my
meditations; for my letters are either above or under all such offices,
*yet I write very affectionately, and I chide and accuse my self of dimin-
ishing that affection, which sends them, when I ask my self why.* Only I
am sure, that I desire that you might have in your hands letters of
mine of all kinds, as conveyances and deliverers of me to you, whether
you accept me as a friend, or as a patient, or as a penitent, or as a
beads-man; for I decline no jurisdiction, nor refuse any tenure. I
would not open any door upon you, but look in, when you open it.
Angels have not, nor affect not other knowledge of one another, than
they list to reveal to one another. It is then in this only, that friends
are angels, that they are capable and fit for such revelations, when
they are offered. If at any time I seem to study you more inquisitively,
it is for no other end, but to know how to present you to God in my
prayers, and what to ask of him for you; for even that holy exercise
may not be done inopportunely, no nor importunely. I find little error
in that Grecian's counsel, who says, If thou ask any thing of God,
offer no sacrifice, nor ask elegantly, nor vehemently; but remember, that
thou would'st not give to such an asker. Nor in his other countryman,
who affirms sacrifice of blood to be so unproportionable to God, that
perfumes, though much more spiritual, are too gross; yea, words, which
are our subtilest and delicatest outward creatures, being composed of
thoughts and breath, are so muddy, so thick, that our thoughts themselves are so; because (except at the first rising) they are ever leavened
with passions and affections. And that advantage of nearer familiarity
with God, which the Act of Incarnation gave us, is grounded upon
God's assuming us, not our going to him: and our accesses to his
presence are but his descents into us. And when we get anything by
prayer, he gave us beforehand the thing and the petition; for I scarce
think any ineffectual prayer free from both sin and the punishment of
sin. Yet as God seposed a seventh of our time for his exteriour worship,
and as his Christian Church early presented him a type of the whole
year in a Lent, and after imposed the obligation of canonique hours,
constituting thereby moral Sabbaths every day, I am far from dehorting
those fixed devotions; but I had rather it were disposed upon thanksgiving than petition, upon praise than prayer; not that God is endeared

[1] MS notes of Coleridge in the books of Charles Lamb, printed in "Coleridgiana
III. Coleridge on the Poet Donne's Letters," *The Literary World*, XII (May 14,
1853), p. 393, and in *Notes Theolog.*, pp. 255-60.

by that, or wearied by this; all is one in the receiver, but not in the lender; and thanks doth both offices; For nothing doth so innocently provoke new graces, as gratitude. I would also rather make short prayers than extend them, though God can neither be surprised nor besieged; for long prayers have more of the man, as ambition of eloquence, and a complacency in the work, and more of the devil by often distractions; for after in the beginning we have all intreated God to hearken, we speak no more to him. Even this letter is some example of such infirmity; which being intended for a letter, is extended and strayed into a homily; and whatsoever is not what it was purposed, is worse. Therefore it shall at least end like a letter, by assuring you, I am, &c.

A noble letter in that *next* to the best style of correspondence, in which friends communicate to each other the accidents of their meditations, and baffle absence by writing what, if present, they would have talked. Nothing can be tenderer than the sentence I have lined.

Donne, LETTERS. *"To the Countess of Bedford."*

Happiest and Worthiest Lady:—I do not remember that ever I have seen a petition in verse; I would not therefore be singular, nor add these to your other papers. I have yet adventured so near as to make a petition for verse, it is for those your ladyship did me the honour to see in Twicknam Garden, except you repent your making, and have mended your judgment by thinking worse, that is, better, because more justly, of their subject. They must needs be an excellent exercise of your wit, which speak so well of so ill. I humbly beg them of your ladyship, with two such promises, as to any other of your compositions were threatenings: that I will not shew them, and that I will not believe them; and nothing should be so used which comes from your brain or heart. If I should confess a fault in the boldness of asking them, or make a fault by doing it in a longer letter, your ladyship might use your style and old fashion of the Court towards me, and pay me with a pardon. Here, therefore, I humbly kiss your ladyship's fair learned hands, and wish you good wishes and speedy grants.
Your ladyship's servant,
John Donne.

A truly elegant letter, and a happy specimen of that dignified courtesy to sex and rank, of that white flattery in which the wit unrealizes the falsehood, and the sportive exaggeration of the thoughts, blending with a delicate tenderness, faithfully conveys the truth as to the feelings.

Donne, LETTERS. *"To the Lady G."*

Madam:—I am not come out of England, if I remain in the noblest part of it, your mind; yet, I confess, it is too much diminution to call your mind any part of England, or this world, since every part even of your body deserves titles of higher dignity. No prince would be loath to die, that were assured of so fair a tomb to preserve his memory:[2] but I have a greater advantage than so: for since there is a religion in friendship, and a death in absence, to make up an entire friend, there must be an heaven too; and there can be no heaven so proportional to that religion, and that death, as your favour; and I am gladder that it is heaven, than that it were a court or any other high place of this world, because I am likelier to have a room there than here, and better cheap; Madam, my best treasure is time, and my best employment of that (next my thoughts of thankfulness for my Redeemer) is to study good wishes for you, in which I am by continual meditation so learned, that any creature (except your own good angel), when it would do you most good, might be content to come and take instructions from

                                       Your humble and affectionate servant,

Amiens, the 7 Feb., 1611   J. D.

Contrast this letter with that to the Countess of Bedford. There is perhaps more wit and more vigor in this, but the thoughts played upon are of so serious a nature, and the exception in the parenthesis so awful, that the art, instead of carrying off, aggravates the flattery, and Donne must either have been literally sincere, or adulatory to extravagance, and almost to blasphemy.

Donne, LETTERS. *"To my honored friend, G. G., Esq."*

Of my Anniversaries, the fault that I acknowledge in myself, is to have descended to print anything in 'verse, which though it have excuse even in our own times by men who profess and practise much gravity; yet I confess I wonder how I declined to it, and do not pardon myself; but for the other part of the imputation of having said too much, my defence is, that my purpose was to say as well as I could: for since I never saw the gentlewoman, I cannot be understood to have bound myself to have spoken just truths, but I would not be thought to have gone about to praise her, or any other, in rhyme; except I took such a person as might be capable of all that I could say: if any of those ladies think that Mistress Drewry was not so, let that lady make herself fit for all those praises in the book, and they shall be hers.

This excuse reminds me of Sallust's (the Greek Platonic Philosopher's) apology for the Pagan mythology, viz. that the fables are so excessively silly and absurd, that they are incapable of imposing on any man in his senses, and therefore to be acquitted of falsehood. To be sure, these Anniversaries were the strangest caprices of genius upon

[2] Coleridge's note: " 'Thou in our wonder and astonishment
                  Hast built thyself a live-long monument;
                  And, there sepulchred, in such state dost lie,
                  That Kings for such a tomb might wish to die.'
                  Milton's Lines on Shakespeare."

record. I conjecture that Donne had been requested to write something on this girl, whom he had never seen, and having no other subject in contemplation, and Miss Drewry herself supplying materials, he threaded upon her name all his thoughts as they crowded into his mind, careless how extravagant they became, when applied to the best woman on earth. The idea of degradation and frivolity which Donne himself attached to the character of a professed poet, and which was only not universal in the reigns of Elizabeth and James, which yet exhibited the brightest constellation of poets ever known, gives a *settling* answer to the fashionable outcry about patronage—nothing but patronage wanting to Midasize their Herr Füssly into Michael Angelo Buonaroti, Mister Shee to a Raphael, and Rat Northcote into a Titian.[3]

Donne, LETTERS. *"To my honored friend G. G., Esq., Jan. 7, 1630."*

It hath been my desire (and God may be pleased to grant it) that I might die in the pulpit; if not that, yet that I might take my death in the pulpit, that is, die the sooner by occasion of those labours.

This passage seems to prove that Donne retained thro' life the same opinions defended in his Biathanatos; at least this, *joined* with his dying command that the treatise should not be destroyed, tho' he did not think the age ripe for its publication, furnishes a strong presumption of his perseverance. in the defensibility of suicide in certain cases.

Robert Burton

My anger and disgust at the malevolent and disgraceful attacks levelled daily against the Church are absolutely without bounds. I am weary of looking out and crying, *Watchman, what of the night?* In reading the *Anatomy of Melancholy* the other morning, I was amused at the wrath which calumnies of a similar character had kindled in the breast of the learned scholar of Christchurch. The passage is worth quoting. He is inveighing against the ignorance of these malevolent antagonists, and he continues,

[3] Coleridge refers to three contemporaries: Henry Fuseli (1741-1825) and James Northcote (1746-1831), painters encouraged by Sir Joshua Reynolds, and Sir Martin Archer Shee (1769-1850), portrait-painter and poet, who became president of the Royal Academy in 1830 and was knighted in the same year.

But though they should read, it would be to small purpose,—*clames,
licet, et mare cælo confundas;* thunder, lighten, preach hell and damnation, tell them 'tis a sin, they will not believe it: denounce and terrify;
they have cauterized consciences; they do not attend; as the enchanted
adder, they stop their ears: call them base, irreligious, profane, barbarous, Pagans, Atheists, epicures (as some of them surely are),
they cry, *Euge! optime;* and applaud themselves with that *miser,
simul ac nummos contemplor in arca:* say what you will, as a dog barks
at the moon, to no purpose are your sayings; take your heaven, let
them have money,—a base, profane, epicurean, hypocritical rout. For
my part, let them pretend what they will, counterfeit religion, blear the
world's eyes, bombast themselves, and stuff out their greatness with
church spoils, shine like so many peacocks,—so cold is my charity,
so defective in their behalf, that I shall never think better of them,
than that they are rotten at core, their bones are full of epicurean
hypocrisy and atheistical marrow.[1]

Does not this smack of what Cowper calls the Diabolical Dictionary.
One fancies that when the author broke into so violent an invective, he
must have forgotten to sweeten his rooms with juniper, which he says
was in great request at Oxford for that purpose. Let me say a word
in praise of this admirable book, which could draw Johnson from his
bed two hours before he was willing to rise. The quaintness of his
style, sometimes rising into strains of wonderful dignity and eloquence,
—the fertility of his invention, the extent of his learning, the multitude
of his illustrations,—all contribute to render the *Anatomy of Learning*
one of the most entertaining books in the language. The independence
of his character, I confess, offers an additional attraction to me.[2]

[1] Burton, *Anatomy of Melancholy,* Part II, Sec. 2, ''Ayre Rectified.''
[2] Willmott, *C. at Trinity,* pp. 30-31. The *Anatomy of Melancholy* annotated by
Coleridge was given to Ludwig Tieck by Mr. Gillman. In a letter to Coleridge, 1818,
Tieck said, ''Mr. Gillman's valued present 'The Anatomy of Melancholy,' gives me
the greatest pleasure.'' This letter is in the possession of A. H. B. Coleridge, who
has given me permission to quote from it.

John Barclay

Barclay, Argenis,[1] *flyleaves and front cover.*

Heaven forbid! that this work should not exist in it's present form
and Language! Yet I cannot avoid the wish, that it had been, during
the reign of James the first, moulded into an heroic poem in English
Octavo Rima; or *epic* blank verse which, however, at that time had
not been invented, and which alas! still remains the sole property of the
Inventor—as if the Muses had given him an unevadible Patent for it!
Of dramatic Blank Verse we have many and various Specimens—ex-gr.,
Shakespere's as compared with Massinger's, both excellent in their
kind—of lyric, and of what may be called the Orphic, or philosophic,
Blank Verse, perfect Models may be found in Wordsworth—of colloquial
Blank Verse excellent, tho' not perfect, examples in Cowper &c.—but
of epic, since Milton, not one. S. T. C.

It absolutely *distresses* me when I reflect that this work, admired as
it has been by great men of all ages, and lately, I hear, by the Poet
Cowper, should be only not *unknown* to general Readers. It has been
translated into English two or three times—how, I know not—wretched-
ly, I doubt not. It affords matter for Thought that the last Translation
(or rather, in all probability, miserable and faithless Abridgement of
some former) was given under another name. What a mournful proof
of the Incelebrity of this great, and amazing Work among both the
Public and the *People!* For as Wordsworth, the greater of the two
great men of this Age,—(at least, except Davy and him, I have *known,*
read* of, *heard* of, no others) for as W. did me the honor of once observing to me, the *People* and the *Public* are two distinct classes, and (as
things go) the former is likely to retain a better Taste, the less it is acted
on by the Latter. Yet *Telemachus* is in every mouth, in every school-
boy's and school-girl's Hand.—It is awful to say of a work, like the
Argenis, the style and Latinity of which, judged not according to classical pedantry, which pronounces every sentence right which can be
found in any book prior to Boetius, however vicious the age, or affected
the author; and every sentence wrong, however natural and beautiful,

---

[1] These marginalia are transcribed from the copy of *Argenis* (Amsterdam: 1659)
in the library of Harvard University and show variations from *Lit. Rem.,* I, 255-58,
communicated by Rev. Derwent Coleridge. An entirely different set of notes occurs
in Southey's copy now in the British Museum.

which has been of the author's own combination, but according to the universal Logic of Thought as modified by feeling, is equal to Tacitus in energy and genuine conciseness, is as perspicuous as Livy, and is free from the affectations, obscurities, and lust to *surprize* of the former, and forms a sort of antithesis to the slowness and prolixity of the Latter. This remark does not however impeach even the classicality of the Language, which, considering the freedom and originality, the easy motion and perfect command of the Thoughts, is truly wonderful—of such a work it is aweful to say, that it would have been well if it had been written in English or Italian verse! Yet the Event seems to justify the Notion.—Alas! it is now too late. What modern work even of the size of Paradise Lost,—much less of the Faery Queen—(N. B. are even these read?) would be read in the present day, or even *bought,* or likely to be *bought,* unless it be an *instructive* work, like Roscoe's 5 quartos of Leo X.—or Boswell's 3 of Dr. Johnson's pilfered brutalities of wit? It may be fairly objected, what work of surpassing merit has given the proof?—Certainly, none. Yet still there are ominous facts, sufficient, I fear, to afford a certain prophecy of its reception, if such were produced. S. T. C.

Barclay, ARGENIS,[2] *note on front board and first flyleaf, recto and verso. "Vide p. 93."*

That Charles the first commanded the Translation of this excellent work, & was so *impatient* for it's early appearance (vide Sir Robt. Le Grice's Preface) is itself no mean proof of his Leaning towards *Catholicism*—at least, that he abhorred the tenets of the Reformed Churches, & was most charitable to the whole corrupt mass of Popery—making certain Tenets of the Puritans, i. e. Predestination, Election, Reprobation, Final Perseverance, &c., the *pretexts*—while the Love of Liberty & the superior knowledge of the Puritans were his true Motives. These purely *theological* Tenets had and still have their Advocates among the Romanists—& I question, whether a single Instance can be found in which their Belief & Disbelief had any practical consequences—except as far as that any serious exercise of the reasoning Faculties accompanied with moral Zeal tends to wean & unsensualize the human mind. But this it is! Men dispute about Cricket, & *Fives*—& forget, that both

---

[2] *John Barclay, his Argenis Translated out of Latin: the Prose upon His Maiestie's Commands,* by Sir Robert LeGrys, Knight; and the Verses by Thomas May, Esquire . . . 1629. British Museum, C. 44. d. 34. This was Southey's book and has his autograph on the title page. These notes were transcribed from the original, but they have been printed by Will T. Brooke, "Unpublished fragments of Coleridge and Lamb," *Newberry House Magazine,* VI (January, 1892), 68-70.

are valuable only for that which is common to both—i. e. employment, exercise, health & agility & strength. S. T. C.

Judge from this of the sincerity of Charles in his Relief of *Rochelle*. I verily am inclined to believe, that their Destruction was *designed, planned*, & rejoiced in by Charles—such a Bigot was he to Arbitrary Rule! S. T. Coleridge

The most important Deduction from this great work (for a great work it is!), we may fairly deem to be the degeneracy of Genius, when it unnaturally weds itself with Cunning, Despair of Human Kind, & (that worst Pest of civilized Man!) the base Calculation of consequences as the grain of morality. Cowards & Traitors! listening with half an ear to the plain, positive Injunction of Conscience, while their eyes are fixed on a Demon in the Distance, now flattering, now threatening them with obscure gestures, the interpretation of which forms their daily & hourly Superstition. Is it right? He who says, I cannot tell, till I calculate the consequences, is already an Atheist in it's worst, nay, in it's only sense. To know the effects of this state of mind, compare the moral Breathings of even the mistaken Patriots of Charles the First & the Republic with the Loyalists (many of them men of superior Talents & amiable characters, as Cowley)—Think of Milton, Ludlow, Colonel Hutchinson, Harrington—in short, compare only in one feeling, the suspicion & hatred of God's Creatures with the Love & Hope of them. For this is the true Difference between the Philo-despotist, & the Republican—the latter of whom may, & under certain circumstances such as that of G. Britain at present, *will*, of necessity, be the most Zealous & faithful Partizan of his King & the Constitution of his Country. A Republican is he, who under any constitution hopes highly of his fellow-citizens, attributes their vices to their circumstances, & takes the proper means (such as are in his power) to ameliorate them—gradually indeed, & not by placing children in the *first Form* or gifting Russian Slaves with the British Constitution—but still looking on & hoping. The Despotist always assumes every vice of any of the People as common to all—& the present vices as essential & irremovable.

Barclay, ARGENIS, *p. 93 [Barclay's account of the Huguenot interpretation of the doctrines of Election and Reprobation].*

A fine instance this of *saying* Truth, and *conveying* Falsehood. It is true, that these Tenets are *Calvinistic*, but most false, that to them the Spread of Calvinism was owing, or the characteristics of their Theology (i. e. the point in which they are unique) are or were characteristic of the *Sect* in France. No! the severity of their morals, & in their opinions not what they held, but what they did *not* hold, what they were emancipated from—Idolatry, Ignorance of the Scriptures, &c. &c.—these were the characters of the Huguenots. It is always suspicious when the opinions of a numerous sect are attacked, omitting their moral conduct—if the latter be bad, the former cannot be good, if good, it proves that the opinions are not as bad as they seem.

John Selden

Selden (that genuine *English* mind whose erudition, broad, deep, and manifold as it was, is yet less remarkable than his robust healthful common sense).[1]

Selden, TABLE TALK,[2] *p. 1.*

There is more weighty bullion sense in this book, than I ever found in the same number of pages of any uninspired writer.

Opinion

Opinion and affection extremely differ. I may affect a woman best, but it does not follow I must think her the handsomest woman in the world. . . . Opinion is something wherein I go about to give reason why all the world should think as I think. Affection is a thing wherein I look after the pleasing of myself.

Good! This is the true difference betwixt the Beautiful and the Agreeable, which Knight and the rest of that πλῆθος ἄθεον have so *beneficially* confounded, *meretricibus videlicet et Plutoni.*

O what an insight into a wise man's *heart!* who has been compelled to act with the Many, as one of the Many! It explains Sir T. More's Zealous Romanism, &c., &c.

Parliament

Excellent! O to have been with Selden over his glass of wine, making every accident an outlet and a vehicle of wisdom!

---

[1] *Statesman's Manual*, Appendix E, p. xlv.

[2] "Literary Journal," Feb. 24, 1814, of Henry Francis Cary, in Rev. Henry Cary, *Memoir of the Rev. Henry Francis Cary with his Literary Journal and Letters* (2 vols.; London: 1847), I, 323-24. Cary says, "There are several other of his remarks, but these are the best. This book is in the Westminster Library." I have not, however, been able to locate it. The notes are also in *Lit. Rem.*, II, 361-63, where *videlicet* appears as *scilicet*.

Poetry

The old poets had no other reason but this, their verse was sung to music; otherwise it had been a senseless thing to have fettered up themselves.

No one man can know all things. Even Selden here talks ignorantly. Verse is in itself a music, and the natural symbol of that union of Passion with Thought and Pleasure, which constitutes the *Essence* of all *Poetry*, as contradistinguished from Science, and distinguished from History, civil or natural. To Pope's Essay on Man, in short to whatever is mere *metrical* good sense and wit the remark applies.

Verse proves nothing but the quantity of syllables; they are not meant for logic.

True; they (*i. e.*, verses) are not logic: but they are, or ought to be, the envoys or representatives of that vital passion which is the practical cement of logic, and without which logic must remain inert.

It should be remembered that Melanchthon regarded Philosophy as a *discipline* for the intellectual powers, not as a store-house of Truths. These were to be sought for in the Inspired Books. Now in this sense and for this purpose, M. seems to have judged rightly—for assuredly in no one of the Greek Philosophers could a Student of Theology acquire the knowledge and habit of distinct conceptions and appropriate *Terms* with a quickness in the detection of equivocations and false consequences so well as in the Logical Works of Aristotle. It should be considered likewise, that the well-founded Scruples as to the Objective validity of conceptual distinctions are in a much less degree applicable to the Doctrines of Religion in which Faith and Revelation supply the place which the Senses and outward experience occupy in natural science, not forgetting, that they are Doctrines revealed for and addressed to, the conceptions of the human mind. It is true, that some of these doctrines *transcend* our Conceptions; but in the theological Disquisitions the main object and most frequent use of Logic and Dialectic are by just distinctions so to expound Doctrines as that they shall not contradict the Conceptions in respect of the proper objects of the Understanding or Conceptive Faculty, ex. gr. by asserting of phænomena what is rendered impossible by all the conditions of their existence, as phænomena. The Reasoning on Theology is almost always apagogic—the truth being proved not by *direct* insight, but by the absurdity of the contrary—a falsity by the absurdity of the consequences or their contrariety to some admitted **Truth**.

Selden, that Prince of robust good Sense, expresses a very different opinion of the value of the School divinity, the study of which he holds indispensable to a sound Divine in the defence of the orthodox faith. See his Table Talk. And when I hear a Theologian speak of the emptiness, and poverty of Thought, of all the Schoolmen, I shall venture to tell him, that he has never read the Summa Theologiæ of Thomas Aquinas, or the Collectorium of Gabriel Biel.[3]

Sir Thomas Browne

Browne, RELIGIO MEDICI,[1] *first flyleaf, recto.*

Strong Feeling & an active Intellect conjoined, lead necessarily to Spinosism. T. Brown was a Spinosist without knowing it—and so indeed are almost all sincerely pious and generous minds.[2]

Browne, RELIGIO MEDICI, *second flyleaf, recto and verso.*

S. T. Coleridge

If I have not all the *Faith* that the author of the Religio Medici possessed, I have all the *inclination* to it. It gives me pleasure to *believe.* N. B. The Post-script at the very End of the Book is well worth Reading. Excepting that there is nothing particularly good after p. 176—where the Religio Medici ends.[3] Sir K. Digby's observations are those of a pedant in his own system & opinion. He ought to have considered the Religio Medici in a *dramatic* & not in a metaphysical View— as a sweet Exhibition of character & passion, & not as an Expression or Investigation of positive Truth. The Religio Medici (i. e. Religion

---

[3] Marginal note from Tennemann, *Geschichte der Philosophie* (12 vols.; Leipzig: 1798-1817), IX, 164-66. British Museum, C. 43. c. 24. Printed for the first time. Gabriel Biel (d. 1495) was a philosopher and a follower of William of Occam.

---

[1] Sir Thomas Browne, *Religio Medici* (London: 1669). This edition with notes in Coleridge's hand and with his name on the second flyleaf is in the John Rylands Library. I am indebted to this library for permission to reproduce the notes. The notes in *Lit. Rem.,* I, 241-48, are said to be from the 1802 edition and to be ''Communicated by Mr. Wordsworth.'' With few exceptions, however, the notes are identical except for editing. Important omissions in *Lit. Rem.* concern Coleridge's private life.

[2] The comment following the dash was omitted in *Lit. Rem.*

[3] This sentence omitted in *Lit. Rem.*

of a Physician) is a fine Portrait of a handsome[4] man in his *best* Cloathes
—it is much of what he *was* at *all* times, a good deal [of what] he was
only in his *best* moments. I have never read a book, in which I felt
greater similarity to my own *make* of mind—active in enquiry, & yet
with an appetite to believe,—in short, an affectionate & elevated *Visionary!* But then I should tell a different Tale of my own heart; for I
would not only endeavor to tell the Truth, (which I doubt not, Sir
T. B. has done) but likewise to tell the *whole* Truth, which most assuredly he has not done. However, it is a most delicious Book.

His own character was a fine mixture of humourist, genius, and
pedant. A library was a living world to him, and every book a man,
absolute flesh and blood! and the gravity with which he records contradictory opinions is exquisite.[5]

Browne, RELIGIO MEDICI, *Part I, beneath title.*

　　i e. a Physician's Religion[6]

Browne, RELIGIO MEDICI, *Part I, sec. 3, p. 3.*

　　Yet I have not so shaken hands with those desperate Resolutions, who
　　had rather venture at large . . .

　　"Resolutions" changed to "Resolvers."

Browne, RELIGIO MEDICI, *Part I, sec. 3, p. 5.*

　　My common conversation I do acknowledge austere, my behaviour full
　　of rigour, sometimes not without morosity.

　　So much the worse.

Browne, RELIGIO MEDICI, *Part I, sec. 3, p. 6.*

　　Those unstable judgements that cannot consist in the narrow point
　　and centre of vertue without a reel or stagger to the circumference.

　　excellent!

Browne, RELIGIO MEDICI, *Part I, sec. 6, p. 10.*

　　Every man is not a proper Champion for Truth.

　　Godwin, for Instance.

Browne, RELIGIO MEDICI, *Part I, sec. 6, p. 11.*

　　I must confess my greener studies have been polluted with two or three,
　　not any begotten in the latter Centuries, but old and obsolete, such

────────
[4] Coleridge has deleted "good" and substituted "handsome."
[5] This paragraph from *Lit. Rem.*, I, 245, does not appear in the 1669 edition.
[6] This explanation and the seven short notes which follow below are not given in
Lit. Rem. In fact, none of the definitions appear. Although these are minor, they
are reproduced for completeness wherever they occur.

as could never have been revived, but by such extravagant and irregular heads as mine.

I sympathize—'tis excellent.

Browne, RELIGIO MEDICI, *Part I, sec. 7, p. 13.*

The second was that of *Origen,* that God would not persist in his Vengeance for ever, but after a definite time of his wrath, he would release the Damned souls from torture: Which error I fell into upon a serious contemplation of the great Attribute of God, his Mercie.

To call this opinion *an error!* Merciful God! how thy creatures blaspheme thee!

Browne, RELIGIO MEDICI, *Part I, sec. 8, p. 16*

. . . general breach or *dichotomy* with their Church.

division

Browne, RELIGIO MEDICI, *Part I, sec. 9, p. 17.*

I love to lose myself in a Mystery, to pursue my reason to an *Oh altitudo!*

"O! the Depth!" So say I: so says dear W. W.[7]

Browne, RELIGIO MEDICI, *Part I, sec. 10, p. 20.*

"Pucellage" defined in margin as "maidenhood."

Browne, RELIGIO MEDICI, *Part I, sec. 12, p. 23.*

"Stenography" defined in margin as "Shorthand."

Browne, RELIGIO MEDICI, *Part I, sec. 15, pp. 30-31.*

I could never content my contemplation with those general pieces of wonder, the flux and reflux of the Sea, the increase of *Nile,* the conversion of the Needle to the North; and have studied to match and parallel those in the more obvious and neglected pieces of Nature, which without further travel I can do in the Cosmography of my self; we carry with us the wonders we seek without us: There is all *Africa* and her prodigies in us; we are that bold and adventurous piece of nature, which he that studies, wisely learns in a *compendium,* what others labour at in a divided piece and endless volume.

This is the true characteristic of Genius—our destiny & instinct is to unriddle the world, & he is the man of Genius who feels this instinct fresh and strong in his nature—who perceives the riddle & the mystery

---

[7] The passage given in *Lit. Rem.* is not the passage commented upon; the substitution for "altitudo" and the reference to Wordsworth are not given in the note.

of all things even the commonest & needs no strange and out of the way Tales or Images to stimulate him into wonder & a deep Interest.

Browne, RELIGIO MEDICI, *Part I, sec. 16, pp. 31-32. Note on p. 32.*

Thus there are two Books from whence I collect my Divinity; besides that written one of God, another of his servant Nature, that universal and publick Manuscript, that lies expans'd unto the eyes of all; those who never saw him in the one, have discovered him in the other: This was the Scripture and Theologie of the Heathens . . . surely the Heathens knew better how to joyn and read these mystical Letters, than we Christians, who cast a more careless eye on these common Hieroglyphicks, & disdain to suck Divinity from the flowers of Nature. . . .

All this is very fine Philosophy, & the best & most ingenious Defence of Revelation.

Browne, RELIGIO MEDICI, *Part I, sec. 16, p. 33.*

I hold there is a general beauty in the works of God, and therefore no deformity in any kinde or species of creature whatsoever: I cannot tell by what Logick we call a Toad, a Bear, or an Elephant, ugly . . .

So do I hold—& believe that a Toad is a comely animal. But nevertheless, a Toad *is* called ugly by almost all men; & it is the Business of a Philosopher to explain the Reason of this.

Browne, RELIGIO MEDICI, *Part I, sec. 18, p. 41.*

An easie Logick may conjoyn Heaven and Earth, in one argument, and with less than a *Sorites** resolve all things into God.

* accumulated argument.

Browne, RELIGIO MEDICI, *Part I, sec. 19, p. 42.*

There is, as in Philosophy, so in Divinity, sturdy doubts, and boisterous objections, wherewith the unhappiness of our knowledge too neerly acquainteth us. More of these no man hath known than my self . . .

This is exceedingly striking! Had Sir T. Brown lived now-a-days, he would probably have been a very ingenious & bold Infidel (in his *real* opinions) tho' the kindness of his nature would have kept him aloof from vulgar prating obtrusive Infidelity.

Browne, RELIGIO MEDICI, *Part I, sec. 25, p. 55.*

Ethnick Superstition.

heathenish. [?]

Browne, RELIGIO MEDICI, *Part I, sec. 32, p. 68.*

The fire and *scintillation* of that noble and mighty Essence.

Sparkling

Browne, RELIGIO MEDICI, *Part I, sec. 33, p. 72.*

single *Hypostasis*

person of the Trinity

Browne, RELIGIO MEDICI, *Part I, sec. 35, p. 77.*

> God being all things, is contrary unto nothing, out of which were made all things, and so nothing became something, and *Omneity* informed *Nullity* into an Essence.

An excellent *Burlesque* on some parts of the Schoolmen, tho' I fear an unintentional one.

Browne, RELIGIO MEDICI, *Part I, sec. 36, p. 80.*

> Thus we are men, and we know not how; there is something in us that can be without us, and will be after us, though it is strange that it hath no history, what it was before us, nor cannot tell how it entred in us.

Truly sublime and in Sir T. Brown's best manner.

Browne, RELIGIO MEDICI, *Part I, sec. 39, p. 85.*

> . . . that other world, the truest Microcosm, the womb of our mother; for besides that general and common existence we are conceived to hold in our Chaos, and whilst we sleep within the bosome of our causes, we enjoy a being and life in three distinct worlds, wherein we receive most manifest graduation.

This is the most admirable passage! Yes! the History of a man for the 9 months preceding his Birth, would probably be far more interesting & contain events of greater moment than all the 3 score & 10 years that follow it.

Browne, RELIGIO MEDICI, *Part I, sec. 41, p. 90.*

> I perceive I do anticipate the vices of age; the worst to me is but a dream or mock-show, and we all therein but Pantalones and Anticks, to my severer contemplation.

One almost thinks Byron's affectation in this particular was copied from the above passage.[8]

Browne, RELIGIO MEDICI, *Part I, sec. 48, p. 105.*

> This is made good by experience, which can from the Ashes of a plant revive the plant, and from its cinders recal it into its stalks and leaves again.

[8] Omitted in *Lit. Rem.*

Moll Row!![9] This was, I believe, some lying Boast of Paracelsus, which the good Sir T. Brown has swallowed for a Truth.

Browne, RELIGIO MEDICI, *Part I, sec. 59, p. 124.*

Again, I am confident, and fully perswaded, yet dare not take my oath of my Salvation: I am as it were sure, and do believe without all doubt, that there is such a City as *Constantinople;* yet for me to take my Oath thereon, were a kinde of Perjury, because I hold no infallible warrant from my own sense to confirm me in the certainty thereof.

Dr. Johnson adopted this argument and I think, gave it as his own. See Boswell—Col. B. quoted it to mean Johnson's.[10]

Browne, RELIGIO MEDICI, *Part II, sec. 1, p. 127.*

Idio-syncrasie.

peculiar temperament.

Browne, RELIGIO MEDICI, *Part II, sec. 2, p. 131.*

It is a happiness to be born and framed unto vertue, and to grow up from the seeds of nature, rather than the inoculation and forced graffs of education.

A just thought well expressed.

Browne, RELIGIO MEDICI, *Part II, sec. 2, p. 131.*

I give no alms to satisfie the hunger of my Brother, but to fulfil and accomplish the Will and Command of my God.

Consider "God" as the word that expresses the *whole* of *all things* & this is just.[11] We ought not to relieve a poor man merely because our feelings impel us; but because these feelings are *just* & *proper* feelings. My *feelings* might impel me to revenge with the same force, with which they urge me to charity. I must therefore have some rule by which I may *judge* my feelings—& this Rule is *"God."*

Browne, RELIGIO MEDICI, *Part II, sec. 5, p. 146. Note continued on blank page pasted in.*

I never yet cast a true affection on a woman, but I have loved my friend as I do vertue, my soul, my God.

I have loved—& still do love—*truly* i. e. not in a fanciful attributing of certain ideal perfections to an existing Being, who possesses perhaps

[9] Possibly "witchcraft" is the implication of "Moll Row," for around Ottery St. Mary there was a superstition that Moll Row was a witch who had a black cat as her familiar. Coleridge told an amusing story of her on the Hartz excursion. See Clement Carlyon, *Early Years and Late Reflections* (4 vols.; London: 1836-58), I, 132-35.

[10] Omitted in *Lit. Rem.*

[11] This sentence does not appear in *Lit. Rem.*, and the final sentence is modified.

no one of them; but in a true & palpable sympathy of manners, sentiments, & affections. So have I loved *one* Woman; & believe that such
a Love of such a Woman is the highest Friendship[12]—for we cannot love
a Friend as a Woman, but we can love a Woman as a Friend. Friendship satisfies the *highest* parts of our nature; but a wife, who is capable
of friendship, satisfies *all*. The great business of real unostentatious
Virtue is—not to eradicate any genuine instinct or appetite of human
nature; but—to establish a concord and unity betwixt all parts of our
nature, to give a Feeling & a Passion to our purer Intellect, and to in-
tellectualize our feelings & passions. This a happy marriage, blessed
with children, effectuates, in the highest degree, of which our nature
is capable, & is therefore chosen by St. Paul, as the symbol of the Union
of the Church with Christ; that is, of the Souls of all good men with
God, the soul of the Universe. "I scarcely distinguish," said once a
good old man, "the wife of my old age from the wife of my youth;
for when we were both young, & she was beautiful, for *once* that I
caressed her with a meaner passion, I caressed her a thousand times
with *Love*—& *these* caresses still remain to us!" Besides, there is another Reason why Friendship is of somewhat less Value, than Love which
includes Friendship—it is this—we may love many persons, all *very*
dearly; but we cannot love many persons, all *equally* dearly. There
will be differences, there will be *gradations*—our nature, imperiously
asks a *summit,* a *resting-place*—it is with the affection in Love as with
the Reason in Religion, we cannot diffuse & *equalize*—we must have a
SUPREME—a *One the highest*. All languages express this sentiment.
What is more common than to say of a man in love, "he idolizes her,"
"he makes *a god* of her?" Now, in order that a person should *continue*
to love another, better than all others, it seems necessary, that this feeling should be reciprocal. For if it be not so, Sympathy is broken off
in the very highest point. A. (we will say, by way of illustration)
loves B. above all others, in the best and fullest sense of the word, love;
but B. loves C. above all others. Either, therefore, A. does not sympathize with B. in this most important feeling; & then his Love must
necessarily be incomplete, & accompanied with a *craving* after something that *is not,* & yet *might be;* or he does sympathize with B. in
loving C. above all others—& then, of course, he loves C. better than
B. Now it is selfishness, at least it seems so to me, to desire that your
Friend should love you better than all others—but not to wish that a
Wife should.

[12] This portion of the note is omitted in *Lit. Rem.*

Browne, RELIGIO MEDICI, *Part II, sec. 6, p. 147.*

> Another misery there is in affection, that whom we truely love like our own, we forget their looks, nor can our memory retain the Idea of their faces; and it is no wonder: for they are our selves, and our affection makes their looks our own.

A Thought I have often had, and once expressed it almost in the same language; the *Fact is* certain, but the explanation here given is very unsatisfactory. For *why* do we never have an image of our own faces? an image of Fancy, I mean? S. T. C.

Browne, RELIGIO MEDICI, *Part II, sec. 7, p. 149.*

> I can hold there is no such thing as injury; that if there be, there is no such injury as revenge, and no such revenge as the contempt of an injury; that to hate another, is to maligne himself, and that the truest way to love another, is to despise ourselves.

I thank God, that I can with a full & unfeigning Heart, utter AMEN to this passage.

Browne, RELIGIO MEDICI, *Part II, sec. 9, p. 156. Note continued on p. 157.*

> I could be content that we might procreate like trees without conjunction, or that there were any way to perpetuate the world without this trivial and vulgar way of coition . . .

He says, he is a Batchelor, but he talks as if he had been a married man, & married to a Woman who did not love him, & whom he did not love. Taken by itself, no doubt, the act is both foolish, & debasing. But what a misery is contained in those words, "taken by itself."? are there not thoughts, & affections, & Hopes, & a *Religion* of the Heart, that lifts & sanctifies all our bodily actions where the union of the Bodies is *but* a language & *conversation* of united Souls![13]

Browne, RELIGIO MEDICI, *Part II, sec. 10, p. 163. Note continued on p. 164.*

> In brief, there can be nothing truely alone, and by its self, which is not truely one; and such is onely God.

O I feel this! & feel myself *alone!* & suffer the painful craving Void of *Solitude!* I want some being, that should be *the dearest,* the very dearest to me—& this can not be unless by the circumstance of *my* being the *very* dearest to that Being! And this, alas! I can not be![14] Reciprocity is that, which alone gives a *stability* to Love! It is not

[13] Omitted in *Lit. Rem.*
[14] The above portion of the note is omitted from *Lit. Rem.*

mere selfishness, that impels all kind natures to desire, that there should be some one human Being, to whom they are *most* dear—it is because they wish some one being to exist, who shall be the resting-place or summit of their Love! & this in human nature is *not possible,* except the two affections coincide—the reason is, that the object of the highest Love will not otherwise be the same in both parties.

Browne, RELIGIO MEDICI, *Part II, sec. 11, p. 165.*

> I thank God for my happy dreams, &c.

I am quite different: for all, or almost all, the painful & fearful Thoughts that I know, are in my Dreams! So much so that when I am wounded by a friend, or receive a painful Letter, it throws me into a state very nearly resembling that of a Dream.

Browne, RELIGIO MEDICI, *Part II, sec. 12, p. 169.*

> Keep still in my Horizon; for to me
> The Sun makes not the day, but *thee*
> Thou whose nature cannot sleep.

thou, says the *grammar;* THEE, says the *Rhyme,* and a Poet of course is naturally *partial* to the latter.

Browne, RELIGIO MEDICI, *Part II, sec. 13, p. 173.*

> Statists that labour to contrive a Common-wealth without our poverty, take away the object of charity, not understanding onely the Commonwealth of a Christian, but forgetting the prophecie of Christ.

O, for shame! for shame!—is there no object of charity but abject Poverty? And what sort of a Charity must that be, which wishes misery, in order that it may have the credit of relieving a small part of it? Pulling down the comfortable cottages of independent Industry to build alms' houses out of the Ruins!

Browne, RELIGIO MEDICI, *"The Annotator to the Reader." Note on blank page opposite.*

> *And* Seneca *saith, some such there* are, Qui patri obstetricem parturienti filiæ accercenti [*sic*] moram injicere possint.

"Which would detain a father that was running to fetch a midwife for his Daughter in labor-pangs"—no bad Hyperbole of Master Seneca's![15]

---

[15] Omitted from *Lit. Rem.*

Browne, RELIGIO MEDICI, *end-page, recto.*[16]

11
17
31
33
39
69
77 for it's exquisite absurdity!
80-81 Divine!
85-86-87 best of all!
204 good quot. *for my Locke Book*
205
206 Poem on the Death of Homer

This book paints certain parts of my moral and intellectual being, (the best parts, no doubt,) better than any other book I have ever met with;—and the style is throughout delicious.[17]

Browne, VULGAR ERRORS,[18] *letter to Sara Hutchinson, 2½ flyleaves.*

Sir Thomas Brown is among my first favourites. Rich in various *knowlege;* exuberant in conceptions and conceits, contemplative, imaginative; often truly great and magnificent in his style and diction, tho' doubtless, too often big, stiff, and hyperlatinistic—: thus I might, without admixture of falsehood, describe Sir. T. Brown, and my description would have only this Fault, that it would be equally, or *almost* equally applicable to half a dozen other Writers, from the beginning of

[16] These citations and comments are omitted from *Lit. Rem.* A final note in pencil appears to be by someone else: "Descartes (Discours de Monde) says, It is one thing to believe, & another for man to imagine that he believes—S. T. C. in one of these MS notes adopts the idea."

[17] Not in the edition of 1669, but given in *Lit. Rem.*, I, 248.

[18] Sir Thomas Browne, *Vulgar Errors, Religio Medici, Hydriotaphia,* and *Garden of Cyrus* (London: 1658). There are separate title pages for *Vulgar Errors* and "*Religio Medici* whereunto is added *Hydriotaphia* and the *Garden of Cyrus.*" The title page of *Vulgar Errors* is inscribed at the top, "Mr. Wordsworth, Rydal Mount," but the fifth flyleaf bears the following note in Lamb's hand: "C. Lamb 9th March 1804, bought for S. T. Coleridge." Under this in Coleridge's writing appears: "Given by S. T. C. to S. Hutchinson March 1804. N. B. It was the 10th; on which day I dined and punched at Lamb's—& exulted in his having procured the Hydriotaphia & all the rest lucro posito. S. T. C." The letter to Sara Hutchinson is dated "March 10th, 1804. Saturday night, 12 o'clock." It begins, "My dear Sara!"

This volume is now in the Berg Collection, the New York Public Library, which has given me permission to reproduce the notes. The notes have been printed with some omissions and changes in *Lit. Rem.*, II, 398-416. Another edition of the letter is found in "Character of Sir Thomas Browne as a Writer," *Blackwood's Magazine*, VI (November, 1819), 197-98.

He is indeed all this, & what he has more than all this, & what he has the reign of Elizabeth to the end of the reign of Charles the Second. peculiar to himself, I seem to convey to my own mind in some measure, by saying, that he is a quiet and sublime Enthusiast with a strong tinge of the Fantast, the Humorist constantly mingling with & flashing across the Philosopher, as the darting colours in shot silk play upon the main dye. In short, he has brains in his Head, which is all the more interesting for a *little Twist* in the Brains. He sometimes reminds the reader of Montaigne; but from no other than the general circumstance of an Egotism common to both, which in Montaigne is too often a mere amusing Gossip, a chit-chat story of Whims & Peculiarities that lead to nothing; but which in Sir Thomas Brown is always the result of a feeling Heart conjoined with a mind of active curiosity—the natural & becoming egotism of a man, who loving other men as himself, gains the habit & the privilege of talking about himself as familiarly as about other men. Fond of the Curious, and a Hunter of Oddities & Strangenesses, while he conceived himself with quaint & humorous gravity, a useful enquirer into physical Truth & fundamental Science, he loved to contemplate & discuss his own Thoughts & Feelings, because he found by comparison with other men's that *they,* too, were curiosities, & so, with a perfectly graceful & interesting Ease, he put *them* too into his Museum & Cabinet of Rarities. In very truth, he was not mistaken—so completely does he see every thing in a light of his own, reading Nature neither by Sun, Moon or Candle-light, but by the Light of the faery Glory around his own Head, that you might say, that Nature had granted to him in perpetuity, a Patent and Monopoly for all his Thoughts. Read his Hydriotaphia above all—& in addition to the peculiarity, the exclusive *Sir Thomas Brown-ness* of all the Fancies and modes of Illustration, wonder at and admire his *entireness* in every subject, which is before him—he is totus in illo—he follows it, he never wanders from it, and he has no occasion to wander—for whatever happens to be his subject, he metamorphoses all Nature into it. In that Hydriotaphia, or Treatise on some Urns dug up in Norfolk—how *earthy,* how redolent of graves & sepulchres is every Line! You have now dark mould, now a thigh-bone, now a skull, then a bit of mouldered Coffin, a fragment of an old tombstone with moss in it's Hic Jacet—a ghost, or a winding-sheet, or the echo of a funeral Psalm wafted on a November wind—& the gayest thing you shall meet with shall be a silver nail, or gilt Anno Dominis, from a perished Coffin Top! The very same remark applies in the same force to the interesting,· though far less interesting, Treatise on Quincuncial Plantations of the Ancients— the same attention to oddities, the same to the minutenesses, & minutiæ of vegetable forms—the same entireness of subject—Quincunxes in Heaven above, Quincunxes in Earth below, & Quincunxes in the water beneath the Earth; Quincunxes in Deity, Quincunxes in the mind of man; Quincunxes in bones, in optic nerves, in Roots of Trees, in leaves, in petals, in every thing! In short just turn to the last Leaf of this volume, & read out aloud to yourself, the 7 last Paragraphs of Chapter V, beginning with the words, "More considerables"—But it is time for me to be in bed; in the words of Sir Thomas, which will serve you, my darling Sara! as a fair specimen of his manner. "But the Quincunx of Heaven (the Hyades or 5 Stars about the Horizon, at midnight at that time) runs low, and tis time we close the five Ports of Knowledge! we are unwilling to spin out our waking Thoughts into the Phantasms of Sleep, which often continueth præcogitations, making Cables of Cobwebs, and wildernesses of handsome Groves. To keep our eyes open longer were to *act* our Antipodes. The Huntsmen are up in America, and they have already past their first Sleep in Persia." Think you, my dear Sara! that there ever was such a reason given before for going to bed at midnight, to wit, that if we did not, we should be acting the part of our ANTIPODES!! And then, "The Huntsmen are up in America" —what Life, what Fancy! Does the whimsical Knight give us thus a dish of strong green Tea, & call it an *Opiate?* I trust that you *are* quietly asleep,

> And all the Stars hang bright above your Dwelling,
> Silent as tho' they watch'd the sleeping Earth!
> S. T. Coleridge

7. Barnard's Inn, Holborn, London.

N. B. On page 48 of "Enquiries into common & vulgar Errors" there is a Plate of Urns & the figure of the Quincunx bound up by mistake, instead of being placed p. 48 of the two last Treatises, which is the opening of the "Cyrus Garden, &c."

N. B. In the marginal symbols, which I have made ⊙ points out a profound or at least solid and judicious observation; = signifies that the sentence or passage in a line with it contains *majesty* of Conception or Style: ⁂ signifies *Sublimity;* || *brilliance* or *ingenuity;* Q signifies characteristic Quaintness; and F, that it contains an *error* in fact or philosophy.

> S. T. Coleridge

Browne, VULGAR ERRORS, *third flyleaf.*

It is not common to find a Book of so early date, at least among those of equal neatness of Printing, that contains so many gross typographical Errors:[19] with the exception of our earliest dramatic writers, some of which appear to have been never corrected; but worked off at once as the Types were first arranged by the Compositors. But the grave & doctrinal works are, in general, exceedingly correct; and form a striking contrast to modern publications, of which the late Edition of Bacon's Works would be paramount in the infamy of mutiplied unnoticed Errata, were it not for the unrivalled Slovenliness of Anderson's British Poets, in which the Blunders are at least as numerous as the pages, and many of them perverting the sense or killing the whole beauty, and yet giving or affording a meaning, however low, instead. These are the most execrable of all typographical Errors. 1808.

Browne, VULGAR ERRORS, *"To the Reader," A₃.*

> For though not many years past Dr. *Primrose* hath made a learned and full Discourse of vulgar Errors in Physick.

Is not this the same person as the Physician mentioned by Mrs. Hutchinson? See the Life of Colonel Hutchinson by his Widow.

Browne, VULGAR ERRORS, *Book I, chap. ii, p. 4. [Text marked with critical symbols described under the second "N. B." following the letter to Sara Hutchinson.]*

> For thinking by this retirement to obscure himself from God, he infringed the omnisciency and essential ubiquity of his Maker, Who as
> = he created all things, so is he beyond and in them all, not only in power, as under his subjection, or in his presence, as being in his cognition,
> = but in his very Essence, as being the soul of their causalties, and the essential cause of their existencies. Certainly, his posterity at this distance and after so perpetuated an impairment, cannot but condemn
> || the poverty of his conception, that thought to obscure himself from his Creator in the shade of the garden, who had beheld him before in the darkness of Chaos, and the great obscurity of nothing; That thought to flie from God, which could not flie himself, or imagined that one
> ※ tree should conceal his nakedness from God's eye as another had revealed it unto his own. Those tormented spirits that wish the mountains to cover them, have fallen upon desires of minor absurdity, and chosen waies of less improbable concealment.

Browne, VULGAR ERRORS, *Book I, chap. ii, p. 4.*

> For although we now do hope the mercies of God will consider our degenerated integrities unto some minoration of our offences.

Minoration, i. e. the Lessening, or extenuation.

Browne, VULGAR ERRORS, *Book I, chap. v, p. 13.*

> Surely that man was constituted for *Anticera.* . . .

[19] Coleridge frequently corrects the errors in the text throughout. Such corrections have not been incorporated in these notes.

Anticera, a place famous for the growth of Hellebore, a place supposed to cure madness.

Browne, VULGAR ERRORS, *Book I, chap. v, p. 13.*

And truth which wise men say doth lye in a well is not recoverable but by exantlation.

The act of drawing up, as a bucket from a well, from ἐξ from, and ἄντλον, a sewer, & thence any deep place containing water.

Browne, VULGAR ERRORS, *Book I, chap. v, p. 13.* *[Marked text.]*

It were some extenuation of the curse, if *in sudore vultus tui* were confinable unto corporal exercitations, and there still remained a Para-
※ dise or unthorny place of knowledge. But now our understandings being eclipsed, as well as our tempers infirmed, we must betake ourselves to waies of reparation, and depend upon the illumination of our
※ endeavours. For thus we may in some measure repair our primary ruines, and build our selves men again.

Browne, VULGAR ERRORS, *Book I, chap. v, p. 14.* *[Marked text.]*

For not obeying the dictates of reason, and neglecting the cries of truth, we fail not only in the trust of our undertakings, but in the intention of man it self. Which although more venial in ordinary constitutions, and such as are not framed beyond the capacity of beaten notions, yet will it inexcusably condemn some men, who having received
= excellent endowments, have yet sat down by the way, and frustrated the intention of their habilities. For certainly some men have sinned in the principles of humanity, and must answer, for not being men, so others offend if they be not more.

O me!!

Browne, VULGAR ERRORS, *Book I, chap. vi, p. 18.* *[Marked text.]*

F They [the ancients] understood not the motion of the eighth sphear from West to east, and so conceived the longitude of the stars invariable.

Browne, VULGAR ERRORS, *Book I, chap. vii, pp. 18-19.* *[Marked text.]*

Q Yet are their Authorities but temporary, and not to be imbraced beyond the minority of our intellectuals.

Browne, VULGAR ERRORS, *Book I, chap. vii, p. 20.*

Of no illation in the negative. . . .

i. e. *can have no argument brought from it to prove the negative.*

Browne, VULGAR ERRORS, *Book I, chap. vii, p. 20.* *[Marked text and note.]*

Whereas indeed the reason of man hath not such restraint; concluding not only affirmatively but negatively; not only affirming there is no

F magnitude beyond the last heavens, but also denying there is any
vacuity within them. Although it be confessed, the affirmative hath
the prerogative illation, and *Barbara* engrosseth the powerful demonstration.

Barbara, one of jargon words in a Latin verse, formed as an instrument of technical memory of the divisions or sorts of Syllogisms in the
old Systems of Logic.

Browne, VULGAR ERRORS, *Book I, chap. viii, p. 22.*
> The first in order, as also in time shall be *Herodotus* of *Halicarnassus.*

The Veracity and Credibility of Herodotus has increased, and increases with the increase of our Discoveries. Several relations deemed
fabulous have been authenticated within the last 30 years from this
present 1808.

Browne, VULGAR ERRORS, *Book I, chap. viii, p. 22.*
> [Sir John Mandeville] left a book of Travels: . . . herein he often
> attesteth the fabulous relations of *Ctesias.*

Many, if not most of these Ctesian Fables in Sir. J. Mandevill were
monkish interpolations.

Browne, VULGAR ERRORS, *Book I, chap. viii, p. 25.*
> [Cardanus] is of singular use unto a prudent Reader; but unto him
> that only desireth *Hoties,* or to replenish his head with varieties, . . .
> he may become no small occasion of error.

Hoties—i. e. ὅτι, *whatevers,* that is whatever is written, no matter
what, true or false,—*omniana;* "all sorts of varieties," as a dear young
Lady once said to me.

Browne, VULGAR ERRORS, *Book I, chap. viii, p. 25.   [Marked text.]*
> And seeing the lapses of these worthy pens [of the learned], to cast
> a wary eye on those diminutive, and pamphlet Treatises daily published
> ※ amongst us. Pieces maintaining rather Typography then verity; Authors
> presumably writing by commonplaces, wherein for many years pro
> ⊙ miscuously amassing all that makes for their subject, they break forth
> at last, in trite and fruitless Rhapsodies; doing thereby not only open
> injury unto learning, but committing a secret treachery upon truth.

Browne, VULGAR ERRORS, *Book I, chap. ix, p. 29.*
> Nothing is not appetible. . . .

> *capable of being wished for*

Browne, VULGAR ERRORS, *Book I, chap. ix, p. 35.*
> If *Heraclitus* with his adherents will hold the Sun is no bigger than it
> appeareth.

It is not improbable, that Heraclitus meant only to imply, that we *perceive* only our own sensations, and they of course are what they are; that the *Image* of the Sun is an appearance, or sensation in our eyes &c, and of course, an appearance can be neither more [nor] less than what it *appears* to be; that the *notion* of the *true Size* of the Sun is *not* an *Image*, or belonging either to sense, or the sensuous fancy, but is an imageless Truth of the understanding, obtained by intellectual Deductions. He could not possibly mean what Sir T. B. supposes him to have meant: for if he had believed the Sun to be no more than a mile distant from us, every Tree and House must have shewn it's absurdity. S. T. C.

Browne, VULGAR ERRORS, *Book I, at end, p. 36.*

In the following Books I have endeavoured (wherever the author himself is in "a vulgar Error") as far as my knowledge extends, to give in the margin, either the demonstrated Discoveries, or more probable opinions, of the present Natural Philosophy: so that, independent of the entertainingness of the Thoughts and Tales, and the force & splendor of Sir T. Brown's Diction and Manner, you may at once learn *from him* the history of human Fancies & Superstitions, both when he detects them & when he himself falls into them—& from my notes, the real Truth of Things, or at least the highest degree of Probability, at which human Research has hitherto arrived. S. T. C.

Browne, VULGAR ERRORS, *Book II, chap. i, p. 37.* [*Production of crystal.*]

Cold = the attractive or astringent power, comparatively uncounteracted by the dilative, the diminution of which is the proportional increase of the contractive. Hence the astringent or power of negative Magnetism is the proper agent in cold, and the contractive, or Oxygen, an allied and consequential power. *Chrystallum, non ex aquâ, sed ex substantiâ metallorum communi confrigoratum.* As the Equator, or mid-point of the equatorial hemispherical Line to the Center, so Water to Gold. Hydrogen = electrical Azot: Azot = Magnetic Hydrogen.

Browne, VULGAR ERRORS, *Book II, chap. i, p. 39.*

[Crystal] will strike fire upon percussion like many other stones; and upon collision with steel actively send forth its sparks, not much inferiourly unto a flint.

It being, indeed, nothing else but pure Flint.

Browne, VULGAR ERRORS, *Book II.* [*Plate opposite p. 48.*]

Misplaced = See p. 48, Garden of Cyrus—towards the end of Vol.

Browne, VULGAR ERRORS, *Book II, chap. iii, p. 58. Note continued on p. 59.*

And the Magick thereof [the lodestone] not safely to be believed, which was delivered by *Orpheus,* that sprinkled with water it will upon a question emit a voice not much unlike an Infant.

i. e. To the twin counterforces of the Magnetic Power, the equilibrium of which is revealed in magnetic Iron, as the substantial, add the twin counterforces, or $+$ and $-$ poles, of the Electrical Power, the indifference of which is realized in Water, as the Superficial (whence Orpheus employed the term *sprinkled,* or rather affused or superfused) and you will hear the voice of infant Nature; i. e. you will understand the rudimental products and elementary Powers and Constructions of the phænomenal World. An Enigma not unworthy of Orpheus, & therefore not improbably ascribed to him. S. T. C.
P. S. $-$ & $+$ Magn. Attraction and Repulsion: or Cohesion and Dispersion. $-$ and $+$ Elect. $=$ Contraction and Dilation.

Browne, VULGAR ERRORS, *Book II, chap. vi, p. 74.*

Many Mola's and false conceptions there are of *Mandrakes,* the first from great Antiquity, conceiveth the Root thereby resembleth the shape of Man.

See Donne's Metempsych.

Browne, VULGAR ERRORS, *Book II, chap. vii, p. 82.*

That Camphire or Eunuchates begets in Men an impotency unto venery observation will hardly confirm.

There is no doubt of the Fact as to a *temporary* effect: and Camphire is therefore a strong and immediate antidote to an overdose of Cantharides. Yet there are, doubtless, sorts & cases of *Imp.* which Camphire might relieve. Opium is occasionally Aphrodisaic, but far oftener Antiaphrodisaic. The same is true of *Bang,* or powdered Hemp leaves, and I suppose of the whole tribe of narcotic Stimulants.

Browne, VULGAR ERRORS, *Book II, chap. vii, p. 83.*

The Yew and the berries thereof are harmless, we know.

The berries are harmless, but the leaves of the yew are undoubtedly poisonous. Vide *Withering,* British Plants. Taxus.

Browne, VULGAR ERRORS, *Book III, chap. xiii, p. 111.*

Snails, a soft and exosseous Animal.

boneless.

Browne, VULGAR ERRORS, *Book III, chap. xiii, p. 111.*

For although *Lapidaries* and questuary enquirers affirm it.
Questuary—having Gain or money for their object.

Browne, VULGAR ERRORS, *Book III, chap.' xvii, p. 119.*

As for the mutation of the sexes or transition into one another, we cannot deny it in Hares, it being observable in Man.

A mere [?] Disease of the κλειτορίς is here taken for a *Transexion.*

Browne, VULGAR ERRORS, *Book VI, chap. viii, p. 264.*

The river Gihon, a branch of *Euphrates* and River of Paradise.

The rivers from Eden were meant to symbolize, or rather meant only, the great primary Races of Mankind. Sir. T. B. was the very man to have seen this, but the superstition of the *Letter* was then culminant.

Browne, VULGAR ERRORS, *Book VI, chap. x, p. 272. Note continued on pp. 273-74.*

The *Chymists* have laudably reduced their causes [of colors] unto Sal, Sulphur, and Mercury.

Even now, after all the brilliant discoveries from Scheele, Priestly and Cavendish, to Borzelius, and Sir. H. Davy, no improvement has been made in this division, not of primary Bodies (those idols of the modern atomic chemistry), but of *causes,* as Sir T. B. rightly expresses them—i. e. of elementary Powers manifested in Bodies. Mercury standing for the bi-polar Metallic Principle, best imaged as a line or axis from N. to S., the North or Negative Pole being the cohesive or coherentific Force, and the South or Positive Pole being the dispersive or incoherentic Force, the first predominant in and therefore represented by Carbon, the second by Nitrogen—the Series of metals being the primary and hence indecomponible Syntheta and proportions of both. In like manner the Sulphur represents the active and passive Principle of Fire: i. e. the contractive Force = negative Electricity, Oxygen, Flame; and the dilative Force = Warmth + El. and Hydrogen, and lastly Salt as the Equilibrium or Compound of the two former. So taken, Salt, Sulphur, and Mercury are equivalent to the Combustive, the combustible, and the Combust, under one or other of which all known Bodies or ponderable Substances may be classed and distinguished.

Browne, VULGAR ERRORS, *Book VII, chap. xvi, p. 314.*

Generations by the devill very improbable. . . .

Sir T. Brown's doubts.

Browne, RELIGIO MEDICI, *Part I, sec. 1, p. 1. Note at end of "To the Reader."*

> For my Religion, though there be several circumstances that might perswade the world I have none, at all, as the generall scandall of my profession . . .

The *historical* origin of this scandal, which in nine cases out of ten is the honor of the medical Profession, may perhaps be found in the fact, that Ænesidemus and Sextus Empiricus, Sceptics, were both Physicians—about the close of the second Century. A fragment from the former has been preserved by Photius, and such as would leave a painful regret for the loss of the work, had not the invaluable work of Sextus Empiricus been still extant.

Browne, RELIGIO MEDICI, *Part I, sec. 7, p. 2. Note continued on p. 7 [so numbered].*

> A third there is which I did never positively maintaine, or practice, but have often wished it had been consonant to Truth, and not offensive to my Religion, and that is, the prayer for the dead, &c.

Our church with her characteristic Christian Prudence does not enjoin Prayer for the Dead, but neither does she prohibit it. In its own nature it belongs to a private aspiration; and being conditional, like all religious acts not expressed in Scripture, and therefore not combinable with a perfect faith, it is something between prayer and wish—an act of natural piety sublimed by Christian Hope, that shares in the light and meets the diverging rays, of Faith, though it be not contained in the Focus.

Browne, RELIGIO MEDICI, *Part I, sec. 13, p. 8.*

> He holds no Counsell, but that mysticall one of the Trinity, wherein though there be three persons, there is but one mind that decrees without contradiction, &c.

Sir T. B. is very amusing. He confesses his past Heresies, which are mere opinions: while his orthodoxy is full of heretical errors. *His* Trinity is a mere *trefoil,* a $3a = 1B$, which is no mystery at all, but a common object of the senses. The mystery is, that One is Three, i. e. each Being the whole God.

Browne, RELIGIO MEDICI, *Part I, sec. 18, p. 10. Note continued on p. 11.*

> 'Tis not a ridiculous devotion to say a prayer before a game at Tables, &c.

But a great profanation, methinks: and a no less absurdity. Would Sir T. Brown before weighing two pigs of Lead, *a* and *b,* pray to God that *a* might weigh the heavier? Yet if the result of the Dice be at the time equally believed to be a settled & predetermined Effect, where lies the Difference? Would not this apply against all petitionary prayer?—St. Paul's injunction involves the answer:—Pray *always*.

Browne, RELIGIO MEDICI, *Part I, sec. 22, p. 12. Note continued on p. 13.* [*End of note cut.*]

> They who to salve this would make the Deluge particular, proceed upon a principle that I can no way grant, &c.

But according to the Scripture, the Deluge was so gentle as to leave uncrushed the green leaves on the Olive Tree. If then it was universal, and if (as admitting the longevity of the ante-diluvians it must have been) the Earth was fully peopled, is it not strange that no Buildings remain in the since then uninhabited parts—in America for instance? That no human skeletons are found may be solved from the circumstances of the large proportion of Phosphoric acid in human Bones. But Cities and Traces of Civilization? I do not know what to think—unless we might be allowed to consider Noah a Homo repræsentatus, [or the last and nearest of a series taken for the whole.]

Browne, RELIGIO MEDICI, *Part I, sec. 33, p. 15.* [*End of note cut.*]

> They that to refute the Invocation of Saints, have denied that they have any knowledge of our affaires below, have proceeded too farre, and must pardon my opinion, till I can thoroughly answer that piece of Scripture, *At the conversion of a sinner the Angels of Heaven rejoyce.*

Take any moral or religious book, and instead of understanding each sentence according to the main purpose and intention, interpret every phrase in its literal sense as conveying, and intended to convey, a metaphysical verity or historical Fact:—what a strange Medley of Doctrines should we not educe? And yet this is [the way in which we are constantly in the habit of treating the books of the New Testament.]

Browne, RELIGIO MEDICI, *Part. I, sec. 34, p. 15.*

> And, truely, for the first chapters of *Genesis* I must confesse a great deal of obscurity; though Divines have to the power of humane reason endeavoured to make all go in a literall meaning, yet those allegoricall interpretations are also probable, and perhaps, the mysticall method of *Moses* bred up in the Hieroglyphicall Schooles of the Egyptians.

The 2nd C. Gen. from v. 4, is as evidently symbolical as the 1st Chap. is literal. The first is by Moses himself; the 2nd of far greater antiquity, and probably translated into words from graven stones.

Browne, RELIGIO MEDICI, Part I, sec. 48, p. 19.

This ¶ is a series of ingenious paralogisms.

Browne, RELIGIO MEDICI, Part I, sec. 49, p. 20.

Moses that was bred up in all the learning of the *Egyptians,* committed a grosse absurdity in Philosophy, when with these eyes of flesh he desired to see God, and petitioned his Maker, that is, truth itself, to a contradiction.

Bear in mind the Jehovah Logos, the ὁ ῏Ων ἐν κόλπῳ πατρός, the Person ad extra and few passages in the O. T. are more instructive, or of profounder Import. Overlook this, or deny it, and none so perplexing, or so irreconcilable with the known character of the inspired Writer.

Browne, RELIGIO MEDICI, Part I, sec. 50, p. 20.

For that mysticall metall of Gold, whose solary & celestiall nature I admire, &c.

Rather "anti-solar and terrene nature." For Gold, most of all Metals, repelleth Light, and resisteth that power and portion of the common Air, which of all ponderable bodies is most akin to Light, and it's surrogate in the realm of Antiphos or Gravity: viz. Oxygen. Gold is *Tellurian* κατ' ἐξοχήν: and if solar, yet as in the solidity and dark Nucleus of the Sun. Iron terrestrial or Earthy the [cut?]

Browne, RELIGIO MEDICI, Part I, sec. 52, p. 20. Note on p. 21.

I thank God that with joy I mention it, I was never afraid of Hell, nor never grew pale at the description of that place! I have so fixed my contemplations on Heaven, that I have almost forgot the Idea of Hell, &c.

¶ 52. Excellent throughout. The fear of Hell, may, indeed, in some desperate cases, like the Moxa, give the first *rouse* from a moral Lethargy, or like the green Venom of Copper, evacuating poison or a dead load from the inner man, prepare it for nobler ministrations and medicines from the realm of Light and Life, that nourish while they stimulate.

Browne, RELIGIO MEDICI, Part I, sec. 54, p. 21. [Note cut at end.]

There is no salvation to those that believe not in Christ, &c.

This is plainly confined to such as have had Christ preached unto them—but the doctrine, that Salvation is in and by Christ only, is a most essential Verity, and an article of unspeakable grandeur and consolation. Name, Nomen, that is, νούμενον, in its spiritual interpretation, is the same as power, or intrinsic Cause. What? Is it a few Letters of the Alphabet, the Hearing of which [in a given succession, that saves?]

Browne, RELIGIO MEDICI, *Part I, sec. 59, p. 22.*

> *Before Abraham was, I am,* is the saying of Christ; yet is it true in some sense if I say it of my self, for I was not only before my self, but *Adam,* that is, in the idea of God, and the decree of that Synod held from all Eternity. And in this sense, I say, the world was before the Creation, and at an end before it had a beginning; and thus was I dead before I was alive, though my grave be *England,* my dying-place was Paradise, and *Eve* miscarried of me before she conceived of *Cain.*

Compare this with p. 8 and the judicious remark on the mere accommodation in the *præ* of predestination. But the subject was too *tempting for the Rhetorician.*

Browne, RELIGIO MEDICI, *Part II, sec. 1, p. 23.*

> But as in casting account, three or four men together come short in account of one man placed by himself below them, &c.

Thus, 1,965. But why is the 1, said to be placed *below* the 965?

Browne, RELIGIO MEDICI, *pp. 23, 25. Note on blank page, end of* GARDEN OF CYRUS.

Religio Medici, p. 23. Column the first, on the Multitude—an admirable ¶. P. 25 full of *fine* observations, especially Sect. 6 on the difficulty of recollecting the images of those we most dearly love.

Browne, RELIGIO MEDICI, *Part II, sec. 7, p. 26.*

> Let me be nothing, if within the compass of myself, I do not finde the battaile of *Lepanto,* passion against reason, reason against faith, faith against the Devill, and my Conscience against all.

It may appear whimsical, but I really feel an impatient regret, that this good man had so misconceived the nature of both Faith and of Reason as to affirm their contrariety to each other.

Browne, RELIGIO MEDICI, *Part II, sec. 7, p. 26. [Note cut at end.]*

> For my originall sin, I hold it to bee washed away in my Baptisme; for my actual transgressions, I compute & reckon with God, but from my last repentance, &c.

This is most true as far [as] the imputation of the same is concerned. For where the means of avoiding it's consequences have been afforded, each after transgression is actual, by a neglect of those.

Browne, RELIGIO MEDICI, *Part II, sec. 14, p. 29.*

> *God,* being all goodnesse, can love nothing but himself; he loves us but for that part, which is as it were himselfe, and the traduction of his holy Spirit.

This recalls a sublime thought of Spinosa. Every true virtue is a part of that Love, with which God loveth himself.

Browne, GARDEN OF CYRUS, *chap. iii, p. 54.*

> That bodies are first spirits, *Paracelsus* could affirm, &c.

Effects purely relative from properties merely comparative, such as edge, point, grater, &c. are not proper Qualities: for they are indifferently producible ab extra, by grinding, &c., and ab intra from growth. In the latter instance, they *suppose* Qualities as their antecedents. Now, therefore, since Qualities cannot result from Quantity, but Quantity from Qual.,—and as matter ✕ spirit is shape by modification of extension, or pure Quantity,—Paracelsus's *dictum* is defensible.

Browne, GARDEN OF CYRUS, *chap. iii, p. 54.*

> The Æquivocall production of things under undiscerned principles, makes a large part of generation, &c.

Written before Harvey's ab ovo omnia. Since his work, and Leuenhoek's microscopium, the question is settled in Physics; but whether in Metaphysics, is not quite so clear.

Browne, GARDEN OF CYRUS, *chap. iv, p. 58.*

> And mint growing in glasses of water, until it arriveth at the weight of an ounce, in a shady place, will sometimes exhaust a pound of water.

How much did B[rown] allow for evaporation?

Browne, GARDEN OF CYRUS, *chap. iv, p. 61.*

> Things entering upon the intellect by a Pyramid from without, and thence into the memory by another from within, the common decussation being in the understanding as is delivered by a *Bovillus.*[20]

This nearly resembles Kant's intellectual Mechanique.

Browne, GARDEN OF CYRUS, *blank page opposite p. 64.*

The Platonists held three Knowledges of God 1. παρουσία his own incommunicable self-comprehension—2. κατὰ νόησιν —of pure inner life, unmixed with sensuous—3. κατ' ἐπιστήμην—or discursive intelligential knowledge. Thus a Greek philosopher:— τοὺς ἐπιστημονικοὺς λόγους μύθους ἡγήσεται συνοῦσα τῷ πατρὶ καὶ συνεστιωμένη ἡ ψυχὴ ἐν τῇ ἀληθείᾳ τοῦ ὄντος, καὶ ἐν αὐγῇ καθαρᾷ=

Those notions of God which we attain by processes of intellect, the soul will consider as mythological allegories, when it exists in union with the Father, and is feasting with him in the Truth of *very*

[20] ''Car. Bovillus de intellectu.'' Coleridge's note.

Being, and in the pure (= the unmixed, absolutely simple & elementary) Splendor. Thus expound Exod. 33. 20. By the face of God, Moses meant the ἰδέα νοητική which God declared incompatible with human Life—κατὰ νόησιν=ἐπαφὴν τοῦ νοητοῦ, the contact &c. S. T. Coleridge

At the end of entire work, end-page.

The difference between a great mind's and a little mind's use of History. The Latter would consider, for instance, what Luther did, taught, or sanctioned: the former, what Luther, *a* Luther, would *now* do, teach, and sanction.

Occurred to me midnight, Tuesday, 16 March, 1824, as I was stepping into bed, my eye having glanced on Luther's Table Talk.

Mem. If you would be well with a great Mind, leave him with a favourable opinion of *You;* if with a little mind, leave him with a favourable opinion of himself.

Nov. 22, 1804. I have memorandum—my past self—In fine, too, on a large scale, take up the Idea of a Swedenborgian called on Sir Thomas Brown, & talking over Christianity with him, or Sir Thomas Moore—& on all odd fellows whom I love & who ought to have thought less slavishly quod humilitatem, &c.—This idea haunted me, as I was reading the Vulgar Errors & Rel. Med. of Sir T. Brown.[21]

Sir T. Brown, Quincunx mystically considered. 200. O to write a character of this man.[22]

Is this a mere random flight in etymology,[23] hunting a bubble and bringing back the film? I cannot think so contemptuously of the attempt to fix and restore the true import of *any* word; but, in this instance, I should regard it as neither unprofitable, nor devoid of rational interest, were it only that the knowledge and reception of the import here given, as the etymon, or *genuine* sense of the word, would save Christianity from the reproach of containing a doctrine so repugnant to the best feelings of humanity, as is inculcated in the following passage, among a hundred others to the same purpose, in earlier and

[21] Notebook 21, fol. 108 verso. British Museum, Add. MSS, 47,518. Printed for the first time.
[22] Notebook 9, fol. 21 verso. British Museum, Add. MSS, 47,506. Printed for the first time.
[23] That is, seeking the true meaning of the word *name.*

in more recent works, sent forth by professed Christians. "Most of the men, who are now alive, or that have been living for many ages, are Jews, Heathens, or Mahometans, strangers and enemies to Christ, in whose *name* alone we can be saved. This consideration is extremely sad, when we remember how great an evil it is, that *so many millions of sons and daughters are born to enter into the possession of devils to eternal ages.*"—Taylor's Holy Dying, p. 28. Even Sir T. Browne, while his heart is evidently wrestling with the dogma grounded on the trivial interpretation of the word, nevertheless receives it in this sense, and expresses most gloomy apprehensions "of the ends of those honest worthies and philosophers," who died before the birth of our Saviour: "It is hard," says he, "to place those souls in hell, whose worthy lives did teach us virtue on earth. How strange to them will sound the history of Adam, when they shall suffer for him they never heard of!" Yet he concludes by condemning the insolence of reason in daring to doubt or controvert the verity of the doctrine, or "to question the justice of the proceeding," *which verity,* he fears, the woeful lot of *"these great examples of virtue must confirm."*[24]

So the Loadstone preserved in the Salt of a Lemon has power to attract Gold out of the deepest wells—"Certainly (says Sir Thomas Brown) a studied absurdity, not casually cast out but plotted for perpetuity: for the strangeness of the effect ever to be admired and for the difficulty of the Trial never to be convicted."—(A good specimen of that grave Humour that renders Sir T. B. so delightful to a learned Reader.) But doubtless it is an intended allegory—attractive manners ✗ cautious Delay & Tenacity &c.[25]

[24] Ashe, *Miscellanies,* pp. 253-54.
[25] Notebook 3½, fol. 116 verso. British Museum, Add. MSS, 47,499. Printed for the first time.

Thomas Fuller

Fuller, WORTHIES,[1] *I, v.*

Much might be said, if it were necessary in vindication of the language of Dr. Fuller.

Fuller's language!—Grant me patience, Heaven! A tythe of his beauties would be sold cheap for a whole library of our classical writers from Addison to Johnson and Junius inclusive. And Bishop Nicolson, a painstaking old charewoman in the Antiquarian and Rubbish concern—The venerable Rust and Dust of the whole Firm are not worth an ounce of Fuller's Earth!

Fuller, WORTHIES, *I, vii: "Memoirs of the Author."*

Shakspear! Milton! Fuller! De Foe! Hogarth! As to the remaining mighty Host of our great Men, other countries have produced something like them—but these are uniques. England may challenge the World to shew a correspondent name to either of the Five. I do not say that with the exception of the First, names of equal Glory may not be produced *in a different kind.* But these are *genera,* containing each only one individual.—S. T. C.

Fuller, WORTHIES, *I, vii, viii.*

His fortune upon this occasion was very singular. He had before preached and published a sermon in London upon "the new-moulding Church-reformation," which caused him to be censured as too hot a Royalist; and now from his sermon at Oxford, he was thought to be too lukewarm!

Poor Fuller! with too strong a leaven of University Prejudice not to be warped in favor of the worser of the two Factions, too enlightened not to see it's abuses and errors, and too honest not to admit the truth and force of sundry complaints urged by the other party!—nothing but a miracle of attraction and amiableness in his personal Disposition and

---

[1] Fuller, Thomas, *The History of the Worthies of England* (2 vols.; London: 1811). These notes are printed from a transcription made in a notebook by Sara Coleridge when H. N. Coleridge was collecting material for *Literary Remains.* The notebook is in the possession of A. H. B. Coleridge. They have also been printed by T. A. Trollope, *"Marginalia by S. T. Coleridge," Notes and Queries* (7th ser.), VI, 501.

Demeanor could have saved him, in such a conflict[2] from being stoned by both Factions! To have been abused and slandered—this was merely a powdered Coat from the dust and dirt thrown up by the Shot that had passed him,—and may be fairly accounted as part and sign of his wonderful preservation.

Fuller, WORTHIES, *I, 285.*

> GEORGE MONCK. . . . It is better that I should be *censured,* than he not *commended.*

I remember no other instance of flattery in this not less wise than witty, and (for one speck in a luminary does not forfeit the name) not less honest than liberal Writer, tho' liberal and *sensible* to a degree unprecedented in his age, and unparalleled. These paragraphs, however, form a glaring exception. The flattery is rancid. A more thoroughly worthless Wretch than Monck, or of meaner talents could[3] History furnish wherewith to exemplify the caprice of Fortune. Or shall I not say rather the Judgement of Providence in righteous scorn by chastisement of a thankless and corrupt Nation, bringing in one reptile by the instrumentality of another, a lewd, lazy, mean Tyrant by a brainless avaricious perjured Traitor—and to this hateful Ingrate alone Charles II. shewed himself not an Ingrate! See Clarendon, last Oxford Edition.

Fuller, WORTHIES, *I, 287.*

> SIR WALTER RAWLEIGH . . . found some hopes of the Queen's favours reflecting upon him. This made him write in a glasse window, obvious to the Queen's eye,
> "Fain would I climb, yet fear I to fall."
> Her Majesty, either espying or being shown it, did underwrite,
> "If thy heart fail thee, climb not at all."
> More commonly written
> Fain would I climb, but O! I fear to fall;
> If thy heart fail thee, climb not then at all.

But I prefer Fuller's as more quippish and *adagy.*

Fuller, WORTHIES, *I, 288.*

> I believe that *bilious Bale* would have been sick of the *yellow* Jaundies, if not venting his *choller* in such expressions. [Bale, Cent. iii, Num. 23.]

How happened it, that Fuller is so bitter against Bale?[4] Bale's rest-

---

[2] Sara Coleridge notes, "Conflux seems to be the word," but there seems no objection to the word as written.

[3] Trollope notes, "Apparently 'not' has been omitted here by a slip of the pen." S. C. in copying the notes did not add the negative.

[4] John Bale (1495-1563), a controversialist during the Reformation. His learning was very broad, but his attacks were often coarse and severe.

less and calamitous life (driven as he was from Dan to Beersheba), which renders his voluminous labors a marvel, ought to have shielded him from all severity of censure. And in this instance, and, I think, in some other frowned at by Fuller, Bale was clearly right.

Fuller, WORTHIES, *I, 376.*

> If any demand why the *Thames* hath not an *Higre* as well as the *Severne,* where we find the same cause, and therefore why meet we not with the same effects? I re-demand of them why is there not an *Euripus* with the same reciprocation of Tides, as well about the other *Cyclides,* as *Eubœa* alone?

A single look at two good County Maps in which the course of the Severn from the mouth, and of the width and then the reaches of the Thames, would have explained the existence of the Higre or Boar in the Severn, the Trent, and the Parrot, and it's absence in the Thames without a voyage to the Eubœan Cyclides [*sic*].

Fuller, HOLY STATE,[5] *p. 4 above the picture of St. Monica.*

O what a temptation to wed!

Fuller, HOLY STATE, *Book I, chap. 9, "Life of Eliezer," p. 21.*

> He will not truant it now in the afternoon, but with convenient speed returns to Abraham, who onely was worthy of such a Servant, who onely was worthy of such a Master.

On my word, Eliezer did his business in an orderly and sensible manner; but what there is to call forth this super-economiastic—"who only"—I cannot see. S. T. C.

Fuller, HOLY STATE, *Book I, chap. 10, "The Good Widow," p. 21.*

> She is a woman whose head hath been quite cut off, and yet she liveth, and hath the second part of virginity.

What? was the former in her *head?*

Fuller, HOLY STATE, *Book I, chap. 10, "The Good Widow," pp. 21-22.*

> Excessive was the sorrow of King Richard the second, beseeming him neither as a King, man, or Christian, who so fervently loved Anna of Bohemia his Queen, that when she dyed at Shean in Surrey, he both cursed the place, and also out of madness overthrew the whole house.

I do not remember whether Shakespear hath availed himself of this trait in Rich. II[nd's] Character.

---

[5] Thomas Fuller, *The Holy State* (London: 1663). From Anne Gillman's copy, Ashley Library, British Museum, Ashley, 4775. All but the first, third, and fourth notes appear with minor changes in *Lit. Rem.,* II, 381-84.

Fuller, HOLY STATE, *Book II, chap. 3, "Life of Paracelsus," p. 51. Note on first flyleaf, verso.*

It is a matter of regret with me, that Fuller, (whose wit alike in quantity, quality, and perpetuity, surpassing that of the wittiest in a witty age, robbed him of the praise not less due to him for an equal superiority in sound, shrewd, good sense, and freedom of intellect) had not looked thro' the two Latin Folios of Paracelsus's Works. It is not to be doubted that a rich and delightful Article would have been the result. For who like Fuller could have brought out, and set forth, this singular compound of true philosophic Genius with the morals of a Quack and the manners of a King of the Gypsies! Nevertheless, Paracelsus belonged to his Age, viz. the Dawn of Experimental Science; and a well-written critique on his Life & writings would present thro' the magnifying glass of a Caricature, the distinguishing features of the Helmonts, Kirchers, &c. in short, of the host of Naturalists of the 16th Century. The Period might begin with Paracelsus and end with Sir Kenelm Digby. S. T. C.

N.b. The potential, (= Λόγος θεάνθρωπος) the ground of the Prophetic, directed the first Thinkers, (= Mystæ) to the metallic bodies, as the Key of all natural Science. The *then* Actual blended with this instinct all the fancies, and fond desires, and false perspective, of the childhood of Intellect. The *essence* was truth, the *form* was folly: and this is the definition of Alchemy. Nevertheless, the very terms bear witness to the veracity of the original Instinct. The world of Sensible Experience cannot be more luminously divided than into the modifying powers. τò ἄλλο —that which *differences,* makes this *other* than that; and the μετ' ἄλλο, that which is beyond or deeper than the modification. Metallon is strictly "the Base of the Mode": and such have the metals been determined to be by modern Chemistry. And what are now the great problems of chemistry? The difference of the Metals themselves, their origin, the causes of their locations, of their co-existence in the same ore (ex. gr. of Iridium, Osmium, Palladium, Rhodium, and Iron with Platinum). Were these problems solved, the results who dare limit? In addition to the Celeste Mechanique we might have a new department of Astronomy, the Celeste Chemique, i.e. a philosophic Astrology. And to this I do not hesitate to refer the old connection between Alchemy and Astrology—the same divinity in the idea, the same childishness in the attempt to realize it. Nay, the very invocations of Spirits were not without a ground of truth. The light was for the greater part suffocated and the rest fantastically refracted; but still it was Light struggling in the darkness. And I am persuaded, that to the full triumph of Science, it will be necessary that Nature should be commanded more *spiritually* than hitherto i.e. more directly in the power of *the Will*.

Fuller, HOLY STATE, *Book IV, chap. 19, "The Prince," p. 323. Note on first end-page.*

> He sympathizeth with him that by a proxy is corrected for his offence.

See Sir W. Scott's Fortunes of Nigel. In an oriental Despotism one would not have been surprized in finding such a custom—but in a Christian Court, and under the light of Protestantism, it is marvellous. It would be well to ascertain, if possible, the earliest date of this contrivance—whether it existed under the Plantagenets, or whether first under the Tudors—or lastly, whether it was a precious import from Scotch-land with the gentle King Jamie.

Fuller, HOLY STATE, *Book IV, chap. 21, "The King." Note on first end-page, recto.*

> He is a mortal god . . .

Pp. 334-35 &c. Compare the fulsome flattery of these and other passages in this volume (tho' modest to the common language of James's Priestly Courtiers) with the loyal but free and manly tone of Fuller's later works, towards the close of Charles 1st's reign & under the Commonwealth & Protectorate. And doubtless this was not peculiar to Fuller: but a great and lasting change was effected in the mind of the Country generally. The Bishops and other Church Dignitaries tried for a while to renew the old king-godding *Mumpsimus*—But the Second Charles laughed at them; and they quarrelled with his Successors, and hated the Hero who delivered them from him too thoroughly to have flattered with any unction, even if William's Dutch Phlegm had not precluded the attempt by making it's failure certain.

Fuller, PROFANE STATE,[6] *Book V, chap. 2, p. 387. Note on first end-page, recto.*

> God gave magistrates power to punish them, else they *bear the sword in vain*. They may command people to serve God, who herein have no cause to complain.

P. 387—and elsewhere. The only serious Macula in Fuller's mind is his uniform support of the right and duty of the Civil Magistrate to punish errors in belief. Fuller would indeed recommend *moderation*

---

[6] Thomas Fuller, *The Profane State* (London: 1663). This note appears, with editing in capitals and punctuation, in *Lit. Rem.*, II, 384. It is here given from British Museum, Ashley, 4775.

in the practice; but of Upas, Woorara, and Persecution there are no *moderate* doses possible.

Fuller, CHURCH HISTORY,[7] *Book I, Cent. 5, sec. 1, p. 27.*

> Pelagius:—Let no Foreiner insult on the infelicity of our Land in bearing this Monster.

It raises or ought to raise our estimation of Fuller's good sense & the general Temperance of his Judgement when we see the heavy weight of prejudices, the universal code of his Age, incumbent on his Judgement —and which nevertheless left sanity of opinion : the general character of his writings : This remark was suggested by the term "Monster" attached to the worthy Cambrian, Pelagius—the Teacher *Arminianismi ante Arminium.*

Fuller, CHURCH HISTORY, *Book II, Cent. 5, sec. 5, p. 54.*

> Whereas in Holy Writ, when Apostles (and Papists commonly call *Augustine* the *English Apostle,* how properly we shall see hereafter) went to a Forreign Nation, God gave them the Language thereof, &c.

What a loss, that Fuller had not made reference to his *authorities* for this assertion—I am sure he could have found none in the New Testament—but facts that imply, & in absence of all such proof, *prove* the contrary.

Fuller, CHURCH HISTORY, *Book II, Cent. 6, sec. 6, p. 55. Note on second flyleaf, recto.*

> Thus we see the whole Week bescattered with *Saxon* Idols, whose Pagan-Gods were the God-fathers of the Dayes, and gave them their Names. This some Zealot may behold as the Object of a necessary Reformation, desiring to have the Dayes of the Week new dipt, and called after other Names. Though indeed this Supposed Scandall will not offend the wise, as beneath their Notice, and cannot offend the Ignorant, as above their Knowledge.

Book II. p. 55 § 6 [——?]. A curious prediction fulfilled a few years after in the Quakers; and well worthy of being extracted and addressed to the present *Friends.* Mem. Error of the Friends, but natural & common to almost all sects, the perversion of the Wisdom of the

[7] Thomas Fuller, *The Church History of Brittain* (London: 1655). British Museum, Ashley, 4774. This volume originally belonged to Basil Montagu and bears his name. It was presented by him to James Gillman, Aug. 24, 1826 (see inscription on first flyleaf). Lamb borrowed this book and returned it in 1830 with this note: "Dear Gillman, Pray do you, or S. T. C., immediately write, to say you have received back the golden works of the dear, fine, silly old angel, which I part from bleeding." The notes, with the exception of one on p. 136 of Book XI, are printed with some editorial changes in *Lit. Rem.,* II, 386-90.

first Establishers of their Sect into their own Folly by not distinguishing between the conditionally right and the permanently and essentially
so. Ex. gr. It was *right* conditionally in the Apostles to forbid black
puddings even to the Gentile Christians, and it was wisdom in them—
but to continue the prohibition would be folly & Judaism in us. The
elder Church very sensibly distinguished Episcopal from Apostolic Inspiration—the Episcopal Spirit, i.e. that which dictated what was fit
and profitable for a particular Community or Church at a particular
period from the Apostolic & Catholic Spirit, which dictated Truth and
Duties of permanent and universal Obligation. S. T. C.

Fuller, CHURCH HISTORY, *Book II, Cent. 7, p. 59.*

Latin Dedication—remarkably pleasing and elegant—Milton in his
classical Youth, the æra of his Lycidas, might have written it—only he
would have given it in Latin Verse.

Fuller, CHURCH HISTORY, *Book X, Cent. 17, sec. 20, p. 11.*

Bp. of Lond. May your majesty be pleased, that the ancient Canon
may be remembered, *Schismatici contra Episcopos non sunt audiendi.*
And, there is another Decree of a very ancient Council, That no man
should be admitted to speak against that whereunto he hath formerly
subscribed.
And as for you Doctor Reynolds, and your Sociates, how much are ye
bound to his Majestie's Clemency, permitting you, contrary to the
Statute *primo Elizabethæ,* so freely to speak against the Liturgie, and
Discipline established. Faine would I know the end you aime at, and
whether you be not of Mr. Cartwright's minde, who affirmed, That we
ought in Ceremonies rather to conforme to the Turks than to the
Papists. I doubt you approve his Position, because here appearing
before his Majesty in Turkey-Gownes, not in your Scholastick habits,
according to the order of the Universities.

If any man, who like myself hath attentively read the Church History of the reign of Elizabeth, and the Conference before and with her
pedant Successor (see Bish. of London's reply to or rather interruption
of Dr. Reynolds, X Book, p. 11) can shew me any essential difference
between Whitgift and Bancroft during their rule, and Bonner and
Gardner in the reign of Mary, I will be thankful to him in my heart
and for him in my prayers. One difference I see, viz. that the former
professing the New Testament to be their rule & guide, and making the
fallibility of all Churches and Individuals an article of faith, were more
inconsistent and therefore less excusable, than the Popish Persecutors.
S. T. C. 30 Aug. 1824. N.B. The crimes, murderous as they were,
were the vice and delusion of the *Age,* and it is ignorance to lack charity

towards the persons, Papist, or Protestant; but the *tone,* the *spirit,* characterizes, and belongs to, the Individual—ex. gr., the bursting spleen of this Bancroft, not so satisfied with this precious Arbitrator for having precondemned his opponents, as fierce and surly with him for not hanging them up unheard!

Fuller, CHURCH HISTORY, *Book XI, Cent. 17, sec. 3, p. 136.*

> During the sitting of the last *Parliament,* one *Leighton* a *Scotish-man,* presented a Book unto them: had he been an *Englishman,* we durst call him a *furious,* and will terme him a *fiery* (whence *kindled* let other ghess) *Writer.* His Book consisted of a continued railing, from the beginning to the end; exciting the Parliament and People to kill all the Bishops, and to smite them under the *fifth Rib.* He bitterly enveyed against the *Queen,* calling hir a *Daughter* of *Heth,* a *Canaanite* and *Idolatress,* and ZIONS PLEA *was* the specious Title of his *Pamphlet.* . .

Did Fuller copy this Lie from Heylin or H. from F.? For a wicked *Lie* it is. Leighton recommending some act of Reform adds that this would be the way to smite Prelacy under the 5th Rib. He had before expressly and affectionately disclaimed every evil wish against the Persons whose Learning & Virtues as Individuals he extols.

Fuller, CHURCH HISTORY, *second flyleaf, recto and continued on verso.*

Next to Shakespeare I am not certain whether Thomas Fuller, beyond all other writers, does not excite in me the sense and emotion of the Marvellous; the *degree,* in which any given faculty or combination of faculties is possessed and manifested, so far surpassing what one would have thought *possible* in a single mind, as to give one's Admiration the flavor and quality of Wonder! Wit was the Stuff and Substance of Fuller's Intellect—it was the Element, the earthen base, the material which he worked in—& this very circumstance has defrauded him of his due praise for the practical wisdom of the Thoughts, for the beauty and variety of the Truths, he shaped the Stuff into. T. Fuller was incomparably the most *sensible,* the *least* prejudiced, great man of an Age that boasted a Galaxy of great men. He is a very voluminous writer, and yet in all his numerous Volumes on so many different subjects, it is scarcely too much to say, that you will hardly find a page in which some one sentence out of every three does not deserve to be quoted for itself, as motto or as maxim,—*God bless thee,* dear Old Man!! May I meet with thee!—which is tantamount to—may I go to heaven! S. T. Coleridge July, 1829, Grove, Highgate.

John Milton

This edition of Milton therefore by the excellent and laborious BIRCH, corrected with a care worthy of the praise of Milton himself, cannot but rise in value; and I dare prophecy that in less than twenty years, it will be sold at not less than ten guineas. I greatly prefer this folio to the quarto edition of Milton, which some have bought in order to have his prose Works uniform with the fourth edition of his poetical Works, even for the opposite reason. Admirable to the very height of praise as Milton's prose works are, yet they are of a party, in country, in religion, in politics, and even in MORALS (the Treatise on the Power of Divorce), a party indeed, to which in all respects, I cleave with head, heart, and body; but yet, it is a *party.* But his poetry belongs to the whole world! It is alike the property of the Churchman and the dissenter, the Protestant and the Catholic, the Monarchist and the Republican, and of every country on earth except the kingdom of Dahomey in Africa, for the PRESENT at least, and of France (as long as it shall be inhabited by Frenchmen) FOR EVER! A mine of lead could sooner take wing and mount aloft at the call of the sun, with the dews and with the lark, than the witty, discontinuous intellect, and sensual sum-total of a Frenchman could soar up to religion, or to Milton and Shakespeare. It is impossible.[1]

In Pindar, Chaucer, Dante, Milton, &c. &c. we have instances of the close connection of poetic genius with the love of liberty and of genuine reformation.[2]

"A Learned Plainness." Inquisitions Scotic.,[3] *p. 60.* BIOG. SCOT., *157-60.*

The Vindication of Cromwell's Ejection of the Republican Parliament grounded on mere Railings against the members is the only Passage of Milton's Life or Writings I find it impossible to defend and (with

[1] [Mary Stuart], *Letters from the Lake Poets to Daniel Stuart, 1800-1838* (Printed for private circulation: 1889), pp. 80-81.

[2] *Biog. Lit.,* I, 205.

[3] *Biographia Scoticana; or a brief Historical Account of the Lives, Characters, and Memorable Transactions of the Most Eminent Scots Worthies* (Leith: 1816).

scarcely less anguish than if I were speaking of some dear Friend, whose
Bier I had just been following, do I say it) difficult even to palliate. I
might indeed refer to Milton's political Principles, viz. that the settling
of Liberty must necessarily be effected by a Dictature, that Liberty consisted in the government of the Wise and Godly—to his Confidence in
Cromwell from the utter incapability of conceiving how such a man
should turn from so full a Glory to the toys of vulgar Ambition &c.
but instead of stammering excuse I will rather make use of this ominous
Sun-spot as a Warning to Men, who have drawn down a faithful *Genius*
with them in their descent from Heaven, not to sink from their fixed
sphere of contemplation into the orbit of wandering Stars & personal
Interests—which their very Excellences prevent them from understanding—for Likeness is the only organ of true perception.[4]

We spoke of Milton. He was, said Coleridge, a most determined
aristocrat, an enemy to popular elections, and he would have been
most decidely hostile to the Jacobins of the present day. He would
have thought our popular freedom excessive. He was of opinion that
the government belonged to the wise, and he thought the people fools.
In all his works there is but *one* exceptionable passage,—that in which
he vindicates the expulsion of the members from the House of Commons
by Cromwell. Coleridge on this took occasion to express his approbation of the death of Charles . . .
Coleridge remarked on the lesson of tolerance taught us by the
opposite opinions entertained concerning the death of Charles by such
great men as Milton and Jeremy Taylor.[5]

I have seldom felt greater indignation than at finding in a large
manufactory a sixpenny pamphlet, containing a selection of inflammatory paragraphs from the prose-writings of Milton, without a hint
given of the time, occasion, state of government, &c. under which they
were written—not a hint, that the Freedom, which we now enjoy, exceeds all that Milton dared hope for, or deemed practicable; and that
his political creed sternly excluded the populace, and indeed the majority
of the population, from all pretensions to political power. If the manifest bad intention would constitute this publication a seditious Libel, a
good intention equally manifest can not justly be denied its share of influence in producing a contrary verdict.[6]

[4] Notebook 30, fol. 64 verso-63 recto (written back to front). Printed for the
first time.
[5] Dec. 23, 1810. Robinson, *Diary*, p. 199, 200.
[6] *The Friend*, General Introduction, Essay XI, I, 129-30.

It was the error of Milton, Sidney, and others of that age, to think it possible to construct a purely aristocratical government, defecated of all passion, and ignorance, and sordid motive. The truth is, such a government would be weak from its utter want of sympathy with the people to be governed by it.[7]

THE QUARTERLY REVIEW, X (October, 1813), 94.

Even Milton has joined in this ill-deserved reproach. "I persuade myself," says he, "if our zeal to true religion, and the brotherly usage of our truest friends were as notorious to the world as our prelatical schism, and captivity to *pocket apothegms,* we had ere this seen our old conquerors, and afterwards liegemen, the Normans, together with the Britains, our proper colony, and all the Gascoins that are the rightful dowry of our ancient Kings, come with cap and knee, desiring the shadow of the English sceptre to defend them from the hot persecutions and taxes of the French. But when they come hither and see a tympany of Spaniolised bishops, swaggering in the foretop of the state, and meddling to turn and dandle the royal ball with unskilful and pedantic palms, no marvel though they think it as unsafe to commit religion and liberty to their arbitrating as to a synagogue of Jesuits."
But against the opinion of those who think that we ought to have departed as widely as possible from all the forms and institutions of the Romish church, and that the general cause of Protestantism was injured because the change was not sufficiently broad and striking, there is the weighty testimony of Sully. When that distinguished statesman came over to congratulate James upon his accession, and saw our Church Service, he remarked, that if the French Protestants had retained the same advantages of order and decency, there would at that time have been thousands more Protestants in France.

I will yield to no man in attachment to the Church of England, yet I dare justify this passage of Milton's as equally wise and accurate as it is forcible. Had the Church adopted Usher's plan of moderate Episcopacy by anticipation, all the Protestant Churches of Europe might have gathered under her wings. There is nothing in the assertion of Sully at all irreconcilable with this.

By the by, what stronger proof can we desire than the known fact, that Laud's and Hammond's tenet concerning the *jus divinum* of Bishops &c. is obsolete; at least, *inter inusitatissima—dogma omnimodo insolens?* So that the Church is lumbered with the huge machinery without the power—a steam-engine without the steam.[8]

I have endeavored in a previous discourse to persuade the more highly gifted and educated part of my friends and fellow-christians,

[7] May 21, 1832. *Table Talk S,* VI, 396. Cf. *Essays,* II, 547. ''Milton was a pure republican, and yet his notions of government were highly aristocratic.''
[8] *Notes Theolog.,* pp. 143-44.

that as the *New* Testament sets forth the means and conditions of spiritual convalescence, with all the laws of conscience relative to our future state and permanent Being; so does the *Bible* present to us the elements of *public* prudence, instructing us in the true causes, the surest preventives, and the only cures, of public evils. The authorities of Raleigh, Clarendon, and Milton must at least exempt me from the blame of singularity, if undeterred by the contradictory charges of paradoxy from one party and of adherence to vulgar and old-fashioned prejudices from the other, I persist in avowing my conviction, that the inspired poets, historians, and sententiaries of the Jews, are the clearest teachers of political economy; in short, that their writings are the STATEMAN'S BEST MANUAL, not only as containing the first principles and ultimate grounds of state-policy whether in prosperous times or in those of danger and distress, but as supplying likewise the details of their *application,* and as being a full and spacious repository of precedents and facts in proof.[9]

John Bunyan

Plato's Republic is like Bunyan's Town of Man-Soul,—a description of an individual, all of whose faculties are in their proper subordination and inter-dependence; and this it is assumed may be the prototype of the state as one great individual. But there is this sophism in it, that it is forgotten that the human faculties, indeed, are parts and not separate things; but that you could never get chiefs who were wholly reason, ministers who were wholly understanding, soldiers all wrath, labourers all concupiscence, and so on through the rest. Each of these partakes of, and interferes with, all the others.[1]

Take from History it's impertinences—& it differs from the Pilgrims Progress only in the coincidence of the Proper Names with those of the particular Time & Country.[2]

Narrative allegory is distinguished from mythology as reality from symbol; it is, in short, the proper intermedium between person and per-

[9] Introduction to *"Blessed are ye,"* pp. xiii-xv.

<hr>

[1] "Notes on Richard II," *Lit. Rem.,* II, 179.
[2] British Museum, MSS Egerton, 2800, fol. 169.

sonification. Where it is too strongly individualized, it ceases to be allegory; this is often felt in the Pilgrim's Progress, where the characters are real persons with nicknames.[3]

. . . in that admirable Allegory, the first Part of Pilgrim's Progress, which delights every one, the interest is so great that spite of all the writer's attempts to force the allegoric purpose on the Reader's mind by his strange names—Old Stupidity of the Town of Honesty, &c. &c.— his piety was baffled by his genius, and the Bunyan of Parnassus had the better of the Bunyan of the Conventicle—and with the same illusion as we read any tale known to be fictitious, as a novel,—we go on with his characters as real persons, who had been nicknamed by their neighbours.[4]

Southey, OMNIANA, *II, 162.*

"He[5] soon begins to imitate John Bunyan in his nomenclature;—but oh! what an imitation of that old king of the tinkers!" R.S.

False, cruelly false! Again and again I puzzle myself to guess in what most un-Southeyan mood Southey could have been, when he thought and wrote the above!—And the phrase, old king of the Tinkers! applied to the author of the inimitable Pilgrim's Progress, that model of beautiful, pure, and harmonious English, no less than of still higher merits, outrages my moral taste.—C. MS.[6]

The Pilgrim's Progress is composed in the lowest style of English, without slang or false grammar. If you were to polish it, you would at once destroy the reality of the vision. For works of imagination should be written in every plain language; the more purely imaginative they are the more necessary it is to be plain.

This wonderful work is one of the few books which may be read over repeatedly at different times, and each time with a new and a different pleasure. I read it once as a theologian—and let me assure you, that there is great theological acumen in the work—once with devotional feelings—and once as a poet. I could not have believed be-

[3] Lecture III, Course of Lectures, 1818. Shedd, IV, 247-48. See also Raysor, *Misc. Crit.,* p. 33.
[4] British Museum, MSS Egerton, 2800, fol. 49 verso, but also printed by Raysor, *Misc. Crit.,* p. 31.
[5] Henry More in the "Song of the Soul."
[6] *Table Talk A,* pp. 392-93.

forehand that Calvinism could be painted in such exquisitely delightful colors.[7]

I know of no book, the Bible excepted, as above all comparison, which I, according to my judgment and experience, could so safely recommend as teaching and enforcing the whole saving truth according to the mind that was in Christ Jesus, as the Pilgrim's Progress. It is, in my conviction, incomparably the best *Summa Theologiæ Evangelicæ* ever produced by a writer not miraculously inspired. June 14, 1830.

It disappointed, nay surprised me, to find Robert Southey express himself so coldly respecting the style and diction of the Pilgrim's Progress. I can find nothing homely in it but a few phrases and single words. The conversation between Faithful and Talkative is a model of unaffected dignity and rhythmical flow.[8]

PILGRIM'S PROGRESS, *Part I, p. 11.*[9]

As I walked through the wilderness of this world.

That in the Apocalypse the wilderness is the symbol of the world, or rather of the worldly life, Bunyan discovered by the instinct of a similar genius. The whole Jewish history, indeed, in all its details is so admirably adapted to, and suggestive of, symbolical use, as to justify the belief that the spiritual application, the interior and permanent sense, was in the original intention of the inspiring Spirit, though it might not have been present, as an object of distinct consciousness, to the inspired writers.

PILGRIM'S PROGRESS, *Part I, p. 11.*

—where was a den.

The jail. My Bunyan wrote this precious book in Bedford jail, where he was confined on account of his religion. The following anecdote is related of him. A Quaker came to the jail, and thus addressed him: "Friend Bunyan, the Lord sent me to seek for thee, and I have been through several counties in search of thee, and now I am glad I have found thee." To which Mr. Bunyan replied, "Friend, thou dost not speak the truth in saying the Lord sent thee to seek me; for the Lord well knows that I have been in this jail for some years; and if he had sent thee, he would have sent thee here directly." [*Note in Edwards*]

[7] May 31, 1830. *Table Talk S*, VI, 326. In commenting on Southey's *Life of Bunyan*, p. lxxix, however, Coleridge says, "Bunyan may have been one [a Calvinist], but I have met with nothing in his writings (except his Anti-pædobaptism, to which he assigns no saving importance) that is not much more characteristically Lutheran." *Lit. Rem.*, III, 398.

[8] *Lit. Rem.*, III, 391-92.

[9] John Bunyan, *The Pilgrim's Progress*, ed. R. Edwards (London: 1820). These notes are taken from *Lit. Rem.*, III, 399-415.

This is a valuable ancedote, for it proves, what might have been concluded *a priori*, that Bunyan was a man of too much genius to be a fanatic. No two qualities are more contrary than genius and fanaticism. Enthusiasm, indeed, ὁ θεὸς ἐν ἡμῖν, is almost a synonyme of genius; the moral life in the intellectual light, the will in the reason; and without it, says Seneca, nothing truly great was ever achieved by man.

PILGRIM'S PROGRESS, *Part I, p. 12.*

> And not being able longer to contain, he brake out with a lamentable cry, saying, "What shall I do?"
> Reader, was this ever your case? Did you ever see your sins, and feel the burden of them, so as to cry out in the anguish of your soul, What must I do to be saved? If not, you will look on this precious book as a romance or history, which no way concerns you; you can no more understand the meaning of it than if it were wrote in an unknown tongue, for you are yet carnal, dead in your sins, lying in the arms of the wicked one in false security. But this book is spiritual; it can only be understood by spiritually quickened souls who have experienced that salvation in the heart, which begins with a sight of sin, a sense of sin, a fear of destruction and dread of damnation. Such and such only commence Pilgrims from the City of Destruction to the heavenly kingdom.
> [*Note in Edwards*]

Most true. It is one thing to perceive and acknowledge this and that particular deed to be sinful, that is, contrary to the law of reason or the commandment of God in Scripture, and another thing to feel sin within us independent of particular actions, except as the common ground of them. And it is this latter without which no man can become a Christian.

PILGRIM'S PROGRESS, *Part I, p. 39.*

> Now whereas thou sawest that as soon as the first began to sweep, the dust did so fly about that the room by him could not be cleansed, but that thou wast almost choked therewith; this is to show thee, that the Law, instead of cleansing the heart (by its working) from sin, doth revive, put strength into, and increase it in the soul, even as it doth discover and forbid it; for it doth not give power to subdue.

See Luther's Table Talk. The chapters in that work named ''Law and Gospel,'' contain the very marrow of divinity. Still, however, there remains much to be done on this subject; namely, to show how the discovery of sin by the Law tends to strengthen the sin; and why it must necessarily have this effect, the mode of its action on the appetites and impetites through the imagination and understanding; and to exemplify all this in our actual experience.

PILGRIM'S PROGRESS, *Part I, p. 40.*

> Then I saw that one came to Passion, and brought him a bag of treasure, and poured it down at his feet; the which he took up, and rejoiced therein, and withal laughed Patience to scorn; but I beheld but awhile, and he had lavished all away, and had nothing left him but rags.

One of the not many instances of faulty allegory in The Pilgrim's Progress; that is, it is no allegory. The beholding "but awhile," and the change into "nothing but rags," is not legitimately imaginable. A longer time and more interlinks are requisite. It is a hybrid compost of usual images and generalized words, like the Nile-born nondescript, with a head or tail of organized flesh, and a lump of semi-mud for the body. Yet, perhaps, these very defects are practically excellencies in relation to the intended readers of The Pilgrim's Progress.

PILGRIM'S PROGRESS, *Part I, p. 43.*

> The Interpreter answered, "This is Christ, who continually, with the oil of his grace, maintains the work already begun in the heart; by the means of which, notwithstanding what the Devil can do, the souls of his people prove gracious still. And in that thou sawest that the man stood behind the wall to maintain the fire, this is to teach thee, that it is hard for the tempted to see how this work of grace is maintained in the soul."

This is beautiful; yet I cannot but think it would have been still more appropriate, if the waterpourer had been a Mr. Legality, a prudentialist offering his calculation of consequences as the moral antidote to guilt and crime; and if the oil-instillator, out of sight and from within, had represented the corrupt nature of man, that is, the spiritual will corrupted by taking up a nature into itself.

PILGRIM'S PROGRESS, *Part I, p. 43.*

> What, then, has the sinner who is the subject of grace no hand in keeping up the work of grace in the heart? No! It is plain Mr. Bunyan was not an Arminian. [*Note in Edwards*]

If by metaphysics we mean those truths of the pure reason which always transcend, and not seldom appear to contradict, the understanding, or (in the words of the great Apostle) spiritual verities which can only be spiritually discerned—and this is the true and legitimate meaning of metaphysics, μετὰ τὰ φυσικά— then I affirm, that this very controversy between the Arminians and the Calvinists, in which both are partially right in what they affirm, and both wholly wrong in what they deny, is a proof that without metaphysics there can be no light of faith.

PILGRIM'S PROGRESS, *Part I, p. 45.*

> I left off to watch and be sober; I laid the reins upon the neck of my lusts.

This single paragraph proves, in opposition to the assertion in the preceding note in Edwards, that in Bunyan's judgment there must be at least a negative co-operation of the will of man with the divine grace, an energy of non-resistance to the workings of the Holy Spirit. But the error of the Calvinists is, that they divide the regenerate will in man from the will of God, instead of including it.

PILGRIM'S PROGRESS, *Part I, p. 49.*

> So I saw in my dream, that just as Christian came up with the Cross, his burden loosed from off his shoulders, and fell from off his back, and began to tumble; and so continued to do, till it came to the mouth of the sepulchre, where it fell in, and I saw it no more.

We know that the Son of God is come, and hath given us an understanding (or discernment of reason) *that we may know him that is true, and we are in him that is true, even in his son Jesus Christ. This is the true God and.eternal life. Little children, keep yourselves from idols.* 1. John, v. 20, 21. Alas! how many Protestants make a mental idol of the Cross, scarcely less injurious to the true faith in the Son of God than the wooden crosses and crucifixes of the Romanists!—and this, because they have not been taught that Jesus was both the Christ, and the great symbol of Christ. Strange, that we can explain spiritually, what to take up the cross of Christ, to be crucified with Christ, means;—yet never ask what the Crucifixon itself signifies, but rest satisfied in the historic image. That one declaration of the Apostle, that by wilful sin we *crucify the Son of God afresh,* might have roused us to nobler thoughts.

PILGRIM'S PROGRESS, *Part I, p. 52.*

> And besides, say they, if we get into the way, what matters which way we get in? If we are in, we are in. Thou art but in the way, who, as we perceive, came in at the gate: and we are also in the way, that came tumbling over the wall: wherein now is thy condition better than ours?

The allegory is clearly defective, inasmuch as 'the way' represents two diverse meanings;—1. the outward profession of Christianity, and 2. the inward and spiritual grace. But it would be very difficult to mend it. 1830.

In this instance (and it is, I believe, the only one in the work,) the allegory degenerates into a sort of pun, that is, in the two senses of the word 'way,' and thus supplies Formal and Hypocrite with an

argument which Christian cannot fairly answer, or rather one to which
Bunyan could not make his Christian return the proper answer without
contradicting the allegoric image. For the obvious and only proper
answer is: No! you are not in the same 'way' with me, though you are
walking on the same 'road.' But it has a worse defect, namely, that
it leaves the reader uncertain as to what the writer precisely meant, or
wished to be understood, by the allegory. Did Bunyan refer to the
Quakers as rejecting the outward Sacraments of Baptism and the Lord's
Supper? If so, it is the only unspiritual passage in the whole beautiful
allegory, the only trait of sectarian narrow-mindedness, and, in Bunyan's
own language, of legality. But I do not think that this was Bunyan's
intention. I rather suppose that he refers to the Arminians and other
Pelagians, who rely on the coincidence of their actions with the Gospel
precepts for their salvation, whatever the ground or root of their
conduct may be; who place, in short, the saving virtue in the stream,
with little or no reference to the source. But it is the faith acting in
our poor imperfect deeds that alone saves us; and even this faith is not
ours, but the faith of the Son of God in us. *I am crucified with Christ:
nevertheless I live; yet not I, but Christ liveth in me; and the life which
I now live in the flesh I live by the faith of the Son of God, who loved
me and gave himself for me.* Gal. ii. 20. Illustrate this by a simile.
Labouring under chronic *bronchitis*, I am told to inhale chlorine as a
specific remedy; but I can do this only by dissolving a saturated solution of the gas in warm water, and then breathing the vapour. Now
what the aqueous vapour or steam is to the chlorine, that our deeds, our
outward life, βίος, is to faith.

PILGRIM'S PROGRESS, *Part I, p. 55.*

> And the other took directly up the way to Destruction, which led him
> into a wide field, full of dark mountains, where he stumbled and fell,
> and rose no more.

This requires a comment. A wide field full of mountains and of
dark mountains, where Hypocrite stumbled and fell! The images here
are unusually obscure.

PILGRIM'S PROGRESS, *Part I, p. 70.*

> They showed him Moses' rod, the hammer and nail with which Jael
> slew Sisera.

I question whether it would be possible to instance more strikingly
the power of a predominant idea (that true mental kaleidoscope with
richly-coloured glass) on every object brought before the eye of the
mind through its medium, than this conjunction of Moses' rod with

the hammer of the treacherous assassin Jael, and similar encomiastic references to the same detestable murder, by Bunyan and men like Bunyan, good, pious, purely-affectioned disciples of the meek and holy Jesus; yet the erroneous preconception that whatever is uttered by a Scripture personage is, in fact, uttered by the infallible Spirit of God, makes Deborahs of them all. But what besides ought we to infer from this and similar facts? Surely, that the faith in the heart overpowers and renders innocent the errors of the understanding and the delusions of the imagination, and that sincerely pious men purchase, by inconsistency, exemption from the practical consequences of particular errors.

PILGRIM'S PROGRESS, *Part I, p. 76.*

> All this is true, and much more which thou hast left out, &c.
>
> This is the best way; to own Satan's charges, if they be true; yea, to exaggerate them also, to exalt the riches of the grace of Christ above all, in pardoning all of them freely. [*Note in Edwards*]

That is, to say what we do not believe to be true! *Will ye speak wickedly for God, and talk deceitfully for him?* said righteous Job.

PILGRIM'S PROGRESS, *Part I, p. 83.*

> One thing I would not let slip: I took notice that now poor Christian was so confounded, that he did not know his own voice; and thus I perceived it: just when he was come over against the mouth of the burning pit, one of the wicked ones got behind him, and stepped up softly to him, and whisperingly suggested many grievous blasphemies to him, which he verily thought had proceeded from his own mind.

There is a very beautiful letter of Archbishop Leighton's to a lady under a similar distemperature of the imagination. In fact, it can scarcely not happen under any weakness and consequent irritability of the nerves to persons continually occupied with spiritual self-examination. No part of the pastoral duties requires more discretion, a greater practical psychological science. In this, as in what not? Luther is the great model; ever reminding the individual that not he, but Christ, is to redeem him; and that the way to be redeemed is to think with will, mind, and affections on Christ, and not on himself. I am a sin-laden being, and Christ has promised to loose the whole burden if I but entirely trust in him. To torment myself with the detail of the noisome contents of the fardel will but make it stick the closer, first to my imagination and then to my unwilling will.

PILGRIM'S PROGRESS, *Part I, p. 83.*

> For that he perceived God was with them, though in that dark and dismal state; and why not, thought he, with me, though by reason

of the impediment that attends this place, I cannot perceive it? But it may be asked, Why doth the Lord suffer his children to walk in such darkness? It is for his glory: it tries their faith in him, and excites prayer to him: but his love abates not in the least towards them, since he lovingly inquires after them, *Who is there among you that feareth the Lord and walketh in darkness, and hath no light?* Then he gives most precious advice to them: *Let him trust in the Lord, and stay himself upon his·God.*

Yes! even in the sincerest believers, being men of reflecting and inquiring minds, there will sometimes come a wintry season, when the vital sap of faith retires to the root, that is, to atheism of the will. *But though he slay me, yet will I cling to him.*

PILGRIM'S PROGRESS, *Part I, p. 85.*

And as for the other (Pope), though he be yet alive, he is, by reason of age, and also of the many shrewd brushes that he met with in his younger days, grown so crazy and stiff in his joints, that he can now do little more than sit in his cave's mouth, grinning at pilgrims as they go by, and biting his nails because he cannot come at them.

O that Blanco White would write in Spanish the progress of a pilgrim from the Pope's cave to the Evangelist's wicket-gate and the Interpreter's house! 1830.

PILGRIM'S PROGRESS, *Part I, p. 104.*

And let us assure ourselves that, at the day of doom, men shall be judged according to their fruit. It will not be said then, "Did you believe?" but "Were you doers or talkers only?" and accordingly shall be judged.

All the doctors of the Sorbonne could not have better stated the Gospel *medium* between Pelagianism and Antinomian-Solifidianism, more properly named Sterilifidianism. It is, indeed, faith alone that saves us; but it is such a faith as cannot be alone. Purity and beneficence are the *epidermis,* faith and love the *cutis vera* of Christianity. Morality is the outward cloth, faith the lining; both together form the wedding-garment given to the true believer in Christ, even his own garment of righteousness, which, like the loaves and fishes, he mysteriously multiplies. The images of the sun in the earthly dew-drops are unsubstantial phantoms; but God's thoughts are things: the images of God, of the Sun of Righteousness, in the spiritual dew-drops are substances, imperishable substances.

PILGRIM'S PROGRESS, *Part I, p. 154.*

Fine-spun speculations and curious reasonings lead men from simple truth and implicit faith into many dangerous and destructive errors. The Word records many instances of such for our caution. Be warned to study simplicity and godly sincerity. [*Note in Edwards on Doubting Castle*]

And pray what does implicit faith lead men into? Transubstantiation and all the abominations of priest-worship. And where is the Scriptural authority for this implicit faith? Assuredly not in St. John, who tells us that Christ's life is and manifests itself in us as the light of man; that he came to bring light as well as immortality. Assuredly not in St. Paul, who declares all faith imperfect and perilous without insight and understanding; who prays for us that we may comprehend the deep things even of God himself. For the Spirit discerned, and the Spirit by which we discern, are both God; the Spirit of truth through and in Christ from the Father.

Mournful are the errors into which the zealous but unlearned preachers among the dissenting Calvinists have fallen respecting absolute election, and discriminative, yet reasonless, grace:—fearful this divorcement of the Holy Will, the one only Absolute Good, that, eternally affirming itself as the I AM, eternally generateth the Word, the absolute Being, the Supreme Reason, the Being of all Truth, the Truth of all Being:—fearful the divorcement from the reason; fearful the doctrine which maketh God a power of darkness, instead of the God of light, the Father of the light which lighteth every man that cometh into the world! This we know and this we are taught by the holy Apostle Paul; that without will there is no ground or base of sin; that without the law this ground or base cannot become sin; (hence we do not impute sin to the wolf or the tiger, as being without or below the law;) but that with the law cometh light into the will; and by this light the will becometh a free, and therefore a responsible will. Yea! the law is itself light, and the divine light becomes law by its relation and opposition to the darkness; the will of God revealed in its opposition to the dark and alien will of the fallen Spirit. This freedom, then, is the free gift of God; but does it therefore cease to be freedom? All the sophistry of the Predestinarians rests on the false notion of eternity as a sort of time antecedent to time. It is timeless, present with and in all times. There is an excellent discourse of the great Hooker's, affixed with two or three others to his Ecclesiastical Polity, on the final perseverance of Saints; but yet I am very desirous to meet with some judicious experimental treatise, in which the doctrine, with the Scriptures on which it is grounded, is set forth more at large; as likewise the rules by which it may be applied to the purposes of support and comfort, without danger of causing presumption and without diminishing the dread of sin. Above all, I am anxious to see the subject treated with as little reference as possible to the divine predestination and foresight; the argument

from the latter being a mere identical proposition followed by an assertion of God's prescience. Those who will persevere, will persevere, and
God foresees; and as to the proof from predestination, that is, that he
who predestines the end necessarily predestines the adequate means, I
can more readily imagine logical consequences adverse to the sense of
responsibility than Christian consequences, such as an individual may
apply for his own edification. And I am persuaded that the doctrine
does not need these supports, according, I mean, to the ordinary notion
of predestination. The predestinative force of a free agent's own will
in certain absolute acts, determinations, or elections, and in respect of
which acts it is one either with the divine or the devilish will; and if
the former, the conclusions to be drawn from God's goodness, faithful-
ness, and spiritual presence; these supply grounds of argument of a
very different character, especially where the mind has been prepared
by an insight into the error and hollowness of the antithesis between
liberty and necessity.

PILGRIM'S PROGRESS, *Part I, p. 178.*

> But how contrary to this is the walk and conduct of some who pro-
> fess to be pilgrims, and yet can wilfully and deliberately go upon the
> Devil's ground, and indulge themselves in carnal pleasures and sinful
> diversions. [*Note in Edwards on the Enchanted Ground*]

But what pleasures are carnal,—what are sinful diversions,—so I
mean as that I may be able to determine what are not? Shew us the
criterion, the general principle; at least explain whether each individual
case is to be decided for the individual by his own experience of the
effects of the pleasure or the diversion, in dulling or distracting his
religious feelings; or can a list, a complete list, of all such pleasures be
made beforehand?

PILGRIM'S PROGRESS, *Part III, at the beginning.*

I strongly suspect that this third part, which ought not to have been
thus conjoined with Bunyan's work, was written by a Roman Catholic
priest, for the very purpose of counter-acting the doctrine of faith so
strongly enforced in the genuine Progress.[10]

PILGRIM'S PROGRESS, *Part III, p. 443.*

> Against all which evils fasting is the proper remedy.

It would have been well if the writer had explained exactly what
he meant by the fasting, here so strongly recommended; during what

---

[10] See note on Southey's ''Life of Bunyan,'' prefixed to his edition of *Pilgrim's
Progress* (London: 1830), p. xcvii, *Lit. Rem.*, III, 398. ''It is remarkable that
Southey should not have seen, or having seen, have forgotten to notice, that this
third part is evidently written by some Romish priest or missionary in disguise.''

period of time abstinence from food is to continue and so on. The effects, I imagine, must in good measure depend on the health of the individual. In some constitutions, fasting so disorders the stomach as to produce the very contrary of good;—confusion of mind, loose imaginations against the man's own will, and the like.

PILGRIM'S PROGRESS, *Part III, at the end.*

One of the most influential arguments, one of those the force of which I feel even more than I see, for the divinity of the New Testament, and with especial weight in the writings of John and Paul, is the unspeakable dfference between them and all other the earliest extant writings of the Christian Church, even those of the same age (as, for example, the Epistle of Barnabas,) or of the next following,—a difference that transcends all degree, and is truly a difference in kind. Nay, the catalogue of the works written by the Reformers and in the two centuries after the Reformation, contain many many volumes far superior in Christian light and unction to the best of the Fathers. How poor and unevangelic is Hermas in comparison with our Pilgrim's Progress!

Edwards' LIFE OF BUNYAN, *prefixed to edition of* PILGRIM'S PROGRESS.[11]

The early part of his life was an open course of wickedness.

Southey, in the Life prefixed to his edition of the Pilgrim's Progress, has, in a manner worthy of his head and heart, reduced this oft-repeated charge to its proper value. Bunyan was never, in our received sense of the word, wicked. He was chaste, sober, honest; but he was a bitter blackguard; that is, damned his own and his neighbor's eyes on slight or no occasion, and was fond of a row. In this our excellent Laureate has performed an important service to morality. For the transmutation of actual reprobates into saints is doubtless possible; but like many recorded facts of corporeal alchemy, it is not supported by modern experiments.

Southey, LIFE OF BUNYAN, *prefixed to edition of* PILGRIM'S PROGRESS, *p. xli.*[12]

But the wickedness of the tinker has been greatly overcharged; and it is taking the language of self-accusation too literally, to pronounce of John Bunyan that he was at any time depraved. The worst of what he was in his worst days is to be expressed in a single word . . . he had been a blackguard . . .

[11] *Lit. Rem.,* III, 398-99.
[12] *Lit. Rem.,* III, 394. Only those notes on Southey's *Life of Bunyan* which comment directly on Bunyan have been included here. See *Lit. Rem.,* III, 392-98.

All this narrative, with the reflections on the facts, is admirable and worthy of Robert Southey: full of good sense and kind feeling—the wisdom of love.

Southey's Life of Bunyan is beautiful. I wish he had illustrated that mood of mind which exaggerates, and still more, mistakes, the inward depravation, as in Bunyan, Nelson, and others, by extracts from Baxter's Life of himself. What genuine superstition is exemplified in that bandying of texts and half-texts, and demi-semi-texts, just as memory happened to suggest them, or change brought them before Bunyan's mind! His tract, entitled, "Grace abounding to the Chief of Sinners," is a study for a philosopher. Is it not, however, an historical error to call the Puritans dissenters? Before St. Bartholomew's day they were essentially a part of the church, and had as determined opinions in favor of a church establishment as the bishops themselves.[13]

Southey, LIFE OF BUNYAN, *p. xxi.*

In an evil hour were the doctrines of the Gospel sophisticated with questions which should have been left in the Schools for those who are unwise enough to employ themselves in excogitations of useless subtlety.

But what, at any rate, had Bunyan to do with the Schools? His perplexities clearly rose out of the operations of his own active but unarmed mind on the words of the Apostle. If anything is to be arraigned, it must be the Bible in English, the reading of which is imposed (and, in my judgment, well and wisely imposed) as a duty on all who can read. Though Protestants, we are not ignorant of the occasional and partial evils of promiscuous Bible reading; but we see them vanish when we place them beside the good.[14]

Samuel Pepys

DIARY,[1] *I, 84.*

From fourth line beginning "went by water to my Lord . . ." to the fifteenth line, "which I was not so convinced of before."

Exquisite specimen of dry, grave, irony.

[13] June 10, 1830. *Table Talk S,* VI, 332-33.
[14] *Lit. Rem.,* III, 393-94.

[1] *Memoirs of Samuel Pepys,* ed. Richard, Lord Braybrook (2 vols.; London:

DIARY, *I, 189.*

> Falling into discourse of a new book of drollery in use, called Hudibras, I would needs go find it out: . . . it is so silly an abuse of the Presbyter Knight going to the warrs, that I am ashamed of it.

At p. 167 Pepys pronounces the *Midsummer Night's Dream* the most insipid ridiculous Play he had ever seen.

DIARY, *II, 10.*

> Beginning at line 11, "Among other discourse," and ending at line 20, "which if true is strange." ["Sir G. Carteret did tell a story, how at his death he did make the town swear that he should never be dug up— they after sixty years do it—found a plate of brasse, saying, &c.—which *if* true, is very strange."]

If ! ! ! but still more strange would be the *truth* of the story. Yet only suppose the *precise date* an addition of the reporters: and nothing more natural.—Mem. The good old story of a jealous Husband's sending his confidential servant to his wife, forbidding her to see a certain Gentleman during his absence, and bring back her solemn oath & promise that she would not: & how the shrewd fellow, instead of this took her oath not to ride on Neptune's Back, their huge Newfoundland Yard-dog.

DIARY, *II, 13.*

> Line 15, "Mrs. Turner do tell me very odde stories," to line 18, "do the business."

Most valuable on many, various, and most important accounts, as I hold this Diary to be, I deem it invaluable, as a faithful Portrait of enlightened (*i. e.* calculating) Self-love and Self-interest in its perihelion to Morality or its nearest possible neighborhood to, or least possible distance from Honour & Honesty. And yet what a cold and torpid Saturn with what a sinister & leaden Shine, spotty as the Moon, does its appear, compared with the principles & actions of the Regicide, Colonel Hutchinson, or those of the Puritan, Richard Baxter (in the autobiography edited by Sylvester), both the Contemporaries of Pepys.

DIARY, *II, 46.*

> He tells me the King of France hath his mistresses, but laughs at the foolery of our King, that makes his bastards princes, &c.

1825). These notes are from a contemporary transcription made when materials were being collected for *Literary Remains* and now in the possession of A. H. B. Coleridge. The notes, with the exception of the first three, were printed by the owner of the volumes: Bonsall, ''Coleridge's Notes in Pepys's *Diary*'' (*Notes and Queries*, 1st ser., VI, 213-15). They also appear in *Notes Theolog.*, pp. 178-89.

Mem. Earl of Munster. This, with Wit and Condescension, was all that was wanting to a perfect parallelism in the character of George IV. with that of Charles II., and this he left to be supplied by his worthy Brother & Successor.

DIARY, *II, 55.*

> Engaged under hand and seal to give the man that obtained it so much in behalf of my Lord Chancellor.

And this was one of the three Idols of our Church—for Clarendon ever follows Charles the Martyr, & the Martyr, Laud! Alas!—What a strange thing the Conscience seems to be, when such actions & deliberate falsehoods as have been on strong grounds imputed to Lord Clarendon,— among others, the suborning of Assassination,—could be made compatible in his own mind with professions of Religion & habitual religious meditations & exercises.

DIARY, *II, 62*

> From the beginning of line 25, "And all this through the negligence of our Prince" to the end of the sentence.

There were good grounds for the belief, that more & yet worse causes than sensuality and sensual sloth were working in the King's mind & heart, viz the readiness to have the French King *his* Master, & the Disposer of his Kingdom's power, as the means of becoming himself the uncontrolled Master of it's wealth. He would fain be a Despot, even at the cost of being another's Underling. Charles IInd. was willing, nay anxious, to reduce his Crown and Kingdom under the domination of the Grand Monarque, provided he himself might have the power to shear & poll his subjects without leave, and unchecked by the interference of a Parliament. I look on him as one of the moral Monsters of History.

DIARY, *II, 108.*

To initiate a young Student into the mystery of appreciating the value of modern History, or the books that have hitherto passed for such,—First, let him carefully peruse this Diary! and then, while it is fresh in his mind, take up and read Hume's History of England, Reign of Charles the 2nd. Even of Hume's Reign of Elizabeth, generally rated as the best and fullest of the work, I dare assert: that to supply the omissions alone, would form an appendix occupying twice the space alloted by him to the whole Reign, and the necessary rectification of his statements half as much. What with omissions, and what with perversions, of the most important incidents, added to the false portraiture of the Character, the work from the Reign of Henry VIIth. is a Mis-

chievous Romance. But alike as Historian and as Philosopher, Hume
has meo saltem judicio, been extravagantly over-rated. Mercy on the
Age, & the People, for whom Locke is profound, and Hume is subtle.

DIARY, *II, 110.*

> Sixth line from bottom: Cowley lamented as "the best poet of our
> nation."

! !—Yet Cowley *was* a Poet, which with all my unfeigned admiration of his vigorous sense, his agile logical wit, and his high excellencies
of diction and metre, is more than (in the strict use of the term Poet)
I can conscientiously say of DRYDEN. Only if Pope was a *Poet,* as Lord
Byron swears, then Dryden, I admit was a very *great* Poet. W. Wordsworth[2] calls Lord Byron the Mocking Bird of our parnassian Ornitholo-
gy; but the Mocking Bird, they say, has a very sweet song of his own, in
true Notes proper to himself. Now I cannot say, I have ever heard any
such in his Lordship's Volumes of Warbles; & spite of Sir W. Scott, I
dare predict that in less than a century, the Baronet's & the Baron's
Poems will lie on the same shelf of Oblivion, Scott be read and remembered as a Novelist and the Founder of a new race of Novels—&
Byron not remembered at all, except as a wicked Lord who from morbid
& restless vanity pretended to be ten times more wicked than he was.

DIARY, *II, 125.*

> Sixth line from the bottom concerning bear-baiting—"The sport was
> very good."

Certainly Pepys was blest with the queerest & most omnivorous
taste that ever fell to the lot of one man!

DIARY, *II, 151.*

> Line 15 from the top, "And there saw Henry the Fourth."

This is, I think, the fifth of Shakspear's Plays, which Pepys found
silly, stupid trash, & among them Othello! Macbeth indeed he com-
mends for the *shews* & music, but not to be compared with the 'Five
Hours' Adventures'!!! This and the want of *Wit* in the Hudibras, is
very amusing—nay, it is seriously instructive. Thousands of shrewd, and
intelligent men, in whom and in S. Pepys, the *Understanding* is *hyper-
trophied* to the necrosis or morasmus of the Reason and Imagination,
while far-sighted (yet oh! how short-sighted) Self-Interest fills the place
of Conscience, could say the same, if they dared.

[2] The remainder of this paragraph does not appear in *Notes Theolog.*

DIARY, *II, 254.*

> Line 22: "a very excellent & persuasive, good & moral sermon . . .
> He shewed, like a wise man, that righteousness is a surer moral way
> of being rich, than sin and villany."

Highly characteristic. Pepys' only ground of morality was Prudence, a shrewd Understanding in the service of Self-love, his Conscience. He was a *Pollard* man, without the *Top* (i. e. the Reason, as the source of Ideas, or immediate yet not sensuous truths, having their evidence in themselves; or, the Imagination or idealising Power, by symbols mediating between the Reason & the Understanding), but on this account more broadly and luxuriantly branching out from the upper Trunk. For the sobriety and stedfastness of a worldly self-interest substitute inventive Fancy, Will-wantonness (*stat pro ratione voluntas*) and a humorous sense of the emptiness and dream-likeness of human pursuits —and Pepys would have been the *Panurge* of the incomparable Rabelais. *Mem.* It is incomprehensible to me that this great and general Philosopher should have been a Frenchman, except on my hypothesis of a continued dilution of the Gothic Blood from the reign of Henry IVth. Des Cartes, Malbranche, Pascal, and Moliere, being the *ultimi Gothorum*, the last in whom the Gothic predominated over the Celtic.

DIARY, *II, 260.*

> To the fair to see the play 'Bartholomew Fair'; and it is an excellent
> play. . . . [Line 5] only the business of amusing the Puritans begins
> to grow stale and of no use, they being the people that at last will
> be found the wisest.

Pepys was always a Commonwealth's man in his heart. N. B. Not a Democrat, but even more than the Constitutional Whigs, the very Antipodes of the modern Jacobins, or *Tail-up, Head-down* politicians. A Voluptuary, and without a spark of bigotry in his nature, he could not be a Puritan; but of his free choice he would have preferred Presbyterianism to Prelacy, and a mixed Aristocracy of Wealth and Talent, to a Monarchy or even a mixed Government—such at least as the latter was in his time. But many of the more enlightened Jacobites were Republicans who despaired of a Republic. *Si non Brutus, Cæsar.*

DIARY, *II, 319.*

Can a more impressive proof be desired of the truth and wisdom of the E. of Carnarvon's recent remark in the House of Lords—that before the reign of Anne, the Constitution had but a sort of uterine life, or but partially appeared as in the birth throes and that it is unworthy of a British Statesman to quote any precedent anterior to the Revolution

of 1688! Here, an honest, high principled, and patriotic Senator, crim-
inates Lord Clarendon for having prevented Charles the 2nd from
making the Crown independent of the Parliament, & this when he knew
& groaned under the infamous vices & folly of the KING! Sick & weary
of the factious and persecuting temper of the H. of Commons, many,
true Lovers of their Country and its freedom, would gladly have dispensed with Parliaments, & have secured for the King a Revenue which
wisely & economically managed, might have sufficed for all ordinary demands, could they have discovered any other way of subjecting the
Judges to a periodical rigorous account for their administration of the
Law. In the *Laws* and the Rights established by Law, these men placed
the proper liberty of the Subject. Before the Revolution a Parliament
at the commencement of a Reign, and of a War, under an economic &
decorous law would have satisfied the people generally.

DIARY, *II, 342.*

From line 4 to line 11: "Thence walked a little with Creed, who tells
me he hears how fine my horses and coach are, and advises me to avoid
being noted for it . . . . being what I feared, &c."

This struggle between the prudence of an Atticus, and the *Sir-Piercy-
Shafton*-Taylor-blood working as an instinct in his veins, with extreme
sensitiveness to the *opinions* of men as the combining medium, is very
amusing.

DIARY, *II, 348, at the conclusion.*

Truly may it be said that, this was a greater & more grievous loss to
the mind's eye of his posterity, than to the bodily organs of Pepys himself. It makes me restless & discontented to think, what a Diary equal
in minuteness and truth of portraiture to the preceding from 1669 to
1688 or 90, would have been for the true causes, process, and character
of the Revolution.

DIARY: CORRESPONDENCE, *II, 65.* [*Correspondence is printed at the end
of the* DIARY.]

Lines 8 and 9 from bottom: "It is a common position among these
factious sectaries, that there is no medium between a true Churchman
of England and a Roman Catholic, &c."

! ! It is only too probable, that James's bigotry alone baffled his
despotism—and that he might have succeeded in suppressing the liberties
of his country, if he would—for a time at least—have kept aloof from
it's Religion. It should be remembered in excuse for the supporters of
James II. that, the practicability of conducting the affairs of the State

with and by a Parliament, had not yet been demonstrated—nay, seemed incompatible with the theoretic division—of the Legislative from the Executive—and indeed only by blending the two *in fact*, & preserving the division in words & appearance, was this effected:—and even now the practicability of governing the Empire with & by a perfectly free & freely elected Parliament, remains to be demonstrated.

DIARY: CORRESPONDENCE, *II, 71.*

Citrine trees.

That Lady of masculine intellect, with all the woman's sense of Beauty (Mrs. *Emerson,* was that the name?—but long a botanical correspondent & contributor to Nicholson's Phil. Magazine, O! Mrs. Ibbetson), believed herself to have discovered the principle of this precious Citrine wood, and the means of producing it—and I see no reason for doubting it—tho' of her phytological anatomy, by help of the Solar Miscroscope I am Skeptical. The engravings instantly call up in my mind the suspicion of some Kaleidoscope delusion—from the singular *symmetry* of all the forms. But she was an excellent and very remarkable Woman, and her contributions in the *Phil. Magazine* worth studying even for the style.

DIARY: CORRESPONDENCE, *II, 73.*

Burnet's *Theory of the Earth.* The whole hypothesis so ingenious and so rational, [that I both admire and believe it at once.]

! Strange! Burnet's book is a grand Miltonic Romance; but the contrast, between the Tartarean Fury, and Turbulence of the Burnetian, and the almost supernatural tranquillity of the Mosaic Deluge, is little less than comic.

DIARY: CORRESPONDENCE, *II, 198.*

Second sight, so called in Scotland. "She's a handsome lady indeed," said the gentleman, "but I see her in blood," &c.

It would have been necessary to cross-examine this Scotch Deuteroptes, whether he had not seen the duplicate or spectrum of other persons in blood. It might have been the result of an inflammatory condition of his own brains, or a slight pressure on the region of the optic Nerves. I have repeatedly seen the phantasm of the page I was reading all spotted with blood, or with the letters all blood.

John Asgill

My only objection, the only possible objection that I can have, to the submitting of my "Asgill's Tracts," and my intended Prae-illa, Pastilla, and Marginalia, or rather the scheme thereof, to either Mr. Lockhart or Mr. Croker[1] or both, is—the difficulty of conveying to any one, who had not conversed with me on the subject, either by the tracts themselves, or by the few MSS Notes, which the paucity and scant dimension of the Blank Leaves, & the lankness of the Margins allowed me to incorporate or rather inatramentate with this papyrus cacatilis [*sic*] of the Volume itself—All I can say is that first, I shall prefix a Life of Asgill, the facts of which I must take wholly from the Biogr. Brit. and Dr. Keppis (Books, I have never read) but, I gather from Mr. Carey's account of these Biographies, make a very, very different interpretation of the said facts, moral, spiritual, and political. 2. a critical & philosophical Essay on Whiggism, from Dryden's Achitophel (Ashly Cooper) the first Whig to Lord Grey, who, I trust in God's Mercy, will be the last) considering the last years of Queen Anne's Reign, as the Zenith or palmy State of Whiggism, in it's divinest Avatar of Common Sense, or of the Understanding vigorously exerted in the right direction on the right & proper Objects of the Understanding (Mr. Croker, not having seen, or if he has, not very likely having had either the leisure or the inclination to read, either my "Aids to Ref." or my Essay on the Constitution in Ch. and State according to the Idea (i. e. Ultimate Aim) will not apprehend the antithesis here implied of the Underst. to the Reason. 3. Asgill's Political Tracts, which (reversing the present Order) I place first—with numerous notes, of which those in the printed Vol. are but the specimen handful. 4. a brief History or philosophico-theologico-ethical Sketch of the History of the Clergy of the Church of England, from Cranmer to Bishop Blomefield, Maltby & Wheatly. In both Whiggism & the Church Clergy-system (mem. *not* the *Church*, whether National or as Christian) wide as the differences are in other respects—I trace the rise, & occasion, progress, and necessary degeneration of this Spirit of *Compromise*—"Councils begun in *fear* shall end in folly." 5. A summary, with the proofs from Divines of the Church, after the Restoration, of the points assumed by Asgill, which were & had

[1] Coleridge proposed to reprint Asgill's *Treatises* with marginalia.

been assumed by & were in fact admitted as orthodox & true, by his Enemies. 6. Then—Asgill's *"famous* Tract or Argument against the base & cowardly Custom of *Dying"*—than which a more incomparable Reductio ad absurdum of a Religion of the Understanding cannot, I hold, be conceived, whether considered as sound Logic or as original Humor, rendered exquisite by Asgill's evident uncertainty as to his own being in Jest or in earnest. 7. His Defense in the House of Commons previous to his Expulsion under the pretext of this Tract—with my notes—8. & 9. My Marginalia & Post-illa on Baxter, Southey's Life of Wesley—Supposing the Anthropoid, Mr. Murray, should deem the extension of two Volumes instead of one too thick to be advisable. This is all the explanation, I can offer, either to Mr. L. or Mr. Croker—with the Tracts themselves—which, pray take care of that whatever may be the Result or M's final decision, I may have this book back. *Mem.* If M. thinks it worth his while, let him assign me a price—for I won't work for nothing, or what is = to nothing, i. e. as possibility of an *Author's Half* of the by the Publisher admitted net profits, after the sale of the very last copy—which a wise Publisher will take good care shall never be sold—unless he sanguinely ventures on the success of a Second edition . . .[2]

Asgill was an extraordinary man, and his pamphlet[3] is invaluable. He undertook to prove that man is literally immortal; or, rather, that any given living man might probably never die. He complains of the cowardly practice of dying. He was expelled from two Houses of Commons for blasphemy and atheism, as was pretended—I really suspect because he was a stanch Hanoverian. I expected to find the ravings of an enthusiast, or the sullen snarlings of an infidel; whereas I found the very soul of Swift—an intense, half self-deceived humorism. I scarcely remember elsewhere such uncommon skill in logic, such lawyer-like acuteness, and yet such a grasp of common sense. Each of his paragraphs is in itself a whole, and yet a link between the preceding and following;

[2] Letter to H. N. Coleridge, ''May 5? or 6? 1832.'' This letter is among the papers in the possession of A. H. B. Coleridge and is reproduced by his kind permission. In a letter of May 9, 1832, to Henry Nelson, Coleridge said: ''But as to this Asgill business, I have no objection at *all* to its being submitted to Lockhart, and since his noble exertions against the Catilinarian riffraff reform Bill, no other objection to Mr. Archer but my knowledge from one of his pamphlets of mutually exclusive contrariety of his opinion to mine, respecting the National Clerisy.'' Griggs, *Unp. Letters,* II, 444.

[3] *An Argument proving that according to the covenant of eternal life revealed in the Scriptures, Man may be translated from hence into that eternal life without passing through death,* etc. (London: 1700).

so that the entire series forms one argument, and yet each is a diamond in itself.[4]

I know no genuine Saxon English superior to Asgill's. I think his and De Foe's irony often finer than Swift's.[5]

Samuel Johnson,[6] whom, to distinguish him from the Doctor, we may call the Whig, was a very remarkable writer. He may be compared to his contemporary De Foe, whom he resembled in many points. He is another instance of King William's discrimination, which was so much superior to that of any of his ministers. Johnson was one of the most formidable advocates for the Exclusion Bill, and he suffered by whipping and imprisonment under James accordingly. Like Asgill, he argues with great apparent candor and clearness till he has his opponent within reach, and then comes a blow as from a sledge-hammer. I do not know where I could put my hand upon a book containing so much sense and sound constitutional doctrine as this thin folio of Johnson's Works; and what party in this country would read so severe a lecture in it as our modern Whigs?

A close reasoner and a good writer in general may be known by his pertinent use of connectives. Read that page of Johnson; you can not alter one conjunction without spoiling the sense. It is a linked strain throughout. In your modern books, for the most part, the sentences in a page have the same connection with each other that marbles have in a bag; they touch without adhering.

Asgill evidently formed his style upon Johnson's, but he only imitates one part of it. Asgill never rises to Johnson's eloquence. The latter was a sort of Cobbett-Burke.[7]

I have a thought by way of a light *prelude,* a sort of unstiffening of my long dormant joints and muscles, to give a reprint as nearly as possible, except in quality of the paper, a facsimile of John Asgill's tracts with a life and copious notes, to which I would affix Pastilla et Marginalia. See my MSS. notes, blank leaf and marginal, on Southey's "Life of John Wesley," and sundry other works. Now can you direct me to any source of information respecting John Asgill, a prince darling of mine, the most honest of all Whigs, whom at the close of Queen Anne's

[4] July 30, 1831. *Table Talk S*, VI, 363-64.
[5] April 30, 1832. *Table Talk S*, VI, 394.
[6] A clergyman (1649-1703).
[7] May 15, 1833. *Table Talk S*, VI, 454-55.

reign the scoundrelly Jacobite Tories twice expelled from Parliament, under the pretext of his incomparable, or only-with-Rabelais-to-be-compared argument against the base and cowardly custom of ever dying? And this tract is a very real treasure, and never more usable as a medicine for our clergy, at least all such as the Bishop of London, Archbishops of Canterbury and of Dublin, and Paleyans and Mageeites,[8] any one or all of whom I would defy to answer a single paragraph of Asgill's tract, or unloose a single link from the chain of logic. I have no biographical dictionary, and never saw one but in a little sort of one-volume thing. If you can help me in this, do.[9]

ASGILL'S ARGUMENT.[10] *Note on first flyleaf, recto and verso, and on title page.*

> An Argument proving that according to the Covenant of Eternal Life reveal'd in the Scriptures, Man may be translated from hence into that Eternal Life, without passing through Death, altho the Human Nature of Christ himself could not be thus translated till he had passed through Death.

If I needed an illustrative example of the distinction between Reason and the Understanding, between Spiritual *Sense,* and *Logic,* this first treatise of Asgill would supply it. Excuse the defect of all *Idea,* or Spiritual Institution of God—and allow yourself to bring him as Plaintiff or Defendant into a common Law-court,—and *then* I cannot conceive a more clear & clever piece of Special pleading than Asgill has here given. The language EXCELLENT—idiomatic, simple, perspicuous, at once significant & lively, i.e. expressive of *the* thought, and of a manly proportion of *feeling* appropriate to it. In short, it is the ablest attempt to exhibit a Scheme of Religion without Ideas, that the inherent contradiction in the thought renders possible.

It is of minor importance *how* a man represents to himself his Redemption by the Word Incarnate, within what scheme of his Understanding he concludes it, or by what supposed analogies (tho' actually no better than metaphors) he tries to conceive it, provided he has a lively

---

[8] Magee, Bishop of Raphoe, 1819, and Archbishop of Dublin, 1822.

[9] To Rev. H. F. Carey, April 22, 1832. Coleridge, E. H., *Letters,* II, 761-62. *See also* Rev. Henry Cary, *Memoir of the Reverend Henry Francis Cary* (2 vols. in ·1; London: Moxon, 1847), II, 194-95.

[10] This tract is in *A Collection of Tracts written by John Asgill, Esq; from the Year 1700 to the Year 1715* (London: 1715). On the title page is written: "2ᵈ Jan.ʸ 1827. This Book given me by Mr. Kirkpatrick—together with the Spes Israel by R. Menasset Ben Israel. S. T. Coleridge." This volume, formerly in the library of Lord Coleridge, is now in the British Museum. The notes have been previously printed in *Lit. Rem.,* II, 380-96.

Faith in Christ, the Son of the living God, and his Redeemer. The
Faith may and must be the same in all who are thereby saved; but
every man, more or less, construes it into an intelligible *Belief* thro' the
shaping and colouring Optical Glass of his individual Understanding.
Mr. Asgill has given a very ingenious Common-Law Scheme. *Valeat
quantum valebit!* It would make a figure among the Benchers of the
Temple. I prefer the belief, that Man was made to know that a finite
free Agent could not stand by the coincidence & independent harmony
of a separate Will with the Will of God. Only by the Will of God can
he obey God's Will. Man fell as a *Soul* to rise a *Spirit.* The first Adam
was a living *Soul;* the last a life-making Spirit. S. T. C.

In him is Life: and that Life is the *Light* of Men. And as long as
the Light abides within it's own sphere, i. e. appears as Reason; so long
it is commensurate with the Life, and it's adequate Representative. But
not so when this Light shines downward into the Understanding of the
Individual.[11] Here it is always more or less refracted, and differently
in every different Individual, and it must be re-converted into *Life* to
rectify itself, and regain it's universality, (*all-commonness,* as the German more expressively says). Hence in Faith and Charity the Church
is Catholic. So likewise in the fundamental Articles of Belief, which
constitute the Right *Reason* of Faith. But in the minor *dogmata,* &
in modes of exposition, & the vehicles of Faith and Reason to the Understandings, Imaginations, and Affections of Men, the Churches may differ,
and in this difference supply one object for Charity to exercise itself on
by mutual forbearance.

O! there is a deep philosophy in the proverbial phrase,—"His Heart
sets his Head right!" In our commerce with Heaven, we must cast
our local Coins and Tokens into the Melting-pot of Love, to pass by
weight of Bullion. And where the Balance of Trade is so immensely
in our favor, we have little right to complain, tho' they should not pass
for half the nominal value, they go for in our own Market. S. T. C.

ASGILL'S ARGUMENT, *"Preface," p. 3. Note on blank page opposite.*
To them that knew not the reason, it looked like a Whym. . . .

Whym; whim— und *der?* Is it the same with the German wahn?

ASGILL'S ARGUMENT, *p. 46. Note continued on p. 47.*

And I am so far from thinking this Covenant of Eternal Life to be
an Allusion to the forms of Title amongst Men, that I rather adore it
as the Precedent for them all, from which our imperfect Forms are

[11] Here Coleridge directed, "turn over the title page." On the verso of the
title page he wrote, "Continued from line 6th of p. 2 blank leaf."

taken: Believing with that great Apostle, that *the things on Earth are but the Patterns of things in the Heavens, where the Originals are kept.*

Aye! this, *this* is the Pinch of the Argument, which Asgill should have *proved,* not merely asserted. Are these Human Laws, and these Forms of Law, *absolutely* good and wise, or only *conditionally,* i. e. the limited powers & intellect, and the corrupt will of men being considered. S. T. C.

ASGILL'S ARGUMENT, *p. 64. Note continued on pp. 65-67.*

> And hence, tho the Dead shall not arise with same Identity of Matter with which they died, yet being in the same Form, they will not know themselves from themselves, being the same to all Uses, Intents, and Purposes. . . . But then as God (in the Resurrection) is not bound up to use the same Matter, neither is he obliged to use a different Matter.

The great objection to this part of Asgill's Scheme, which has had, & still, I am told, has many advocates among the chief Dignitaries of our Church, is—that it either takes Death, as the utter extinction of Being—or it supposes a continuance, or at least a renewal of consciousness after Death. The former involves all the irrational, and all the immoral, consequences of Materialism. But if the latter be granted, the proportionality, adhesion, and symmetry, of the whole Scheme are gone, and the infinite Quantity, (i. e. immortality under the Curse of estrangement from God) is rendered a mere supplement tacked on to the finite, and comparatively insignificant, if not doubtful, evil, namely, the dissolution of the organic Body. See what a poor hand Asgill makes of it, p. 26:

ASGILL'S ARGUMENT, *p. 66.*

> *Thou will not leave my Soul in the Grave . . .*
> And that it is translated *Soul,* is an *Anglicism,* not understood in other languages, which have no other word for *Soul* but the same which is for Life.

? Seele,χ Leben, German: Ψυχή χ Ζωή, Greek.

ASGILL'S ARGUMENT, *p. 67.*

> Then to this Figure God added Life, by breathing it into him from himself, whereby this inanimate Body became a living one.

And what was *Life?* Something? or Nothing? And had not, first, the Spirit, and next the Word, of God infused Life into the *Earth,* of which Man as an animal & all other animals were made— & then, *in addition* to this, breathed into *Man* a living *Soul,* which he did *not* breathe into the other Animals?

ARGILL'S ARGUMENT, *pp. 75-81, ad finem. First paragraph of note on first blank page pasted to cover. Second paragraph on blank page before tract on the "Succession of the House of Hanover."*

> I have a great deal of business yet in this world, without doing of which heaven itself would be uneasy to me.
> And therefore do depend, that I shall not be taken hence in the midst of my days, before I have done all my heart's desire.
> But when that is done, I know no business I have with the dead, and therefore do as much depend that I shall not go hence by *returning to the dust,* which is the sentence of that law from which I claim a discharge: but that I shall make my *exit* by way of translation, which I claim as a dignity belonging to that degree in the science of eternal life, of which I profess myself a graduate, according to the true intent and meaning of the covenant of eternal life revealed in the Scriptures.

A man so κατ' ἐξοχήν clear-headed, so remarkable for the perspicuity of his Sentences, and the luminous Orderliness of his Arrangement— in short, so consummate an Artist in the statement of his Case, and in the inferences from his Data, as John Asgill must be allowed by all competent Judges to have been,—*was he in earnest or in jest* from p. 75 to the end of the first treatise?—*My* belief is, that He himself did not know.

Asgill was a thorough *Humorist:* and so much of WILL, with a spice of THE WILFUL, goes to the making up of a Humorist's Creed, that it is no easy matter to determine, how far such a man might not have a pleasure in humming his own mind, and believing in order to enjoy a dry laugh at himself for the Belief. S. T. C.

That Asgill's Belief, professed and maintained in the first of these tracts, is unwise and odd, I can more readily grant than that it is altogether *irrational* and absurd. I am even strongly inclined to conjecture, that so early as St. Paul's Apostolate there were persons (whether sufficiently numerous to form a sect or party, I cannot say), who held the same tenet as Asgill's, and in a more intolerant and exclusive a Sense; and that it is to such Persons that St. Paul refers in the justly-admired 15th C. of the Corinthians; and that the inadvertence to this has led a numerous class of Divines to a misconception of the Apostle's Reasoning, and a misinterpretation of his words, in behoof of the Socinian notion, that the Resurrection of Christ is the only Argument of Proof for the Belief of a Future State, and that this was the great end and purpose of this Event. Now this assumption is so destitute of support from the other writers of the N. T., and so discordant with the whole spirit and gist of St. Paul's Views and Reasoning every where else, that it is a priori probable, that the apparent exception in Corinth. xvth is only apparent. And this the hypothesis, I have here advanced, would enable one to show, and to exhibit the true bearing of the Texts. Asgill contents himself with maintaining that Translation without Death is *one*, & the best, mode of passing to the Heavenly State. *Hinc itur ad astra*. But his earliest Predecessors contended that it was the *only* mode, and to these St. Paul justly replies:—If in this Life only we have Hope, we are of all men most wretched. S. T. Coleridge. Feb.ʸ 2. 1827.

INTRODUCTION TO ASGILL'S DEFENCE UPON HIS EXPULSION FROM THE HOUSE OF COMMONS *(1712), p. 28.*[12] *Note continued on p. 29 and endpage, verso.*

> For as every Faith, (or Credit) that a Man hath attain'd to, is the Result of some Knowledg [*sic*] or other; so that whoever hath attain'd that Knowledg, hath that Faith (for whatever a Man knows, he cannot but believe:)
> So this *All* Faith being the Result of all Knowledg, 'tis easy to to conceive that whoever had once attain'd to all that Knowledg, nothing could be difficult to him.
> And thus, tho this extreme Notion in the Science of Faith be intelligible only and not imitable; yet the lesser degrees of Knowledg in that Science are both intelligible and imitable.

This discussion on Faith is one of the very few instances in which Asgill has got out of his Depth. According to all usage of words, Science & Faith are incompatible in relation to the same object—while, according to Asgill, Faith is merely the power, which Science confers on the Will. A. says—What we know, we must believe. I retort—What we only *believe*, we do not know. The *minor* here is excluded by, and not included in, the *major*. Minors by difference of Quantity are included in their Majors; but Minors by difference of quality are excluded by them, or superseded. Apply this to Belief and Science, or certain Knowleges. On the confusion of the second, (minors by difference of QUALITY) with the first, rests Asgill's erroneous exposition of Faith.

In my Noetic, or Doctrine and Discipline of Ideas = *logice, Organon* —I purpose to select some four, five or more instances of the sad effects of the absence of ideas in the use of words and in the understanding of truths, in the different departments of life; for example, the word *body*, in connection with resurrection-men, &c.—and the last instances, will (please God!) be the sad effects on the whole system of Christian divinity. I must remember Asgill's book.[13]

---

[12] From *A Collection of Tracts* described in n. 10. Previously printed in *Lit. Rem.*, II, 397.

[13] *Notes Theolog.*, p. 60.

POETRY

George Chapman

Notes on Chapman's Homer[1]

Chapman I have sent in order that you might read the Odyssey; the Iliad is fine, but less equal in the translation, as well as less interesting in itself. What is stupidly said of Shakspeare, is really true and appropriate of Chapman; mighty faults counterpoised by mighty beauties. Excepting his quaint epithets which he affects to render literally from the Greek, a language above all others blest in the happy marriage of sweet words, and which in our language are mere printer's compound epithets—such as quaffed divine *joy-in-the-heart-of-man-infusing* wine (the under-marked is to be one word, because one sweet mellifluous word expresses it in Homer);—excepting this, it has no look, no air, of a translation. It is as truly an original poem as the Faery Queene;—it will give you small idea of Homer, though a far truer one than Pope's epigrams, or Cowper's cumbersome most anti-Homeric Miltonism. For Chapman writes and feels as a poet,—as Homer might have written had he lived in England in the reign of Queen Elizabeth. In short, it is an exquisite poem, in spite of its frequent and perverse quaintnesses and harshnesses, which are, however, amply repaid by almost unexampled sweetness and beauty of language, all over spirit and feeling. In the main it is an English heroic poem, the tale of which is borrowed from the Greek. The dedication to the Iliad is a noble copy of verses, especially those sublime lines beginning,—

> O! 'tis wondrous much
> (Though nothing prisde) that the right vertuous touch
> Of a well written soule, to vertue moves.
> Nor haue we soules to purpose, if their loves
> Of fitting objects be not so inflam'd.
> How much then, were this kingdome's maine soule maim'd,
> To want this great inflamer of all powers
> That move in humane soules! All realmes but yours,
> Are honor'd with him; and hold blest that state
> That have his workes to reade and contemplate.

[1] "Extract of a letter sent with the Volume. 1807." Notes "communicated through Mr. Wordsworth." *Lit. Rem.*, I, 259-63. An unpublished letter from Sara Hutchinson to J. H. Green, Jan. 10, 1835, requests the return of the book, which had been sent from Rydal Mount in her absence. This letter is in the possession of A. H. B. Coleridge.

In which, humanitie to her height is raisde;
Which all the world (yet, none enough) hath praisde.
Seas, earth, and heaven, he did in verse comprize;
Out sung the Muses, and did equalise
Their king Apollo; being so farre from cause
Of princes light thoughts, that their gravest lawes
May finde stuffe to be fashioned by his lines.
Through all the pompe of kingdomes still he shines
And graceth all his gracers. Then let lie
Your lutes, and viols, and more loftily
Make the heroiques of your Homer sung,
To drums and trumpets set his Angels tongue:
And with the princely sports of haukes you use,
Behold the kingly flight of his high Muse:
And see how like the Phœnix she renues
Her age, and starrie feathers in your sunne;
Thousands of yeares attending; everie one
Blowing the holy fire, and throwing in
Their seasons, kingdomes, nations that have bin
Subverted in them; lawes, religions, all
Offerd to change, and greedie funerall;
Yet still your Homer lasting, living, raigning.—

and likewise the 1st, the 11th, and last but one, of the prefatory sonnets
to the Odyssey. Could I have foreseen any other speedy opportunity, I
should have begged your acceptance of the volume in a somewhat hand-
somer coat; but as it is, it will better represent the sender,—to quote
from myself—

A man disherited, in form and face,
By nature and mishap, of outward grace.

Dedication to Prince Henry

Chapman in his moral heroic verse, as in this dedication and the
prefatory sonnets to his Odyssey, stands above Ben Jonson; there is
more dignity, more lustre, and equal strength; but not midway quite between him and the sonnets of Milton. I do not know whether I give
him the higher praise, in that he reminds me of Ben Jonson with a sense
of his superior excellence, or that he brings Milton to memory notwithstanding his inferiority. His moral poems are not quite out of books
like Jonson's, nor yet do the sentiments so wholly grow up out of his
own natural habit and grandeur of thought, as in Milton. The sentiments have been attracted to him by a natural affinity of his intellect,
and so combined;—but Jonson has taken them by individual and successive acts of choice.

Epistle Dedicatorie to the Odyssey

All'this and the preceding is well felt and vigorously, though harshly, expressed, respecting sublime poetry *in genere;* but in reading Homer I look about me, and ask how does all this apply here? For surely never was there plainer writing; there are a thousand charms of sun and moonbeam, ripple, and wave, and stormy billow, but all on the surface. Had Chapman read Proclus and Porphyry?—and did he really believe them,—or even that they believed themselves? They felt the immense power of a Bible, a Shaster, a Koran. There was none in Greece or Rome, and they tried therefore by subtle allgorical accomoda-tions to conjure the poem of Homer into the βιβλίον θεοπαράδοτον of Greek faith.

Epistle Dedicatorie to the Batrachomyomachia

Chapman's identification of his fate with Homer's and his complete forgetfulness of the distinction between Christianity and idolatry, under the general feeling of some religion, is very interesting. It is amusing to observe, how familiar Chapman's fancy has become with Homer, his life and its circumstances, though the very existence of any such indi-vidual, at least with regard to the Iliad and the Hymns, is more than problematic. N. B. The rude engraving in the page was designed by no vulgar hand. It is full of spirit and passion.

End of the Batrachomyomachia

I am so dull, that neither in the original nor in any translation could I ever find any wit or wise purpose in this poem. The whole humor seems to lie in the names. The frogs and mice are not frogs or mice, but men, and yet they do nothing that conveys any satire. In the Greek there is much beauty of language, but the joke is very flat. This is always the case in rude ages;—their serious vein is inimitable,— their comic low and low indeed. The psychological cause is easily stated, and copiously exemplifiable.[2]

Chapman had translated Homer excellently in some parts, but he did not agree in Lamb's wholesale applause of the verse, and wished that the old poet had continued, as he had begun, in the ten-syllable heroic measure: it would have been more readable, and might have saved us from Pope. Chapman had failed, where he had not succeeded, by en-deavouring to write English as Homer had written Greek; Chapman's was Greekified English,—it did not want vigour, or variety, but smooth-ness and facility. Detached passages could not be improved: they were Homer writing English.[3]

[2] *Lit. Rem.,* I, 259-63.
[3] Collier, "Diary," Oct. 10, 1811, in Collier, *Seven Lect.,* pp. xxxi-xxxii.

Samuel Daniel

Men of great Genius find in new words & new combinations the sin that most easily besets them—a strong feeling of originality seems to receive a gratification by new Terms—hence the all too often useless nomenclatures in the philosophical writings of all men of originality— some quite overlayed by it, as Jac. Boehmen, but if a *Daniel* whom Gower & Lidgate were so much below, & Chaucer so much above, had lived in the age of Chaucer, I doubt not we should have been as much struck by the contrast of Daniel's Language with Spencer's, & even the later Shakespere.[1]

Daniel's incomparable Epistle to the Lady Margaret, Countess of Cumberland, is written in Stanzas of eight lines, Iambic Pentameter: the two last a couplet, the other six corresponding, the 1st to the 4th, 2nd to the 5th, the 3rd to the 6th—And this metre certainly has a good effect in a poem of stately moral sentences, and seems a serviceable medium between rhyme & blank verse, attuned as it here is, by the rhymes of the last couplet. But in the Epistle preceeding, where metre is adopted *without* the couplet, it becomes a mere waste of rhymes, the poet having all their restraint and trouble, while the reader has none of the effect, unless indeed now and then an obscure sense of a *jingle* in the monotonous blank verse.[2] Yet I rather am disposed to alter this metre: whether I make the lines tetrameter or pentameter, in one or other of the following ways—either by transposing the rhymes from the 3rd & 6th to the 3rd and 5th, or from the first & 4th to the first and 6th— breath, grave, men; death, when, gave: flew, renew: or grave, breath, men; death, when, gave: flew, renew: or grave, when, breath, death, men, gave, flew, renew. And I seem to anticipate, that for a moral poem all four modes may be adopted. In short, I would always preserve the final couplet as the always anticipable burthen of the metre, & which with the same number of lines in all would make the whole poem

---

[1] Notebook 16, fol. 66 recto. British Museum, Add. MSS, 47,513. Printed for the first time.

[2] For a similar statement see marginal note on ''To the Lord Henry Howard,'' p. 517.

sufficiently uniform, but the first six I would [say?] ad libitum, i. e. ring the changes.[3]

In Daniel's Sonnets there is scarcely one good line; while his Hymen's Triumph, of which Chalmers says not one word, exhibits a continued series of first-rate beauties in thought, passion and imagery, and in language and metre is so faultless, that the style of that poem may without extravagance be declared to be imperishable English. 1820.[4]

Read Daniel—the admirable Daniel—in his "Civil Wars," and "Triumphs of Hymen." The style and language are just such as any very pure and manly writer of the present day—Wordsworth, for example—would use; it seems quite modern in comparison with the style of Shakspeare.[5]

Both in respect of this[6] and of the former[7] excellence, Mr. Wordsworth strikingly resembles Samuel Daniel, one of the golden writers of our golden Elizabethian [sic] age, now most causelessly neglected: Samuel Daniel, whose diction bears no mark of time, no distinction of age, which has been, and as long as our language shall last, will be so far the language of the to-day and for ever, as that it is more intelligble to us, than the transitory fashions of our own particular age: A similar praise is due to his sentiments. No frequency of perusal can deprive them of their freshness. For though they are brought into the full day-light of every reader's comprehension; yet are they drawn up from depths which few in any age are priviledged [sic] to visit, into which few in any age have courage or inclination to descend. If Mr. Wordsworth is not equally with Daniel alike intelligible to all readers of average understanding in all passages of his works, the comparative difficulty does not arise from the greater impurity of the ore, but from the nature and uses of the metal. A poem is not necessarily obscure, because it does not aim to be popular. It is enough, if a work be perspicuous to those for whom it is written, and,
"Fit audience find, though few."[8]

[3] Notebook 22, fol. 85 verso-86 recto. British Museum, Add. MSS, 47,520. Printed for the first time.
[4] "Chalmer's Life of Daniel," Ashe, Miscellanies, p. 293. Cf. Lit. Rem., II, 360.
[5] March 15, 1834. Table Talk S, VI, 505.
[6] "Correspondent weight and sanity of the Thoughts and Sentiments,—won not from books; but from the poet's own meditative observation."
[7] "An austere purity of language both grammatically and logically; in short a perfect appropriateness of the words to the meaning."
[8] Biog. Lit. C, II, 166-67.

Drayton is a sweet poet, and Selden's notes to the early part of the Polyolbion are well worth your perusal. Daniel is a superior man; his diction is pre-eminently pure;—of that quality which I believe has always existed somewhere in society. It is just such English, without any alteration, as Wordsworth or Sir George Beaumont might have spoken or written in the present day.

Yet there are instances of sublimity in Drayton. When deploring the cutting down of some of our old forests, he says, in language which reminds the reader of Lear, written subsequently, and also of several of Mr. Wordsworth's poems:—

> ". . . Our trees so hack'd above the ground,
> That where their lofty tops the neighboring countries crown'd,
> Their trunks (like aged folks) now bare and naked stand,
> *As for revenge to heaven each held a wither'd hand.*"

That is very fine.[9]

On the contrary to how many passages, both in hymn books and in blank verse poems, could I (were it not invidious) direct the reader's attention, the style of which is most *unpoetic, because,* and only because, it is the style of *prose?* He will not suppose me capable of having in my mind such verses, as

> "I put my hat upon my head
> And walk'd into the strand;
> And there I met another man,
> Whose hat was in his hand."

To such specimens it would indeed be a fair and full reply, that these lines are not bad, because they are *unpoetic;* but because they are empty of all sense and feeling; and that it were an idle attempt to prove that an ape is not a Newton, when it is evident that he is not a man. But the sense shall be good and weighty, the language correct and dignified, the subject interesting and treated with feeling; and yet the style shall, notwithstanding all these merits be justly blameable as *prosaic,* and solely because the words and the order of the words would find their appropriate place in prose, but are not suitable to *metrical* composition. The "Civil Wars" of Daniel is an instructive, and even interesting work; but take the following stanzas (and from the hundred instances which abound I might probably have selected others far more striking)

[9] Sept. 11, 1831. *Table Talk S,* VI, p. 372-73.

"And to the end we may with better ease
Discern the true discourse, vouchsafe to shew
What were the times foregoing near to these,
That these we may with better profit know.
Tell how the world fell into this disease;
And how so great distemperature did grow;
So shall we see with what degrees it came;
How things at full do soon wax out of frame."

"Ten kings had from the Norman conqu'ror reign'd
With intermixt and variable fate,
When England to her greatest height attain'd
Of power, dominion, glory, wealth, and state.
After it had with much ado sustain'd
The violence of princes with debate
For titles, and the often mutinies
Of nobles for their ancient liberties."

"For first the Norman, conqu'ring all by might,
By might was forced to keep what he had got;
Mixing our customs and the form of right
With foreign constitutions, he had brought;
Mastering the mighty, humbling the poorer wight,
By all severest means that could be wrought;
And making the succession doubtful rent
His new-got state and left it turbulent."

B. I. St. vii. viii. & ix.

Will it be contended on the one side, that these lines are mean and senseless? Or on the other, that they are not prosaic, and for *that* reason unpoetic? This poet's well-merited epithet is that of the "*well-languaged Daniel;*" but likewise and by the consent of his contemporaries no less than of all succeeding critics, the "prosaic Daniel." Yet those, who thus designate this wise and amiable writer from the frequent incorrespondency of his diction to his metre in the majority of his compositions, not only deem them valuable and interesting on other accounts, but willingly admit, that there are to be found throughout his poems, and especially in his *Epistles* and in his *Hymen's Triumph,* many and exquisite specimens of that style which, as the *neutral ground* of prose and verse is common to both.[10]

Daniel, POETICAL WORKS,[11] *Vol. II, first flyleaf.*

[10] *Biog. Lit. C,* II, 80-82.

[11] Samuel Daniel, *Poetical Works* (2 vols.; London: 1718). This copy from the library of Charles Lamb is now in the Houghton Library, Harvard University. The volumes at one time belonged to William Carew Hazlitt, who wrote in Vol. I: "This copy is particularly interesting as having belonged to Charles Lamb and having been enriched by him and S. T. Coleridge with MSS notes. It also contains two or three letters by S. T. C. which are not published." Only the notes on the *Civil Wars* are by Coleridge.

Tuesday, Feb. 10th, 1808 (10th or 9th)
Dear Charles,
I think more highly, far more, of the "Civil Wars" than you seemed
to do (on Monday night, Feb. 9th, 1808)—the verse does not teaze *me;*
and all the while I am reading it, I cannot but fancy a plain England-
loving English Country Gentleman, with only some dozen Books in his
whole Library, and at a time when a "Mercury" or "Intelligencer" was
seen by him once in a month or two, making this his Newspaper and
political Bible at the same time, & reading it so often as to store his
Memory with it's aphorisms. Conceive a good man of that kind, diffident
and passive, yet *rather* inclined to Jacobitism; seeing the reasons of the
Revolutionary Party, yet by disposition and old principles leaning, in
quiet nods and sighs, at his own parlour fire, to the hereditary Right—
(and of these characters there must have been many)—& then read this
poem, assuming in your heart his character—conceive how grave he
would look, and what pleasure there would be, what unconscious, harmless, humble self-conceit, self-compliment in his gravity; how *wise* he
would feel himself—& yet after all, how forbearing, how much calmed
by that most calming reflection (when it is really the mind's own reflection)[12]—aye it was just so in Henry the 6th's Time, always the
same passions at work—&c.[13] Have I injured thy Book—? or wilt thou
like it the better there*fore?* But I have done as I would gladly be done
by—thee, at least.

S. T. Coleridge

Daniel, POETICAL WORKS, *Vol. II, second flyleaf.*
p. 217. V. a fine Stanza.[14]

Hazlitt lent the volumes to the editor of *Notes and Queries*, who published the
two letters and some of the notes: "Coleridge: Letters to Lamb, and Notes on
Samuel Daniel's Poems," *Notes and Queries* (1st ser.), VI, 117-18. The letters
have been reprinted elsewhere and are included in Raysor's *Misc. Crit.*, pp. 235-38.
When Hazlitt's library was offered for sale, some additional notes were printed in
the *Athenæum*, Nov. 18, 1893, pp. 697-98. A transcript of the original notes with
only one or two omissions is in William Godwin's hand among Godwin's papers in
Lord Abinger's library. Duke University has the microfilm of these papers, and I
am indebted to Professor Lewis Patton for sharing with me his discovery of the
notes on Daniel and to the Duke University Library for permission to collate these
notes with the printed versions and the original. Harvard University has kindly
given permission for the use of the original notes which, since my MS went to
press, have been transcribed and edited by Cecil C. Seronsy, "Coleridge Marginalia
in Lamb's Copy of Daniel's *Poetical Works*," *Harvard Library Bulletin*, VII
(Winter 1953), 105-12.

[12] Parenthetical comment omitted in the Godwin transcript.
[13] Quotation marks, "Aye, . . . at work &c." in the Godwin transcript.
[14] In *Notes and Queries* this reference was erroneously printed as Vol. V, p. 217,
and followed by a note on the *Civil Wars*, Book VI, st. xciii, which is on p. 206.

Second Letter / 5 hours after the First.
Dear Charles,
You must read over these Civil Wars again. We both know what
a *mood* is. And the genial[15] mood will, it shall come for my sober-
minded Daniel. He was a Tutor and a sort of Steward in a noble Family
in which Form was religiously observed, and Religion formally; & yet
there was such warm blood & mighty muscle of substance within, that
the moulding Irons did not distort tho' they stiffened the vital man
within. Daniel caught & recommunicated the Spirit of the great
Countess of Pembroke, the glory of the North (he *formed* her mind, &
her mind inspirited him. Gravely sober in all ordinary affairs, & not
easily excited by any—yet there is one, on which his Blood boils—whenever he speaks of English Valour exerted against a foreign Enemy. Do
read over—but some evening when we are quite comfortable, at your
fire-side—& O! where shall I ever be, if I am not so there—that is the
last Altar, on the horns of which my old Feelings hang, but alas! listen
& tremble) Nonsense!—well! I will read it to you & Mary. The 205,
206, and 207th page (above all, that 93rd ※ Stanza)[16] what is there in
description superior even in Shakspere? only that Shakespere would
have given one of his *Glows* to the first Line, and flatter'd the mountain
Top with his sovran Eye—instead of that poor "a marvellous advantage
of his years"—but this however is Daniel—and he must not be read
piecemeal. Even by leaving off, & looking at a Stanza by itself, I find
the loss.
S. T. Coleridge
※ and in a different style the 98th stanza, p. 208: and what an Image
in 107, p. 211. Thousands even of educated men would become more
sensible, fitter to be members of Parliament or Ministers, by reading
Daniel—and even those few who, quoad intellectum only gain refreshment of notions already their own, must become better Englishmen.

Raysor therefore surmised a printer's error for volume and page (*Misc. Crit.*, p.
236 n.). It is clear from both the original notes and Godwin's transcript that the
two notes are separate and pertain to two different stanzas. Furthermore, st. v, p.
217, Book VII includes the "polysyllables—such as Eminence, Obedience, Reverence"
to which Coleridge refers on the fourth flyleaf, *infra*.
[15] "genial" is omitted in the Godwin transcript.
[16] Book VI, st. xciii, p. 206.
   Whilst *Talbot* (whose fresh Ardor having got
   A marvelous Advantage of his Years)
   Carries his unfelt Age as if forgot,
   Whirling about where any Need appears.
   His Hand, his Eye, his Wits all present, wrought
   The Function of the Glorious Part he bears:
   Now urging here, now cheering there, he flies;
   Unlocks the thickest Troops, where most Force lies.

O, if it be not too late, write a kind note about him.

S. T. Coleridge

Daniel, POETICAL WORKS, *Vol. II, fourth flyleaf.*[17]

Is it from any hobby-horsical Love of our old writers (& of such a passion respecting Chaucer, Spenser, and Ben Jonson's Poems I have occasionally' seen glaring proofs in one the string of whose Shoe I am not worthy to unloose) or is it a real Beauty, the interspersion, I mean, (in stanza poems) of rhymes from polysyllables—such as Eminence, Obedience, Reverence? To my ear they convey not only a relief from variety, but a *sweetness* as of repose—and the Understanding they gratify by reconciling Verse with the whole wide extent of good Sense. Without being distinctly conscious of such a Notion, having it rather than reflecting it (for one may think in the same way as one may see and hear), I seem to be made to know, that I need have no fear; that there's nothing excellent in itself which the Poet cannot express accurately & naturally, nay, no good word.

Daniel, POETICAL WORKS: CIVIL WARS, *Book V, st. ci, p. 171.*[18]

Considering the style of this poem, & how it is pitched, it is unpardonable in the author to have put the particulars of Suffolk's Death in a *Note,* and yet have inserted a stanza unintelligible without it. Concerning the abuse of *Notes* in modern works an Essay might be written usefully.

Daniel, POETICAL WORKS: CIVIL WARS, *Book V, st. cii-cv, pp. 172-73. Note continued on pp. 174, 175.*

This is the most inappropriate Speech in the whole Work: it is indeed so very much out of character, that I should not be surprized if something of nearly the same import were to be in our old English or Latin Chronicles, for Daniel is a man of excellent good sense, and had he had to *invent* a speech for the Queen, would, I would fain think, have entered decently, at least *Racinishly,* if not Shakspearianly, into her character—and yet, meeting the speech in the shape of history, would have [been] seduced by it's coincidence with his own modes of reflection to have inserted & versified it. The recommencement of the narration, "Thus *storms* the Lady,"[19] is truly *humorous.* Like a Phlegmatist, who conversing with his Lip-brother, the Pipe, in his mouth, observed—"I know, I'm too-apt-to speak—pre-cip-cipi-cipitately."

[17] Not in the Godwin transcript.
[18] This comment and the one on sts. cii-cv are not in either set of printed notes but are in the Godwin transcript.
[19] St. cvi.

Daniel, POETICAL WORKS: CIVIL WARS, *Book V, st. cxiii, p. 175.*[20]

It is perhaps worth noticing as an excellence suited to the style of the Poetry (whatever may be thought of that) that the accents and scansion of Daniels Lines more assist the reading & the sense, than in any work, I know. If the Line runs ill to you, you may be sure, you have not read it in it's exact sense. The whole represents a grave, easy man talking seriously to his friends. Sometimes, too, he breaks up, for a moment, the feeling of versification; but never by a *contradiction to* it, but by heightening the feeling of conversation—*ex. gr.,* by putting 3 important words in the most important Line of an aphorism, as if at each of the three words the speaker gave a wise nod aided by the motion of the forefinger—[21]

⁜ To *Greatness,* who *Love,* and *Opinion* hath. [Book V, st. cxiv, 1.8.]

p. 192, l. 14—where there are 3 emphatic and 3 subemphatic words.

Daniel, POETICAL WORKS: CIVIL WARS, *Book VI, st. xlvi, l. 4. [p. 192, l. 14]*

⁜ Powers betray'd, Princes slain, Kings massacred

See 175. l. 20th & the note.

Daniel, POETICAL WORKS: CIVIL WARS, *Book VI, st. cvi, l. 6, p. 211.*

Some for Revenge, some for Wealth, some for Delight.[22]

p. 192 & 175. ∪∪∪—/∪∪—/∪∪∪—: two Pæon quarts with an anapest interposed, 14 instead of 15, the pause more than making up the deficient time, so very much more indeed that I cannot but admire the metrical judgement of the Poet.

Daniel, POETICAL WORKS: CIVIL WARS, *Book VI, st. ii, l. 5, p. 178.*

When as the King thereof ascertained.

I do not recollect to have seen this word elsewhere, accented as a Pæon Secundus ∪—∪∪, but it gives the meaning & brings out the sensorium-syllable far better than the present anapestic or Pæon-tertius emphasis. What is *"tain'd"* or *"tained"*?

[20] This comment and the next two were printed in the *Athenæum* but not in *Notes and Queries.* Only the first two were copied in the Godwin transcript.
    Then as for those who were his Followers,
    (Being all Choice Men for Virtues, or Deserts)
[21] The first reference is omitted in the *Athenæum* but is correctly given in the Godwin transcript as ''st. 114, 1. 8.''
[22] This example does not appear in the Godwin transcript. The next reference is ''B. VI, st. 14, l. 6,'' which is the second quotation in the *Athenæum,* and is immediately followed by the comment.

Daniel, POETICAL WORKS: CIVIL WARS, *Book VI, st. xiv, p. 182.*

[Warwick]
Laments the State, the People's Misery,
And (that which such a Pitier seldom mends)
Oppression, that sharp two-edged Sword,
That others wounds, and wounds likewise his Lord.

We can not too highly praise the strain of political morality thro'
this Work. No Success, no Heroism ever makes the author forget the
immutable Right & Wrong. And if it be objected, that the right to
the Throne is confounded with the right to common property, to an
estate or house, yet still this was the Creed of those Ages, as much the
Creed of Henry the IVth & Vth as Richard the Second—yet Daniel was
not blinded by it, so as to overlook the guilt of involving a nation in
civil war on an old tho' *rightful* claim. See p. 155, Stanza 46.[23]

Daniel, POETICAL WORKS: CIVIL WARS, *Book VI, st. xvi, p. 182. Note on
p. 183.*

Anjou and *Main,* (the Maim that foul appears;
Th'eternal Scar of our dismember'd Land)

In the first Line of Stanza 16 of this Book is a Pun in it's right place
& passion. Had Puns never been used less judiciously than in this
sentence & that of the fallen angels in the 6th Book of Paradise Lost,
they would still have been considered as Beauties.

Daniel, POETICAL WORKS CIVIL WARS, *Book VI, sts. xxxii-xlvii, pp. 188-
92. Note continued on p. 193. [Speech of Nemesis to Pandora]*

But the passage vexes me: it has spoilt and discharactered the poem,
the best of its kind in any language: for, spite of a few dazzling passages in the Pharsalia, it is as much superior to Lucan's (meâ quidem
sententiâ) as the steady staid gait of manhood to the all-sorts-of-mo-
tions of a Hobbitihoy, or a plain and often deep sense to Stoical declamations. The Pharsalia is really a Hobbitihoy poem—neither man nor
boy. It is to me just what I should have expected from a youth well-
educated & of strong natural Talents at 19: and great works might have
followed if he had lived, but more probably, if this work had been composed in his head & forgotten by himself. For no man is proof against
the popularity of his own writings.—But in this long [speech] what
vexes one, is that the whole might so well have been said in the author's
own person, the philosophy being shallow, indeed, and short-sighted (a
cowardice of present evil is the character of the writers of that age) but
it is of a piece, it harmonizes, and in the morally, tho' not *intellectually*

[23] Book VI, st. xlvi.

(for that is scarcely possible) nobler æra that succeeded even Milton fell into the nonsense of abusing Fire-arms.

Daniel, POETICAL WORKS: CIVIL WARS, *Book VI, st. xxxiv, ll. 7-8, note on p. 189.*

> And that abused[24] Pow'r which thus hath wrought,
> Shall give her self the Sword to cut her Throat.

The Poets of Elizabeth & still more of James's time had a half in half hankering for Popery—we see it in Spenser, in Drayton, in Massinger. In dignity of moral character they were wofully inferior to the succeeding age—a fact honorable to Liberty & therefore to human nature.

Daniel, POETICAL WORKS: CIVIL WARS, *Book VI, st. xliii, l. 8, p. 191.*

> . . . and all her People toss'd
> With unkind Tumults, and almost lost.

[Coleridge underlines unkind] the etymon of *Kinde* is here preserved & unkind = unnatural.

Daniel, POLITICAL WORKS: CIVIL WARS, *Book VI, st. xcix, p. 208.*

> Yet happy-hapless Day, blest ill-lost Breath,
> Both for our better Fortune, and your own!
> For what foul Wounds, what Spoil, what shameful Death,
> Had by this forward Resolution grown;
> If at St. *Albans, Wakefield, Barnet-Heath,*
> It should unto your Infamy been shown?
> Blest you, that did not teach how great a Fault
> Ev'n Virtue is in Actions that are naught.

A Stanza obscure from mismanagement of syntax—a defect, of which there is scarce a second example in our "well-languaged Daniel," as Spenser most appropriately, as to the fact, calls him, tho' the phrase stands in contrast to the sense.

Southey! rarely will the English Tongue admit of participles of substantives.

Daniel, POETICAL WORKS: CIVIL WARS, *Book VI, st. ci, p. 209.*

> The wŏrkĭng Spĭrĭt cēas'd nŏt, thŏ' work dĭd cēase,

A whole Book might be written, neither diffuse or uninstructive, on the metrical excellence of the 5th line of the CIst Stanza. The pause after Spirit compels a stress on ceas'd, & so makes ceas'd not, by addition of the pause after not, = to a spondee—a fine effect after the Tribrach, or ⌣⌣⌣. Spirit, Body, money, honey, & two or 3 more perhaps

[24] Daniel's note: "The Church."

which I do not recollect, are remnants of genuine *metre* in our language
—they are, at least always may be, Pyrrhics, i. e. �‿�‿ = – : as a delicate
ear may instantly perceive & prove that accent, contrary to the almost
universal opinion, shortens the syllable on which it rests; for in these
words there is an equal accent in both syllables—hence they are both
short. The wōrkīng Spĭrĭt (a pause equal to ˘) ceas'd nŏt, thŏ' Wōrk
dĭd cease. N.B. This is a valuable Remark.

Daniel, POETICAL WORKS: CIVIL WARS, *Book VI, st. cv, l. 4, p. 210.*

Those Peace-spilt Times, weary of being well:

better (or = to) spoilt.

Daniel, POETICAL WORKS: CIVIL WARS, *Book VII, st. ii, p. 216. Note*
continued on p. 217.

> The Queen abroad, with a revenging Hand
> (Arm'd with her own Disgrace, and others Spite,
> Gath'ring th' Oppressed Party of the Land)
> Held over him the threatening Sword of Might;
> That forc'd him in the Terms of Awe to stand,
> (Who else had burst-up Right, to come t'his Right)
> And kept him so confus'd, that he knew not
> To make use of the Means which he had got.

In the mind of a man like Daniel, neither Priest or Lawyer, too
honest to falsify a notion of Duty and too good by nature to stifle a sense
of general misery, this mistake (common to all his Contemporaries except Buchanan, Knox, & Raleigh) (I speak of authors) of the Jus Individui de re individuâ for the Munus Individui *propter* rem publicam
occasioned a civil war, bloodless indeed, yet as perplexed as that which
the same mistake called into action by ambition produced in the *real*
world. See Judge Foster's excellent animadversions on Hale's obs.
concerning Kings de jure & de facto.[25]

Daniel, POETICAL WORKS: CIVIL WARS, *Book VII, st. viii, p. 218.*

These Machines of Ambition, and high Pride;

The word was pronounced sometimes, *Matchins,* sometimes Mackins,
from machĭnă.

[25] Sir Matthew Hale (1609-76) wrote concerning kings *de jure* and *de facto* in
Pleas of the Crown; or a Methodical Summary of the Principal Matters Relating to
That Subject. His opinions were refuted by Sir Michael Foster (1689-1763), ''Dis-
course IV. Observations on Some Passages in the Writings of Lord Chief Justice
Hale, relative to the Principles on which the Revolution and present happy Estab-
lishment are founded,'' *A Report of Some Proceedings on the Commission for the*
Trial of the Rebels in the Year 1746, in the County of Surry; and of Other Crown
Cases: to Which Are Added Discourses upon a Few Branches of the Crown Law
(2d ed.; Dublin: 1791), pp. 379-412 (1st ed., 1762).

Daniel, POETICAL WORKS: CIVIL WARS, *Book VII, st. xiv, p. 220.*

Wrapt in a strong and curious Ordinance
Of many Articles, bound solemnly.

Curious = careful in the extreme, solicitously guarded.

Daniel, POETICAL WORKS: CIVIL WARS, *Book VI, st. xxviii.*[26]

It was the time when fair Europa sat
With many goodly diadems address'd,
And all her parts (in flourishing estate)
Lay beautiful, in order, at their rest.
No swelling member unproportionate,
Grown out of form, sought to disturb the rest:
The less subsisting by the greater's might;
The greater by the less kept upright.

A theory framed in Fancy (in strictness, not θεωρία but ἀθεωρία, *or* at best ἡμιθεωρία) never fails to produce a distortion of Fact. Consult the contemporary Historians of the 12 & 13 Centuries, & compare them with Daniel's flattering statement.

Daniel, POETICAL WORKS: CIVIL WARS, *Book VI, st. xxx ff.* [*Nemesis calls for Pandora to spread evils.*]

Nothing can be more *out of keeping,* as the Painters say, than the introduction of these fictions in so grave & prosaic, tho' rhymed, History. They read like a stupid Lie, told in cold blood, for Lying's sake.

Daniel, TO THE LORD HENRY HOWARD.[27]

A curious instance how rhymes may be *wasted,* and the poet have all the restraint and trouble, while the reader has none of the effect— except now and then a perplexed suspicion of a *jingle* in the monotonous blank verse.

Daniel, TO THE LADY MARGARET.

A noble poem in all respects.

[26] This comment and the next following, are here transcribed from the set of Robert Anderson's *The Poets of Great Britain* (13 vols.; Edinburgh: 1793-1807) in the Victoria and Albert Museum, South Kensington, VI, 165-67, but they were printed by Raysor, *Misc. Crit.,* pp. 238-39.

[27] The notes on Daniel's poems below are taken from the set of Anderson's *British Poets* in the Folger Shakespeare Library, IV, 204, 206, 208-9. Many of the notes in this set are by Hartley Coleridge, but some are in the hand of S. T. C. The notes here quoted were printed by Derwent Coleridge in his edition of Hartley Coleridge's *Essays and Marginalia* (London: 1851), II, 14-16, where all were attributed to S. T. C. except the one on "To the Lady Lucy, Countess of Bedford." I agree with Raysor, who also prints the notes, that the hand is Coleridge's for this comment as for the others. See Raysor, *Misc. Crit.,* pp. 239-40.

Daniel, TO THE LADY LUCY, COUNTESS OF BEDFORD.
> And though books, madam, cannot make this mind,
> Which we must bring apt to be set aright;
> Yet they do rectify it in that kind,
> And touch it so, as that it turns that way
> Where judgment lies . . .

Annex these lines as a note and modest answer to the lines in Milton's *Paradise Regained* in Christ's reply—*Paradise Regained,* B. IV:
> "However, many books
> Wise men have said, are wearisome," etc.

Daniel, THE PASSION OF A DISTRESSED MAN.

This "Resumption" has done away the chief possible merit of this moot case, by destroying its only possible moral—viz., that for our lives we are not answerable, but for our actions. If, therefore, life be offered me at the price of a bad action, let it be one or twenty, the murder is with the offerer. I die not only innocent, but virtuous. Better a thousand die than one commit a crime; for what a *crime* is, it were impiety to pretend to be ignorant; what death is, it were presumptuous to pretend to know.

Davies still more than even Daniel is a proof that our Language has made no steps, endured no real alteration since the Time of Elizabeth at least. Every 5 years, has it's affectation; but he who writes simply well, must write now, both words & construction as our ancestors, two or even three hundred years ago.[28]

To the Editor of the *Courier,* December 7, 1809.

If you should have no verses in your Poet's corner for the day, permit me to recommend the following quotations, the latter from an obscure poet of the reign of Charles the First; the former from a poet of Elizabeth's days, whose name indeed is better known, but whose works are almost as little read. The excellent good sense of the first, sufficiently atones for the languour of the metre, and the prosaic character of the diction: the application of both is too striking to need any comment.
> Here Irish discontents and fears of France,
> Urged with the present times' necessity,
> Brought forth in a subtly-shadow'd countenance
> Of quiet PEACE, resembling amity;
> Wrapt in a strong and curious ordinance

[28] Notebook 22, fol. 75 recto and 76 verso. Printed for the first time.

Of many articles bound solemnly.
As if these gordian knots could be so tied
That no ambitious sword could them divide!

Especially, whereas the self-same ends
Concur in no one point of like respect,
But that each party covertly intends
Thereby its own designment to effect.
Such Peace with more endangering wounds offends
Than War can do, which stands upon suspect;
And never can be tied with other chain
Than intermutual benefit and gain.
                    Daniel's *Civil Wars*, B. 7. Stan. 14, 15.

Fear never wanted arguments: you do
Reason yourself into a careful bondage,
Circumspect only to your misery.
I could urge Freedom, Charters, Country, Laws,
Gods, and Religion, and such precious names,
Nay, what you value higher, WEALTH; but that
You sue for bondage, yielding to demands
As treacherous as they are insolent, and have
Only this sluggish praise—to PERISH FULL!
                    Love's Convert, by Cartwright.[29]

John Donne

Notes of Coleridge on the Poet Donne[1]
Versification of Donne

To read Dryden, Pope, &c., you need only count syllables; but to read Donne you must measure *Time*, and discover the *Time* of each word

[29] *Essays*, II, 599-600.

---

[1] MSS notes of Coleridge in the books of Charles Lamb, May 2, 1811. Printed in the *Literary World* as "Coleridgiana II," XII (April 30, 1853), 349-50, and "Coleridgiana IV," May 28, 1853, p. 435. These notes also appear in *Notes Theolog.*, pp. 249-55, 260-61. In both sources they were communicated by Mr. George T. Strong of New York. The Houghton Library, Harvard University has a manuscript entitled *The Songs and Sonnets of Dr. John Donne with critical Notes by the Late Samuel Taylor Coleridge. Edited by Barron Field, Esq.* This volume was prepared for the Percy Society but was never printed. Field says:
  "The following Notes were written by the Poet Coleridge in his and my friend Charles Lamb's copy of Donne; and Mr. Lamb permitted me to transcribe them into mine, thirty years ago. I expected that they would be published, with the

by the sense of[2] Passion. I would ask no surer test of a Scotchman's *substratum* (for the turf-cover of pretension they all have) than to make him read Donne's satires aloud. If he made manly metre of them and yet strict metre, then,—why, then he wasn't a Scotchman,[3] or his soul was geographically slandered by his body's first appearing there.

Doubtless, all the copies I have ever seen of Donne's Poems are grievously misprinted. Wonderful that they are not more so, considering that not one in a thousand of his readers have any notion how his lines are to be read—to the many, five out of six appear anti-metrical. How greatly this aided the compositor's negligence or ignorance, and prevented the corrector's remedy, any man may ascertain by examining the earliest editions of blank verse plays, Massinger, Beaumont and Fletcher, &c. Now, Donne's rhythm was as inexplicable to the many as blank verse, spite of his rhymes—ergo, as blank verse, misprinted. I am convinced that where no mode of rational declamation by pause, hurrying of voice, or apt and sometimes double emphasis, can at once make the verse metrical and bring out the sense of passion more prominently, that[4] there we are entitled to alter the text, when it can be done by simple omission or addition of *that, which, and,* and such 'small deer;' or by mere placing[5] of the same words—I would venture nothing beyond.[6]

> And by delighting many, frees again
> Grief which Verse did restrain.
> The Triple Fool, v. 15

A good instance how Donne read his own verses. We should write 'The Grief, verse did restrain;' but Donne roughly emphasized the two

---

rest of such things, in the 'Literary Remains' of our wise and good philosopher; but the learned Editor of that work has lamentedly died without collecting them. They are carelessly written, and were intended only for the eye of the author's dear friend, but few as they are they are too precious to be lost to the world; and the Poems of Donne are so little read, that there will be no harm in affording the Members of the Percy Society with opportunity of refreshing their acquaintance with this learned and fanciful poet. It is true that the whole of his poetical works are in the collections of Bell, Anderson and Chalmers; but these editions were abandoned to literary hackneyman and printers, and are full of errors.''

There are only slight differences between these notes and those communicated by Mr. Strong. Supplementary use of Barron Field's transcription is made with the kind permission of the Houghton Library, Harvard University, and of Professor Roger Bennett, who first discovered the material among uncatalogued MSS. Differences in capitalization and punctuation are not recorded.

[2] Field writes ''and,'' reading ''sense and passion.''

[3] Field writes, ''then he was no Scot.'' He cancels this comment on the Scots. and it is also omitted by Derwent Coleridge in *Notes Theolog.*, etc.

[4] Field writes ''then.''

[5] Field and *Notes Theolog.* give ''mere new-placing.''

[6] Field does not give the comments between this point and the notes on ''Songs and Sonnets.''

main words, Grief and Verse, and, therefore, made each the first syllable
of a trochee or dactyl:—

> Grief, which / verse did re / strain.
> And we join to't our strength,
> And we teach it art and length.

Song.

The anapest judiciously used, in the eagerness and haste to confirm
and aggravate. This beautiful and perfect poem proves, by its title
"Song," that *all* Donne's Poems are equally *metrical* (misprints allowed
for) though smoothness (i.e., the metre necessitating the proper reading) be deemed appropriate to *songs;* but in poems where the writer
thinks, and expects the reader to do so, the sense must be understood in
order to ascertain the metre.

Satire III

If you would teach a scholar in the highest form how to *read*, take
Donne, and of Donne this satire. When he has learnt to read Donne,
with all the force and meaning which are involved in the words, then
send him to Milton, and he will stalk on like a master *enjoying* his walk.

Notes on "Songs and Sonnets."[7]

On Donne's First Poem

[The Flea]

> Be proud as Spaniards. Leap for pride, Ye Fleas!
> In Nature's *minim* realm ye're now grandees.
> Skip-jacks no more, nor civiller skip-johns;
> Thrice-honored Fleas! I greet you all as *Dons*.
> In Phœbus's Archives registered are ye.
> And this your patent of nobility.

The Good Morrow.

> What ever dies is not mixt equally;
> If our two loves be one, both thou and I
> Love just alike in all; none of these loves can die.

Too good for mere wit. It contains a deep practical truth, this
triplet.[8]

[7] Field adds a note: "Not one of these poems is a Legitimate sonnet; but
such was the popular phraseology of those times—'Songs and Sonnets.'"

[8] Field writes, "The last triplet contains a deep practical truth." Following
this note, Field gives two comments omitted elsewhere: on the Song "Go and
catch . . .": "Life from crown to sole"; on "The Undertaking": "A grand poem;
and yet the tone, the *riddle* character, is painfully below the dignity of the main
thought. Addressed to those who understand and feel it, it finds sympathy and
admiration, no wonderment. To the rest, it is a lie; and it was meant therefore to
turn the discourse to them."

To Woman's Constancy

After all, there is but one Donne! and now tell me yet, wherein, in *his own kind*, he differs from the similar power in Shakspeare? Shakspeare was all men, potentially, except Milton; and they differ from him by negation, or privation, or both. This power of dissolving orient pearls, worth a kingdom, in a health to a whore!—this absolute right of dominion over all thoughts, that dukes are bid to clean his shoes, and are yet honored by it! But, I say, in this lordliness of opulence, in which *the* positive of Donne agrees with *a* positive of Shakspeare, what is it that makes them *homoiousian*, indeed: yet not homoousian?

To the Sun Rising

Busie old fool, unruly Sun,
    Why dost thou thus
    Through windows and through curtains look on us?
Must, to thy motions, Lovers' seasons run?
Saucy, pedantique wretch, goe chide
    Late school-boys, or sour 'prentices;
Go tell court-huntsmen that the King will ride;
Call country ants to harvest offices:
Love, all alike, no season knows nor clime;
Nor hours, days, months, which are the rags of time.
Thy beams, so reverend and strong,
    Dost thou not think
    I could eclipse and cloud them with a wink,
But that I would not lose her sight so long?

Fine vigorous exultation, both soul and body in full puissance!

To the Indifferent

I can love both fair and brown;
Her whom abundance melts, and her whom want betrays;
Her who loves loneness best, and her who sports and plays;
Her whom the country formed, and whom the town;
Her who believes, and her who tries;
Her who still weeps with spungy eyes,
And her who is dry cork and never cries;
I can love her, and her, and you, and you;
I can love any, so she be not true.

How legitimate a child was not Cowley of Donne; but Cowley had a soul-*mother* as well as a soul-*father*, and who was she? What was that?[9] Perhaps, sickly court-loyalty, conscientious per[10] accident—a discursive intellect, *naturally* less vigorous and daring, and then *cowed* by king-worship. The populousness the activity, is as great in C. as in D.;

[9] "What was that?" is omitted by Field.
[10] Field writes "par."

but the *vigor*, the insufficiency to the poet of active fancy without a substrate of profound, tho' mislocate thinking,—the will-worship, in squandering golden hecatombs on a Fetisch,[11] on the first stick or straw met with at rising—this pride of doing what he likes with his own, fearless of an immense surplus to pay all lawful debts to self-subsisting themes, that rule, while they cannot create, the moral will[12]—this is Donne! He was an orthodox Christian only because he could have been an infidel *more* easily; and, therefore willed to be a Christian: and he was a Protestant, because it enabled him to lash[13] about to the right and to the left, and without a *motive,* to say better things for the Papists than they could say for themselves. It was the impulse[14] of a purse-proud opulence of innate power! In the sluggish pond the waves roll this or that way; for such is the wind's direction: but in the brisk spring or lake, boiling at bottom, wind this way, that way, all ways, most irregular in the calm, yet inexplicable by the most violent ab extra tempest.

To Canonization

One of my favorite poems. As late as ten years ago, I used to seek and find out grand lines and fine stanzas; but my delight has been far greater since it has consisted more in tracing the leading thought thro'out the whole. The former is too much like coveting your neighbor's goods; in the latter you merge yourself in the author, you *become He.*

A Fever

Yet I had rather owner be
Of thee one hour, than all else ever.

Just and affecting, as *dramatic,* i.e., the outburst of a transient feeling, itself the symbol of a deeper feeling, that would have made *one* hour, *known* to be *only* one hour (or even one year), a perfect hell! All the preceding verses are detestable. Shakspeare has nothing of this. He is never positively bad, even in his Sonnets. He may be sometimes worthless (N.B., I don't say he *is*), but nowhere is he *unworthy.*[15]

To a Valediction forbidding Mourning

An admirable poem which none but Donne could have written. Nothing was ever more admirably made out than the figure of the Compass.

[11] Field omits ''on a Fetisch.''
[12] Field writes, ''while they create the moral will.''
[13] Field writes ''cast'' instead of ''lash.''
[14] Field writes ''influence'' instead of ''impulse.''
[15] In Field the following comment on ''Air and Angels'' is given below:
''The first stanza is able, and reminds one of Wordsworth's apparition-poem; the second I do not understand.''

Our two souls, therefore, which are one,
  Though I must go, indure not yet
A breach, but an expansion,
  Like gold to airy thinness beat.

If they be two, they are two so
  As stiff twin Compasses are two;
Thy soul, the fixt foot, makes no show
  To move, but doth, if th'other do.

And, though it in the centre sit,
  Yet, when the other far doth roam,
It leans and harkens after it,
  And grows erect, as that comes home.

Such wilt thou be to me, who must,
  Like th'other foot, obliquely run;
Thy firmness makes my circle just,
  And makes me end where I begun.

To The Extacy

I should never find fault with metaphysical poems, were they all
like this, or but half as excellent.[16]

To the Primrose

I am tired of expressing my admiration; else I could not have passed
by the Will, the Blossom, and the Primrose, with the Relique.[17]

Notes on the Elegies upon Dr. Donne

To the Memory of my ever desired Friend, Dr. Donne

To have lived eminent, in a degree
Beyond our lofty flights, *that is,* like thee,
Or t'have had too much merit, is not safe;
For such excesses find no epitaph.
At common graves we have poetic eyes,
Can melt themselves in easy elegies:
Each quill can drop his tributary verse,
And pin it, like the hatchments to the hearse:
But at thine, poem or inscription
(Rich soul of wit and language) we have none.
Indeed, a silence does that tomb befit,
Where is no herald left to blazon it.
Widowed invention justly doth forbear
To come abroad, knowing thou art not here,
Late her great patron: whose prerogative
Maintained and clothed her so, as none alive
Must now presume to keep her at thy rate,

[16] Following this note, Field gives this comment on ''Love's Deity''—''But for
the last stanza, I would use this poem as my Love-creed.''
[17] Field does not give this note.

Though he the *Indies* for her dowry' estate.
Or else that awful fire, which once did burn
In thy clear brain, now fall'n into thy urn,
Lives there to fright rude empyricks from thence,
Which might profane thee by their ignorance.
Who ever writes of thee, and in a style
Unworthy such a theme, does but revile
Thy precious dust, and wake a learned spirit,
Which may revenge his rapes upon thy merit.
For all, a low-pitched fancy can devise,
Will prove, at best, but hallowed injuries.
Thou, like the dying swan,[18] didst lately sing
Thy mournful dirge in audience of the King;
When pale looks, and faint accents of thy breath,
Presented so to life *that piece of death,*
That it was feared and prophesied by all,
Thou thither cam'st to preach thy funeral.
O! hadst thou, in elegiac knell,
Rung out unto the world thine own farewell,
And in thy high victorious numbers beat
The solemn measure of thy grieved retreat;
Thou might'st the poet's service now have missed,
As well as then thou didst prevent the priest;
And never to the world beholden be,
So much as for an epitaph for thee.
  I do not like the office. Nor is't fit,
Thou who didst lend our age such sums of wit,
Shouldst not re-borrow from her bankrupt mine
That ore to bury thee, which once was thine;
Rather still leave us in thy debt; and know,
(Exalted soul), more glory 'tis to owe
Unto thy hearse, what we can never pay,
Than with embased coin those rites defray.
  Commit me, then, thee to thyself; nor blame
Our drooping loves, which thus to thy own fame
Leave thee executor; since, but thy own,
No pen could do thee justice, nor bays crown
Thy vast desert: save that we nothing can
Depute, to be thy ashes' guardian.
  So jewellers no art or metal trust
To form the diamond, but the diamond's dust.
                                        H. K.

We cannot better illustrate the weight and condensation of metal
in the old English Parnassian Guinea, or the immense volume of French
writing which it would cover and ornament, if beat into gold leaf, than
by recurrence to the funereal poems of our elder writers, from Henry
VIII to Charles II. These on Donne are more than usually excellent,

[18] "His last Sermon at Court."

their chief, and, indeed, almost only fault, being want of smoothness, flow, and perspicuity, from too great compression of thought—too many thoughts, and, often, too much thought in each.

There are occasions, in which a regret expresses itself, not only in the most manly but likewise in the most natural way, by intellectual effort and activity, in proof of intellectual admiration. This is one; and with this feeling should these poems be read. This fine poem has suggested to me many thoughts for 'An Apology for Conceits,' as a sequel to an Essay I have written called 'An Apology for Puns.'

The careful perusal of modern Latin verses is not without its use. They furnish instances of every species of nice characteristic of modern English poetry; and in some measure, are, perhaps, a cause. But even Virgil and Horace (in his serious Odes) will do the same, though in a less glaring way. Yet compare them, or the best of their successors, with Lucretius, Catullus, Plautus, and even Terence, the difference is as between Rome, Dr. Johnson, &c., and the writers of Elizabeth and James.

Born in London, 1573.———Died, 1631.[19]

I.

With Donne, whose muse on dromedary trots,
Wreathe iron pokers into true-love knots;
Rhyme's sturdy cripple, fancy's maze and clue,
Wit's forge and fire-blast, meaning's press and screw.

II.

See lewdness and theology combin'd,—
A cynic and a sycophantic mind;
A fancy shar'd party per pale between
Death's heads and skeletons, and Aretine!—
Not his peculiar defect or crime,
But the true current mintage of the time.
Such were the establish'd signs and tokens given
To mark a loyal churchman, sound and even,
Free from papistic and fanatic leaven.

The wit of Donne, the wit of Butler, the wit of Pope, the wit of Congreve, the wit of Sheridan—how disparate things are here expressed by one and the same word, Wit!—Wonder-exciting vigour, intenseness and peculiarity of thought, using at will the almost boundless stores of a capacious memory, and exercised on subjects, where we have no right

[19] These notes are reprinted from *Lit. Rem.*, I, 148-50, where the editor, Henry Nelson Coleridge, gives the source as "some notes written by Mr. Coleridge in a volume of Chalmer's Poets, belonging to Mr. Gillman" and indicates that Coleridge is the author of only the first stanza of the verses.

to expect it—this is the wit of Donne! The four others I am just in the mood to describe and inter-distinguish;—what a pity that the marginal space will not let me!

> My face in thine eye, thine in mine appears,
> And true plain hearts do in the faces rest;
> Where can we find two fitter hemispheres
> Without sharp north, without declining west?
> > Good-Morrow, v. 15, &c.

The sense is:—Our mutual loves may in many respects be fitly compared to corresponding hemispheres; but as no simile squares (*nihil simile est idem*), so here the simile fails, for there is nothing in our love that corresponds to the cold north, or the declining west, which in two hemispheres must necessarily be supposed. But an ellipse of such length will scarcely rescue the line from the charge of nonsense or a bull. *January*, 1829.

Woman's Constancy

A misnomer. The title ought to be—

Mutual Inconstancy.

> Whether both th' Indias of spice and *mine*, &c.
> > Sun Rising, v. 17.
> And see at night the western land of *mine*, &c.
> > Progress of the Soul, 1 Song, 2. st.

This use of the word mine specifically for mines of gold, silver, or precious stones, is, I believe, peculiar to Donne.

The 3rd—perhaps the 2nd—the 4th and the 7th—are wholes and need not the Filter. The sixteenth supplies the Stuff for

A SONG
Break of Day

> Stay, O sweet! and do not rise
> The Light, that shines, comes from thine eyes
> 'Tis not the Day breaks but my heart,
> Because that you and I must part.
>
> 'Tis here, 'tis day. What tho' it be,
> O wilt thou therefore rise from me?
> Why should we rise, because 'tis Light?
> Did we lie down because 'twas Night?
>
> Must Business then from hence remove?
> O that's the worst disease of Love!
> The poor, the plain, the false, Love can
> Admit but not the busied Man!

20th

Here Love's Divines (since all Divinity
Is Love or Wonder) may find all they seek

22nd—influence of Spring on Love

Gentle Love dead as Blossoms on the Bough
From Love's awaken'd Root do bud not now.

23rd   Extravaganza truly *Donnesque*

This Face by which Love could command
And change the Idolatry of any Land,
This face which whereso'er it comes
Can call wood men from Cloisters, dead from Tombs
And melt both Poles at once.

On Parting

requires an introductory stanza, easily supplied—then

2

Our souls are two indeed but so
As stiff twin compasses are two.[20]

The vividness of the descriptions or declamations in DONNE, or
DRYDEN, is as much and as often derived from the force and fervour
of the describer, as from the reflections forms or incidents which constitute their subject and materials. The wheels take fire from the mere
rapidity of their motion.[21]

The *rules* of the IMAGINATION are themselves the very powers of
growth and production. The *words,* to which they are reducible, present
only the outlines and external appearance of the fruit. A deceptive
counterfeit of the superficial form and colors may be elaborated; but
the marble peach feels cold and heavy, and *children* only put it to
their mouths. We find no difficulty in admitting as excellent, and
the legitimate language of poetic fervor self-impassioned, DONNE's
apostrophe to the SUN in the second stanza of his "Progress of the
Soul:"

"Thee, eye of heaven! this great soul envies not:
By thy male force is all, we have, begot.
In the first East thou now beginn'st to shine,
Suck'st early balm and island spices there;

[20] Notebook 43, fol. 79-78 verso (written from back to front). British Museum,
Add. MSS, 47,538. Printed for the first time.
[21] *Biog. Lit. S,* II, 75.

> And wilt anon in thy loose-rein'd career
> At Tagus, Po, Seine, Thames, and Danow dine,
> And see at night this western world of mine:
> Yet hast thou not more nations seen, than she,
> Who before thee one day began to be,
> And, thy frail light being quench'd, shall long,
>   long out-live thee!"

Or the next stanza but one:

> "Great destiny, the commissary of God,
> That hast mark'd out a path and period
> For ev'ry thing! Who, where we offspring took,
> Our ways and ends see'st at one instant: thou
> Knot of all causes! Thou, whose changeless brow
> Ne'er smiles or frowns! O vouchsafe thou to look,
> And shew my story in thy eternal book, &c."

As little difficulty do we find in excluding from the honors of un-affected warmth and elevation the madness prepense of Pseudo-poesy, or the startling *hysteric* of weakness over-exerting itself, which bursts on the unprepared reader in sundry odes and apostrophes to abstract terms. Such are the Odes to Jealousy, to Hope, to Oblivion, and the like in Dodsley's collection and the magazines of that day, which seldom fail to remind me of an Oxford copy of verses on the two SUTTONS, commencing with

"INOCULATION, heavenly maid! descend!"[22]

In the evening with B. Montagu to Coleridge's. He had been seized with a fit of enthusiasm for Donne's poetry, which I think somewhat un-accountable. There was great strength, however, in some passages which he read. One stanza or rather division of his poem, on the "Progress of the Soul," struck me very much; it was, I think, the fourth, in which he addresses Destiny as the "Knot of Causes." The rest of the poem seemed the effusion of a man very drunk or very mad.[23]

Donne's poetry must be sought in his prose; yet some of his verses breathe an uncommon fervency of spirit, and when he looked in his heart and wrote, his manner is delightful. The following poem, for sweetness and tenderness of expression, chastened by a religious thought-fulness and faith, is, I think, almost perfect. It is, you see, the address of a lover, or friend, to one whom he leaves behind;—mark the exquisite

[22] *Biog. Lit. S*, II, 87-88.
[23] *A Memoir of Baron Hatherly*, ed. W. R. W. Stephens (2 vols.; London: 1883), I, 51-52. Jan. 29, 1829.

allusion in the conclusion of the second and fourth stanzas: [Quotes "Sweetest love, I do not go.]²⁴

Bishop Richard Corbet

I almost wonder that the inimitable humour, and the rich sound and propulsive movement of the verse, have not rendered Corbet a popular poet. I am convinced that a reprint of his poems, with illustrative and chit-chat biographical notes, and cuts by Cruikshank, would take the public uncommonly well. September, 1823.¹

George Wither

I will, by way of compromise, and for the amusement of the reader, sum up in the rhyming prose of an old Puritan Poet, consigned to contempt by Mr. Pope, but whose writings, with all their barren flats and dribbling common-place, contain nobler principles, profounder truths, and more that is properly and peculiarly *poetic* than are to be found in his* own works. The passage in question, however, I found occupying the last page on a flying-sheet of four leaves, entitled *England's Misery and Remedy, in a judicious Letter from an Utter-Barrister to his Special Friend, concerning Lieut-Col. Lilburne's Imprisonment in Newgate,* Sept. 1745; and I beg leave to borrow the introduction, together with the extract, or that part at least, which suited my purpose.

"Christian Reader, having a vacant place for some few Lines, I have made bold to use some of Major GEORGE WITHERS his verses out of VOX PACIFICA, *page* 199.

"Let not your King and Parliament in *One,*
Much less apart, mistake themselves for that
which is most worthy to be thought upon:
Nor think they are, essentially, the STATE.
Let them not fancy, that th'Authority
And Priviledges upon them bestown,

---

²⁴ Willmott, *C. at Trinity,* pp. 15-16.

¹ *Lit. Rem.,* II, 360-61.

Conferr'd are to set up a MAJESTY,
A POWER, or a GLORY, of their own!
But let them know, 'twas for a deeper life,
Which they but *represent*—
That there's on earth a yet auguster Thing,
Veil'd tho' it be, than Parliament and King.

* If it were asked whether the Author then considers the works of the one of equal value with those of the other, or holds George Withers as great a writer as Alexander Pope? his answer would be that he is as little likely to do so, as the Querist would be to put no greater value on a highly wrought vase of pure silver from the hand of a master, than of an equal weight of Copper Ore that contained a small per centage of separable Gold scattered through it.   The Reader will be pleased to observe, that in the stanza here cited, the "STATE" is used in the largest sense, and as synonimous with the Realm, or entire Body Politic, including Church and *State* in the narrower and special sense of the latter term.   S. T. C.[1]

Francis Quarles

Between the *thinking* of a Harvey or Quarles, and the thinking of a Bacon or a Fenelon, many are the degrees of difference, and many the differences in degree of depth and originality; but not such as to fill up the chasm *in genere* between thinking and no-thinking, or to render the discrimination difficult for a man of ordinary understanding, not under the same contagion of vanity as the writer.   Besides, there are shallows for the full-grown, that are the maxims of safe depth for the younglings.   There are truths, quite *commonplace* to you and me, that for the uninstructed many would be new and full of wonder, as the common daylight to the Lapland child at the re-ascension of its second summer.   Thanks and honor in the highest to those stars of the first magnitude that shoot their beams downward, and while in their proper form they stir and invirtuate the sphere next below them, and natures preassimilated to their influence, yet call forth likewise, each after its own *form* or model, whatever is best in whatever is susceptible to each, even in the lowest.   But, excepting these, I confess that I seldom look at

[1] *Church and State*, pp. 127-29.

Hervey's Meditations, or Quarles' Emblems,[1] without feeling that I
would rather be the author of those books—of the innocent pleasure,
the purifying emotions, and genial awakenings of the *humanity* through
the whole man, which those books have given to thousands and tens of
thousands—than shine the brightest in the constellation of fame among
the heroes and *Dii minores* of literature. . . .[2]

Unusually great earnestness, intension and devotion to any one thing
in and for itself necesarily weakens or precludes the disturbing force of
associations. Quarles, Withers, and others have been unkindly under-
rated on this account—their want of Taste was from fullness of Appetite, their sound Hunger and Thirst after religion. But old Fuller had
not—but χ not a deficiency, but the positively opposite, of this φιλοπρεπῇ
—& would have given, first an Edipus Ægyptiacus identification of
Hermes with the Logos, Mercury Χρῖσμα with the Χέρσῳ —Salvation
from Salivation, and conversely Sal/vation from Salve-ation, in proper
gout.[3]

Quarles' Emblems—Even in the present Rage for our old poets, how
much under-rated! N.B. Those of inferior merit, yet meriting praise, I
mark by the numeral cyphers χ numeral Letters.

Books I. IV.–5—X—5th of 12–XIII
Book II. III. IV—V—VI (p. 93. 7th 11-18 lines) XII. 1.2 (!!) XIV.
[Twice under lined] XV. p. 122, the last 16 lines
Book III, p. 125. & 126 last 14 lines, erasing 9 & 10th. IX. very
spirited.[4]

(Epitaph of Drayton said to be written by Jonson or Quarles)
Doe pious marble, let thy Readers know
What they and what their children owe

[1] A full collection, a *Bibliotheca Specialis*, of the books of emblems and symbols,
of all sects and parties, moral, theological, or political, including those in the
Centenaries and Jubilee volumes published by the Jesuit and other religious orders, is
a *desideratum* in our library literature that would well employ the talents of our
ingenious masters in wood-engraving, etching, and lithography, under the superin-
tendence of a Didbin, and not unworthy of royal and noble patronage, or the attention of a Longman and his compeers. Singly or jointly undertaken, it would do
honor to these princely merchants in the service of the muses. What stores might
not a Southey contribute as notes or interspersed prefaces? I could dream away an
hour on the subject. [Coleridges' note.]
[2] Letter IV, "To a Junior Soph at Cambridge," Shedd, IV, 426-27. Cf. Ashe,
Miscellanies, pp. 249-50.
[3] Notebook 21½, p. 94. Printed for the first time.
[4] Notebook 25, fol. 85 recto. British Museum, Add. MSS, 47,523. Printed for
the first time.

To Drayton's name; whose sacred dust
We recommend unto thy trust;
Protect his memory and preserve his story,
Remain a lasting monument of his glory;
And when thy ruins shall disclaime
To be the treasurer of his name;
His name, that cannot fade, shall be
An everlasting monument to thee.

A noble epitaph, more sweet and rhythmical than Jonson commonly is, and more robust and dignified than Quarles.[5]

George Herbert

I find more substantial comfort now in pious George Herbert's "Temple," which I used to read to amuse myself with his quaintness, in short, only to laugh at, than in all the poetry since the poems of Milton. If you have not read Herbert I can recommend the book to you confidently. The poem entitled "The Flower" is especially affecting; and to me such a phrase as "and relish versing" expresses a sincerity and reality, which I would willingly exchange for the more dignified "and once more love the Muse," &c. and so with many other of Herbert's homely phrases.[1]

The best and most forcible sense of a word is often that, which is contained in its Etymology. The Author of the Poems (*The Synagogue*) frequently affixed to Herbert's TEMPLE, gives the original purport of the word Integrity, in the follwing lines (fourth stanza of the eighth Poem:)[2]

Next to Sincerity, remember still,
Thou must resolve upon *Integrity*.
God will have *all* thou hast, thy mind, thy will,
Thy thoughts, thy words, thy works.

[5] MS note by Coleridge in Anderson's *British Poets*, Vol. III, quoted by S. C. Hall, *Book of Gems*, (1st ser.; 3 vols.; London: 1836-38), II, 96, and Raysor, *Misc. Crit.*, p. 241.

[1] To W. Collins, Esq. A. R. A., December, 1818, in Coleridge, E. H., *Letters*, II, 694-95. Cf. Shedd, IV, 394.
[2] "Church-Porch."

And again, after some verses on Constancy and Humility, the poem concludes with—

> He that desires to see
> The face of God, in his religion must
> Sincere, *entire,* constant, and humble be.

Having mentioned the name of *Herbert,* that model of a man, a Gentleman, and a Clergyman, let me add, that the quaintness of some of his thoughts (not of his diction, than which nothing can be more pure, manly, and unaffected,) has blinded modern readers to the great general merit of his Poems, which are for the most part exquisite in their kind.[3]

Notes on Herbert's Temple and Harvey's Synagogue[4]

G. Herbert is a true poet, but a poet *sui generis,* the merits of whose poems will never be felt without a sympathy with the mind and character of the man. To appreciate this volume, it is not enough that the reader possesses a cultivated judgment, classical taste, or even poetic sensibility, unless he be likewise a *Christian,* and both a zealous and an orthodox, both a devout and a *devotional* Christian. But even this will will not quite suffice. He must be an affectionate and dutiful child of the Church, and from habit, conviction, and a constitutional predisposition to ceremoniousness, in piety as in manners, find her forms and ordinances aids of religion, not sources of formality; for religion is the element in which he lives, and the region in which he moves.

The Church, say rather, the Churchmen of *England,* under the first two Stuarts, have been charged with a yearning after the Romish fopperies, and even the Papistic usurpations, but we shall decide more correctly, as well as more charitably, if for the Romish and Papistic we substitute the *Patristic* leaven. There even was (natural enough from their distinguished learning, and knowledge of ecclesiastical antiquities) an overrating of the Church and of the Fathers, for the first five or even six centuries; the lines on the Egyptian monks, "Holy *Macarius* and great *Anthony"* [p. 220] supply a striking instance and illustration of this.

P. 12
> If thou be single, all thy goods and ground
> Submit to love; but yet not more than all.
> Give one estate as one life. None is bound

---

[3] *The Friend,* General Introduction, Essay VI, I, 67 n.

[4] *Works of George Herbert* (London: 1859), Vol. II, notes on the *Temple* and *Synagogue* by S. T. Coleridge, pp. 379-84. Also printed in Shedd, IV, 388-94.

> To work for two, who brought himself to thrall.
> God made me one man; love makes me no more.
> Till labor come, and make my weakness score.

P. 12, last stanza. I do not understand this stanza.

P. 43.
> My flesh began unto my soul in pain,

Either a misprint, or a noticeable idiom of the word "began?"
Yes! and a very beautiful idiom it is;—the first colloquy or address of
the flesh.

P. 47.
> What though my body run to dust?
> Faith cleaves unto it, counting every grain,
> With an exact and most particular trust,
> Reserving all for flesh again.

"With an exact and most particular trust," &c. I find few historical facts so difficult of solution as the continuance, in Protestantism,
of this anti-Scriptural superstition.

P. 57
> "This verse marks that, &c.
> Unto a third that ten Leaves off doth lie.

The spiritual unity of the Bible = the order and connexion of organic
forms in which the unity of life is shown, though as widely dispersed
in the world of sight as the text.

P. 57.
> Then as dispersed herbs do *watch* a potion,"

Some misprint.

P. 93.
> Sweet Spring, full of sweet days and roses,
> A *box* where sweets compacted lie.

"A *box* where," &c. Nest.

P. 97. *Man.*
> Each thing is full of duty:
> Waters united are our navigation:
> *Distinguished, our habitation;*
> *Below, our drink; above, our meat:*
> *Both are our cleanliness. Hath one such beauty?*
> Then how are all things neat!

"Distinguished." I understand this but imperfectly. Distinguished
—they form an island? and the next lines refer perhaps to [the] then

belief that all fruits grow and are nourished by water? But then how is the ascending sap "our cleanliness"?

> P. 151.
> But he doth bid us take his blood for wine.

Nay, the contrary; take wine to be blood, and *the* blood of a man who died 1800 years ago. This is the faith which even the church of *England* demands; for the Consubstantiation only *adds* a mystery to that of Transubstantiation, which it implies.

> P. 189. *The Flower.*

A delicious poem.

> P. 189.
> How fresh, O Lord, how sweet and clear
> Are thy returns! e'en as the flowers in the spring;
> To which, besides their own we demean,
> The late past frosts tributes of pleasure bring.
> Grief melts away
> Like snow in May,
> As if there were no such cold thing.

"The late past frosts tributes of pleasure bring."

Epitritus primus + Dactyl + Trochee + a long monosyllable, which, together with the pause intervening between it and the preceding trochee, equals ˘ ˘ ˘ , for a pleasing variety in the Pentameter Iambic with rhymes. Ex gr.

> The late past frosts | tributes of pleasure | bring.

N. B. First, the difference between — ˘ | — and an amphimacer — ˘ — | and this is not always or necessarily arising out of the latter being one word. It may even consist of three words: yet the effect be the same. It is the pause that makes the difference. Secondly, the expediency, if not necessity, that the first syllable both of the Dactyl and the Trochee should be short by quantity, and only long by force of accent or position—the Epitrite being true *lengths*. Whether the last syllable be long or short the force of the rhymes renders indifferent.

"As if there *were no such cold thing.*" Had been no such thing.

> P. 195.
> Thou who condemnest Jewish hate, &c.
> Call home thine eye (that busy wanderer),
> *That* choice may be thy story.

"That choice," &c. Their.

P. 198.
Nay, thou dost make me sit and dine
E'en in my *enemies'* sight.

Foemen's

P. 216. *Judgment.*
"Almighty Judge, how shall poor wretches brook
Thy dreadful look, &c.
What others mean to do, I know not well;
Yet I here tell,
That some will turn thee to some leaves therein
So void of sin,
That they in *merit* shall excel."

I should not have expected from *Herbert* so open an avowal of *Romanism* in the article of *merit*. In the same spirit is *holy Macarius* and great *Anthony*, p. 220.

P. 317. *The Communion Table.*
And for the matter whereof it is made,
The matter is not much,
"Although it be of *tuch*,"
Or wood, or metal, what will last, or fade;
So vanity
And superstition avoided be.

Tuch rhyming to *much*, from the German *tuch*, cloth; I never met with before, as an English word. So I find *platt* for *foliage* in *Stanley's* Hist. of Philosophy, p. 22.

P. 332. *The Synagogue*, by Christopher Harvey. *The Bishop.*
But who can show of old that ever any
Presbyteries without their bishops were:
"Though bishops without presbyteries many,"

An instance of *proving too much*. [If Bishop without Presb. B. = Presb. i.e. no Bishop.]

P. 333.
To rule and to be ruled are distinct,
And several duties, severally belong
To several *persons*.

Functions of times, but not of persons, of necessity? Ex. Bishop to Archbishop.

P. 335. *Church Festivals*
Who loves not you, doth but in vain profess
"That he loves God, or heaven, or happiness."

Equally unthinking and uncharitable;—I approve of them;—but yet remember Roman Catholic idolatry, and that it originated in such high-flown metaphors as these.

P. 335. *The Sabbath, or Lord's Day.*

Hail	Vail
Holy	Wholly
King of days, &c.	To thy praise, &c.

Make it sense and lose the rhyme; or make it rhyme and lose the sense.

P. 339. *The Nativity, or Christmas Day.*
Unfold thy face, unmask thy ray,
Shine forth, bright sun, double the day,
Let no malignant misty fume, &c.

The only poem in *The Synagogue* which possesses *poetic* merit; with a few changes and additions this would be a striking poem. Substitute the following for the fifth to the eighth line.

To sheath or blunt one happy ray,
That wins new splendour from the day.
This day that gives the power to rise,
And shine on hearts as well as eyes:
The birth-day of all souls, when first
On eyes of flesh and blood did burst
That primal great lucific light,
That rays to thee, to us gave sight.

P. 348. *Whit-Sunday.*

The spiritual miracle was on the descent of the Holy Ghost: the outward the wind and the tongues; and so St. *Peter* himself explains it. That each individual obtained the power of speaking all languages, is neither contained in, nor fairly deducible from, St. *Luke's* account.

P. 351.
The Trinity
In Unity,
And Unity
In Trinity,
"All reason doth *transcend.*"

Most true but not *contradict.* Reason is to faith, as the eye to the telescope.

Another exquisite master of this species of style, where the scholar and the poet supplies the material, but the perfect well-bred gentleman, the expressions and the arrangement, is George Herbert. As from the nature of the subject, and the too frequent quaintness of the thoughts, his "Temple; or Sacred Poems and Private Ejaculations" are comparatively but little known, I shall extract two poems. The first is a Sonnet, equally admirable for the weight, number, and expression of the thoughts, and the simple dignity of the language. (Unless indeed a fastidious taste should object to the latter half of the sixth line.) The second is a poem of greater length, which I have chosen not only for the present purpose, but likewise as a striking example and illustration of an assertion hazarded in a former page of these sketches; namely, that the characteristic fault of our elder poets is the reverse of that, which distinguishes too many of our more recent versifiers; the one conveying the most fantastic thoughts in the most correct and natural language; the other in the most fantastic language conveying the most trivial thoughts. The latter is a riddle of words; the former an enigma of thoughts. The one reminds me of an odd passage in Drayton's IDEAS:

SONNET IX.

As other men, so I myself do muse,
Why in this sort I wrest invention so;
And why these *giddy metaphors* I use,
Leaving the path the greater part to go!
I will resolve: *I am lunatic!*

The other recalls a still odder passage in the "SYNAGOGUE: *or the Shadow of the Temple*," a connected series of poems in imitation of Herbert's "TEMPLE," and in some editions annexed to it

O how my mind
Is gravell'd!
Not a thought,
That I can find
But's ravell'd
All to nought!
Short ends of threds
And narrow shreds
Of lists,
Knots snarled ruffs,

Loose broken tufts
Of twists;
Are my torn meditation's ragged clothing,
Which wound and woven shape a sute for nothing:
One while I think, and then I am in pain
To think how to unthink that thought again!

Immediately after these burlesque passages I cannot proceed to the extracts promised, without changing the ludicrous tone of feeling by the interposition of the three following stanzas of Herbert's.[5] [Quotes "Virtue," and then follows with "The Bosom Sin" and "Love Unknown."]

[5] *Biog. Lit.,* II, 98-99.

Prayer—A sort of Tune which all things hear and fear.
                                        Herbert

Every time I read Herbert anew, the more he grows in my liking.
I admire him greatly.—14 June, 1826.

			Antiphon Men & Angels
— ◡ — — ◡ — — —	a	Chorus.	Praised be the God of Love
— ◡ —	b	M.	Here below
◡ — ◡ —	a	A.	And here above
— ◡ — ◡ — ◡ —	b	Ch.	Who hadth dealt his mercies so
— ◡ —	c	A.	To his Friend
◡ — ◡ —	b	M.	And to his foe
— ◡ — ◡ — ◡ —	c		That both Grace & Glory tend
— ◡ —	d	A.	Us of old
◡ — ◡ —	c	M.	And us in th' end
— ◡ — ◡ — ◡ —	d	※	The great Shepherd of the Fold
— ◡ —	e	A.	We did make
◡ — ◡ —	d	M.	For us was sold.

The last syllable of the penultimate line of each stanza rhyming to
the 1st & 3rd line of the following stanza.

※ The licenses are bidden by the tune. Such must be *read tuning.*

> He our foes in pieces brake. Him we touch
> And him we take. Wherefore since that he is such,
> We adore And we do crutch (crouch)[6]

My dear old friend Charles Lamb and I differ widely (and in point
of taste and moral feeling this is a rare occurrence) in our estimation
and liking of George Herbert's sacred poems. He greatly prefers
Quarles, nay, he *dis*likes Herbert. But if Herbert had only written the
two following stanzas[7]—and there are a hundred other that in one mood
or other of my mind have impressed me—I should be grateful for the
possession of his works. The stanzas are especially affecting to me; because the folly of overvaluing myself in any reference to my future lot
is *not* the sin or danger that besets me, but a tendency to self-contempt,
a sense of the utter disproportionateness of all I can call *me,* to the
promises of the Gospel—*this* is *my* sorest temptation: the promises,
I say, not to the *threats.* For in order to the fulfilment of these, it
needs only that I should be left to myself to sink into the chaos and
lawless productivity of my own still perishing yet imperishable nature.[8]

[6] Notebook 26, fol. 81 verso-82 recto. British Museum, Add. MSS, 47,524. Printed
for the first time. The quotation is from ''Antiphon.''
[7] These are not given in the source.
[8] Letter to Lady Beaumont, Saturday, March 18, 1826. Knight, *Memorials of
Coleorton,* II, 248-49. The conclusion of this letter is cut away.

John Milton

INTRODUCTION

THE MILTON LECTURES

Coleridge found in Milton a poet to whom he could turn as a lifelong resource. His annotations show extensive study of the early poetry, the prose, the three great poems, and furthermore of Hayley's *Life of Milton*. Much of this material was utilized in lectures on Milton given as part of various lecture series—first in 1808 at the Royal Institution; then in 1811-12 for the London Philosophical Society at Scot's Corporation Hall, Crane Court, Fleet Street; next in 1812-13 at the Surrey Institution; again in 1813-14 at Clifton and at Bristol; and in 1818 and 1818-19 back in London in two series at Fleur-de-Luce Court.

Coleridge planned to write out at least half the 1808 series before he started the lectures, and in a letter to Humphrey Davy, says he has "all my materials ready, and can rapidly reduce them into form."[a] Apparently he did write out some of the lectures and read them, but he must not have written the lecture on Milton, for Henry Crabb Robinson reported that he did not mention "Milton's name till ten minutes before the close."[b] Robinson adds that this was "the least interesting lecture I have heard." Edward Jerningham refers to a letcure on Milton in which Coleridge discussed Milton's "Treatise on Education" and then took up the Lancaster plan.[c] Raysor thinks, however, that this was the special additional lecture on education given by Coleridge on May 3 and not a lecture purporting to be on Milton.[d]

We know more about the series of 1811-12 given for the London Philosophical Society, for J. P. Collier's *Seven Lectures on Shakespeare and Milton* gives a full report of the lecture on Milton, and Robinson's *Diary* entrance for January 16, 1812, says that after reviewing Johnson's Preface (treated in the preceding lecture), Coleridge gave a lecture on Milton in which he "vindicated Milton's moral and political character," and then took up the minor poems and "the nature of blank

---

[a] Griggs, *Unp. Letters*, I, 384.
[b] Quoted by Raysor, *Shakes. Crit.*, II, 14.
[c] The *Jerningham Letters* (1780-1843), ed. Edgerton Castle (2 vols.; London: 1896), I, 316.
[d] Raysor, *Shakes. Crit.*, II, 20 n. 2.

verse.''[e] The lecture on January 20 was supposed to conclude his remarks on Milton but fortunately Coleridge, no doubt aware that (as Robinson said) this was ''not one of his happiest lectures,'' returned to Milton in his brilliant lecture concluding the series on January 27. Robinson wrote enthusiastically to Mrs. Clarkson on January 28 that ''Coleridge's explanation of the character of Satan, his vindication of Milton against the charge of falling below his subject where he introduces the Supreme Being, and his illustration of the difference between poetic and abstract truth, and the *diversity in identity* between the philosopher and the poet were equally wise and beautiful.''[f]

The Syllabus for the lectures of 1812 at the Surrey Institution announced that Lectures XI and XII would be on Milton. In his *Diary* Robinson only briefly records attending ten of the lectures and says that he missed the seventh and eighth by being in the country. The slight indication of content which he sometimes gives would indicate that Coleridge kept fairly well to the syllabus. Lecture XI was, however, on the general character of Shakespeare, the subject announced for Lecture X. It seems likely that the concluding lecture was on Milton. Robinson says of this lecture: ''During the evening he gained great applause by some eloquent *moral* reflections; and he *this* evening, as well as on the three or four preceding nights, redeemed the reputation he lost at the commencement of the course.''[g] This lecture also received great applause at the end and seems to fit Coleridge's recollection that ''the favourite lecture of those give at the Surrey Institution'' was on ''the *Paradise Lost,* with the character of Milton.''[h]

In the late fall of 1813 Coleridge went to Bristol to give a series of lectures on Shakespeare and was persuaded also to offer a series at Clifton, where among the subjects announced two were on Milton: ''the construction, metre, and characteristic beauties of the *Paradise Lost,* with illustrative readings; on Milton in general, as a man, and a poet.''[i] In spite of the fact that these lectures were poorly attended there was ''so general a wish that I should give the Miltonian lectures at Bristol''[j] that Coleridge announced a new series to begin in December and to include four lectures on Milton. Illness delayed these lectures, and though they were reannounced to begin in January, 1814, no reports

[e] *Ibid.,* II, 219-20.

[f] *Ibid.,* II, 229-30.

[g] *Ibid.,* II, 250. Jan. 26, 1812.

[h] Letter to J. Britton. British Museum, Add. MSS, 36,532, fol. 3-4, but quoted by Raysor, *Shakes. Crit.,* II, 327.

[i] *The Bristol Gazette,* Nov. 4, 1813. Also quoted by Raysor, *Shakes. Crit.,* II, 254.

[j] Letter to Mrs. John Morgan, Nov. 22, 1813. Griggs, *Unp. Letters,* II, 103.

have been located. There is some question of their having been delivered, for again on April 2, 1814, a series of six lectures, four on
Milton, was announced in *Felix Farley's Bristol Journal.*[k] These were:

> 1st.—On the Life, Character, and Prose
> Writings of MILTON.
> 2d.—on the Minor Poems of MILTON.
> 3d. and 4th.—on the Plan, Metre, Characters
> and distinguishing Beauties of the
> PARADISE LOST.

These lectures were all mentioned in the Bristol papers, and the audience
was said to be "numerous and respectable."[l]

In the syllabus for the lectures of 1818 at Fleur-de-Luce Court the
topic for Lecture X was given as "Of Donne, Dante, and Milton," but
in the announcement in the *Morning Chronicle*, February 27, Donne's
name was omitted. It seems, however, that the material on Donne had
been prepared, for in writing H. F. Cary on February 2, 1818, he said:

> I am vain enough to set an unusual value on the critique I have devoted
> to the names of Dante, Donne, and Milton (the middle name will,
> perhaps, puzzle you) and I mean to publish it singly in the week follow-
> ing its delivery.[m]

When, however, he wrote to Blackwood, September 19, 1821, about con-
densing certain lectures for articles, he mentioned the Dante and Milton
lecture, again omitting the name of Donne.[n] Robinson considered the
Milton lecture one of his very best and said, "He digressed less than
usually and really gave information and ideas about the poets he professed to criticise."[o]

Coleridge gave two series of literary lectures in 1818-19 concurrent
with the philosophical lectures at the Crown and Anchor. In the second
series the fourth lecture was again on Milton and was advertised in the
Morning Chronicle, March 4, 1819, as "Paradise Lost, and the Character of Milton."[p] This lecture with the heading "March 4, 1819," is
in a Coleridge notebook in the Berg Collection, New York Public Library. The material is much the same as Collier's report of Lecture X
for the London Philosophical Society in 1812. In the Collier report
there is some material which does not appear in the notebook. The
notebook, on the other hand, provides the only record which has yet
been discovered of the illustrative passages from *Paradise Lost* used

---

k See also Raysor, *Shakes. Crit.*, II, 256.
l *Felix Farley's Bristol Journal*, April 16, 1814.
m Griggs, *Unp. Letters*, II, 230.
n Griggs, *Unp. Letters*, II, 297.
o Raysor, *Shakes. Crit.*, II, 317.
p *Ibid.*, II, 320.

in the lectures. Coleridge cites page, book, and lines and adds enough comment for one to have some idea how the passages were to be used.

On February 28, 1819, Coleridge replied to the letter previously mentioned from Britton inviting him to come to the Russell Institution to give the lectures which he had presented at the Surrey Institution in 1812-13. Coleridge answered that he "did not *have* the lectures" and therefore could not repeat them, but he offered several subjects on which he could lecture, among them "the *Paradise Lost*, with the character of Milton." No record has been discovered to show whether he gave these lectures. In connection with the invitation it is interesting to note that Hazlitt had lectured on Shakespeare and Milton at the Surrey Institution on January 27, 1819, a month before Britton's invitation to Coleridge for the Russell Institution.

No report of the content of Coleridge's lectures on the early poetry or the prose has been found, and for the criticism of these we must rely on the notes made in 1823 upon reading Warton's second edition of the poems, and upon scattered comments. Admiration of Milton both as man and poet is evidenced in many and varied connections, and the assembled materials here presented form a valuable commentary.

GENERAL COMMENTS

To MILTON's trump
The high Groves of the renovated Earth,
Unbosom their glad echoes: inly hush'd
Adoring NEWTON his serener eye
Raises to heaven.[1]

Let England be Sir. P. Sidney, Shakespere, Spenser, Milton, Bacon, Harrington, Swift, Wordsworth; and never let the names of Darwin, Johnson, Hume, *furr* it over!—If these too must be England, let them be another England,—or rather let the first be old England, the spiritual, platonic, old England & the second with Locke at the head of the Philosophers & Pope of the poets, with the long list of Priestleys, Payleys, Hayleys, Darwins, Wm. Pitts, Dundasses, &c. &c. be representative of commercial G. Britain; these have their merits but are as alien to me, as the Mandarin Philosophers & Poets of China.[2]

[1] "Religious Musing," *Poems* (1797), ll. 370-74. Coleridge's note: "The Millenium: in which I suppose that man will continue to enjoy the highest glory of which his human nature is capable. That all who in past ages have endeavoured to ameliorate the state of man, will rise & enjoy the fruits & flowers, the imperceptible seeds of which they had sown in their former life."

[2] Notebook 17, fol. 80 verso. British Museum, Add. MSS, 47,514. It also appears in *Anima*, p. 151.

Such is the inherent dignity of human nature, that there belong to it sublimities of virtues which all men may attain, and which no man can transcend: and though this be not true in an equal degree, of intellectual power, yet in the persons of Plato, Demosthenes, and Homer, —and in those of Shakspeare, Milton, and Lord Bacon,—were inshrined as much of the divinity of intellect as the inhabitants of this planet can hope will ever take up its abode among them.[3]

In the next world the Souls of the Dull Good men serve for Bodies to the Souls of the Shakspers & Miltons—& in the course of a few Centuries, when the Soul can do without it's vehicle, the Bodies will by advantage of good Company have refined themselves into Souls fit to be clothed with like Bodies.[4]

Not only Chaucer and Spenser, but even Shakespere and Milton have as yet received only the earnest, and scanty first gatherings of their Fame—This indeed it is, which gives it's full dignity and more than mental grandeur to Fame, this which at once distinguishes it from Reputation, and makes it's attainment a fit object of pursuit to the good, and an absolute duty to the Great; that it grows with the growth of Virtue & Intellect, and co-operates in that growth; it becomes wider and deeper, as their country, and all mankind are the countrymen of the man of true and adequately exerted Genius, becomes better and wiser.[5]

It is saying less than the truth to affirm, that an excellent book (and the remark holds almost equally good of a Raphael as of a Milton) is like a well-chosen and well-tended fruit tree. Its fruits are not of one season only. With the due and natural intervals, we may recur to it year after year, and it will supply the same nourishment and the same gratification, if only we ourselves return with the same healthful appetite.[6]

Take the immediate Predecessors of Shakespear—note the general Taste of Milton's age—and then deduce the *ungroundedness* of the

[3] *The Friend*, Introduction, Section II, III, 34.

[4] Notebook 16, p. 60. Cf. *Anima*, p. 161.

[5] Notebook 22, fol. 27 recto. British Museum, Add. MSS, 47,520. Printed for the first time.

[6] Prospectus of the 1818 lectures. *Canterbury Magazine*, I (September, 1834), 124.

supposition, that a great Genius produced dull works on account of the *age* in which he lived. It is the royal prerogative of genius to out-run, and to form the Taste of the Age.[7]

Great Injury that has resulted from the supposed Incompatability of one talent with another, Judgment with Imagination, and Taste, Good sense with strong feeling &c.—if it be false, as assuredy it is, the opinion has deprived us of a test which every man might apply. Locke's opinions of Blackmore, Hume of Milton, Shakspere, &c.[8]

To judge with fairness of an Author's works, we must observe, firstly what is essential, and secondly, what arises from circumstances. It is esential, as in Milton, that poetry be *simple, sensuous,* and *impassionate. Simple,* that it may appeal to the elements and the primary laws of our nature: *sensuous,* since it is only by sensuous images that we can elicit truth as at a flash: *impassionate,* since images must be vivid, in order to move our passions and awaken our affections.[9]

I think nothing can be added to Milton's definition or rule of poetry, —that it ought to be simple, sensuous, and impassioned; that is to say, single in conception, abounding in sensible images, and informing them all with the spirit of the mind.[10]

Thus, to express in one word what belongs to the senses or the recipient and more passive faculty of the soul, I have reintroduced the word *sensuous,* used, among many other of our elder writers, by Milton, in his exquisite definition of poetry, as "simple, sensuous, passionate": because the term *sensual* is seldom used at present, except in a bad sense, and *sensitive* would convey a different meaning. Thus too I have restored the words, *intuition* and *intuitive,* to their original sense—"an intuition," says Hooker, "that is, a direct and immediate beholding or presentation of an object to the mind through the senses or the imagination."[11]

[7] Carl Friedrich Flögel, *Geschichte der komischen Litteratur* (4 vols.; Liegnitz und Leipzig: 1784-87), IV, 313. The volumes with the Coleridge notes are in the Houghton Library at Harvard, and this comment is transcribed from the original. It has been previously printed by Buxton Forman in *Cosmopolis,* X (April, 1898), 66.

[8] Notebook 21, p. 81. Cf. *Anima,* p. 24.

[9] Report of Milton's First Lecture in 1813. Bristol *Gazette,* Nov. 4, 1813, p. 3.

[10] May 8, 1824. *Table Talk S,* VI, 276.

[11] "On the Principles of Genial Criticism," Essay Third. *Biog. Lit. S,* II, 229-30. See also Cottle, *Recollections,* p. 247.

Milton in three incidental words has implied all which for the purpose of more distinct apprehension, which at first must be slow-paced in order to be distinct, I have endeavored to develope in a precise and strictly adequate definition. Speaking of Poetry, he says, (as in a parenthesis) which is—"simple, sensuous, passionate"—How awful is the power of words!—how fearful often in their consequences when merely felt, not understood! most awful when both felt and understood!—Had these three words only been properly understood [by], and present in the minds of general Readers, not only almost a Library of false Poetry would have been either precluded or still-born, but, what is of more consequence, works truly excellent, and capable of enlarging the understanding, warming & purifying the heart, and placing in the centre of the whole Being the Germs of noble & manlike Actions, would have been the common Diet of the Intellect instead. For the first condition namely, simplicity, while it distinguishes Poetry from the arduous processes of Science, laboring towards an end not yet arrived at, & supposes a smooth and finished Road on which the reader is to walk onward easily, with streams murmuring by his side, & Trees & Flowers, & human dwellings to make his journey as delightful as the object of it is desirable, instead of having to toil with the Pioneers, & painfully make the road, on which others are to travel, precludes every affectation —& so on.[12] The second condition, sensuousness, insures that framework of objectivity, that definiteness and articulation of imagery, and that modification of the images themselves, without which poetry becomes flattened into mere didactics of practice, or evaporated into a hazy, unthoughtful day-dreaming; and the third condition, passion, provides that neither thought nor imagery shall be simply objective, but that the *passio vera* of humanity shall warm and animate both.[13]

As to harmony, it is all *association*. Milton is *harmonious* to me, and I absolutely nauseate Darwin's poems.[14]

As characteristic of Spenser, I would call your particular attention in the first place to the indescribable sweetness and fluent projection of his verse, very clearly distinguishable from the deeper and more inwoven harmonies of Shakspeare and Milton.[15]

[12] Notebook 25, fol. 9-10. British Museum, Add. MSS, 47,523.
[13] The latter part of the excerpt is from *Lit. Rem.*, II, 10, where the whole appears, pp. 9-10. Cf. Raysor, *Shakes. Crit.*, I, 164-66.
[14] To John Thelwall, May 13, 1796. Coleridge, E. H., *Letters*, I, 164.
[15] *Lit. Rem.*, I, 91. Lecture III, 1818 series, on Spenser.

In Spenser, indeed, we trace a mind constitutionally tender, delicate, and, in comparison with his three great compeers, I had almost said *effeminate;* and this additionally saddened by the unjust persecution of Burleigh, and the severe calamities, which overwhelmed his latter days. These causes have diffused over all his compositions "a melancholy grace," and have drawn forth occasional strains, the more pathetic from their gentleness. But no where do we find the least trace of irritability, and still less of quarrelsome or affected contempt of his censurers.

The same calmness, and even greater self-possession, may be affirmed of Milton, as far as his poems, and poetic character are concerned. He reserved his anger for the enemies of religion, freedom, and his country. My mind is not capable of forming a more august conception, than arises from the contemplation of this great man in his latter days: poor, sick, old, blind, slandered, persecuted,

"Darkness before, and danger's voice behind,"

in an age in which he was as little understood by the party, *for* whom, as by that, *against* whom he had contended; and among men before whom he strode so far as to *dwarf* himself by the distance; yet still listening to the music of his own thoughts, or if additionally cheered, yet cheered only by the prophetic faith of two or three solitary individuals, he did nevertheless

—"Argue not
Against Heaven's hand or will, nor bate a jot
Of heart or hope; but still bore up and steer'd
Right onward."

From others only do we derive our knowledge that Milton, in his latter day, had his scorners and detractors; and even in his day of youth and hope, that he had enemies would have been unknown to us, had they not been likewise the enemies of his country.[16]

That a true poem must give "as much pleasure in each part as is compatible with the greatest sum of pleasure in the whole." We must not look to parts merely, but to the whole, and to the effect of that whole. In reading Milton, for instance, scarcely a line can be pointed out which, critically examined, could be called in itself good: the poet would not have attempted to produce merely what is in general understood by a good line; he sought to produce glorious paragraphs and systems of harmony, or, as he himself expresses it,

[16] *Biog. Lit. C,* I, 34-36.

"Many a winding bout
Of linked sweetness, long drawn out."
L'Allegro.[17]

He [Klopstock] then talked of Milton and Glover, and thought Glover's blank verse superior to Milton's. W— and myself expressed our surprise; and my friend gave his definition and notion of harmonious verse, that it consisted (the English iambic blank verse above all) in the apt arrangement of pauses and cadences, and the sweep of whole paragraphs,

—"with many a winding bout
Of linked sweetness, long drawn out."

and not in the even flow, much less in the prominence or antithetic vigour, of single lines, which were indeed injurious to the total effect, except where they were introduced for some specific purpose. Klopstock assented, and said that he meant to confine Glover's superiority to single lines. He told us that he had read Milton, in a prose translation, when he was fourteen. I understood him thus myself, and W— interpreted Klopstock's French as I had already construed it. He appeared to know very little of Milton—or indeed of our poets in general.[18]

To-day he [Klopstock] informed me that he had finished his plan before he read Milton. He was enchanted to see an author who before him had trod the same path. This is a contradiction of what he said before.[19]

At the same time that we were studying the Greek Tragic Poets, he[20] made us read Shakspeare and Milton as lessons; and they were lessons too, which required most time and trouble to *bring up,* so as to escape his censure. I learnt from him, that Poetry, even that of the loftiest and, seemingly, that of the wildest odes, had a logic of its own, as severe as that of science; and more difficult, because more subtle, more complex, and dependent on more, and more fugitive causes. In the truly great poets, he would say, there is a reason assignable, not only for every word, but for the position of every word; and I well remember that

[17] Collier, *Seven Lect.,* pp. 19-20.
[18] Satyrane's Letters, IV. *Biog. Lit. C,* II, 239-40.
[19] *Biog. Lit. C,* II, 247.
[20] Boyer, his teacher at Christ's Hospital.

availing himself of the synonimes to the Homer of Didymus, he made us attempt to show, with regard to each, *why* it would not have answered the same purpose; and *wherein* consisted the peculiar fitness of the word in the original text.

In our own English compositions (at least for the last three years of our school education) he showed no mercy to phrase, metaphor, or image, unsupported by a sound sense, or where the same sense might have been conveyed with equal force and dignity in plainer words.[21]

I was wont boldly to affirm, that it would scarcely be more difficult to push a stone out from the pyramids with the bare hand, than to alter a word, or the position of a word, in Milton or Shakspeare, (in their most important works at least) without making the author say something else, or something worse, than he does say. One great distinction, I appeared to myself to see plainly, between, even the characteristic faults of our elder poets, and the false beauty of the moderns. In the former, from DONNE to COWLEY, we find the most fantastic out-of-the-way thoughts, but in the most pure and genuine mother English; in the latter, the most obvious thoughts, in language the most fantastic and arbitrary.

Our faulty elder poets sacrificed the passion and passionate flow of poetry to the subtleties of intellect and to the starts of wit; the moderns to the glare and glitter of a perpetual, yet broken and heterogeneous imagery, or rather to an amphibious something, made up, half of image, and half of abstract meaning. The one sacrificed the heart to the head; the other both heart and head to point and drapery.[22]

The collocation of words is so artificial in Shakspeare and Milton, that you will as well think of pushing a brick out of a wall with your forefinger, as attempt to remove a word out of any of their finished passages.[23]

The excellence of verse, he said, was to be untranslatable into any other words without detriment to the beauty of the passage;—the position of a single word could not be altered in Milton without injury.[24]

---

[21] "This, indeed, is worthy of being ranked as a maxim—*regula maxima*—of criticism. Whatsoever is translatable in other and simpler words of the same language without loss of sense or dignity, is bad. By dignity I mean the absence of ludicrous or debasing associations. 1825." *Biog. Lit. C*, I, 8-9.

[22] *Biog. Lit. C*, I, 23-24.

[23] July 3, 1833. *Table Talk S*, VI, 467.

[24] April 21—Richmond. From "Recollections of Mr. Coleridge"—communicated by Mr. Justice Coleridge. Shedd, VI, 527.

The acquaintance with so many languages has likewise made me too often *polysyllabic*—for these are the words which are possessed in common by the English with the Latin and its south European offspring, and those into which, with the least *looking roundabout,* one can translate the *full* words of the Greek, German, etc. Still there are not so many as the work has been charged with, if it be judged by what I have tried to impose on myself as the ordeal—that is, to reject whatever can be translated into other words of the same language without loss of any meaning—i. e. without change either in the conception or the feeling appropriate to it—under which latter head I do *not* place the feeling of self-importance on the part of the Author or that of *wonderment* on the part of the Readers.

Dr. Johnson's

> Let observation with extensive view
> Survey mankind from China to Peru

i. e. Let observation with extensive observation observe mankind extensively (besides this ἀναιμόσαρκος ἀπαθής printer's devil's *Person.— observation.*) contrasted with Dryden's "Look round the world"—is a good instance. Compare this with Milton's "Yet Virgin of Proserpina from Jove"—which you may indeed easily translate into simple English as far as the *Thought* is concerned, or Image, but not without loss of the delicacy, the sublimation of the ethereal part of the thought with a compleat detachment from the grosser *caput mortuum.*[25]

And compare this[26] with the language of ordinary men; or with that which I can conceive at all likely to proceed, in *real* life, from *such* a narrator, as is supposed in the note to the poem; compare it either in the succession of the images or of the sentences, I am reminded of the sublime prayer and hymn of praise, which MILTON, in opposition to an established liturgy, presents as a fair *specimen* of common extemporary devotion, and such as we might expect to hear from every self-inspired minister of a conventicle![27]

In referring various lines in Gray to their original in Shakspeare and Milton; and in the clear perception how completely all the propriety was lost in the transfer; I was, at that early period, led to a conjecture, which, many years afterwards was recalled to me from the same thought having been started in conversation, but far more ably,

---

[25] To Hugh J. Rose, Sept. 25, 1816. Griggs, *Unp. Letters,* II, 188-89.
[26] "The Thorn," by Wordsworth.   [27] *Biog. Lit. C,* II, 59.

and developed more fully, by Mr. WORDSWORTH; namely, that this
style of poetry, which I have characterised above, as translations of
prose thoughts into poetic language, had been kept up by, if it did not
wholly arise from, the custom of writing Latin verses, and the great
importance attached to these exercises, in our public schools . . . In my
defence of the lines running into each other, instead of closing at each
couplet; and of natural language, neither bookish, nor vulgar, neither
redolent of the lamp, or of the kennel, such as *I will remember thee;*
instead of the same thought tricked up in the rag-fair finery of,

> —thy image on her wing
> Before my FANCY'S eye shall MEMORY bring.—

I had continually to adduce the metre and diction of the Greek Poets
from Homer to Theocritus inclusive; and still more of our elder English poets from Chaucer to Milton.[28]

THE EARLY POEMS

You may find a few minute faults in Milton's Latin verses; but you
will not persuade me that, if these poems had come down to us *as*
written in the age of Tiberius, we should not have considered them to
be very beautiful.[29]

Milton's Latin style is, I think better and easier than his English.[30]

Milton, "De Idea Platonica quemadmodum Aristoteles Intellexit."

This is not, as has been supposed, a Ridicule of Plato; But of the
gross Aristotelian misinterpretation of the Platonic Idea, or Homo
Archetypus.[31]

Milton, "The Nightingale, l. 13: "Most musical, most melancholy . . ."

This passage in Milton possesses an excellence far superior to that
of mere description: it is spoken in the character of the melancholy Man,
and has therefore a *dramatic* propriety. The author makes this remark,
to rescue himself from the charge of having alluded with levity to a line
in Milton: a charge than which none could be more painful to him, except perhaps that of having ridiculed his Bible.[32]

[28] *Biog. Lit. C*, I, 20, 21-22.
[29] Oct. 23, 1833. *Table Talk S*, VI, 492.
[30] May 8, 1824. *Table Talk S*, VI, 276.
[31] From the set of Anderson's *British Poets* in the Victoria and Albert Museum,
V, 193. The note above is transcribed from the original Coleridge note, but it
has been printed by Raysor, *Misc. Crit.*, p. 190.
[32] *Lyrical Ballads* (1798), p. 64 n.

I know nothing that surpasses the vileness of deciding on the merits of a poet or painter (not by characteristic defects; for where there is genius, *these* always point to his characteristic *beauties;* but) by accidental failures, or faulty passages; except the impudence of defending it, as the proper duty, and most instructive part, of criticism. Omit or pass slightly over, the expression, grace, and grouping of Raphael's *figures;* but ridicule in *detail* the knitting-needles and broom-twigs, that are to represent trees in his back grounds; and never let him hear the last of his *galli-pots!* Admit, that the Allegro and Penseroso of Milton are not *without merit;* but repay yourself for this concession, by reprinting at length the *two poems on the University Carrier!* As a fair specimen of his Sonnets, quote *"A Book was writ of late called Tetrachordon;"* and, as characteristic of his rhythm and metre cite his literal translation of the first and second psalm! In order to justify yourself, you need only assert, that had you dwelt chiefly on the beauties and excellencies of the poet, the admiration of these might seduce the attention of future writers from the objects of their love and wonder, to an imitation of the few poems and passages in which the poet was most unlike himself.[33]

He for whom Ideas are constitutive, will in effect be a Platonist—and in those, for whom they are regulative only, Platonism is but a hollow affectation. Dryden *could* not have been a Platonist—Shakespear, Milton, Dante, Michael Angelo & Rafael could not have been other than Platonists.[34]

How little the commentators of Milton have availed themselves of the writings of Plato, Milton's darling! But alas, commentators only hunt out verbal parallelisms—*numen abest.* I was much impressed with this in all the many notes on that beautiful passage in "Comus" from l. 629 to 641. All the puzzle is to find out what plant Hæmony is; which they discover to be the English spleenwort, and decked out as a mere play and license of poetic fancy with all the strange properties suited to the purpose of the drama. They thought little of Milton's platonizing spirit, who wrote nothing without an interior meaning. "Where more is meant than meets the ear," is true of himself beyond all writers. He was so great a man that he seems to have considered fiction as profane unless where it is consecrated by being emblematic of some truth. What an unthinking and ignorant man we must have

[33] *Biog. Lit. C,* I, 62-63.
[34] To J. Gooden, Jan. 14 (1820). Griggs, *Unp. Letters,* II, 266.

supposed Milton to be, if, without any hidden meaning, he had described it as growing in such abundance that the dull swain treads on it daily, and yet as never *flowering*. Such blunders Milton of all others was least likely to commit. Do look at the passage. Apply it as an allegory of Christianity, or, to speak more precisely, of the Redemption by the Cross, every syllable is full of light! *"A small unsightly root."*— "To the Greeks folly, to the Jews a stumbling-block"—*"The leaf was darkish and had prickles on it"*—If in this life only we have hope, we are of all men the most miserable," and a score of other texts. *"But in another country, as he said, Bore a bright golden flower"*—"The exceeding weight of glory prepared for us hereafter"—*"But not in this soil; unknown and like esteemed and the dull swain Treads on it daily with his clouted shoon"*—The promises of Redemption offered daily and hourly, and to all, but accepted scarcely by any—*"He called it Hæmony."* Now what is Hæmony? αἱμα οἶνος Blood-wine. "And he took the wine and blessed it and said, 'This is my Blood,' "—the great symbol of the Death on the Cross. There is general ridicule cast on all allegorising poets. Read Milton's prose works, and observe whether he was one of those who joined in this ridicule. There is a very curious passage in Josephus [De Bello Jud. 6, 7, cap. 25 (vi. 3)] which is, in its literal meaning, more wild and fantastically absurd than the passage in Milton. . . . But the passage in Josephus, I have no doubt, is wholly allegorical.[35]

I remember a strange fantastic legend somewhere in Josephus (but in Mr. Gillman's villainous English Josephus I cannot find it) of a certain Root of wondrous efficacy in strengthening the Brain & purging the eyesight; but which no man can pull up without imminent hazard, alienation of mind & so forth—But that if it be fastened by a string to a Dog, and the Dog be made to draw it up into light, then it may with proper precaution, be used, &c. At the time, I read it, I thought of the root, Hæmony, in Milton's Comus—which that it should have been left to *me* to discover the meaning of, viz. that it is an allegory of the Gospel Dispensation Redemption by Christ as represented in the Eucharist— αἱμα οἶνος surprizes me to this hour—(& and in like manner I conjectured, I remember, that this root of Josephus's meant Philosophy, and the *Dog,* the Pagan Greeks—i. e. the σοφὸς τῶν ἐθνῶν, the wise man of the Gentiles, generally.[36]

[35] To W. Sotheby, Sept. 10, 1802. Coleridge, E. H., *Letters*, I, 406-07.

[36] Letter to Reverend Edward Irving, not dated but stamped 1826. Pierpont Morgan Library. Here first published by the kind permission of the library.

"I laid me down and slept. I awaked: for the Lord sustained me" (Psalm 112). The Moments of our Life are the Pulses, that measure the divine Mercy, that sustains and repairs us and is the Life of our Life. It is indeed our Hæmony, the true Bloodwine which circulates *in* us, *received as wine & becoming the Life-blood* without which we cannot live.[37]

. . . spiritual partaking of the Redeemer's Blood, of which, mysterious as the symbol may be, the sacramental Wine is no mere or arbitrary, memento. This is the only certain, and this is the universal preventive of all debasing superstitions, this is the true HÆMONY (αἷμα blood: οἶνος wine) which our Milton has beautifully allegorized in a passage strangely overlooked by all his commentators. Bear in mind, Reader! the character of a militant christian, and the results (in this life and the next) of the Redemption by the Blood of Christ: and *so* peruse the passage!

> Amongst the rest a small unsightly root,
> But of divine effect, he culled me out:
> The leaf was darkish, and had prickles on it,
> But in another country, as he said,
> Bore a bright golden flower, but not in this soil!
> Unknown and like esteem'd, and the dull swain
> Treads on it daily with his clouted shoon;
> And yet more med'cinal is it than that moly
> That Hermes once to wise Ulysses gave.
> He called it HAEMONY, and gave it me,
> And bade me keep it as of sovr'an use
> 'Gainst all enchantments, mildew, blast, or damp,
> Or ghastly furies' apparition.
>   MILTON'S COMUS

These lines might be employed as an amulet against delusions: for the man who is indeed a Christian, will as *little* think of informing himself concerning the future by dreams or presentiments, as of looking for a distant object at broad noon-day with a lighted taper in his hand.[38]

Homer is the Poet for the Warrior—Milton for the Religionist— Tasso for Women, Robert Southey for the Patriot.[39]

[37] Notebook 45, June, 1830, fol. 19 recto. Printed for the first time.
[38] *Statesman's Manual*, Appendix C, pp. xxv-xxvi.
[39] To John Thelwall, Nov. 19, 1796. From the original in the Morgan Library, but printed in Coleridge, E. H., *Letters*, I, 178.

C. R. Maturin, BERTRAM, OR THE CASTLE OF ST. ALDOBRAND, *Act V, scene 3.*

> *Imog.* (*with a frantic laugh*)
>   The forest fiend hath snatched him—[40]
>   He rides the night-mare thro' the wizzard woods.

Now these two lines consist in a senseless plagiarism from the counter-feited madness of Edgar in Lear, who, in imitation of the gipsey incantations, puns on the old word Mair, a Hag; and the no less senseless adoption of Dryden's forest-fiend, and the wizzard-stream by which Milton, in his Lycidas, so finely characterises the spreading Deva, fabulosus Amnis.[41]

Found Mr. G[illman] with Hartley in the Garden, attempting to explain to himself and to Hartley a feeling of a something not present in Milton's works, i. e., the Par[adise] Lost, Par[adise] Reg[ained,] & Samson Agon[istes]—which he *did* feel so delightedly in the Lycidas —& (as I added afterwards, in the Italian sonnets compared with the English)—& this appeared to me *the Poet* appearing & wishing to appear *as the Poet*—a man likewise? For is not *the Poet* a man? as much as, tho' more rare than the Father, the Brother, the Preacher, the Patriot? Compare with Milton, Chaucer's Fall of the Leaf, &c. &c., & Spenser throughout, & you cannot but *feel* what Mr. Gillman meant to convey—What is the solution? This I believe—but I will premise, that there is a *synthesis* of intellectual Insight including the mental object, or *anschauung.* The organ & the correspondent being indivisible, and this (O deep truth!), because the Objectivity consists in the universality of it's Subjectiveness—as when A *sees,* and Millions *see,* even so—and the Seeing of the millions is what constitutes to A & to each of the million the *objectivity* of the sight, the *equivalent* to a Common Object—(a synthesis of *this,* I say), and of a proper external Object, which we call *Factors.* Now this it is, which we find in Religion, & the Contents of Religion—it is more than philosophical Truth, it is other & more than Historical Fact; it is not made up by the addition of the one to the other—but it is *the Identity* of both—the co-inherence.

Now this being understood, I proceed to say in using the term, *Objectivity* (arbitrarily I grant), for this identity of Truth and Fact— that Milton hid the Poetry in or *transformed* (not transubstantiated) the Poetry into the objectivity while Shakspeare, in all things, the divine opposite, or antithetic Correspondent of the divine Milton, transformed the *Objectivity* into *Poetry.*

[40] The Child.   [41] *Biog. Lit. C,* II, 290-91.

Even so the styles of M[ilton] & Sh[akespeare] the same *weight* of effect from the exceeding *felicity* (subjectivity) of Sh. & the exceeding *propriety* (*extra arbitrium*) of M.[ilton] Char. Friday evening, Sept. 18, 1820.[42]

Of all men I ever knew, Wordsworth himself not excepted, I have the faintest pleasure in things contingent and transitory . . . I am not certain whether I should have seen with any Emotion the Mulberry Tree of Shakspere. If it were a Tree of no notice in itself, I am sure, that I should feel by an effort with self-reproach at the dimness of the Feeling—if a striking Tree, I fear that the Pleasure would be diminished rather than increased, that I should have no unity of Feeling & find in the constant association of Shakspere's having planted it an intrusion that prevented me from wholly (as a whole man) losing myself in the flexures of it's Branches and interweaving of it's Roots. No doubt, there are Times & conceivable circumstances, in which the contrary would be true . . . or here, on this Bank Milton used to lie, in late May, when a young man, & familiar with all it's primroses, made them yet dearer than their dear selves, by that sweetest line in the Lycidas, "And the rathe primrose that forsaken dies;"[43] or from this Spot the immortal Deer Stealer, on his Escape from Warwickshire, had the first View of London, and asked himself, And what am I to do there? at certain times, uncalled & sudden, subject to no bidding of my own or others', these Thoughts would come upon me like a Storm, & fill the Place with something more than Nature. But these are not contingent or transitory, they are Nature, even as the Elements are Nature—yea, more to the human mind, for the mind has the power of abstracting all agency from the former, & considering as mere effects & instruments. But a Shakspere, a Milton, a Bruno, exist in the mind as *pure Action*, defecated of all that is material and passive—And the great moments that formed them—it is a kind of impiety against a Voice within us, not to regard them as predestined, & therefore things of Now & For Ever, and which were Always.[44]

[42] Clasped Vellum Notebook, pp. 265 (writing back to front), 264. The entire comment with relatively few changes except in format is found in *Anima*, pp. 296-98.

[43] Coleridge quotes this line again in a note to *Winter's Tale*, Act IV, Scene 4, 122-23: "pale primroses That die unmarried." *Shakespeare's Plays*, ed. Lewis Theobold. (8 vols.; London: 1773 ——), III, 302. British Museum, C. 45. a. 21. Printed by Raysor, *Shakes. Crit.*, I, 120.

[44] Notebook 15, pp. 6-10. Also in *Anima*, "Thursday, April 19, 1804," pp. 71, 72, 73.

The authority of Milton and Shakespeare may be usefully pointed out to young authors.[45] In the Comus, and earlier Poems of Milton there is a superfluity of double epithets; while in the Paradise Lost we find very few, in the Paradise Regained scarce any. The same remark holds almost equally true of the Love's Labour Lost, Romeo and Juliet, Venus and Adonis, and Lucrece compared with Lear, Macbeth, Othello, and Hamlet of our great Dramatist. The rule for the admission of double epithets seems to be this: either that they should be already denizens of our Language, such as blood-stained, terror-stricken, self-applauding: or when a new epithet, or one found in books only, is hazarded, that it, at least, be one word, not two words, made one by mere virtue of the printer's hyphen. A language which, like the English, is almost without cases, is indeed in its very genius unfitted for compounds. If a writer, every time a compounded word suggests itself to him, would seek for some other mode of expressing the same sense, the chances are always greatly in favor of his finding a better word. "Tanquam scopulum sic vites, insolens verbum," is the wise advice of Cæsar to the Roman Orators, and the precept applies with double force to the writers in our own language. But it must not be forgotten, that the same Cæsar wrote a treatise for the purpose of reforming the ordinary language by bringing it to a greater accordance with principles of Logic or universal Grammar.[46]

Had a wretched day till near Tea-Time—& did nothing but doze over Warton's Edition of Milton's Juvenile Poems—a capital Edition on the whole; but this (the 2nd Ed.) infamously misprinted, the Greek and Latin quotations often unconjecturable—Spite of Warton's Eulogistic Compliments to Judge Jenkins, Milton plainly subjected to posthumous persecution in the annulling of his Will. Good Heavens! What a melancholy picture of his domestic state—as Jupiter to his least Moon, so M. to S. T. C.—as M. to S. T. C., so θυγατέρες to ———? Mem. not to forget to preserve some where my Detection of Warton's & the general mis-interpretation of Milton's first Latin Elegy. Strong proof of the perverting & blinding power of party prejudice, for the passage is even school-logically false-construed by Warton.—n.b. Warton's unfledged criticism, but it was quite as much as his age could bear, & we owe fervent thanks to him.

Thursday, 16th October, 1823[47]

[45] Coleridge is discussing "new coined double epithets."

[46] *Biog. Lit. C,* I, 5 n. Henry Nelson Coleridge gave the Latin as *Ut tanquam scopulum sic fugias insolens verbum,* from A. Gellius, Noct. Att. I. 10.

[47] Notebook 30, fol. 62 recto and 61 verso. Printed for the first time.

Warton, MINOR POEMS,[48] *on the flyleaf.*

Of Criticism we may perhaps say, that these divine Poets, Homer, Eschylus, and the two Compeers, Dante, Shakespeare, Spencer, Milton, who deserve to have Critics, ϰριταί, are placed above Criticism in the vulgar sense, and move in the sphere of Religion while those who are not such, scarcely deserve Criticism, in any sense.—But speaking gen‑erally, it is far, far better to distinguish Poetry into different Classes; and instead of fault-finding to say, this belongs to such or such a class—thus noting inferiority in the *sort* rather than censure on the particular poem or poet. We may outgrow certain *sorts* of poetry (Young's Night-thoughts, for instance) without arraigning their excellence *proprio genere.* In short, the wise is the genial; and the genial judgement is to distinguish accurately the character and characteristics of each poem, praising them according to their force and vivacity in their own kind—and to reserve Reprehension for such as have no *character*—tho' the wisest reprehension should be not to speak of them at all.

Warton, MINOR POEMS, *p. iii. A general note at the head of the Preface.*

Most shamefully incorrect. The Errata in the Latin Quotations are so numerous and so whimsical, as to puzzle the ingenuity of the best Latinist. I suspect that this is one of old Lackington's pirate editions. The paper seems too bad for such respectable Publishers, as the Robin-sons, who did not deal in this *charta* [?] *cacatilis* [*sic.*]

Warton, MINOR POEMS, *p. iii.*

After the Publication of the Paradise Lost, *whose* acknowledged merit and increasing celebrity . . .

Can Tom Warton have been guilty of this offence against prose English? Whose instead of "of which."

Warton, MINOR POEMS, *p. iv.*

It was late in the present century, before they [Milton's early poems] attained their just measure of esteem and popularity. Wit and rhyme, sentiment and satire, polished numbers, sparking couplets, and pointed periods, having so long kept undisturbed possession in our poetry, would not easily give way to fiction and fancy, to picturesque descrip-tion, and romantic imagery.

[48] John Milton, *Poems on Several Occasions*, ed. Thomas Warton (London: 1791). The original is in the Houghton Library, Harvard, and these notes have been directly transcribed from this source. They have been previously printed by John Drinkwater in *The London Mercury*, XIV (September, 1926), 491-505, and in *A Book for Bookmen* (London: 1926), pp. 63-91, and by Raysor *Misc. Crit.*, pp. 170-90.

It is hard to say which of the two kinds of metrical composition are here most unfaithfully characterized that which Warton opposes to the Miltonic, or the Miltonic asserted to have been eclipsed by the former. But a marginal note does not give room enough to explain what I mean.

Warton, MINOR POEMS, *p. xx.*

> Te bibens arcus Jovis ebriosus
> Mille formosus *removit* colores

"removit" corrected to read "renovat"

> Lucidum trudis properanter agmen :
> Sed resistentum super ora rerum
> Lonitur stagnas, liquidoque inundas
> Cuncta colore :

"lonitur" corrected to read "leniter."

Warton, MINOR POEMS: LYCIDAS, *p. 1, l. 1.*

> *Yet once more, &c.*] The best poets imperceptibly adopt phrases and formularies from the writings of their contemporaries or immediate predecessours. An Elegy on the death of the celebrated Countess of Pembroke, Sir Philip Sydney's sister, begins thus:
>
> Yet once againe, my Muse—

This, no doubt, is true; but the application to particular instances is exceedingly suspicious. Why, in Heaven's name! might not "once more" have as well occurred to Milton as to Sydney? On similar subjects or occasions some similar Thoughts *must* occur to different Persons, especially if men of resembling genius, quite independent of each other. The proof of this, if proof were needed, may be found in the works of contemporaries of different Countries in books published at the very *same time,* where neither *could* have seen the work of the other—perhaps ignorant of the language. I gave my lectures on Shakespear two years before Schlegel *began* his at Vienna, and I was myself startled at the close even verbal Parallelisms. S. T. Coleridge.

Warton, MINOR POEMS: LYCIDAS, *p. 2, l. 5.*

> *mellowing year.*] Here is an inaccuracy of the poet: *The Mellowing Year* could not affect the leaves of the laurel, the myrtle and the ivy; which last is characterized before as *never sere.*

If this is not finding fault for fault-finding sake, Maister Tummas! I do not know what it is. The young and diffident poet tells us, that the Duty to his Friend's memory compels him to produce a poem before his poetic Genius had attained it's full development, or had received the due culture and nourishment from Learning and Study. The faculties

appertaining to Poetic Genius he symbolizes beautifully and appropriately by the Laurel, the Myrtle and the Ivy—all three berry-bearing
Plants: and these Berries express here the *actual* state, degree and
quality of his poetic Powers, as the Plants themselves express the potential—the Leaves of the Ivy are "never sere," both because this is
the general character of Ivy and of Verse, and by a natural and graceful Prolepsis in reference to his own future productions—now if Warton
had thought instead of criticized, he must have seen that it was the
Berries which were to be plucked, but that in consequence of their un-
ripeness and the toughness of the pedicles, he was in danger of *shatter-
ing* the Leaves in the attempt. It was the *Berries*, I repeat, that the
more advanced Season was to have *mellowed;* and who indeed ever
dreamt of *mellowing* a Leaf?! The autumn may be said to mellow the
tints of the Foliage; but the word is never applied to the Leaves themselves. S. T. C.

Warton, MINOR POEMS: LYCIDAS, *p. 3, l. 11.*

  To sing, and build the lofty rhyme.] . . . I cannot however admit bishop
  Pearce's reasoning, who says, "Milton appears to have meant a different
  thing by RHIME here from RIME in his Preface, where it is six times
  mentioned, and always spelled without an *h*: whereas in all the Editions,
  RHIME in this place of the poem was spelled with an *h*. Milton probably meant a difference in the thing, by making so constant a difference
  in the spelling; and intended we should here understand by RHIME not
  the *jingling sound of like Endings, but Verse in general.*" Review of the
  Text of Paradise Lost, Lond. 1733, p. 5.

I am still inclined to think Bishop Pearce in the right. It is the
tendency of all Languages to avail them of the opportunities given by
accidental differences of pronunciation and spelling to make a word
multiply on itself: ex. gr. Propriety, Property; Mister and Master.—
Besides, we can prove that this was Milton's plan. In the first Edition
of the Par. Lost in *Twelve* Books, called the second Edition, Heè, Sheè
are systematically thus distinguished from He, and She; and her, their
from hir, thir, where they are to convey a distinct image to the mind,
and are not merely grammatical adjuncts, such as would be *understood*
in Latin.

Warton, MINOR POEMS: LYCIDAS, *p. 5, l. 18.*

  Hence with denial vain, and coy excuse:] The epithet, COY, is at present
  restrained to Person. Antiently, it was more generally combined. Thus
  a shepherd in Drayton's Pastorals,

>   Shepherd, these things are all too COY for me,
>   Whose youth is spent in jollity and mirth.

  That is, "This sort of knowledge is too *hard,* too difficult for me, &c."

Why, Warton! dear Tom Warton! wake up, my good fellow! You are snoring. Even in Drayton's Pastoral the *"coy"* is poorly explained into *"hard"*; but here it is evidently *personal*—excuse showing coyness in the Sisters.

But this is nothing to the want of Tact, Taste, and Ear—yea, of Eye and Sagacious nostril—in the evidenced preference given to the Edit. 1638.—The § ph. begins anew with, Together etc. After shroud there should be a colon only.[49]

Warton, MINOR POEMS: LYCIDAS, *p. 5, l. 25.*

> *Together both, &c.*] Here a new paragraph begins in the edition of 1645, and in all that followed. But in the edition of 1638, the whole context is thus pointed and arranged.

> > For we were nurst upon the self-same hill,
> > Fed the same flock by fountain, shade, and rill;
> > Together both, ere the high lawns appear'd, &c.
> > Under the opening eye-lids of the morn,

It is astonishing to me, that Warton should not have felt, the couplet,

> For we were nurst upon the self-same Hill,
> Fed the same flock by fountain, shade and rill!

is manifestly the Base or Pedestal of the Stanza or Scheme of verse, commencing with "Begin then, Sisters," and that it is divided from the 8th line of the Scheme by a colon: i. e. a full stop intended but with the *cadence* revoked, as it were, by a sudden recollection of some appertaining matter, confirming, enforcing or completing the preceding thought. Then follows a Pause, during which the Thought last started and expressed generally, unfolds itself to the poet's mind—and he begins anew with the proof and exposition of it by the particulars.—Another, and for a poet's ear convincing, proof that the couplet belongs to the third stanza is, that the 8th line like the first is *rhymeless* and was left so, because the concurring rhymes of the concluding Distich were foreseen as the compensation. Mem. This applicable to Sonnets, viz: under what circumstances the Sonnet should be 8 + 6, 12 + 2 or 14.[50]

Warton, MINOR POEMS: LYCIDAS, *p. 8, ll. 37-44.*

> But, O the heavy change, now thou art gone,
> Now thou art gone, and never must return!
> Thee, Shepherd, thee the woods, and desert caves
> With wild thyme and the gadding vine o'ergrown,
> And all their echoes mourn:

[49] This note on 1.25 follows immediately the note on 1.18.
[50] This note on 1.25 appears on the flyleaf.

> The willows, and the hazel copses green,
> Shall now no more be seen
> Fanning their joyous leaves to thy soft lays.

There is a delicate beauty of sound produced by the floating or oscillation of assonance and consonance, in the rhymes gone, return, caves, o'ergrown, mourn, green, seen, lays. Substitute flown for gone in the first line: and if you have a Poet's Ear, you will feel what you have lost and understand what I mean. I am bound, however, to confess that in the five last lines of this Stanza I find more of the fondness of a classical scholar for his favorite Classics than of the self-subsistency of a Poet destined to be himself a Classic,—more of the Copyist of Theocritus and *his* Copyist, Virgil, than of the free Imitator, who seizes with a strong hand whatever he wants or wishes for his own purpose and justifies the seizure by the improvement of the material or the superiority of the purpose, to which it is applied.

Warton, MINOR POEMS: LYCIDAS, *pp. 11-12, l. 5.*

> *Ay me! I fondly dream!*
> *Had ye been there—for what could that have done?*

So these lines stand in editions 1638, 1645, and 1673, the two last of which were printed under Milton's eye. Doctor Newton thus exhibits the passage:

> Ay me! I fondly dream
> Had ye been there, for what could that have done?

and adds this note: "We have here followed the pointing of Milton's manuscript in preference to all the editions: and the meaning plainly is, 'I fondly *dream of your having been there,* for what would that have signified?' But surely the words, *I fondly dream had ye been there,* will not bear this construction. The reading which I have adopted, to say nothing of its authority, has an abruptness, which heightens the present sentiment, and more strongly marks the distraction of the speaker's mind. 'Ah me! I am fondly dreaming! I will suppose you had been there—*but why should I suppose it,* for what would that have availed?' The context is broken and confused, and contains a sudden elleipsis which I have supplied with the words in Italics."

Had this been Milton's intention, he would have written *but,* as W. has done; and not *for.* Newton's is clearly the true Reading.

Warton, MINOR POEMS: LYCIDAS, *p. 13, l. 63.*

> *Down the swift Hebrus to the Lesbian shore.*] In calling Hebrus SWIFT, Milton, who is avaricious of classical authority, appears to have followed a verse in the Æneid, i. 321.

> VOLUCREMQUE fuga prævertitur Hebrum.

> But Milton was misled by a wrong although very antient reading . . .

"Smooth" would have suited M.'s purpose even better than "swift,"
even tho' the latter had now been inappropriate as poetically contrasting
with the vehemence and turbulence of the preceding Lines.—Possibly,
Milton was at this period of his life too predominantly a Poet to have
read Servius. Mem. The Virgilian Line might not unhappily be applied to the Hon. Mr. B****, who has made a more hasty "Cut and
run" than his *past* friend, H-r- Volucremque fugâ prævertitur Hebrum,
i. e.:

> Prick't from behind by Fear, his Legs his Bail,
> Outruns swift *Heber* following at his *Tail.*

Warton, Minor Poems: l'allegro, *p. 44, l. 23.*

> *Fill'd her,* &c.] Mr. Bowle is of opinion that this passage is formed
> from Gower's song in the Play of pericles prince of tyre. A. I. s.i. . . .

Perhaps, no more convincing proof can be given that the power of
poetry is from a *Genius,* i. e. not included in the faculties of the human
mind common to all men, than these so frequent "opinions," that this
and that passage was formed from, or borrowed, or stolen, &c. from
this or that other passage, found in some other poet or poem, three or
300 years older. In the name of common sense, if Gower could write
the lines without having seen Milton, why not Milton have done so tho'
Gower had never existed? That Mr. Bowle or Bishop Newton, or Mr.
Cory etc. should be unable to imagine the origination of a fine thought,
is no way strange; but that *Warton* should fall into the same dull
cant—!!

Warton, Minor Poems: l'allegro, *p. 64, ll. 133-34.*

> Or sweetest Shakespeare, Fancy's child,
> Warble his native wood-notes wild.

> "Milton shews his judgment here, in celebrating Shakespeare's *Comedies,*
> rather than his Tragedies. For models of the latter, he refers us rightly,
> in his penseroso to the Grecian scene, V. 97. H.[urd]

Be damn'd!—An Owl!

H. thou Right Reverend Aspirate! What hadst thou to do with
sweetest Shakespeare? Was it not enough to *merder* the Prophets?
But to be serious—if by Tragedies Hurd means "Song of the Goat,"
and if there were any pagans that had to make such, they would have
to look to the Ancient Greeks for Models. But what Shakespear proposed to realize was—an Imitation of human actions in connection with
sentiments, passions, characters, incidents, and events for the purpose
of pleasurable emotions; so that whether this be shewn by Tears of

Laughter or Tears of Tenderness, they shall still be Tears of Delight, and united with intellectual Complacency. Call such a work a Drama: and then I will tell the whole Herd of Hurdite Critics, that the Dramas of Shakespear, whether the lighter or the loftier emotions preponderate, are all, this one no less than the others, *Models*, with which it would be cruel and most unjust to the Names either of Eschylus, Sophocles, Euripides, or of Aristophanes to compare the *Tragedies* of the former or the Comedies of the latter. Shakespere produced Dramatic Poems, not Tragedies nor Comedies. If the Greek Tragedies, or as H. affectedly expresses it, "The Greek Scene" be a Model for anything modern, it must be for the Opera Houses. S.T.C.

Warton, MINOR POEMS: IL PENSEROSO, *pp. 67-76, ll. 1-60.*

The first 60 lines are (with unfeigned diffidence I add) in my humble judgement not only inferior to the Allegro, but such as many a second-rate Poet, a Pygmy compared with Milton, might have written.

Warton, MINOR POEMS: IL PENSEROSO, *pp. 88-89, l. 47.*

> *And let some strange mysterious dream*
> *Wave at his wings in aery stream*
> *Of lively portraiture display'd,*
> *Softly on my eye-lids laid.*

I do not exactly understand the whole of the context. Is the Dream to wave at Sleep's wings? Doctor Newton will have *wave* to be a verb neuter: and very justly, as the passage now stands. But let us strike out *at,* and make *wave* active.

> —Let some strange mysterious dream
> Wave his wings, in airy stream, &c.

"Let some fantastic DREAM put the wings of SLEEP in motion, which shall be *displayed,* or expanded, in an *airy* or soft *stream* of visionary imagery, gently falling or settling on my eye-lids." Or, *his* may refer to DREAM, and not to SLEEP with much the same sense. In the mean time, supposing *lively* adverbial, as was now common, *displayed* will connect with *pourtraiture,* that is "pourtraiture lively displayed," with this sense, "Wave his wings, in an airy stream of rich pictures so *strongly displayed* in vision as to resemble real *Life.*" Or, if *lively* remain an adjective, much in the same sense, *displayed* will signify *displaying* itself. On the whole, we must not here seek for precise meanings of parts, but acquiesce in a general idea, resulting from the whole, which I think is sufficiently seen.

A winged Dream upon a winged Sleep on the Poets eyelids! More sacks on the Mill! Warton must have written these notes in a careless hurry.

Explain the four lines as you will and tinker them how you can, they will remain a confused and awkwardly arranged period. But the *construing* I take to be this—and at his wings (dewy-feather'd) softly laid on my eye-lids let some strange mysterious Dream flow wavingly in aery stream of lively portraiture—*display'd* being a rhyme to "laid," and therefore not quite superfluous. S. T. C.

P. S. If any conjectural Reading were admissible, I should prefer

> Weave on his wings it's aery scheme (or theme)
> In lively, &c.

Warton, MINOR POEMS: IL PENSEROSO, *p. 93, note at the end.*

—"Of these two exquisite little poems [*L'Allegro* and *Il Penseroso*] I think it clear that this last is the most taking; which is owing to the subject. The mind delights most in these solemn images, and a genius delights most to paint them." H.[urd]

I feel the direct opposite, almost painfully. But I suspect, that this contrariety would go thro' all my decisions in reference to Bishop Hurd's.

Warton, MINOR POEMS: COMUS, *p. 152, l. 108.*

> *And Advice with scrupulous head.*

"The manuscript reading, *And quick Law* is the best. It is not the essential attribute of *Advice* to be Scrupulous: but it is of *Quick Law,* or *Watchful Law,* to be so." W.[arburton]

Bless me! Who would have expected a remark so tasteless or so shallow a reason from Warton? It is not the essential character of Advice, but it is the very character, by which the God of Riot and Wassail would ridicule him. And then the sound and rhythm—*Quick Law*—and the confusion of executive (Quick) with Judicial Law (Scrupulous). In short the wonder is that it should be found in the MSS. —as having occurred to Milton.

Warton, MINOR POEMS: COMUS, *p. 155, l. 140.*

> *From her cabin'd loop-hole peep.*] Warton here refers to Milton's use of the loop-holes in the Indian fig-tree in *Paradise Lost*, Book IX, saying "Milton was a student in botany. He took his description of this multifarious tree from the account of it in Gerard's HERBALL."

If I wished to display the charm and *effect* of metre and the *art* of poetry, independent of the Thoughts and Images—the superiority, in short of *poematic* over *prose* Composition, the poetry or no-poetry being the same in both—I question, whether a more apt and convincing instance could be found, than in these exquisite lines of Milton's compared with the passage in Gerard of which they are the organized version. Shakespeare's Cleopatra on the Cydnus, compared with the original in North's Plutarch is another almost equally striking example. S. T. C. 22nd Ocbr: 1823. Ramsgate.

Warton, MINOR POEMS: COMUS, *p. 168, l. 238.*

> *O, if thou have,*
> *Hid them in some flow'ry cave.*] Here is a seeming inaccuracy for the sake of the rhyme. But the sense being hypothetical and contingent, we will suppose an elleipsis of *shouldest* before *have.*

Could W. have been so ignorant of English Grammar? His Brother[51] would have flogged a Winchester Lad for an equivalent ignorance in a Latin Subjunctive.

Warton, MINOR POEMS: COMUS, *p. 168, l. 380.*

> *Were all to ruffled.*—] ALL-TO, or AL-TO, is, *Intirely.*

Even this is not the exact meaning of to—or all-to which answers to the German *Zer,* as our *for* in forlorn to ver, pronounced fer.

Warton, MINOR POEMS: COMUS, *pp. 241-42, ll. 892-95.*

> *My sliding chariot stays,*
> *Thick set with agat, and the azurn sheen*
> *Of turkis blue, and emrald green,*
> *That in the channel strays.*]

L. 895. The word "strays" *needed* a Note—and therefore it is the only part of the sentence left unnoticed. First of all, Turquoises and Emeralds are not much addicted to *straying* anywhere; and the last place, I should look for them, would be in channels; and secondly, the verb is in the singular number and belongs to Sheen, i. e. Lustre, Shininess, as it's nominative case. It may therefore bear a question, whether Milton did mean the wandering flitting tints and hues of the Water, in my opinion a more poetical as well as a much more appropriate Imagery. He particularizes one precious stone, the Agate, which often occurs in brooks and rivulets, and leaves the *substance* of the other *ornaments* as he had of the chariot itself undetermined, and describes them by the effect on the eye / thickset with agate and that transparent, or humid, shine of (turquoise-like) Blue, and (emeraldine) Green that strays in the channel. For it is in the water immediately above the pebbly Bed of the Brook, that one seems to see these lovely glancing Water-tints. N.B. This note is in the best style of Warburtonian perverted ingenuity.

[51] Joseph Warton, headmaster of Winchester, 1766-93.

Warton, MINOR POEMS: COMUS, *p. 255, ll. 946-56.*

> And not many furlongs thence
> Is your Father's residence,
> Where this night are met in state
> Many a friend to gratulate
> His wish'd presence and beside
> All the swains that near abide,
> With jigs and rural dance resort;
> We shall catch them at their sport,
> And our sudden coming there
> Will double all their mirth and chear.

With all prostration of reverence at the feet of even the Juvenal, [*sic.*][52] Milton, I must yet lift up my head enough to pillow my chin on the Rose of his shoe, and ask him in a timid whisper whether Rhymes and Finger-metre do not render poor flat prose ludicrous, rather than tend to elevate it, or even to hide it's nakedness.

Warton, MINOR POEMS: ODE ON THE MORNING OF CHRIST'S NATIVITY, *p. 722, l. 116.*

> With unexpressive notes . . .

It is strange that *Milton* should have held it allowable to substitute the active Aorist *ive* for the passive adjective *ible.* It was too high a compliment even to Shakspear. What should we think of undescriptive for indescribable? Surely, no authority can justify such a Solecism.

Warton, MINOR POEMS: ODE ON THE MORNING OF CHRIST'S NATIVITY, *p. 274, st. xv.*

> Yea, Truth and Justice then
> Will down return to men,
>   Orb'd in a rainbow; and like glories wearing
> Mercy will sit between,
> Thron'd in celestial sheen,
>   With radiant feet in the tissued clouds down steering:
> And heav'n, as at some festival,
> Will open wide the gate of her high Palace hall.

xv. A glorious subject for the Ceiling of a princely Banquet room, in the style of Parmeggiano, or Allston. S. T. C. Stanz. XXIII. I think I have seen—possibly, by Fuseli.

Warton, MINOR POEMS: ON THE MORNING OF CHRIST'S NATIVITY, *p. 281, l. 231.*

> *Pillows his chin upon an orient wave.*] The words *pillows* and *chin,* throw an air of burlesque and familiarity over a comparison most exquisitely conceived and adapted.

[52] The meaning is obviously "juvenile."

I have tried in vain to imagine, in what other way the Image could be given. I rather think, that it is one of the Hardinesses permitted to a great Poet. Dante would have written it: tho' it is most in the Spirit of Donne.

Warton, MINOR POEMS: THE PASSION, *p. 286, st. viii.*

This subject the author finding to be above the years he had, when he wrote it, and nothing satisfied with what was begun, left it unfinished.

I feel grateful to Milton, that instead of preserving only the VIth and the first five lines of the VIIIth Stanza, he has given us the whole Eight. The true solution of 1st, 2nd, 3rd, 4th, vth, and 7th Stanzas is, that Milton has not yet *un*taught himself the looking up to inferior minds, which he had been taught to consider as Models. He did not yet dare to know, how great he was.

Warton, MINOR POEMS: AT A VACATION EXERCISE, *p. 307, ll. 3-6.*

And mad'st imperfect words with childish trips,
Half unpronounce'd, slide through my infant-lips, ※
Driving dumb silence from the portal door,
Where he had mutely sat two years before.※

※ "Slide" seems to me not quite the right word. Perhaps "stumble" or "struggle" would be better? omitting "my"
   Half unpronounced, stumble through infant lips.
※ Well might He speak late who spoke to such purpose!

Warton, MINOR POEMS: AT A VACATION EXERCISE, *p. 312, l. 59.*

—*For at thy birth*
The faery ladies danc'd upon the hearth.] This is the first and last time that the system of the Fairies was ever introduced to illustrate the doctrine of Aristotle's ten categories. It may be remarked, that both were in fashion, and both exploded, at the same time.

Exploded? The Categories? Aristotle's *Table* of the Categories was corrected and improved, but even this not till long after the Date of this Exercise.

Warton, MINOR POEMS: AT A VACATION EXERCISE, *p. 314, l. 83.*

To find a foe it shall not be his hap.] *Substantia, substantiæ nova contrariatur*, is a schoolmaxim.

It is curious that on this purely logical conception or rather *form* of conceiving, Spinoza re-codified the Pantheism of the old Greek Philosophy. S. T. C.

Warton, Minor Poems: on the university carrier, *pp. 318-19 (two poems).*

"I wonder Milton should suffer these two things on Hobson to appear in his edition of 1645. He, who at the age of nineteen, had so just a contempt for

> Those new-fangled toys, and trimming slight,
> Which take our new fantastics with delight." H.[urd.]

It is truly edifying to observe, what value and importance certain Critics attach to a farthing's worth of paper. One *wonders*—another *regrets*—just as if the two poor copies of verses had been a Dry-rot, threatening the whole life and beauty of the Comus, Lycidas, and other work in their vicinity! I confess that I have read these *Hobsons* 20 times, and always with amusement, without the least injury to the higher and very different Delight afforded by Milton's *poetry.*—These are the Junior Soph's very learned Jocularitys.—S. T. C.

And why should not Milton as well as other Cantabs like to chuckle over his old College Jokes and crack them anew?

Warton, Minor Poems: sonnet iv, *p. 330, ll. 1-2.*

> Diodati, e te'l dirò con maraviglia   meraviglia
> Quel ritroso io ch'ampor spreggiar soléa   ch'amor

Warton, Minor Poems: sonnet to mr. h. lawes, *p. 340.*

It is rather singular that the compliment to a musician by the most musical of all poets and who loved the man as well as his Art, should be the least musical of all the Sonnets—notwithstanding the sweetness of the three last lines. S. T. C.

Warton, Minor Poems: translation of psalm vii, *p. 376.*

This is a very pleasing stanza, and which I do not elsewhere recollect.

A B A B B A. A more pleasing stanza might I think be constructed for a *shorter* poem by extending it to eight lines

A B A B B A B A

ire rage fire cage page sire wage lyre.

Warton, Minor Poems: translation of psalm viii, *p. 378, second stanza.*

> Out of the mouths of babes and sucklings thou
> Hast founded strength because of all thy foes,
> To stint th' enemy, and slack th'avenger's brow,
> That bends his rage thy providence t'oppose.

A truly majestic composition. Milton pronounced Jē hŏ văh, as an amphimacer. S. T. C.

Miltons ear taught him that accent even with emphasis, provided the latter be slight, quickens the sound. I doubt not, that Milton meant that there should be no elision of the e final of the definite article, but intended thĕ ĕnĕmȳ for a discretic or tetrabrach isochronous only to an emphasized Iambic. I find it easy to read the line so as to give it a good and striking metrical effect, by at once rapidly and yet emphatically pronouncing "the enemy" with a smart stroke on the "en." S. T. Coleridge.

Warton, MINOR POEMS: TRANSLATION OF PSALM VIII, *p. 379, fifth stanza, ll. 17-18.*

> O'er the works of thy hand thou mad'st him Lord,
> Thou hast put all under his lordly feet . . .

The two first lines of the 5th stanza are more difficult. Yet even here there needs only an educated ear. In the first line the two last feet properly read are almost spondees instead of iambics; the others, a trochee and a choriambic. Now count the four last syllables as equal to six breves, and you have the same number of times, as in pure Iambics, and the spondaic character of the two last feet compensating for the quickened utterance of the 3 former.

Wharton, MINOR POEMS: TRANSLATION OF PSALM LXXXII, *pp. 385-86.*

With a few alterations this Psalm might be adopted in a new church version, or at least a revision of Sternhold.

Warton, MINOR POEMS: TRANSLATION OF PSALM LXXXII, *p. 386, l. 24.*

> As other Princes *die.*

Other? Ought not the word to have been in italics? This is the only passage or verse in the Old Testament in which I can imagine any allusion to the fall of the Spirits, the Thrones, or Potentates = Ἰδέαι ἤ Ἀριθμοί. Our Lord plainly interpreted the verse in this sense.

Warton, MINOR POEMS: LATIN ELEGY TO CHARLES DIODATI, *p. 421, l. 12.*

Nec dudum vetiti me laris angit amor.] The words *vetiti Laris,* and afterwards *exilium,* will not suffer us to determine otherwise, than that Milton was sentenced to undergo temporary removal or rustication from Cambridge . . .

I cannot agree with Warton. It seems to me far more probable that Diodati in a pedantic fit had called Milton's vacation an Exile from

POETRY/JOHN MILTON

the Muses—and that Milton tacitly or rather implicitly, reproves his friend's Pedantry. But how Warton could have so utterly mistaken the sense of the 11 and 12 Lines is astonishing.

Warton, MINOR POEMS: LATIN ELEGY TO CHARLES DIODATI, *p. 429, l. 70.*

Jactet, et Ausoniis plena theatra stolis

Remarkable, that a man of so fine an ear as Milton, should have endured a short syllable before *st.*—theatra *st*olis.

Warton, MINOR POEMS: SYLVARUM LIBER, *p. 533, l. 6.*

Adesdum, et haec s'is verba pauca Salsillo. *hanc?*

PARADISE LOST
Lecture on Milton[53]
and the
Paradise Lost
4 March, 1819

If we divide the period from the ascension of Elizabeth to the Protectorate of Cromwell into two unequal portions, the first ending with the Death of James the First, the other comprehending the reign of Charles and the brief glories of the Republic, we are forcibly struck with a difference in the character of the illustrious Actors, by whom each period is severally memorable. Or rather, the difference in the characters of the great men in each leads us to make this division. Eminent as the intellectual Powers were, that were displayed in both, yet in the number of great men, in the various sorts of excellence, and not merely the variety but almost diversity of talents united in the same Individual, the age of Charles falls short of it's predecessor; and the Stars of the Parliament, keen as their radiance was, yet in fullness and richness of lustre yield to the constellation at the Court of Elizabeth. To be equalled only by Greece at time of her Epaminondas [viz.?], Pericles, Zenophon, Thucydides, when the Poet Philosopher, Historian, Statesman, and General formed a garland around the same head—Sir W. Ralegh.[54] But on the other hand, there is a vehemence of Will, an enthusiam of principle, a depth and an earnestness of Spirit, which the charm of individual fame and personal aggrandizement could not

[53] The text of more than half the lecture on Milton as published with some omissions in *Lit. Rem.*, I, 166-78, is here reproduced from the original in the Clasped Vellum Notebook, pp. 292-85, pagination numbered backwards. The illustrative passages from *Paradise Lost* to be used in the lecture are printed for the first time.

[54] This sentence, marked for insertion at this point, appears at the bottom of the first page of the notebook.

pacify, an aspiration after reality, permanence, and general Good—in short, a moral Grandeur in the latter æra, with which the law intrigues, Macchiavelian [sic] maxims, and the selfish and servile ambition of the former stand in painful contrast.

The causes of this it belongs, not to the present occasion to detail at full—the quick succession of Revolutions in Religion, breeding a political indifference in the mass of men to Religion itself, the enormous increase of the Royal Power from the humiliation of the Nobility & the Clergy, and the transference of the Papal Powers to the Crown, and especially the unfixed state of Elizabeth's Opinions, whose inclinations were as papal as her interests were Protestant, and the controversial extravagance and practical imbecillity [sic] of her successor, explain the former period—and the persecutions, that had given a life and soul interest to the Disputes imprudently fostered by James, the ardour of a conscious increase of Power in the minority and the greater austerity of manners & maxims which is the natural product and the most formidable weapon of religious Minorities, not merely in conjunction but in closest combination with new-awakened political and republican Zeal— these account for the latter.

In the close of the former period and during the bloom of the latter the Poet, Milton, was educated and formed—survived the latter and all the fond hopes & aspirations which had been it's life, and in evil days standing as the representative of the combined excellence of both produced the Paradise Lost, as by an after-throe of Nature. "There are some persons (observes a Divine, a Contemporary of Milton!) of whom the Grace of God takes early hold, and the good Spirit inhabiting them carries them on in an even constancy thro' innocence into virtue: their Christianity bearing equal date with their manhood, and reason and religion like warp and woof running together, make up one web of a wise and exemplary life. This (he adds) is a most happy case, wherever it happens—for besides that there is no sweeter or more lovely thing on earth than the early Buds of Piety, which drew from our Savior signal affection to the beloved Disciple, it is better to have no wound than to experience the sovereign Balsam, which if it work a cure yet usually leaves a scar behind." Tho' it was and is my intention to defer the consideration of Milton's own character to the conclusion of this address, yet I could not prevail on myself to approach to the Paradise without impressing on your minds the *conditions* under which such a work was producible, the original Genius having been assumed as the immediate agent and efficient cause—and these conditions I was to find in the character of his times and in his own character. The age, in

which the foundations of his mind were laid, was congenial to it, as our
golden æra of profound Erudition and original[55] Genius—that in
which it's superstructure was carried up, no less congenial by a
sterness [sic] of it's discipline and a shew of self-control highly flattering to the imaginative dignity of "an heir of Fame"—and which won
him over from the dear-loved delights of academic Groves, and Cathedral Aisles, to the anti-prelatic Party—and it acted on him, no doubt,
and modified his studies by it's characteristic controversial spirit,[56] no
less busy indeed in political than in theological & ecclesiastical dispute,
but the former always more or less in the guise of the latter—and as
far as Pope's censure of our Poet, that he makes God the Father a
School-divine is Just, we must attribute it to the character of his Age,
from which the men of Genius, who escaped, escaped by a worse disease,
the licentiousness of the French Court.   Such were the nidus or soil
in which he was, in the strict sense of the word, the circumstances of
his mind—in the mind itself purity, piety, an imagination to which
neither the Past nor the Present were interesting except as far as they
called forth and enlived [sic] the great Ideal, in which and for which
he lived, a keen love of Truth which after many weary pursuits found
an harbour in a sublime listening to the low still voice in his own
spirit, and as keen a love of his Country which after disappointment,
still more depressive at once expanded and sobered[57] into a love of Man
as the Probationer of Immortality, these were, these alone could be, the
conditions under which such a work could be conceived and accomplished.   By a life-long study he had known

> what was of use to know
> What best to say could say, to do had done—
> His actions to his words agreed, his words
> To his large Heart gave utterance due, his heart
> Contain'd of good, wise, fair, the perfect Shape—

and left the imperishable Total, as a bequest to Ages, in the PARADISE
LOST (not perhaps *here*, but towards or as the conclusion to chastise the
fashionable notion that Poetry is a relaxation, amusement, one of the
superfluous Toys & Luxuries of the Intellect!)[58]

   Difficult as I shall find it to turn over these Leaves without catching
some passage which would tempt me, I propose to consider first, the
general plan and arrangement of the work—2nd the subject with it's
difficulties and advantages—3rd the Poet's *Object*, the Spirit in the
Letter, the ἐπιμύθιον ἐν μύθῳ the true school-*divinity* and lastly, the

[55] *Lit. Rem.* reads "individual."
[56] *Lit. Rem.* inserts a parenthetical comment.
[57] *Lit. Rem.* reads "soared" but the MS is clear.
[58] In *Lit. Rem.* this remark appears as a footnote with another sentence added.

characteristic excellences, of the poem, & in what they consist and by what means they are produced.

First then, the plan and ordonnance,

1. Compared with the Iliad, many of the books of which might change places without any injury to the thread of the story[59]—and 2ndly with both the Iliad and more or less in all epic Poems where subjects are from History, they have no *rounded* conclusion—they remain after all but a single chapter from the volume of History tho' an ornamented Chapter.[60] In Homer too the importance of the subject, namely, as the first effort of confederated Greece, an after thought of the critics—& the interest, such as it is, derived from the events as distinguished from the manner of representing them, languid to all but Greeks.[61] The superiority of the Paradise Lost is obvious, but not dwelt on because it may be attributed to Christianity itself, tho' in this instance it comprehends the whole Mohamedan World as well as Xtndom—and as the origin of evil and the combat of Evil and Good, a matter of such interest to all mankind as to form the basis of all religions, and the true occasion of all Philosophy.[62]

Next the exquisite simplicity. It and it alone really possesses the Beginning, Middle, and End—the totality of a Poem or circle as distinguished from the ab ovo birth, parentage, &c. or strait line of History. An exquisite Propriety in the narration by Raphael & Adam—et artis est celare artem, the propriety of beginning as he does.[63]

Quotations and Passages referred to.

P. 4 - to 5.   "thus began"—in proof of fore figure preserved fore-
L. 26 to 83.   most—and of *ascent*.

P. 11 "He scarce had ceased" to 12. of Hell resounded. L. 283 to 315. 364 to 520—judgement in humanizing the Spirits to the imagination.

P. 20 (587) further proof—and of the increased humanity of Satan.

P. 48. 1. 666—of allegory, and the difference of Poetry from Painting.

P. 63. Beginning of the Third Book—it's utility in the construction of the poem, as a connecting link, in addition to it's beauty—besides, the whole subjective character of the Poem.

[59] In *Lit. Rem.* the following sentence is inserted: "Indeed, I doubt the original existence of the Iliad as one poem; it seems more probable that it was put together about the time of the Pisistratidæ."

[60] In *Lit. Rem.* the paragraph below on simplicity is here inserted.

[61] In *Lit. Rem.* is inserted here, "It is a Greek poem."

[62] This material has minor changes in wording in *Lit. Rem.*

[63] This sentence is omitted in *Lit. Rem.* The remainder of the lecture as given in *Lit. Rem.* is from some other source. In the notebook Coleridge sets down a number of references from which the nature of the discussion can be inferred.

78. Limbo very *entertaining* but out of character.
91. Minute Landscape of Paradise—no attempt to describe Heaven: judgement.
95. (B. IV. 270) Judicious conclusion with fables of human forms prior to the introduction of the first human Pair.
96. She as a Veil—Dress. So 101, l. 492, So p. 235 (B. IX. 425)— and again of the Angel (Book V. 276) p. 127.
108. Love in Paradise. No Rosicrusianism, but far removed as Heaven from Hell, from Dryden's degradation. Explain. The difference in the Like, or correspondent opposites—all the images which preclude passion collected & last the Prayers.

Book VI.
P. 173. 324. After the justification of the Book VI. on the grounds stated by Raphael—(Book V. l. 560) P. 135—& the philos p. 133.
Book IX. What could not be escaped, how well overcome in the *fall* before the *fall*—and still more magnificently, p. 237. l. 495.
Book X. The Pathos of p. 287. l. 915.
Why the XIth and XIIth Books are less interesting, owing in great measure to the habit of reading Poetry for the story. If read in connection as the History of mankind nothing can be finer. The Beauty of the two last Lines, as presenting *a picture*—and so representative of the state of man, at best, in the fallen world.
P. 304. Book XI. 248. Michal finally contrasted with Rafael p. 214.
P. 274. (l. 425. B. X-& l. 505)[64]

The FALL of Man is the subject; Satan is the cause; man's blissful state the immediate object of his enmity and attack; man is warned by an angel who gives him an account of all that was requisite to be known, to make the warning at once intelligible and awful, then the temptation ensues, and the Fall; then the immediate sensible consequence; then the consolation, wherein an angel presents a vision of the history of man with the ultimate triumph of the Redeemer. Nothing is touched in this vision but what is of general interest in religion; any thing else would have been improper.

The inferiority of Klopstock's Messiah is inexpressible. I admit the prerogative of poetic feeling, and poetic faith; but I can not suspend the judgment even for a moment. A poem may in one sense be a dream, but it must be a waking dream. In Milton you have a religious faith combined with the moral nature; it is an efflux; you go along with it. In Klopstock there is a wilfulness; he makes things so and so. The

[64] At this point the material in the notebook ends, and the remainder of the lecture is printed from *Lit. Rem.*, I, 172-78.

feigned speeches and events in the Messiah shock us like falsehoods; but nothing of that sort is felt in the Paradise Lost, in which no particulars, at least very few indeed, are touched which can come into collision or juxtaposition with recorded matter.

But notwithstanding the advantages in Milton's subject, there were concomitant insuperable difficulties, and Milton has exhibited marvellous skill in keeping most of them out of sight. High poetry is the translation of reality into the ideal under the predicament of succession of time only. The poet is an historian, upon condition of moral power being the only force in the universe. The very grandeur of his subject ministered a difficulty to Milton. The statement of a being of high intellect, warring against the supreme Being, seems to contradict the idea of a supreme Being. Milton precludes our feeling this, as much as possible, by keeping the peculiar attributes of divinity less in sight, making them to a certain extent allegorical only. Again poetry implies the language of excitement; yet how to reconcile such language with God? Hence Milton confines the poetic passion in God's speeches to the language of Scripture; and once only allows the *passio vera,* or *quasi humana* to appear, in the passage, where the Father contemplates his own likeness in the Son before the battle:—

> Go then, thou Mightiest, in thy Father's might,
> Ascend my chariot, guide the rapid wheels
> That shake Heaven's basis, bring forth all my war,
> My bow and thunder; my almighty arms
> Gird on, and sword upon thy puissant thigh;
> Pursue these sons of darkness, drive them out
> From all Heaven's bounds into the utter deep:
> There let them learn, as likes them, to despise
> God and Messiah his annointed king.
>
> B. vi. v. 710

3. As to Milton's object:

It was to justify the ways of God to man! The controversial spirit observable in many parts of the poem, especially in God's speeches, is immediately attributable to the great controversy of that age, the origination of evil. The Arminians considered it a mere calamity. The Calvinists took away all human will. Milton asserted the will, but declared for the enslavement of the will out of an act of the will itself. There are three powers in us, which distinguish us, from the beasts that perish:—1, reason; 2, the power of viewing universal truth; and 3, the power of contracting universal truth into particulars. Religion is the will in the reason, and love in the will.

The character of Satan is pride and sensual indulgence, finding in self the sole motive of action. It is the character so often seen *in little* on the political stage. It exhibits all the restlessness, temerity, and cunning which have marked the mighty hunters of mankind from Nimrod to Napoleon. The common fascination of men is, that these great men, as they are called, must act from some great motive. Milton has carefully marked in his Satan the intense selfishness, the alcohol of egotism, which would rather reign in hell than serve in heaven. To place this lust of self in opposition to denial of self or duty, and to show what exertions it would make, and what pains endure to accomplish its end, is Milton's particular object in the character of Satan. But around this character he has thrown a singularity of daring, a grandeur of sufferance and a ruined splendor, which constitute the very height of poetic sublimity.

Lastly, as to the execution:—

The language and versification of the Paradise Lost are peculiar in being so much more necessarily correspondent to each than those in any other poem or poet. The connexion of the sentences and the position of the words are exquisitely artificial; but the position is rather according to the logic of passion or universal logic, than to the logic of grammar. Milton attempted to make the English language obey the logic of passion as perfectly as the Greek and Latin. Hence the occasional harshness in the construction.

Sublimity is the pre-eminent characteristic of the Paradise Lost. It is not an arithmetical sublime like Klopstock's, whose rule always is to treat what we might think large as contemptibly small. Klopstock mistakes bigness for greatness. There is a greatness arising from images of effort and daring, and also from those of moral endurance; in Milton both are united. The fallen angels are human passions, invested with a dramatic reality.

The apostrophe to light at the commencement of the third book is particularly beautiful as an intermediate link between Hell and Heaven; and observe, how the second and third book support the subjective character of the poem. In all modern poetry in Christendom there is an under consciousness of a sinful nature, a fleeting away of external things, the mind or subject greater than the object, the reflective character predominant. In the Paradise Lost the sublimest parts are the revelations of Milton's own mind, producing itself and evolving its own greatness; and this is so truly so, that when that which is merely entertaining for its objective beauty is introduced, it at first seems a discord.

In the description of Paradise itself, you have Milton's sunny side as a man; here his descriptive powers are exercised to the utmost, and he draws deep upon his Italian resources. In the description of Eve, and throughout this part of the poem, the poet is predominant over the theologian. Dress is the symbol of the Fall, but the mark of intellect; and the metaphysics of dress are, the hiding what is not symbolic and displaying by discrimination what is. The love of Adam and Eve in Paradise is of the highest merit—not phantomatic, and yet removed from every thing degrading. It is the sentiment of one rational being towards another made tender by a specific difference in that which is essentially the same in both; it is a union of opposites, a giving and receiving mutually of the permanent in either, a completion of each in the other.

Milton is not a picturesque, but a musical, poet; although he has this merit, that the object chosen by him for any particular foreground always remains prominent to the end, enriched, but not encumbered, by the opulence of descriptive details furnished by an exhaustless imagination. I wish the Paradise Lost were more carefully read and studied than I can see any ground for believing it is, especially those parts which, from the habit of always looking for a story in poetry, are scarcely read at all,—as for example, Adam's vision of future events in the 11th and 12th books. No one can rise from the perusal of this immortal poem without a deep sense of the grandeur and the purity of Milton's soul, or without feeling how susceptible of domestic enjoyments he really was, notwithstanding the discomforts which actually resulted from an apparently unhappy choice in marriage. He was, as every truly great poet has ever been, a good man; but finding it impossible to realize his own aspirations, either in religion or politics, or society, he gave up his heart to the living spirit and light within him, and avenged himself on the world by enriching it with this record of his own transcendent ideal.

I have a continual Dream, representing visually & audibly all Milton's Paradise Lost.[65]

To understand fully the mechanism, in order fully to feel the incomparable Excellence, of Milton's Metre, we must make four Tables, or a four fold compartment: the first for the Feet, single & composite, for which the whole 26 feet of the ancients will be found necessary; the second, to note the construction of the Feet, whether from different or from single words: for who does not perceive the difference to the ear between

[65] Notebook 10, fol. 50 recto. British Museum, Add. MSS, 47,507. Printed for the first time.

"Inextricable Disobedience," and

"To love or not: in this we stand or fall."

yet both lines are composed of five Iambics. The Third, of the strength and position, the concentration or diffusion of the *emphasis.* Fourth, the Length and Position of the Pauses. Then compare his Narrative with the Harrangues. I have not noticed the Ellipses, because they either do not affect the Rhythm, or are not Ellipses, but comprehended in the Feet.[66]

Semi-breve; Breve; Plusquam breve; Long; Plusquam long.

In the Iambic Pentameter of the *Paradise Lost,* I assume fifteen breves as the total quantity of each line—this isochrony being the identity or element of sameness, the varying quality of the isochronous feet constituting the difference; and from that harmony or fine balance of the two opposite (N. B. *not* contrary) forces, viz., identity and difference, results the likeness; and again, this likeness (*quicquid simile est, non est idem*) [is] reducible to a law or principle and therefore anticipable, and, in fact, tho perhaps unconsciously expected by the reader or auditor, constitutes poetic metre. Each line is a metre—*ex. gr.,* we should not say, that an hexameter is a line of six metres, but that it is a metre of six feet. But the harmonious relation of the metres to each other, the fine medium between division and continuity, distinction without disjunction, which a good reader expresses by a pause without a cadence, constitutes rhythm. And it is this harmonious opposition and balance of metre and rhythm, superadded to the former balance of the same in quantity with the difference in quality, the one belonging to the lines, the other to the paragraphs, that makes the peculiar charm, the *excellency,* of the Miltonic poesy. The Greek epic poets left rhythm to the orators. The metre all but precluded rhythm. But the ancients *sang* their poetry. Now for a nation who, like the English, have substituted *reading,* impassioned and tuneful reading, I grant, but still *reading,* for *recitative,* this counter-action, this inter-penetration, as it were, of metre and rhythm is the dictate of a sound judgment and like all other excellencies in the fine arts, a postulate of common sense fulfilled by genius, the *needful* at once contained and [———?] in the beautiful. S. T. Coleridge.

P. S. Milton must be scanned by the *Pedes Compositæ,* as the Choriambus, Ionics, Pæons, Epitrites, etc., taking the five meters ˘|˘ ˘| ˘ ˘ ˘ | – | ˘ – | as the ground.[67]

[66] Notebook 17, p. 240. Also in *Anima,* p. 253.

[67] Sir Walter Scott, *Novels and Romances* (7 vols.; Edinburgh: 1825), flyleaves, Vol. I. Given in Raysor, *Misc. Crit.,* pp. 337-38.

(= means *equal to*)

◡ = short syllable

‒ = ◡◡

◡◡ = a Pyrrhic or Dibrach, as bŏdў, spĭrĭt

◡◡◡ = a Tribrach, as nŏbŏdў, when hastily pronounced

◡ ‒ an Iambic, as dēlight

‒ ◡ a Trochee, as Līghtlў

‒ ‒ a Spondee, as Gōd spāke

N. B. The fewness of Spondees in single words in our and indeed in the modern Languages in general makes perhaps the greatest distinction between them & the Greek and Latin, at least metrically considered.

‒ ◡ ◡ a Dactyl, as mērrĭlў

◡ ◡ ‒ an Anapæst, as āprŏpōs, or the first syllables of cĕrĕmōnĭă

◡ ‒ ◡ an Amphibrach, as dĕlīghtfŭl

‒ ◡ ‒ an Amphimacer, as ōvĕr Hīll

‒ ‒ ◡ a Bacchius, as Hēlvēllўn

◡ ‒ ‒ an Anti-bacchius, as thĕ Lōrd Gōd

‒ ‒ ‒ a Molossus, as Jōhn, Jāmes, Jūde

These which are called Simple Feet may suffice for understanding the metres of Shakespear, for the greater part; but Milton cannot be made harmoniously intelligible without the composite feet (Ionics, Pæons, & Epitrites—brachus in Greek means short, and makros long: amphi on each side. Therefore amphibrach means short on both sides with a long syllable between, and amphimacer long on both sides with a short syllable between. So Dibrach means twice short, and Tribrach thrice short. The Spondee and the Molossus might analogically have been named Dimacer and Trimacer. Anapæst from a Greek word signifying to strike descending, i. e. to lay the stress on the last syllable of three.[68]

P. S. The pause after the second syllable in pentameter iambic blank verse is frequent in the poems of Mr. Southey and his imitators. But should it be imitated? Milton uses it, when the weight of the first iambic, trochee, or spondee of the second line requires a pause of preparation at the last foot of the preceding.[69]

[68] This note is from Theobald's edition of Shakespeare, in the British Museum, Vol. I., second flyleaf. It appears in the notes on *Midsummer Night's Dream* in *Lit. Rem.*, II, 113, and is given in part by Raysor, *Shakes. Crit.*, I, 252-53. In both the latter sources there are slight variations from the original.

[69] Barry Cornwall, *Dramatic Scenes and Other Poems* (London: 1819). From Lamb's copy in the Victoria and Albert Museum, South Kensington, flyleaves at end.

But for some defect in the metre, [i. e. in Sotheby's *Saul*] arising
from the shortness of the Periods in part, and in part from the pausing
so often at the second Syllable which Milton never does, as far as I have
examined, except when he means to give an unusual Importance to the
words—and even then most often a trochaic, not a spondee, or an
Iambic—

> "And now his Heart
> Distends with pride, and hard'ning, in his strength
> *Glories:*" Book I, 571.—

But when it is an Iambic, it always has and is meant to have some great
effect—see Book I. from Line 585 to 615—after all the grand preparation of the imaginative power.

> "He now prepared
> To speak:—whereat their doubted ranks they bend, etc."

Of course, I do not apply this remark in all it's force to Lines beginning
periods or paragraphs; tho' even here, it ought to have some attention
paid it . . . yet to my *feelings* the metre alone prevents the poem from
being *wholly* delightful.[70]

Hayley, MILTON, *pp. 69-70, comment continued on p. 71.*[71]

> [Hayley quotes:] "Time serves not now, and, perhaps, I might seem too
> profuse to give any certain account of what the mind at home, in the
> spacious circuits of her musing, hath liberty to propose to herself,
> though of highest hope and hardest attempting; whether that epic
> form, whereof the two poems of Homer, and those other two of Virgil
> and Tasso, are a diffuse, and *the book of Job a brief, model.*"

These words deserve particular notice. I do not doubt, that Milton
intended his Paradise Lost, as an Epic of the first class, and that the
poetic Dialogue of Job was his model for the general scheme of his
Paradise Regained. Readers would not have been disappointed in this
latter poem, if they had proceeded to it with a proper preconception of
the kind of interest intended to be excited in that admirable work.
In it's kind, it is the most *perfect* poem extant; tho' it's *kind* may be inferior Interest, being in it's essence didactic, to that other sort, in which
Instruction is conveyed more effectively, because more indirectly, in
connection with stronger & more pleasurable Emotions, & thereby in

H. N. Coleridge does not include this note in *Lit. Rem.*, but Raysor, *Misc. Crit.*, p.
344, gives it as transcribed by Alice D. Snyder.
[70] Letter to William Sotheby, postmarked April 28, 1808. Griggs, *Unp. Letters*,
I, 412-13.
[71] William Hayley, *Life of Milton* (London: 1796). The 1796 edition with notes
by Coleridge is in the Huntington Library, and these notes have been transcribed
from the original. They also appear in *Lit. Rem.*, I, 179-84, communicated by
Poole to H. N. Coleridge.

a closer affinity with action. But might we not as rationally object to an accomplished Woman's conversing, however agreeably, because it has happened that we have received a keener pleasure from her singing to the Harp? Si genus sit probo et sapienti homine haud indignum, et si poema sit in suo genere perfectum, satis est. Quod si hoc auctor idem altioribus numeris et carmini diviniori ipsum pene divinum superadderit, mehercule satis est, et plus quam satis. I cannot, however, but wish, that the answer of Jesus to Satan in the fourth book, l. 205, et sequentia,[72] had breathed the spirit of this noble quotation rather than the narrow bigotry of Gregory the Great. The passage indeed, is excellent, & is partially true; but partial Truth is the worse [sic] mode of conveying falsehood. S. T. C.

Hayley, MILTON, p. 75.

> The sincerest friends of Milton may here agree with Johnson, who speaks of *his controversial merriment as disgusting.*

The man who reads a work meant for immediate effect on one age, with the notions & feelings of another, may be a refined gentleman, but must be a sorry critic. Who posseses imagination enough to *live* with his forefathers and leaving comparative reflection for an after moment, to give himself up during the first perusal to the feelings of a contemporary, if not a partizan, will, I dare aver, rarely find any part of M.'s prose works *disgusting.*

Hayley, MILTON, p. 100-1, comment continued on p. 102.

> The odium which the president *justly* incurred in the trial of Charles seems to have prevented even our liberal historians from recording with candour the great qualities he possessed: he was undoubtedly not only an intrepid but a sincere enthusiast in the cause of the commonwealth.

Why *justly?* What would the contemptible Martyr-worshippers, (who yearly apply to this fraudulent would-be despot the most aweful phrases of holy writ concerning the Saviour of Mankind, concerning the Incarnate *Word* that is with *God* & is *God,* in a cento of ingenious blasphemy, that has no parallel in the annals of impious Adulation) what would even these men have? Can they, as men, expect that Bradshaw & his Peers, should give sentence against the Parliament & Armies of England, as guilty of all the blood that had been shed—as Rebels and Murderers! Yet there was no other alternative. That he or his peers were influenced by Cromwell is a gross Calumny, sufficiently confuted

---

[72] The lines referred to are:
Think not but that I know these things; or think
I know them not, not therefore am I short
Of knowing what I ought.

by their after lives & by their death-hour—& has been amply falsified by
Mrs. Hutchinson in her incomparable Life of her Incomparable Husband, Colonel Hutchinson. O that I might have such an action to remember on my Death-bed! The only enviable parts of Charles's Fate
& Life is that his name is connected with the greatest names of ancient
and modern times—Qui cum victus erat, *tantis* certasse feretur?[73] S. T.
Coleridge

Hayley, Milton, *pp. 103-4.* [*Concerning Milton's answer to* Icon
Basilice.]

> . . . for though he was certainly no imposter in imputing the prayer
> in question to the king, yet his considering the king's use of it as an
> offence against heaven, is a pitiable absurdity; an absurdity as glaring
> as it would be to affirm, that the divine poet is himself profane in assign-
> ing to a speech of the Almighty, in his poem, the two following verses:
>
> > Son of my bosom, son who art alone
> > My word, my wisdom, and effectual might—
>
> Because they are partly borrowed from a line in Virgil, addressed by a
> heathen goddess to her child:
>
> > Nate, meæ vires, mea magna potentia solus.

Assuredly, I regret that Milton should have written the passage
alluded to and yet the adoption of a prayer from a Romance on such an
occasion does not evince a delicate or deeply sincere Mind. We are the
creatures of association—there are some excellent moral & even serious
Lines in Hudibras, but what if a Clergyman should adorn his Sermon
with a quotation from that Poem? Would the abstract propriety of
the Lines leave him *"honorably acquitted?"* The Xtian Baptism of
a Line of Virgil is so far from being a parallel, that it is ridiculously
inappropriate, "an absurdity as glaring" as that of the bigoted puritans,
who objected to some of the noblest & most scriptural prayers ever dictated by wisdom & piety simply because the Catholics had used them.
S. T. C.

Hayley, Milton, *p. 107.*

> The *ambition* of Milton was as pure as his genius was sublime.

I do not approve of the so frequent use of this word relatively to
Milton. Indeed, the fondness of ingrafting a good sense on the word
"ambition," is not a Christian Impulse in general.

Hayley, Milton, *p. 110.*

> It was the opinion of Johnson, and Milton himself seems to have enter-
> tained the same idea, that it was allowable in literary contention to

---

[73] This is a modified version of Ovid's *Met.* 13, 1. 20.

ridicule, vilify, and depreciate as much as possible the character of an opponent. Surely this doctrine is unworthy of the great names who have endeavoured to support it . . .

If ever it were allowable, in this case it was especially so. But these general observations, without meditation on the particular times & genius of the times, are most often as unjust as they are always superficial.

Hayley, MILTON, p. 133.

With a mind full of fervid admiration for his [Cromwell's] marvellous atchievements, and generally disposed to give him credit for every upright intention, Milton hailed him as the father of his country, and delineated his character.

Besides, however, Milton might & did regret the immediate necessity, yet what alternative was there? Was it not better that Cromwell should usurp power to protect religious freedom at least, than that the Presbyterians should usurp it to introduce an accursed religious persecution; extending indeed the notion of spiritual concerns so far, as to leave no freedom even to a man's bedchamber?

Hayley, MILTON : CONJECTURES ON THE ORIGIN OF PARADISE LOST, p. 250.

In the course of this discussion we may find, perhaps, a mode of accounting for the inconsistency both of Dryden and Voltaire; let us attend at present to what the latter has said of Andreini!—If the Adamo of this author really gave birth to the divine poem of Milton, the Italian dramatist, whatever rank he might hold in his own country, has a singular claim to our attention and regard.

If Milton borrowed a hint from any writer, it was more probably from Strada's Prolusions, in which the fall of the Angels &c. is pointed out as the noblest subject for a Christian Poet. The more dissimilar the detailed images are, the more likely it is that a great genius should catch the general idea. S. T. C.

Hayley, MILTON : APPENDIX, Containing Extracts from the ADAMO of Andreini, p. 295. ADAMO, Act I, scene 2.

> Lucifer. Who from my dark abyss
> Calls me to gaze on this *excess of light?*

This is unfair & may suggest that Milton really had read & did imitate this Drama. The original is, "on so great Light." Indeed the whole translation is affectedly & inaccurately Miltonic.

> Forming thy works *of dust,*

of dirt.

      Let him unite above
      Star upon star, moon, sun.
Let him weave star to star
Then join both moon & sun!
      Since in the end division
      Shall prove his works, and all his efforts, vain.
derision.

      Since finally with censure and disdain
      Vain shall the work be, & his Toil be vain—

word for word

N. B. To procure & read Mirandola de Ente et Uno. In this book is found the Expression adopted by Milton Divini Splendoris caligine exoculati.[74]

Sol. p. 229 [Petrarch's Vit. Sol.] Compare Milton, P. L. Book the 5th—lines 350-355.[75]

Petrarch: Vit. Sol. p. 229. "Iste vero vel paucis, vel uno, &c.—pulchro fine concludat." *Might* possibly have suggested some thoughts in the Adam of Milton—tho' what noble Petrarch abstracted from his own Heart, why should not nobler Milton, in nobler Times, have received from the same Oracle—nothing can be baser than Parallelisms, when brought to invalidate the originality of a certainly original mind— nothing more pleasing than when they are merely to shew how the hearts of great men have sympathized in all ages.[76]

Luther's TABLE TALK, *chap. xxxii (1652), p. 364.*

> For they entred into the Garden about the hour at noon-daie, and having appetite to eat, shee took delight in the Apple, then about two of the clock (according to our accompt) was the fall.

Milton has adopted this notion in the Par. Lost—not improbably from this book.[77]

  In extension of the argument that all modern literature is but an imitation of the ancients, we find the commentators of our own Milton,

[74] Notebook 3½, fol. 4 recto. British Museum, Add. MSS, 47,499. Printed for the first time.

[75] Notebook 3½, p. 124. British Museum, Add. MSS, 47,499. Printed for the first time.

[76] Notebook 20, fol. 4 verso. British Museum, Add. MSS, 47,517. Printed for the first time.

[77] Martin Luther, *Colloquia Mensalia*, trans. Capt. Henry Bell (London: 1652). British Museum copy with Coleridge's notes, Ashley, 4773.

tracing each thought to some higher original and asserting because his subject had engaged a former pen that Genius does not belong and that at best he can claim no other merit than that of copyist—continue these truly absurd speculations and you may convince yourself that thought has not or never had an existence.[78]

Of the absurdity of tracing the growth of poetic Genius by ancestry: as if Dante or Milton were *creatures* of *wandering* Bards— Ritson & other Dullards are full of this nonsense.[79]

In the Paradise Lost—indeed, in every one of his poems—it is Milton himself whom you see; his Satan, his Adam, his Raphael, almost his Eve—are all John Milton; and it is a sense of this intense egotism that gives me the greatest pleasure in reading Milton's works. The egotism of such a man is a revelation of spirit.[80]

Shakspeare is the Spinozistic deity—an omnipresent creativeness. Milton is the deity of prescience; he stands *ab extra,* and drives a fiery chariot and four, making the horses feel the iron curb which holds them in. Shakspeare's poetry is characterless; that is, it does not reflect the individual Shakspeare; but John Milton himself is in every line of the Paradise Lost . . . There is a subjectivity of the poet, as of Milton, who is himself before himself in every thing he writes; and there is a subjectivity of the *persona,* or dramatic character, as in all Shakspeare's great creations, Hamlet, Lear, &c.[81]

What then shall we say?—Even this, Shakspear, no mere child of Nature, no Automaton of Genius, possessed by the Muse not possessing, first studied, deeply meditated, understood minutely—tho' knowledge became habitual gradually, added itself to his habitual feelings, & at length gave him that wonderful Power by which he stands alone, with no equal or second in his own class any where. It seated him on one of the two Golden Thrones of the English Parnassus, with Milton on the other. The one darting himself forth & passing into all the forms of human character & passion; the other attracting all forms and things to himself, into the unity of his own grand Ideal.—Sh. becomes all things, yet for ever remaining himself—while all things & forms be-

[78] Report of the Philosophical Lectures, 1819, Lecture X, March 1, pp. 2-3. MSS Egerton, 3057. Cf. Coburn, *Phil. Lect.*, p. 297.
[79] Notebook 14, fol. 6 verso-7 recto. British Museum, Add. MSS, 47,511. Printed for the first time.
[80] Aug. 18, 1833. *Table Talk S,* VI, 479.
[81] May 12, 1830. *Table Talk S,* VI, 312, 313.

come Milton. O what great men hast thou not produced, England, my country! Truly indeed—

> We must be free or die, who speak the tongue,
> Which SHAKSPEARE spake; the faith and morals hold,
> Which MILTON held. In every thing we are sprung
> Of earth's first blood, have titles manifold.
>
> WORDSWORTH[82]

If I could judge others by myself, I should not hesitate to affirm, that the most interesting passages in our most interesting Poems are those, in which the Author developes his own feelings. The sweet voice of Cona never sounds so sweetly as when it speaks of itself; and I should almost suspect that man of an unkindly heart, who could read the opening of the third book of the Paradise Lost without peculiar emotion.[83]

The destruction of Jerusalem is the only subject now remaining for an epic poem; a subject which, like Milton's Fall of Man, should interest all Christendom, as the Homeric War of Troy interested all Greece. There would be difficulties, as there are in all subjects; and they must be mitigated and thrown into the shade as Milton has done with the numerous difficulties in the Paradise Lost.[84]

Many Scriptural poems have been written with so much of Scripture in them, that what is not Scripture appears to be not true, and like mingling lies with the most sacred revelations. Now Milton, on the other hand, has taken for his subject that one point of Scripture of which we have the mere fact recorded, and upon this he has most judiciously constructed his whole fable. So of Shakespeare's "King Lear:" we have little historic evidence to guide or confine us, and the few facts handed down to us, and admirably employed by the poet, are sufficient, while we read, to put an end to all doubt as to the credibility of the story. It is idle to say that this or that incident is improbable, because history, as far as it goes, tells us that the fact was so and so. Four or five lines in the Bible include the whole that is said of Milton's story, and the Poet has called up that poetic faith, that conviction of

[82] Few ideas have been more often repeated by Coleridge than this famous comparison. It was given almost verbatim in the lectures on Milton and so impressed the reporters that they took it down with unusual accuracy for the newspapers. See the newspaper reports of the fourth lecture of the 1811-12 series, Raysor, *Shakes. Crit.*, II, 202-3. For other occurrences see *ibid.*, II, 95-96 and 278-79. *Biog. Lit. C*, II, 2 appears to be a variant of the above note which was given me by Miss Katheleen Coburn from her photograph of Notebook 1810, pp. 57-58.

[83] Preface to Coleridge's *Poems* (2d ed.; 1797), pp. xiv-xv.

[84] April 28, 1832. *Table Talk S*, VI, 392-93.

the mind, which is necessary to make that seem true, which otherwise might have been deemed almost fabulous.[85]

Among the conceptions, of the mere ideal character of which the philosopher is well aware, and which yet become necessary from the necessity of assuming a beginning; the original fluidity of the planet is the chief. Under some form or other it is expressed or implied in every system of cosmogony and even of geology, from Moses to Thales, and from Thales to Werner. This assumption originates in the same law of mind that gave rise to the *prima materia* of the Peripatetic school. In order to *comprehend,* and *explain* the *forms* of things, we must imagine a state *antecedent* to form. A chaos of heterogeneous substances, such as our Milton has described, is not only an *impossible* state (for this may be equally true of every other attempt), but it is *palpably* impossible. It presupposes, moreover, the thing it intended to solve; and makes *that* an *effect* which had been called in as the explanatory *cause.* The requisite and only serviceable fiction, therefore, is the representation of CHAOS as one vast homogeneous drop! In this sense it may be even justified, as an appropriate symbol of the great fundamental truth that all things spring from, and subsist in, the endless strife between indifference and difference. The whole history of Nature is comprised in the specification of the transitional states from the one to the other. The symbol only is fictitious: the thing signified is not only grounded in truth—it is the law and actuating principle of all other truths, whether physical or intellectual.[86]

PARADISE LOST, *V. 469-70; Anderson's* BRITISH POETS,[87] *V, 45. Note continued on pp. 46-47.*

> O Adam, one Almighty is, from whom
> All things proceed, and up to him return.

There is nothing wanting to render this a perfect enunciation of the only true system of Physics, but to declare the *"one first matter all"* to be a one Act or Power consisting in two Forces or opposite Tendencies, φύσις διπλοειδής potentialiter sensitiva; and all that follows, the same in different Potencies. For matter can neither be *ground* or distilled into spirit. The Spirit is an Island harbourless, and every way inaccessible: all it's contents are it's products, all it's denizens indigenous. Ergo, as matter could exist only for the Spirit, and as for the Spirit,

---

[85] Collier, *Seven Lect.,* Lecture IX, pp. 117-18.

[86] *Hints towards the Formation of a More Comprehensive Theory of Life,* ed. Seth B. Watson (London: 1848), pp. 67-68.

[87] From the set with Coleridge's notes in the Victoria and Albert Museum. See also Raysor, *Misc. Crit.,* p. 189.

it cannot exist, Matter as a *principle* does not exist at all; but as mode of Spirit, and derivatively, it may and does exist: it being indeed the intelligential act in it's first potency.

The most doubtful position in Milton's ascending series is the Derivation of Reason from the Understanding—without a medium. S. T. C.

The *story* of Milton might be told in two pages—it is this which distinguishes an *Epic Poem* from a *Romance in metre.* Observe the march of Milton—his severe application, his laborious polish, his deep metaphysical researches, his prayers to God before he began his great poem, all that could lift and swell his intellect, became his daily food. I should not think of devoting less than 20 years to an Epic Poem. Ten to collect materials and warm my mind with universal science. I would be a tolerable Mathematician, I would thoroughly know Mechanics, Hydrostatics, Optics, and Astronomy, Botany, Metallurgy, Fossilism, Chemistry, Geology, Anatomy, Medicine—then the *mind of man*—then the *minds* of *men*—in all Travels, Voyages and Histories. So I would spend ten years—the next five to the composition of the poem—and the five last to the correction of it.[88]

In my judgment, an epic poem must either be national or mundane. As to Arthur, you could not by any means make a poem on him national to Englishmen. What have *we* to do with him? Milton saw this, and with a judgment at least equal to his genius took a mundane theme —one common to all mankind. His Adam and Eve are all men and women exclusively. Pope satirizes Milton for making God the Father talk like a school divine. Pope was hardly the man to criticize Milton. The truth is, the judgment of Milton in the conduct of the celestial part of this story is very exquisite. Wherever God is represented as directly acting as Creator, without any exhibition of his own essence, Milton adopts the simplest and sternest language of the Scriptures. He ventures upon no poetic diction, no amplification, no pathos, no affection. It is truly the Voice or the Word of the Lord, coming to, and acting on, the subject Chaos. But, as some personal interest was demanded for the purposes of poetry, Milton takes advantage of the dramatic representation of God's address to the Son, the Filial Alterity, and in *those addresses* slips in, as it were by stealth, language of affection, or thought, or sentiment. Indeed, although Milton was undoubtedly

[88] To Joseph Cottle (Spring, 1797), Griggs, *Unp. Letters,* I, 71-72. This letter is given with many alterations by Cottle in *Reminiscences,* p. 77; and by Turnbull, *Biog. Epist.,* I, 130-31. Coleridge also says, "A Parliament of Poets could never have written the Paradise Lost." Notebook 22, fol. 18. British Museum, Add. MSS 47,520.

a high Arian in his mature life, he does in the necessity of poetry give a greater objectivity to the Father and the Son than he would have justified in argument. He was very wise in adopting the strong anthropomorphism of the Hebrew Scriptures at once. Compare the Paradise Lost with Klopstock's Messiah, and you will learn to appreciate Milton's judgment and skill quite as much as his genius.[89]

Notes on A Barrister's Hints on Evangelical Preaching *(1810), Part II, p. 47.*

. . . certain metaphysical dogmas concerning free will, or free will forfeited, *de libero vel servo arbitrio*—of grace, predestination, and the like;—dogmas on which, according to Milton, God and the Logos conversed, as soon as man was in existence, they in heaven, and Adam in paradise and the devils in hell . . .[90]

I have already received a hint that my "idol, *Milton,* has represented metaphysics as the subject which the bad spirits in hell delight in discussing."[91]

The addition of Fiction, such as that of the Quarrel between Satan and Beelzebub, could not have been blamed (unless we blame the Paradise Lost) had it been written before the Paradise Lost. But as all your Readers have learnt from Milton alone, that Satan and Beelzebub were different Persons (in the Scriptures they are different names of the same Evil Being) it produces an effect too light, too much savoring of capricious Invention, for the exceeding Solemnity of the Subject.[92]

But in its utmost abstraction and consequent state of reprobation, the Will becomes satanic pride and rebellious self-idolatry in the relations of the spirit to itself, and the remorseless despotism relatively to others; the more hopeless as the more obdurate by its subjugation of

[89] Sept. 4, 1833. *Table Talk S*, VI, 490. This point was also made in the lectures on Milton: see lecture above. Henry Crabb Robinson wrote to Mrs. Clarkson, Jan. 28, 1812, concerning the lecture in that series: "Coleridge's explanation of the character of Satan, and his vindication of Milton against the charge of falling below his subject, where he introduces the Supreme Being, and his illustration of the difference between poetic and abstract truth, and of the *diversity* in *identity* between the philosopher and the poet, were equally wise and beautifully demonstrated." Quoted by Raysor, *Shakes. Crit.*, II, 229-30.
[90] *Lit. Rem.*, IV, 347.
[91] *The Friend*, General Introduction, Essay XV, I, 180.
[92] To Joseph Cottle, March 7, 1815. Griggs, *Unp. Letters*, II, 129. The reference is to Cottle's poem, "Messiah."

sensual impulses, by its superiority to toil and pain and pleasure; in
short, by the fearful resolve to find in itself alone the one absolute
motive of action, under which all other motives from within and from
without must be either subordinated or crushed.

This is the character which Milton has so philosophically as well as
sublimely embodied in the Satan of his *Paradise Lost*.[93]

ROBINSON CRUSOE *(1812), II, 261, 263.*

> I entered into a long discourse with him about the devil, the original
> of him, his rebellion against God, his enmity to man, the reason of it,
> his setting himself up in the dark parts of the world to be worshipped
> instead of God, and as God, and the many stratagems he made use of
> to delude mankind to their ruin; how he had a secret access to our
> passions and to our affections and to adapt his snares to our inclina-
> tions, so as to cause us ever to be our own tempters, and run upon
> our destination by our own device.

I presume that Milton's "Par. Lost" must have been bound up with
one of Crusoe's Bibles, or I should be puzzled to know where he found
all this history of the Old Gentleman. Not a word of it in the Bible itself
I am quite sure. But to be serious, De Foe does not reflect that all
these difficulties are attached to a mere fiction or at best an allegory,
supported by a few popular phrases and figures of speech used incidentally or dramatically by the Evangelists and that the existence of a
Personal intelligent evil Being the counterpart and antagonist of God
is in direct contradiction to the most express declarations of Holy
Writ! Is there evil in the city and I have not done it? saith the Lord.
I do the evil and I do the good.[94]

The great defect of Houyhnhnms is not its misanthropy, and those
who apply this word to it must really believe that the essence of human
nature, that the *anthropos misoumenos,* consists in the shape of the
body. Now, to shew the falsity of this was Swift's great object; he
would prove to our feelings and imaginations, and thereby teach *practically* that it is Reason and Conscience which give all the loveliness
and dignity not only to Man, but to the shape of Man; that deprived
of these, and retaining the understanding, he would be the most loathsome and hateful of all animals; that his understanding would manifest

---

[93] *Statesman's Manual,* Appendix C, p. ix.

[94] Henry B. Wheatley, "Coleridge's Marginalia in a Copy of *Robinson Crusoe,*"
The Hampstead Annual (Hampstead, Eng.: 1902), pp. 104-5. Wheatley suggests:
"Coleridge appears to be quoting from memory the passage in Amos (iii: 6) 'Shall
there be evil in a city, and the Lord hath not done it.'" A. S. P. Woodhouse sug-
gested to the editor that Coleridge might be combining memories of Amos 3:6 and
Isaiah 45:7, "I form the light and create darkness; I make peace and create evil.
I the Lord do all these things."

itself only as malignant cunning, his free will as obstinacy and un-teachableness. And how true a picture this is every madhouse may convince any man; a brothel where highwaymen meet will convince every philosopher. But the defect of the work is its inconsistency; the Houyhnhnms are not rational creatures, *i. e.* creatures of perfect reason; they are not progressive; they have servants without any reason for their natural inferiority or any explanation how the difference acted [?]; and, above all, they—*i. e.* Swift himself,—has a perpetual affectation of being wiser than his Maker, and of eradicating what God gave to be subordinated and used; *ex. gr.* the maternal and paternal affection (στοργή). There is likewise a true Yahooism in the constant denial of the existence of Love, as not identical with Friendship, and yet distinct always and very often divided from Lust. The best defence is that it is a Satyr; still, it would have been felt a thousand times more deeply if Reason had been truly pourtrayed, and a finer imagination would have been evinced if the author had shewn the effects of the possession of Reason and the moral sense in the outward form and gestures of the Horses. In short, critics in general complain of the Yahoos; I complain of the Houyhnhnms.

As to the *wisdom* of adopting this mode of proving the great truths here exemplified, that is another question, which no feeling mind will find a difficulty in answering who has read and understood the Para-dise scenes in the 'Paradise Lost,' and compared the moral effect on his heart and his virtuous aspirations of Milton's Adam with Swift's horses; but different men have different turns of genius; Swift's may be good, tho' very inferior to Milton's; they do not stand in each other's way. S. T. C.[95]

I feel that it is impossible to defend Shakespeare from the most cruel of all charges,—that he is an immoral writer—without entering fully into his mode of pourtraying female characters, and of displaying the passion of love. It seems to me, that he has done both with greater perfection than any other writer of the known world, perhaps with the single ex-ception of Milton in his delineation of Eve.[96]

The latter part of your letter made me truly happy. Uriel himself should not be half as welcome; and indeed he, I must admit, was never any great favourite of mine. I always thought him a bantling of zoneless

[95] "Coleridge in *Gulliver's Travels*," *Athenæum* (Aug. 15, 1896), II, 224. See also Raysor's transcript in *Misc. Crit.*, pp. 128-30.
[96] Collier, *Seven Lect.*, Lecture VII, pp. 68-69.

Italian muses, which Milton heard cry at the door of his imagination and took in out of charity.[97]

I can understand and allow for an effort of the mind, when it would describe what it cannot satisfy itself with the description of, to reconcile opposites and qualify contradictions, leaving a middle state of mind more strictly appropriate to the imagination than any other, when it is, as it were, hovering between images. As soon as it is fixed on one image, it becomes understanding; but while it is unfixed and wavering between them, attaching itself permanently to none, it is imagination. Such is the fine description of Death in Milton:—[98]

> "The other shape,
> If shape it might be call'd, that shape had none
> Distinguishable in member, joint, or limb,
> Or susbtance might be call'd, that shadow seem'd,
> For each seem'd either; black it stood as night;
> Fierce as ten furies, terrible as hell,
> And shook a dreadful dart: what seem'd his head
> The likeness of a kingly crown had on."
>
> *Paradise Lost,* Book II.

The grandest efforts of poetry are where the imagination is called forth, not to produce a distinct form, but a strong working of the mind,[99] still offering what is still repelled, and again creating what is again rejected; the result being what the poet wishes to impress, namely, the substitution of a sublime feeling of the unimaginable for a mere image. I have sometimes thought that the passage just read might be quoted as exhibiting the narrow limit of painting, as compared with the boundless power of poetry: painting cannot go beyond a certain point; poetry rejects all control, all confinement. Yet we know that sundry painters have attempted pictures of the meeting between Satan and Death at the gates of Hell; and how was Death represented? Not as Milton has described him, but by the most defined thing that can be imagined—a skeleton, the dryest and hardest image that it is possible to discover; which, instead of keeping the mind in a state of activity, reduces it to the merest passivity,—an image, compared with which a square, a triangle, or any other mathematical figure, is a luxuriant fancy.[100]

I should guess that the minister was in the author's mind at the moment of composition, as completely ἀπαθής ἀναιμόσαρκος, as Anac-

[97] To W. Sotheby, July 13, 1802. Coleridge, E. H., *Letters*, I, 370.

[98] There is a similar comment in *A Diary of Thomas De Quincey*, ed. H. A. Eaton (London: Noel Douglas Replica, 1927), pp. 169-70.

[99] In Lecture IX, Series 1811-12, Coleridge said: "The Power of poetry is, by a single word perhaps, to instil that energy into the mind, which compels the imagination to produce the picture." Collier, *Seven Lect.*, p. 116.

[100] *Ibid.*, Lecture VII, pp. 64-66.

reon's grasshopper, and that he had as little notion of a real person of flesh and blood,

"Distinguishable in member, joint, or limb,"

as Milton had in the grim and terrible phantoms (half person, half allegory) which he has placed at the gates of Hell.[101]

Sonnetto
Sotto caliginose ombre profonde . . .
O invisible Sol, ch'a noi ti celi
Dentro abisso luminoso e fosco

Note the luminous *and* dark (or dusky black) gives an apparent incompatibility without any notice of the author's consciousness of it, or of it's intentionality—luminoso e fosco—it should at least be "yet" instead of "and"—& even thus how inferior to "dark with excess of light" in which the very wonder involves it's own explication, and while they excite that striving of thought and feeling of difficulty in the reader, which it is the Author's Object to do, yet reconcile it to his understanding by the very same words; words at once expressing and explaining an approximation to Incompatibility.[102]

The Imagination modifies images, and gives unity to variety; it sees all things in one, *il più nell' uno.* There is the epic imagination, the perfection of which is in Milton; and the dramatic, of which Shakspeare is the absolute master. The first gives unity by throwing back into the distance; as after the magnificent approach of the Messiah to battle, the poet, by one touch of himself—

——"far off their coming shone!"—

makes the whole one image. And so at the conclusion of the description of the appearance of the entranced angels, in which every sort of image, from all the regions of the earth and air is introduced to diversify and illustrate,—the reader is brought back to the single image by—

"He call'd so loud, that all the hollow deep
Of Hell resounded."

The dramatic imagination does not throw back, but brings close; it stamps all nature with one, and that its own, meaning, as in Lear throughout.[103]

---

[101] The reference is to Pitt in An Apologetic Preface to "Fire, Famine, and Slaughter," *Sib. Leaves*, p. 96.

[102] Notebook 18, fol. 98. British Museum, Add. MSS, 47,515. Printed for the first time.

[103] June 23, 1834. *Table Talk S*, VI, 518-19.

What can be finer in any poet than that beautiful passage in Milton—

"——Onward he moved
And thousands of his saints around."

This is grandeur, but is grandeur without completeness: but he adds—

"Far off their coming shone;"

which is the highest sublime. There is *total* completeness.

So I would say that the Saviour praying on the Mountain, the Desert on one hand, the Sea on the other, the city an immense distance below, was sublime. But I should say of the Saviour looking towards the City, his countenance full of pity, that he was majestic, and of the situation that it was grand.

When the whole and the parts are seen at once, as mutually producing and explaining each other, as unity in multiety, there results shapeliness—*forma formosa*. Where the perfection of *form* is combined with pleasurableness in the sensations, excited by the matters or substances so formed, there results the beautiful.

Corollary.—Hence colour is eminently subservient to beauty, because it is susceptible of forms, *i. e.* outline, and yet is a sensation. But a rich mass of scarlet clouds, seen without any attention to the *form* of the mass or of the parts, may be a delightful but not a beautiful object or colour.

When there is a deficiency of unity in the line forming the whole (as angularity, for instance), and of number in the plurality or the parts, there arises the formal.

When the parts are numerous, and impressive, and predominate, so as to prevent or greatly lessen the attention to the whole, there results the grand.

Where the impression of the whole, *i. e.* the sense of unity, predominates, so as to abstract the mind from the parts—the majestic.

Where the parts by their harmony produce an effect of a whole, but there is no seen form of a whole producing or explaining the parts, *i. e.* when the parts only are seen and distinguished, but the whole is felt—the picturesque.

Where neither whole not parts, but unity, as boundless or endless *allness*—the sublime.[104]

In my opinion the picturesque power displayed by Shakespeare, of all the poets that ever lived, is only equalled, if equalled, by Milton and Dante.[105]

[104] *Table Talk A*, pp. 323-24.
[105] Collier, *Seven Lect.*, Lecture IX, p. 115.

Is not Milton a sublimer poet than Homer or Virgil? Are not his personages more sublimely clothed, and do you now know that there is not perhaps *one page* in *Milton's* Paradise Lost in which he has not borrowed his imagery from the *Scriptures?* I allow and rejoice that *Christ* appealed only to the understanding and the affections; but I affirm that after reading Isaiah, or St. Paul's "Epistle to the Hebrews," Homer and Virgil are disgustingly *tame* to me, and Milton himself barely tolerable. . . . *You* may prefer to all this the quarrels of Jupiter and Juno, the whimpering of wounded Venus, and the jokes of the celestials on the lameness of Vulcan. Be it so (the difference in our tastes it would not be difficult to account for from the different feelings which we have associated with these ideas) ; I shall continue with Milton to say that

> "Zion Hill
> Delights me more, and Siloa's brook that flow'd
> Fast by the oracle of God!"[106]

The Poet should paint to the imagination, not to the fancy; and I know no happier case to exemplify the distinction between these two faculties. Master-pieces of the former mode of poetic painting abound in the writings of Milton, ex. gr.

> "The fig-tree; not that kind for fruit renown'd,
> But such as at this day, to Indians known
> In Malabar or Decan spreads her arms
> Branching so broad and long, that in the ground
> The bended twigs take root, *and daughters grow*
> *About the mother-tree, a pillar'd shade*
> *High over-arch'd, and* ECHOING WALKS BETWEEN:
> *There oft the Indian Herdsman, shunning heat*
> *Shelters in cool, and tends his pasturing herds*
> *At loop-holes cut through thickest shade."*
> MILTON, *P. L.* 9, 1100

This is *creation* rather than *painting*, or if painting, yet such, and with such co-presence of the whole picture flash'd at once upon the eye, as the sun paints in a camera obscura. But the poet must likewise understand and command what Bacon calls the *vestigia communia* of the senses, the latency of all in each, and more especially as by a magical *penna duplex*, the excitement of vision by sound and the exponents of sound. Thus, "THE ECHOING WALKS BETWEEN," may be almost said to reverse the fable in tradition of the head of Memnon, in the Egyptian statue. Such may be deservedly entitled the *creative words* in the world of imagination.[107]

[106] To John Thelwall, Dec. 17, 1796. Coleridge, E. H., *Letters*, I, 199-200.
[107] *Biog. Lit.*, II, 141-42.

'Shakespeare,' said Coleridge, 'is full of these familiar images and illustrations: Milton has them too, but they do not occur so frequently, because his subject does not so naturally call for them. He is the truest poet who can apply to a new purpose the oldest occurrences, and most usual appearances: the justice of the images can then always be felt and appreciated.'[108]

It is very remarkable that in no part of his writings does Milton take any notice of the great painters of Italy, nor, indeed, of painting as an art; while every other page breathes his love and taste for music. Yet it is curious that, in one passage in the Paradise Lost, Milton has certainly copied the *fresco* of the Creation in the Sistine Chapel at Rome. I mean those lines,—

> "now half appear'd
> The tawny lion, pawing to get free
> His hinder parts, then springs as broke from bonds,
> And rampant shakes his brinded mane;—" &c.

an image which the necessities of the painter justified, but which was wholly unworthy, in my judgment, of the enlarged powers of the poet. Adam bending over the sleeping Eve, in the Paradise Lost, and Dalilah approaching Samson, in the Agonistes, are the only two proper pictures I remember in Milton.[109]

I have said, that a combination of poetry with doctrines, is one of the characteristics of the Christian muse; but I think Dante has not succeeded in effecting this combination nearly so well as Milton . . .

By way of preparation to a satisfactory perusal of the Divina Commedia, I will now proceed to state what I consider to be Dante's chief excellences as a poet. And I begin with

I. Style—the vividness, logical connexion, strength and energy of which cannot be surpassed. In this I think Dante superior to Milton; and his style is accordingly more imitable than Milton's, and does to this day exercise a greater influence on the literature of his country. . . .

Nor have I now room for any specific comparison of Dante with Milton. But if I had, I would institute it upon the ground of the last canto of the Inferno from the 1st to the 69th line, and from the 106th to the end. And in this comparison I should notice Dante's occasional fault of becoming grotesque from being too graphic without imagination; as in his Lucifer compared with Milton's Satan. Indeed he is sometimes horrible rather than terrible—falling into the μισητόν instead of the δεινόν

---

[108] Nov. 1, 1811. Collier, *Seven Lect.*, p. xxxvi.
[109] Aug. 7, 1832. *Table Talk S*, VI, 409-10.

of Longinus;[110] in other words, many of his images excite bodily disgust, and not moral fear. But here, as in other cases, you may perceive that the faults of great authors are generally excellencies carried to an excess.[111]

The translator of the Bagavat Geeta [sic] finds, in the story of churning the ocean for the fourteen jewels, a wonderful affinity to— Milton! I could not I confess, help inferring from this remark that taste does not resemble the wines, that improve by a voyage to & from India. For if there be one character of genius predominant in Milton, it is this, that he never passes off bigness for greatness. Children can never make things big enough, and exactly so it is with the poets of India.[112]

Does the following Passage from p. 257 of Hill's Review of the Works of the R. Society[113] at all elucidate the phrase of living Sapphires, i. e. Stars, in Milton?[114]—"But the same Salmasius has proved very sufficiently the truth of our assertion, &c"—then—"then as to our Sapphire, it was unknown to them under that name, they called it the sky-blue Beryl. What they called Cyanus, is our Lapis Lazuli—and what they called Sapphire, the same stone, only that it had the gold-coloured marks disposed in Spots, in forms of *Stars*, in it, not in veins." Mem. to consult Salmasius, Plin. Exercit:[115]—which will doubtless quote it or it must refer to the passage in Theophrastus &c.[116]

Yet on the other hand I could readily believe that the mood and Habit of mind out of which the Hymn[117] rose, that differs from Milton's and Thomson's and from the Psalms, the source of all three, in the Author's addressing himself to *individual* objects as actually present to his Senses, while his great Predecessors apostrophize *classes* of things,

[110] *De. Subl.* 1. ix.   [111] *Lit. Rem.*, I, 157, 159, 165-66.
[112] Coleridge, *On the Divine Ideas*, Huntington Library MS, HM 8195, p. 269. Printed for the first time.
[113] John Hill, M.D., *Review of the Works of the Royal Society of London* (London: 1751).
[114] *Paradise Lost*, Book IV, l. 605:
      Silence was pleased: now glowed the Firmament
      With living Sapphires.
[115] C. Salmasii *Plinianæ exercitationes* in C. Julii Solini *Polyhistoria (Trajecta ad Rhenum*, 1689). Pliny, *The Natural History*, trans. John Bostock and H. G. Riley (Bohn Library; London: 1850-57), VI, 432, 437. "For sapphiros, too, is refulgent with spots like gold." The Asteriated sapphire is called "Star-stone." See also Theophrastus, *History of Stones*, with an English version by John Hill (London: 1746), Sec. 4, 23-24.
[116] Notebook 24, fol. 16 recto. British Museum, Add. MSS, 47,522. Printed for the first time.
[117] "A Hymn before Sunrise in the Vale of Chamouny." Cf. *Paradise Lost*, Book V, ll. 153 ff.

presented by the memory and generalized by the Understanding—I can readily believe, I say, that in this there may be too much of what the learned Med'ciners call the *Idiosyncratic* for true Poetry.[118]

It is not necessary that A or B should judge *at all* concerning poetry; but *if* he does, in order to a just taste, such and such faculties *must have* been developed in his mind. If a man, upon questioning his own experience, can detect no difference in *kind* between the enjoyment derived from the eating of turtle, and that from the perception of a new truth; if in his feelings a taste *for* Milton is essentially the same as the taste *of* mutton, he may still be a sensible and valuable member of society; but it would be a desecration to argue with him on the Fine Arts; and should he himself dispute on them, or even publish a book (and such books *have* been perpetrated within the memory of man) we can answer him only by silence, or a courteous waiving of the subject.   To tell a blind man, declaiming concerning light and color, "you should wait till you have got eyes to see with," would indeed be telling the truth, but at the same time be acting a useless as well as an inhuman part.   An English critic, who assumes and proceeds on the identity in kind of the pleasures derived from the palate and from the intellect, and who literally considers *taste* to mean one and the same thing, whether it be the taste of venison, or a taste for Virgil, and who, in strict consistence with his principles, passes sentence on Milton as a tiresome poet, because he finds nothing amusing in the Paradise Lost (i. e. damnat Musas, quia animum a musis non divertunt)—this taste-meter to the fashionable world gives a ludicrous portrait of an African belle, and concludes with a triumphant exclamation, "such is the ideal of beauty in Dahoma!"   Now it is curious, that a very intelligent traveller, describing the low state of the human mind in this very country, gives as an instance, that in their whole language they have no word for beauty, or the beautiful; but say either it is nice, or it is good; doubtless, says he, because this very sense is as yet dormant, and the idea of beauty as little developed in their minds, as in that of an infant.— I give the substance of the meaning, not the words; as I quote both writers from memory.[119]

Anderson's LIFE OF MILTON, BRITISH POETS,[120] *V, iv. Note continued on pp. v and vi.*

[118] To an Unknown Correspondent, 1820. Griggs, *Unp. Letters,* II, 262.
[119] "Principles of Genial Criticism," *Biog. Lit. S,* II, 225-26. Cf. Ashe, *Miscellanies,* pp. 12-13; Cottle, *Recollections,* p. 211.
[120] From the set with Coleridge's notes in the Victoria and Albert Museum. This note is from the original, but it has been printed by Raysor, *Misc. Crit.,* pp. 188-89.

He sold the copy [of *Paradise Lost*] to Samuel Simmons for Five Pounds in hand, Five pounds more when 1300 should be sold, and the same sum on the publication of the second and third Editions, for each edition. Of this agreement Milton received in all Fifteen Pounds; and his widow afterwards sold the claim for Eight.

In the nature of things this is impossible. Say rather that it is contradictory, as illustrating what it is meant to illustrate, the paltry payment for the P. L. I do not doubt the Fact, that is too well established! but I as little doubt that these 5 pounds were means to transfer the Property legally, & I could venture to determine that they were devoted by Milton to charitable purposes: a man might incautiously sell any Copy-right for £5; but would any man in his senses who wished to sell it, have bargained that after 1300 Copies, he should have 5£ more? If the sum was greater than now was not likewise Paper Printing &c., cheaper in the same proportion? I do not know the price at which the first Edition of Paradise Lost was sold—say only five Shillings— yet 1300 × 5 = 6500 s. = 325£. Say that the expenses of Publication, Paper, Printing, &c., cost an 100£ (in all probability not above 50£) still the net profit would be 225£; & this a man with his eyes open (for he states the number of the edition, 1300) *sells* for 10£. Nay, and nothing more was demanded, even tho' by the Sale of the first Edition the success of the Poem must have been then proved! and this too by Milton, who remained *the admired* of all parties, & the revered of a very numerous one, and with whose name "all Europe rung from side to side." Even so, I doubt not that it was Milton's injunction to his Widow to pursue the same course & not degrade the divine Muse by Merchandize. S. T. C.

Hacket, SCRINIA RESERATA *(1693), first page of flyleaf.*

A contemporary of Bishop Hacket's designates Milton as the author of a profane and lascivious poem entitled Paradise Lost. The biographer of our divine bard ought to have made a collection of all such passages. A German writer of a Life of Salmasius acknowledges that Milton had the better in the conflict in these words: 'Hans (Jack) von Milton— not to be compared in learning and genius with the incomparable Salmasius, yet a shrewd and cunning lawyer,' &c. *O sana posteritas!*[121]

I saw an old book at Coleorton in which Paradise Lost was described as an "obscene Poem."[122]

[121] See p. 220 n. 7. Taken from *Lit. Rem.*, III, 200-1.
[122] To Southey, February, 1819. Griggs, *Unp. Letters*, II, 247.

Let us suppose Milton in company with some stern and prejudiced Puritan, contemplating the front of York Cathedral, and at length expressing his admiration of its beauty. We will suppose it too at that time in his life, when his religious opinions, feelings, and prejudices most nearly coincided with those of the rigid Anti-prelatists.—P. Beauty; I am sure, it is not the beauty of holiness.—M. True; but yet it is beautiful.—P. It delights not me. What is it good for? Is it of any use but to be stared at?—M. Perhaps not! but still it is beautiful.—P. But call to mind the pride and wanton vanity of those cruel shavelings, that wasted the labor and substance of so many thousand poor creatures in the erection of this haughty pile.—M. I do. But still it is very beautiful.—P. Think how many score of places of worship, incomparably better suited both for prayer and preaching, and how many faithful ministers might have been maintained, to the blessing of tens of thousands, to them and their children's children, with the treasures lavished on this worthless mass of stone and cement.—M. Too true! but nevertheless it is *very* beautiful.—P. And it is not merely useless; but it feeds the pride of the prelates, and keeps alive the popish and carnal spirit among the people.—M. Even so! and I presume not to question the wisdom, nor detract from the pious zeal, of the first Reformers of Scotland, who for these reasons destroyed so many fabrics, scarce inferior in beauty to this now before our eyes. But I did not call it *good,* nor have I told thee, brother! that if this were levelled with the ground and existed only in the works of the modeller or engraver, that I should desire to reconstruct it. The GOOD consists in the congruity of a thing with the laws of the reason and the nature of the will, and in its fitness to determine the latter to actualize the former: and it is always discursive. The Beautiful arises from the perceived harmony of an object, whether sight or sound, with the inborn and constitutive rules of the judgement and imagination: and it is always intuitive. As light to the eye, even such is beauty to the mind, which cannot but have complacency in whatever is perceived as pre-configured to its living faculties. Hence the Greeks called a beautiful object καλόν quasi καλοῦν, i. e. *calling on* the soul, which receives instantly, and welcomes it as something connatural. . . .[123]

How the heart opens at the magic name of Milton! yet who shall, in our day, hang another garland upon his tomb? Eloquence has exhausted its treasures in his praise, and men of genius have rivalled each other in the splendour of their offerings at the shrine of the Bard. He

[123] "On the Principals of Genial Criticism," *Biog. Lit. S,* II, 242-43. Cf. Ashe, *Miscellanies,* pp. 30-31; Cottle, *Recollections,* p. 234.

has long ago taken his seat with Homer and with Shakspeare, one of the Poets of the World.

It belongs only to the noblest intellect thus to identify itself with all nations, and to find countrymen wherever the spirit of humanity dwells. Into the remotest seclusion of the civilized world, the voice of the "old man eloquent" has penetrated. Even the lone Icelander, placed,

> Far amid the melancholy main,

has listened in his own tongue to the Story of Paradise. As a poet, his genius was universal. He has left us models of excellence in every branch of his art. In the sublime epic, the noble drama, the picturesque mask, the graceful elegy, the vigorous sonnet,—in all he is equally great, equally beyond the reach of rivalry. His genius ripened with his years; and every poem he wrote was a step of purer gold to his Temple of Fame. His element was sublimity,—but he possessed, in an eminent degree, the opposite qualities of tenderness and grace. He who, with the power of heroic song, could stir the soul, as with the sound of a trumpet, knew also the "tender stops" of the pastoral flute; and the same hand that armed the rebellious legions, and built up the radiant domes of Pandemonium, mingled also the cup of enchantment in *Comus,* and strewed the flowers on the hearse of Lycidas.

But to Milton, far higher praise is due than mere genius, however, mighty, can demand. He has brought the Muse to the aid of piety, and confuted, in every line of his noble epics, the assertion of Gibbon, that his powers were "cramped by the system of our Religion, and never appeared to so great an advantage as when he shook it a little off." We may well glory, that:

> Piety has found
> Friends in the friends of science, and true prayer
> Has flowed from lips wet with Castalian dews.
> *The Task*[124]

PARADISE REGAINED

I object from principle to all fictions grounded on Scripture History —and more than all to any introduction of our Lord. Even the Paradise Regained offends my mind. Here what is not historic truth, is a presumptuous falsehood.[125]

[124] Willmott, *C. at Trinity,* pp. 5-6.
[125] Notebook 41, fol. 72 recto. British Museum, Add. MSS, 47,536. Printed for the first time.

The execution of Par. Regained is superior to that of Par. Lost, and that is all Milton meant in giving it a preference to the Par. Lost.[126]

Whoever was your Informer, can likewise tell you that the immediately preceding part of the Lecture[127] had been of a (*for me*) unusually cheerful and even mirth-exciting nature—and in speaking of a sublime Invention of Milton, unsupported by the natural and obvious sense of the Text (for had it been a mere quotation, like that of "Let there be Light! etc.," where had been *his* Sublimity?)   I said in previous explanation these very words: "*for Milton has been pleased to represent Satan as a sceptical Socinian.*"

Now had I said, that Milton had represented Satan as convinced of the prophetic and Messianic character of Christ, but sceptical concerning any higher claims, I should have stated the mere matter of fact—and can I think it possible that you should for ever withhold your affection and esteem from me merely because most incautiously and with improper Levity, I confess and with unfeigned sorrow, I conveyed the very same thoughts or fact in a foolish Phrase?[128]

Dr. Estlin, I found, is raising the city against me, as far as he and his friends can, for having stated a mere matter of fact, viz.—that Milton had represented Satan as a sceptical Socinian—which is the case, and I could not have explained the excellence of the sublimest single Passage in all his writings had I not previously informed the Audience, that Milton had represented Satan as knowing the prophetic and Messianic Character of Christ, but was sceptical as to any higher Claims—and what other definition could Dr. E. himself give of a sceptical Socinian?   Now that M. has done so, please to consult Par. Regained, Book IV from line 196—and then the same. book from line 500.[129]

Dr. Estlin has contrived not only to pick a gratuitous quarrel with me, but by his female agents to rouse men who should be ashamed of such folly, for my saying in a Lecture on the Paradise Regained, that Milton had been pleased to represent the Devil as a sceptical Socinian. Alas! if I *should* get well—wo' to the poor Doctor and to his Unitarians!

[126] Henry Crabb Robinson's Diary, Dec. 23, 1810.   From MS volume of *Reminiscences*, 1834, p. 433.   In Dr. Williams's Library, Sadler (I, 200) expanded the comment, changed the meaning somewhat, at least by implication, and added a sentence.

[127] A lecture on Milton given at Bristol.   Cf. Cottle, *Reminiscences*, p. 249.

[128] To the Rev. John P. Estlin, April 9, 1814.   Griggs, *Unp. Letters*, II, 105.

[129] To Joseph Cottle, April 26, 1814.   Griggs, *Unp. Letters*, II, 109.

They have treated me so ungenerously that I am by the allowance of all my friends let loose from all bonds of delicacy. Estlin has behaved downright cruel and brutal to me.[130]

PARADISE REGAINED, *Book IV, ll. 563-81. Anderson's* BRITISH POETS,[131] *V, 123.*

> But Satan with amazement fell.
> As when Earth's son Antæus (to compare
> Small things with greatest) in Irassa strove
> With Jove's Alcides . . .

O that these eighteen lines had been omitted. Here, as in one other Instance in the Par. Lost, Power & Fertility injure Strength & Majesty.

> "And what he brings, what needs he elsewhere seek?"
> PARADISE REGAINED

A sophism, which I fully agree with Warburton, is unworthy of Milton; how much more so of the awful person, in whose mouth he has placed it?[132]

SAMSON AGONISTES

Milton's Introduction to SAMSON AGONISTES; *Anderson's* BRITISH POETS,[133] *V, 125-56.*

> Division into act and scene, referring chiefly to the stage (to which this Work never was intended) is here omitted.
> It suffices if the whole drama be found not produced beyond the fifth act.

The submission of Milton's mind to the Ancients indiscriminately (spite of the declaration, in Par. Reg. B. IV (in this Vol., p. 121) is here curiously exemplified.

The play has *no* acts: for Aristotle prescribes none, & the Greek Tragedies knew of no such division—But yet it is not extended beyond the 5th act—for a line of Horace (a mere *ipse dixit* without one reason assigned & therefore probably founded on some accident of the Roman Stage) enjoins the *non quinto productior actu.* Into such contradictions could overweening Reverence of Greek & Latin authorities seduce the greatest & most judicious of men. And from the same cause must

---

[130] To John J. Morgan, Sunday, May 15, 1814. Griggs, *Unp. Letters*, II, 113.

[131] From the set in the Victoria and Albert Museum. The above note is transcribed from the original note by Coleridge, but it has been printed by Raysor, *Misc. Crit.*, p. 189.

[132] *Biog. Lit.*, I, 143. The line quoted is from *Paradise Regained*, Book IV, l. 325. H. N. C. substitutes "thinking Being" for "awful person."

[133] From the set in the Victoria and Albert Museum. This note is transcribed from the original, but it has been printed by Raysor, *Misc. Crit.*, p. 190.

we explain the stern censure on the Heterogeneous (comic Stuff with Tragic Gravity) as applied to Shakespear. Milton had not reflected, that Poetry is capable of subsisting under two different modes, the Statuesque—as Sophocles—and the Picturesque, as Shakespear—the former producing a Whole by the separation of Differents, the latter by the balance, counteraction, inter-modification, & final harmony of Differents. Of this latter, Shakespear is the only Instance. In all other writers Tragi-comedy merits all, that Milton has here affirmed concerning it. S. T. C.

Milton's "Samson Agonistes" being introduced as a topic, Coleridge said, with becoming emphasis, that it was the finest imitation of the ancient Greek drama that ever had been, or ever would be written. One of the company remarked that Steevens (the commentator on Shakespeare) had asserted that "Samson Agonistes" was formed on the model of the ancient Mysteries, the origin of our English drama; upon which Coleridge burst forth with unusual vehemence against Steevens, asserting that he was no more competent to appreciate Shakespeare and Milton than to form an idea of the grandeur and glory of the seventh heavens . . .[134]

This is the Logical Pentad; Prothesis, Thesis, Antithesis, Mesothesis (Or the *Indifference* of Thesis and Antithesis, *i. e.* that which is both in either, but in different Relations; while the Prothesis is both as one in one and the same relation) and lastly the Synthesis. . . .

Painting is the Mesothesis of thing and thought. A coloured wax peach is one *thing* passed off for another thing—a practical lie, and not a work appertaining to the Fine Arts—a delusion—not an imitation. Every imitation as contra-distinguished from a copy, is a Mesothesis, but which according to the variable propiority to the Thesis or the Antithesis may be called the librating Mesothesis. Thus, Real and Ideal are the two poles, the Thesis and Antithesis. The Sophoclean drama, or the Samson Agonistes is the Mesothesis in its propiority or comparative proximity to the ideal—the tragedies of Heywood, Ford, &c. (*ex. gr.*, The Woman killed by Kindness,) is the Mesothesis in comparative proximity to the Real, while the Othello, Lear, &c., is the *Mesothesis* as truly as possible ἐν μέσῳ though with a *clinamen* to the ideal.[135]

The styles of Massinger's plays and the Samson Agonistes are the two extremes of the arc within which the diction of dramatic poetry

[134] Collier, *Seven Lect.*, p. xxvii. Report of a conversation. From his diary, Oct. 17, 1811.
[135] *Notes Theolog.*, pp. 402, 404.

may oscillate. Shakspeare in his great plays is the midpoint. In the Samson Agonistes, colloquial language is left at the greatest distance, yet something of it is preserved, to render the dialogue probable: in Massinger the style is differenced, but differenced in the smallest degree possible, from animated conversation, by the vein of poetry.

There's such a divinity doth hedge our Shakspeare round, that we can not even imitate his style. I tried to imitate his manner in the Remorse, and, when I had done, I found I had been tracking Beaumont and Fletcher and Massinger instead. It is really very curious. At first sight, Shakspeare and his contemporary dramatists seem to write in styles much alike; nothing so easy as to fall into that of Massinger and the others; while no one has ever yet produced one scene conceived and expressed in the Shaksperian idiom. I suppose it is because Shakspeare is universal, and, in fact, has no *manner;* just as you can so much more readily copy a picture than Nature herself.[136]

Samson Agonistes—Choruses of, ˘ – &c. = common blank verse line.

Samson

1. ˘ – &c.

2. ˘ ˘ – ˘ ˘ ˘ | – | – ˘ | ˘ –

3. ˘ – | ˘ – | – | ˘ – | –

4, 5, 6. ˘ – &c.

7. ˘ – | ˘ – | ˘ –

8. ˘ – | ˘ – | ˘ –

9. ˘ – | ˘ – | ˘ –

10. – ˘ | ˘ – | ˘ – ˘ – ˘ – –

11, 12. ˘ – – &c.

13. ˘ – | ˘ – | ˘ –

From 13 to 28 ˘ – &c. except 25 = 3 Iambics. 28, 29, 30 = 25. Then concludes with 5 ˘ – &c.

Chorus

– – – – – ˘ ˘ –
– ˘ – ˘ – ˘ – ˘
˘ – ˘ – ˘ – | – ˘ ˘ –
– – – – ˘ – ˘ | – ˘ ˘ | ˘ –
˘ – ˘ – ˘ –
˘ – | – – | ˘ – ˘

[136] Feb. 17, 1833. *Table Talk S*, VI, 426-27 n.

˘ − | ˘ − | ˘ − ˘

˘ − ˘ | − ˘ | − − ˘ | −

˘ − ˘ −

˘ − | ˘ − | ˘ − | ˘ − | ˘ − | ˘ −   N. B. Hexameter Iambic

− ˘ | − ˘ − ˘ −

− ˘ | − ˘ ˘ | − − | − | ˘ −

3 Hexameter Iambics

˘ − ˘ − ˘ −

− − ˘ − ˘ − | − ˘ ˘ − ˘ ˘

Pentameter Iambic hyperacatalectic
Pentam. Iamb. acatalectic

$$\left. \begin{array}{l} \text{˘ ˘ − | − ˘ | −} \\ \text{˘ − ˘ − ˘ − ˘ −} \end{array} \right\} \text{rhymes}$$

Then 15 Pentam. & Hexameter Iambics mixt.[137]

It is especially with reference to the drama, and its characteristics in any given nation, or at any particular period, that the dependence of genius on the public taste becomes a matter of the deepest importance. I do not mean that taste which springs merely from caprice or fashionable imitation, and which, in fact, genius can and by degrees will, create for itself; but that which arises out of wide-grasping and heart-enrooted causes, which is epidemic, and in the very air that all breathe. This it is which kills, or withers, or corrupts. Socrates, indeed, might walk arm and arm with Hygeia, whilst pestilence, with a thousand furies running to and fro, and clashing against each other in a complexity and agglomeration of horrors, was shooting her darts of fire and venom all round him. Even such was Milton; yea, and such, in spite of all that has been babbled by his critics in pretended excuse for his damning; because for them too profound excellencies,—such was Shakspeare. But alas! the exceptions prove the rule. For who will dare to force his way out of the crowd,—not of the mere vulgar,—but of the vain and banded aristocracy of intellect, and presume to join the almost supernatural beings that stand by themselves aloof?[138]

I understand why the ancients called Euripides the most tragic of their dramatists: he evidently embraces within the scope of the tragic poet many passions,—love, conjugal affection, jealousy, and so on, which

[137] Notebook 12, fol. 30 verso-32 recto.   British Museum, Add. MSS, 47,509. Printed for the first time.
[138] ''Lectures upon Shakespeare and other Dramatists,'' *Lit. Rem.*, II, 47-48.

Sophocles seems to have considered as incongruous with the ideal statu-
esqueness of the tragic drama . . .

There is nothing very surprising in Milton's preference of Euripides,
though so unlike himself. It is very common—very natural—for men
to *like* and even admire an exhibition of power very different in kind
from any thing of their own. No jealously arises. Milton preferred Ovid
too, and I dare say he admired both as a man of sensibility admires a
lovely woman, with a feeling into which jealousy or envy cannot enter.
With Æschylus or Sophocles he might perchance have matched himself.

In Euripides you have oftentimes a very near approach to comedy,
and I hardly know any writer in whom you can find such fine models
of serious and dignified conversation.[139]

Knight, TASTE,[140] *pp. 122-23. Comment continued on p. 124. [Quota-
tions from* PARADISE LOST, *Book IX, ll. 1026-38, and Pope's translation
of the* ILIAD, *Book III, ll. 549-54.]*

> Adam's argument in this case, is certainly more pointed and logical,
> than that of the young Trojan; but pointed and logical argument is
> not what the case required. The rapturous glow of enthusiastic passion,
> with which the latter addresses his mistress, would have much more
> influence upon the affections of an amorous lady, though it may be
> less satisfactory to the understanding of a learned critic . . .

What a Booby; Milton is describing sinful appetite the evidence &
seal of the highest guilt: what had this to do with the rapturous glow of
enthusiastic passion! his versification is perturbed like the feelings of
our degraded parent. Contrast the movement of the verse here with
those passages when it is really his aim to describe rapturous admiration
& so forth—Sweet is the breath of morn &c. [several words crossed out]
—Or when he describes to Raphael his nuptials with Eve, though there
is more perturbation than to the Angel appeared consistent with his
dignity as a sinless creature and accordingly he warns Adam against
it.

Knight, TASTE, *pp. 128-29.*

> The collocation of words, according to the order of desire or imagination,

[139] July 1, 1833. *Table Talk S*, VI, 464, 466.

[140] The marginalia in Richard Payne Knight's *An Analytical Inquiry into the
Principles of Taste* (3d ed.; London: 1806) have been considered as the joint
work of Coleridge and Wordsworth, with the larger number of the notes in Wordsworth's hand. See "Wordsworth and Coleridge Marginalia in a Copy of Richard
Payne Knight's *Analytical Inquiry into the Principles of Taste*," *Huntington
Library Quarterly*, I (October, 1937), 63-99. See also Julian Lindsay's "A Note
on the Marginalia," *ibid.*, pp. 95-99. Certainly, however, the ideas are those of
Coleridge and the handwriting is no worse than, say, that of Coleridge's note on the
board of *Osorio*.

it is easy to perceive, must have been much better adapted to the purposes of poetry, than the collocation of them according to the order
of the understanding; but a variety of flexible terminations is absolutely
necessary to make words, so arranged, intelligible; and, in these, all
the polished languages of modern Europe are defective: wherefore it is
impossible that they should ever rival those of the Greeks and Romans
in poetical diction and expression.

It is so far from being impossible that the writings of Shakespear
and Milton infinitely transcend those of the Greeks and for reasons which
might easily *be given.*

Knight, TASTE, *p. 130.*

> . . . but Milton and other epic and moral writers in blank verse, who
> viewed nature through the medium of books, and wrote from the head
> rather than the heart, have often employed the inverted order merely
> to stiffen their diction, and keep it out of prose; an artifice, of all others,
> the most adverse to the genuine purposes of a metrical or poetical style.

Milton wrote chiefly from the Imagination which you may place
where you like in head heart liver or veins. *Him* the Almighty Power
hurled headlong &c. see one of the most wonderful sentences ever formed
by the mind of man. The instances of imaginative and impassioned
inversion in Milton are innumerable. Take for instance the first sentence
of his Poem. Of mans first Disobedience &c.

Knight, TASTE, *p. 400.*

> Our blank verse, though used as an heroic metre, and appropriated
> to the most elevated subjects, is, like the Greek iambic, too near to the
> tone of common colloquial speech to accord well with such flights; nor do
> I believe that it would be possible to translate the above cited passage
> of Virgil [the formation of the thunder-bolts of Jupiter] into it, with-
> out losing all its poetical spirit, and consequently making it appear
> nonsensical as well as insipid.

What nonsense Does this Prater pour out. Let him read the sixth
Book of Paradise Lost, and he will find that almost every line gives the
lie to this libel—But it is little less than blasphemy in me to think of
comparing this trash of Virgil, with the Chariot of the Messiah, or his
advance toward the rebel Angels; or with the first shock of the en-
countering armies.[141]

Knight, TASTE, *p. 402.*

> The imagery of Milton, as before observed, is often confused and
> obscure; and so far it is faulty: but, nevertheless, I can find neither
> confusion nor obscurity in the passage, which has been so confidently
> quoted [i. e. by Burke] as an instance of both.

[141] Cf. Coleridge's comment, June 23, 1834, *Table Talk S*, VI, 518-19, for similar comment on this passage.

> He above the rest,
> In shape and gesture proudly eminent,
> Stood like a tower: his form had yet not lost
> All its original brightness, nor appeared . . .
> Perplexes monarchs.

You Rogue—*hêr*—this little blunder lets out the whole secret if any there had been; viz that Mr. K. is incapable of the slightest relish of the appropriate grandeur of Milton's poetry.

Knight, TASTE, *pp. 403-4. Comment continued on p. 405.*

The imagery in the description of the allegorical personage of death by the same great author must, however, be admitted to be indistinct, confused, and obscure; and, by being so, loses much of its sublimity:
> —the other shape,
> If shape it might be call'd, that shape had none,

is a confused play of words in Milton's worst manner.

This author confounds indeterminateness with dimness or inadequacy of communication. He perceives in the Fell Thirst of Gray an instance of this latter; but here in Milton is no inadequacy of dimness but the utmost liveliness in conveying the Idea which was that of a shape so perpetually changing upon the eye of the spectator and so little according in any of its appearances with Forms to which we are accustomed that the poet cannot without hesitation apply the familiar word shape to it at all—in like manner with substance. The Phantom had a *likeness* to a head & to a kingly crown but a likeness only—all which beautifully accords with our author concerning death.[142]

Knight, TASTE, *p. 404.*

> Fierce as ten Furies, terrible as hell,

are comparisons that mean nothing; as we know still less of the fierceness of furies or terrors of hell, than we do those of death; and fierceness is a mental energy, and not a positive quality, that can be measured by a scale of number. Ten furies may have collectively more strength than one; because the mechanic strength of many individuals may be concentered into one act or exertion; but this is not the case with fierceness.

That is false because the fierceness of one may animate that of another.

Knight, TASTE, *p. 408.*

Virgil has perhaps hurt the effect by making them actually engage in the mighty attempt instead of merely designing or aiming at it—

[142] Cf. Collier, *Seven Lect.*, Lecture VII, pp. 64-66, for comment on same passage.

Ter sunt conati imponere Pelio Ossam
Scilicet, atque Ossæ frondosum involvere Olympum:
Ter Pater extructos disjecit fulmine montes—

and Claudian has quite spoiled it by making his giants complete the attempt, in which he has been followed by Milton in his battle of the angels, a part of the Paradise Lost, which has been more admired, than, I think, it deserves.

The fact is that as far as Physical Power goes Homer's Achilles his Giants and his Jupiters and Neptunes are contemptible Creatures compared with the Angels of Milton, as is strikingly illustrated by the close of the fourth Book of Paradise Lost, where the Poet does not trust them to a conflict in this visible universe, for the whole would have gone to wrack before them.

Haec quicunque legit certem circumesse putabit
Mementur Priapus Virgilium inlicis.

Richard Crashaw

Crashaw seems in his poems to have given the first ebullience of his imagination, unshapen into form, or much of, what we now term, sweetness. In the poem Hope, by way of question and answer, his superiority to Cowley is self-evident. In that on the name of Jesus equally so; but his lines on St. Theresa are the finest.

Where he does combine richness of thought and diction nothing can excel,[1] as in the lines you so much admire—

Since 'tis not to be had at home,
She'l travel to a martyrdome.
No home for her confesses she,
But where she may a martyr be.
She'l to the Moores, and trade with them
For this invalued diadem,
She offers them her dearest breath,
With Christ's name in't, in change for death.
She'l bargain with them, and will give
Them God, and teach them how to live
In Him, or if they this deny,
For Him she'l teach them how to die.

[1] Coleridge gives the text of the first edition of *Steps to the Temple* (London: 1646). For "she offers" the edition of 1652 substitutes "she'l offer," and "Her Lord's" for "The Lord's" below.

> So shall she leave amongst them sown
> The Lord's blood, or, at least, her own.
> Farewell then, all the world—adieu,
> Teresa is no more for you;
> Farewell all pleasures, sports and joys,
> Never till now esteemed toys—
> Farewell whatever dear'st may be,
> Mother's arms or father's knee;
> Farewell house, and farewell home,
> She's for the Moores and martyrdom.

These verses were ever present to my mind whilst writing the second part of Christabel; if, indeed, by some subtle process of the mind they did not suggest the first thought of the whole poem.—Poetry, as regards small poets, may be said to be, in a certain sense, conventional in its illustrations; thus Crashaw uses an image:—

> As sugar melts in tea away;

which, although *proper then*, and *true now*, was in bad taste at that time equally with the present. In Shakspeare, in Chaucer there was nothing of this.[2]

Anderson, BRITISH POETS:[3] LIFE OF CRASHAW, *IV, 706.*

With the exception of only two lines ("Yet doth not stay To ask the windows leave to pass that way") I recollect few Poems of equal length so perfect in suo genere, so passionately supported, & closing with so grand a Swell, as that (719) *On a Prayer-book, sent to Mrs. M. R.* S. T. C.

Anderson, BRITISH POETS, *"The Weeper," st. vi, IV, 707.*

> Not in the evening's eyes
> When they red with weeping are.

Better—Tho' they red with weeping were.

Who but must regret, that the Gift of Selection, and, of course, of Rejection, had not been bestowed on this sweet poet in some proportion to his Power and Opulence of Invention! I have ventured throughout to mark the Stanzas,[4] by the mere omission of which the finer Poems would have increased in weight, no less than Polish. However justly the modern Chemists may triumph over the doctrine of Phlogiston or

[2] Allsop, *Letters*, I, 194-96. Cf. *Table Talk A*, pp. 321-22.
[3] From the set in the Victoria and Albert Museum. The notes are transcribed from the original, but they have been printed by Raysor, *Misc. Crit.*, pp. 277-79. Only the notes which contribute to the criticism of Crashaw's poems are reproduced here.
[4] Sts. 3, 4, 5, 10, 17 in this poem are so marked.

positive Levity, there exists undeniably a poetic Phlogiston which adds by being abstracted and diminishes by it's presence.

S. T. Coleridge

Anderson, BRITISH POETS, *"A Hymn to the Name and Honour of the Admirable Saint Teresa," IV, 721.*

An admirable Poem; but the two first ¶s *most* admirable. Here indeed præcipitatur liber Spiritus.

Anderson, BRITISH POETS, *"In the Glorious Epiphany of Our Lord God," IV, 741.*

Crashaw is far too apt to weary out a Thought.

Samuel Butler

Is this the land of liberal Hearts!
Is this the land, where Genius ne'er in vain
Pour'd forth her soul-enchanting strain?
Ah me! yet Butler 'gainst the bigot foe
    Well-skill'd to aim keen Humour's dart,
    Yet Butler felt Want's poignant sting;
    And Otway, Master of the Tragic art,
    Whom Pity's self had taught to sing,
    Sank beneath a load of Woe;
This ever can the generous Briton hear,
And starts not in his eye th'indignant Tear?[1]

I shall shortly publish a second Volume of Poems—
    My Poverty, & not my will consenting.
I have likewise written a Tragedy & a Farce, & have planned out a long comic Poem, of regular & epic construction, as long as Hudibras; but tho' with infinitely less wit, yet I trust with more humour, more variety of character, & a far, far more entertaining, & interesting Tale. Each book will be in a different metre, but all in rhyme—& each Book a regular metre. It seems to me, that a comic Epic Poem lies quite new and untouched to me—Hudibras is rather a series of Satires than a comic

---

[1] "Monody on the Death of Chatterton," ll. 13-23.

Poem.—My plan does not exclude the utmost beauty of Imagery & poetic Diction, and some parts will be serious and pathetic.[2]

Perhaps the most important of our intellectual operations are those of detecting the difference in similar, and the identity in dissimilar, things. Out of the latter operation it is that wit arises; and it, generically regarded, consists in presenting thoughts or images in an unusual connection with each other, for the purpose of exciting pleasure by the surprise. This connection may be real; and there is, in fact, a scientific wit; though where the object, consciously entertained, is truth, and not amusement, we commonly give it some higher name. But in wit popularly understood, the connection may be, and for the most part is, apparent only, and transitory; and this connection may be by thoughts, or by words, or by images. The first is our Butler's especial eminence; the second, Voltaire's; the third, which we oftener call fancy, constitutes the larger and more peculiar part of the wit of Shakspere . . . When serious satire commences, or satire that is felt as serious, however comically drest, free and genuine laughter ceases; it becomes sardonic. This you experience in reading Young, and also not unfrequently in Butler. The true comic is the blossom of the nettle.[3]

Were it my task to form the mind of a young man of Talent, desirous to establish his belief on solid principles, and in the light of distinct understanding, I would commence his theological studies, or, at least, that most important part of them respecting the aids which Religion promises in our attempts to realize the ideas of Morality, by bringing together all the passages scattered throughout the Writings of Swift and Butler, that bear on Enthusiasm, Spiritual Operations, and pretences to the Gifts of the Spirit, with the whole train of New Lights, Raptures, Experiences, and the like. For all that the richest Wit, in intimate union with profound Sense and steady Observation, can supply on these Topics, is to be found in the works of these Satirists; though unhappily alloyed with much that can only tend to pollute the Imagination.

Without stopping to estimate the degree of caricature in the Portraits sketched by these bold Masters, and without attempting to determine in how many of the Enthusiasts, brought forward by them in proof of the influence of false Doctrines, a constitutional Insanity,

[2] To Samuel Purkis, Feb. 1, 1803. From the original MS in the Huntington Library, HM 12,109. Cf. Griggs, *Unp. Letters*, I, 245.

[3] "Wit and Humor," Ashe, *Miscellanies*, pp. 121, 122. In British Museum, Add. MSS, 34,225, fol. 75 the final section above reads: "When serious satire commences or satire that is felt as serious however comically drest, the *free* Laughter ceases—it becomes Sardonic—Felt in Young's Satire—not uninistanced in Butler—the truly Comic in the *Blossom of the Nettle*."

that would probably have shown itself in some other form, would be the truer Solution, I would direct my Pupil's attention to one feature common to the whole Group—the pretence, namely, of possessing, or a Belief and Expectation grounded on other men's assurances of their possessing, an immediate Consciousness, a sensible Experience, of the Spirit in and during its operation on the soul. It is not enough that you grant them a consciousness of the Gifts and Graces infused, or an assurance of the Spiritual Origin of the same, grounded on their correspondence to the Scripture *Promises,* and their conformity with the *Idea* of the divine Giver. No! They all alike, it will be found, lay claim (or at least look forward) to an inward perception of the Spirit itself and its operating.

Whatever must be misrepresented in order to be ridiculed, is in fact *not* ridiculed; but the thing substituted for it. It is a Satire on something else, coupled with a Lie on the part of the Satirist, who knowing, or having the means of knowing the truth, chose to call one thing by the name of another. The Pretentions to the Supernatural, *pilloried* by Butler, sent to Bedlam by Swift, and (on their re-appearance in public) *gibbeted* by Warburton, and *anatomized* by Bishop Lavington, one and all, have *this* for their essential character, that the Spirit is made the immediate Object of Sense or Sensation . . .[4]

The definition of good Prose is—proper words in their proper places —of good Verse—the most proper words in their proper places. The propriety is in either case relative. The words in prose ought to express the intended meaning, and no more; if they attract attention to themselves, it is, in general, a fault. In the very best styles, as Southey's, you read page after page, understanding the author perfectly, without once taking notice of the medium of communication; it is as if he had been speaking to you all the while. But in verse you must do more; there the words, the *media,* must be beautiful, and ought to attract your notice—yet not so much and so perpetually as to destroy the unity which ought to result from the whole poem. This is the general rule, but, of course, subject to some modifications, according to the different kinds of prose or verse. Some prose may approach towards verse, as oratory, and therefore a more studied exhibition of the *media* may be proper; and some verse may border more on mere narrative, and there the style should be simpler. But the great thing in poetry is, *quocunque modo,* to effect a unity of impression upon the whole; and a too great fulness and profusion of point in the parts will prevent this. Who can read with pleasure more than a hundred lines or so of Hudibras at one time?

[4] *Aids,* pp. 76-77. Cf. Shedd, I, 155-57.

Each couplet or quatrain is so whole in itself, that you can't connect them. There is no fusion—just as it is in Seneca.[5]

I never regarded the character of a mere linguist with any admiration. Butler has hit it off with great spirit. He that has many languages to express his thoughts, and none worth expressing, he compares to one that can write all hands, but never the better sense; or can cast any sum of money, but has none.[6]

Henry More

Who is ignorant of Homer's Πήλιον εἰνοσίφυλλον? Yet in some Greek Hexameters (MSS) we have met with a compound epithet, which may compete with it for the prize of excellence in *"flashing* on the mental eye" a complete image. It is an epithet of the brutified archangel, (see p. 12) and forms the latter half of the Hexameter.

Κερκοκερώνυχα Σατᾶν.

Ye youthful bards! compare this word with it's literal translation, "Tail-horn-hoofed Satan," and be shy of compound epithets, the component parts of which are indebted for their union exclusively to the printer's hyphen. Henry More indeed would have naturalized the word without hesitation, and CERCOCERONYCHOUS would have shared the astonishment of the English reader in the glossary to his Song of the Soul with ACHRONYCUL, ANAISTHÆSIE, &c., &c.[1]

Whenever an attempt is made, as in H. More's, n. b. *not Hannah,* "Song of the Soul" to popularize Philosophy, Ideas must perforce be represented by Words, but Words in their primary import always referring to *Things* and *Images,* and here in order to be rendered attractive & interesting to be supported by Images of Things, as Similitudes or Allegories. What wonder that Platonism at least should appear to sober-minded Men, who have become acquainted with it by such Books,

[5] July 3, 1833. *Table Talk S,* VI, 468.
[6] Willmott, *C. at Trinity,* p. 28.

[1] Coleridge in Southey's *Omniana,* I, 197; printed also in *Notes Theolog.,* p. 299. Cf. *Table Talk A,* p. 353.

the veriest Romance or Faery Tale!—It is one of my Objects to prove the difference of the Christian Faith from Platonism even in it's purest form—but so is the Xtian Moral System different from the Stoic—but as no one on this account denies the resemblances & coincidences in the latter, so rather ought we to do in the former.[2]

And for the other visitors of Prometheus, the elementary powers, or spirits of the elements, *Titanes pacati,* θεοὶ ὑπονόμιοι, vassal potentates, and their solicitations, the noblest interpretation will be given, if I repeat the lines of our great contemporary:—

> Earth fills her lap with pleasures of her own:
> Yearnings she hath in her own natural kind,
> And even with something of a mother's mind,
> And no unworthy aim,
> The homely nurse doth all she can
> To make her foster-child, her inmate, *Man,*
> Forget the glories he hath known,
> And that imperial palace whence he came!
> Wordsworth.

which exquisite passage is prefigured in coarser clay, indeed, and with a less lofty spirit, but yet excellently in their kind, and even more fortunately for the illustration and ornament of the present commentary, in the fifth, sixth, and seventh stanzas of Dr. Henry More's poem on the Pre-existence of the Soul:

> "Thus groping after our own center's near
> And proper *substance,* we grew dark, contract,
> Swallow'd up, of earthly life! Ne what we were
> Of old, thro' ignorance can we detect.
> Like noble babe, by fate or friends' neglect
> Left to the care of sorry salvage wight,
> Grown up to manly years cannot conject
> His own true parentage, nor read aright
> What father him begot, what womb him brought to light!
>
> So we, as stranger infants elsewhere born,
> Cannot divine from what spring we did flow;
> Ne dare these base alliances to scorn,
> Nor lift ourselves a whit from hence below;
> Ne strive our parentage again to know,
> Ne dream we once of any other stock
> Since foster'd upon RHEA'S knees we grow
> In SATYRS' arms with many a mow and mock
> Oft danced and hairy PAN our cradle oft hath rock'd!
>
> But Pan nor Rhea be our parentage!
> We been the offspring of the all seeing NOUS," &c.

[2] Notebook 18, p. 302. Printed for the first time.

To express the supersensual character of the reason, its abstraction from sensation, we find the Prometheus ἀτεϱπῆ, while in the yearnings accompanying with the remorse incident to and only possible in consequence of the NOUS, as the rational, self-conscious, and therefore responsible will, he is γυπὶ διαχναιόμενος.[3]

The incomparable Passage[4] in W. Wordsworth's incomparable Ode
—Our birth is but a sleep—Earth strews her lap—And even with something of a Mother's Mind and no unworthy Aim The homely Nurse—&c. is pre-figured in coarser clay, by a less mastering hand & with a less lofty Spirit, yet excellent in it's own kind by Henry More. Stanz. 5. 6. 7. of his Poem on The Preexistency of the Soul.

5

Thus groping after our own Center's near
partic. passim.   And proper substance, we grew dark, contract
swal'd up   Swallow'd (up) of earthly life, ne what we were
⌣ ⌣ — ' for ⌣ —   Of old, thro' ignorance can we detect.
Like Noble Babe by fate or friend's Neglect
Left to the care of sorry Salvage Wight,
Grown up to manly years cannot conject
His own true parentage, nor read aright
What Father him begot, what Womb him brought to light.

6

So we as stranger Infants elsewhere born
Cannot divine from what spring we did flow,
Ne dare these base alliances to scorn
Nor lift ourselves a whit from hence below;
Ne strive our parentage again to know,
Ne dream we once of any other stock
Since foster'd upon RHEA'S *knees we grow,*
In Satyrs' arms with many a mow and mock
Oft danc'd and hairy Pan our Cradle oft hath rock'd.

7

But Pan nor Rhea be our parentage!
We been the offspring of all-seeing Jove
&c

Rhea, the Earth as the transitory ever-flowing Nature—the sum of Phænomena or objects of the outward Senses—in contra-dist. from

[3] *On the Prometheus of Aeschylus* (London: 1825) in British Museum, Ashley, 2868, pp. 19-20. Printed in *Transactions of the Royal Society of Literature* (London: 1825) Vol. II, Part II, and in Ashe, *Miscellanies*, pp. 80-81.
[4] The first part of this comment differs very little from the comments above on the *Prometheus,* but thereafter is new material from the Clasped Vellum Notebook, pp. 146-51.

the Earth as Vesta = the eternal Law from ῥέω, fluo. Satyrs, the Sports and desires of the sensuous Nature. Pan = the total Life of the Earth, the presence of all in each, Universal Organismus of bodies & bodily life.

Whĕthĕr = whēhr in old poets frequent—and the forcible use of the verb, been, not as an Elleipsis for *have been*, but as a tense containing in one the force of are and were or Præteritum adhuc Presens or Præteritum continuum.

The renitence against employing in it's several and primary sense a word of frequent and almost hourly occurrence in a secondary and particular sense—for instance, Passion as simply the antithesis of Action. More uses *perpession*

> All ear, all eye—Sphere of pure Sense which no perpessions curb
> Nor uncouth shapen Spectres ever can disturb.
> Stanz. 14—

Our particle *fore* an unfortunate equivocalizing pseudography for ver (pronounced fer) having the force of fahren or fahren lassen—*to make away*—Kochen, to boil verkochen, to boil away—Reissen to rend, verreissen, to rend away—Thus foreslow their flight—to make the flight *slow* away, diminish into a slowness—. In the common sound of forget, I *hear* that it was originally *fer*get.

Stanza 17—Asserting the same theory of earthly-minded Souls haunted their sepulchres and linger [*sic*] near Their wonted homes, and oft themselves they show—very ingeniously in

Stanza 18. Illustrates this by Somnambulists—there being no other difference than that the latter Souls have a dead-asleep body to lug about, instead of hover over.

> For Men that wont to wander in their Sleep
> By the fixt light of inward Phantasie
> Tho' a short fit of Death fast bounden keep
> Their outward sense, and all their organs tie;
> Yet forth they fare, steared right steadily
> By that internal guide, even so the Ghosts
> Of men deceased, bedewed with the sky
> And night's cold influence, *in sleep yclos'd*
> *Awake within,* and walk in their forewonted Coach.

This might be made physiologically *plausible* by placing the difference in the total death of the Sepulchral body—so that there is no life to serve as a copula or magic block between it and the life of the Soul— whereas in the Sleep-walker, tho' the Idiozoic Life be dead pro tempore, yet the zoïe entomöides, instinctive, insectiform Life (the Irritability or Arteris muscular Life, and the ζωὴ φυτοειδής, or vegetable Life (vis

vegeta) or parenchymatous and veno-glandular Vitality, are alive—and
in fact the idiozoic, with the exception of the *æsthetic*—Qy. In cases
of proper Neurolepsia where the Body's highest Life is deprived of her
lower instrumental parts, we find the secretions approach to simple &
elementary natures—Gas, Water—But is not secretion = attraction?
Analogia! might not the Soul be imagined to have the power of attracting Air or vapor—or when not that, as too complex yet perhaps *aura
electrica*—so as to produce visible motion tho' she could not produce
visible forms? Answer, O yes! you may imagine, what you look—not
contradicting geometry—i. e. you may bring words together without
perceiving their incongruity.

Were there no other operative Causes, as there are many, for the
partial diffusion and sudden decay of Platonism in the 16th and 17th
Centuries, it's obscure and in part erroneous explanation of *Matter,* and
the frequency with which the Platonists confounded Matter with Body,
would have sufficed. In Henry More who blended the doctrine of Des
Cartes (viz. that matter is mere extension and that Body and Soul or
Spirit are especially heterogeneous) with the Notions of Plotinus, which
are built, on the assumption of their being differences in degree, Body
being the dying away of Spirit, and it's last vibrations & echoes, this
incongruity is especially prominent and revolting. Matter is mere
Potentiality, Potentiality mere non-entity, & yet this non-entity plays
the part of a most energetic Figurante in all possible forms, attracts
and is attracted, exerts magic influences, bird-limes Spirits &c. In short,
the πρῶτον ψεῦδος of all these Schemes is that they commence with an
Abstraction, that is, an *Object.* Hence whatever is in it's nature incapable of being contemplated objectively, as the I, We, with all the
Affections and Passions, are not explained at all, or with more than
Stoical Bravado called Nothings, that require and permit no explanation—tho' in every Object these Subjects are supposed, in order to it's
being an Object.—And yet from the same cause Explanations are end-
lessly sought for, in lieu of that insight which Ideas alone can afford—
for an Abstraction quoad Abstraction is necessarily incomplete, and
supposes a something from which it is abstracted; but this again is an
Abstraction, and so on ad infinitum. This, however, is an evil common
to the Pseudo-Platonists with the Epicurean-Naturalists; but it is
peculiar to the former, that their Objects being either properly Subjective, as the Soul, or Transcendent, as Deity, their Explanations are
all not so much Suppositions or hypotheses, as *Suffixions* or hypopoieses
ex. gr. the Eight orbs, orbs Monadical, Intellectual, Psychical, Imaginative, Sensitive, Spermatical, Quantitative, and Hyle or Coactive.[5] And

[5] See st. 23 of *Psychathanasia,* Book I, canto iii.

yet the Attention of the Soul being throughout intentionally and pro-
fessedly directed to her highest Interests, these Writers have and cannot but have a charm for minds, that feel and struggle up against the
insight and witchery of Custom and yearn for an evidence and a reality
beyond what the flux of the Senses can afford: and after all, if there
be not some third better than either, it is nobler and perhaps wiser to
dream about realities than to be grave-awake about dreams!

More, POEMS,[6] *written on the flyleaf at the beginning of the volume.*

Ah! what strength might *I* gather, what comfort might *we* derive,
from these Proclo-plotinian Platonists' doctrine of the Soul, if only
they or their Spinozistic imitators, the Natur-philosophers of present
Germany, had told or could tell us what they meant by *I* and *we*, by
Pain and Remorse. Poor *we* are nothing in *act* but everything in suffering.

*(A manuscript note in a different hand, with Coleridge's added re-
mark)*

> Dr. More uses many words that are obsolete, many that are provincial,
> and many that are entirely his own coinage, which the novelty of the
> subject may in some degree have rendered necessary. His elisions
> appear to be more licentious than have either been adopted before or
> since.
> Spenser he acknowledges in his Dedication was a favourite author with
> him from childhood, and his partiality is sufficiently obvious from follow-
> ing his antiquated diction, and from writing in the same octave stanza,
> which Spenser borrowed from the Italian poets.

Which is not an octave but an ennead (*i. e.* a stanza of nine lines)
and which Spenser did *not* borrow from the Italians, but after many
and various experiments invented for himself, as a perfect ※ whole, as
it is indeed, and it only.

※ That I mean, to which nothing can be added and from which nothing can be removed.

More, POEMS: PSYCHOZOIA, *canto iii, l. 55.*

> "So bravely went he on withouten dread,
> Till at the last we came *whereas* a hill
> With steep ascent highly lift up his head."

Of very ancient usage for *to where.*

---

[6] These notes were communicated to T. Ashe by H. J. Roby, M.A., and appear in
Miscellanies, pp. 332-36.

More, POEMS: PSYCHOZOIA, *notes to canto i, including the following passage.*

"Ahad, Aeon, Psyche, the Platonick Triad, is rather the τὸ θεῖον than θεός, the Divinity rather than the Deity. For God is but one indivisible immovable self-born Unity, and his first born creature is wisdome, Intellect, *Aeon, On* or *Autocalon*, or in a word the intellectual world, whose measure himself is, that is, simple and perfect Goodnesse. Τὸ δέ ἐστιν ἀνενδεές, ἱκανὸν ἑαυτῷ, μηδενὸς δεόμενον, μέτρον πάντων καί, πέρας, δοὺς ἐξ αὐτοῦ νοῦν καὶ οὐσίαν καὶ ψυχήν; that is,—for he is without need, self sufficient, wanting nothing, the measure and term of all things, yielding out of himself Intellect or On and Psyche."

The 3 or 4 preceding pages convince me that H. More was a poetical philosophist who amused himself in calling Aristotelian abstractions by the names of Platonic Ideas; but by no means a philosophic poet, framing in the life-light of a guiding Idea. The very phrase, a first-*born creature*, which is a contradiction in terms, and the applying of creature to the Logos, sophia, and ὁ ὤν are * * * [*sic*],

More, POEMS: PSYCHATHANASIA, *Preface.*

"So a tender mother if she see a knife stuck to her child's heart, would shreek and swound as if her selfe had been smit; when as if her eye had not beheld that spectacle, she had not been moved though the thing were surely done. So I do verily think that the mind being taken up in some higher contemplation, if it should please God to keep it in that ecstasie, the body might be destroyed without any disturbance to the soul, for how can there be or sense or pain without animadversion?"

Doubtless! but what is that in the body which enforceth the soul to attend? and where is the middle term between the *act* of attention and the *pass* of Pain or Pleasure?

More, POEMS: PSYCHATHANASIA, *Book I, canto iii, st. 23-26.*

23

"This number suits well with the *universe.*
The number's eight of the Orbs general,
From whence things flow or wherein they converse,
The first we name *Nature Monadicall*,
The second hight *Life Intellectuall*,
Third *Psychicall;* the fourth *Imaginative,*
Fifth *Sensitive*, the sixth *Spermaticall*,
The seventh be fading forms *Quantitative*,
The eighth *Hyle* or *Ananke* perverse, coactive.

24

That last is nought but potentiality,
Which in the lower creature causeth strife,
Destruction by incompossibility

In some, as in the forms *Quantitative.*
All here depend on the Orb *Unitive,*
Which also hight Nature *Monadicall;*
As all those lights and colours did derive
Themselves from lively Phœbus life centrall.
Nought therefore but vain sensibles we see caducall.

25

And that the first *Every-where-Unitie*
Is the true root of all the living creatures,
As they descend in each distinct degree,
That God's the sustentacle of all Natures;
And though those outward forms & gawdy features
May quail like rainbowes in the roseid sky,
Of glistring Parelies or other meteors;
Yet the clear light doth not to nothing flie;
Those six degrees of life stand sure, and never die.

26

So now we plainly see that the dark matter
Is not that needful prop to hold up life;
And though deaths engins this grosse bulk do shatter
We have not lost our Orb conservative,
Of which we are a ray derivative.
The body sensible so garnished
With outward forms these inward do relieve,
Keep up in fashion and fresh lively-hed;
But this grosse bulk those inward lives stands in no sted."

What mere logomachy! All is first assumed in the definition of body, and then proved by applying the impossible of the definition to 6 or 7 particular instances of this impossibility. The Materialist need make no other answer than: Aye! but this is not what I mean by matter of body: or I defy the truth of your definition.

More, POEMS, PSYCHATHANASIA, *Book III, canto i, st. 21.*

"But if't be so, how doth Psyche hear or see,
That hath not eyes nor eares? she sees more clear
Than we that see but secondarily.
We see at distance by a *circular*
Diffusion of that spright of this great sphear
Of th'universe: Her sight is tactuall.
The Sun and all the Starres that do appear
She feels them in herself, can distance all,
For she is at each one purely presentiall."

Still *we:* and in contradistinction from our *Soul.*

More, POEMS, *written on the flyleaf at the end of the volume.*

It would be no trifling convenience in close reasoning on metaphysical subjects if we might dare coin the word *pass* or *pasch*, as the antithet or corresponding opposite of *act*.

The 5 main faults characteristic of our elder poets not of the first class, and of none more than of H. More, are:

1. That in the pursuit of strength and vigour they fall into, may eagerly rush upon, the hateful and loathsome, and particularly the offensive to the sense of smell, aggravated by moral disgust and associations of disease, "fed with stinking gore suck'd from corrupted corse" (*Psychathanasia*, Bk. 1., cant. 1. v. 5).

2. That from a predilection for the lively and exact in similitudes and descriptions, they recur to the mean, the ludicrous, and the odd.

3. That generally they are regardless of the influence of associations, not merely such as are the accidental growth of a particular age and fashion, but of those that are grounded on the nature of man and his circumstances.

4. That they sacrifice the grand keeping and total impression to particular effects, and if it only be *bene* sonans per se, care not though it should be dissonant in the concert.

5. That they construct their metre in correspondence to their own passionate humouring and often peculiar and mannered mode of reading or reciting their verses—a mode always more influenced by what they intended the words to mean than by the necessary or obvious sense of the words themselves.

On the SONG OF THE SOUL.

"There is perhaps no other poem in existence, which has so little that is good in it, if it has anything good."—R.S.

27 Decr. 1819. Mr. (J. H.) Frere, of all men eminently φιλόκαλος, of the most exquisite Taste, observed this very day to me—how very grossly Southey had wronged this Poem. I cannot understand in what mood S. could have been: it is so unlike him.[7]

"The following extract is the best specimen that can be given of the strain of feeling, which Henry More could express in no better language than an inharmonious imitation of Spenser's, barbarized by the extremes of carelessness the most licentious, and erudition the most pedantic."
—R. S.

After so very sharp a censure, of the justice of which the following extract is to be the proof, who would have expected a series of

[7] Coleridge's MS note in Southey's *Omniana*, II, 157. Printed in *Table Talk A*, p. 392.

Stanzas for the greater part at least so chaste in language, and easy in versification? Southey must have wearied himself out with the Poem, till the Mist from it's swamps and stagnants had spread over its green and flowery Plots and Bowers.[8]

Did Henry More precede Milton, Harington, and Jeremy Taylor in the advocation of universal Toleration—The *second* greatly enlarged and corrected Edition of his Song of the Soul in 1647—Two questions are to be answered—1. The date of the first Edition? 2. Whether the Episode commencing at Stanza 33, Canto ii, is to be found in the first Edition. The Sentiments are throughout Miltonic.

That Presbyter is but Old Priest writ large—&c. More's contempt and aversion are poured out equally on the Church of Rome, the Prelatic High-Church of England Men, and their antagonists, the Geneva & Puritan Divines. Some passages might have suggested a hint to Butler's Ralpho and Hudibras.[9]

Abraham Cowley

The seductive faults, the dulcia vitia of Cowley, Marini, or Darwin might reasonably be thought capable of corrupting the public judgement for half a century, and require a twenty years war, campaign after campaign, in order to dethrone the usurper and re-establish the legitimate taste.[1]

Repeated Meditations led me first to supect, (and a more intimate analysis of the human faculties, their appropriate marks, functions, and effects matured my conjecture into full conviction) that fancy and imagination were two distinct and widely different faculties, instead of being, according to the general belief, either two names with one

[8] Coleridge's MS note in Southey's *Omniana*, II, 168-69. Printed in *Table Talk A*, p. 393.
[9] This comment is in notes on *Memoirs of Mr. Halyburton's Life*, pp. 19, 20, in the MS volume *On the Divine Ideas*, p. 2, The Huntington Library, HM 8195. Printed for the first time.

---

[1] *Biog. Lit. C*, I, 78.

meaning, or at furthest, the lower and higher degree of one and the same power. It is not, I own, easy to conceive a more opposite translation of the Greek φάντασις[2] than the Latin Imaginatio; but it is equally true that in all societies there exists an instinct of growth, a certain collective, unconscious good sense working progressively to desynonymize those words originally of the same meaning, which the conflux of dialects supplied to the more homogeneous languages, as the Greek and German: and which the same cause, joined with accidents of translation from original works of different countries, occasion in mixt languages like our own. The first and most important point to be proved is, that two conceptions perfectly distinct are confused under one and the same word, and (this done) to appropriate that word exclusively to one meaning, and the synonyme (should there be one) to the other. But if (as will be often the case in the arts and sciences) no synonyme exists, we must either invent or borrow a word. In the present instance the appropriation has already begun, and been legitimated in the derivative adjective: Milton had a highly *imaginative*, Cowley a very *fanciful* mind. If therefore I should succeed in establishing the actual existence of two faculties generally different, the nomenclature would be at once determined. To the faculty by which I had characterized Milton, we should confine the term *imagination;* while the other would be countradistinguished as *fancy*.[3]

There have been works, such as Cowley's Essay on Cromwell, in which prose and verse are intermixed (not as in the Consolation of Boetius, or the Argenis of Barclay, by the insertion of poems supposed to have been spoken or composed on occasions previously related in prose, but) the poet passing from one to the other as the nature of the thoughts or his own feelings dictated. Yet this mode of composition does not satisfy a cultivated taste. There is something unpleasant in the being thus obliged to alternate states of feeling so dissimilar, and this too in a species of writing, the pleasure from which is in part derived from the preparation and previous expectation of the reader.[4]

Classically too, as far as consists with the allegorizing fancy of the *modern*, that still *striving to project* the inward, contra-distinguishes itself from the seeming ease with which the poetry of the ancients re-

---

[2] *Phantasia.*   [3] *Biog. Lit. C.*, I, 86-88.
[4] *Biog. Lit. C.*, II, 134-35.

flects the world without.   Casimir[5] affords, perhaps, the most striking
instance of this characteristic difference.—For his *style* and *diction*
are really classical: while Cowley, who resembles Casimir in many respects, compleatly barbarizes *his* Latinity, and even his metre, by the
heterogeneous nature of his thoughts.   That Dr. Johnson should have
passed a contrary judgement, and have even preferred Cowley's Latin
Poems to Milton's, is a caprice that has, if I mistake not, excited the
surprize of all scholars.   I was much amused last summer with the
laughable *affright,* with which an Italian poet perused a page of Cowley's Davideis, contrasted with the enthusiasm with which he first ran
through, and then read aloud, Milton's Mansus and Ad Patrem.[6]

For competitors in barbarism with Cowley's Latin Poem De Plantis,
or even his *not quite so bad* Davideid Hexameters, we must go, I fear,
to the Deliciæ Poetarum Germanorum or other Warehouses of Seal-fat,
Whale Blubber and the like Boreal Confectionaries, selected by the
delicate Gunter.[7]

[In Cowley's Preface to the MISCELLANIES[8] *there are two notes by
Coleridge.   Cowley remarks disparagingly on some of his youthful
poems.   But Coleridge evidently understood him to mean that he lightly
regarded all of his Miscellany, for Coleridge wrote in the margin:]*

Strange that a respect for the subject of two of these poems viz—that
on his Friend Harvey & the other on the Poet Crashaw, both funereal
Poems, should not have preserved him from speaking in this manner.
But there is here a deal of affection.

[After he had read the MISCELLANY, *however, he came to the following
conclusion:]*

I have fallen into a mistake in the above.   The contemptuous tone
in which he spoke is not the one to apply to the whole *Miscellany* but
only to the juvenile part of it.   It gives pleasure to have observed this
& to correct the mistakes in this manner rather than erase the Note.[9]

⁵ Matthias Sarbieuski Casimir (1595-1640).   His Latin poems are often ranked
with those of the ancient classical poets.   Coleridge owned Barbou's edition (1759)
and considered translating the poems.
⁶ *Biog. Lit. C,* II, 295 n.
⁷ MSS Egerton, 2800, fol. 54.   Printed for the first time.
⁸ London: 1681.
⁹ Warren E. Gibbs, ''Two Unpublished Notes by S. T. Coleridge,'' *MLN,*
XLVIII (1933), 22.

Cowley's Ode "Upon his Majesty's Restoration and Return," st. 8, ll. 11f., Anderson's BRITISH POETS, *V, 290.*[10]

Cromwell's Exploits, the intimate connection of his name with vast Events, might easily have blended in the mind of a Genius, his name & the idea of magnanimous Liberty conquered and enforced—and in such a spirit is Milton's panegyric of Cromwell conceived. But how is it possible not to feel the degradation of a man of mind who could submit thus to flatter the wretched progeny of the Stuarts.

Charles Cotton

Sammlung Einiger Abhandlungen von Christian Garve, Garve's comment on Gellert.

It was a strange and curious phenomenon, and such as in Germany had been previously unheard of, to read verses in which everything was expressed, just as one would wish to talk, and yet all dignified, attractive, and interesting; and all at the same time perfectly correct as to the measure of the syllables and the rhyme. It is certain, that poetry when it has attained this excellence makes a far greater impression than prose. So much so indeed, that even the gratification which the very rhymes afford becomes then no longer a contemptible or trifling gratification.

However novel this phenomenon may have been in Germany at the time of Gellert, it is by no means new, nor yet of recent existence in our language. Spite of the licentiousness with which Spencer occasionally compels the orthography of his words into a subservience to his rhymes, the whole Fairy Queen is an almost continued instance of this beauty. Waller's song "Go, lovely Rose, &c." is doubtless familiar to most of my readers; but if I had happened to have had by me the Poems of COTTON, more but far less deservedly celebrated as the author of the Virgil travestied, I should have indulged myself, and I think have gratified many who are not acquainted with his serious works, by selecting some admirable specimens of this style. There are not a few poems in that volume, replete with every excellence of thought, image, and passion, which we expect or desire in the poetry of the milder

[10] From the set in the Victoria and Albert Museum. This note is transcribed from the original, but it has been printed by Raysor, *Misc. Crit.*, p. 280. For another comment on Cowley see the note on p. 489.

muse; and yet so worded that the reader sees no one reason either in the selection or the order of the words, why he might not have said the very same in an appropriate conversation, and cannot conceive how indeed he could have expressed such thoughts otherwise, without loss or injury to his meaning.[1]

I think there is something very majestic in Gray's Installation Ode; but as to the Bard and the rest of his lyrics, I must say I think them frigid and artificial. There is more real lyric feeling in Cotton's Ode on Winter.[2]

The 6th Edit. of Cotton's Trans. of Montaigne, 1743, the Editor says he has altered Cotton's English in 3000 places; it would be very well worth while getting an early Edition of Cotton, & comparing the alterations.[3]

John Dryden

You will find this a good gauge or criterion of genius,—whether it progresses and evolves, or only spins upon itself. Take Dryden's Achitophel and Zimri,—Shaftesbury and Buckingham; every line adds to or modifies the character, which is, as it were, a-building up to the very last verse; whereas, in Pope's Timon, &c., the first two or three couplets contain all the pith of the character, and the twenty or thirty lines that follow are so much evidence or proof of overt acts of jealousy, or pride, or whatever it may be that is satirized. In like manner compare Charles Lamb's exquisite criticisms on Shakspeare, with Hazlitt's round and round imitations of them.[1]

Dryden's genius was of that sort which catches fire by its own motion; his chariot wheels *get* hot by driving fast.[2]

[1] *Biog. Lit. C*, II, 95-96.
[2] Oct. 23, 1833. *Table Talk S*, VI, 493.
[3] Notebook 16, fol. 67 verso. British Museum, MSS, 47,513. Printed for the first time.

[1] Aug. 6, 1832. *Table Talk S*, VI, 409.
[2] Nov. 1, 1833. *Table Talk S*, VI, 494.

He [i. e. Klopstock] asked whether it was not allowed, that Pope had written rhyme poetry with more skill than any of our writers—I said, I preferred Dryden, because his couplets had great variety in their movement. He thought my reason a good one; but asked whether the rhyme of Pope were not more exact. This question I understood as applying to the final terminations, and observed to him that I believed it was the case; but that I thought it was easy to excuse some inaccuracy in the final sounds, if the general sweep of the verse was superior. I told him that we were not so exact with regard to the final endings of lines as the French. He did not seem to know that we made no distinction between masculine and feminine (i. e. single or double,) rhymes: at least he put inquiries to me on this subject. He seemed to think, that no language could ever be so far formed as that it might not be enriched by idioms borrowed from another tongue. I said this was a very dangerous practice; and added that I thought Milton had often injured both his prose and verse by taking this liberty too frequently. I recommended to him the prose works of Dryden as models of pure and native English.[3]

They [the Gothic Tribes] in all their habits discovered a connexion without combination. They were belinked together, but no part would lose its own integrity and individuality . . . And this which marked the whole political character disclosed itself likewise in their poetry: we find no remnants of any poem which can be said to have a beginning, a middle and an end, and in which all the parts are means to some one great end, with a number of successive highly interesting narrations following each other in the order of time and going to one purpose. It is, in truth, the same character which afterwards appeared and has given rise to the couplet verse, which is precisely what I mean—if we take for instance, the writings of Dryden, or Ben Jonson's poems, you will find a series of distinct couplets, all upon the same subject but each having a wholeness of itself.[4]

A pernicious opinion that of Dr. Johnson's & Dryden's & Adam Smith's &c. that Authors by compulsion in the profession are likely to be the best, i. e. professional musicians &c.[5]

. . . and the ever-recurring blunder of using the possessive case "*compassion's* tears" &c. for the preposition "of"—a blunder of which

[3] *Biog. Lit. C*, II, 251.
[4] Philosophical Lecture X, March 1, 1819. Coburn, *Phil. Lect.*, pp. 289-90.
[5] Notebook 10, fol. 1 recto. British Museum, Add. MSS, 47,507. Printed for the first time.

I have found no instances earlier than Dryden's slovenly verses written for the Trade. The rule is—that the case is always personal—either it modifies a person, or a personification, as "Who for their Belly's sake" in Lycidas—Belly-Gods, Worshippers of their Belly—the Belly will make himself heard &c.[6]

> *Virgil,* as a familiar occurrence, by way of simile, describes a dove haunting the cavern of a rock in such engaging numbers, that I cannot refrain from quoting the passage; and *John Dryden* has rendered it so happily in our language, that without further excuse I shall add his translation also:
> "Qualis speluncâ subitò commota Columba,
> Cui domus, et dulces, latebroso in pumice nidi,
> Fertur in arva volans, plausumque exterrita pennis
> Dat tecto ingentem—mox aere lapsa quieto,
> Radit iter liquidum, celeres neque commovet alas."
>
> "As when a dove her rocky hold forsakes,
> Rous'd, in a fright her sounding wings she shakes;
> The cavern rings with clattering:—out she flies,
> And leaves her callow care, and cleaves the skies;
> At first she flutters:—but at length she springs
> To smoother flight, and shoots upon her wings."

Curiosa felicitas, indeed a very *odd* way of translating a passage *happily,* except the 4 last words, and it wants 5 only of having as many faults as words, and many of them gross & glaring faults.—S. T. C. (Of course, I leave the "in," "with," "and," "she," "her," "a," and "the" out of the reckoning.)[7]

I confess that I have ever felt the Spotted Panther, &c., as pleasing marks of the tranquil feeling in which this ingenious poem[8] was written, and possibly intended as such by Dryden.[9]

I recollect writing a very long letter to Mr. Owen, and conjuring him, with tears in my eyes, to avoid this rock; this vexed question of Fate and Freewill; of which less seems to be known, by those who argue upon it, than of any other subject of difference.

[6] Letter to H. C. Robinson, MS volume, 1809-17, p. 140. Dr. Williams's Library. Cf. Coleridge, E. H., *Letters,* II, 672-73, where slight differences occur.

[7] Gilbert White, *The Works in Natural History* (2 vols.; London: 1802), I, 194-95 and p. 194 n. British Museum, C. 61. b. 20.

[8] "The Hind and the Panther."

[9] Hartley Coleridge, *Northern Worthies,* III, 300 n.

"The Priesthood grossly cheat us with free-will;
Will to do what, but what Heaven first decreed?
Our actions then are neither Good nor Ill,
Since from eternal causes they proceed:
Our passions, fear and anger, love and hate,
Mere senseless engines that are moved by fate;
Like ships on stormy seas without a guide,
Tost by the winds, are driven by the tide."

These lines of Dryden seem to me to express the doctrine and its results better than any other I recollect. It is true the illustrations are now varied, but nothing has been added to the argument either in force or variety.[10]

We should form a very inaccurate as well as mean idea, and blind ourselves to the natural connection of tragedy with these Hymns of the Goat, if we imagine the ancients to have sung the praise of Bacchus in the words which Dryden has given to Timotheus in his celebrated Ode on Alexander's Feast. Whether or no the drinking song introduced is to be justified by the general plan of this ode, and the effect which the poet wished to produce, I do not pretend to decide—but in itself it is a very gross impropriety. Timotheus must have been a dull and awkward flatterer, if before Alexander, proud to be considered as the son of Jupiter by a mortal, and at the same time full of the conquest of India, he in singing the praise of Bacchus, of Bacchus likewise the Son of Jove by a mortal, and likewise the Conquerer of India, had forgotten the God and substituted a commonplace panegyric on the joys of drinking. No! with the ancients Bacchus, or Dionysius, [sic] was among the most awful and mysterious deities—in his earthly character, &c., to such passions. In the hymns of celebration the different voices would sometimes sing in chorus, sometimes separately, and in responses. The narrative parts of the hymns, containing accounts either of the God's own actions, or of those effected by him either in reward or vengeance, would be sung in notes less removed from animated dialogue, than in devotional and lyric addresses—etc.[11]

[10] Allsop, *Letters*, II, 233.
[11] *Catalogue of the Collection of Autograph Letters and Historical Documents*, formed by Alfred Morrison, compiled and annotated under the direction of A. W. Thibaudeau (Printed for private circulation; London: 1883 ff., 2d ser., 1883-93), II (1895), 267-68. Also printed by Raysor, *Shakes. Crit.*, I, 185.

Sir Richard Blackmore

It may be assumed, as a critical axiom, that no man who, during his life-time has obtained a very large share of applause, is deserving of total oblivion. This is emphatically true of Cowley, of Herbert, of Crashaw, and even of Blackmore, who though, in general, writing quite bad enough for a physician, has, in one or two places, in defiance, as it were, of his nature, risen into true poetry. You will see my meaning in the description of Satan's journey:—

> From afar
> I did with wondrous joy descry at last
> Some streaks of light which darted on the waste,
> Pale beams that on the face of chaos lay;
> Mounting this way, I reached the lightsome sky,
> And saw the beauteous world before me lie.
> The fresh creation looked all charming, mild,
> *And all the flowery face of Nature smiled.*
> What odours, such as heavenly zephyrs blow,
> *From the sweet mouth of the infant world did flow!*

So again, we perceive a very uncommon ingenuity and beauty in the application of the legendary invasion of heaven by the giants, to the fervent and unceasing prayers of penitence, which are called,—

> The only giants that assail
> The throne of heaven, and in the end prevail.[1]

[1] Willmott, *C. at Trinity*, p. 7.

DRAMA

Ben Jonson

Humor, as Ben Jonson has well set forth in his admirable Comedy, is a term grounded on, and borrowed from the humoral Physiology, which supposed health of Body, and implicite Sanity of Mind to consist in, or depend on, a due *temperament, proportion,* and, as it were, balance & adjustment of the four prime *Humors,* or Seri-fluids, the Blood, the Phlegm, the χολή or Bile, and the Gall or Black Bile. As absolute proportionateness was for fallen Man an *Ideal,* in each man *actually* it being a case of more or less *dis*temperament, the supposed predominance of either of these four was deemed to constitute the distinguishing *Character* of the Individual—either as *Sanguine,* the blood predominating, or Phlegmatic, or Choleric, or Melancholic. Thence et Lucens a non Crescendo, so *a Temper* from the disturbance of the *Temperament,* and the undue excess of some one of the four, as applied to the momentary effect: while *Humor* meant the same relatively to the *Habit,* the Whole Life. A Humorist, therefore, implies a so far *insane* mind, when applied to the mind & consequently, the Doctor's Conclusion is involved in, is a mere repetition of the Premise. The Question should have been—Is the individual, who condemns and opposes "the World and the World's Law," necessarily a Humorist. Was John the Baptist a *Humorist?* Simon Stylites was. Yes, they both defied the World and the World's Law. But this is the prominent fault of the Author, that in order to give zest and seeming novelty to Commonplace Thoughts, he turns Truth into Falsehood by raising Generals into *Universals.* The old adage, "Extremes meet," might have saved him from this.[1]

Mr. C., in deciphering the character of Falstaff, was naturally led to a comparison of the wit of Shakespeare with that of his contemporaries (Ben Jonson, &c. &c), and aptly remarked, that whilst Shakespeare gave us wit as salt to our meat, Ben Jonson gave wit as salt instead of meat. After wit, Mr. C. proceeded to define *humor,* and entered into a curious

[1] Robert Southey, *The Doctor* (7 vols.; London: 1834-37), II, 281-83. The passage to which this note refers is: "And the Doctor's knowledge of human nature led him to conclude that solitary humourists are far from being happy." This annotated volume is in the British Museum, C. 43. b. 22.

history of the origin of the term, distinguishing the sanguine, the temperate, the melancholy, the phlegmatic. Where one fluid predominated over the other, a man was said to be under the influence of that particular *humour*. Thus a disproportion of *black bile* rendered a man melancholy. But when nothing serious was the consequence of a predominance of one particular fluid, the actions performed were humorous, and a man capable of describing them termed a humorist.[2]

Ben Jonson, Beaumont and Fletcher, and Massinger[1]

A contemporary is rather an ambiguous Term, when applied to Authors. It may simply mean that one man lived and wrote while another was yet alive, however deeply the former may have been indebted to the latter as his model. There have been instances in the literary world that might remind a Botanist of a singular sort of parasite Plant, which rises above ground, independent and unsupported, an apparent Original; but trace it's roots and you will find the fibres all terminating in the root of another plant at an unsuspected distance—which perhaps from want of sun and genial soil, and the loss of sap, has scarcely been able to peep above ground. —Or it may mean whose compositions were contemporaneous in such a sense as to preclude all likelihood of the one having borrowed from the other. In the latter sense, I should call Ben Jonson a contemporary of Shakespeare, tho' he long survived him—while I should prefer the phrase of immediate Successors for Massinger & B. & F.—tho' they too were his contemporaries in the former sense.

Ben Jonson[2]
Born, 1574.—Died, 1637

Ben Jonson is original; he is, indeed, the only one of the great dramatists of that day who was not either directly produced, or very greatly modified, by Shakspeare. In truth, he differs from our great master in every thing—in form and in substance—and betrays no tokens of his proximity. He is not original in the same way as Shakspeare is original; but after a fashion of his own, Ben Jonson is most truly original.

[2] Lecture VI, Bristol lectures of 1813-14. Reported in the *Gazette*, Nov. 18, 1813. Coleridge gave the lecture on Tuesday, Nov. 16. Quoted by Raysor, *Shakes. Crit.*, II, 286.

---

[1] From British Museum, Add. MS 34,225, fol. 57 recto.

[2] "Course of Lectures, Lecture VII," *Lit. Rem.*, I, 97-113. The section on Jonson comprises pp. 97-100. Note that the date of Jonson's birth has now been established as 1572.

The characters in his plays are, in the strictest sense of the term, abstractions. Some very prominent feature is taken from the whole man, and that single feature or humour is made the basis upon which the entire character is built up. Ben Jonson's *dramatis personæ* are almost as fixed as the masks of the ancient actors; you know from the first scene—sometimes from the list of names—exactly what every one of them is to be. He was a very accurately observing man; but he cared only to observe what was external or open to, and likely to impress, the senses. He individualizes, not so much, if at all, by the exhibition of moral or intellectual differences, as by the varieties and contrasts of manners, modes of speech, and tricks of temper; as in such characters as Puntarvolo, Bobadill, &c.

I believe there is not one whim or affectation in common life noted in any memoir of that age which may not be found drawn and framed in some corner or other of Ben Jonson's dramas; and they have this merit, in common with Hogarth's prints, that not a single circumstance is introduced in them which does not play upon, and help to bring out, the dominant humour or humours of the piece. Indeed I ought very particularly to call your attention to the extraordinary skill shown by Ben Jonson in contriving situations for the display of his characters. In fact, his care and anxiety in this matter led him to do what scarcely any of the dramatists of that age did—that is, invent his plots. It is not a first perusal that suffices for the full perception of the elaborate artifice of the plots of the Alchemist and the Silent Woman:—that of the former is absolute perfection for a necessary entanglement, and an unexpected, yet natural, evolution.

Ben Jonson exhibits a sterling English diction, and he has with great skill contrived varieties of construction; but his style is rarely sweet or harmonious, in consequence of his labour at point and strength being so evident. In all his works, in verse or prose, there is an extraordinary opulence of thought; but it is the produce of an amassing power in the author, and not of a growth from within. Indeed a large proportion of Ben Jonson's thoughts may be traced to classic or obscure modern writers, by those who are learned and curious enough to follow the steps of this robust, surly, and observing dramatist.

(Stockdale) WORKS,[3] *I, flyleaves.*

It would be amusing to collect from our Dramatists from Eliz. to Charles I. proofs of the manners of the Times. One striking symptom

[3] From the original marginalia in *The Dramatic Works of Ben Jonson and Beaumont and Fletcher* (4 vols.; London: 1811), printed for John Stockdale. These volumes, formerly in the library of Lord Coleridge, are now in the British Museum.

of general Coarseness (*i. e.,* of *manners,* which may co-exist with great
refinement of morals, as, alas! vice versâ), is to be seen in the very frequent allusions to the olfactories and [?] their most disgusting Stimulants, and these, too, in the Conversation of virtuous Ladies. This
would not appear so strange to one who had been on terms of familiarity
with Sicilian and Italian Women of Rank; and bad as they may, too
many of them, *actually be,* yet I doubt not, that the extreme grossness
of their Language has imprest many an Englishman of the present
æra with far darker notions, than this same language would have produced in one of Eliz. or James Ist's Courtiers. Those who have read
Shakespear only, complain of occasional grossness in *his* plays—Compare him with his Contemporaries, & the inevitable conviction is that
of the exquisite purity of his imagination.

The observation I have prefixed to the *Volpone,* is the Key to the
faint Interest that these noble efforts of intellectual power excite—with
the exception of the Sad Shepherd—because in that fragment only is
there any character, in whom you are morally interested. On the other
hand, the Measure for Measure is the only play of Shakespear's in which
there are not some one or more characters, generally many, whom you
follow with an affectionate feeling. For I confess, that Isabella of all
Shakespear's female Characters, interests me the least; and the M. for
Meas. is the only one of his genuine Works which is painful to me.

Let me not conclude this Remark, however, without a thankful ac-
knowlegement to the Manes of Jonson, that the more I study his
writings, the more I admire them—and the more the study resembles
that of an ancient Classic, in the minutiæ of his rhythm, metre, choice
of words, forms of connection, &c, the more numerous have the points of
admiration become. I may add too, that both the Study and Admiration cannot but be disinterested—for to expect any advantage to the
present Drama were ignorance. The latter is utterly heterogeneous from
the Drama of the Shakespearian Age—with a diverse Object and a contrary *principle.* The one was to present a model by *imitation* of real
life, to take from real life all that is what it ought to be, and to supply
the rest—the other to *copy* what *is,* and as it *is*—the best a tolerable,
the worst a blundering, *Copy.* In the former the Difference was an
essential Element—in the latter an involuntary Defect. We should think
it strange, if a Tale in *Dance* were announced, and the actors did not
dance at all! Yet such is modern comedy.

Notes primarily textual are omitted. For a complete transcription of the notes see
Raysor, *Misc. Crit.,* pp. 48-64. My reading differs occasionally from that of Raysor.

(Stockdale) Works: preface *by Whalley, I, xii.*

But Jonson was soon sensible, how inconsistent this medley of names and manners was in reason and nature; and with how little propriety it could ever have a place in a legitimate and just picture of real life.

But did Jonson reflect that the very Essence of a Play, the very language in which it is written, is a Fiction to which all the parts must conform—Surely, Greek manners in English are a still grosser improbability than a Greek name transferred to English manners.

(Stockdale) Works: preface *by Whalley, I, xiv.*

Jonson's Personæ are too often not Characters, but derangements; the hopeless Patients of a Mad-doctor rather than exhibitions of Folly betraying itself spite of existing Reason and Prudence. He not poetically but painfully exaggerates every trait i. e., not by the drollery of the circumstance, but by the excess of the originating Feeling.

(Stockdale) Works: preface *by Whalley, I, xvi.*

But to this we might reply, that far from being thought to build his characters upon abstract ideas, he was really accused of representing particular persons then existing; and that even those characters which appear to be the most exaggerated, are said to have had their respective archetypes in nature and life.

This degrades Jonson into a Libeller, instead of justifying him as a Dramatic Poet. Non quod verum est, sed quod verisimile, is the Dramatist's Rule. At all events, the Poet who chooses transitory manners, ought to content himself with transitory Praise—if his object be Reputation, he ought not to expect Fame. The utmost he can look forwards to, is to be quoted by, and to enliven the writings of, an Antiquarian. Pistol, Nym, &c. do not please us as Characters, but are endured as fantastic Creations, Foils to the native Wit of Falstaff.—I say *wit:* for this so often extolled as the masterpiece of Humor, contains, and was not meant to contain, *any* humor at all.

(Stockdale) Works: life of jonson *by Whalley, I, xxxv.*

It is to the honour of Jonson's judgment, that the greatest poet of our nation had the same opinion of Donne's genius and wit; and hath preserved part of him from perishing, by putting his thoughts and satire into modern verse.

Viz., Pope

(Stockdale) Works: life of jonson *by Whalley, I, xxxv.*

He said further to Drummond, Shakespeare wanted art, and sometimes sense; for in one of his plays he brought in a number of men saying

they had suffered shipwreck in Bohemia, where is no sea near by an
hundred miles.

I have often thought Shakespear justified in this seeming anachro-
nism. In Pagan times a single name of a German Kingdom might well
be supposed to comprise a 100 miles more than at present. These notes
of Drummond ought never to have been published. They are more disgraceful to himself than to Jonson. It would be easy to conjecture
Jonson's comments on them—how grossly he had been misunderstood,
and what he had said in jest (as of Hippocrates) interpreted in earnest.
But this is characteristic of a Scotchman. He has no notion of a jest,
unless you tell him—*This is a joke!* still less of that shade of feeling,
the half-and-half.[4]

(Stockdale) WORKS: POETASTER, *Introduction.*

> Light! I salute thee, but with wounded nerves,
> Wishing thy golden splendour pitchy darkness.

There is no reason to suppose Satan's address to the Sun in Par.
Lost more than a mere coincidence with these Lines; but, were it otherwise, it would be a fine Instance, what usurious Interest a great genius
pays in borrowing.[5] It would not be difficult to give a detailed psychological proof from these constant outbursts of anxious Self-assertion,
that Jonson was not a *Genius*—a creative Power. Subtract that, and
you may safely accumulate on his name all other excellencies of a
capacious, vigorous, agile, and richly-stored Intellect.[6]

(Stockdale) WORKS: POETASTER, *Act V, scene 3.*

> Cris. O—oblatrant-furibund—fatuate—strenuous . . .
>   O—conscious—damp.

It would form an interesting Essay, or rather series of Essays, in a
periodical work, were all the attempts to ridicule new phrases brought
together, to observe the proportion of the words ridiculed that have
been adopted, and are now common (as strenuous, conscious, &c)—&
how far any grounds can be detected, so that one might determine beforehand whether a word was invented under the conditions of Assimi-
lability to our Language. Thus much is certain, that the Ridiculers
were as often wrong as right; and Shakespear himself could not prevent the naturalization of Accommodation, Remuneration, &c—or Swift
the *abuse* even of *Idea.*

[4] The one note on *Every Man Out of His Humour* is omitted.
[5] Similar statements occur in Notebook 21, fol. 37 recto; *Table Talk A,* p. 366;
Southey, *Omniana,* I, 239; and *Lit. Rem.,* I, 305.
[6] One note is omitted.

(Stockdale) WORKS: FALL OF SEJANUS, *Act I, scene 1.*

> *Arr[untius]*. The name Tiberius,
> I hope, will keep, howe'er he hath foregone
> The dignity and power.
> *Sil[ius]*. Sure, while he lives.
> *Arr.*   And dead, it comes to Drusus. Should he fail,
> To the brave issue of Germanicus;
> And they are three: too many (ha?) for him
> To have a plot upon?
> *Sil.*   I do not know
> The heart of his designs; but, sure, their face
> Looks farther than the present.
> *Arr.*   By the gods,
> If I could guess he had but such a thought,
> My sword should cleave him down from head to heart.

This *anachronic* mixture of the Roman Republican, to whom Tiberius must have appeared as much a Tyrant as Sejanus, with the *James-and-Charles-the-1st* Zeal for legitimacy of Descent, is amusing. Of our great names Milton was, I think, the first who could properly be called a Republican. My recollections of Buchanan's Works are too faint to enable me to decide whether the Historian is not a fair exception.

(Stockdale) WORKS: FALL OF SEJANUS, *Act II, scene 1 (speech of Sejanus).*

> Adultery! it is the lightest ill
> I will commit. A race of wicked acts
> Shall flow out of my anger, and o'erspread
> The world's wide face, which no posterity
> Shall e'er approve, not yet keep silent, etc.

The more we reflect and examine, examine and reflect, the more astonished are we at the immense Superiority of Shakspear over his contemporaries—& yet what contemporaries! Giant minds! Think of Jonson's Erudition, & the force of learned authority in that age—& yet in no genuine part of Shakespear is to be found such an absurd rant & *ventriloquism* as this, & too, too many other passages ferruminated from Seneca's Tragedies and the later Romans by Jonson. Ventriloquism, because Sejanus is a Puppet, out of which the poet makes his own voice appear to come.[7]

(Stockdale) WORKS: FALL OF SEJANUS, *Act V, scene 1 (scene of the sacrifice to Fortune).*

This scene is unspeakably irrational. To believe, and yet to scoff at a present miracle is little less than impossible. Sejanus should have been made to suspect Priestcraft & a secret Conspiracy against him.

[7] Two notes are omitted.

(Stockdale) WORKS: VOLPONE, *title page.*

This admirable, indeed, but yet more wonderful than admirable Play is from the fertility and vigor of Invention, Character, Language, and Sentiment, the strongest proof, how impossible it is to keep up any pleasurable Interest in a Tale, in which there is no goodness of heart in any of the prominent characters. After the 3rd act, this Play becomes not a dead but a painful weight on the Feelings. F. C. Fathom and Zelucco[8] are instances of the same truth. Bonario and Celia should have been made in some way or other *principals* in the Plot—which they might be, and the objects of Interest, without being made characters—in Novels, the Person, in whose fate you are most interested, is often the least marked character of the whole. If it were practicable to lessen the paramouncy [*sic*] of Volpone, a most delightful Comedy might be produced, Celia being the Ward or Niece instead of the Wife of Corvino, & Bonario her Lover.

(Stockdale) WORKS: EPICÆNE, *title page.*

The Epicæne is to my feeling the most entertaining of old Ben's Comedies—and more than any other would admit of being brought out anew, if under the management of a judicious and stage-understanding Play-wright; and an Actor, who had *studied* Morose, might make his fortune.[9]

(Stockdale) WORKS, *I, 326, Whalley's note at the end of* EPICÆNE. *Note continued on title page of* ALCHEMIST.

> Some criticks of the last age imagined the character of Morose to be wholly out of nature. But to vindicate our poet, Mr. Dryden tells us from tradition, and we may venture to take his word, that Jonson was really acquainted with a person of this whimsical turn of mind: and as humour is a personal quality, the poet is acquitted from the charge of exhibiting a monster, or an extravagant or unnatural caricatura.

If Dryden had not made all additional proof superfluous by his own Plays, this very vindication would evince that he had formed a false and vulgar Conception of the nature and conditions of the Drama and dramatic Personation. Ben Jonson would himself have rejected such a Plea:

> For he knew, Poet never credit gain'd
> By writing Truths; ※ but things, like Truth, well feign'd!
> Prologue 2nd to this Play

[8] Smollet's *Ferdinand Count Fathom* (1753) and Dr. John Moore's *Zeluco* (1786). [Raysor's note, *Misc. Crit.*, p. 55.]
[9] Two notes are omitted.

※ I.e. Facts. Caricatures are not less so because they are found existing in real life. But Comedy demands Characters, and leaves Caricatures to Farce. The safest & truest defence of old Ben were to call the Epicæne the best of Farces. The defect in the Morose, as in other of Jonson's Dr. Personæ, lies in this: that the accident is not a Prominence growing out of and nourished by the *character* which still circulates in it, but the Character rises out of the accident—say rather, consists in the Accident. Shakespear's comic Personages have exquisitely characteristic Features—however awry, disproportionate, & laughable, yet like his Bardolph's nose, still Features. But Jonson's are, either a man with a huge *Wen*, having a circulation of it's own, & which we might conceive amputated, and the Patient thereby losing all his *character;* or they are mere Wens instead of Men, Wens personified or with eyes, nose & mouth cut out, mandrake-fashion.

P. S. All the above, and more, will have been justly said, if and whenever the drama of Jonson is brought into *"comparisons of rivalry"* with the Shakespearian. But this should not be. Let it's inferiority to the Shakespearian be at once fairly owned; but at the same time as the inferiority of an altogether different *Genus* of the Drama. On this ground, old Ben would still maintain his proud Height. He, no less than Shakespear, stands on the summit of his Hill, & looks round him like a Master: tho' his be Lattrig, and Shaksp's Skiddaw.[10]

(Stockdale) WORKS: CATILINE, *opposite title page.*

A fondness for judging one work by comparison with others, perhaps altogether of a different Class, argues a vulgar Taste. Yet it is chiefly on this Principle that the Catiline has been rated so low. Take it and Sejanus as compositions of a particular Kind—viz. as a mode of relating great historical Events in the liveliest and most interesting manner, and I cannot help wishing that we had Whole Volumes of such Plays. We might as rationally expect the excitement of the Vicar of Wakefield from Goldsmith's History of England, as that of Lear, Othello &c. from the Sejanus & Catiline.

(Stockdale) WORKS: CATILINE, *Act I, scene 4.*

This is either an unintelligible, or (in *every* sense) a most *unnatural* passage—improbable, if not impossible—at the very moment of signing and swearing such a Conspiracy for the most libidinous satyr. The very presence of the Boys is an outrage to probability. I suspect that these Lines should be removed so as to follow the 5th Line of the second Column, p. 381. "On this part of the House—Sirrah! what ail you?

[10] Notes on *The Alchemist* omitted.

P.[age] Nothing. B.[estia] Aye, nothing—only somewhat modest. Cat. Slave, I will strike &c." A total erasure, however, would be the best, or, rather the *only* possible, amendment.

(Stockdale) WORKS: CATILINE, *Act II, scene 2 (Sempronia's speech).*

. . . He is but a new fellow,
An inmate here in Rome (as Catiline calls him).

A *Lodger* would have been a happier imitation of the inquilinus [of Sallust].

(Stockdale) WORKS: CATILINE, *Act IV, scene 6 (speech of Cethegus).*

Can these or such be any aids to us, etc.

What a strange notion Ben must have formed of a determined, re-morseless, all-daring, Foolhardiness, to have represented it in such a mouthing Tamburlane, and bombastic Tongue-Bully as this Cethegus of his!

(Stockdale) WORKS: BARTHOLOMEW FAIR, *Induction (Scrivener's speech).*

If there be never a servant-monster i' the Fair,[11] who can help it, he says, nor a nest of antiques? he is loth to make nature afraid in his plays, like those that beget tales, tempests, and such like drolleries, to mix his head with other men's heels . . .[12]

The best excuse that can be made for Jonson, and in a somewhat less degree for Beaumont & Fletcher, in respect of these base and silly Sneers at Shakespear, is, that his Plays were present to men's minds chiefly as acted. They had not a neat *Edition* of them, as we have—so as by comparing the one with the other to form a just notion of the mighty mind that produced the whole. At all events, & in every respect, Jonson stands far higher in a moral Light than B. & F. He was a fair con-temporary & in *his* way & as far as respects Shakespear, an Original. But B. & F. were always imitators, often borrowers, and yet sneer at him with a spite far more malignant than Jonson, who has besides made noble compensation by his Praises.

(Stockdale) WORKS: BARTHOLOMEW FAIR, *Act II, scene 3.*

Just. I mean a child of the horn-thumb, a babe of booty, boy, a cut-purse.

Confirms what the passage itself cannot but suggest the propriety of substituting Booty for Beauty in the first Act of Henry 4th, first Part.

[11] A reference to Caliban. [Raysor's note, *Misc. Crit.*, p. 59.]
[12] A reference to the dance of satyrs in *The Winter's Tale*, IV. iv. [Raysor's note, *Misc. Crit.*, p. 59.]

Falstaff. Let not us that are [squires of the night's body be called thieves of the day's beauty].

It is not often that old Ben condescends to imitate a *modern;* but Master Dan Knockhum Jordan and his vapours are manifest Replicas of Nym and Pistol.[13]

(Stockdale) WORKS: STAPLE OF NEWS, *Act IV, scene 3 (Pecunia's speech).*[14]

No, he would ha' done,
That lay not in his power: he had the use
Of our bodies, Band and Wax, and sometimes Statute's.
[*Coleridge deletes "Of" at the beginning of the third line and adds it to the end of the second line; and he indicates the alteration of "our" to "your."*]

I doubt the Legitimacy of my transposition of the "of" from the 4th[15] (Of your bodies) to this preceding line—for tho' it facilitates the metre and reading of the 4th line, and is frequent in Massinger, yet this disjunction of the preposition from its case seems to have been disallowed by Jonson. Better, for the reasons above assigned, read "O' *your*"—the two syllables slurred into one, or rather snatched or sucked up into the emphasized *Your*. In all points of view, therefore, Ben's Judgement is just—for in this way the Line cannot be read as *metre* without that strong and quick emphasis on *your* which the *Sense* requires: and had not the sense required an emphasis on *your*, the tmesis of the sign of it's cases "of," "to," &c., would destroy almost all boundary between the dramatic verse and *prose* in Comedy. A lesson not to be rash in conjectural amendments. S. T. C.[16]

It is worth noticing that Jonson uniformly prefers a slurring of the signs of the Cases at the beginning of a line, so as to form but one syllable with the noun, pronoun, or article, to placing the sign at the end of the preceding line, even where it would only make the last trochaic of the 11-syllable dramatic blank verse line—I think, judiciously. Indeed, his verse throughout well deserves studying.[17]

It was not possible, that so bold and robust an Intellect as that of Ben Jonson could be devoted to any form of intellectual Power vainly or even with mediocrity of Product. He could not but be a Species of

[13] Five notes omitted and *The Devil Is an Ass* omitted.
[14] One note above and two following are omitted.
[15] Fourth on the page; third in the reference as quoted. [Raysor's note, *Misc. Crit.*, p. 62.]
[16] The last paragraph of this note comes from the first flyleaf of the volume with the reference, "See p. 550," which is the page of the preceding paragraph.
[17] Two notes following are omitted. *The New Inn* is omitted.

himself: tho' like the Mammoth and Megatherion fitted & destined to
live only during a given Period, and then to exist a Skeleton, hard, dry,
uncouth perhaps, yet massive and not to be contemplated without that
mixture of Wonder and Admiration, or more accurately, that middle
somewhat between both for which we want a term—not quite even with
the latter, but far above the mere former. In this Light, a Heretic as
to the ordinary Notion (if words echoed sine noscendo can be called
Notions) but in compleat sympathy with the practical Feeling of my
contemporary, I regard B. Jonson, the Play-wright—& hold his Dramas
of worth far inferior to his Poems, and the Plays themselves chiefly
valuable for the many & various passages which are not dramatic. In
Harmony of metre, in rhythm, in sweetness of words, he is indeed
greatly inferior to Juvenal; but in all other excellencies superior—and
in none more so, than those which (in *kind*) they both possessed in
common—Jonson's philosophy more profound, his morality more pure,
his observation more acute & active, and his Figures more alive and
individual. S. T. C.[18]

He said that Shakespeare was almost the only dramatic poet, who
by his characters represented a class, and not an individual: other
writers for the stage, and in other respects good ones too, had aimed
their satire and ridicule at particular foibles and particular persons,
while Shakespeare at one stroke lashed thousands: Shakespeare struck
at a crowd; Jonson picked out an especial object for his attack.[19]

For a young Author's first work almost always bespeaks his recent
Pursuits, and his first observations of Life are either drawn from the
recent employments & from the characters & images most impressed on
his mind in the situations, in which these Employments had placed him
—or else they are fixed on such objects & occurrences in the World, as
are easily connected with & seem to bear upon his studies & the hitherto
subjects of his meditation. Thus Lessing's earliest Comedies were placed
in the Universities and the events & characters conceivable in Academic
Life—Ben Jonson, who applies himself to the Drama after having served
in Flanders, fills his earliest plays with true or pretended soldiers, the
wrongs & neglects of the former, and the absurd Boasts & knavery of
their Counterfeits.[20]

[18] Anderson, *British Poets*, IV, blank page opposite the *Life* and verse of the title
page. This note is taken from the original in the Victoria and Albert Museum, but
it has previously been printed by Raysor in *Misc. Crit.*, pp. 47-48.
[19] Collier, *Seven Lect.*, pp. xxi-xxii.
[20] "Notes on Love's Labor's Lost," Notebook, 1810, pp. 37-38. Given with
some variations in *Lit. Rem.*, II, 108. The sentence on Lessing is transposed. This
note is given me by Miss Kathleen Coburn from her photograph of the material.

In this same epoch [i. e. the first] I should place the Comedy of Errors, remarkable as being the only specimen of poetical farce in our language, that is, intentionally such . . . I say intentionally such; for many of Beaumont and Fletcher's plays, and the greater part of Ben Jonson's comedies are farce-plots.[21]

I am inclined to consider The Fox as the greatest of Ben Jonson's works. But his smaller works are full of poetry.[22]

In Ben Jonson you have an intense and burning art. Some of his plots, that of the Alchymist, for example, are perfect. Ben Jonson and Beaumont and Fletcher would, if united, have made a great dramatist indeed, and yet not have come near Shakspeare; but no doubt Ben Jonson was the greatest man after Shakspeare in that age of dramatic genius.[23]

Beaumont and Fletcher

Beaumont. Born, 1586.—Died, 1616.

Fletcher. Born, 1576.—Died, 1625.[1]

Mr. Weber, to whose taste, industry, and appropriate Erudition, we owe, I will [not] say the best (for that would say little), but a good Edition of Beaumont and Fletcher, has compliment[ed] the Philaster, which he himself speaks of as inferior to the Maid's Tragedy by the same writers, as but little inferior to the noblest of Shakspears, the Lear, and Macbeth—consequently implying the equality at least of the Maid's Tragedy—''and another living critic of deserved eminence,'' who in his original works and in the manly wit, strong, sterling sense, and robust style had presented the best possible credentials of office,

[21] *Lit. Rem.*, II, 90.
[22] June 24, 1827. *Table Talk S*, VI, 287.
[23] Feb. 17, 1833. *Table Talk S*, VI, 426.

---

[1] The majority of the notes for the lecture on Beaumont and Fletcher are found in the British Museum, Add. MSS, 34,225, fol. 57 verso-62. These notes are taken direct from this source, but Raysor has also printed them in *Misc. Crit.*, pp. 41-45. Coleridge repeats the phrase, saying, ''An eminent living critic.''

as chargé d'affaires of Literature in general; and who by his Edition of Massinger, a work in which there was more for an Editor to do, and in which more was actually done and well done, than in any similar work within my knowledge, has proved an especial right of authority in the appreciation of dramatic poetry, and hath, in it's effect, potentially a double voice with the public as well as in the critical Synod where as princeps senatus he posesses it by his prerogative—has affirmed that Shakspear's superiority to his Contemporaries rests on his superior wit alone, while in all of the other and as I should deem higher excellencies of the Drama, Character, Pathos, Depth of Thought, &c. he is equalled by B. and F., B. J., and Massinger.

Of Wit I am engaged to treat in my IXth Lecture—it is a genus of many species—and at present I shall only say, that the species, which is predominant in Shakspear, is so completely Shakspearian, and in it's essence so interwoven with all his other characteristic excellencies that I am equally incapable of comprehending, both how it can be detached from his other Powers and how being disparate in kind from the Wit of contemporary Dramatists, it can be compared with them in degree. Again, supposing both the detachment and the comparison practicable, I should, I confess, be rather inclined to concede the contrary, and in the most common species of Wit, and in the ordinary application of the term, to yield the palm to Beaumont and Fletcher whom here and henceforward I take as one Poet, with two names—leaving undivided what a rare Love and still rarer congeniality had united—at least, I have never been able to distinguish the presence of Fletcher during the life of Beaumont, nor the absence of Beaumont during the survival of Fletcher.

But waiving, or rather deferring, this question, I protest against the remainder of the position in toto—and while I shall not I trust, shew myself blind to the various merits of Jonson, Fletcher, and Massinger, or insensible of the greatness of the merits which they possess in common, or to the specific excellencies which give to each of the three a worth of his own; but I confess, that one main object of this Lecture was to prove that Shakspear's eminence is his own, and [not] his age's—as the Pine Apple, the Melon, and the Gourd may grow on the same bed—nay the same circumstances of warmth and soil may be necessary to their full development—but does not account for the golden hue, the ambrosial flavor, the perfect shape of the Pine Apple, or the tufted Crown on it's head. Would that those, who would twist it off could but promise us in this instance to make it the germ of an equal Successor!

What had a grammatical and logical consistency for the Ear, what could be put together and represented to the Eye, these Poets took from the Ear and Eye, unchecked by any intuition of an inward impossibility —just as a man might put together a quarter an Orange, a quarter an Apple, and the like of a Lemon and of a Pomegranate, and make it look like one round diverse colored fruit—but Nature who works from within, by evolution and assimilation according to a Law, cannot do it—nor could Shakspear: for he too worked in the spirit of nature, by evolving the Germ within by the imaginative Power according to an Idea—For as the power of seeing is to Light, so is an Idea in mind to a Law in nature—they are correlatives that suppose each other.[2]

Doubtless, from mere observation, or from the occasional similarity of the writer's own character, more or less will happen to be in correspondence with nature, and still more in apparent compatibility—but yet the false source is always discoverable, first by the gross contradictions to nature in so many other parts, and secondly, by the want of the impression, which Shakspear makes, that the thing said not only might have been said but that nothing else could be substituted, so as to excite the same sense of it's exquisite propriety—illustrated from Iago when brought into Othello's sight. [I have always thought the conduct and expressions of Othello and Iago in the last scene, when Iago is brought in prisoner, a wonderful instance of Shakspeare's consummate judgment:—

> *Oth.* I look down towards his feet;—but that's a fable.
> If that thou be'st a devil, I cannot kill thee.
> *Iago.* I bleed, Sir; but not kill'd.
> *Oth.* I am not sorry neither.

Think what a volley of execrations and defiances Beaumont and Fletcher would have poured forth here!][3]

Hence Massinger and Ben Jonson both more perfect in their kind than Beaumont & Fletcher—the former more to story and affecting incidents, the latter more to manners and pecularities & whims in language —and vanities of appearance.

But there is a diversity of the most dangerous kind here. S. shaped his characters out of the nature within—but we can not so safely say, out of *his own* Nature, as an *individual person*. No! this latter is itself but a *natura naturata*—an effect, a product, not a *power*. It was S's prerogative to have the *universal*, which is potentially in each *par-*

---

[2] In *Lit. Rem.* a paragraph which is not in the MS follows. The first of it is from a folio now in the E. E. Lewis Library. See below, p. 671.

[3] The briefer statement in the MS has been expanded and the quotation included in *Lit. Rem.*, I, 105.

ticular, opened out to him—the *homo generalis* not as an abstraction of observation from a variety of men, but as the substance capable of endless modifications of which his own personal existence was but one, and to use this *one* as the eye that beheld the other, and as the Tongue that could convey the discovery. No greater or more common vice in Dramatic Writers than to draw out of themselves—how *I* (alone & in the self-sufficiency of my study, as all men are apt to be proud in their Dreams) should like to be talking—King? I am the King who would bully the Kings—Tut! Shakspear, in composing had no *I* but the I representative. Bertholdo in Massinger &c. &c.

B. & F.—the Fair Maid of the Inn.

Thierry & Theodoret—Another!—a *case* for a Mad doctor. [In Beaumont and Fletcher[4] you have descriptions of characters by the poet rather than the characters themselves: we are told, and impressively told, of their being; we rarely or never feel that they actually are.

There is, occasionally, considerable license in their dramas; and this opens a subject much needing vindication and sound exposition, but which is beset with such difficulties for a Lecturer, that I must pass it by. Only as far as Shakspeare is concerned, I own,] I can with less pain admit a fault in Shakspear than beg an excuse for it. I will not therefore attempt to palliate the grossness that actually exists by the customs of his age or by the far greater coarseness of all his Contemporaries—excepting Spencer—who is himself not wholly blameless tho' nearly so—for I have placed his merits on being of no age. But I would clear away what is clearly not his (as the porter in Macbeth)— what is in manners only—& what is derived from association with Crimes (foul thoughts—mean words).

The vile comments and aidances offensive & defensive of Pope's

Lust thro' some gentle strainers once refined,
Is Love[5]

contrasted with Shakespeare & even with the dogmatic [?] of M. &c. Hence Stern a favorite with the French.

The injuriousness of this because they cannot be answered where an answer would be most desirable from the painful nature of one part of the position; but this very pain is demonstrative of the falsehood.[6]

[4] From this point to "I can with less pain" are not in the MS, but are included in *Lit. Rem.* After the first paragraph, a part of a comment from the folio in the E. E. Lewis Library follows. In the present edition the entire comment appears in the general criticism after the notes.

[5] *Pope's Essay on Man,* canto ii, ll. 189-90. Not accurately quoted by Coleridge.

[6] Raysor restores the two paragraphs above to their place in the discussion of Sterne (*Misc. Crit.,* p. 122), but since the comment is also on the dramatists it is here incorporated as in *Lit. Rem.,* I, 107, with a minor difference. Raysor reads "injuriousness" as "unfairness."

(Stockdale) WORKS: PREFACE *by Seward (1750), I, xxi.*[7]

The King And No King too is extremely spirited in all its characters; Arbaces holds up a mirror to all men of *virtuous principles,* but *violent passions.* Hence he is as it were at once *magnanimity* and *pride, patience* and *fury, gentleness* and *rigor, chastity* and *incest,* and is one of the finest mixtures of virtues and vices that any poet has drawn . . .

These are among the endless instances of the abject state to which Psychology had sunk from the reign of Charles the I. to the middle of the present reign—George 3—& even now it is but awaking.[8]

(Stockdale) WORKS: PREFACE *by Seward, I, xl.*

[*Seward's classification of the plays according to relative excellence.*]

These four [*Monsieur Thomas, The Chances, Beggar's Bush,* and *The Pilgrim*] should surely have been placed in the very first class! But the whole attempt ends in a woeful failure.

(Stockdale) WORKS, *Harris's commendatory poem on Fletcher, I, lxxiv.*

I'd have a state of wit convok'd, which hath
A power to take up on common faith.

This is an instance of that modifying of quantity by Emphasis, without which our elder Poets can not be scanned. "Power," here, instead of being one—(Pow'r), must be not indeed – –, nor yet – ◡, but – ◡ ◡. The first syllable is 1¼.

(Stockdale) WORKS, *flyleaves of Vol. II.*

We can never expect an authentic Edition of our Elder *dramatic Poets* (for in those times a Drama was a Poem) until some man undertakes the work who has studied the philosophy of metre. This has been the main Torch of sound Restoration in the Greek Dramatists by Bentley, Porson, and their followers: how much more, then, in our own Tongue! It is true that *Quantity,* an almost iron Law with the Greek, is in our language rather a subject for a peculiarly fine ear, than any law or even rule; but then we, instead of it have first, accent; 2ndly, emphasis; and lastly, retardation & acceleration of the Times of Syllables according to the meaning of the words, the passion that accompanies

[7] The notes from this preface and from other sources are selected for general interest. Textual notes and minor comments have been omitted since complete transcriptions appear in Raysor, *Misc. Crit.,* pp. 65-93. See also *Lit. Rem.,* II, 289-322. The notes re-edited are my own reading from the original in Stockdale's edition (see p. 639 n. 3), or as designated in several cases, from *Fifty Comedies and Tragedies* (London: 1679), British Museum, C. 45, i. 7. The latter have also been printed by William Taylor, *Crit. Annot.,* pp. 13-19.

[8] Three notes are omitted.

them, and even the character of the Person that uses them. With due attention to these, above all to that, which requires the most attention & the finest taste, the last; *Massinger, ex. gr.*, might be reduced to a rich and yet regular metre. But then the *Regulæ* must be first known—tho' I will venture to say, that he who does not find a line (not corrupted) of Massinger's flow to the *Time total* of an Iambic Pentameter Hyperacatalectic, i. e. four Iambics ($\smile -$) and an Amphibrach ($\smile -- \smile$) has not read it aright. By power of this last principle (ret[ardation] and accel[eration] of time) we have even proceleusmatics and dispondœuses— proceleusmatics ($\smile \smile \smile \smile$) and Dispondœuses ($----$)—not to mention the Choriambics, the Ionics, the Pæons, and the Epitrites. Since Dryden, the metre of our Poets leads to the Sense: in our elder and more genuine Poets, the Sense, including the Passion, leads to the metre. Read even Donne's Satires as he meant them to be read, and as the sense & passion demand, and you will find in the lines a manly harmony.

(Stockdale) WORKS: LIFE OF JOHN FLETCHER, *II, 7.*

In general their plots are more regular than Shakspeare's . . .

This is true, if true at all, only before a Court of Criticism which judges one scheme by the Laws of another and a diverse. Shakespear's Plots have their own laws or regulæ—and according to these they are *regular.*

(Stockdale) WORKS: MAID'S TRAGEDY, *Act I, scene 1 (Melantius's speech).*[9]

> These soft and silken wars are not for me:
> The music must be shrill, and all confus'd
> That stirs my blood; and then I dance with arms.

What strange self-trumpeters and tongue-bullies all the brave Soldiers of B. and F. are! Yet I am inclined to think it was the fashion of the age, from the Soldier's speech in the Counter Scuffle—& deeper than the fashion B. and F. did not fathom.

(Stockdale) WORKS: MAID'S TRAGEDY, *Act I, scene 1 (Lysippus's speech).*

> Yes, but this lady
> Walks discontented, with her wat'ry eyes
> Bent on the earth, etc.

Opulent as Shakespear was, and one of his opulence prodigal, he yet would not have put this exquisite piece of Poetry in the mouth of a

* The first note is omitted.

no-character, or as addressed to Melantius.   I wish that B. and F. had
written Poems instead of *Tragedies.*[10]

(Stockdale) WORKS: MAID'S TRAGEDY, *Act II, scene 1 (Amintor's speech).*

> Oh, thou hast nam'd a word, that wipes away
> All thoughts revengeful!   In that sacred name,
> "The king," there lies a terror.

It is worth noticing that of the three greatest tragedians, Massinger
was a Democrat, B. & F. the most servile jure divino Royalists, Shakespear a Philosopher—if anything, an Aristocrat.[11]

(Stockdale) WORKS: THE CUSTOM OF THE COUNTRY, *Act I, scene 1
(Rutilio's speech).*[12]

> Yet if you play not fair, and above-board too,
> I have a foolish engine here:—I say no more.
> I'll tell you what, and, if your honours guts are not
> enchanted . . .

Evidently transposed—

> Yet if you play not fair, above-board too,
> I'll tell you what—
> I've a foolish engine here:—I say no more—
> But if your Honour's guts are not enchanted—

Licentious as the comic metre of B. and F. is, far more lawless and
yet a far less happy imitation of the rhythm of animated Talk in real
life, than Massinger's—Still it is made worse than it really is by ignorance of the halves, thirds, and two-thirds of [a] Line which B. and
F. adopted from the Italian & Spanish Dramatists.   Thus in Rutilio's

> . . . any man would
> Desire to have her, & by any means,
> At any rate too, yet this common Hangman
> Who hath whipt off a thousand maids' heads already—
> That he &c.

In all comic metres the Gulping of short syllables, and the abbreviation
of syllables ordinarily long by the rapid pronunciation of eagerness and
vehemence is [*sic*] not so much a license, as a Law—a faithful copy
of nature, & let them be read characteristically, the *Times* will be found
nearly the same.   Thus "a thousand maids' heads" is a choriambus, or
even perhaps a Pæon primus _ ‿ ‿ _ (a dactyl, by virtue of comic rapid-

[10] Five notes omitted.
[11] One note omitted.   *A King and No King* and *The Scornful Lady* omitted.
[12] One note preceding this omitted.

ity, being equal to an Iambic when the Iambic is distinctly pronounced).
I have no doubt, that all B. and F.'s works might be safely corrected
by attention to this rule—and that the Editor is entitled to transpositions
of all kinds, & to not a few omissions. For the rule of the metre lost,
what was to restrain the actors from interpolation?[13]

(Stockdale) WORKS: THE LOYAL SUBJECT, *page opposite title page; continued on title page.*

It is well worthy of notice, and yet has not been (I believe) noticed
hitherto, what a marked difference there exists in the dramatic writers of
the *Elizabetho-Jacobaean* age—(mercy on me! *what* a phrase for "during the reigns of Eliz. and James I!") in respect to political Opinions.
Shakespear, in this as in all other things, himself and alone, gives the
permanent Politics of Human Nature, and the only Predilection, which
appears, shews itself in his contempt of Mobs and the Populace.
Massinger is a decided Whig: B. and Fletcher high-flying, passive-obedience Tories. The Spanish Dramatists furnished them with this as
with many other Ingredients.[14] By the bye, an accurate and familiar
acquaintance with all the productions of the Spanish Stage prior to
1620, is an indispensable qualification for an Editor of Beaumont and
Fletcher—and with this qualification a most interesting and instructive
Edition might be given. This Edition is below Criticism.

P.S.—In the metre of the Drama, B. and F. are inferior to Shakespear on the one hand, as expressing the poetic part of the Drama, and
to Massinger on the other, in the art of reconciling metre with the
natural rhythm of Conversation: in which Massinger is, indeed, unrivalled. *Read* him aright, and measure by Time, not syllables, and no
lines can be more legitimate, none in which the substitution of equipollent Feet, and the modifications by emphasis, are managed with such
exquisite judgment. B. & F. are fond of the 12 syllable (not Alexandrine) line, as—

Too many Fears 'tis thought too: and to nourish those—

This has often a good effect. It is one of the varieties most common
in Shakespear.[15]

[13] The following are omitted: *The Elder Brother, The Spanish Curate, Wit without Money, The Humorous Lieutenant, The Mad Lover.*
[14] Cf. note on *The Tempest, Lit. Rem.*, II, 101. "In other writers we find the particular opinions of the individual; in Massinger it is rank republicanism; in Beaumont and Fletcher even *jure divino* principles are carried to excess;—but Shakspeare never promulgates any party tenets."
[15] *Rule a Wife and Have a Wife* omitted.

FIFTY COMEDIES:[16] THE LAWS OF CANDY, *Part I, p. 314.*

This Play has (to my feelings) a defect which is uncommon in B. and F. It is not even *entertaining.* The Story is as dull, as the characters are unnatural and the incidents improbable & revolting. The diction indeed is perhaps purer & more simple than in several other of the Dramas: but there are fewer poetic lines and passages, & such as there are or were intended to be such seem to me an old coat new turned, the mere parodies of the same thoughts & passions better exprest in their other plays—as Cassilane's Harangues, for instance, compared with Memnon in the Mad Lover, Archas in the Loyal Subject with Theodore, & with Caratach in Bonduca.—It is remarkable that Fletcher so exquisite in his Comedies, should so universally fail in all the Comic scenes of his Tragedies. They not only do not re-act upon & finally fuse with the tragic Interest, an excellence peculiar to Shakspere and Hogarth (see Lamb's Essay on Hogarth, in the Reflector) but they are dull & filthy in themselves.[17]

(Stockdale) WORKS, *flyleaves of Vol. III.*

Mem. To note how many of the Plays are founded on rapes—how many on unnatural incestuous passions—how many on mere lunacies. Then their virtuous women, either crazy superstitions of a merely bodily negation of a having been acted on, or Strumpets in their imaginations and wishes—or as in The Maid of the Mill, both at the same time.

In the men, the Love is merely Lust in one direction—exclusive preference of one Object. The Tyrant's speeches are mostly taken from the mouths of indignant Denouncers of the Tyrant's character, with the substitution of I for He, and the omission of *He acts as if he thought or said,* Know I am far above the faults I do, and those I do I'm able to forgive too. Nor dare the gods be angry at my Actions. The only feelings they can possibly excite are disgust at the Aeciuses, and other Loyalists or ire [?], or compassion, as Bedlamites. So much for their Tragedies.

But even their comedies are most of them disturbed by the fantasticalness or gross caricature of the persons or incidents. There are few characters that you can like (even tho' you should have had erased for you all the *filth* that bespatters the most likeable, as Piniero [in *The Island Princess*] for instance), scarcely any you can love. How different from Shakespear, who makes one have a sort of sneaking affection for even his Barnardines, whose very Iagos and Richards are aweful, and, by the counteracting power of profound Intellects, ren-

[16] See p. 653 n. 7.　　　　[17] *The Little French Lawyer* omitted.

dered fearful rather than hateful—and even the exceptions, as Goneril and Regan, proofs of superlative Judgment & the finest moral tact, in being utter monsters, nulla virtute redemptæ, and kept out of sight as much as possible—they being indeed only means for the excitement and deepening of noblest emotions toward the Lear, Cordelia, &c.—and employed with the severest economy. But even his grossness—that which is really so independent of the increase of vicious associations with things indifferent (for there is a state of manners conceivable so pure, that the language of Hamlet at Ophelia's feet might be harmless rallying, or playful teazing, of a Shame that would exist in Paradise)—yet at the worst, how different from B. & F.'s! In Shakespear the mere generalities of Sex, mere words oftenest, seldom or never distinct images— all head-work, and fancy-drolleries—no sensation supposed in the Speaker, no itchy wriggling. In B. and F. the minutiæ of a lecher.

(Stockdale) WORKS: VALENTINIAN, *Act I, scene 3.*

It is a real Trial for Charity to read this Scene with tolerable Charity towards Fletcher. So very slavish, so reptile are the feelings and sentiments represented as duties. And yet remember, he was a Bishop's Son—and the Duty to God was the supposed Basis.

Personals (including 1. body, 2. house, 3. home, 4. religion[18])—Property—Subordination—Inter-community—these are the Fundamentals of society. Now no one of these can be rightfully attacked except when it's Guardian has abused it to subvert one or more of the rest. Charles I. *deserved* death.

The reason is, that the guardian, as a Fluent, is less than the PERMANENT which he is to guard. He is the temporary and mutable *mean*—and derives his whole value from the *end*. In short, as *robbery* is not High Treason, so neither is every unjust act of a King the converse—*all* must be attached and endangered. Why? Because the King, as a to A, is a means of A = subordination in a far higher sense, than a proprietor b is to Property B.[19]

[18] I.e. negative so that the Person be not compelled to do or utter in relation of the Soul to God what would be in *that* Person, a Lie—such as to force a man to go to Church, to swear that he believes what he does not believe, &c. The *positive* may be a great and useful Privilege; but cannot be a *right;* were it for this only, that it can not be predefined. The ground of this distinction between negative and *positive* is plain. No one of my fellow-citizens is encroached on by my *not* declaring to him what I believe respecting the supersensual—but should every man be entitled to preach against the preacher, who could hear *any* preacher? Now it is different in Loyalty. There we have *positive* Rights, but not *negative* Rights. For every pretended negative would be in effect positive, as if a Soldier had a right to keep to himself, whether he would, or would not, fight. [*Coleridge's note*]

[19] One note omitted.

(Stockdale) WORKS: VALENTINIAN, *Act III, scene 1.*

B. & F. always write as if Virtue or Goodness were a sort of Talisman or Strange Something that might be lost without the least fault on the part of the Owner. In short, their chaste Ladies value their chastity as a material thing, not as an act or state of being—and this mere *thing* being merely imaginary, no wonder that all his [*sic*] Women are represented with the minds of Strumpets, except a few irrational Humorists, far less capable of exciting our sympathy than a Hindoo, who had had a basin of Cow-broth thrown over him—for this, tho' a debasing superstition, is still real, and we might pity the poor wretch, though we cannot help despising him. But B. & F.'s Lucinas are clumsy *Fictions.* It is too plain that the Authors had no one idea of Chastity as a virtue—but only such a conception as a blind man might have of the power of seeing, by handling an Ox's Eye. In the Queen of Corinth, indeed, they *talk* differently—but it is all *Talk*, for nothing is real but the dread of losing a reputation. Hence the frightful contrast between their women (even those who are meant for virtuous) and Shakespear's. So, for instance, the Maid of the Mill—a female must not merely have grown old in brothels, but have chuckled over every abomination committed in them with a rampant sympathy of imagination, to have had her fancy so [———?] drunk with the minutiæ of Lechery as this icy chast Virgin, the Maid of the Mill.[20]

FIFTY COMEDIES: VALENTINIAN, *Part I, p. 380 (the sick Emperor Valentinian).*[21]

It is strange that a man of Genius should have thought it worth while to steal, in this [?] parody[22] line, the rants of Shakspeare's poisoned King John.

FIFTY COMEDIES: VALENTINIAN, *Part I, pp. 384-85.*

A noble subject for the few noble minds capable of treating it would be this: What are the probable, what the possible defects, of *Genius* & of each given *sort* of Genius? And of course, what defects are psychologically impossible? This would comprize—what Semblance of *Genius* can *Talent* supply? And what *Talent* united with strong feeling for poetry & aided by Taste & Judgement? and how in the effects to be distinguished from those of Genius? Lastly, what degree of Talent may

---

[20] Henry Nelson Coleridge (*Lit. Rem.*, II, 310) added, "evinces hers to have been." Raysor inserts the paragraphs from the flyleaves of Vol. III at this point.

[21] See p. 653 n. 7.

[22] *Parody* is used in the sense of "weak imitation." See King John, Act V, scene 7. Taylor, *Crit. Annot.*, p. 14, gives a long note on the subject.

be produced by an intense desire of the End (*e. g.*, to be and to be thought, a Poet) without any *natural, more than* general, aptitude for the means?[23]

Be it not presumptuous or taken as a proof of Self-conceit, I will affirm that no man can have formed a just idea of possible *tragic* Drama, as opposed to possible *comic* Drama & not find in this Trag. of *Valent[inian]* a convincing proof, that the Writer was utterly incapable of Tragedy—and that such instances ad contra as may be brought, must be attributed to lucky Imitation of Shakspere, tho' blind to the *essential* excellence (which easily may be, notwithstanding the mind is struck with *accidental* beauties) of what he has imitated. In short, I scarcely *recollect* any scene or passage in B. & F. that is exclusively tragic, that is not in a higher degree poetic—*i. e.*, capable of being narrated by the Poet in his own person in the same words, with strict adherence to the character of the Poet. There is a kind of Comedy which whoever produces, must be capable of Tragedy (Cervantes, Shakspere)—but there is another kind & that too highly amusing, which is quite heterogeneous. Of this latter Fletcher was a great master. The surface and all it's flowers and open pleasures, serious or light, were his Property—all his eye can see, ear hear—nothing more.

A beautiful effect produced by the mixture of Trochaic with Iambic feet, of Lulling &, as it were, sleep-like Despondency in the Song over the poisoned Valentinian—

Care-charming Sleep, thou easer of all woes.

This Line introduces the Subject & supplies the general Notion which is to give distinct & enlivening individualizing power to the feelings excited by the Music—an ordinary Composer would begin in the most lulling strain, a great Composer in an Andante, soberly sad, & with a dignified monotonous solemn Distinctness. ⌣ signifies slow as a long-syllable but yet as little emphasized from it's comparative prominence of meaning, as a short syllable, therefore the symbol unites them ⌣ & –, i.e. ⌣⌣, better ⊣– = both long & short, or ⌣ or ⌟ , or rather without mark ⌟⌟ long.

Care-charming Sleep, thou easer of all woes,
Brother to Death, sweetly thyself dispose

[Note] thyself in mere pronunciation an iambic; but in emphasis no more than a cretic ⌣⌣ or rather ⌣⌣.

[23] Cf. other remarks on Genius and Talent: May 21, 1830, and Aug. 20, 1833, *Table Talk S*, pp. 319 and 481.

On this afflicted (yes! that will be the best way, only to mark by –
the syllables dwelt on with emphasis).

> On this afflicted Prince fall like a cloud
> In gentle showers, give nothing that is loud
> Or painful to his Slumbers, easy, sweet
> And as a purling stream, thou Son of Neit (night)
> Pass by his troubled Senses! sing his pain
> Like hollow murmuring wind, or silver Rain
> Into this Prince gently, O gently slide
> And kiss him into Slumbers, like a Bride.

An exquisite example of the power of a Poet to make his verse capable of scanning as iambics, & yet so to place the words that if the Reader has sense & feeling, they must have all the effect of Trochees. This pursued through all the single and composite Feet is the charm of Butler—and might perhaps be shown by Ratios in Time, ½, 1, 2, 3. The chief defect in metrical notation is that we have no symbols to make those influences and modifications, which the *sense* occasions in the same syllables in different Lines—This distinction, however, throws no light on the accent and quantity of the Ancients: since the former was no less invariable than the Latter. It belongs to the Poet's self-known Laws to make the Line *readable* by being scannable into certain allowed feet— not that they *should* be so read, or *ought* not to be otherwise scanned.[24]

(Stockdale) WORKS: ROLLO, *title page.*

This is, perhaps, the most energetic of Fletcher's tragedies. He evidently aimed at a new *Richard the Third* in *Rollo;* but as in all his other imitations of Shakespeare, he was not philosopher enough to *bottom* his original. Thus, in Rollo, he has produced a mere personification of outrageous Wickedness, with no fundamental characteristic impulses to make either the Tyrant's words or actions philosophically intelligible. Hence, the most pathetic situations border on the *horrible,* and what he meant for the Terrible, is either hateful, (μισητέον) or ludicrous. The scene of Baldwin's Sentence in the Act the IIId is probably the grandest working of Passion in all B. and F.'s Works; but the very magnificence of filial affection given to Edith in this noble scene renders the after-scene—(in imitation of one of the least Shakespearian of all Shakespear's works, (if it BE his) that between Richard and Lady Anne), in which

[24] This metrical note is from MSS Egerton, 2800, fol. 59. It is interesting in the light it throws on Coleridge's conception of metrics, and it shows Coleridge's mind at work in the effort to convey what he himself feels to be the correct reading. Printed for the first time.

Edith is yielding to a few words and Tears, not only unnatural, but disgusting. Queen Anne is described as a weak, vain, *very* woman throughout.

(Stockdale) WORKS: ROLLO, *Act I, scene 1.*

> *Gis.* He is indeed the perfect character
> Of a good man, and so his actions speak him.

This character of Aubrey, and the whole spirit of this and several other plays of the same Author, are interesting as traits of the morals which it was fashionable to teach in the reigns of James I, and his Successor, who died a martyr to them . Stage, Pulpit, Law, Fashion— all conspired to enslave the Realm. Massinger's plays breathe the opposite spirit; Shakespear's the spirit of wisdom that is for all ages. By the bye, the Spanish Dramatists (Calderon in particular) had some influence in this respect, (i. e., romantic Loyalty to the greatest monsters), as well as in the busy intrigues of B. & Fletcher's Plays.

FIFTY COMEDIES:[25] ROLLO, *Part I, p. 432 (Act II, scene 1).*

Tho' Single Facts in History would poorly justify a Poet's introduction of anomalous varieties, accidental monsters, Lusus Naturæ—were it only that they cannot represent an *Idea*, and whatever is not ideal (*i. e.*, partaking of the τὸ καθόλον) cannot be poetry: Yet even in genuine History, such as Froissard, Comines, &c. I remember no instance of Villains talking to their Sovereigns, in the character of Counsellors, as professed Villains.

FIFTY COMEDIES: ROLLO, *Part I, p. 432 (Act II, scene 1).*

> *Rollo.* Conscience Latorch! whats that?

That men have reasoned thus to themselves after a guilty deed in order to blunt the sting of Remorse, I doubt not; but that it is natural to reason thus as an inducement to perpetrate a crime, I find no evidence in History, or my own experience of Men, no slim presentiments, no *germ* of it's possibility in my own Heart.

FIFTY COMEDIES: ROLLO, *Part I, p. 433 (Act II, scene 2—the Drinking Song).*

> Drink to day and drown all sorrow,
> You shall perhaps not do it to morrow
> Best while you have it use your breath,
> There is no drinking after death.
>
> Wine works the heart up, wakes the wit,
> There is no cure 'gainst age but it—

[25] See p. 653, n. 7.

> It helps the head-ach, cough and tissick,
> And is for all diseases Physick.
> Then let us swill boyes for our health,
> Who drinks well, loves the commonwealth.
> And he that will to bed go sober,
> Falls with the leaf still in October.

This is the original of the excellent Song, "Punch cures the Gout, the Colic, and the Phthysic," the Imitation is an Improvement![26]

(Stockdale) WORKS: THE PILGRIM, *Act IV, scene 2.*

Alinda's interview with her Father is lively and happily hit off; but *this* scene with Roderigo is truly excellent. Altogether indeed this Play holds the first place in Fletcher's romantic Entertainments *(Lustspiele)* which collectively are his happiest performances, and is inferior only to the romance of Shakespear, As You Like It, Twelfth Night, &c.[27]

FIFTY COMEDIES:[28] THE PROPHETESS, *Part I, p. 578.*

Were I to choose a play, that most realized the Ideal of Anti-Shakesperianism, I should fix, I think on this: tho' perhaps half a dozen others of the same writer might be perilous Competitors. A witch, possessed of all powers & comprizing in herself all the Gods; yet an every-day old Aunt, & only a Witch, but by whose powers no one knows—working neither for good or for evil, but to secure her *Niece* a reluctant Husband —& all the rest, pasteboard puppets, ducking heads, lifting arms, & sprawling legs, as she pulls the thread—nothing from within, all from without—sincere conversions to virtue produced in an instant by unmanly terrors—no characters, no men, no women—but only mouthing Vices, or interlocutory *Entia Narrationis*—Explanations personified by Hat, Coat, Waistcoat, & Breeches—of course, no *Interest* (for a vulgar curiosity about—not what is to *happen* next—but about what the Witch will *do* next, whether Thunder or a Brimstone She Devil, or an Earthquake,[29] cannot be called *Interest*)—Miserable parodies & thefts of fine

---

[26] The first verse of the song alluded to is as follows:—
> Come, landlord, fill a glowing bowl, until it does run over,
> For to night we all will merry be, tomorrow will get sober.

The line quoted by Coleridge is in the third verse.
> Punch cures the Gout, the colic, and the tisic [*sic*]
> And is to all men, the every best of physic.

Taylor's note, p. 15.
The Wild Goose Chase and *Wife for a Month* are omitted.
[27] One note omitted. [28] See p. 653 n. 7.
[29] Taylor read the word "earwigmaker."

lines in Shakespere—and the compound, a senseless Day-dream, with all
the wildness without any terror of a Night-mair, in short Stupidity from
malice (of self-conceit) prepense, aping Madness. The proper compliment is to open one's mouth in *wonder* and lo! it was only a Yawn.

(Stockdale) WORKS: THE QUEEN OF CORINTH, *Act II, scene 1 (Merione's
speech).*

Had the scene of this Tragi-comedy been laid in Hindostan instead
of Corinth, and the gods here addressed been the Vishnoo and Co. of the
Indian Pantheon, this Rant would not have been much amiss.

FIFTY COMEDIES:[30] THE QUEEN OF CORINTH, *Part II, p. 8.*

Exquisite specimen of the μισητέον substituted for the φοβερόν.

FIFTY COMEDIES: THE QUEEN OF CORINTH, *Act II, scene 3 (Merione
expresses her gratitude to Agenor).*

This is pretty; but it is false, & made up of incompatibles, natural
feelings, & abstract notions, wch being, such feelings can not exist.[31]

(Stockdale) WORKS: THE QUEEN OF CORINTH, *Act III, scene 1, note at the
end.*

In respect of Style and Versification, this Play and the Bonduca
may be taken as the best, and yet as *characteristic,* specimens. Particularly, the first Scene of Bonduca. Take the Richard the Second of
Shakespear, and having selected some one scene of about the same
number of Lines, and consisting mostly of long Speeches, compare it
with the first scene of Bonduca—not for the idle purpose of finding out
which is the better, but in order to see and understand the difference.
The latter (B. and F.) you will find a well arranged bed of Flowers, each
having it's separate root, and it's position determined aforehand by the
will of the Gardener—a fresh plant, a fresh Volition. In the former an
Indian Fig-tree, as described by Milton—all is growth, evolution, γένεσις
each Line, each word almost, begets the following—and the Will of the
writer is an interfusion, a continuous agency, no series of separate
Acts. Sh. is the height, breadth, and depth of Genius. B. and F. the
excellent mechanism, in juxtaposition and succession, of Talent.[32]

(Stockdale) WORKS: THE NOBLE GENTLEMAN, *title page.*

Why have the dramatists of the times of Elizabeth, James I, and the
first Charles become almost obsolete? excepting Shakespear? Why do

---

[30] See p. 653 n. 7.   [31] One personal note omitted.
[32] *Bonduca* omitted.

they no longer belong to the English People, being once so popular?
And why is Shakespear an exception? One thing among 50 necessary
to full solution is, that they all employed *poetry* and poetic diction on
unpoetic Subjects, both Characters & Situations—esecially in their Comedy. Now Shakespear is all all, ideal—of no time, & therefore of all
times. Read for instance, *Marine's* panegyric on the Court, p. 108,
Column 2nd. [in the first scene of this play—

> Know
> The eminent court, to them that can be wise,
> And fasten on her blessings, is a sun
> That draws men up from coarse and earthly
> being, etc.]

What can be more unnatural & inappropriate (not only is, but must be
felt as such) than such poetry in the mouth of a silly Dupe? In short,
the scenes are mock dialogues, in which the Poet Solo plays the ventrilo-
quist, but can not suppress his own way of expressing himself. Heavy
complaints have been made respecting the transprosing of the old
plays by Cibber—but it never occurred to these critics to ask, how it
came that no one ever attempted to transprose a comedy of Shakespear's.[33]

(Stockdale) WORKS: THE FAIR MAID OF THE INN, *Act II, scene 1 (Albertus's speech).*

> But, sir,
> By my life, I vow to take assurance from you,
> That right-hand never more shall strike my son, . . .
> Chop his hand off!

In this (as indeed in all other respects, but most in this) it is that
Shakespear is so incomparably superior to Fletcher & his Friend—in
Judgement! What can be conceived more unnatural & motiveless
than this brutal resolve? How is it possible to feel the least interest
in Albertus afterwards? or in Cesario?

(Stockdale) WORKS: THE TWO NOBLE KINSMEN, *Act, II, scene 1.*

On comparing the prison scene in this act = II, with the dialogue
between the same speakers in the First, I can scarcely retain a doubt
as to the First Act's having been written by Shakspear: assuredly not
by B. or F. I hold Jonson more probable than either of these two.

The main presumption for Shakespear's share in this play rests
on a point, to which both these sturdy critics[34] (and indeed all before

---

[33] *The Coronation* and *Wit at Several Weapons* omitted.

[34] Colman, and Seward, whom Colman quotes at length. [Raysor's note.]

them) were blind—the construction of the Blank Verse, which proves beyond all doubt an intentional imitation, if not the proper hand, of Shakespear. Now, whatever improbability there is in the former (which supposes Fletcher conscious of the inferiority, the too poematic minus-dramatic nature, of his versification, and of which there is neither proof nor likelihood) adds so much to the probability of the latter. On the other hand, the *harshness* of many of these very passages, and a harshness unrelieved by any lyrical interbreathings, and still more the want of profundity in the thoughts, keep me fluctuating. S. T. Coleridge.[35]

Being asked whether he included the "Two Noble Kinsmen," among the doubtful plays, he answered, "Decidedly not: there is the clearest internal evidence that Shakespeare importantly aided Fletcher in the composition of it. Parts are most unlike Fletcher, yet most like Shakespeare, while other parts are most like Fletcher, and most unlike Shakespeare. The mad scenes of the Jailor's daughter are coarsely imitated from 'Hamlet': those were by Fletcher, and so very inferior, that I wonder how he could so far condescend. Shakespeare would never have imitated himself at all, much less so badly. There is no finer, or more characteristic dramatic writing than some scenes in "The Two Noble Kinsmen."[36]

I have said nothing of Anacreon, for he is known and admired by all. His joyousness of heart, his festivity of fancy, his grace and richness of expression, glow with an oriental fervour. His garments breathe of myrrh, as if he had been made glad in ivory palaces. He has no un-meaning expletives to swell out a halting line. Every word, like the flowers of an Eastern love-letter, is a symbol of some tender and romantic sentiment. You will meet with much of this picturesque beauty in those "dainty devices," which abounded in the early part of the seventeenth century. Shakspeare, too, who combined the highest strains of the Muse with the humblest, enjoyed this delightful vein. But the most charming passage with which my memory furnishes me, occurs in the *Noble Kinsmen,* of Beaumont and Fletcher. The lover is indulging in one of those bursts of enthusiasm to which lovers in all ages have been prone.

> Blessed garden,
> And fruits and flowers more blessed, that
> still blossom
> As her bright eyes shine on ye! would I were,

[35] One note omitted. *The Woman Hater* omitted. The marginal notes end with the latter play.
[36] Collier, "Diary," Oct. 13, 1811, *Seven Lect.*, p. xx.

> For all the fortune of my life hereafter.
> *Yon little tree, yon blooming Apricot,*
> *How I would spread, and fling my wanton arms*
> *In at her window.* I would bring her fruit,
> Fit for the gods to feed on. Youth and pleasure,
> Still as she tasted, should be doubled on her.[37]

We have indeed two poets who wrote as one, near the age of Shakespeare, to whom (as the worst characteristic of their writings), the Coryphæus of the present Drama may challenge the honour of being a poor relation, or impoverished descendant. For if we would charitably consent to forget the comic humor, the wit, the felicities of style, in other words, *all* the poetry, and nine-tenths of all the genius of Beaumont and Fletcher, that which would remain becomes a Kotzebue.[38]

It is well worthy notice, that Lear is the only serious performance of Shakespear, the interest & situations of which are derived from the assumption of a gross Improbability; whereas Beaumont and Fletcher's Tragedies are, almost all, founded on some out-of-the-way Accident or Exception to the general Experience 'of mankind. But observe the matchless Judgment of our Shakespear. First, improbable as the conduct of Lear is, in the first Scene, yet it was an old Story, rooted in the popular Faith—a thing taken for granted already, & consequently, without any of the *effects* of Improbability. 2ndly it is merely the canvass for the Characters and passions, a mere *occasion*—and not (as in B. and F), perpetually recurring as the cause & sine quâ non of the Incidents and Emotions. Let the first Scene of Lear have been lost, and let it be only understood that a fond father had been duped by hypocritical professions of Love and Duty on the part of two Daughters to disinherit a third, previously, & deservedly, more dear to him, & all the rest of the Tragedy would retain it's Interest, undiminished, & be perfectly intelligible. The *accidental* is no where the ground-work of the Passions: but that which is καθόλου, that which in all ages has been & ever will be, close & native to the heart of man—Parental Anguish from filial Ingratitude, the genuineness of worth, though coffered in bluntness, and the vileness of a smooth Iniquity. Perhaps, I ought to have added the Merchant of Venice; but here too the same remarks apply. It was an old Tale; & substitute any other danger, than that of the Pound of Flesh (the circumstance in which the improbability lies) yet all the situations & the emotions appertaining to them remain equally excellent & appropriate. Whereas take away from "the Mad Lover" the fantastic

---

[37] Willmott, *C. at Trinity*, pp. 32-33.
[38] *Biog. Lit. C*, II, 260.

hypothesis of his engagement to cut out his own Heart, and have it presented to his mistress, & all the main Scenes must go with it. Kotzebue is the German B. & F., without their poetic powers, & without their vis comica. But, like them he always deduces his situations & passions from marvellous accidents, & the trick of bringing one part of our moral nature to counteract another—as our pity for misfortune & admiration of generosity & courage to combat our condemnation of Guilt, as in Adultery, Robbing, &c., & like them too, he excels in his mode of telling a story clearly, & interestingly, in a series of dramatic Dialogues. Only the trick of making Tragedy-Heroes & Heroines out of Shopkeepers & Barmaids was too low for the age, & too unpoetic for the genius, of Beaumont & Fletcher, inferior in every respect as they are to their great Predecessor & Contemporary! *How* inferior would they have appeared, had not Shakespear existed for them to *imitate?*— which in every play, more or less, they do, & in their Tragedies most glaringly—and yet—(O Shame! Shame!)—miss no opportunity of sneering at the divine Man, and sub detracting from his Merits.[39]

Lamb led Coleridge on to speak of Beaumont and Fletcher: he highly extolled their comedies in many respects, especially for the vivacity of the dialogue, but he contended that their tragedies were liable to grave objections. They always proceeded upon something forced and unnatural; the reader never can reconcile the plot with probability, and sometimes not with possibility. One of their tragedies[40] was founded upon this:—A lady expresses a wish to possess the heart of her lover, terms which that lover understands, all the way through, in a literal sense; and nothing can satisfy him but tearing out his heart, and having it presented to the heroine, in order to secure her affections, after he was past the enjoyment of them. Their comedies, however, were much superior, and at times, and excepting in the generalisation of humour and application, almost rivalled those of Shakespeare. The situations are sometimes so disgusting, and the language so indecent and immoral, that it is impossible to read the plays in private society. The difference in this respect between Shakespeare and Beaumont and Fletcher (speaking of them in their joint capacity) is, that Shakespeare always makes vice odious and virtue admirable, while Beaumont and Fletcher do the very reverse—they ridicule virtue and encourage vice: they pander to the lowest and basest passions of our nature.[41]

[39] From the original note in Theobald's edition of *Shakespeare's Plays*, VI, second flyleaf verso, third flyleaf and fourth flyleaf recto. Note signed and dated Jan. 1, 1813. A note, IV, 239, says, "That B. and F. have more than once been guilty of sneering at their great master, cannot I fear be denied." The passage above appears with a few minor variations from my reading in Raysor, *Shakes. Crit.*, I, 59-60.
[40] *The Mad Lover.*   [41] Collier, *Seven Lect.*, pp. xxii-xxiii.

The next character belonging to Shakespeare as Shakespeare, was the *keeping at all times the high road of life.* With him there were no innocent adulteries; he never rendered that amiable which religion and reason taught us to detest; he never clothed vice in the garb of virtue, like Beaumont and Fletcher, the Kotzebues of his day.[42]

The writings of Beaumont and Fletcher bear no comparison; the grossest passages of Shakespeare were purity to theirs; and it should be remembered that though he might occasionally disgust a sense of delicacy, he never injured the mind: he caused no excitement of passion which he flattered to degrade, never used what was faulty for a faulty purpose; carried on no warfare against virtue, by which wickedness may be made to appear as not wickedness, and where our sympathy was to be entrapped by the misfortunes of vice; with him vice never walked, as it were, in twilight. . . .[43]

. . . . the pardon and marriage of Angelo not merely baffles the strong indignant claim of Justice—(for cruelty, with Lust and damnable Baseness, cannot be forgiven, because we cannot conceive them as being *morally* repented of) but it is likewise degrading to the character of Woman. Beaum[ont] and Fletcher, who can follow Shakespeare in his errors only, have presented a still worse, because more loathsome & contradictory instance of the same kind in the Night-Walker, in the marriage of Alathe to Algripe.[44]

I believe it possible that a man may, under certain states of the moral feeling, entertain something deserving the name of love towards a male object—an affection beyond frendship, and wholly aloof from appetite. In Elizabeth's and James's time it seems to have been almost fashionable to cherish such a feeling; and perhaps we may account in some measure for it by considering how very inferior the women of that age, taken generally, were in education and accomplishment of mind to the men. Of course there were brilliant exceptions enough; but the plays of Beaumont and Fletcher—the most popular dramatists that ever wrote for the English stage—will show us what sort of women it was generally pleasing to represent. Certainly the language of the two friends, Musidorus and Pyrocles, in the Arcadia, is such as we could

[42] Lecture I, Lectures of 1813-14. Raysor, *Shakes. Crit.*, II, 266. A somewhat different version is found in *Lit. Rem.*, II, 79.

[43] Raysor, *Shakes. Crit.*, II, 268. A similar statement occurs in the lecture on Beaumont and Fletcher.

[44] From the original note in Theobald's edition of *Shakespeare's Plays*, I, 305, title page for *Measure for Measure*, but also printed by Raysor, *Shakes. Crit.*, I, 113-14.

not now use except to women; and in Cervantes the same tone is sometimes adopted, as in the novel of the Curious Impertinent. And I think there is a passage in the New Atlantis of Lord Bacon, in which he speaks of the possibility of such a feeling, but hints the extreme danger of entertaining it, or allowing it any place in a moral theory.[45]

It has been remarked, I believe by Dryden,[46] that Shakespeare wrote for men only, but Beaumont and Fletcher (or rather "the gentle Fletcher") for women.[47]

Shakespeare, RICHARD II, *Act I, scene 2.*

> *Gaunt.* Heaven's is the quarrel; for heaven's substitute,
> His deputy annointed in his sight,
> Hath caus'd his death: the which if wrongfully,
> Let heaven revenge; for I may never lift
> An angry arm against his minister.

Without the hollow extravagance of Beaum. and Fletch.'s Ultra-royalism, how carefully does Shakspear acknowledge and reverence the eternal distinction between the mere Individual, and the Symbolic or representative: on which all genial Law no less than patriotism, depends.[48]

I would once more remark upon the exalted idea of the only true loyalty developed in this noble and impressive play. We have neither the rants of Beaumont and Fletcher, nor the sneers of Massinger ; . . . .[49]

In Beaumont and Fletcher priests are represented as a vulgar mockery; and, as in others of their dramatic personages, the errors of a few are mistaken for the demeanour of the many: but in Shakespeare they always carry with them our love and respect.[50]

Shakspeare's intellectual action is wholly unlike that of Ben Jonson

[45] May 14, 1833. *Table Talk S*, VI, 451-52.
[46] Preface to *Troilus and Cressida.*
[47] Lecture VI, Lectures of 1811-12. Collier, *Seven Lect.*, p. 50. Cf. p. 69. In the notes on the *Tempest*, *Lit. Rem.*, II, 96-97, the following version of the same idea appears:
"The opinion once prevailed, but, happily, is now abandoned, that Fletcher alone wrote for women;—the truth is, that with very few, and those partial, exceptions, the female characters in the plays of Beaumont and Fletcher are, when of the light kind, not decent; when heroic, complete viragos."
[48] From the original note in *Shakespeare's Plays*, printed for John Stockdale (2 vols.; London: 1807), I, 415. Note on blank page opposite passage. British Museum, C. 61. h. 7. Printed also by Raysor, *Shakes. Crit.*, I, 147.
[49] *Ibid.*, at end of notes on *Richard II*, but cf. Raysor, *Shakes. Crit.*, I, 151.
[50] Lecture VIII, 1811-12, Collier, *Seven Lect.*, p. 75.

or Beaumont and Fletcher. The latter see the totality of a sentence or passage, and then project it entire. Shakspeare goes on creating, and evolving B. out of A., and C. out of B., and so on, just as a serpent moves, which makes a fulcrum of its own body, and seems forever twisting and untwisting its own strength.[51]

Beaumont and Fletcher are the most lyrical of our dramatists. I think their comedies are the best part of their work, although there are scenes of very deep tragic interest in some of their plays. I particularly recommend Monsieur Thomas for good pure comic humor. The plays of Beaumont and Fletcher are mere aggregations without unity: in the Shakesperian drama there is a vitality, which grows and evolves itself from within—a key note which guides and controls and harmonies throughout.[52]

In Beaumont and Fletcher's tragedies the comic scenes are rarely so interfused amidst the tragic as to produce a unity of the tragic on the whole, without which the inter-mixture is a default. In Shakspeare, this is always managed with transcendent skill. The Fool in Lear contributes in a very sensible manner to the tragic wildness of the whole drama. Beaumont and Fletcher's serious plays or tragedies are completely hybrids,—neither fish nor flesh,—upon any rules, Greek, Roman, or Gothic; and yet they are very delightful notwithstanding. No doubt, they imitate the ease of gentlemanly conversation better than Shakspeare, who was unable *not* to be too much associated to succeed perfectly in this.[53]

Too many of B. and Fletcher's Com. Trag. and Trag. Comedies and the greater number of Jonson's Comedies are Farce-Plots.[54]

Monsieur Thomas and The Little French Lawyer are great favorites of mine among Beaumont and Fletcher's plays. How those plays overflow with wit! And yet I scarcely know a more deeply tragic scene anywhere than that in Rollo, in which Edith pleads for her father's

[51] March 5, 1834. *Table Talk S*, VI, 503.
[52] Folio 1679, in the E. E. Lewis Library, Sioux City, Iowa. This note is transcribed in ''Coleridge the Commentor,'' by John Louis Haney, *Coleridge: Studies by Several Hands on the Hundredth Anniversary of His Death*, ed. Edmond Blunden and E. L. Griggs (London: 1934), p. 123. It was, however, sent to me by the Librarian. It has also been printed by Raysor, *Misc. Crit.*, p. 44.
[53] July 1, 1833. *Table Talk S*, VI, 464.
[54] Notebook 24, p. 6. Printed for the first time.

life, and then, when she can not prevail, rises up and imprecates vengeance on his murderer.[55]

In the romantic drama, Beaumont and Fletcher are almost supreme. Their plays are in general most truly delightful. I could read the Beggar's Bush from morning to night. How sylvan and sunshiny it is! The Little French Lawyer is excellent. Lawrit is conceived and executed from first to last in genuine comic humor. Monsieur Thomas is also capital. I have no doubt whatever that the first act and the first scene of the second act of the Two Noble Kinsmen are Shakspeare's. Beaumont and Fletcher's plots are, to be sure, wholly inartificial; they only care to pitch a character into a position to make him or her talk; you must swallow all their gross improbabilities, and, taking it all for granted, attend only to the dialogue. How lamentable it is that no gentleman and scholar can be found to edit these beautiful plays! Did the name of criticism ever descend so low as in the hands of those two fools and knaves, Seward and Simpson? There are whole scenes in their edition which I could with certainty put back into their original verse, and more that could be replaced in their native prose. Was there ever such an absolute disregard of literary fame as that displayed by Shakspeare and Beaumont and Fletcher?[56]

As for editing Beaumont and Fletcher, the task would be one *immensi laboris*. The confusion is now so great, the errors so enormous, that the editor must use a boldness quite unallowable in any other case. All I can say as to Beaumont and Fletcher is, that I can point out well enough where something has been lost, and that something so and so was probably in the original; but the law of Shakspeare's thought and verse is such, that I feel convinced that not only could I detect the spurious, but supply the genuine, word.[57]

Unwisely perhaps, I mentioned to Mr. Arnold, Mr. Rae, and some others connected with the Theatres my intention & plans for preparing for the stage three plays: the one, Richard II, into which I had intended to introduce a female character, & to have attempted the giving of *theatrical* Interest to a Play, which for the *closet* is already among the most perfect of Shakespear's—the second Beaumont & Fletcher's Pilgrim, almost wholly re-written, and the scene placed in Ireland, under the name of Love's Metamorphoses. The third, of the success of which I had the greatest hopes, & which I described most at large, with it's

[55] June 24, 1827. *Table Talk S*, VI, 287.
[56] Feb. 17, 1833. *Table Talk S*, VI, 425-26.
[57] March 15, 1834. *Table Talk S*, VI, 506.

peculiar *ten-penny*[58] advantages, was the Beggar's Bush, of B. & F. It is, assuredly, an odd coincidence, if it be mere coincidence, that these three, the only ones I ever mentioned or thought of, should be the two of them brought out, with what success I know not—& the third spoken of in the Newspapers, as about to be brought out. Things irremediable I make point not to complain of—but as to this latter play, I have made great progress with, so that I could compleatly fit it for the stage in a fortnight. I have taken little more than the outline of the Plot, and not more than half of the Characters: and of the Language and Speeches more than half are compleatly original:— and I had purposely given a prominence to one character (& the want of a *prominent* Character is one grievous Defect, both of this & some other of Beaumont & Fletcher's best plays) with a view to Mr. Kean . . .[59]

Philip Massinger

Born at Salisbury, 1584.—Died, 1640[1]

1. Massinger—Vein of Satire on the Times—*i. e.* not as in Shakspear —the Natures evolve themselves according to their incidental dispro-portions, from excess, deficiency, or mislocation of one or more of the component elements—but what is attributed to them by others.

2. His excellent metre—a better model for dramatists in general— even tho' a dramatic Taste existed in the Frequenters of the Stage, and could be gratified in the present size and management (or rather man-agerment) of the two patent Theatres. [I do not mean that Massinger's verse is superior to Shakespeare's or equal to it. Far from it; but it is much more easily constructed, and may be more successfully adopted by writers in the present day. It is the nearest approach to the language of real life at all compatible with a fixed metre. In Massinger, as all our poets before Dryden, in order to make harmonious verse in

---

[58] Miss Stuart read the word as "temporary."

[59] Letter to Daniel Stuart, Oct. 7, 1835. British Museum, Add. MSS, 34,046, no. 68, fol. 88. Printed without the names of Arnold and Rae in Stuart, *Lake Poet Letters*, pp. 242-43, and with "Mrs." for "Mr." Kean.

---

[1] The comments on Massinger from Lecture VII are from my reading of British Museum, Add. MSS, 34, 225, fol. 64-67. Previously printed in Raysor, *Misc. Crit.*, pp. 93-97. Cf. the section on Massinger in *Lit. Rem.*, I, 108-112. Some comments appear only in the latter source.

the reading, it is absolutely necessary that the meaning should be understood;—when the meaning is once seen, then the harmony is perfect. Whereas in Pope and in most of the writers who followed in his school, it is the mechanical metre which determines the sense.][2]

3. Impropriety, indecorum of Demeanor in his favorite characters: as in Bertoldo [in the Maid of Honour] who is a swaggerer—who talks to his Sovereign what no Sovereign could endure, & to gentlemen what no gentlemen would answer but by pulling his nose.

4. Shakespear's Sir Andrew Ague-cheek, & Osric [are] displayed by others—in the course of social intercourse, as by the mode of their performing some office in which they are employed—but Massinger['s] *Sylli* comes forward to declare himself a fool ad arbitrium aucthoris, and so the diction always needs the *subintelligitur* ('the man looks *as if he thought* so and so,') expressed in language of the satirist—not of the man himself—*ex. gr.* v. 3. p. 29. Astutio to Fulgentio. The Author mixes his own feelings and judgements concerning him—but the man himself, till mad, fights up against them & betrays by the attempt to modify an activity & copiousness of thought, Image and expression which belongs not to Sylli, but to a man of wit making himself merry with his character.

5. Utter want of preparation—as in Camiola, the Maid of Honour— Why? because the Dramatis Personæ were all planned, *each by itself* but in Sh. the Play is a *syngenesia*—each has indeed a life of it's own, & is an *individuum* of itself: but yet an organ to the whole—as the Heart & the Brain, &c.—the Heart &c. of *that* particular Whole. Sh. [was] a comparative anatomist.

Hence Massinger & all, indeed, but Sh., take a dislike to their own characters, and spite themselves upon them by making them *talk like fools* or *monsters:* so Fulgentio in his visit to CAMIOLA [Act ii, sc. 2]. Hence too the continued Flings at Kings, Courtiers, and all the favorites of Fortune, like one who had enough of intellect to see the injustice of his own inferiority in the share of the good things of life, but not genius enough to rise above it & forget himself—envy demonstrated.[3] B. & F. the same vice in the opposite Pole—Servility of Sentiment—partizanship of the monarchical Faction.

6. From the want of character, of a guiding Point in Massinger's Characters, you never know what they are about.

7. Soliloquies,—with all the connectives and arrangements that have

[2] The section in brackets does not appear in the MS, but is taken from *Lit. Rem.,* I, 108-9.

[3] Raysor, *Misc. Crit.,* p. 95, reads ''democratic'' with a question, but the word is clear.

no other purpose from fear lest the person to whom we speak should not understand us.

8. Neither a one effect produced by the spirit of the whole, as in the "As You Like It"—nor by any one indisputably prominent as the Hamlet—"Which you like, Gentlemen!"

9. Unnaturally irrational passions that deprive the Reader of all sound interest in the characters—as in Mathias in the Picture—

10. The comic Scenes in Massinger not only do not harmonize with the tragic, not only interrupt the feeling, but degrade the characters that are to form any Part in the action of the Piece so as to render them unfit for any *tragic interest*—as when a gentleman is insulted by a mere Black-guard—it is the same as if any other accident of nature had occurred, as if a Pig had run under his legs, or his horse threw him.[4]

[I like Massinger's comedies better than his tragedies, although where the situation requires it, he often rises into the truly tragic and pathetic. He excells in narration, and for the most part displays his mere story with skill. But he is not a poet of high imagination; he is like a Flemish painter, in whose delineations objects appear as they do in nature, have the same force and truth, and produce the same effect upon the spectator. But Shakspeare is beyond this: he always by metaphors and figures involves in the thing considered a universe of past and possible experiences; he mingles earth, sea, and air, gives a soul to every thing, and at the same time that he inspires human feelings, adds a dignity in his images to human nature itself:—

> Full many a glorious morning have I seen
> Flatter the mountain tops with sovereign eye;
> Kissing with golden face the meadows green,
> Gilding pale streams with heavenly alchymy, &c.
>   33rd Sonnet][5]

Have I not over-rated Gifford's Edition of Massinger? *Not* if I have, as but just is, main reference to the rectification of the Text; but yes perhaps, if I were Talking of the *Notes*. These are more often wrong than right. See Vol. 3, p. 6. "A Gentleman yet no Lord." Gifford supposes a transposition of the Press for No Gentleman yet a Lord. But this would have no connection with what follows—and we have only to recollect that Lord means a Lord of Lands—to see that the after lines are explanatory. He is a man of high birth, but no landed Property. As to [the] former, he is a distant branch of the Blood Royal—as to the latter, his whole Estate lies "In a narrow compass, the King's Ear."

[4] *Ibid.*, p. 96, gives a slightly different reading.
[5] The section in brackets does not appear in the MS, but is taken from *Lit. Rem.*, I, 111-12.

My ear deceives me if Mason's "initiation" be not the right word. In short imitation is utterly impertinent to all that follows—he tells Antonio that he had been initiated with manners suited to the Court by two or three sound beatings & that a similar experience would be greatly useful for his initiation to the Camp—not a word of his imitation.[6]

Two or three tales, each in itself independent of the others, and united only by making the persons that are the agents in the story the *relations* of those in the other, as when a bind-weed or thread is twined round a bunch of flowers, each having its own root—and this novel narrative in *dialogue*—such is the *character* of Massinger's plays.—That the juxtaposition and the tying together by a common thread, which goes round this and round that, and then round them all, twine and intertwine, are contrived ingeniously—that the component tales are well chosen, and the whole well and conspicuously told; so as to excite and sustain the mind by kindling and keeping alive the curiosity of the reader—that the language is most pure, equally free from bookishness and from vulgarism, from the peculiarities of the School, and the transiencies of fashion, whether fine or coarse; that the rhythm and metre are incomparably good, and form the very model of dramatic versification, flexible and seeming to rise out of the passions, so that whenever a line sounds immetrical, the speaker may be certain he has recited it amiss, either that he has misplaced or misproportioned the emphasis, or neglected the acceleration or retardation of the voice in the pauses, (all which the mood or passion would have produced in the real Agent, and therefore demand from the Actor or $\left\{ \begin{array}{l} \text{translator} \\ \text{emulator} \end{array} \right\}$) and that read aright the blank verse is not less smooth than varied, a rich harmony, puzzling the fingers, but satisfying the ear—these are Massinger's characteristic merits.

Among the varieties of blank verse Massinger is fond of the anapæst in the first and the third foot, as:

[6] The *Maid of Honour*, Act I, scene 1:
Bertol.   But when you had been
          Cudgell'd, twice or thrice, and from the doctrine
     Made profitable uses, you concluded
     The sovereign means to teach irregular heirs.
     Civility, with conformity of manners,
     Were two or three sound beatings.
Ant.   I confess
     They did much good upon me.
Gasp.   And on me.
Bertol.   You'll find
     The like instruction in the Camp.
     Gifford criticized Mason's reading of "initiation" for "imitation" in the quarto.

"To your more | than mas | culine rea | son
that commands 'em || —"
The Guardian, Act i. sc. 2.

Likewise of the second Pæon (˘ – ˘ ˘) in the first foot followed by four trochees (˘ –) as:

"So greedily | long for, | know their |
titill | ations."
Ib. ib.

The emphasis too has a decided influence on the metre, and, contrary to the metres of the Greek and Roman classics, at least to all their more common sorts of verse, as the hexameter and hex and pentameter, Alchaic, Sapphic, &c. has an essential agency on the character of the feet and power of the verse. One instance only if this I recollect in Theocritus:

τα μη καλα καλα πεφανται

unless Homer's "῎Αρες, ῎Αρες" may (as I believe) be deemed another —For I can not bring my ear to believe that Homer would have perpetrated such a cacophony as "῏Ωρες, ῎Αρες,"

"In fear | my chaasteetee | may be | suspected."
Ib. ib.

In short, musical notes are required to explain Massinger—metres in addition to prosody. When a speech is interrupted, or one of the characters speaks aside, the last syllable of the former speech and first of the succeeding Massinger counts but for one, because both are supposed to be spoken at the same moment.
"And felt the sweetness *of't.*"

"*How* her mouth runs over."
Ib. ib.

Emphasis itself is twofold, the *rap* and the *drawl,* or the emphasis by quality of sound, and that by quantity—the hammer, and the spatula —the latter over 2, 3, 4 syllables or even a whole line. It is in this that the actors and speakers are generally speaking defective, they can not equilibrate an emphasis, or spread it over a number of syllables, all emphasized, sometimes equally, sometimes unequally.[7]

The first act of the Virgin Martyr is as fine an act as I remember in any play. The Very Woman is, I think, one of the most perfect plays we have. There is some good fun in the first scene between Don John, or Antonio, and Cuculo, his master; and can any thing exceed the

[7] Shedd, IV, 262-63, from notes in a copy of Massinger's works belonging to Mr. Gillman. The Theocritus quotation is Idyll 6, l. 19.

skill and sweetness of the scene between him and his mistress, in which
he relates his story? The Bondman is also a delightful play. Massinger
is always entertaining; his plays have the interest of novels.

But, like most of his contemporaries, except Shakspeare, Massinger
often deals in exaggerated passion. Malefort senior, in the Unnatural
Combat, however he may have had the moral will to be so wicked, could
never have actually done all that he is represented as guilty of, without
losing his senses. He would have been in fact mad . . . .[8]

Except in Shakspeare, you can find no such thing as a pure conception of wedded love in our old dramatists. In Massinger, and Beaumont and Fletcher, it really is on both sides little better than sheer
animal desire. There is scarcely a suitor in all their plays, whose
abilities are not discussed by the lady or her waiting-woman. In this,
as in all things, how transcendent over his age and his rivals was
our sweet Shakspeare![9]

Flögel, GESCHICHTE DER KOMISCHEN LITERATUR, II, 24.

> Er hat die Satire des Lucils verfeinert und veredelt; seine wesentliche
> Veränderung bestand darinn, dass er der Satire ein gewisses bestimmtes
> Sylbenmaass, nämlich das heroische gab.

Whoo! had not Lucilius done this in 21 books out of 30? And are not
many of Horace's Epodes Iambic and Lyric Satires? No! Horace
invented a style and metre, "sermoni propiora," of which no Imitation is extant. The style of Persius is half sophistic, i. e. abrupt, jagged,
thorny; and half declamatory—: and the metre corresponds. Juvenal
again is altogether rhetorical, a flow of impassioned Declamation: and
the correspondent metre is as unlike Persius, and Horace, as their
schemes of metre are unlike each other. All three wrote Hexameters,
it is true; and so did Shakespear, Milton, and Young all three write
blank verse in Lines of ten syllables! But O the asinine luxuriance
of Ear that does not perceive that they are 3 perfectly distinct and
different forms of metre and rhythm. Perhaps, the Horation Hexameter
may be compared to the blank verse of Massinger, the Persian to that
of Young, and the Juvenalian to Cowper's.[10]

Ben Jonson's blank verse is very masterly and individual, and perhaps Massinger's is even still nobler. In Beaumont and Fletcher it is
constantly slipping into lyricisms.[11]

[8] April 5, 1833. *Table Talk S*, VI, 433-34.
[9] April 24, 1833. *Table Talk S*, VI, 445.
[10] Flögel (see p. 546 n. 7), II, 24-25. Note transcribed from the original. Cf.
Cosmopolis, IX (March, 1898), 642-43.
[11] March 15, 1834. *Table Talk S*, VI, 506.

John Dryden

Coleridge afterwards made some remarks upon more modern dramatists, and was especially severe upon Dryden, who could degrade his fine intellect, and debase his noble use of the English language in such plays as 'All for Love,' and 'Sebastian,' down to 'Limberham,' and 'The Spanish Friar.'[1]

In this scene [*The Tempest*, I. 2], as it proceeds, is displayed the impression made by Ferdinand and Miranda on each other; it is love at first sight;—

> at the first sight
> They have chang'd eyes:—

and it appears to me, that in all cases of real love, it is at one moment that it takes place. That moment may have been prepared by previous esteem, admiration, or even affection,—yet love seems to require a momentary act of volition, by which a tacit bond of devotion is imposed,—a bond not to be thereafter broken without violating what should be sacred in our nature. How finely is the true Shakspearian scene contrasted with Dryden's vulgar alteration of it, in which a mere ludicrous psychological experiment, as it were, is tried—displaying nothing but indelicacy without passion.[2]

Sir George Etherege

Thus too with regard to the comedies of Wycherly, Vanbrugh, and Etherege, I used to please myself with the flattering comparison of the manners universal at present among all classes above the lowest with those of our ancestors even of the highest ranks. But if for a moment I think of those comedies, as having been acted, I lose all sense of comparison in the shame, that human nature could at any time have endured such outrages to its dignity; and if conjugal affection and the sweet

[1] Collier, *Seven Lect.*, p. xxiii.
[2] Notes on *The Tempest*, *Lit. Rem.*, II, 98-99.

name of sister were too weak, that yet Filial Piety, the gratitude for a
Mother's holy love, should not have arisen and hissed into infamy these
traitors to their own natural gifts, who lampooned the noblest passions
of humanity in order to pander for its lowest appetites.

As far, however, as one bad thing can be palliated by comparison
with a worse, this may be said, in extenuation of these writers; that the
mischief, which they can do even on the stage, is trifling compared with
that stile of writing which began in the pest-house of French literature,
and has of late been imported by the *Littles* of the age, which consists in a perpetual tampering with the *morals* without offending the
decencies. And yet the admirers of these publications, nay, the authors
themselves, have the assurance to complain of Shakspear, (for I will not
refer to one yet far deeper blasphemy)—Shakspear, whose most objectionable passages are but *grossnesses* against lust, and these written
in a gross age; while three-fourths of *their* whole works are *delicacies*
for its support and sustenance. Lastly, that I may leave the reader in
better humour with the name at the head of this article [i. e. Etherege],
I shall quote one scene from Etherege's Love in a Tub, which for
exquisite, genuine, original humour, is worth all the rest of his plays,
though two or three of his witty contemporaries were thrown in among
them, as a make-weight. The scene might be entitled, "the different
ways in which the very same story may be told, without any variation
in matter of fact:" for the least attentive reader will perceive the
perfect identity of the Footboy's account with the Frenchman's own
statement in contradiction to it. . . .[1]

William Congreve

The thought of confining a novel to the *unities* was something original
. . . and Congreve, a precocious mind, might hope to gain a laurel by
applying the French rules to a species of composition never before made
amenable to them; as if one should make tea or brew small beer in
chemical nomenclature.

A most infelicitous illustration! And why *might* not a novel, and
a very good one in its kind, be written on such a plan? I am sure that
the "Pilgrim," "Beggar's Bush," and several others of B. and F.'s
dramas might be turned into very interesting novels. Had Congreve

¹ "Sir George Etherege," No. 175 in Southey, *Omniana*, II, 23-28. See also
Table Talk A, pp. 387-88.

said that a good novel must be so written, then indeed H. might have stopped him.[1]

> There are degrees of wickedness too bad to laugh at . . .

Wickedness is no subject for comedy. This was Congreve's great error, and almost peculiar to him. The Dramatis Personæ of Dryden, Wycherly, &c., are often *vicious,* obscene, &c., but not, like Congreve's wicked.[2]

> But there is another and more serious obstacle to the success of the "Way of the World," as an acting play. It has no moral interest. There is no one person in the *dramatis personæ* for whom it is possible to care. Vice may be, and too often has been, made interesting; but cold hearted, unprincipled villainy never can.

Virtue and wickedness are *sub eodem genere.* The absence of *Virtue* is no deficiency in a genuine comedy, but the presence of wickedness a great defect.[3]

> Poor John Aubrey's Miscellanies—the probable original of Congreve's old omen-monger.[4]

George Farquhar

But whatever play of Shakespeare's we had selected there is one preliminary point to be first settled, as the indispensable condition not only of just and genial criticism, but of all consistency in our opinions. This point is contained in the words, probable, natural. We are all in the habit of praising Shakespeare or of hearing him extolled for his fidelity to Nature. Now what are we to understand by these words, in their applications to the Drama? Assuredly, not the ordinary meaning of them. Farquhar, the most ably,[1] and if we except a few sentences in one of Dryden's Prefaces (written for a partic[ular] purp[ose] and

[1] Hartley Coleridge, ''William Congreve,'' *Northern Worthies,* III, 296 n.
[2] *Ibid.,* pp. 318-19 n.   [3] *Ibid.,* p. 333 n.
[4] Notebook 22, fol. 41 recto. British Museum, Add. MSS, 47,520. Printed for the first time.

[1] In *A Discourse Upon Comedy.*

in contrad[iction] to the opinions elsewhere supported by him) first exposed the ludicrous absurdities involved in the supposition, and demolished as with the single sweep of a careless hand the whole edifice of French Criticism respecting the so-called Unities of Time and Place.[2]

[2] Stockdale's edition of *Shakespeare's Plays*, I, first flyleaf, recto. Also in Raysor, *Shakes. Crit.*, I, 127.

APPENDIX

Reason and Understanding

Let me by all the labors of my life have answered but one end, if I shall have only succeeded in establishing the diversity of Reason and Understanding, and the distinction between the *Light* of Reason in the Understanding, viz. the absolute Principle presumed in all Logic and the condition under which alone we draw universal and necessary Conclusion from contingent and particular facts, and the Reason itself, as the source and birthplace of *Ideas,* and therefore its conversion to the Will the power of *Ultimate* Ends, of which Ideas only can be the subjects; and I shall have thus taught[1] as many as have in themselves the conditions of learning the true import and legitimate use of the term, Idea, and directed the nobler and loftier minds of the rising Generation to the incalculable *Value* of Ideas (and therefore of Philosophy which is but another name for the manifestation and application of Ideas) in *all* departments of Knowlege, not merely technical and mechanic, and their indispensable presence in the Sciences that have a worth as well as a value to the Naturalist no less than to the Theologian, to the States·man no less than to the Moralist—in Philology, in Organology, in Psychology, as *subjective,* and physiological Anatomy as *Objective,* Analytique, in Chemistry as the constructive Science de Minimis and Astronomy as the correspondent Science de Maximis I shall have deserved the Character which the fervid Regard of my friend, Irving,[2] has claimed for me, and fulfilled the high Calling which he invokes me to believe myself to have received.[3]

THE FRIEND, *"First Landing Place," Essay V.*[4]

> Man may rather be defined a religious than a rational character, in regard that in other creatures there may be something of Reason, but there is nothing of Religion.
>
> Harrington

[1] Negatively—i.e. what is not an Idea, and what the term, Idea, does *not* mean, for *all* who have sufficient power *of* Thought to ask the question; but positively for those to whom it is given, the *occasion* of their turning themselves toward the East. [*Coleridge's note*]

[2] Edward Irving (1792-1834), an eloquent and very popular preacher and friend of Carlyle as well as of Coleridge.

[3] Snyder, *Logic,* p. 135.

[4] *The Friend,* I, 263-77.

If the Reader will substitute the word "Understanding" for "Reason," and the word "Reason" for "Religion," Harrington has here completely expressed the Truth for which the Friend is contending. [Man may rather be defined a rational than an intelligent creature, in regard that in other creatures there may be something of understanding, but there is nothing of reason.[5]] But that this was Harrington's meaning is evident. Otherwise instead of comparing two faculties with each other, he would contrast a faculty with one of its own objects, which would involve the same absurdity as if he had said, that a man might rather be defined an astronomical than a seeing animal, because other animals possessed the sense of Sight, but were incapable of beholding the satellites of Saturn, or the nebulæ of fixed stars. If further confirmation be necessary, it may be supplied by the following reflections, the leading thought of which I remember to have read in the works of a continental Philosopher. It should seem easy to give the definite distinction of the Reason from the Understanding, because we constantly imply it when we speak of the difference between ourselves and the brute creation. No one, except as a figure of speech, ever speaks of an animal *reason;*[6] but that many animals possess a share of Understanding, perfectly distinguishable from mere Instinct, we all allow. Few persons have a favorite dog without making instances of its intelligence an occasional topic of conversation. They call for our admiration of the *individual* animal, and not with exclusive reference to the Wisdom in Nature, as in the case of the storgè or maternal instinct of beasts; or of the hexangular cells of the bees, and the wonderful coincidence of this form with the geometrical demonstration of the largest possible number of rooms in a given space. Likewise, we distinguish various *degrees* of Understanding there, and even discover from inductions supplied by the Zoologists, that the Understanding appears (as a general rule) in an inverse proportion to the Instinct. We hear little or nothing of the instincts of the "half-reasoning elephant," and as little of the Understanding of Caterpillars and Butterflies. N.B. Though REASONING does not in our language, in the lax use of words natural in conversation or popular writings, imply scientific conclusion, yet the phrase "half-reasoning" is evidently used by Pope as a poetic hyperbole.) But Reason is wholly denied, equally to the highest as to ·the lowest of the brutes; otherwise it must be wholly attributed to them, and with it therefore Self-consciousness, and *personality*, or Moral Being.

[5] This sentence does not appear in the 1818 edition.
[6] In a note on p. 264 Coleridge mentions a translation of Blumenbach's *Physiology* by Dr. Elliotson in which an error in presenting Blumenbach's opinion seems to form an exception.

I should have no objection to define Reason with Jacobi,[7] and with his friend Hemsterhuis, as an organ bearing the same relation to spiritual objects, the Universal, the Eternal, and the Necessary, as the eye bears to material and contingent phænomena. But then it must be added, that it is an organ identical with its appropriate objects. Thus, God, the Soul, eternal Truth, &c., are the objects of Reason; but they are themselves *reason*. We name God the Supreme Reason; and Milton says, "Whence the Soul *Reason* receives, and Reason is her Being."[8]

Whatever is conscious *Self*-knowledge is Reason; and in this sense it may be safely defined the organ of the Super-sensuous; even as the Understanding wherever it does not possess or use the Reason, as another and inward eye, may be defined the conception of the Sensuous, or the faculty by which we generalize and arrange the phænomena of perception: that faculty, the functions of which contain the rules and constitute the possibility of outward Experience. In short, the Understanding supposes something that is *understood*. This may be merely its own acts or forms, that is, formal Logic; but *real* objects, the materials of *substantial* knowledge, must be furnished, we might safely say *revealed*, to it by Organs of Sense. The understanding of the higher Brutes has only organs of outward sense, and consequently material objects only; but man's understanding has likewise an organ of inward sense, and therefore the power of acquainting itself with invisible realities or spiritual objects. This organ is his Reason. Again, the Understanding and Experience may exist without Reason. But Reason cannot exist without Understanding; nor does it or can it manifest itself but in and through the understanding, which in our elder writers is often called *discourse*, or the discursive faculty, as by Hooker, Lord Bacon, and Hobbes: and an understanding enlightened by reason Shakespear gives as the contra-distinguishing character of man, under the name *discourse of reason*. In short, the human understanding possesses two distinct organs, the outward sense, and "the mind's eye" which is reason: wherever we use that phrase (the mind's eye) in its proper sense, and not as a mere synonyme of the memory or the fancy. In this way we reconcile the promise of Revelation, that the blessed will see God, with the declaration of St. John, God hath no one seen at any time.

We will add one other illustration to prevent any misconception, as if we were dividing the human soul into different essences, or ideal persons. In this piece of *steel* I acknowledge the properties of hardness,

[7] Friedrich Heinrich Jacobi (1743-1819), *Von den Göttlichen Dingen*, Beilage A, and Frans Hemsterhuis (c. 1722-90), a Dutch philosopher.
[8] *Paradise Lost*, Book V, l. 486.

brittleness, high polish, and the capability of forming a mirror. I find all these likewise in the plate glass of a friend's carriage; but in *addition* to all these, I find the quality of transparency, or the power of transmitting as well as of reflecting the rays of light. The application is obvious.

If the reader therefore will take the trouble of bearing in mind these and the following explanations, he will have removed beforehand every possible difficulty from the Friend's political section. For there is another use of the word, Reason, arising out of the former indeed, but less definite, and more exposed to misconception. In this latter use it means the understanding considered as using the Reason, so far as by the organ of Reason only we possess the ideas of the Necessary and the Universal; and this is the more common use of the word, when it is applied with *any* attempt at clear and distinct conceptions. In this narrower and derivative sense the best definition of Reason, which I can give, will be found in the third member of the following sentence, in which the understanding is described in its three-fold operation, and from each receives an appropriate name. The Sense, (vis sensitiva vel intuitiva) *perceives*: Vis regulatrix (the understanding, in its own peculiar operation) *conceives*: Vis rationalis (the Reason or rationalized understanding) *comprehends*. The first is impressed through the organs of sense; the second combines these multifarious impressions into individual *Notions*, and by reducing these notions to Rules, according to the analogy of all its former notices, constitutes *Experience:* the third subordinates both these notions and the rules of Experience to ABSOLUTE PRINCIPLES or necessary LAWS: and thus concerning objects, which our experience has proved to have *real* existence, it demonstrates moreover, in what way they are *possible,* and in doing this constitutes *Science.* Reason therefore, in this secondary sense, and used, *not* as a spiritual *Organ* but as a *Faculty* (namely, the Understanding or Soul *enlightened* by that organ)—Reason, I say, or the *scientific* Faculty, is the Intellection of the *possibility* or *essential* properties of things by means of the Laws that constitute them. Thus the *rational* idea of a Circle is that of a figure constituted by the circumvolution of a straight line with its one end fixed.

Every man must feel, that though he may not be exerting different faculties, he is exerting his faculties in a different way, when in one instance he begins with some one self-evident truth, (that the radii of a circle, for instance, are all equal,) and in consequence of this being true sees at once, without any actual experience, that some other thing must be true likewise, and that, this being true, some *third* thing must be equally true, and so on till he comes, we will say, to the properties of the lever, considered as the spoke of a circle; which is capable of having all its marvellous powers demonstrated even to a savage who had never seen a lever, and without supposing any other previous knowledge in his mind, but this one, that there is a conceivable figure, all possible lines from the middle to the circumference of which are the same length: or when, in the second instance, he brings together the facts of experience, each of which has its own separate value, neither encreased nor diminished by the truth of any other fact which may have preceded it; and making these several facts bear up on some particular project, and finding some in favour of it, and some against it, determines for or against the project, according as one or the other class of facts preponderate: as, for instance, whether it would be better to plant a particular spot of ground with larch, or with Scotch fir, or with oak in preference to either. Surely every man will acknowledge, that his mind was very differently employed in the first case from what it was in the second; and all men have agreed to call the results of the first class the truths of *science*, such as not only are true, but which it is impossible to conceive otherwise: while the results of the second class are called *facts*, or things of *experience*: and as to these latter we must often content ourselves with the greater *probability*, that they are so, or so, rather than otherwise—nay, even when we have no doubt that they are so in the particular case, we never presume to assert that they must continue so always, and under all circumstances. On the contrary, our conclusions depend altogether on contingent *circumstances*. Now when the mind is employed, as in the case first-mentioned, I call it *Reasoning,* or the use of the pure Reason; but, in the second case, the *Understanding* or *Prudence.*

This reason applied to the *motives* of our conduct, and combined with the sense of our moral responsibility, is the conditional cause of *Con-science,* which is a spiritual sense or testifying state of the coincidence or discordance of the FREE WILL with the REASON. But as the Reasoning consists wholly in a man's power of seeing, whether any two ideas, which happen to be in his mind, are, or are not in contradiction with each other, it follows of necessity, not only that all men have reason, but that every man has it in the same degree. For Reasoning (or Reason, in this its *secondary* sense) does not consist in the Ideas, or in their clearness, but simply, when they *are* in the mind, in seeing whether they contradict each other or no.

And again, as in the determinations of Conscience the only knowledge required is that of my own *intention*—whether in doing such a thing, instead of leaving it undone, I did what I should think right if any other person had done it; it follows that in the mere question of guilt or innocence, all men have not only Reason equally, but likewise all the materials on which the reason, considered as *Conscience,* is to work. But when we pass out of ourselves, and speak, not exclusively of the *agent as meaning* well or ill, but of the action in its consequences, then of course experience is required, judgment in making use of it, and all those other qualities of the mind which are so differently dispensed to different persons, both by nature and education. And though *the reason itself* is the same in all men, yet the means of exercising it, and the materials (i. e. the facts and ideas) on which it is exercised, being possessed in very different degrees by different persons, the *practical Result* is, of course, equally different—and the whole ground work of Rousseau's Philosophy ends in a mere Nothingism.—Even in that branch of knowledge, on which the *ideas,* on the congruity of which with each other, the Reason is to decide, are all possessed alike by all men, namely, in Geometry, (for all men in their senses possess all the component images, viz. *simple* curves and straight lines) yet the power of *attention* required for the perception of linked Truths, even of *such* Truths, is so very different in A and in B, that Sir Isaac Newton professed that it was in this power only that he was superior to ordinary men. In short, the sophism is as gross as if I should say—The *Souls* of all men have the *faculty* of sight in an *equal* degree—forgetting to add, that this faculty cannot be exercised without *eyes,* and that some men are blind and others short-sighted, &c.—and should then take advantage of this my omission to conclude against the use or necessity of spectacles, and microscopes, &c.—or of chusing the sharpest-sighted men for our guides.

Having exposed this gross sophism, I must warn against an opposite error—namely, that if Reason, as distinguished from Prudence, consists merely in knowing that Black cannot be White—or when a man has a clear conception of an inclosed figure, and another equally clear conception of a straight line, his Reason teaches him that these two conceptions are incompatible in the same object, i. e. that two straight lines *cannot* include a space—the said Reason must be a very *insignificant* faculty. But a moment's steady self-reflection will shew us, that in the simple determination "Black is not White"—or, "that two straight lines can not include a space"—all the powers are implied; that distinguish Man from Animals—first, the power of *reflection*—2d. of *comparison*—3d. and therefore of *suspension* of the mind—4th. therefore of a controlling will, and the power of acting from *notions,* instead of mere images exciting appetites; from *motives,* and not from mere dark *instincts.* Was it an insignificant thing to weigh the Planets, to determine all their courses, and prophecy every possible relation of the Heavens a thousand years hence? Yet all this mighty chain of science is nothing but a *linking* together of truths of the same kind, as, *the whole is greater than its part:*—or, if A and B = C, then A = B—or 3 + 4 = 7, therefore 7 + 5 = 12, and so forth. X is to be found either in A or B, or C, or D: it is not found in A, B, or C; therefore it is to be found in D.—What can be simpler? Apply this to an animal—a Dog misses his master where four roads meet—he has come up one, smells to two of the others, and then with his head aloft darts forward to the fourth road without any examination. If this was done by a conclusion, the Dog would have *Reason*—how comes it then, that he never shews it in his *ordinary* habits? Why does this story excite either wonder or incredulity?— If the story be a fact, and not a fiction, I should say—the Breeze brought his Master's scent down the fourth Road to the Dog's nose, and that *therefore* he did not put it down to the Road, as in the two former instances. So aweful and almost miraculous does the simple act of concluding, that *take 3 from 4, there remains one,* appear to us when attributed to one of the most sagacious of all animals.

The unspeakable importance of the Distinction between the Reason, and the Human Understanding, as the only Ground of the Cogency of the Proof a posteriori of the existence of a God from the order of the known Universe. Remove or deny this distinction, and Hume's argument from the Spider's proof that Houses &c. were spun by Men out of their Bodies seems valid.[9]

Mem. to enforce and expound the distinction between the Systematic Unity, which the Understanding made intelligential by the *Light* of Reason strives after and the Identity in all Alterity, or absolute Unity, peculiar to Reason in it's own Sphere—to Reason as opposed to Understanding and distinct from even the Light of Reason in the Understanding. Perhaps *Union* or Totality would be more appropriate to the Systematizing Tendency of the Understanding: while Unity might be reserved for the higher Gift, Reason as the Source and Seat of Ideas or Spiritual Verities. In short, this most important Principle of the essential difference of Reason and Understanding cannot be presented to the Mind of the Pupil in too great a detail of instances, examples and illustrations. 'Tis in the circle of Wicks in an Argand's Lamp, if any one takes light, it kindles all the rest. So any one instance of the diversity of the R. and U. clearly apprehended and thoroughly mastered

---

[9] Moses Mendelssohn, *Morgenstunden* (Frankfurt: 1790), British Museum, C. 43. a. 5. (1), 3d flyleaf verso. Also quoted by Alice D. Snyder, ''Coleridge's Reading of Mendelssohn's *Morgenstunden* and *Jerusalem*,'' *JEGP*, XXVIII (October, 1929), **510.**

(and which of the number may be successful one depends so much on the accident of constitution and experiences in the individual Pupil's Mind that it cannot be known beforehand) all the other instances will become luminous on each.side, till the whole blend in a circle of Light.[10]

What is wanting to complete my exposition of the diversity of Reason and Understanding, is to translate the truths out of the language of Abstract or General Terms into that of Reality. The first Step is already secured in the establishment of the Identity of Reason & Being, and of both with the Eternal WORD, the Only-begotten Son—and in the necessity of the fraile mind to distinguish the One Absolute Being with Person, the Manifestative focal or Central Subsistence, and the *Sphere,* in which he is every where present operatively. Hence Reason is the Sphere, the Light of the Son, the Light which the Son *is*—and this the Light, that lighteth every man that cometh into the World.

Now the Understanding is the Man himself, contemplated as an intelligent Creature—and the Light shineth down into his natural darkness (= blind instinct) and by it's presence converts the vital instinct into Understanding—or the Understanding as modified by this Light may be distinguished from the Reason itself, as *Lumen* from Lux. It is *Lumen* Humanum or Luce Divina—and the implanted susceptibility of this *Illumination* so that the Light is present *for* him as well as in him, is present as *Light*—constitutes him a *Man,* and is truly the *Image* of God—for Lumen est *imago* Lucis.

The Understanding then *is* the Man—whose rationality consists in the innate susceptibility of the Lumen a Luce—but the Reason is not the Man, but πρὸς ἄνθρωπον, which, however, as far as he is a Spirit, might be named an *Attribute* of his Humanity by the Virtue of the perpetual presence of the never-setting Light & Sun—but because he is a fallen Spirit ὃ ἐγένετο σάρξ,the necessity of Sleep reminds him of his Fall by the periodical eclipse of the Light—thro' the unfitness of his bodily organism to continue unintermittently to be the *Medium.*[11]

The true Mystic Philosophy may be divided into three parts—first, the introductory and purifying, which Gerson[12] rightly describes as consisting of *abnegation,* or a watchful repelling and setting aside the intrusive images of Sense, and the conceptions of the Understanding,

[10] Notebook 26, fol. 8-9 recto. British Museum, Add. MSS, 47,524. Printed for the first time.

[11] Notebook 47 ("Fly-catcher No. xv"), Oct. 21, 1830, fol. 22 verso-24 recto. Printed for the first time.

[12] Jean Charlier de Gerson (1363-1429), French theologian.

both these generalized from the Data of the Senses or formed by reflection on it's (the Understanding's) own processes. Secondly, the contemplation of the Ideas, or Spiritual truths, that present themselves, like the Stars, in the silent Night of the Senses and the absence of the animal Glare. That these Ideas have a true Objectivity is, as Gerson seems to have seen, implied in the Soul's Self-knowledge. To these solemn Sabbaths of Contemplation we must add the work-days of Meditation on the interpretation of the Facts of Nature and History by the Ideas; and on the fittest organs of Communication by the symbolic use of the Understanding, which is the function of the Imagination. (See the MSS on the inner cover at the end of this Volume). Now these two parts comprize the actual attainments of the true Mystic, as what in a greater or less degree he holds it not boastful to say, he possesses. The third part he hopes and waits for—*confident* only, that it will exist for the spirit after he has been delivered "from the body of this death["]; but yet willing to believe it neither impossible, nor out of the analogy of the ways of God with man, that even in this life certain antepasts, and Foretastes of the marriage feast may be vouchsafed to the pure in heart. This is what the followers of Plotinus named, the knowledge of the Supreme Good by spiritual contact—the Christian Mystics—the fruition of God—& it's philosophic Validity rests on the Position of Life, as an eternal distinct Form.[13]

Gerson's & St. Victore's Contemplation is in my System = *Positive* Reason, or R. in her own sphere as distinguished from the merely *formal* Negative Reason, R. in the lower sphere of the Understanding. The + R. = Lux: − R. = Lumen a Luce. By the one the Mind contemplated Ideas: by the other it meditates on conceptions. Hence the distinction might be expressed by the names, Ideal Reason ✗ Conceptual Reason.

The simplest yet practically sufficient order of the Mental Powers is, beginning from the[14]

[13] Tennemann, *Geschichte der Philosophie*, VIII (2nd half), 2d flyleaf recto and verso. British Museum C. 43. c. 24. Printed for the first time.

[14] *Ibid.*, p. 900. Note on back board. Printed for the first time.

Cf. first flyleaf recto: "The *Idea* of *a* Supreme Being is a misuse of the term, Idea. We may have *conceptions* of *a* man, perceptions and images of *this* man; but the Idea of *Man*. Equally improper is the phrase, *an* Idea of—. It is either no Idea, or not at all; *or* it is *the* Idea."

Also cf. p. 96: "What G. [Gerson] calls Contemplation is what I call Positive Reason. Reason in her own Sphere, as distinguished from Negative or merely *formal* Reason, Reason in the Sphere of the Understanding."

Fancy and Imagination are Oscillations, *this* connecting R. and U.; *that* connecting Sense and Understanding.

lowest	highest
Sense	Reason
Fancy	Imagination
Understanding	Understanding
Understanding	Understanding
Imagination	Fancy
Reason	Sense

The Reason in that highest sense, in which the speculative is united with the practical, not the reason as the mere collective of necessary & universal theoretic principles, but the Reason[15] as the living source of living & substantial verities, presents the Idea to the individual mind, and subjective intellect, which receives & employs it to its own appropriate ends, namely to understand thereby both itself and all its objects— receives it I say, uncomprehended, by it to comprehend the universe, the world without & the yet more wonderful world within.[16]

[15] I here use the word in it's highest as well as most comprehensive Sense,— and not for the mere Collectaneum of *theoretic* principles or of such speculative truths as are accompanied with the sense of unconditional necessity and absolute universality. [*Coleridge's note*]

[16] *On the Divine Ideas*, Huntington Library MS, HM 8195, p. 249. The above note is on the page opposite, p. 248. Printed for the first time.

Index

Addison, Joseph, xxiii, xxv, 415, 463
Aeschines, 287
Aeschylus, 559, 565, 609
Anacreon, 594, 666
Andreini, Giovanni Battista, 585, 600-601, 604-5, 613, 614
Andrewes, Lancelot, 163, 204, 226
Anne, Queen of England, xxx, 384, 415, 493, 495
Apostles' Creed, 156, 198, 225, 295, 297-98, 363
Aquinas, Thomas, 70, 204, 438
Arianism, 89, 166, 352, 357, 380, 383, 389
Aristophanes, 565
Aristotelian, xxxviii, 74, 102, 103 n., 148, 552
Aristotle, xxxviii, 5, 40, 41, 45, 46, 47, 48, 53, 58, 60 n., 61, 70, 71, 82, 85, 99, 100, 102, 103, 103 n., 104, 105, 106, 116, 146, 148, 191, 256, 437, 569, 605
Arminianism, 10, 206, 266, 267, 287, 289, 290, 307, 329, 348, 352, 355, 478, 480, 577
Astronomy, 158, 395, 396
"At a Vacation Exercise" (Milton), 569
Aubrey, John, 681
Augustine, St., 147, 167, 170, 179, 185, 196, 198, 199, 200, 243, 267, 297, 301, 373, 379, 387, 389, 468

Bacon, Francis, xxiv, xxv, xxxii, 5, 75, 102, 132, 138, 159, 173, 211, 212, 358, 396, 397, 412, 413, 417-18, 420, 425, 426, 450, 531, 544, 545, 597, 670, 687; anticipation of Kant in, 102, 109-10, 114-16, 173, 317; character, 56-57; error in method, 46; Kepler contrasted with, 46-47; Platonism in, xxxiv-xxxv, 40, 41-58, 235, 396
Bale, John, 464, 465
Bancroft, Richard, 469, 470
Barrow, Isaac, 368-69, 412, 415, 421, 423, 425
Baxter, Richard, 20, 111-12, 134, 138-39, 153, 274, 278, 298, 313, 318, 321-64, 487, 494; influence of Schoolmen on,

359; the king as individual and executive not distinguished by, 337-38; marginalia in *Life of Himself*, 321-57; marginalia in *Catholic Theologie*, 359-64; "idea" and "conception" not distinguished by, 363; Coleridge's agreement and disagreement with, 321; principle of trichotomy discovered by, xxxvi, 111-12, 118-21; value of reading his works, 331-32
Beaumont, Francis, and John Fletcher, ix, x, xxviii, xxix, 520, 607, 638, 646, 649-73, 678, 680. *See also* under titles of plays
Beaumont, Lady, 368
Beaumont, Sir George, 508
Beggars Bush (Beaumont and Fletcher), 653, 672, 673, 680
Bellarmine, Robert Cardinal, 107
Belsham, Thomas, 298, 344
Bentham, Jeremy, 187
Bentley, Richard, 133
Berkeley, George, xxxiv, 87, 90, 98, 105, 107, 281, 375
Black, Joseph, 398
Blackmore, Sir Richard, 546, 634
Boccaccio, Giovanni, 413, 420
Bonduca (Beaumont and Fletcher), 664
Bonner, Edmund, 27, 345, 469
Boswell, James, 434, 443
Boyle, Robert, 106, 399, 406
Brown, Tom, 424, 425
Browne, Sir Thomas, 158, 371, 438-62; active faith enjoyed by, 113; Copernican system rejected by, 395; likeness of Coleridge to, 439, 447; marginalia in his works, 438-61; character revealed in *Religio Medici*, 438-39; style, 414, 420-21, 447-49
Bruno, Giordano, xxxi, 119, 557
Buchanan, George, 516
Buckingham, George Villiers, 1st Duke of, 56, 57, 153, 209, 210, 216, 217, 218, 227
Bull, George, Bishop, 128, 138, 166, 266, 380, 381, 382, 383, 387, 388, 390

Bunyan John, 474-86; allegory, sometimes faulty, 474, 475, 478, 479-80; character, 485; Christian teaching, 476; effectiveness of his language, 475, 476; marginalia on, 476-85; superstitious use of Scriptural texts, 486

Burke, Edmund, 265, 310 n., 412

Burnet, Gilbert, 3, 9-10, 134-35, 243, 244, 247, 258, 274, 369-75; Bedell's attack on Wotton criticized by, 369-71; evaluation of *Life*, 375; marginalia in *Life of Bedell*, 369-74

Burnet, Thomas, *Telluris Theoria Sacra*, 263, 368, 492

Burton, Robert, x, 211, 431-32

Butler, Samuel, 145, 526, 614-17, 661; *Hudibras*, 489, 614, 616-17

Byron, George Gordon, Lord, 442, 489

Calamy, Edmund, 153, 278, 350, 353, 355

Calvin, John, 10, 158, 161, 185, 188, 189, 228, 289, 293, 297, 357

Calvinism, 266, 289

Cambridge Platonists, xxxii, xxxiii, xxxvi, 109 n., 128, 366, 622

Cary, Lucius, Lord Falkland, 13, 25, 27, 219, 230

Casimir, Matthias Sarbieuski, 628

Catholicism, permeation of century by, 8, 9, 35, 144-45, 149-50, 156, 157, 159-60, 162, 185, 188, 206, 213, 217, 224, 228, 229-30, 242, 266, 268, 273, 279, 292, 297, 300, 306, 307, 308, 314, 315, 319, 325, 327, 353, 357, 370-71, 373, 434-35, 469-70, 479, 534, 537

Catullus, Gaius Valerius, 526

Cavendish, Henry, 398, 455

Cavendish, William, Duke of Newcastle, 20, 21

Cervantes Saavedra, Miguel de, 660

Chances, The (Beaumont and Fletcher), 653

Chapman, George, x, 259; translation of Homer, 503-5

Charles I, xxv, 3, 4, 7, 10, 11, 12, 13, 16, 19, 20, 25, 26, 27, 28, 29, 30, 31, 53, 66, 139, 208, 210, 212, 216, 217, 219, 221, 228, 281, 300, 326, 332, 336, 337, 338, 346, 348, 356, 374, 434, 435, 467, 488, 518, 572; the church in the reign of, 324; justice of execution of, 14-15, 335, 336-37, 351-52, 472, 658; lying, 24, 34, 220, 294, 350; reign of, compared with Elizabeth's, 5-6

Charles II, 7, 63, 89, 153, 235, 237, 268, 281, 316, 322, 324, 331, 359, 366, 395, 413, 415, 423, 424, 464, 467, 488, 491, 525; plot to introduce Catholicism in reign of, 9; restoration of, 31-34, 349-50

Chaucer, Geoffrey, 416, 420, 421, 471, 506, 512, 545, 552, 556, 613

Chillingworth, William, 134, 165, 230-32; arguments against Romanism, 230-31; evaluation of *Religion of Protestants*, 232

Church and State, 143, 144-45, 181-82, 217-18, 356, 361

Church Fathers, 17th-century reverence for, 137, 163, 170, 171, 180, 185, 206, 207, 208, 256, 267-68, 279, 287, 295, 297, 298, 300, 308, 389-90, 485, 534

Church of England: definition, 266-67; rank, 387; three evil epochs, 355-56; two interpretations, 354-55

Cicero, 71, 94, 263, 287, 358, 416

Clarendon, Edward Hyde, 1st Earl of, 3, 13, 15, 25, 26-27, 31, 34, 335, 464, 474, 488, 491

Clark, Samuel, 381, 389

Coleridge, Alwyne H. B., xi, 153, 463 n., 494 n., 503 n.

Coleridge, Derwent, 153, 160

Coleridge, Hartley, 13, 15, 209, 556

Coleridge, Henry Nelson, viii

Coleridge, Lord, xi

Coleridge, Samuel Taylor, vii, viii, ix, x, xi, xxi-xxxviii, 2, 3, 4, 5, 39, 40, 109, 110, 111, 112, 125, 126, 127, 128, 129, 130, 131, 132, 133, 134, 348-49, 381, 393, 394, 472, 529, 541, 542, 543, 544, 558, 606

Coleridge, Sara, 131

Collier, Jeremy, 421

Collyer, Joseph, 415, 424

Compound epithets, 558, 617

"Comus" (Milton), 566-68; "haemony" in explained, 553-55

Condillac, Etienne Bonnot de, 59, 138

Congreve, William, 526, 680-81

Corbet, Bishop Richard, 530

Cotton, Charles, 629-30

Cowley, Abraham, x, 65, 154, 203, 415, 421, 435, 550, 612, 626-29, 634; characteristics of his poetry, 489; comparison with Donne, 522; fanciful mind, 626-27

Cowper, William, 432, 433, 503, 678

Crashaw, Richard, 612-14, 628, 634; "Christabel" influenced by, 613; lack of selective power, 613
Croker, J. W., 493, 494
Cromwell, Oliver, 4, 11, 12, 15, 22, 26, 28-29, 65, 221, 222, 322, 340, 343, 351, 421, 471, 472, 572, 583-84, 585, 627, 629
Cudworth, Ralph, 357, 366
Custom of the Country (Beaumont and Fletcher), 655-56
Cyprian, St., 206, 297, 360, 373

Daniel, Samuel, 506-19; Civil Wars, 512-17; criticism of rhymes, 506, 517; letters to Lamb concerning, 510-12; "The Passion of a Distressed Man," 518; "prosaic" applied to, 509; quoted, 518-19; scansion of his poems, 513, 515-16; style and language, 507, 518; "To the Lady Lucy, Countess of Bedford," 518; "To the Lady Margaret," 506, 517; "To the Lord Henry Howard," 517
Dante Alighieri, xxxi, 55, 259, 310, 310 n., 471, 543, 553, 559, 569, 587, 596, 598
Darwin, Erasmus, 358, 547, 626
Davy, Sir Humphrey, 53, 248, 393, 398, 433, 455, 541
De Foe, Daniel, 463, 495, 592
Demosthenes, 263, 287, 545
Descartes, René, 40, 59, 60 n., 61, 67-68, 70-74, 75, 76-88, 92-94, 98, 99, 100, 103, 105, 106, 187, 397, 490, 621. See John Locke
Dichotomy, errors through, 18
Donne, John, x, xi, xxvii, xviii, xxxvii, 125, 137, 163-205, 252, 266, 268, 428-31, 454, 519-30, 543, 550, 569, 641; art of orator found in, 205; claims of the church sustained by, 181; confusion of "reason" and "understanding", 172-73, 197; elegant division of subject illustrated by, 191; exaggeration, 199; insight not always steady, 184; legends accepted by, 171, 185; marginalia: in Sermons, 163-205; marginalia on Letters, 428-31; marginalia in Poems, 519-28; misunderstanding of act of faith, 184; opulence of power, 522-23; patristic leaven in, 163, 170, 171, 180, 185, 188; play on words, 195, 203; poetic fervor, 523; poetry in prose, 205, 529; quality of sermons, 135, 205;

rhythms suited to sense, 519-21, 654; tenderness expressed, 529-30; wit displayed, 526-27; words not always clearly defined, 190
Drayton, Michael, xxviii, 508, 515, 532, 539, 561, 562
Drummond, William, 641-42
Dryden, John, xxii, xxviii, xxxv, 5, 416, 421, 422, 489, 493, 519, 528, 551, 553, 585, 630-33, 644, 654, 670, 673, 679, 681; ability degraded in some plays, 679; couplets marked by variety, 631; drinking song inappropriately introduced in "Alexander's Feast," 633; genius evolved from itself, 630; impersonal possessive first used by, 631-32; second period of English prose introduced by, 425
Dundas, Henry, Viscount Melville, 544

Edward VI, xxiii, xxv, 135, 156, 166, 173, 268, 277, 331, 413, 420, 426
Eichhorn, Johann Albrecht Friedrich, 153, 341
"Elegy I" (Milton), 558, 571, 572
Elizabeth, Queen of England, 4, 5, 6, 7, 8, 18, 21, 35, 56, 143, 160, 163, 181, 216, 218, 235, 238, 277, 316, 355, 412, 420, 431, 448, 469, 488, 503, 515, 518, 526, 572, 573, 639, 640, 656, 664, 669
Epictetus, 257, 377
Epicurus, 375, 378
Estlin, Dr. John, 604, 605
Etherege, Sir George, 679-80
Euripides, 310, 565, 609

Faerie Queene, The, 434
Fair Maid of the Inn, The (Beaumont and Fletcher), 665
Faith, 180, 482, 483, 536; accepted in contradiction to understanding, 173, 197, 481, 497; confused with belief, 183-84, 252, 341, 500; revealed by deeds, 480; restricted to ideas, 296
Falkland, Lord. See Cary, Lucius
Fame, distinguished from reputation, 545
Farquhar, George, 681
Felix Farley's Bristol Journal, April 16, 1814, 543
Fichte, Johann Gottlieb, 116
Field, Richard, 137, 166; free will discussed by, 160-61; marginalia in Of the Church, 153-62; Ptolemaic theory retained by, 158; recommendation to Derwent Coleridge of, 153, 160; "syn-

agogue'' and ''church'' distinguished by, 154-55; ''understanding'' and ''reason'' understood by, 117

Fletcher, John, and Francis Beaumont, ix, x, xxvii, xxix, 520, 607, 638, 646, 649-73, 678, 680. *See also* Francis Beaumont and plays

Free will, 160, 161, 225, 483, 633

Fuller, Thomas, x, 54, 232-43, 258, 463-70, 532; the Bible considered as one book, 241; a ''call'' to the ministry upheld, 239-40, 241; characteristics, 238, 463-64, 466, 468; despotism of Presbyterian clergy illustrated, 235, 236-37; elegance of dedication of *A Triple Reconciler*, 233; infant baptism supported, 236; Lamb's appreciation of, x; language, 463; marginalia in *A Triple Reconciler*, 232-43; marginalia in *Life out of Death, a Sermon*, 241; marginalia in *The Appeal of Injured Innocence*, 242; marginalia in *The Worthies*, 463-65; marginalia in *The Holy and the Profane State*, 465-68; marginalia in *Church History*, 468; private interpretation of the Bible opposed, 237-38; text of sermon fully explicated, 234; uniqueness, 463; wonder excited by, 470

Galileo, 5, 6, 46, 399
Gardiner, Stephen, 27, 325, 345, 469
Gassendi, Pierre, 70, 88, 98, 418
George I, 381, 384
George III, 381, 384, 653
Gerard, John, 566, 567
Gerson, Jean Charlier de, 692
Gibbon, Edward, xxiv, 282, 416, 427, 603
Gifford, William, 675
Gilbert, Humphrey, 46, 47, 394, 397
Gillman, James, 554, 556
Glover, Richard, 549
Goethe, Johann Wolfgang von, 44, 394, 403, 404, 411
Gordon, George. *See* Byron
Gower, John, 506, 564
Gray, Thomas, 99, 101, 551, 638
Grindal, Edmund, 145
Grotius, Hugo, 153, 319, 320, 326, 327, 330, 337, 345, 359, 366

Hacket, John, 10, 163, 205-22, 247, 601; contradictions in his reasoning, 222; contrasted features in his sermons, 207; definition of wisdom, 210-11; margi-nalia in *Scrinia Reserata*, 209-22; marginalia in *Sermons*, 205-8; Romish tendencies, 206, 208, 217; *Sermons* contrasted with *Scrinia Reserata*, 208-9

Hall, Joseph, xxiv, 298, 313, 315, 371, 372, 374, 376, 427

Hammond, Henry, 266, 313, 331, 332, 473

Hampden, John, 11, 313, 352

Harrington, James, 26, 435, 544, 626, 685, 686

Harriot, Thomas, 397

Hartley, David, xxxi, 5, 39, 58, 59, 60, 61, 75, 78, 84, 108, 397, 402

Harvey, Christopher, x, 531, 534

Helvetius, Claude Adrien, 138

Henry VII, 354, 488

Henry VIII, 209, 210, 355, 418, 525

Heraclitus, 54, 452, 453

Herbert, Edward, 1st Baron of Cherbury, 71, 128, 366

Herbert, George, x, xxviii, 275, 533-40, 634; marginal notes on *Works*, 534-39; metrical variations, 536, 540; quaintness, 533, 538, 544; reader's qualifications for enjoyment of, 534

Heylin, Peter, 223-30; bitter spirit, 224, 227, 228; intentional misrepresentation, 224-25; marginalia in *Life of Archbishop Laud*, 223-28; Protestant neglect of Luther and Calvin stated by, 228-34

History of the 17th century, 3-36

Hobbes, Thomas, xxxvii, xxxviii, 5, 39, 40, 58-67, 72, 75, 80-81, 88-89, 98, 112, 418, 687; contrast of Spinoza with, 64; synonymous use of ''compelled'' and ''obliged,'' 62-63; source of ideas in: Aristotle, 61-62, 70, Descartes, 59-60, Locke, 40; translation of Homer, 65-67

Hogarth, William, 463, 657

Homer, 55, 65, 503-05, 545, 550, 552, 555, 559, 575, 597, 603, 612, 617, 677

Hooke, Robert, 46

Hooker, Richard, xxii xxiv, xxv-xxvi, xxxii, xxxiii, xxxiv, 5, 52, 129, 134, 140-52, 204, 206, 266, 368, 412, 413, 414, 483, 546, 687; antecedence of law to thing meant by, 145-46; Aristotelian philosophy, 147-48; Christian faith clearly propounded by, 150-51; conception of faith similar to Coleridge's, 141; distinction of ''reason'' and ''understanding'' clear to, 116-17, 173;

error in comparing things differing in kind, 142; intellectual superiority abused, 148-49; later periods influenced by, 127; marginalia in *Works*, 141-52; metaphysical genius, 144; redemptive process clarified, 151-52; style, 140-41, 415, 420, 421, 425; value of reading his works, 331-32

Horace, 526, 605, 678

Howe, John, 353

Hume, David, xxviii, 39, 40, 41, 43, 59, 60, 60 n., 68, 70, 89, 90, 91, 95, 98, 104, 105, 111, 138, 488, 489, 544, 546, 691

Hutchinson, Lucy, *Life of Colonel Hutchinson*, 3, 16-23, 351, 359, 413, 435, 450, 487, 584

Hutchinson, Sara, x, 447, 449

Hyde, Edward. *See* Clarendon, 1st Earl of

Iamblichus, 54, 71

Icon Basilice, discussed, 24-25

"Idea," meaning clarified, 143, 146, 183, 288, 291, 363, 384, 385, 386

Iliad, 575

"Il Penseroso" (Milton), 553, 565-66

Immortality, 164, 333, 334, 366

Infant baptism, 236, 269, 298

Irenaeus, 171, 321, 390

Ireton, Henry, 313, 351

Irving, Edward, 247, 248, 342

Isocrates, 257

Jacobi, Friedrich Heinrich, 687

James I, 5, 10, 14, 25, 27, 56, 57, 127, 162, 166, 169, 210, 213, 214, 217, 219, 225-26, 355, 356, 366, 369-70, 431, 433, 467, 473, 515, 526, 572, 573, 640, 643, 656, 662, 664, 669; bishoprics weakened by, 7-8; character, 212, 218

James II, 7, 9, 32, 35, 88, 135, 173, 222, 268, 281, 319, 338, 355, 426, 491, 495

Johnson, Dr. Samuel, xxiv, 282, 304, 371, 381, 415, 423, 427, 432, 434, 443, 463, 526, 544, 583, 584, 631; his preference of Cowley's Latin poems to Milton's, 628; his style derived from Bishop Hall, 372; his style translatable, 416, 422, 551

Johnson, Samuel (the Whig), 495

Jonson, Ben, 637-49; as a contemporary of Shakespeare, 638; blank verse, 678; comparison with Beaumont and Fletcher, 651; comparison with Chapman, 504; comparison with Shakespeare,

648, 649, 650, 656; couplets, 631; farce-plots of comedies, 649, 671; genius not organic, xxix, 670; literary qualities, 639, 648; originality, 638; poetry ranked above drama, 648; question of authorship of "Drayton's Epitaph," 532-33; reflection of contemporary manners, 640, 641; his soldiers derived from his service in Flanders, 648; to be studied as a classic, 640; use of "humors," 637-38, 639, 641; works commented on, 642-47, 649—*see also* under titles

Josephus, Flavius, 554

Junius, 282, 416, 423, 463

Kant, Immanuel, xxxi, xxxii, xxxiii, xxxiv, xxxv, xxxvi, 5, 41, 58, 102, 109-21, 130, 256, 288, 291, 317, 366, 460; anticipations of, xxvi; reason and understanding distinguished, 109-10, 111-12, 116-17, 460, 496-97; trichotomy introduced, 118-21

Kepler, Johannes, 46, 47, 58, 75, 158, 394, 396, 397, 399, 400

Klopstock, Friedrich Gottlieb, 411, 549, 576, 578, 591, 631

Knox, John, 203, 516

Kotzebue, August Friedrich Ferdinand von, 667, 668, 669

Laforge, Louis de, 397

Lagrange, Joseph Louis, Count, 381

"L'Allegro" (Milton), 553, 564-65

Lamb, Charles, ix, x, xi, 4, 505 510, 511, 540, 630, 657, 668

Langhorne, John, 205

Laplace, Pierre Simon de, 381

Latimer, Hugh, xxv, 420

Laud, William, 10, 25, 126, 139, 153, 163, 169, 211, 212, 268, 283, 287, 294, 296, 300, 313, 315, 353, 355, 473; character, 34; persecutions by, 278, 290, 297, 347-48; *Life* by Peter Heylin, 223-30

Lauderdale, John Maitland, Duke of, 248

Lavoisier, Antoine Laurent, 398

Laws of Candy (Beaumont and Fletcher), 657

Le Clerc, Jean, 132, 389

Leeuwenhoek, Anton van, 460

Le Grice, Robert, 434

Leibniz, Gottfried Wilhelm, xxxiv, 54, 89, 90, 94, 95, 97

Leighton, Robert, vii, xxxiii, xxxv, 9, 114, 115, 152, 229, 243-58, 291, 294, 315, 316, 352, 353, 481; estimate of his works, 250; faults of "Exhortation to the Students," 250, 257; marginalia in *Works*, 250-57; orthodoxy, 242-45; as "Plato glorified by St. Paul," 252; plan of extracting from his works for *Aids to Reflection*, 245-50; style, 243-44, 246, 250, 255

Le Sage, Alain René, 397

Lessing, Gotthold Ephraim, 648

L'Estrange, Sir Roger, 368, 415, 421, 423, 424, 425

Lindsay, Lady Anne, 344

Little French Lawyer, The (Beaumont and Fletcher), 672

Liturgy, use of, 274-76, 277, 278-79, 321, 352

Livy, 285, 434

Locke, John, xxxii, 39, 60 n., 67-109, 126, 138, 232, 326, 384, 399, 447, 489, 544, 546; Aristotle in relation to, 70, 71-72, 102-6; Descartes as source of ideas, 40, 67-74, 88, 92-94, 98, 99; letters to Wedgwoods on, 68-90; reasons for popularity, 88-90, 91, 94-97, 98, 99-100

Lockhart, J. G., 493, 494

Loyal Subject, The (Beaumont and Fletcher), 656

Lucan, 514

Lucilius, 678

Lucretius, 526

Ludlow, Edmund, 26, 435

Luther, Martin, x, xxv, 10, 53, 90, 130, 138, 147, 152, 158, 161, 163, 170, 174, 175, 183, 184, 185, 224, 225, 228, 229, 268, 292, 297, 328, 332, 334, 385, 395, 396 n., 420, 461, 477, 481, 586

"Lycidas" (Milton), 556, 560-64

Lydgate, John, 506

Macintosh, James, 40, 41, 58, 67, 70, 71, 84, 98, 282

Maclaurin, Colin, 90

Maid of Honour, The (Beaumont and Fletcher), 674

Maid of the Mill, The (Beaumont and Fletcher), 657, 659

Maid's Tragedy, The (Beaumont and Fletcher), 649, 654-55

Maitland, John. *See* Lauderdale

Malebranche, Nicolas de, 84, 85, 90, 490

Mandeville, Sir John, 452

Marini, Giambattista, 626

Mary I, Queen of England, 8, 156, 469

Mason, J. Monck, 676

Massinger, Philip, ix, x, xxvii, xxviii, xxix, 433, 515, 520, 606, 607, 638, 647, 650, 651, 652, 654, 655, 662, 670, 673-78; comments on *The Bondman, The Maid of Honour*, 673, 674; *A Very Woman*, 677; *The Virgin Martyr*, 677; general criticism, 675; outline of lecture on, 673-75; mechanical unity of plays, 676; metre, 656, 673, 676-77, 678

Mazarin, Jules, 31, 351

Melancthon, Philipp, 61, 138, 224, 297, 437

Michelangelo Buonarroti, xxxv, 431, 553

Middleton, Conyers, 319, 345

Milton, John, xxii, xxiv, xxv, xxviii, xxix, xxx, xxxi, xxxii, xxxiii, xxxv, 5, 27, 30, 55, 91, 112, 128, 131, 154, 155, 162, 203, 220, 261, 271, 282, 332, 346, 352, 388, 400, 412, 413, 415, 416, 417, 420, 421, 425, 427, 433, 435, 463, 469, 504, 521, 522, 533, 541-612, 626, 627, 628, 629, 631, 664, 678, 687; comparison with Dante, 598; comparison with Shakespeare, 556, 557, 587, 595, 602; comparison with Jeremy Taylor, 310-16; Cromwell's ejection of Parliament defended by, 22, 471-72; Euripides preferred by, 608; Latin verse, 552; lectures on, 541-44; marginalia in *Minor Poems*, 559-72; marginalia in Hayley's *Life of Milton*, 582-85; marginalia in Knight's *Principles of Taste*, 609-12; party influence shown by, 471; Platonism, 553; poems, 541-612; poetry defined by, 546-47; political principles, 472, 473; range of excellence, 471, 602-3; unchangeable order of words in, 422, 550-51; uniqueness, 463. *See also* separate poems

Molière, Jean Baptiste, 490

Monboddo, James Burnett, Lord, 69

Monk, George, 33, 464

Monsieur Thomas (Beaumont and Fletcher), 653, 671

Montagu, Basil, 55, 529

Montagu, Richard, 163, 227, 355

Montaigne, Michel de, 414, 420, 448

Mordaunt, Charles, 3rd Earl of Peterborough and Monmouth, 88

More, Henry, x, xxviii, 316-21, 357, 366, 376, 617-26; causes of errors in *Theological Works*, 317-18; five main faults

in his poetry, 625; foreshadowing of Wordsworth, 618, 619; marginalia in *Theological Works*, 316-21; marginalia in *Poems*, 622-25; names in poems 617; philosophic and poetic genius, 316-17, 623; poetry, 617-26
More, Sir Thomas, 358, 425, 461
Murray, John, 494

Nelson, Robert, 486
Newcastle, 1st Duke of. *See* William Cavendish
Newton, Isaac, 5, 58, 75, 80, 90, 95, 97, 106, 108, 375, 394, 396, 397, 399-408, 508, 544, 690; Cartesian physics overthrown by, 89, 94; chief error, 404-5; critical estimate, 407; derivation from Kepler, 397, 399-400; difficulties in theory of comets, 405-6; inferiority to Shakespeare and Milton, 400; the *Optics*, 400-403; utility as a test of value, 408
Nicolas, Hendrick, 319, 320
Noble Gentlemen, The (Beaumont and Fletcher), 664-65
North, Roger, 415, 421, 423, 424, 425

"Ode on the Morning of Christ's Nativity" (Milton), 568-69
Oken, Lorenz, 394, 403, 404
Old Divines: beginnings of Broad Church movement, 134; causes of errors in their theological schemes, 316-18; classification, 127, 163; Coleridge's views on their controversial doctrines, 128-32; contemporary divines contrasted with, 204; diffusion of learning through, 125-26, 134-35; interest of audience in, 135-36, 194-95; literary ability, 125, 136-37, 181, 191; reasons for acquaintance with, 331-32
"On the University Carrier" (Milton), 570
Origen, 190-91
Ovid, 609
Owen, John, 353

Paley, William, 376, 544
Pantheism, identified with atheism, 381-82
Paracelsus, 443, 460, 466
Paradise Lost (Milton), 434, 544, 556, 558, 561, 572-82, 585, 586, 587, 588, 589, 590, 591, 592-93, 594, 595, 597, 598, 601, 604, 609, 642; conditions under which produced, 572-74; execution of, 578-79; fable from brief facts, 588; matter as a mode of spirit, 589; metrics, 579-82; object, 577-78; payment for, 600-601; plan and arrangement, 574-76; Satan's aim, 591; subject, 576-77; unfixed image of Death, 593-94
Paradise Regained (Milton), 556, 558, 582, 596, 603-5; execution of, superior to *Paradise Lost*, 603; Satan portrayed as a skeptical Socinian, 604
Parallelisms, 560, 564, 586, 642
Pascal, Blaise, 490
"Passion, The" (Milton), 569
Paulo, Padre, 369, 370, 372, 375
Pearson, John, 198
Penn, William, 107, 320
Pepys, Samuel, 486-92; historical facts important in diary, 490-91, 491-92; literary taste mistaken in, 487, 489; self-interest, 487, 489, 490, 491
Persius, 678
Peterborough, 3rd Earl of. *See* Mordaunt, Charles
Petrarch, 586
Philaster (Beaumont and Fletcher), 649
Philosophy, identified with Christianity, 377; main evils of, 394; two schools—Plato and Aristotle, 147-48
Pilgrim, The (Beaumont and Fletcher), 653, 663, 680
Pindar, 471
Pitt, William, 544
Plautus, 526
Plotinus, 116, 693
Poetry and science, 55
Political economy, source of in Bible, 474
Poole, Thomas, viii, xxiv, 3, 68 n., 393
Pope, Alexander, xxiii, xxvii, 5, 65, 262, 415, 437, 489, 503, 505, 519, 526, 530, 531, 544, 574, 590, 609, 630, 631, 641, 652, 674, 686
Porphyry, 505
Potter, Edward, 132, 133
Prayer: for the dead, 456; question of using set forms of, 274-75, 278
Priestley, Joseph, 108, 298, 398, 399, 455, 544
Proclus, 339, 505
Prophetess, The (Beaumont and Fletcher), 663-64
Prose and verse distinguished, 616-17; poetic prose, 259-63

Prose style: Cavalier, 415, 419, 423, 427; classical, xxv, 413-14, 418, 420; effect of science on, 418; individual variations, 412; influence of 17th-century style on Coleridge, xxiv, 425, 426-27; organic principle, xxvi; rules for forming, 416-17, 422; same words in poetry and prose, 411, 424

Prynne, William, 211, 247, 294

"Psalm VII" (Milton trans.), 570

"Psalm VIII" (Milton trans.), 570-71

"Psalm LXXXII" (Milton trans.), 571

Pythagoras, 80, 101, 102, 144, 198

Quarles, Francis, x, xxviii, 531-33; appeal to the masses, 531-32; reason for underrating, 532

Queen of Corinth, The (Beaumont and Fletcher), 664

Rabelais, François, 490

Raleigh, Sir Walter, 3, 5, 262, 378, 464, 474, 516, 572

Reason and Understanding, xxxii-xxxiv, 685-94; importance of distinction, 114-16; distinguished in the 17th century, 109-11, 116-17, 138, 154-55, 173, 255, 256, 364, 388

Redemption, 151-52, 165-66, 173-74, 200, 295, 306, 360, 481

Republican, definition of, 435

Reynolds, Sir Joshua, 414

Rhenferd, James, 320

Robinson, Henry Crabb, 541, 542, 543

Rollo (Beaumont and Fletcher), 661-63

Roscoe, William, 358

Rousseau, Jean Jacques, 690

Rupert, Prince, 9, 19, 20, 21

Sacrament, the, 158-59, 175, 176, 235, 284, 301, 302, 304, 305-6, 308, 309-10

St. James, 155

St. John, 114-15, 150, 164-65, 168, 169, 171, 174-75, 301, 303, 319, 363, 377, 382, 383, 386, 388, 407, 483, 485, 687

St. Luke, 167, 170, 190, 276, 538

St. Paul 114-15, 150, 158, 161, 162, 166, 167, 168, 169, 170, 171, 172, 173, 174-75, 177, 188, 189, 190, 240, 243, 252, 256, 276, 286, 296, 307, 319, 363, 376, 381, 382, 386, 390, 408, 444, 457, 483, 485, 499, 500, **597**

St. Peter, 158, 179, 245, 246, 250, 538

Sallust, 430

Samson Agonistes (Milton), 556, 598, 605-8; diction, 606; imitation of Greek drama in, 605; metrics of chorus, 607-8

Sanderson, Robert, xxxiii, 216, 266

Scaliger, Joseph, 320

Scheele, Karl Wilhelm, 398, 455

Schelling, Friedrich Wilhelm Joseph von, 116, 394, 404

Schiller, Johann C. F. von, 411

Schlegel, August Wilhelm von, 560

Science, successive predominance of: experimentation, 396-97; magnetism, 397; mechanical system, 397-98; electricity, 398; chemistry, 398

Scott, Sir Walter, 247, 467, 489

Scriptures, the: critical and historical approach, 169-70, 177-78; restatement of inspiration, 16-17, 179, 276, 277, 388; terminology, 132-33; textual study, 132

Selden, John, 137, 209, 328, 436-38, 508

Seneca, xxvi, 257, 377, 424, 426, 446, 477, 617, 643

Shaftesbury, Earl of (Anthony Ashley Cooper) 1st Earl of Shaftesbury, 62, 493

Shakespeare, William, x, xxi, xxii, xxvi, xxviii, xxix, xxxi, xxxii, xxxv, 56, 91, 113, 156, 191, 244, 258, 317, 331, 400, 417, 422, 433, 463, 465, 470, 471, 489, 503, 506, 507, 511, 522, 523, 542, 544, 545, 546, 547, 549, 550, 551, 553, 556, 557, 558, 559, 560, 564, 565, 567, 568, 581, 587, 588, 593, 595, 597, 598, 603, 606, 607, 608, 610, 613, 615, 630, 637, 638, 640, 641, 642, 643, 645, 646, 648, 649, 650, 651, 652, 654, 655, 656, 657-58, 659, 660, 661, 662, 663, 664, 665, 666, 667, 668, 669, 670, 671, 672, 673, 674, 675, 678, 680, 681, 687

Sharp, James, 248

Sheldon, Gilbert, 29, 128, 139, 167, 283, 324, 325, 329, 330, 347, 353

Sheridan, Richard Brinsley, 526

Sherlock, William, 128, 133

Sidney, Algernon, 28, 416, 421, 473

Sidney, Sir Philip, 5, 233, 412, 544, 560

Simmons, Samuel, 601

Simonides, 310

Smith, John, 117, 134, 365-67

Smyth, Henry, *Sermons*, 137

"Sonnet to Mr. H. Lawes" (Milton), 570

Sophocles, 565, 606, 608, 609

South, Robert, 369, 423

Southey, Robert, xxviii, 35, 211, 242, 243, 348, 349, 358, 371, 393, 424, 475, 476, 485, 486, 494, 495, 515, 556, 581, 616, 625

Spenser, Edmund, xxix, 259, 260, 416, 421, 506, 512, 515, 544, 545, 547, 548, 556, 559, 662, 625, 629

Spinoza, 58, 64, 98, 333, 367, 460, 569, 587

Steffens, Henrik, 394, 404

Stillingfleet, Edward, 68, 72, 94, 95, 97, 126, 128, 137, 138, 166, 231, 232, 266, 267, 290, 353, 412; marginalia in *Origines Sacrae*, 375-79

Strada, Famiano, 585

Strafford, Earl of. *See* Thomas Wentworth

Style, loss of dignity after the Restoration, 368

Sunday, observance of, 328

Swift, Jonathan, 65, 416, 421, 494, 544, 593, 615, 616

Tacitus, 416, 434·

Tasso, Torquato, 555

Tatius, Achilles, 418

Taylor, Jeremy, x, xxii, xxiv, xxv, xxvi, xxxv, 58, 60 n., 117, 131, 163, 252, 258-316, 318, 345, 350, 353, 359, 366, 368, 412, 413, 415, 416, 420, 421, 425, 427, 462 (quoted), 472, 626; characteristics as a writer, 265, 278, 279, 280-81, 282, 294; comparison with Milton, 310-16; *Discourse of Confirmation* least judicious work, 299; *Doctrine and Practice of Repentance* criticized, 266, 267; general comments on works, 266-67; inferiority of verse, 261-62; as logician, 264, 283, 284, 298; marginalia on *Polemicall Discourses* (1674), 271-316; original sin, error in explanation of, 130; original sin, reaction against consequences, 263-64; Pelagianism, 290, 293; poetic quality of prose, 259-61, 263; prayers, 275; punctuation, 271-72; quality of sermons, 135; sense of church authority, 268; Socinianism deducible from his scheme, 293, 298; spirit of casuistry, 284-85; toleration disavowed by after Restoration, 294; value of reading his works, 331-32; vocabulary, 262

Terence, 526

Tertullian, 180, 376, 387, 390

Theocritus, 412, 552, 563, 677

Thomson, James, 260, 599

Tillotson, John, 267, 290, 376

Toleration, 331, 358, 626

Tooke, Horne, 103, 154, 423

Trinity, 146, 166-67, 168; classical writers on, 380-81

Tully, 191, 222

Twiss, William, 353

Two Noble Kinsmen, The (Beaumont and Fletcher), 665-66, 672

Ussher, James, 27, 274, 336

Valentinian (Beaumont and Fletcher), 658-60

Vanbrugh, John, 679

Villiers, George. *See* Buckingham, 1st Duke of

Virgil, 526, 563, 584,· 597, 610, 611

Vives, Ludovicus, 40, 61

Voltaire, 90, 94, 95, 97, 138, 585, 615

Voss, Johann Heinrich, 411

Waddesworth, James, 371, 373-74

Walker, George, 355

Waller, Edmund, 629

Walsingham, Sir Francis, 413, 420

Walton, Isaac, x, 135, 142, 194

Warburton, William, 241, 356, 605, 616

Ward, Seth, 353

Warton, Thomas, 544, 558, 559-72

Waterland, Daniel, 128, 131, 132, 266, 379-90; Arianism overcome by, 166, 357; distinction of ''reason'' and ''understanding'' not clear to, 386, 388; *idea* of God vague to, 379-80, 380-81, 382-83, 385, 386; marginalia in *A Vindication of Christ's Divinity*, 380-87; marginalia in *The Importance of the Doctrine of the Holy Trinity*, 387-90; pantheism equal to atheism from arguments of, 381-82

Watson, Seth B., 248

Wedgwood, Josiah, 3, 67, 75, 80, 86

Wedgwood, Thomas, 40, 41, 67, 75, 80, 86, 393

Wellesley, Sir Arthur, Duke of Wellington, 215

Wellington, Duke of. *See* Sir Arthur Wellesley

Wentworth, Thomas, Earl of Strafford, 13, 23-24, 313

Wesley, Samuel, *Life of* by Robert Southey, 242, 243, 494, 495

Whitaker, William, 137, 266
White, Blanco, 482
Whitgift, John, 469
Wieland, Christoph Martin, 411
Will, the: good and evil, 173-74; ground of being, 178, 181, 186, 194, 201-2, 211
William III, 4, 11, 35, 36, 91, 181, 384, 467, 495
Wit, kinds of, 615
Wither, George, x, xxviii, 530-31
Wollaston, William Hyde, 398
Words, importance of exact definition of, 115, 461-63
Wordsworth, Christopher, 24, 25, 139
Wordsworth, Dorothy, 3
Wordsworth, William, xxv, 3, 433, 489, 507, 508, 544, 549, 552, 557, 588, 618 (quoted), 619
Wotton, Sir Henry, 370-71
Writers from Edward VI to Charles II, six reasons for reading, 331-32
Wycherley, William, 679, 681

Xenophon, 257, 358, 418

Young, Edward, 263, 678

Zeno, 116
Zinzendorf, Count Nikolaus Ludwig von, 385
Zwingli, Ulrich, 158, 185, 300